NEW THEATRES FOR OLD

ANTOINE

Forty sous opened a new era

From Le Théâtre

NEW THEATRES FOR OLD

by
Mordecai Gorelik

OCTAGON BOOKS

A DIVISION OF FARRAR, STRAUS AND GIROUX

New York 1975

Reprinted 1975
by special arrangement with Samuel French, Inc.

OCTAGON BOOKS
A DIVISION OF FARRAR, STRAUS & GIROUX, INC.
19 Union Square West
New York, N. Y. 10003

Library of Congress Cataloging in Publication Data

Gorelik, Mordecai, 1899-
New theatres for old.

Reprint of the ed. published by S. French, New York.
Bibliography: p.
Includes index.

1. Theater. 2. Theaters—Stage-setting and scenery. I. Title.
PN2037.G54 1975 792 75-14002
ISBN 0-374-93213-1

Manufactured by Braun-Brumfield, Inc.
Ann Arbor, Michigan

Printed in the United States of America

TO THE THEATRE OF THE AMERICAN AUDIENCE

Fresh come, to a new world indeed, yet long prepared,
I see the genius of the modern, child of the real and ideal,
Clearing the ground for broad humanity, the true America,
                    heir to the past so grand,
To build a grander future.

WHITMAN

ACKNOWLEDGMENTS

Now that this book is finished (or at least as finished as I can reasonably hope), and the time has come to credit those who have helped bring it into existence, I am impressed by the fact that so many people have taken part in some phase of the work. Whether this be evidence of friendship for the aims of the book, or only for myself, how can I ever hope to repay it? I can only fall back on the usual device of listing names as a token of my indebtedness.

Much of the writing was done in spare time snatched from work as a scene designer—during summer months, between shows, even in an occasional hour in hotel bedrooms during tryouts of plays out of town. Under these handicaps it might have become a futile project. It entered the realm of things possible when the John Simon Guggenheim Memorial Foundation appointed me to a fellowship in 1935 (with a renewal in 1937). I feel that I should begin by thanking the Foundation and expressing my personal regard for its secretary, Henry Allen Moe.

My heartfelt appreciation also goes to two men without whose aid this book would lack most of its value—Bertolt Brecht, who helped to clarify the original outline, and Robert Edmond Jones, who discussed the manuscript in its later stages. These artists of the theatre, so far apart in background and temperament, are united in their poetic insight into the meaning of stage technique, their sense of responsibility to the theatre and its audiences, and their power to share their knowledge with those anxious to learn.

It has been my good fortune to be associated since its beginnings with the Group Theatre, which is regarded today as the most distinguished dramatic company in the United States. I wish to acknowledge how much I have learned through this association and to name those Group members, including Harold Clurman, Elia Kazan, Robert Lewis and Molly Thacher, who read the manuscript or made suggestions. It is sad to have to put into a separate category the name of Emanuel Eisenberg, whose sparkling personality was ended in so tragic a manner.

ACKNOWLEDGMENTS

During 1936 I was able to compare my own views (which were still in a formative stage) with those of theatre craftsmen and dramatic critics abroad. I should like to thank the following people for the interviews which they granted:

In Sweden, the designers John Jon-And (Royal Opera); Sven-Erik Skawonius (Royal Dramatic Theatre); Georg Magnusson (Vasa Theatre, Stockholm). Also Dr. Eric Wettergren, curator of the National Museum; Dr. Agne Beijer, curator of the Drottningholm Theatre Museum; Stig Torsslov, of the Royal Dramatic Theatre; Sven Bergvall, secretary of the Svenska Teaterförbund (the actors' union of Sweden); Dr. Matthey Schischkin, artistic director of the Amatörteatern Riksförbund; Dr. Per Lindberg, director of the Vasa Theatre.

In Denmark, the designers Svend Gade (Royal Theatre); Svend Johansen (Royal Theatre, Norrebro Theatre); Kjeld Abell (Royal Theatre, Riddersal. Herr Abell is an internationally known dramatist as well). Also Herr Borchsenius, chief régisseur of the Royal Theatre; Per Knutzon, director of the Theatre of the Riddersal, Copenhagen. In Finland, Nikken Rönngren, director of the Swedish Theatre, Helsinki; Mme. Elli Tompuri, former director of the Free Theatre, Helsinki.

Among German theatre people living in exile I interviewed Brecht in Denmark; the designers Teo Otto and Wolfgang Roth in Zurich; the playwright Friedrich Wolf in Russia; Fräulein Margaret Lode, former secretary of the Workers' Theatre Alliance, in Russia; Hanns Eisler, composer; Dr. Kurt Pinthus, critic; Erwin Piscator, director; Ernst Toller, playwright; Dr. Paul Zucker, critic, all in the United States.

In the Soviet Union I spoke with the designers Nikolai Akimov (Comedy Theatre, Leningrad); V. N. Rindin (Vakhtangov Theatre, Moscow); Alexander Tishler (State Jewish Theatre, Moscow). Later I met, in New York, Isaac Rabinovich, scenic artist of the Bolshoi Opera and of the Moscow Art Theatre's Musical Studio. Other Soviet people whom I interviewed included: Y. Boyarsky, chairman of the Dramatic Section of the All-Union Committee on Art; Mme. Vaneva, director of the Vakhtangov Theatre; Seki Sano, of Meyerhold's Theatre; I. Gremislavsky and V. Sherubovich, in charge of the technical work at the Moscow Art Theatre; V. Vishnevsky, Alexander Afinogenov and Anatoli Glebov, dramatists;

N. Pazhkovsky, secretary of the Central Committee of the Union of Art Workers of the U.S.S.R.; K. A. Skriagin, secretary of the Artists' Section of the same union; Mme. E. N. Kolosova, director of the State Central Theatre Museum, Moscow.

In Czechoslovakia I interviewed the designers Antonín Heythum (National Theatre) and M. Kouřil (Burian Collective). Also J. Voscovec and J. Werich, directors of the V & W Theatre, Prague; and E. F. Burian, director of the Burian Collective, then currently designated as the D 37 Theatre. In Austria, the designer Emil Pirchan (Burgtheater, Vienna); Dr. Joseph Gregor, curator of the Theatre Collections at the National Library. In France, the designers Michèle Larianov and Mme. Nathalie Gontcharova, of the Ballet Russe; Paul Mathos, of the Théâtres Indépendents; Fernand Léger, designer of the Ballet Méchanique and the Ballet Suédois. Also Louis Jouvet, director of the Théâtre Athénée, Paris; Léon Moussinac, stage director and critic. In New York I had the opportunity, later, to consult with two young English directors, André van Gyseghem of the Left Theatre, London; and Rollo Gamble, of the Westminster Theatre, London.

I have since had the cooperation, in New York, of George Freedley, of the Theatre Collection of the New York Public Library; Jay Leyda, of the Film Library of the Museum of Modern Art; Miss Alice Evans, of the New Theatre League; Mark Marvin and Ben Blake, of *Theatre Workshop;* Thurber Lewis, of Amkino; Miss Rose Rubin, of the American-Russian Institute. I owe a special debt to Garrett H. Leverton, of Samuel French, Inc., and to Mrs. Edith J. R. Isaacs, editor of *Theatre Arts,* many of whose valuable suggestions have been incorporated in my writing. My obligation to Mrs. Isaacs and *Theatre Arts* is apparent in the book itself, but it goes back through all the years in which I have read and written for this magazine.

Among the many individuals who have been helpful I wish to name Dr. Kurt Adler; Ralph Berton; Dr. H. W. L. Dana; Barthold Fles; William L. Laurence; Joseph Levine, attorney; Edward Maltz; Erwin Piscator; Herman Shumlin; Oscar Serlin; Barrie Stavis; Ralph Steiner; Lee Strasberg (who gave me access to his fine library of books on theatre), and John Wexley. I am particularly grateful for the aid given by Miss Rita Hassan during the final work on the MS. Among the people who did technical work on the manuscript were Dick Bennett, Miss Rose Morrison, Miss Ariel Bryce, Miss Florence Cohen, and especially my invaluable secretary, Miss Clara Louise Tuckerman.

I wish to acknowledge the kindness of the many publishers who gave permission to quote or to reproduce illustrations from their books and to thank the Royal Dramatic Theatre and the Vasa Theatre, Stockholm; The Royal Theatre and the Riddersal, Copenhagen; the V & W Theatre and the Burian Collective, Prague; the Théâtre Athénée, Paris; the Federal Theatre, New York; and a number of playhouses in Moscow, all of which supplied me with photographs of their productions. The Museum of Modern Art, New York, has permitted the use of a large number of photographs from its files.

Most of my historic research was done at the Stadsbibliothek, Stockholm, and the New York Public Library, with supplementary work at the Bakhrushin State Central Theatre Museum, Moscow; the Nationalbibliothek, Vienna; the Brander Matthews Memorial Library, New York; the Fifty-eighth Street Branch of the New York Public Library, and the Library of the Museum of Modern Art.

Finally let me record that there would still be no book were it not for my wife, Frances Gorelik, whose devoted encouragement and help kept the project alive through arduous times.

Confused terminology, usual in the arts, seems to be especially rampant in the field of the theatre. I have not tried to clarify all the terms used in the text, believing it would hurt the unity of the work if there were too many pauses for definition. Instead I have appended a short glossary of stage terms. I have also thought it advisable to define a few esthetic, economic, scientific and philosophic terms according to their usage in this book. It will be noted that the titles of plays are given throughout in UPPER CASE while the titles of books and articles are in italics. I have capitalized arbitrarily the names of the theatrical styles, in the hope of keeping them more clearly before the mind of the reader.

This book is offered in a spirit of friendly inquiry, with no desire to wound individual feelings or beliefs. My views are my own (although based, I think, on adequate study). They are colored by twenty years of stage experience which I have shared with the other people of the American theatre. If, occasionally, some comments seem severe, I hope they will be seen in the perspective of my admiration for the basic vitality of our theatre and of my optimism about its future.

MORDECAI GORELIK

CONTENTS

ILLUSTRATIONS

ILLUSTRATIONS

ILLUSTRATIONS

NEW THEATRES FOR OLD

Mimicry

The hunter; cave drawing

INTRODUCTION

IMMORTAL THEATRE

INCANDESCENT fire, vivid as the rainbow, blazes before the altar of Dionysus in the western world. Few Americans consider their lives complete without a glimpse of Broadway, dramatic capitol of the new hemisphere, fabulous street of a fantastic, towered city.

Crowds line up before the movie palaces. Customers are turned away at the doors of the "smash hits." Never was our theatre more expert, never were its stage lights more dazzling, its colors more palpitant; never was its tempo swifter or its beauty more alluring. Actors, managers, directors and designers flash into international prominence overnight. Broadway plays go to Hollywood bidders for almost a quarter of a million dollars apiece. Motion pictures and radio, capitalized in sums running up to billions of dollars, reach a larger audience in one day, perhaps, than came to the Baroque theatre in two hundred years.[1]

Possibly, in sight of this stirring picture of stage and screen activity, it comes as a shock to learn that Broadway stage production is only half what it was in the peak season of 1927–28. Yet what remains more than fills the eye; and something tells us that theatre cannot perish no matter what dangers assail it. Behind Broadway and Hollywood stretches a history of three thousand years during which the theatre has lived down wars, persecution, pestilence, hunger and even its own mistakes. The generations of men depart but theatre goes on forever.

> For Dionysus is immortal, and the theatre lives alway.
> (Cheney: *The Theatre*).

What is theatre? What makes it live forever? Why has it been so treasured by men from the stone age to the age of steel?

It is described to us as

> the inundation of the spirit, in beauty and clarity, toward which the art of the theatre gropes. And this, in a world from which divinity and mystery have been unsparingly shorn, this is as near as we are likely to come to the divine and the spiritual. It is the Dionysian experience, our ecstatic participation in the divine life. (Cheney).

We are told that the theatre cannot die because it has the ageless appeal of *magic*. The stage is a magic mirror in which life is reflected in a manner closer to our hearts' desire. We who attend the dramatic ceremony as players or playgoers leave real life, with its pettiness and vexations, behind us; instead we take part in a larger emotional experience which makes us happier or at least wiser.

We learn that the kind of magic which Broadway and Hollywood use today was used by totemistic drama at the beginning of human history. It was present in the mad revels of Cybele in Phrygia and Dionysus in Thrace, in the Alexandrian funeral rites of Aphrodite and Adonis, in the Mexican sacrifice of Tezcatlipoca, whose heart was torn from his living body at the summit of a pyramid. The principle of dramatic magic was already ancient when Aristotle wrote it down over two thousand years ago in his *Poetics,*

> Through pity and terror effecting a purification.[2]

Who has not known this kind of magic? Who has not, in the playhouse, had the sensation of living an unaccustomed, superhuman life? This omnipotence, this godlike power to change life at the behest of a simple wish—is now said to be the essence of theatre. And the belief in stage magic has, if anything, been emphasized in the age of science and mass industry. It remains largely unquestioned even at this moment, when practically everything else is being questioned.

But have there not been changes, important changes, in the nature of theatre during thousands of years? Yes, say our authorities; but only in the theatre's ability to mimic the world more convincingly. Primitive man tried to imitate life with his dance rituals and animal skins. His attempts were pathetic, but they foreshadowed the marvelous techniques of today, when steel machines, electricity and even cathode rays create startling images of life itself. Thus we may picture the long evolution of the forces of theatre, developing harmoniously out of the past until they emerge as the almost perfect mechanism of our own times.

Immortal theatre—a proud and heart-warming conception!

MORTAL THEATRE

But it is a conception which must serve to celebrate the theatre, not to define it.

In practical definition it begins to fail us. All the more so if we are craftsmen anxious to understand the medium with which we work, or if we are teachers who wish to know how the stage can best serve our countrymen in an hour of danger.

In terms of craftsmanship we find that the rhapsodic explanation of the stage is less helpful than it might be. For it is an explanation derived not so much from stage experience as from the good wishes of literary men who have loved the theatre. Many such writers have succeeded in communicating to us their appreciation of the special genius of the stage. Few have lived in the playhouse, smelled the heavy perfume of makeup or the equally heady scent of carpenter's glue.

The literary school of dramatic criticism has a specific way of dealing with the forms of theatre. It proceeds by means of classifications. First dividing the world-history of theatre into separate "periods," it then links together these "period" theatres by means of the idea of the *immortal playscript.*

It begins with the principle (assumed to be self-evident) that theatrical production is a method of staging a script. Looking back into history, and considering the masterpieces of dramatic writing which have come down to us, it concludes that the "spoken word" is the soul of drama while production is the mere outward form, the body of drama. What is eternal about theatre is the tradition of the script of the dramatic poet, which develops on a spiritual plane. On a lower plane the material body of the theatre dies and is reborn in comparatively unimportant (if picturesque) phases.

We must acknowledge the serene beauty of this picture. But births and deaths here below continue to be matters of importance, often attended by stormy circumstances.

In practice it is difficult to separate the activities of the soul from those of the body. When theatrical form changes a living theatre dies and a new one is born. But this is a real death and a real birth. The change takes place not in the serenity of the dramatic critic's study but tumultuously in the theatre districts and on crowded stages.

THEATRICAL TRUTHS

A study of the theatre from the more neglected standpoint of *production* rather than of the playscript (which is only one important element of production), presents us with many new values.

It obliges us to look upon stage history not as a succession of scripts illustrated in various kinds of performances, but as a long-continued search for theatrical truths.

What are theatrical truths? Like truths in any other field, they are accurate, revealing comments on some phase of existence. Only, in the case of theatre, truths are not revealed in print between the covers of a book, or by means of a speech at a lecture, or by means of a demonstration in a laboratory, or by means of a picture recorded with paint on canvas. In the case of the theatre, truths are revealed on a stage platform with the help of actors, dramatist, director, designer, settings, lights, sound effects and all the rest of the personnel and apparatus of the stage. There are many ways in which truths can be revealed to people. The stage provides one of these ways.

It is one of the most vivid ways. Theatre has accompanied

every period of history; every age has used the theatrical medium to express its idea of the truth. By the same token, every age combined the elements of stage production in a manner which seemed best suited to this purpose. The English theatre of the Restoration, convinced of the divine right of kings, revealed this belief on the stage, using for that purpose all its resources of wing settings, tallow candles, chamber music and declamatory actors. Three hundred years later the theatre of the Soviets, convinced that life must be explained in terms of economic struggle, reveals its belief in the playhouse with the help of new modes of acting, directing, scene design and highly mechanized stages.

The historic forms of drama are not mere whimsical changes in fashion. If we look for more than the earmarks of style we shall see that each era of theatre used a hodgepodge of method, in which different elements of production were combined in varying degrees and with varying success. There have been stage formulas in which the script counted for little, others in which the script was of first importance. Sometimes the actor has occupied center stage, sometimes the scene designer, or even the technician.

Nor did these dramatic formulas appear upon the scene full-grown and conveniently labeled. They were milestones along the road of *experiment.*

The theatre has evolved new forms to meet new conditions, sometimes abandoning an old form midway in favor of a new one showing better promise. Yet it has seldom been clear about its objectives. The experimenting has gone on with all too human uncertainty and far too little planning. Over its long span of time the theatre has made progress; but by no means in a simple, continuous forward movement. It has progressed—and regressed—with all its available forces. The forces available to it have also varied a great deal. The drama can call upon technical forces today which it did not have in the days of Shakespeare; and these forces are a potential strength or a potential weakness.

The author of this book holds that dramatic technique is not a goal in itself but a means to an end. This purpose, over centuries of confused experiment, may be summed up as follows: *to influence life by theatrical means.* Primitive theatre thought it could do this directly, by means of magic ceremonies. Later theatres have been satisfied to reveal to audiences what they considered to be the truths of their times. They knew that such revelations have the same effect, even though indirectly.

We may judge the theatre by its own activity. So long as it makes headway toward this goal it is a living institution. It ceases to live in measure as it falls away from its objective.

On the whole there is good reason why theatre may be called immortal. That reason is not the simple fact that plays last indefinitely when printed in books. Not only the playscript, but theatre itself lives forever. Nothing dies more completely than theatre; yet it dies only to return more vigorously alive than before.

Theatre is immortal not because it never dies but because it is always being reborn. When a particular theatre comes to an end because it is no longer useful to its audiences, it is replaced by a newer theatre, which takes up the work where its predecessor left off.

NEW THEATRES FOR OLD

It was Hebbel who declared, "Theatre is the only possible pause in a man's life." This is an arresting statement, made by a dramatist of uncommon power and shrewdness. Yet the message is a cryptic one.

It has been interpreted to mean that theatre is something different from, even opposed to, the activities which we carry on from day to day. Theatre, according to this interpretation, is something which is artistically gratifying, without any other purpose.

But it seems obvious that Hebbel did not have in mind a blank pause, however esthetic. It is a pause for another kind of thought. For theatre in its own province picks up our unclear thoughts and carries them onward to clarity. Healthy theatre is not just a pleasant stupor.

If we look on theatre as stage production rather than as a branch of literature, we begin to see it as a valiant, practical effort to understand and influence life. As something more constructive, *more important,* than mere artistic gratification, although that, too, is an indispensable side of theatre.

Theatre is not something in contrast to the other aims of life. It shares those aims. Like man's other activities it has grown continually in experience. It has moved further and further away from wishful thinking. It has grown in the kind of imagination which is strengthened, not weakened, by contact with reality itself.

Even the very earliest dramatic efforts, fantastically unreal as they appear to us now, had a constructive purpose. We have learned that primitive man did not prance in animal skins just for an emotional holiday. His dance ceremonies were fraught with importance for the welfare of his tribe. To encourage summer to return after winter; to bring rain in arid countries; to make sure of an adequate supply of game; to make himself invulnerable in war; to guide his children safely through puberty and adolescence —these were among the objects of the earliest drama. True, it was not a rational drama. But it was as rational as it knew how to be.

Ages had to go by before theatre could think as logically and effectively as in the Greek tragedies. More centuries had to pass before the Baroque playhouses showed their keen interest in geography, history and the natural sciences. As we enter the domain of modern theatre (which is the principle object of study in this book), we find the drama consciously setting out to present a truthful image of nature and man.

Some fifty years ago a new conception of theatre, cradled in the rationalism of the French Encyclopedists and grown to maturity in a scientific age, was ready to insist that *life itself* be brought to the stage. And so the Naturalistic stage form was integrated, under the brilliant tutelage of men like Ibsen, Strindberg, Zola, Antoine, Brahm, Hauptmann, Chekhov and Stanislavsky.

The Naturalists did not succeed entirely in their aim. A second generation of theatre workers pointed out shortcomings in the Naturalistic practice, rebelled against Naturalistic dogma. People like Appia, Craig, Erler, Fort, Reinhardt, Yeats, Maeterlinck, led their rebellion. Once considered incompetent dreamers, these insurgents finally inherited the theatre. They brought back lyricism to a drama which had lost the power to take wing. They replaced with a poetic stage form another form which had grown hopelessly prosaic. Serene in the strength of its imagination the new theatre created a vision of beauty toward which it invited men to build in peace.

DOWN FROM THE MOUNTAIN PEAKS

For something like thirty years our theatre beheld this vision from its mountain peaks, until it almost forgot the life of men in the valleys far below. In the places where men live, disaster and want also make their homes. Deep down in the valleys the old savage struggle went on, increasing in ferocity, until even from a far distance the flame and smoke of destruction could be seen.

But our theatre clung desperately to its vision, whose outlines were beginning to blur. It insisted that the more terrible the emergency, the greater was the need for the long view; the more bitterly men fought over immediate material things, the more necessary it was to call attention to the immemorial values of the spirit.

Today it begins to look as if there was a fallacy somewhere in this reasoning. Although our theatre has remained lofty in intention, it has lost contact with the needs of its audiences. And thereby it has also lost its freshness.

The theatre which once tried to seize life whole now tends to describe life in terms of anecdotes and vague generalities. The theatre which reproached its predecessor with intellectual bankruptcy today looks askance at new ideas and makes a virtue of drifting. By 1930 it had almost abandoned any serious attempt to understand the tumult of life around it, insisting, on a note of hysteria, that it would not be drawn into anything "controversial." It was no longer interested in new and constructive ideas with which to face the perils which threaten to overwhelm its audiences.

In his summary of American drama since 1918, the discerning critic of *The Nation,* Joseph Wood Krutch, maintains that "a critical discussion of the recent American drama is most fruitful when it is a discussion, not in terms of 'ideas,' but in terms of imagination and literary form." He says, with reference to the successful American dramatists of our times:

> It is, moreover, by no means certain that a single one of their works will continue to be regarded as having permanent value. But the question will be decided on the basis of their excellence in their kind, and if they fail to survive it will be exclusively because they were not good enough, because they did not succeed well enough in what they tried to do, not because their ideas have grown stale.

And yet, if Mr. Krutch is correct, what a mournful summary this is! The value of these plays seems in doubt, their ideas are perhaps stale; one must be careful to appraise them only in terms of craftsmanship and of imagination unrelated to "ideas."

Is it possible to bring creative craftsmanship to stale ideas? The history of art refutes such a belief. New ideas do not necessarily create artists, but artists of real size must have new ideas out of which to create.

By "ideas" is meant, of course, ways of looking at life, not the narrow definition of plots, gestures or color schemes. Shakespeare used stale plots, which were completely transfigured by his own commentary. His ideas were those of a turbulently progressive era, and his own robust personality matched the spirit of his times.

Mr. Krutch's statement becomes possible only in the atmosphere of a theatre whose interest in life has diminished—a theatre whose utterances are no longer as important as the cadence of its intonation. Those stage productions which depend on abstract craftsmanship, on abstract imagination lacking new ideas, will in future be judged both for their ideas and their craftsmanship. It will not be strange if they are found lacking in both.

Let it be recalled that theatre does not exist for the sake of the craftsmanship of playwrights, actors or scene designers. Theatre exists for the sake of its audiences. We who work in the theatre bear a heavy responsibility toward these audiences; our usefulness ends the moment this responsibility is forgotten.

The roar of guns and bombing planes echoes again through the world. The Europe to which we have been accustomed is going down like a sinking continent. Its playhouses are sinking also; they are not exempt from the general catastrophe.

Under such stress the theatres that remain can no longer be passive. The outer world, which some of them have almost forgotten, is battering at their doors, forcing them to a decision. They can mobilize their audiences in defense of human hopes; or they can continue to talk about pure craftsmanship, unalloyed imagination—and fall without a struggle.

If the stage wants to go on serving its audiences it will have to build a dramatic form suited to our times. To do this it must have a thorough knowledge of existing stage technique. But no analysis of such technique will be useful if it is confined to a narrow study of the stage itself. He who would understand theatre at this moment cannot stand only on the stage. He must have one foot in the theatre, one outside.

UP FROM PROPAGANDA

While the established theatre has been descending, unwillingly, from its mountain peaks, a new kind of drama has been struggling up from below.

From primitive times onward theatre has tried to influence reality, to shape it closer to its own desires. Theatre, in this sense, has not always been artistic, but it has been almost continuously propagandist. The primitive war dance was propaganda against the enemy. Greek drama inculcated the principles of religion, as did the Chinese and Japanese drama and the liturgical plays of the Middle Ages in Europe. The Baroque theatre glorified the point of view of autocracy. The Romantic theatre, on the contrary, spread the doctrine of the greatness of every individual soul. The Naturalistic theatre was an advocate of social reform. Even our present-day theatre, which has concentrated so much effort on rising above propaganda to the plane of art, has never given up the effort to influence mankind through what Gordon Craig once called "the inspiration exhaling from its beauty."

These efforts did not come to an end in the twentieth century. In fact, as the stage began to reach ever larger audiences, and as cinema and radio became a necessity for millions of people, the propagandist importance of theatre reached levels never known before. The cleavage between nationalist states, the conflict in interests between capital and labor, the distress caused by economic failure, gave added occasion for the use of theatre as outright propaganda. It is not surprising that the Soviet revolution, one of the severest conflicts of this century, should have made the claim that "Theatre is a weapon." Soviet theatre not only declared openly that it was a weapon in the war of thought; it insisted that, as a proletarian theatre, it was replying in kind to the "capitalist propaganda" of the theatres of other countries.

Whatever might be the merits of this contention, there is no doubt that partisan propaganda had become the order of the day, and not only in Soviet Russia. Theatres which were outspokenly agitational sprang into existence all over the world, from America to the Far East. Propagandist drama did not care, at first, whether it was artistic. What was important was the fact that theatre was once more speaking to its audiences about matters of vital concern.

One might suppose that such a development, as vehement as it was widespread, would mean the end of the drama as an art. That from now on any further discussion of the art of the theatre would be superfluous. In short, that after three thousand years Dionysus was finally and irrevocably dead.

But in fact the theatre as an art did not come to an end. Instead the art of the theatre turned out to be one of the most important problems with which propagandist drama was obliged to deal.

The story of the Soviet stage is one of continuous struggle over questions of artistic form. The building of a new artistic form for its theatre is an official part of the Soviet program—not for abstract artistic reasons, but to increase its effectiveness as propaganda. By 1936 the problem had become so severe that it was illustrated by a whole series of "incidents" in which leading theatre people were involved.

Just as significant was the brief but important cycle of political stage productions in Germany before Hitler. Purely agitational at first, they began by deliberately rejecting the art of the theatre. But the moment this political theatre turned its back on dramatic art as already known, it had to start creating a new art of the theatre on the spot. Even more striking is the fact that this theatre, which started out as fervently partisan, in the end affirmed the need for a kind of drama which would be based not on wishes but on impartial facts.

Other countries have witnessed the birth of stridently class-conscious theatres which, in a short time, lost their "agitprop" outlines and began to find their normal place in progressive stage activity throughout the world.

In sum, we have a two-fold direction in modern drama. The older theatre gradually returns from abstract art to a recognition of the needs of its audiences. The newer theatre moves from the level of topical propaganda to that of enduring art. The older finds that art flowers only when it deals with life. The newer theatre sees that propaganda is effective in proportion as it turns into art.

Perhaps we may hope, then, that the time is coming nearer when the experience of both theatres may become the basis of a theatre of the future. The present writer is not interested in cramming art down the throats of propagandists, nor propaganda down the throats of artists. He asks no one to kneel before the high, thin flame of beauty; neither does he ask anyone to worship a steam shovel. But he does make a plea for calm reasoning—if not tolerance—on both sides. He feels that the adherents of each viewpoint have something to learn and that, in the best interests of the American theatre and its public, they ought to learn it.

The more conservative section of our American theatre, annoyed by the radical propaganda of left-wing drama, has not fully appreciated the amount of artistry that has made its appearance as a by-product, so to speak, of the activities of the newer drama. The more radical theatres, intent on their "message," have tended to lose sight of the fact that content cannot exist without artistic form. They have tended to neglect the problem of form, expecting it to take care of itself.

But form does not arrive spontaneously. Neither does it arrive automatically to express a new message. *Form must be created.*

UNDER FIRE

In recent years the content of drama has received a great deal of attention. In this book we shall ask ourselves whether it is possible to create an adequate new form.

At first glance the times seem anything but favorable. The dangers that require us to build a new stage form are a threat to the future of the stage itself. For the second time in less than twenty-five years Europe is plunged into a "total war." Political storms, of which no one can see the outcome, now rage in the United States.

Never very secure economically, the world's commercial playhouses see grave financial difficulties ahead. The smaller, more experimental dramatic groups look to a future even more precarious. Moreover the time has come when any theatre, great or small, which displeases a particular jack-in-office, will face political persecution.

Thus the most important experimental theatre of western

Europe, the Epic theatre of pre-Hitler Germany, was censored, wrecked financially and finally suppressed. Even Soviet theatres, frankly devoted to propaganda, are under the handicap of keeping pace with the Soviet's continual changes in foreign policy. Elsewhere in Europe those courageous theatres which took the welfare of their audiences seriously, have been wiped out by Nazi conquests or local legislation.

In this type of activity the present German regime is entitled to claim first place, the destruction of the world-famous German liberal and working class theatres having been carried out by a policy of expropriation, terror and exile. It was this regime, also, which perfected the method of destroying progressive theatres under cover of an anti-Semitic campaign, a technique which has been emulated in other countries in Europe.

Still another contribution to theatre-wrecking has now been made in the United States, where our own Congress put an end to the very promising Federal Theatre, whose artistic contributions had been hailed by public and critics alike. Although this was done under cover of a hue and cry over "economy," its real object was political retaliation against the New Deal. Local politicians in different parts of the country have also lent their aid in illegally censoring new kinds of plays whose views do not match their own.

It is clear that if the theatre goes on to perform its vital functions it will not remain unmolested. It will not have the freedom to carry out its experiments on their own merits. Honesty and talent, in fact, are not at all sufficient to guarantee the eventual triumph of a new theatre in our age.

Nor should we overlook the backward pull inside theatre itself. Bad plays and bad movies have had their effect. The present generally low standard of commercial theatre and film tends to set up a corresponding standard in playgoers and in theatre workers. This is an inertia not easy to overcome. We may remember that a new dramatic form is a matter of slow growth. At least two centuries elapsed between the Medieval Church drama and the theatre of the Renaissance. It took the English Moralities a century and a half to flower in the dramas of Shakespeare. Between the Roman stage and the earliest examples of Church drama the theatre lay moribund for nine or ten centuries.

To list all these difficulties, however, is only to show all the more clearly that our theatre must take steps to restore itself to full vigor. Theatre is under fire. But in this ordeal it may find all the strength it needs.

Theatre has always managed to exist in spite of economic insecurity. It is not going through political storms for the first time, either. It will weather those of today, as it did those of the past, even though the present ones are unprecedented in their violence. In the long run the reason for the immortality of theatre is the need of its audiences. Today's audiences need the theatre as never before.

It is true that theatre has never before been "big business," but it will know how to live down even that experience. There may be a small Broadway trade which is satisfied to let its theatres run down until they become utterly futile. But even among the most incorrigible first-nighters there is plenty of healthy judgment left. As for those millions of workers and lower middle class who have entered the world theatre as a new audience since 1900—not even decades of seeing bad movies have convinced them altogether that good drama begins where vital ideas leave off. (Even many Hollywood producers no longer have that conviction.)

We have stressed danger quite enough. It is possible to stress it too much. Let us not forget that the crisis which threatens our playhouses at the same time promises a marvelous rebirth of theatre. A theatre which devotes itself fully to its audiences in the days to come may yet turn into that theatre whose beauty, power and truth once appeared to us in a vision.

Theatre is immortal. Once we could affirm that lyrically. Now it is a dramatic affirmation.

NOTES

1. According to the 1938 Hayes Office report there were some 85 million motion picture admissions per week in the United States and Canada alone.

2. Buckley's translation of Aristotle's *Poetics* reads: "Through pity and fear effecting a purification from such like passions." This is varied significantly by S. H. Butcher in his *Aristotle's Theory of Poetry and*

Fine Art: "Through pity and fear effecting a proper purgation of these emotions." See Chapter IX, Note 10.

REFERENCES

Sheldon Cheney: *The Theatre, Three Thousand Years of Drama, Acting and Stagecraft.* Tudor Publishing Company, New York, 1935. By permission of Longmans, Green & Company, New York.

Joseph Wood Krutch: *The American Drama Since 1918.* Random House, New York, 1939.

Theodore Buckley: *Aristotle's "The Poetic."* From Barrett H. Clark: *European Theories of the Drama.* Appleton, New York, 1926.

S. H. Butcher: *Aristotle's Theory of Poetry and Fine Art.* Macmillan, New York, 1907.

1

ON STAGE

PLAY AND PRODUCTION

A PLAY, according to William Archer, one of the outstanding dramatic critics of the past generation, is "a ship destined to be launched in a given element, the theatre." In Archer's metaphor the dramatic script is something which comes to the theatre. The widespread tendency now is to consider the theatre as something which is placed at the service of the script. Thus in his informative book, *The Stage Is Set,* Lee Simonson arrives at the conclusion that the progress of theatre must wait upon the dramatist. "In the modern theatre, as in every other, the beginning is in the word."

There is even the implication that the forces of production, as distinguished from the script, must be looked upon as a threat to the integrity of drama itself. Mrs. Anita Block, in *The Changing World in Plays and Theatre,* declares:

> *Theatre-consciousness* is the condition of being entranced by the glamour and by the often spurious trappings of the theatre—such as clever acting, smart dialogue, dazzling costumes and effective scenery—into a drugged indifference to the values of the play content. *Play-consciousness* is the condition of being critically alive, in the theatre, to the play as literature. . . . Once a theatre-goer has developed play-consciousness he can never be deceived in the theatre again.

It is curious that this tendency in dramatic theory should now be current in a type of theatre which, when it was younger, insisted that "the Art of the Theatre is neither acting nor the play, it is not scene nor dance, but it consists of all the elements of which these things are composed." (Gordon Craig, 1905). But in fact few present-day American critics are as extreme in their views on this problem as are Lee Simonson or Mrs. Block. It is still generally affirmed that theatre is something bigger than the playscript. "The play's the thing—in the library," says John Mason Brown.[1]

Still, however widely this may be understood in theory, it is just as commonly disregarded in practice. Current dramatic reviews and books on drama are overwhelmingly concerned with the playscript alone. In practice the fundamental belief is simply that dramatic production exists to illustrate a story written by a dramatist (even though it is quite possible that in the process the story may be drastically altered).

It is supposed that theatre begins at some such point as when Maxwell Anderson, having written MARY OF SCOTLAND, sells it to the Theatre Guild for production. The Theatre Guild executive board then meditates: "This is a romantic historical play of a certain calibre. How can it best be transposed to the stage? Obviously by getting Theresa Helburn to direct, Helen Hayes to play Mary, and Robert Edmond Jones to design the settings." And there is no doubt that this was what happened. The Theatre Guild subscribers and the press critics went to the opening night of a play which consisted of a dramatic story concerning Mary Stuart; a story written by Maxwell Anderson and interpreted by a director, stage star and scene designer, as well as by a large supporting cast.

Still we must be permitted some doubts whether the fact that this happened in any way *proves* that dramatic production consists of the staging of a script. It is comparatively easy to think of the dramatic process beginning with the writing of a play. This chronological order, however, is not sufficiently chronological. Before the dramatist can write a play for the theatre, the theatre has to be there. And not only a theatre in the abstract but a very particular kind of theatre—the theatre of the playwright's own epoch.

What comes first, the dramatist's script or the forces of theatre in general? Can it be said that the script alone is truly creative, while the other elements of production are "interpretive"? What is the value of such a distinction? Or is it of no more pressing importance than the question of which came first: the chicken or the egg?

It happens to be a question of great theoretical and practical importance whether the script alone is creative while the other factors of production are interpretive.

The belief that the script alone enters upon new paths, while the other elements of production must wait upon the script because they are "interpretive" has been set forth by Lee Simonson:

> . . . the development of scene-designing as an art must wait upon the arrival, in sufficient numbers, of dramatic poets capable of interpreting life profoundly. Until they appear the scene-designer, whatever his graphic gifts may be, can do little more than mark time. . . . As designers we cannot perform the functions of dramatic poets, but once they enter the theatre we are their indispensable collaborators. We cannot call them forth. It is they who must summon us. Meanwhile we wait and work.

Is the theatre really obliged to wait until the dramatist makes up his mind to change it? Is it only the dramatist who can initiate progress in the theatre? Is it true, as those who think always in terms of playscripts assert: "It is the dramatist who brings about changes, for he calls for innovations which the actors, designers and directors hasten to supply"?

The truth is that all the elements of theatrical production are creative. We have no right to put any of them in an uncreative category. The progressive theatre must make progress in all its branches.

The overwhelming importance attached at present to the factor of the script—at the expense of the other factors—is due to a special condition in the production methods of Broadway and Hollywood. Here production usually revolves around the playscript. The script is the center of the theatre's economic set-up, and productions are assembled by the "casting-office" method. That is to say, the productive forces are assembled temporarily for a specific play, after which they are disbanded.

This method, considered in the light of theatre history, is a radical change in the customary manner of production. It happens to be an injurious change.

THE STORY ON STAGE

The true relationship of the playscript to production is hidden from us today because of certain conditions peculiar to our theatre. These conditions prevail in the Broadway theatre especially.

The Broadway dramatist, unlike his predecessors (who were

usually associated with theatrical companies) as a rule does his work separately. To all appearances he is an independent craftsman who writes his plays in the seclusion of his own study (if he is an established success; in the reading room of a public library if he is rather less fortunate). The product of his labor is thrown on the play-market, where it may be bought by any one of a score of producing managers or producing organizations. As soon as a manager decides on a script and has the necessary funds, the director, designer, actors and technical people are called in. It therefore looks as if dramatic activity always begins with a number of typewritten pages.

But in fact the dramatist's script grows out of the whole apparatus of the theatre as it is available in his own day. More than that, it grows out of the living individual talents available in his own day.

Tradition has it that, over two thousand years ago, Sophocles composed his dramas with the particular talents of his acting company in mind. Shakespeare, on strong evidence, is held to have done the same. The process can be followed today in the work of such a dramatist as Clifford Odets, who, by way of exception to the modern rule, is associated with a definite producing unit, the Group Theatre. When he sets to work on a play Odets can, and does, estimate to a nicety what material the Group has in the way of actors, directors, designers and technical resources; and so he shapes his play.

This does not mean that his talent is hampered. If anything his script becomes weighted with all the talent in the Group. He can work without compulsion but rather with inspiration, to shape a Papa Bonaparte upon the framework of Morris Carnovsky's acting, or a Steve Takis upon the acting possibilities of Elia Kazan. And even if he works at first with other prototypes in mind, he must be prepared to do definite cutting and fitting of the rôles to the actors when the parts are cast. The process of writing a play by no means ends when a manager accepts a script. It is a task which continues far into rehearsals.

This is true whether or not a dramatist is attached to any special producing organization. No experienced (or even inexperienced) dramatist who is honest with himself will deny that every one of his scripts contains memories of specific performances he has witnessed. Often he requires the services of a certain actor or actress whom he "saw" in the part from the first draft of the play. In professional parlance, a rôle may be a Lionel Barrymore part, a Helen Hayes, Ina Claire or George M. Cohan part. The dramatist may or may not visualize his setting as Jo Mielziner would visualize

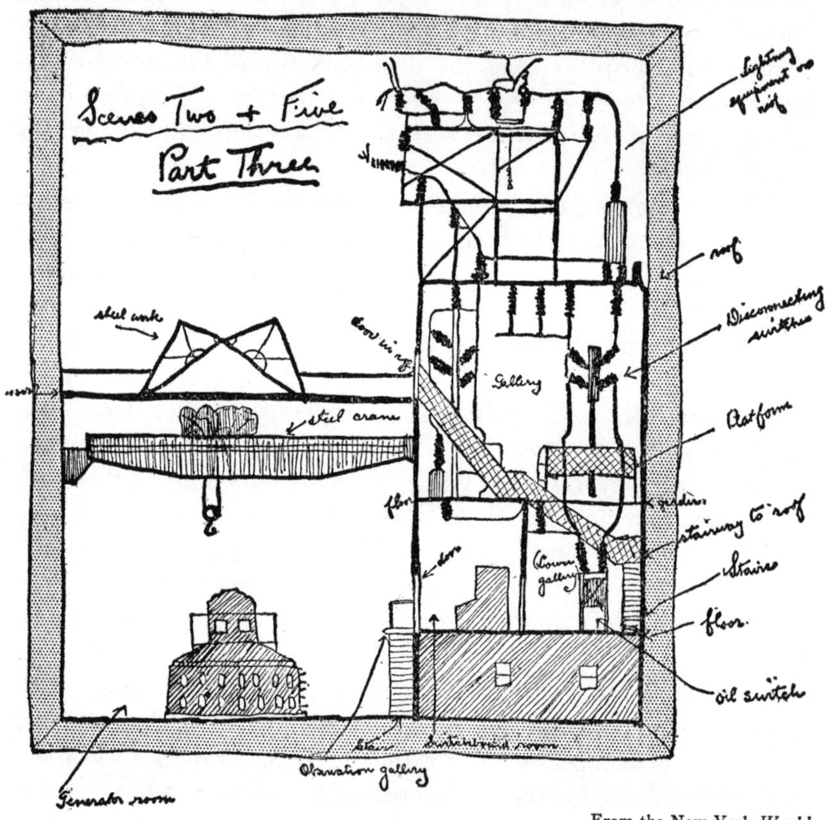

From the New York *World*

DYNAMO (1929)

Drawing by Eugene O'Neill

it; but like Mielziner he would depend upon a technical apparatus which the twentieth century has made available to the theatre, knowing that he can call upon types of plastic form, color and light whose possibilities already exist. What a dramatist writes or does not write may even depend upon the sound equipment which he finds in the theatre:

In a memorandum sent by Eugene O'Neill to the Theatre Guild shortly before his play DYNAMO went into rehearsal, the dramatist wrote: "I cannot stress too emphatically the importance of starting early in rehearsals to get these [sound] effects exactly right. . . . This is a machine age which one would like to express as a background for lives in plays in overtones of characteristic, impelling and governing mechanical sound and rhythm—but how can one, unless a corresponding mechanical perfection in the theatre is a reliable string of the instrument (the theatre as a whole) on which one composes?" (*The Stage Is Set*).

Still more, the dramatist's choice of theme and his treatment of that theme are determined by existing theatrical producers. Dramatists write with the expectation of interesting not just the play-market in general, but specifically George Abbott, the Theatre Guild, Guthrie McClintic, the Playwrights' Producing Company or the Group Theatre. The mere existence of the Group Theatre, for example, causes certain types of plays to be composed which would not otherwise be written. On the other hand, some plays even if independently written would never become stage realities did not an organization exist which was willing to give them life. Sklar and Peters' STEVEDORE (1934), written in the spirit of the workers' theatre movement, remained a sheaf of paper untouched until a newly created organization, the Theatre Union, turned it into a stage success.

If the chronology of production is one apparent reason for the overwhelming emphasis on the script on Broadway, a more solid reason is the economic value of the script. The script, more than any other element, more even than the high-priced star, is the cornerstone of commercial theatre enterprise. It is the script in which the producer invests primarily, for which he gathers his financial and artistic resources and from which he hopes to profit on Broadway and in Hollywood.[2]

Audiences, it is too often forgotten, go to the theatre to see a *show*. This means that, among the things which the spectator goes to see is a Group Theatre cast, a setting by Donald Oenslager, the direction of Lee Strasberg or a solo performance by Katharine Cornell or by Paul Robeson.

It is true at the same time that the spectator is mentally prepared always for a *story* which will take place on the stage. Even revues and burlesque shows are accustomed to have a story, however flimsy, upon which the comic scenes and vaudeville acts are strung together. A story, or at least the rudiments of one, seems to be essential.

Still this fact does not settle the matter. The important question for us is not whether a story is essential to theatre, but whether it *is* theatre. Whether the whole significance of stage production consists in transferring a story to the stage without "hurting" it; or whether the story is no more than an important ingredient of something which, on the stage, becomes more than a story—something which turns into that ceremony, that composite of many art forms, which we call theatre.

THIS TOO, TOO SOLID FLESH

We have seen that in theory—but not in practice—most critics grant that the dramatic performance is something different from, something more than, the playscript which it contains. The performance does not illustrate a script; rather, the script is imbedded in the performance. How do these critics define a dramatic story?

What constitutes a story to some people's notions is not a story to others'. There was a time when a study of private emotions, as the *Sturm und Drang* period saw them, was not a story to the classicists who understood only objective behavior in stage characters. When the Expressionists set to work, audiences accustomed to Naturalistic plots saw no story in the stream-of-consciousness pattern of the newer writers. The plays of Brecht and Piscator were not stories in the opinion of those who did not like politics on the stage. No doubt a well-presented account of drop-forging, which might seem intensely dramatic to some people, would not be considered a story by others.

Again, it becomes evident that a story in its literary form cannot be the same as a story in its form on the stage. The moment the story appears in the theatre it becomes subject to the laws of the theatrical world. A chair has to be placed on the stage. What kind of chair? And where to place it? The stage must be lit up. What kind of light? How much of it, from what direction? Shall it be constant, or shall it change from time to time? At once the story, as such, gives way to more immediate problems, more immediate in a theatrical sense.

There are, of course, certain people who are undeterred by logic and who will hang on like grim death to the belief that the theatre is the script and nothing but the script. In 1908 the Russian dramatist Sologub, who seems to have had the courage of his convictions, called for the elimination of the actor from the theatre. Instead of actors there would be a reader who would sit quietly in some remote corner of the stage reciting the lines of the play. As a sop to those not yet ready for this conception of theatre, the curtain might rise and reveal some actors going through the motions called for in the script.[3]

Eleanora Duse and Gordon Craig also expressed, irascibly, the desire to rid the stage of actors. Finding the human actor too unreliable a medium, Craig wanted to replace him with an Über-marionette, or puppet figure of a superior type. He quoted Duse as follows:

> To save the theatre the theatre must be destroyed, the actors and actresses must all die of the plague. . . . They make art impossible.

During the 1937–38 Broadway season there appeared three successful plays—the Mercury Theatre's JULIUS CAESAR and THE CRADLE WILL ROCK, and OUR TOWN, presented by Jed Harris—in which there was a minimum of scenery or which had stage walls showing. Immediately it was declared that these "no-scenery" shows proved that scenery and scene designers are really an encumbrance to the plays in which they are used. They, too, should be abolished.

A peculiar kind of idealism governs these theories. They stem from the notion that theatre consists of a priceless soul (the script) and a mere body (the production). As Brown expresses it,

> Great plays are great for other reasons than that they are adapted to the stage. They soar above its physical limitations as the spirit transcends the body.

The process of production is regarded as an ordeal through which the playscript is obliged to pass. If the script is fortunate it escapes with comparatively little hurt and can give its message to the audience with almost virginal purity. Freed of the production-mechanism the theatre would be carried back to the paradise of its alleged beginnings in the Word.

There is little ground, however, for the contention that the theatre began with the Word: science has established that gesture came before language. It has also become customary to state that "the origin of tragedy lies in the dithyramb sung in honor of Dionysus." (Nicoll), as if dramatic action followed literature. In reality the dramatic poet was a late comer who added the element of playwriting to a dramatic ritual that was already ancient, one that already included the elements of dance, gesture, music, costume and setting.

Speaking before the International Theatre Congress of the Royal Italian Academy in Rome, 1934, the fascist theoretician Silvio D'Amico declared:

> The theatre's sole salvation can come through the Poet . . . from him who shall recapture and speak the Word.[4]

But even the weight of such authority is not enough to sustain the belief that "the beginning is in the word." Such a belief is in fact a *reductio ad absurdum* of the nineteenth-century tradition of literary dramatic criticism. It is not shared by more temperate theorists.

> Drama is a transliteration of the Greek δρᾶμα, which means a thing done; theatre is a transliteration of the Greek θέατρον, which means a seeing-place. The word audience, meaning those who listen, is derived from the Latin and therefore represents a later idea of play-going. From this use of two Greek words and one Latin a useful hint is given us as to the first dramatic values. Drama begins with action and spectacle; the deed comes before the word, the dance before the dialogue, the play of body before the play of mind. The audience is subsequent to the spectators. (Ivor Brown: *Drama, Encyclopaedia Britannica,* 1938).

> Aristotle maintained that action, not character, is the basic ingredient of drama, and that "Character comes in as a subsidiary to the actions." This is very widely accepted as one of the cornerstones of technical theory. George Pierce Baker says, "History shows indisputably that drama, in its beginnings, no matter where we look, depended most on action." Gordon Craig, rebelling against the wordy theatre of the nineteen hundreds, says that "the father of the dramatist was the dancer." Brander Matthews says: "A wise critic once declared that the skeleton of a good play is a pantomime." (John Howard Lawson: *Theory and Technique of Playwriting*).

Technically considered, the value of a good playscript lies in the fact that it functions on the stage. Otherwise what distinguishes it from any other printed literature? A good script is *stageworthy*, or it is not a good script. The author of a good script knows his way around a stage either by experience or by insight. The playscript is essentially a chart, a definition, of stage action, meaning that it defines something which already exists. It was in this way that Aeschylus constructed upon the ritual of Dionysus. It was in this way that Molière constructed upon the Commedia dell' Arte.

Few laymen understand that, on the stage, dialogue is no substitute for action. Stage dialogue has dramatic worth only when it is another form of action, when it is muted action. Even so, muted, spoken action of this sort is comparatively rare (George Bernard Shaw is one of the few masters of this art). As a rule dialogue functions as a kind of libretto for the stage action.

SARDOUDLEDOM

The phenomenon of the *well-made play* requires a note of its own. It is taken for granted today that the highly exciting, carefully geared dramatic story is an eternal aspect of theatre. Compression in dramatic writing is of course an ancient phenomenon. It did not always have its present deftness. The main outlines of scripts from the Greeks until long after Shakespeare were often impressively unified and logical; but few indeed were without digressions, interpolations and other ragged ends. Our contemporary ideal in expert playmaking does not really go back beyond the dramatist Eugène Scribe (1791–1861).[5]

It was this French classicist who, finding the playscripts of the past as loose in structure as they were solid in ideas, established a veritable technology of dramatic writing. Scribe turned the dramatic story into a well-oiled machine, and then proceeded to bring plays by the hundreds off the assembly-lines. No idea, great or small, could fail to achieve dramatic form from now on if the Scribe machine was properly used. Hollywood might well erect a monument to this pioneer and forebear, who worked with story-originators, dialogue men and gag men. His formula of the well-made play was further perfected by his successors, the younger Alexandre Dumas and Victorien Sardou.

It seems peculiar that a dramatic device of such proven worth could be the object of attack by theatre people. It is true that Scribe and Sardou applied their technique to trivial themes, like many dramatists of our own period. History has already judged adversely the plays which they turned out. Yet there is nothing about the well-made play itself which makes it a menace to clarity or honesty in the theatre. Why, then, did the Naturalistic theatre, in the latter part of the nineteenth century, find the well-made play so reprehensible? It was attacked by Ibsen, labeled "Sardoudledom" by Shaw. As recently as 1938 Shaw declared that "Plot has always been the curse of serious drama, and indeed of serious literature of any kind." Yet Ibsen and Shaw are both expert play-builders on occasion. Since the first World War the well-built play has come under the fire of the Epic theatre. Why?

Because it lends itself readily and effectively to the dramatization of meretricious ideas as well as of creative ones. Without its help the colossal amount of trash turned out by the less scrupulous showmen of Broadway and Hollywood would be impossible. Curiously enough the well-made play, which was originally repudiated by the Naturalists, has since become one of the bulwarks of the contemporary Naturalist-Symbolist theatre of *illusion.*

THE CHANGING FACE OF THEATRE

Here we must pause to define a few terms.

Dramatic historians of the past half-century have made careless use of certain terms. One of these is the word *realism;* another is the word *illusion.* The meaning of "realism," as used theatrically, has become especially confused. It has been used as a synonym for Naturalism, but at the same time has been stretched to such lengths (everything from "Romantic realism" to "Socialist realism") that it can no longer be regarded as synonymous with Naturalism.

In the present book the term realism will not be used to denote any theatrical style. It will designate outer reality—life outside the theatre. Any theatrical style will therefore be called realistic in so far as it tends to approach and examine the realities which exist in life outside the theatre. By this standard, therefore, a fantasy like Ibsen's PEER GYNT may conceivably be more realistic than a Naturalistic play like Sidney Kingsley's DEAD END.

The word *illusion* has also acquired a confused meaning. However, it has a definite technical meaning, and will be used throughout this book in this technical sense. Illusion is defined herewith as one of the two dominant technical methods employed by the theatre, the alternative method being that of *convention.*

The illusory method is one which attempts, fundamentally, to deceive the senses of the audience. It tries to convince the spectator that the stage events which he is witnessing are not really events on the stage having a sequence planned by stage workers, but that they are rather a series of natural or phenomenal events unrelated to the stage and viewed by spectators in a theatre as if by accident.

Thus, if the scene of Terence Ratigan's FRENCH WITHOUT TEARS (1937) is "Monsieur Maingot's villa in a small seaside town in the south of France," the illusory technique bends every effort toward making the spectator believe he is actually looking into the interior of a certain villa located at that very moment on the French Riviera. The spectator must also be made to believe that the actor playing the rôle of M. Maingot is not an actor at all, but M. Maingot himself. The Broadway producers of the play will feel their work artistically rewarded if the spectator at the end of an act is obliged to shake himself out of the conviction that he is inside a French villa, so that he can go for a smoke in the lobby of a New York theatre.

If, on the basis of the definition here given, the production method of today is illusory, it may be that the production method of tomorrow will be non-illusory. It may be that dramatic form right now is starting on one of its historic transitions toward a new goal, leaving the era of Maxwell Anderson and Noel Coward behind it as a memory. There is some reason to believe that at this moment the theatre stands at one of the most important crossroads on its long journey out of the past.

In the past the characteristics of stage production, the whole face of the theatre has sometimes altered beyond recognition from one era to the next. Today the theatre seems about to change once more.

For these reasons it is not an academic question just what part the playscript has in the dynamics of the stage.

"CREATIVE VERSUS INTERPRETIVE"

Is it true that the playscript must be regarded as an original piece of creative work while the other elements of stage production are merely "interpretive"? It is not true. There is no objective basis for the belief that only the script is creative and that the acting, the direction, the setting, must all draw their breath of life from the script.

How often have we not seen scripts without life, scripts which are mere echoes and imitations of previous productions! Such play-scripts are occasionally brought to life by superb performances of actors whose every gesture transcends the play. How often a setting creates a dramatic statement of which the play itself is incapable! How often does not a director take a lifeless script and make it live, to some degree at least, on the stage!

Shakespeare borrowed practically every one of the plots of his plays. Does that make him only an "interpreter"? Nowhere does more "borrowing" of this sort go on than in the drama. Down through the ages playwrights have not hesitated to lift plots, situations or scenes from other dramatic works. William Winter remarks that

> Several of Shakespeare's plays were based by him on plays of earlier date, by other authors. Dryden borrowed freely from Spanish plays and sometimes from Corneille and Molière—a fact which caused Scott to remark (Preface to "The Assignation") that "originality consists in the mode of treating a subject more than in the subject itself." English dramatists, from Wycherly onward, have freely borrowed from Molière. Fielding, there is reason to believe, derived an occasional hint from the great Frenchman, as also from Thomas Murphy. Goldsmith was a little indebted to Wycherly. Hoadley borrowed from Farquhar; Steele from Bickerstaff; Colman from Murphy; Sheridan from both Wycherly and Congreve, and perhaps from his mother's play of "The Discovery" and her novel of "Sidney Biddulph"; Boucicault from many French sources and some English ones.

Many of our contemporary dramatists make a point of not borrowing consciously from any previously known dramatic situation. Does that make them necessarily creative as compared with Shakespeare?

In the course of an article on the principles of directing, the Russian director B. E. Zakhava makes some interesting observations on the question of "creative versus interpretive":

> By what standards then does the work of the actor and director become creative work? The director and the actor work on the basis

of the material given them by the dramatist; this latter in itself does not in any sense or degree lessen their right to create. There is no art where the artist creates out of thin air. Every artist uses that cultural heritage which has accumulated in his particular field. He must inevitably profit by this accumulation in his art. More than this we know that, in the history of art, great artists have created their finest masterpieces by using the work of their predecessors. For instance, it is well known that Shakespeare wrote HAMLET on the framework of a Scandinavian saga preserved in the vaults of the Danish scholar Saxo Grammaticus and revised before Shakespeare by Belleforest and Thomas Kyd. It is also no news that Ostrovsky often borrowed plots from the French comedies. This does not in any way lessen our admiration for Shakespeare or Ostrovsky.

What is wrong with something being "interpretive"? The script itself is interpretive of the other theatrical elements; its story carries along and makes understandable to the average spectator certain nuances of acting or setting which he might not otherwise appreciate. HAMLET and KING LEAR provide great actors with adequate means of expression. From this point of view these plays are "vehicles," in a good sense, for actors of superior calibre.

A great script, like a great rôle or a great scene design, is a valuable achievement. The script has a leading function, moreover, above that of the other elements of production, because it is a *chart* of production, it rallies the forces of production. (Unlike the other factors, also, it is comparatively imperishable in the form of the printed word.) This leading function is an important privilege of the script; but it is a quality which must not be confused with creativeness.

The playwright, like all the other workers in the theatre, has done his share to change the character of the theatre even as he worked in it. Aeschylus is generally known today only for his plays; but his plays were only one department of his dramatic activities. More than a playwright he was a creator of stage form. He is said to have supervised personally the training of his choruses, for whom he devised dances and designed costumes. He is credited with having given definitive form to the strange costume of the Greek tragic actor. It was Aeschylus who cut down the length of the choral odes, stressed dialogue instead and introduced a second actor—changes which transformed the archaic Dionysian ritual into "an essentially dramatic species of art." Like Aeschylus, Sophocles and Euripides also took part actively in the definition of Attic stage form.

Closer to our own times we have the examples of Goethe, Wagner, Victor Hugo, Strindberg and Zola, who were all vehement partisans of scenic reform. They realized that the problems of dramaturgy could not be separated from the other problems of production.

Many dramatists of our own period have been aware of the need for changes in theatrical form. Among American playwrights Eugene O'Neill has been one of the most restless of scenic innovators, calling upon techniques which ranged from Naturalism to Expressionism (as in THE HAIRY APE, 1922) and Constructivism (as in DYNAMO, 1929). In a whole cycle of his plays the actors were called upon to don masks, as in THE HAIRY APE, THE GREAT GOD BROWN (1926), THE RIME OF THE ANCIENT MARINER (1924), LAZARUS LAUGHED (1926). John Howard Lawson has been equally protean in style, from Symbolism in SUCCESS STORY (1932) and GENTLEWOMAN (1934), to Expressionism in ROGER BLOOMER (1923), Theatricalism in PROCESSIONAL (1925) and Constructivism in LOUDSPEAKER (1927).

Beginning with ON TRIAL (1914), Elmer Rice turned to a play-construction of staccato "flash-back" scenes instead of the previous convention of three or four acts. Plays of twelve or more scenes are now a commonplace on modern stages, necessitating new systems of stage mechanics, scene shifting and designing. Marc Connelly, Sidney Howard, George Sklar, Marc Blitzstein, Martin Flavin, Irwin Shaw, Sidney Kingsley, Arnold Sundgaard, are other American dramatists who have shown an active interest in technique. Indeed it can be said that every dramatist who has written more than one play has found it necessary to have definite views on the matter, and to make his wishes known. Contemporary playwrights, like those of the past, have left their impress upon the stage conventions which they found, changing the fate of these conventions.

The privilege of introducing new methods to the theatre is one which attaches to original talents, not to any one department of production. Playwrights can be conservative as well as radical, conformist as well as independent, in their attitude toward style. None of the Attic dramatists, for example, saw anything about the *deus ex machina* which required correction. To bring a god down from Olympus at the end of a rope in order to disentangle a plot seemed a perfectly valid method for centuries, even though it was denounced by Aristotle. For centuries also the Renaissance dramatists adhered slavishly to the supposed "laws" embodied in the Three Unities of Aristotle's *Poetics*. Playwrights like Corneille even boasted of their ability to conform to the Unities. The Bacchanal of Wagner's TANNHÄUSER owes its existence to the fact that, for the Paris Opera performance in 1861 the composer was obliged to write in something approximating a ballet number, which was then considered indispensable in the second act of an opera. (It should be added that Wagner did this as a compromise, after flatly refusing to include a regular ballet.)

In periods of stagnancy in the theatre the dramatists also seem to lose interest in style. It is enough to glance at Broadway at present to see how few of the well-known playwrights are showing more than a languid interest in the development of style. As concerns scenery, few of them will think it a very vital matter even if the producer of their plays orders settings from hack commercial studios.

In the course of history we come regularly upon periods when the initiative was in hands other than those of the dramatist. The eras of the artistic ascendency of the script have been few and far between in the course of more than twenty-five centuries of production. Such periods can be numbered on the fingers of one hand: the Attic theatre; the Baroque theatre of France, Spain and England; the Elizabethan theatre; the Romantic theatre; the Naturalistic theatre of the late nineteenth century. Theatre has managed to flourish for centuries with the merest rudiments of a script, or with no script at all.

> But in past times there were eras when story and poetry weighed heaviest, others when spectacles and trick-effects alone satisfied the audiences; and still others when a vigorous show of virtuoso acting was the *clou* of stage art. . . . In a period covering the late seventeenth and most of the eighteenth century, acting was one of the most conspicuous elements in the theatre's activity, and the only element around which a history of the playhouses of the time could be written. Dramatists of world significance are not met with in France for a long time after Molière, nor in Spain after Calderon, nor in England after Dryden; and Germany won't bring forward any contribution till the star of Goethe and Schiller rises a century hence. (Cheney: *The Theatre*).

In the Greek theatre of the fifth century B. C. it was the dramatic poet who was predominant; but the following century was the age of great actors, and for many centuries thereafter the Hellenic theatres remained important institutions while served by poor dramatists. In the Roman theatre the dramatist was an obscure figure, while the whole life of theatre ran in spectacles, gladiatorial combats and sea-fights staged in the great arenas. The court theatres of the Italian and French Renaissance held their audiences less with the work of the dramatists than with the work of technicians like Sebastiano Serlio, Nicola Sabbattini, Leone de' Somi, Leonardo da Vinci, Giacomo Torelli, Gaspare Vigarani, Léon Mahelot, Burnacini and Mantegna. In the same era the Italian street theatres—the Commedia dell' Arte—and the Comedians who were its French counterpart, were devoted completely to actors—Pasquati, Scala, Fiorillo, Riccoboni, Tommasino, Dominique, Turlupin, Gros-Guillaume, Gautier-Garguille, Tabarin. These players had a huge following although they worked only with rags and tags of plots planned by themselves, with most of the dialogue invented on the spur of the moment. The entire European stage, as Cheney points out, gave first place to the actor throughout the eighteenth century and far into the nineteenth; such names as Adrienne Lecouvreur, David Garrick, Sarah Siddons, John Philip Kemble, Talma, Edmund Kean, Ludwig Devrient, Tommaso Salvini, Eleanora Duse, Rachel, Réjane, Sarah Bernhardt, represented theatre to theatre audiences, even more than did the name of any dramatist.

Opera belongs first of all to the composers; ballet to the dancers. The nineteenth century saw the emergence of professional directors like Saxe-Meiningen, Antoine, Brahm and others, to whom the authority of the dramatist is now subordinated. In the period just before and after the War scene designers like Adolphe Appia and Gordon Craig moved to the forefront. In this way from time to time some element of dramatic production may forge ahead, dragging the other elements, including the playscript, after it.

THE SCRIPT ON STAGE

Few dramatic theorists want to deny all this. They merely assert that in the periods when the script was not predominant the theatre was in a bad way, or at least not up to present standards.

Such theorists should undertake to prove their basic contention. In the meantime we may remain skeptical when we are told that the purity of a script will be harmed by the intrusion of settings or actors.

True enough many of the past periods of the stage are gone never to return; so that we cannot show by actual exhibit that the actors' theatre of the Commedia was a distinguished theatre in its own right, as compared with the dramatists' theatre of Broadway. We can, however, make inferences from more recent examples.

There are, for instance, the examples of the radical theatres in our own day. Following the Soviet revolution the new regime bent every effort to make its theatre an instrument for effective propaganda. One might suppose that without the "spoken word" the new Soviet theatre would be lost. After twenty years the script is still not as brilliant as the other elements in Soviet production. Yet this particular theatre has developed on a gigantic scale and has impressed foreign experts, many of them strongly antipathic to the political views of the Soviets. Nor can it be shown that the comparative lack of experiment of the new Russian scripts has been *caused* by the high standard of the other factors of production.

The productions of Piscator's theatre in Berlin, which brought new life and vigor to the German theatre, had to make use of playscripts which were in most cases makeshift. It was the directing genius of Piscator and the imagination of his designers which, for the most part, created a type of stage form whose influence grows even though its activity in Germany has been suspended.

The American cinema furnishes still another example. Is there anyone who does not know the low level of three-fourths of the Hollywood film scenarios? This is a cruel deficiency. Yet the films cannot be simply dismissed as non-existent. They are a powerful influence on an audience numbered in millions.

And yet, in spite of its great emphasis on scripts, our present system of production really has no genuine solicitude for the script. It is true that a dramatist whose script "goes over" may be fabulously rewarded in royalties from a Broadway run; he may also be hired thereafter by Hollywood to write dialogue at a salary of several thousand dollars per week. This does not alter our conclusion. Broadway and Hollywood, considered as business ventures, are interested in the *business possibilities* of the script, not its cultural excellence. The dramatist is rewarded not for his cultural contribution, but for his sales value. The tale of a movie dramatist who is paid huge sums while his ideas are thrown into the wastebasket is no idle fancy. It is neither unusual nor comic. Difficult as it may be for outsiders to credit, the sincere playwright who is treated in this manner develops a real grievance.

The disregard of some film producers for the writing talent for which they are ready to pay high wages, is too well known to require examples.[6] A dramatist who sells his play to Hollywood is all too often prepared to see the play distorted, perhaps beyond recognition. Harry Alan Potamkin, in his essay *The Eyes of the Movie* gives a number of instances of such distortion. THE TRAIL OF '98, THE COVERED WAGON, CIMARRON, historical pictures conceived by their authors as epic themes, were reduced in their film versions to narratives of attempted rape, "boy meets girl," personal enmity and personal vanity. Theodore Dreiser's AN AMERICAN TRAGEDY became little more than a plot for a murder story. (A circumstance which caused the author to sue, unsuccessfully, the company which had produced the film.) Upton Sinclair's THE MONEYCHANGERS, which named a well-known financier as the cause of the panic of 1907, underwent a film metamorphosis, becoming a melodrama of Chinatown dope traffic. More recently what befell Sean O'Casey's THE PLOW AND THE STARS, Elsie Shauffler's PARNELL, or Remarque's THE ROAD BACK when the movies were through with them, can hardly have satisfied the hopes of the respective dramatists. It is necessary to add, however, that there have been occasions, increasingly frequent, when a novel or a play has been equaled or improved in its movie form, as in GREED, ABE LINCOLN IN ILLINOIS, or THE GRAPES OF WRATH.

The assumption that a script is inviolate is a pedantic one from the point of view of any practical dramatist or director. Every script is a living organism capable of development or adaptation. A play, as all dramatists know, "is not written, but re-written." Ten or more versions are not infrequent before a script receives definitive form. Sometimes the question of which version is the last depends on nothing more sublime than an opening date which has to be met. Drastic re-writing of plays following openings in summer theatre or "out of town" tryouts is common practice in the United States. On Broadway itself, as in ancient Athens, it sometimes happens that a play which fails is rewritten and produced once more.[7]

One of the most professional aspects of a good script is its ability to meet the momentary needs of production. The "Word" of the dramatist when it enters the producer's office is always a fairly tentative word, ready to take account of every kind of accident. It may require changes because a certain actress is not available; because it will be addressed to trade union audiences instead of socialite audiences (something the author may, conceivably, not have anticipated); because the stage of the theatre is not wide enough or the auditorium is too large or too small; because the producer is affluent or poverty-stricken.[8]

Far from handing down his Word on tablets of stone amid thunder over Mount Sinai, the dramatist follows his script into the theatre with a bluepencil handy, and keeps inserting or throwing out lines even after the opening-night curtain.

SCRIPTS THAT ARE EATEN AWAY

The fact that the dramatist is essentially subordinate to production is sometimes a poignant fact, but only in times of weakened theatre. Once institutionalized and rendered stodgy, a theatrical form tends to reduce all dramatic elements, the script included, to its own level. The hardened dramatic form has a tendency to "eat away" any dramaturgy which is foreign to its own nature.

During the inception of the Naturalistic period, plays written in the new style were destroyed by old-style Romantic productions. After three Naturalistic plays had failed at Paris in the established theatres of that day, Antoine, founder of the Naturalistic Théâtre-Libre, wrote to the dramatic critic Sarcey:

> Well, the very simple reason for this three-fold happening in which the actors, as a rule excellent, were judged mediocre for one evening (and for this time only) is that not one of the three works was produced and played according to its true meaning. The fact is that this new (or renewed) drama requires interpreters who are new or renewed. . . . What do you expect will be the fate of a play drawing its effects from life when it is presented in a falsified atmosphere? (Miller).

It must be added that not only new material is stultified when run through an out-of-date theatrical machine. The same thing happens to the classics. It is a truism that the one tragedy greater than HAMLET is the kind of production which HAMLET is usually accorded—a production which that melancholy prince would have used as an object lesson in his famous lecture on the subject of bad theatre.

The "eating away," the blighting of the script by misused forces of dramatic production, comes within the experience of many modern dramatists. Indeed it is this very experience which provides the basis for the mistaken idea that dramatic production, as such, is a menace to the script.

Still it should never be forgotten that the director, the actors, the designer, can be, and often are, equally victimized. For many Broadway designers today Shakespeare consists of a succession of distinguished period interiors. But the fact that a setting for Shakespeare may turn out irrelevant or inadequate is as much the fault of a backward production method as of any particular designer.

THE DRAMATIST ON STAGE

The hiatus which now exists between the work of the dramatist and the work of the other people of the theatre is one result of the radical departure in production method which is practiced by our theatre today. Broadway, except in a few instances, no longer knows the meaning of production by permanent companies. Permanent companies are the genuine tradition, the very life of theatre. In a permanent company the dramatist has his correct place, surrounded by and in daily contact with the other forces of creative theatre. The moment this relationship is abandoned the dramatist's place in production becomes confused.

Simonson inquires:

> Does anyone suppose that if we reconstructed an Elizabethan stage to the last mortise and tennon and baited it like a fox-trap with "tyring-house," an "inner stage" and a "heavens," we would find caught within it one fine morning another Shakespeare or a second Marlowe?

According to this view, dramatists are the only ones who bring freshness to the theatre, and they get it outside. But if ever a dramatist was fashioned by his theatre, it was William Shakespeare, who, as actor and actor-manager, spent almost the whole of his life in stage atmosphere. Molière, like Shakespeare, was a seasoned trouper and hard-working stage manager. All the dramatic poets of the great age of Attic drama were also actors, designers or stage managers.

> During the earlier period of the Athenian drama the principal part in the training and instruction of the chorus was undertaken by the poet himself. . . . The older dramatic writers, such as Thespis, Pratinus, Cratinus, and Phrynichus, were called "dancers," not only because of the prominent part which the chorus and the dancing filled in their plays, but also because they gave instruction in choric dancing. . . . This intimate connexion between the poet and the stage, between the literary and the theatrical part of dramatic production, continued to exist during the great period of Athenian drama. Sophocles appeared personally in some of his plays. In the THAMYRIS he played the harp. In the NAUSICAA he won great applause by the skill with which he played ball in the scene where Nausicaa is sporting with her maidens. Euripides also seems to have superintended the training of his choruses in person, as there is a story in Plutarch which represents him as singing over one of his odes to the choreutae. (A. E. Haigh: *The Attic Theatre*).

The achievements of Shakespeare and Marlowe were part of a dramatic age of great power, part also of a corresponding type of production in the theatre. Is there any doubt that the dynamic stage form of the Elizabethans had its full effect upon Shakespeare's plays? Or that the writings of Aeschylus were both defined and inspired by the form of the Attic theatre? Molière relied upon the pattern of the Baroque stage of his own day. The dramaturgy of Ibsen and Galsworthy was of a piece with the Naturalistic stage of the "fourth wall," a scenic form which became possible in their own era. Today Eugene O'Neill, Clifford Odets, Maxwell Anderson, Robert Sherwood, write plays which are essentially related to the scenic methods of the Symbolist theatres. Even in the highly specialized theatre of today many of our dramatists, like Odets, O'Neill, George Kelly, George M. Cohan, Sidney Kingsley, Rachel Crothers, Clare Boothe, George Abbott, Marc Connelly, Moss Hart, have begun their writing careers after some experience as actors or directors. Others who have become dramatists without previous stage experience have found it necessary to immerse themselves at once in this experience. So long as theatre itself is on the upgrade, you will not find one playwright worth his salt who is not keenly and enthusiastically interested in every nuance of acting, directing and scene design.

It is necessary to study with care the collective basis of stage production—what collective work really means, the type of relationship which exists or should exist therein, the kind of discipline it requires, its tradition throughout the history of theatre, the place of the dramatist, especially, in the permanent company. The greater part of the secret of stage production lies hidden in these relation-

REVISOR (1836)

Drawing by Gogol

ships. Such a study would help to explain why the whole modern progressive movement in the theatre since the breakdown of the Baroque style has gone forward in work done by pioneering companies, among them the company of Duke Georg of Saxe-Meiningen; the Théâtre-Libre, Théâtre d'Art and the Compagnie des Quinze, of Paris; the Freie Bühne, Volksbühne, Tribunal and Tribüne, of Berlin; the Moscow Art Theatre and its numerous studios; the V & W Theatre and the Burian Collective, of Prague; the London Stage Society; the Dublin Gate Theatre; the Washington Square Players, the Provincetown, the Group Theatre and Theatre of Action, of New York.

The study of permanent companies is outside the scope of our present inquiry. The significance of such companies can be inferred, to some extent, from our other material. It should never be lost sight of. It is these independent, more or less permanent troupes which incubate the new life of theatre. Individual talents sometimes arise and develop within the commercial theatre itself. New theatrical styles do not. The casting-office system cannot give theatre new life. When the commercial theatre and film are healthy they show an ability to absorb and use properly the new truths which independent stage groups have revealed. When unhealthy the show business instead merely appropriates the new discoveries, stultifying them in the process.[9]

MEN OF THEATRE

Theatre is production. Dramatic production is a composite art in the hands of people working together in a sustained creative undertaking. The results thus achieved are never accidental. The men who have led the theatre forward, the most creative, intelligent and stubborn fighters in the recent history of drama, have been part of such producing groups or have identified themselves with the new movements initiated by these independent groups. The building of a new theatre is not the responsibility of the dramatist alone. It is the common responsibility of all theatre people, whatever their specialization, who feel the necessity for building an adequate and lucid drama. It is also an individual responsibility—not only of playwrights, but of every worker in the theatre.

Let us not underestimate the worth of an actor-manager like Constantin Stanislavsky, who over most of his lifetime of seventy-five years, devoted himself with tireless optimism and persistence to the creation of a truthful, living mode of stage production. At the time of the founding of the Moscow Art Theatre, when he and Nemirovich-Danchenko outlined the duties which living theatre required of them, he had protested

> . . . against the customary manner of acting, against theatricality, against bathos, against declamation, against overacting, against the bad manner of production, against the habitual scenery, against the star

system which spoiled the ensemble, against the light and farcical repertoire which was being cultivated on the Russian stage at that time.

For forty years, including years of the catastrophes of war, civil war and the turmoil of reconstruction, Stanislavsky and Nemirovich-Danchenko held the Moscow Art Theatre to its great task of carving out an adequate theatre.

Many other people who have not been dramatists have served the theatre just as resolutely, among them André Antoine, Otto Brahm, Max Littmann, Fritz Erler, Georg Fuchs, Eugene Vakhtangov, Adolphe Appia, Gordon Craig, Robert Edmond Jones, Max Reinhardt, Erwin Piscator. And how many thousands of lesser known, historically anonymous stage people—actors, directors, scenic artists, critics, business and office managers, press representatives, technicians!

Forty years of hard practical work did not solve the problems of Stanislavsky's theatre. Neither did they exhaust that great director's will for a solution. He believed, toward the end of his life, that the world stood before the beginning of a new form of drama, whose quality he could not see clearly. "War and suffering have changed people's outlook," he declared. "Although I don't know myself what the new theatre will be, I'm sure there is a general expectancy of a new ideal." [10]

THEATRE AS PRODUCTION

To understand our present-day theatre or the vistas which are opening for the future we must go beyond the study of the playscript for information. It is necessary to follow closely the mutations of style in the theatre, especially in recent years.

In making our inquiry we may learn a great deal from a consideration of the stage setting. The nuances of style in scene design, once they are properly understood, are more obvious than those of acting or directing styles, hence are more readily illustrative. Again, the factor of design is almost at the polar end of production from that of the script; it affords an approach to production which is very different from the one in vogue at this time. Finally the exact connection between scene design and the other factors of production is a question which has provoked much thought among stage workers; it should prove illuminating to bring up the opinions which have been expressed on that subject.

It is our contention that *all* the forces of stage production are creative; that each of these factors can and should make progress; that the fight for a better theatre has to be waged all along the line of production.

In line with this contention we have re-examined the relation of the dramatist's script to the other production elements. We have given instances from dramatic history to show that theatre has not been merely a succession of playscripts. We have tried to show that the progress of the script itself may be frustrated by the backwardness of other elements. It has also been pointed out that in everyday practice the script is not "inviolate," and should not be.

While granting the special importance of the script, we have also tried to show that the script is not something independent of the rest of the theatre. It is, on the contrary, something which arises out of the whole apparatus of theatre.[11]

The American commercial stage employs a casting-office system of assembling its personnel. Yet the whole technique which it has inherited is a product of the creative work of permanent companies; and experience warrants the conclusion that future progress will be made primarily in such companies. For stage production is a composite art, and it is practiced by people working together in creative association—a type of rapport which is unfortunately not encouraged by "casting-office" methods.

We have taken note of some of the personalities in recent stage history who were not dramatists yet devoted their lives to the improvement of theatre in general, a work whose importance justified such devotion. None of these men felt that the perfect technique has already been found, but all of them have believed optimistically that the solution would arrive, perhaps in the near future.

It appears now that before we can go on to the future of which these men have dreamt, we must find the answer to a technical problem that has arisen on our stages. That problem, hitherto vague, is becoming clearer.

It is the question whether the theatre can develop further on the basis of its present form.

NOTES

1. "But in the theatre, the play is not 'the thing.' It is only part of it. It is the hull and cargo of the ship, but not its superstructure or its crew. It is the arrow, but not the bow that sends it on its way; the Constitution, but not its interpretation. It is what the platform of a winning party is to the administration that tries to live up to it.

"Truly viewed, no acted play is the play its author wrote. It may be better. It may be worse. Its merits may be equal. But it cannot be the same thing. It is the play which audiences see; the play which has taken on the dimensions of its actors, which finds its words colored by their voices, its characters modified to fit their personalities, its emphasis subject to the skill and understanding of its director, its backgrounds supplied by a designer." (John Mason Brown: *The Art of Playgoing*).

2. "When an established producer, an author, an actor or literary dilettante; a banker, a racketeer, or a bored manufacturer of woolen underwear decide to produce a play, the first and most important thing to do is to find a suitable manuscript." (Morton Eustis: *B'way, Inc.*).

Between September, 1936 and June, 1937 fifteen or more Broadway scripts were acquired by Hollywood at prices ranging from an estimated $7,500 to just under a quarter of a million dollars for a single script. YOU CAN'T TAKE IT WITH YOU fetched $200,000 from Hollywood bidders, while ROOM SERVICE went for $225,000. According to the figures given by the New York *Times*, a "surprising number" of scripts changed hands for $100,000 or more apiece during that period.

3. B. E. Zakhava: *Principles of Directing*.

4. *New Theatre*, March, 1935.

5. J. Dover Wilson calls attention to this difference in structure as between Shakespearean and modern plays. The Shakespearean play, to give his apt comparison, is "composed of a succession of waves through which the spectator moves like a swimmer." (*What Happens in Hamlet*).

6. The Hollywood attitude toward the script seems to swing between the extremes of overestimation and underestimation. The movies began practically without scripts. The earlier Chaplin and Keystone comedies, like the Italian Commedia dell' Arte, were guiltless of formal dramaturgy. Even some of the feature films of earlier days got along without well-prepared scenarios. Directors like Von Stroheim drew up their own scenarios. Today most Hollywood pictures are "tight-scripted," and the director is expected to carry out the script with almost literal fidelity. This reduces some of the chaos that once existed during production. At the same time it reduces the initiative of the director and begins to stifle the creative work of actors and designers.

7. "At Athens during the fifth century even successful plays were only exhibited once. But if a play was unsuccessful, the poet was al-

lowed to revise and rewrite it, and to compete with it again in its improved shape. . . . Such was the case with the LEMNIAN WOMEN of Sophocles, and the AUTOLYCUS and PHRIXUS of Euripides. The HIPPOLYTUS of Euripides which we at present possess is a revised edition pruned of its original defects. The CLOUDS of Aristophanes on its first appearance was very unsuccessful, and was altered in many important particulars before it reached the form in which it has come down to us. Among the other plays of Aristophanes, the PEACE, the PLUTUS, and the THESMOPHORIAZUSAE were brought out a second time in a corrected form." (A. E. Haigh: *The Attic Theatre*).

8. "I do not select my methods: they are imposed upon me by a hundred considerations; by the physical considerations of theatrical representation, by the laws devised by the municipality to guard against fires and other accidents to which theatres are liable, by the economics of theatrical commerce, by the nature and limits of the art of acting, by the capacity of the spectators for understanding what they see and hear, and by the accidental circumstances of the particular production in hand. . . . In short, all the factors that must be allowed for before the representation of a play on the stage becomes practicable or justifiable: factors which some never comprehend and which others integrate almost as unconsciously as they breathe, or digest their food." (George Bernard Shaw: *On the Principles That Govern the Dramatist*).

9. The value of a permanent company has been realized by producers like George Abbott, Guthrie McClintic or the Theatre Guild, who have tried to keep a nucleus of personnel from one show to another. This is also true of Labor Stage. None of these, with the possible exception of Labor Stage, have tried to create that inner rapport of personnel for which the Group Theatre is famous. Whenever finances have permitted, the Group has conducted rehearsals and classes in the country for its members and invited guests. Legally speaking, the Group is a non-profit-making membership corporation. Its structure has been democratic to a degree unusual in dramatic companies. A large amount of executive power is in the hands of the executive director, who is, however, subject to recall by the members. In the Group Theatre the creative relations that should exist among the different departments of production is not merely a theory. It is embodied in a rapport among living individuals. In the opinion of veteran critics and "hardboiled" showmen the Group Theatre sets the standard of dramatic production in the United States. It does not do so by accident.

10. New York *Times*, August 8, 1938.

11. In recent years a great deal of critical literature has been devoted to playwriting. By comparison dramatic production, a highly complex art with its own laws of artistry, has been neglected as a study —even though modern theorists continue to assert that the script is dependent upon stage production in general.

Thus John Howard Lawson in his *Theory and Technique of Playwriting* observes: "In the theatre the creative process does not stop with the completion of the playwright's script. Every step in the preparation of production is creative, and every step affects the living quality of the play. A line drawn by the scenic artist, an actor's way of smiling, the color of a woman's dress, may mar the completeness of the whole design." This passage, with two others relating to Craig and Appia, and one example of the use of a stage setting, contains practically all of Lawson's comment on the way in which the script is related to production. (Lawson's example of a helpful setting, Jo Mielziner's design for Sidney Howard's YELLOW JACK, is also praised by Eleanor Flexner in her *American Playwrights 1918–1938*. The present writer does not share this opinion. See Chapter IX, p. 432.)

It is sometimes supposed that, as the factors of theatrical production are derived from other fields—acting, the dance, music, painting, architecture, sculpture, lighting—they are fully covered in discussions elsewhere. It is true that these elements can be considered in this manner, just as the playscript can be considered as a literary form. But in their stage use, brought together synthetically, these arts acquire a significance peculiar to drama alone. The Symbolists—Wagner, Appia, Craig—have understood this clearly; but its reality becomes apparent to any experienced worker in the theatre.

For the director the problem is of course paramount. As an instance, Stanislavsky relates that in spite of his admiration for the great Russian scene painters like Korovin, Levitan, Benois or Golovin, he was frustrated by their work when it came into his theatre: "What business have I, an actor, with the fact that behind me hangs a drop curtain painted by a great artist? I don't see it, it does not inspire me, it does not help me. Just the opposite; it only forces me to be as talented as the backdrop against which I am standing and which I do not see. Often this wonderful backdrop only interferes with me, for I have not agreed with the artist beforehand, and in the majority of cases we pull in different directions. Better give me one good armchair around which I will find an endless series of methods for the expression of my emotions." (*My Life in Art*).

No analysis of painting itself would clear up the problem which Stanislavsky presents here. From the theatrical viewpoint one thing that was wrong was that the painters brought on to the stage not their graphic experience but their canvases.

REFERENCES

Lee Simonson: *The Stage Is Set.* Harcourt, Brace & Company, New York, 1932.

Anita Block: *The Changing World in Plays and Theatre.* Little, Brown & Company, Boston, 1939.

Edward Gordon Craig: *On the Art of the Theatre.* Browne's Bookstore, Chicago, 1911.

John Mason Brown: *The Art of Playgoing.* W. W. Norton & Company, New York, 1936.

Morton Eustis: *B'way, Inc.* Dodd, Mead & Company, New York, 1935.

B. E. Zakhava: *Principles of Directing. Theatre Workshop.* April–July, 1937.

Allardyce Nicoll: *The Development of the Theatre.* Harcourt, Brace & Company, New York, 1927.

John Howard Lawson: *The Theory and Technique of Playwriting.* G. P. Putnam's Sons, New York, 1936. Copyright, 1936, by John Howard Lawson.

George Bernard Shaw in the *London Mercury.* February, 1938.

J. Dover Wilson: *What Happens in Hamlet.* Cambridge University Press, 1937.

William Winter: *The Life of David Belasco.* Vol. 2. Jefferson Winter, Staten Island, New York, 1918. By permission of Mr. Morris Gest.

A. E. Haigh: *The Attic Theatre.* Clarendon Press, Oxford, 1907.

Sheldon Cheney: *The Theatre.* Tudor Publishing Co.

Harry Alan Potamkin: *The Eyes of the Movie.* International Pamphlets, New York, 1934.

André Antoine. From Anna Irene Miller: *The Independent Theatre in Europe.* Ray Long & Richard R. Smith, New York, 1931. By permission of Barnes & Noble.

Constantin Stanislavsky: *My Life in Art.* Little, Brown & Company, Boston, 1924. Reprinted by permission of Little, Brown & Company.

George Bernard Shaw: *On the Principles That Govern the Dramatist.* (1902). From Barrett H. Clark: *European Theories of the Drama.* Appleton.

2

PICTURES AND PLATFORMS

NATURAL AND UNNATURAL

IMAGINE yourself in the city of New York (if you are not there at this moment). You have subwayed or taxied to Times Square, and now you make your way through crowds, taxicabs and multicolored electric lights to the Belasco Theatre, to see a modern play dealing with the life of the slums of this enormous American city. The play has a story which carries you along excitedly through its melodramatic events. It has a thesis: that the conditions of slum life breed crime. Before your eyes a gangster is killed by G-men, while an attractive and manly boy finds himself on the way to a so-called reformatory, whence, it is implied, he will one day emerge as another human rat. The story is sinister but plausible. Its plausibility becomes convincing because of the way it has been put on the stage.

The setting is a dead-end street which slopes down to the piers of the river. A standard New York street sign reading *Dead End* is in the middle of the gutter. Over at stage right stands a row of grimy tenements, with littered firescapes in front, washlines in back. Farther downstage the tenements give way suddenly to an elegant modern apartment house, whose back-entrance gate is visible. At left a heavily timbered coal hopper looms over the street. Upstage the gutter is blocked by a stalled paving-machine. These items of environment have been placed there with the keenest sort of observation. The buildings seem almost to have been lifted bodily from a street outside and transplanted to the stage. Everything is three-dimensional. The facets of the cut stones in the apartment-house wall stand out a good three inches. The tenement wash is hung out to dry on washlines, the separate articles of clothing diminishing in perspective. The gutter has an asphalt texture, the sidewalk has the texture of stone. Bits of rubbish litter the street, mudstains run along the curbs, an old newspaper has fluttered along the gutter and stuck under the steamroller. The daylight is the gloomy sort left over from the shadows which New York buildings cast upon each other; the sun appears to strike through a haze of dust and gasoline fumes. The total impression thus made upon the eye is reinforced by an insinuative pattern of noises that reach the ear: the murmur of the city, the lapping of water at the piers, the warning whistles of river traffic; one can even hear the potatoes sizzling in the fire which street urchins have built in a rubbish can.[1]

Or perhaps you, the playgoer, manage to catch a glimpse of the short-lived production CASEY JONES. Casey Jones, the fabulous engineer, sits enthroned in a locomotive almost as legendary in its huge size. A great hulk of steel, it seems to pound the rails at high speed, careening through its own smoke, bellowing hoarsely as it tears through the night.[2]

To the playgoer of today it seems axiomatic that stage settings exist to create an illusion of a particular place or period. Contemporary stage settings and costumes evoke that shrewd copy of life which the theatregoer has come to expect—which he believes, in fact, to be the eternal quality of theatre. For has he not been taught that illusion is the essence of drama? The latest mechanical stage devices, the almost perfect medium of electric light, now help to create stage illusions so marvelous that at rise of curtain the spectator is "carried away" in a kind of trance to other climes and ages. The stage has become a magic box holding infinite space and eternal time. A brilliantly illuminated picture framed in a gilt proscenium—is it not the very image of theatre?

Before you nod almost automatically in agreement, leave Broadway for one evening; go instead to a performance far downtown on Forsythe Street in the exotic vicinity of Chatham Square. A Chinese Opera troupe is playing here. You will not find it advertised in the papers. The theatre, for all it is named New China, is an ancient, dingy relic of a playhouse under the Manhattan Bridge. The audience is not very fashionable. Chinese, practically all of them men, with perhaps a visiting young lady or two in native dress and the latest style in coiffures. The audience munches sunflower seeds and seems to eye the performance with languid interest. We must learn later on what plays we have seen; we are unable to read the large yellow program printed in Chinese.

Take a good look at the stage. There is no front curtain. The sides of the naked proscenium are lined with electric bulbs glaring like Coney Island. There is a setting on the stage—left over, perhaps, by some tenant who could not pay his rent in 1902. The tomato-colored set of flats has painted panels and no ceiling. There

Drawing by Mordecai Gorelik

Chinese theatre, New York

is a door-opening at each end of the back wall, but folds of Chinese silk hang in the doorways instead of doors. The center of the setting is decorated with anti-spitting and no-smoking notices in Chinese, Italian and Yiddish. Just under the proscenium arch hangs a magnificent fringed Chinese drapery. Upstage right sits the orchestra: half a dozen musicians in shirtsleeves, their clothes and jackets hung on a clothes-stand behind them. Don't expect soothing strains of music from this orchestra. You will hear a discordant clash of cymbals, tappings on a wooden block, a cacaphony which will very likely give you a headache after two hours.

Taking courage in spite of this strange atmosphere we ask the elderly Chinese at our right what the play is about. We learn that there are a number of pieces on the bill, which began at seven o'clock and will continue to eleven. We are in time for a drama called THE STRATEGY OF THE UNGUARDED CITY, an ancient favorite. Evidently the play is just starting, because the last character of the previous drama has just gone through the left-hand door, and the first of the new characters is coming in at the right.

A startling apparition walks on: a round white face streaked with black bars; above this tigerish head a boxlike silk headgear with red pompoms; below, a huge black beard. This appalling figure is raised high on padded slippers. A gold silk apron descends almost to the slippers. Jutting out from the shoulders are four pennants, like wings, in heavy silk brocade. The actor who wears this costume represents the renowned General Ma Shu, who lived in the period of the Three Kingdoms (A. D. 190–280). You may be sure that General Ma Shu never looked in the least like his stage representation. He never wore a black, white and gold makeup, an obviously false beard or a gown with four flags tied on behind. It appears that in this theatre all generals have a similar costume and makeup, no matter who they are, or of what historical period. The flags represent the number of armies under General Ma Shu's command. The long-handled instrument, like a mop, which he carries, denotes a horse. The General is supposed to be on horseback leading his troops.

Ma Shu and his cohorts are now leaving behind them their stronghold of Chieh-t'ing, after a disastrous defeat. They have ordered General Chu-kê Liang to hold the fortress with a rearguard consisting of two old soldiers and two servant boys! Ma Shu with his fancied army disappears through the curtain, left. General Chu-kê comes on at right, followed by the two servants. All are clad in silk, with a fantastic richness unrelated to historic accuracy or reality. A property man in a black bellhop uniform and ordinary cloth cap comes over from his "prop" table at stage left, to hand Chu-kê an oriental violin and a drinking-cup. You gather that the dire peril of the city does not overwhelm Chu-kê, even though he knows that the enemy, led by the redoubtable Szŭ-ma, is coming to lay siege.

Chu carouses symbolically but with ostentatious pomp and loud music within the city, which consists of a large blue drapery with a gate and bricks painted on it. This banner, stretched horizontally on a bamboo pole, has been brought in by the property man and his assistant. The cloth gates in the center of the blue banner are looped aside. The two old soldiers come on, from right. They, also, are dressed in silk. They perform a ballet which implies that they are calmly sweeping near the open gates.

Now Szǔ-ma arrives, also from the right entrance door. He wears a priceless costume glittering with embroidery; he too has a great beard and holds a mop in his hand. Coming straight to the footlights he declaims in falsetto: "I can easily tell that this city is well protected by a hidden army! The gates are open and you, Chu-kê, think I will be foolish enough to walk into the trap. Though you believe you are clever, your trap will not catch me. My troops will now retreat forty *li!*" As Szǔ-ma speaks the orchestra accents each phrase with a clashing of the cymbals.

(The end of this story, by the way, is that Szǔ-ma found out too late that he had been tricked after all. By the time he returned to assault the city it had received reinforcements.) [3]

What becomes of our accepted beliefs about stage production as we watch this performance? The show we have witnessed is not the notion of some Chinese lunatic. Its type has endured for thousands of years, has had distinguished audiences, remarkably capable actors. Its strangeness puzzles and repels us in many ways, yet it is not lacking in a beauty which we can also sense. Even the unaccustomed gestures of the players are effective. We watch them with fascination, knowing that, like the falsetto voices and abstract makeup, they are standardized in every detail and used only on the stage.

Here is a production method which contains no magic box of infinite space and eternal time. It is not a painting which comes to life before our eyes. We never forget that we are in a theatre in front of a stage platform.

We are not under the impression that we are living in the days of the Three Kingdoms. We do not behold these ancient generals as if they were resurrected for us in the flesh. We do not feast our eyes upon what seem to be the veritable walls of the city of Chieh-t'ing. The rival armies do not pass before us; not even one squad of soldiers do we see, no spirited chargers, no pageantry of military advance and retreat. We see no steep upland trails; no snow-crowned mountains enclose the horizon. Here is a tradition of theatre very unlike the one which prevails in the modern theatres uptown.

Does this production have any meaning for us today? Is it only something to smile at tolerantly, as a naïve remnant of antiquated theatre?

This style of production does have a meaning for us. It gives us a historical perspective which might not otherwise be possible. For this is the stage of time immemorial as contrasted with our own stage of the moment.

THE UNWORTHY SCAFFOLD

The stage has not always been a magic box. It has not always been a framed picture. For almost twenty-five centuries it was, instead, a trestled platform, the ὀκριβας of the Greeks. Dumas is said to have defined theatre as "three boards and a passion." Shakespeare called the stage an "unworthy scaffold"; [4] and it was upon this scaffold, with its mere tokens of locale, that he built his dramas. Shakespeare's precision in words is notable, as always. His phrase is more than a picturesque metaphor, it is the word of an artisan conveying the sense of dramatic construction.

At some date approximately half a thousand years before the birth of Christ there appeared in Europe the wooden stage platform, an instrument which was to become the hallowed tool of drama as the plow is the tool of agriculture. It must have arrived after the lifetime of Aeschylus (525–456 B. C.), to judge from the stage directions of this first great tragic poet of the Greeks.

Just outside Athens, at the foot of the bare mountain slope of the Acropolis, a space seventy-eight feet in diameter was marked out. The ground within the circle was beaten hard. The origin of the circle was lost in the mists of time even to those far-off Athenians; but there is evidence for the belief that it was once a threshing-floor where the rites of Dionysus, god of the fields and vineyards, were conducted. Originally the audience simply took its place on the hillside; it could look down on the circular area (known as the *orkestra*) with its small altar to Dionysus standing in the center. Beyond the flat plain of the *orkestra* it saw a valley in which grapes ripened, while far to the left lay the harbor of the city. A palisade hemmed in the far side of the *orkestra* to keep it from pitching into the valley.

It is clear today why THE SUPPLIANTS, THE PERSIANS and PROMETHEUS BOUND have their scenes laid in a deserted countryside. The deserted countryside is merely the bare earthen circle of ground. Aeschylus used it for his settings. He is even said to have used the palisade, making Prometheus disappear from view over its edge.[5]

Such was the first European theatre, a space wrested from nature itself. At an indefinite date this space began to be framed in wood. Wooden seats, forming an auditorium somewhat larger than a semicircle, defined the seating space on the hill. A wooden building, the *skene,* serving as a dressing room for the actors, arose at the far side of the *orkestra.* At each end this building returned toward the audience with a short wing. Wedged between the wings and standing a short height above the ground was a long, narrow platform—the first European stage. The wooden walls behind it were pierced by three doors which gave access to the stage from the dressing rooms behind the wall. Like the Roman stage which followed it, this wooden platform and auditorium were later reproduced in enduring stone.[6]

Why was a platform necessary? To elevate the principal actors above the chorus of dancers who stood in the circle, making them fully visible above the chorus. But the mere existence of the platform must have introduced something new in the relationship of play to audience. Like the altar, the stage platform became a place consecrated, set apart by general consent. You could take for granted that the actions which transpired there did not necessarily obey the laws of nature. A new world of perception, of interpretation, was possible on that little, marked-off space.

What kind of actions were possible? We shall come back to the question. Let us go on for the present to see how the stage platform has been put to use throughout history.

In the Middle Ages the Catholic Church dramatized the Passion of Christ. This liturgical drama also erected a platform, usually in the north aisle of the church building. Increasingly secularized, the performances moved into the open air. They lingered for a time on the steps of the west doors of the church, the first outdoor platform of this type of drama.

Passing finally from the hands of the priests into those of the

Iainly Convention: Attic theatre

TWO KINDS OF THEATRE

Mainly Illusion:
A DOLL'S HOUSE at the Moscow Art Theatre

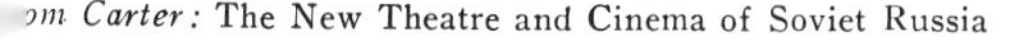

om Carter: The New Theatre and Cinema of Soviet Russia

guildsmen, its mode of production became that of the "mansions." The mansions were small buildings representing some of the familiar halting-places in the life of Jesus, the Stations of the Cross, as well as other localities mentioned in the older and newer Testaments: the house of the Disciples; the palace of Herod; Gethsemane; the Holy Sepulchre; the Pillar of Scourging; even Heaven and Hell. The latter took the popular form of the head of a frightful monster emerging from the earth with open jaws breathing fire and smoke. These scenic edifices, arranged in a line or street, semicircle or circle, were really separate stage platforms upon which actors performed, the ground between them, known as the *platea,* counting as neutral territory or unlocalized stage.[7]

In the fifteenth century the trades guilds of England developed a rather original version of the mansion system. They turned the mansions into flimsy decorated booths mounted on wheeled platforms. The mobile platforms were moved from one square to another in the town, playing an episode at a time.

The so-called Interludes which come next chronologically (15th–16th centuries), were rude one-act farces. They made use of a trestled platform backed by a curtain—a stage-form utterly naïve in its elements. The same arrangement served the Commedia dell' Arte of the Italian Renaissance, the early classic revivals of the same period, the Hanswurst comedians of the later Renaissance in Germany, the student dramas of Bohemia, the "corral" players of Lope de Vega in Spain, the strolling players who were the precursors of Shakespeare's company in England. The mobile popular theatre known as the *carpa,* found today in Mexico, is a living example of this primitive scenic platform.

The prototype of the Italian court theatre was a dais set up at one end of a ballroom, connected with the dance floor by a short flight of steps. The Hôtel de Bourgogne, which housed the French equivalent of the Italian Commedia, contained a platform at the end of a long hall. The more mobile dramatic troupes in France at the time of Racine and Molière were accustomed to set up their acting platforms in indoor tennis courts. At Baroque courts, for masques and private performances, players set up platforms in the larger salons. In summer they gave outdoor shows on temporary platforms or on the grass terraces of garden theatres. The stage of the Elizabethan playhouse was a large wooden-canopied platform which jutted far out into the "pit," where the common spectators, the "groundlings," stood packed around it. Long after the stage curtain came into general use the stage platform remained a feature of theatre architecture as a forestage, or "apron," pushing out toward the audience from the stage proper.

In China the most ancient form of the stage still exists in the popular "mat theatres" of the strolling companies. Platforms erected upon bamboo scaffolding and roofed with thatch provide a stage, a greenroom, loges and tea-pavilions. Matting covers the platforms. Most of the audience stand or sit on the ground close to the stage. In the permanent city playhouses in China there is a gal-

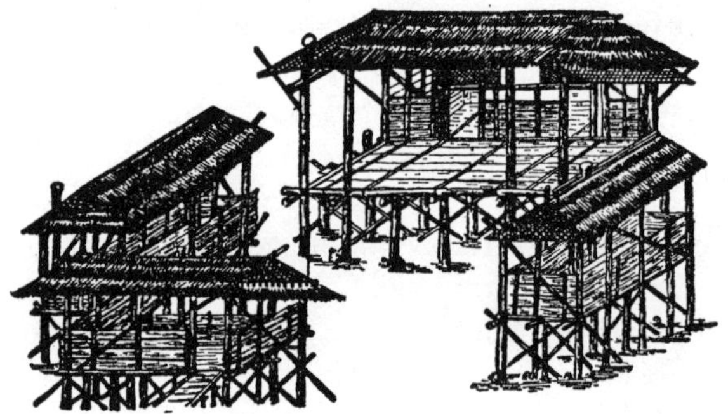

From Kate Buss: *Studies in the Chinese Drama*

Mat theatre

lery opposite the stage and a line of boxes on each side, on a level with the stage. Stage and auditorium are rectangular in shape. The gallery has seats while the orchestra pit contains tables and chairs.

The outthrust platform is disappearing in the modern Chinese playhouses, but its effect on staging remains visible in the present-day Japanese theatres, of which the Chinese is the prototype.

Prints representing the *Bugaku*, one of the most archaic forms of Japanese drama (the *Bugaku* is thought to have reached its highest development about 850 A. D.) show an outdoor, central platform bordered by a wooden railing, with steps leading on from opposite sides. The wooden platform has characterized Japanese staging throughout its history. The present form of the Japanese stage became fixed probably in the early eighteenth century. It consists of a wide platform at the end of a rectangular hall. A wooden canopy, closely resembling the "heavens" which sheltered the Elizabethan stage against rain, stretches over the central portion of the Japanese acting platform, and is supported on ornamental columns. Doors from the stage give access to the greenroom in back, as in the Elizabethan and Greek stages. Around all sides of the hall there runs a narrow shelf of stage, known as the *hana-michi,* or flower path. The flower path is joined to the main stage at either end, so that the stage action may be carried on around the whole auditorium. The audience sits (or rather, kneels) in loges around the walls or below in the central pit enclosed by the stage platforms. The main platform of the Japanese stage usually accommodates both a revolving stage and rising trapdoors; these are operated in the low space (*naraku*), under the platform.

ILLUSIONS AND CONVENTIONS

Surely we are not wrong in the impression that it is the stage platform upon which dramatic form is constructed? Even today in the Broadway playhouse, although we are conscious only of a stage picture, the platform exists. The forestage, that last remnant of platform technique, has been whittled down, or taken away altogether. Yet the rest of the platform is still there, below the picture on the stage. Only, in a fierce attempt to soar beyond immediate experience, we seem to have forgotten it.

Swept away by the dramatist, actors and designer to an infinity of space and an eternity of time, we feel only dimly that it is Wednesday evening, let us say, between 8:45 and 11 P. M., in front of the 27′–0″ x 80′–0″ stage platform of the Belasco Theatre. The *illusory* method of stage production, our contemporary method, has achieved this for us. We must actually be prodded to remember that the aboriginal stage platform still exists.

For the illusory method is only our own particular way of using Shakespeare's scaffold. The Elizabethan dramatic scaffold has become a scaffold framed in steel, incandescently lit, not as "unworthy" as it was in the reign of Queen Bess. It differs most from its predecessors in its psychology, for it prefers to hide itself, disclaiming its own existence as a wooden stand plain for all to see. So well has it succeeded that its audiences are startled when this psychology is dispelled, as in the case of the "no-scenery" plays of a recent Broadway season.

The reminder may be a little unsettling to people who like to imagine that the illusory method as practiced on Broadway is the sanctified method of the theatre since the beginning of time. It is true that illusion has been part of the technique of theatre since theatre began. But the illusory method as a distinct style has developed within a very recent period, one which falls within the memory of many living playgoers. In 1937 the illusory style was exactly fifty years old.

Not a very long time considering the theatre's history of three thousand years! Nor can it be said that illusory production has reigned serenely during its half-century. Mutable, like all living processes, this particular method of bringing life to the stage has at times developed, at times retrogressed; it has had rivals and has more than once been threatened with extinction. Between the time of the inception of the illusory style, and today, we can trace a kind of see-saw of fortune between it and the traditional, or *conventional* method of the drama.

We have already defined these two methods. Let us define them again, since it is essential that we be clear about the terms we use. The *illusory* method wishes to obliterate the stage platform. It wishes, in fact, to entrance its audiences into the belief that they are not in a theatre building at all—that they are hovering, unseen, at the side of events which are taking place in the outer world.

The *conventional* method, on the contrary, emphasizes the presence of the stage platform. This platform it conceives of as an area like a chessboard, where a problem of life may be played through according to certain arbitrary rules accepted by the audience, as the moves of chess are accepted by chessplayers. The conventional method does not seek to *transplant* life to the stage: instead it represents life at a distinct remove, by means of obvious surrogates and tokens.

THE TRADITIONAL STAGE

So far our distinction is fairly clear. But the moment we search for it in practice we run into difficulties. In practice it is not possible to sort out these two methods so easily.

To begin with, no single stage production is ever purely of one type or another. The student of dramatic conventions is struck by the fact that the stage platform is the basic convention; but after that he encounters the most diverse rules for the conduct of the dramatic game.

The Chinese theatre and the Attic theatre are almost equally conventional; both have a general technique which is far removed from the illusory one known to us today. The Attic tragedian wore a mask and clothes sculpturally padded; the Chinese tragic actor makes up his face in non-human designs and wears a special costume which is neither modern nor historically accurate. Other resemblances exist. In spite of these resemblances we may be sure that the Chinese spectator would need to have the conventions of an Athenian performance explained to him, even if he could understand Attic Greek and knew the story of the play. To come back to our metaphor of chess: both the Athenian and Chinese stages may be chessboards, but the moves are different.

Purists would find it even more difficult to show that the conventional stage techniques known to history had no admixture of illusion. There has never been a perfect conventional style, any more than there has ever been a perfect illusory style. In every conventional style there are digressions into the most literal illusion.[8]

Thus the nature of the Attic style was predominantly conventional. A. E. Haigh in his authoritative work *The Attic Theatre* sums up the ancient Athenian stage method as follows: "All those elaborate spectacular illusions, which are rendered practicable by the great depth of the modern stage, were impossible. . . ." No form of staging can be called illusory whose setting consists of a platform emphatically visible and backed by a permanent architectural façade; in which the actors wear masks, appear of supernatural height, walk with measured stride and make arbitrary gestures; in which an altar is a permanent architectural feature of the foreground; in which a god is brought from heaven to earth by means of a rope lowered from a crane; in which a chorus of twelve to fifteen people stands in rows in the *orkestra* continuously.

Yet we must acknowledge that this particular technique shades off continually into an illusory one. Greek productions did not hesitate to use such possibilities of illusion as came their way.

From the beginning the bare *orkestra* supplied the quality of a deserted countryside. The Greek chorus wore costumes intended, to some extent at least, to give illusion. Groups of satyrs were dressed in animal skins and had satyr-masks, beards and wild hair. Birds wore feathers, wings, strange bird-masks. It is believed that for the EUMENIDES Aeschylus himself invented the costumes for the chorus

From Dubech

Scenes from MEDEA (431 B.C.)

Vase drawings

of Furies, who appeared in black garments, frightful masks and streaming, snaky locks, horrifying the audience.

There was undoubted illusory technique in the details of other costumes as well. Kings wore crowns, Persians had oriental turbans, Heracles wore a lion's skin and carried a club. Sophocles' Oedipus was led onto the stage apparently blinded and bleeding —the effect being accomplished by a change in masks. The masks themselves, like the painted makeups of the Chinese stage, consisted of very many different types, or rather stereotypes; there is evidence that at least thirty different masks were used for tragedy. Unlike the Chinese, the Athenian actors did not mount imaginary steeds. It appears to have been fairly common for horses and chariots to be used in performance.[9]

The Attic stage was acquainted with a number of mechanical devices including moveable platforms, trapdoors and cranes. The operation of these units was obviously visible under the conditions of the Greek stage; yet they were associated with dramatic actions definitely illusory in nature. Our phrase *deus ex machina* is derived from the Greek practice of bringing a god down from Olympus on a rope and pulley to untie a dramatic plot which had become too much for the dramatist himself to resolve. There was also a device whereby a god could be swung into view by revolving a shutter, the astonishment of the audience being heightened by means of thunder machines (jars filled with stones and emptied into brass cauldrons). For the comic poets, who customarily burlesqued the tragic ones, the crane was a fertile source of inspiration.[10]

The mechanism known as the *ekkyklema,* or *exostra,* supposedly a low platform on wheels, could apparently be pushed or swung out of any of the main stagedoors. It served the purpose of revealing what had just happened offstage—characteristically a tableau of murdered victims, since scenes of actual killing were proscribed on the Greek stage. The tableaus shown on this platform were illusory in quality.[11]

A type of theatre which erects a platform in the nave of a cathedral, and there, before a drapery hung in folds, enacts scenes from the Bible in choral responses to the accompaniment of organ music, can scarcely be called illusory in the sense that it tries to make its audiences believe they are not witnessing a staged performance. Such a label would be even less appropriate for a theatre whose stages are wheeled around on wagons through the town, as was the practice in the staging of the English Mysteries. But again in the Passion and Mystery plays of the Middle Ages, we find a plentiful admixture of illusion. As an example, the Valenciennes Mystery had a kind of ferris wheel, with angels painted on it, surrounding the mansion of Heaven. When the wheel turned, the angels flew around the throne of God. There is an obvious increase in illusory effects as compared even with the later period of Greek stage production; but we are still a long way from a technique which is predominantly illusory. Only the sensory elements seem capable of comparison.[12]

The Chinese theatre presents us with a further example of mixed conventional and illusory styles. Its conventional nature has already been described. Let us see more clearly how this conventionalism is used, and note how it, too, shades off into illusion.[13]

Extreme as this conventionalism may seem at first glance, upon reflection we find many illusory elements. When characters are represented as in a boat, there is no boat, but there is a swaying motion, and there is an oar for paddling. When a character is represented as on horseback, there is no horse, but the movements used in mounting an imaginary steed correspond closely to those used in reality. A beggar may wear silk rags: still they are rags as compared with the character of other costumes. There is differentiation in makeup and costume so that there are stage garments which approximate the armor of generals, the robes of monks or mandarins. Chairs and tables are used not only symbolically but in their proper character as chairs and tables. Fans, swords, bows and arrows, drums, flutes, tea-urns, are used naturally by the stage characters. It is impossible to draw a line showing which type of property is to be used symbolically, and which is to be used literally. In recent years under the influence of western drama the number of properties literally used has greatly increased, painted settings have been brought into the theatre, actresses are playing women's rôles, which were formerly played by actors.

The Japanese stage closely parallels the Chinese as regards the type and amount of conventions used. The "invisible" property man is also a Japanese institution. Boys robed in black follow the actors around the stage, removing properties or scenery which is no longer required in the course of a scene. Japanese plays are given by daylight, but if a performance should be prolonged until after dark, a row of candles is placed along the front, while an attendant carrying a candle fixed to a rod illuminates in turn the actors who are speaking. Emotions are not expressed "inwardly" but are instead translated into dance movements to the accompaniment of music and the chant of the chorus.

Houses are reproduced on stage in almost exact replica of

those offstage, complete with thatched roofs. This Naturalism is all the more striking because actual Japanese homes, like their stage counterparts, remove whole walls in milder weather, exposing the rooms within. Lamps, tables, entire kitchens, closets with clothes hanging in them are shown. At the same time these houses are placed in front of backdrops on which landscapes have been painted in the conventional style familiar to us on Japanese screens.

The architect Josiah Conder (as quoted by Huntly Carter) gives an account of a Japanese production which is noteworthy for its admixture of convention and illusion. A prince and his retinue enter a boat which is presumably lying on a beach. The beach, however, is only painted on a groundcloth, on which waves are also painted farther upstage. The boat moves off (on the stage turntable); the groundcloth is drawn forward until the beach disappears and only the waves are seen. At the same time additional waves painted on strips of canvas are drawn in on cords around the upper boxes of the theatre. Finally, on the gallery directly opposite the stage, there appears a painting of the distant shore and castle which the voyagers have left behind. In soliloquy the prince at sea addresses his native home, which is fading into distance.

THE ILLUSIONISTS LOOK AT CONVENTION

Those commentators who think in terms of illusion have not found it easy to explain conventional staging.

The type of explanation which they offer has varied somewhat but its basic assumption remains the same. They take for granted that the familiar illusory technique of today is the one and only technique of the theatre. Conventional forms, in their opinion, are only a more primitive attempt to create illusion on the stage.

For Mantzius there was nothing in the form of the Chinese theatre worth serious attention:

> The slight attempts which are nevertheless made by Chinese stage managers to guide the imagination of the public cannot fail to strike European eyes on account of their extreme naïveté. . . . Scenic art in China continues to be what it always was: a systematic, carefully prepared *amusement,* perfect of its kind, but wanting in individual character and the intellectual stamp which ought to raise it to the level of a real art.

Writing about a quarter-century later, Sheldon Cheney is just as severe if apparently more judicious:

> Truth to tell, dramatic literature in China never reached the importance a Sophocles or a Shakespeare endowed it with in the West. The Chinese themselves make no claims for it; and even allowing for the lack of language-embroidery values possibly lost in translation, the Western reader may agree that Chinese plays are little more than melodrama or hack journalistic plays—or grand opera *libretti.* The situations are pretty well standardized, the characters run to obvious types, the "effects" are neither deeply dramatic nor cumulatively emotional. All that the Western mind craves in tragedy is overlooked or dissipated: taut dramatic structure, suspense, psychologic truth. The casual nature of the plot, indeed, explains the apparently shattering confusion in the auditorium, the constant going and coming of spectators, the tea-drinking, the conversations and eating and even games while the actors are going through a particularly important passage. There is no continuity of mood, no built-up tension. The performance probably lasts from late afternoon till after midnight; but the programme includes several plays. As the actors from one go out of the exit door, the players of the next enter by the other, so that action is continuous. And so is the music that sounds so squeaky and clangy to Western ears.

Cheney's objections, summed up, amount to the assertion that the Chinese dramatic technique has no dramatists of any calibre and that it fails to sweep away the audience emotionally. Cheney himself elsewhere has cited centuries of flourishing European theatre in which the dramatist was unimportant. And it is not a legitimate objection to the Chinese technique to say that its music sounds squeaky and clangy to our ears. The insistence that all plays must have an uninterrupted mood and increasing suspense is something which has yet to be proved, although it is undoubtedly a requirement of most western drama. Confusion in the auditorium, the coming and going of spectators, eating and drinking, have characterized the whole history of the European theatre to within a very recent period. To give one instance, the English Restoration theatres were accustomed not only to eating, drinking and card-playing but to duels and assignations as well.

Like Mantzius, Cheney assumes that the conventional dramatic form is a naïve approach to the type of contemporary illusory staging which is held up as the standard of what theatre should be. For Simonson it is clear likewise that the Attic theatre wanted illusion and could not get the perfection we have today only because it did not have modern resources. To make this point he resorts to some odd reasoning:

> The crane that made the descent of a god at the end of a tragedy a literal fact, a blatantly bare piece of machinery on a palace roof, seems to us to destroy illusion rather than to create it. But the point to be stressed is again the fact that the Greek audiences so wanted the descent of the deity actually displayed before their eyes that they could ignore ropes and pulleys in full sunlight. In this they showed a typical Occidental temper, which always tends to elaborate its symbols until they reproduce experience rather than accept symbolic equivalents for it as Oriental audiences do from one century to another. If the Athenians had been as eager for a purely formal art of the theatre as their modern apologists maintain, they would not have hoisted their deities through the air, or demanded a tableau of murder trundled into sight.[14]

Whatever merit there may be in this reference to "typical Occidental temper" as contrasted with the temper of oriental audiences will have to be left to competent anthropologists for discussion; it does not explain the nature of conventional technique. It is undoubtedly true that the Athenians were not eager for a purely formal art of the theatre as visualized by some of the more woolly-minded followers of Gordon Craig. The Athenians were eager for a theatrical form which would best suit their purpose. Whether they were looking for illusion is another matter.

According to Simonson, the Athenian audiences craved illusion, wanted it so badly that they deliberately shut their eyes to the ropes and pulleys which lowered the gods from Olympus. We must assume that these same audiences in a like manner shut their eyes to the masks worn by the actors, seeing hallucinations of supernatural faces; that they ignored the padded clothes, seeing only supernatural physiques; that they ignored the architectural façade of the stage background, seeing instead the temples, palaces, ruins or deserts to which the tragic or comic poet referred. . . . They ignored the choruses standing in formation in the orchestra, and instead saw what?

Why make the tortuous supposition that these audiences shut their eyes to things which were blatantly visible before them? We may assume that they saw just what we should see today; a combination of conventional and illusory technique—conventional in scenic architecture, the use of stage machinery, certain costumes, the use of a chorus; illusory in a number of stage effects, tableaus, certain other costumes, etc.; the conventional aspects far outweighing the illusory ones.

Is the use of the mask part of the technique of illusion? Here again Simonson is not too careful in his use of the term "realism." He asserts that the Greek actor's mask was realistic because the actor required it in order to be visible to the back rows of the amphitheatre and because the mask contained a speaking-trumpet! His point is evidently that the Greek mask was not an "arty" idea but that it served in a utile manner. This fact in no way brings the Attic mask into the tradition of Naturalistic, illusory theatre. The enormous difference between the technique of the Greek mask and even the *comparative* Naturalism of the Elizabethan drama is implied in the comment by Haigh: "It would be difficult to imagine the part of Hamlet played in a mask."

As compared with Mantzius, Cheney and Simonson show a mounting interest in conventional technique while still regarding it as an inferior form of illusion. Still more recently it has been implied by John Mason Brown that the conventional style is not necessarily inferior, but that it is *essentially not different* from the illusory technique:

> None of these conventions is difficult to accept. Nor does the acceptance of most of them require more time than did Mr. O'Neill's use of masks in THE GREAT GOD BROWN or of "the stream of consciousness" in STRANGE INTERLUDE. Yet to varying degrees they are different enough from the conventions of our own theatre to call attention to themselves. Their strangeness compels us to look beyond what is being done in the productions they have shaped and consider both the reason for, and the manner of, its doing. By making us mindful of the importance of other theatrical conventions they may even recall to our minds the importance of those no less artificial but usually ignored conventions, by means of which our realistic theatre is permitted to achieve its illusion of reality.
>
> In spite of all its oaths, its gas-jets, its crunching snow, its family dinners, its Bronx homes and Long Island drawing-rooms, its chatter about the heat and the humidity, and its slouching actors who keep their hands in their pockets, ours is a theatre which is as much at the mercy of its audiences' will to make-believe as was the theatre of the Elizabethans and the Greeks, or as is the superbly stylized and defiantly unreal theatre of Mei Lan Fang. . . . We know, as surely as the Chi-

nese know a real door has a doorstep, that a real room does not have three walls. Yet, like the Chinese, we give our belief to a scenic gesture. . . .

It is worthwhile for us, as playgoers, to recall the unreality of realism if only to realize how inseparably it is linked to the medium it takes such pains to deny.

Thus Brown arrives at a respectful consideration of the conventional style, only to abolish or minimize all that separates the conventional from the illusory. This treatment of the problem clarifies it no better than the patronizing attitude of the earlier writers. The startling difference between these two techniques in the theatre cannot be abolished, even though there is a wide area of middle ground between them. For Mantzius the distinction between the two styles was still clear:

Therefore in the Greek theatre of the classic age we never find a direct imitation of nature; everything—costumes, masks, elocution and movements—is fantastic or conventional. We cannot point out sharply enough this absolute difference between the ancient Greek and our modern theatre; and we may suppose that, if it had been constantly kept in view, people would not have taken so much trouble to invent the multitude of untrustworthy and sometimes quite absurd details of scenic arrangement, which have so long distorted and confused the picture of the ancient Hellenic stage. As a fact it never—at least never in the most ancient times—represented any particular place: it was *the stage* whence the words of the poet were spoken, but it did not show the *image* of the place he described, any more than a lecture hall changes according to the poems declaimed by a reciter, or than a concert hall illustrates the music which is performed in it.

If all stage methods were fundamentally identical, what would explain the historical transitions from one type to another, transitions often made amid bitter dispute?

The facts themselves bring us to the conclusion that any stage technique in practice is *predominantly conventional* or *predominantly illusory.*

PICTURES ON PLATFORMS

Conventional and illusory form meet in practice, not because they are the same, but because the illusory technique rests in turn upon convention.

It has already been pointed out that, however startling a replica of nature may be brought to the stage, it is still enclosed in a conventional frame and rests upon a conventional platform. Indeed, upon close inspection it appears that the quality of Naturalism which the spectator perceives is generally imparted by scenic arrangements and acting performances which are essentially unnatural.

Thus the locomotive in CASEY JONES which gave so convincing an illusion of a real locomotive was actually shaped like half of a

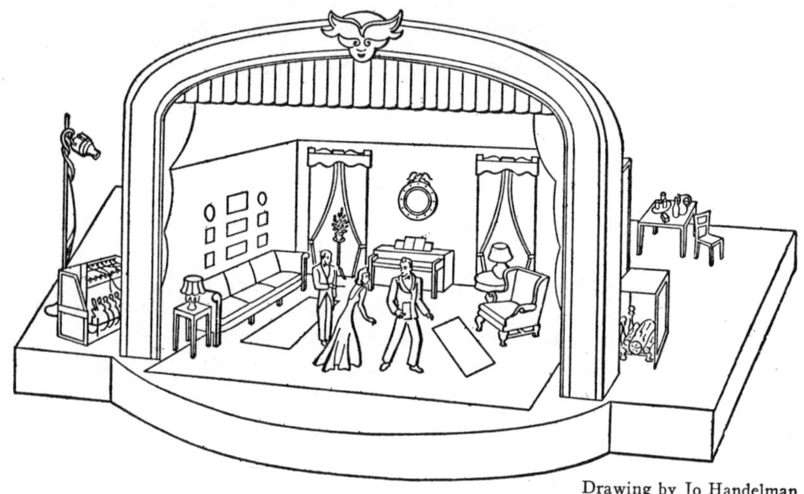

Drawing by Jo Handelman

The picture on the platform

flatiron and was covered with black velour instead of steel. In GOLDEN BOY, Carnovsky as Papa Bonaparte or Garfield as the taxi-driver Siggie seemed perfectly natural on the stage; but if one were to see such characters in an ordinary home alongside real people they would seem demented.

Stanislavsky has given an instance of this phenomenon, citing an event which occurred near Kiev when the Moscow Art Theatre was touring in the provinces. The incident which he describes happened casually, but it made a deep impression on him, an impression which he formulated as a challenge to the scene designer in the theatre:

We walked on the shore of the river and the gates of the old palace were opened to us. We were in a Turgenev-like atmosphere, with ancient flower beds, alleys, summerhouses and benches. One place in the palace park we recognized as the scenery of the second act of Turgenev's A MONTH IN THE COUNTRY, with which we had just ended our season in Kiev. Here there were also benches for spectators. The entire surrounding begged for a performance in the open air, in the midst of nature. We were asked to repeat the second act of the play. We consented and began our improvised performance with a great deal of aplomb. My turn also came, and now Knipper-Chekhova and I, as we are supposed to do in the play, walked along a long alley-path, repeating our text, and then sat down on a bench, according to our usual *mise en scène,* and—I stopped, because I could not continue my false and theatrical pose. All that I had done seemed untrue to nature, to reality. And it had been said of us that we had developed simplicity to a point of naturalism! How far we are from simple human speech, how conventional we saw to be what we had become used to do on the stage, considering our scenic truth to be real truth.

. . . the trees, the air, the sun hinted to us of such real, beautiful and artistic truth which cannot, because of its aestheticism, be compared to that which is created in us by the dead wings of a theatre. Let the artist who paints the scenery for the theatre be great, but there is another, all-powerful Artist who acts in mysteries and ways unknown to us on our superconsciousness. This artistic truth, hinted to us by nature, is incomparably more aesthetic and more beautiful, and what is even more important, more scenic than that relative truth and theatrical conventionality with which it is the habit to limit theatrical creativeness.

By now, perhaps, the reader may agree that convention and illusion are distinct tendencies in stage technique. What establishes the relationship between them? This relationship is something that changes with each period of stage history. The two in varying degrees form the compound out of which each historic stage form has been created.

As we review the stage techniques of the past, two conclusions seem inevitable. First, that until our own era the technique of drama was overwhelmingly conventional. Second, that within conventional technique there has been a slow development of greater and greater illusion-values.

The later Greek, or Hellenic, theatre made increasing use of illusion. Medieval drama was a good deal more illusory than the classic Greek; in addition it used powerful emotional elements to "carry away" its audiences hypnotically. Elizabethan staging combined illusory and conventional elements in a highly dynamic manner. In the Italian Renaissance the trend toward illusion reached a new plane with the introduction of painted perspectives, modulated lighting, complex machinery and elaborate stage effects.

The Italian Renaissance, in fact, saw the beginnings of the Naturalistic technique which flowered centuries later.[15] Yet, in all the intervening centuries, the illusory elements remained subordinate to the conventional ones. Not until the time of Antoine did illusion become the dominant, systematized technique which exists, for example, on Broadway and in Hollywood today.

FORMULAS FOR THEATRE

The work of building up a whole *illusory system* began when the last great conventional stage technique—that of the Baroque—had disintegrated. In our attempt to distinguish between convention and illusion we have learned something from our study of early forms of the theatre. We shall learn more if we follow the later development of the Naturalistic theatre—the form in which the search for stage illusion has found its most complete, perhaps its *final* expression.

For, as we shall see, the illusory form has already been followed by other methods. The principal modes of dramatic production of the past fifty years may be listed for convenience as follows:

BAROQUE	illusory-*conventional*
ROMANTIC	conventional-*illusory*
NATURALISTIC	illusory
SYMBOLIST	illusory
THEATRICALIST	illusory-*conventional*
SOCIALIST REALISTIC	conventional-*illusory*
EPIC	conventional

The above list is far too simplified. Even so, these styles are a bewildering array! Are they to be explained on the basis of the pendulum of fashion swinging from one extreme to another? (That famous pendulum upon which so many theories have been hung and whose alleged motions explain nothing whatever!)

Fortunately we do not need any mythical pendulums with

Alfredo Valente

CASEY JONES (1938). Setting by Mordecai Gorelik
Velvet locomotive

ILLUSION

DEAD END (1934). Setting by Norman Bel Geddes
The wash diminished in perspective

White photo

which to explain these techniques. Each of them had a rational purpose. Each had its theorists and practitioners, and each has represented nothing more or less than a hopeful formula for interpreting life in terms of a stage platform set up in front of an audience.

There are those who say that the purpose of theatre is to teach. Others say, in contradiction, that the purpose of theatre is to amuse, or at most, to interest. The burden of proof is upon those who make this arbitrary division in the nature of theatre. The purpose of living theatre, as we know through our experience with it, is to teach apparently without effort, so that to learn by way of theatre is like playing an exhilarating game. Good theatre, like good art of any sort, is not pedantry; neither is it mere tittilation.

The scaffold of theatre is set up. Upon it a game is played by the actors and spectators, a delightful game both serious and gay, a game of life and death. On a platform before us—in a manner known only to the theatre, perhaps—the confused flow of life about us will be made clearer to our minds and senses. Costumed actors will tread upon the platform, making gestures and speeches. They will play before, or upon, a stage setting. Music and colored lights will accompany the action—

But what, indeed, is this theatrical manner which is known only to the theatre? The definition is not easily found.

Stage form is something whose outlines have become clearer only as the result of centuries of thought, practice and experiment. From time to time it has crystallized temporarily in certain styles. None of these styles has attained perfection. None of them is likely to give us perfection in the immediate future. Let us compare them, admiring their ingenuity and noting the vigor with which they have been proposed and defended. What is more important, let us learn from them.

We have maintained that the traditional, and basic, form of dramatic production is not the illusory but the *conventional* style. Admittedly it is difficult to sort out these two styles, since every historic period has contained a mixture of both.

Still the matter is not settled by denoting the illusory style as the standard of excellence and then concluding that the conventional style is a naïve approximation of the illusory. Neither is it settled by asserting that the two styles are really identical. The tendencies are obviously distinct. We are not likely to learn much about either of them if we name them identical. Past stage techniques have been largely conventional. But the illusory factor has developed until our current technique, in contrast to previous ones, is specifically that of illusion.

What caused this development of illusory technique? We shall try to answer that question later on. For the moment let us take note that the illusory style as we know it in its present systematic form is not the eternal technique of theatre. It is only one of the techniques which the stage has tried out in the course of centuries. Its successors (which have already appeared on the horizon) show a tendency to return to the conventional style.

The technique of illusion is not the theatre's eternal form. It is not even the theatre's habitual form. Unless we are alert to that fact we cannot advance toward an improved technique in the future.

NOTES

1. DEAD END, by Sidney Kingsley. Produced and designed by Norman Bel Geddes. Belasco Theatre, New York, 1934.

2. CASEY JONES, by Robert Ardrey. Produced by the Group Theatre, designed by Mordecai Gorelik. Fulton Theatre, New York, 1937.

3. Although Chinese acting troupes have often visited New York, playing usually in older theatres close to Chinatown, this account of a New York production of THE STRATEGY OF THE UNGUARDED CITY is fictitious. The author vouches for the accuracy of atmosphere and method of production. The story of the play has been derived from Cecilia S. L. Zung's *Secrets of the Chinese Drama.*

4. See Chapter III, Note 9.

5. "It is a fact that up to 465 [B. C.] this simple arrangement endured which explains the settings and some of the conventions in the earliest plays of Aeschylus. Thus the SUPPLIANTS (c. 490 B. C.), the PERSIANS (472 B. C.), and PROMETHEUS BOUND (c. 47 B. C.) are all laid, in contradistinction to later plays, in open, desert countryside unflanked by any building, proving the non-existence then of any background. Aeschylus adapted these early plays to the requirements of the stage, just as later he and other playwrights made use of the scenic wall erected after 465 B. C. Still further, Aeschylus utilized for dramatic purposes the trench or drop formed at the rear edge of the orchestral circle. In

PROMETHEUS BOUND a dummy figure was evidently used for the captive fire-bringer, and this figure at the close of the drama sank into the abyss, to give place to a live actor who ascended at the commencement of the lost PROMETHEUS UNBOUND. . . . In many other ways physical conditions which might well seem at first sight inconvenient or unadaptable to the purposes of dramatic art were freely made use of by the playwrights. Thus the fact that the performance of the dramas commenced usually at sunrise led to time references in the dialogue which made dramatic action and actual surroundings harmonize. In Euripides' IPHIGENIA AT AULIS the setting starts with the last darkness before dawn. 'What star is there sailing?' asks Agamemnon, to whom his attendant replies, 'Sirius, in his middle height near the seven Pleiads riding.' Some time later the dawn begins to break:

> That silver light
> Shows the approach of morn, the harbinger
> Of the sun's fiery steeds.

The rest of the action takes place in the broad light of day. What an effect this synchronization of dramatic setting and actual physical phenomena must have had may well be imagined." (Nicoll: *The Development of the Theatre*).

6. The Dionysian Theatre at Athens was rebuilt in stone following a collapse of the wooden seats in 499 B. C.

7. The famous contemporary picture of the Mystery Play at Valenciennes in 1547 shows a line of mansions standing on a *platea* which is itself a rather high platform.

8. Simonson rightly calls attention to this mixture of styles in historic productions, remarking that "The scenic methods employed by the hallowed past I found to be quite as pragmatic as my own." He then concludes with the surprising non-sequitur that stage technique has always been illusory.

9. "In the AGAMEMNON of Aeschylus, Agamemnon and Cassandra approach the palace in a chariot; Agamemnon remains seated there for a considerable time, while he converses with Clytaemnestra; he then dismounts and enters the palace, leaving Cassandra still in the chariot. In the ELECTRA of Euripides, when Clytaemnestra comes to visit her daughter at the country cottage, she arrives in a chariot, accompanied by Trojan maidens, who assist her to dismount. Animals for riding were occasionally introduced. In the PROMETHEUS there is the winged steed upon which Oceanus makes his entrance; and in the FROGS of Aristophanes Xanthias rides in upon a donkey. " (Haigh).

10. "We have mentioned that the actors sometimes talked from the roof of the *proskenion*, and nothing prevents us from supposing that the gods frequently made their appearances there, simply stepping forth from the upper storey of the edifice, which had an opening in

front . . . but this simple arrangement was not always practicable. Thus in the ORESTES of Euripides it is distinctly indicated that Apollo is soaring with Helena in the air above the roof of the palace (*proskenion*) on which Orestes, Pylades and Hermione find themselves, and that he flies away at last to the 'star-covered' vault, carrying off Helena to the festal hall of Zeus. In the MAD HERCULES Iris and Lyssa (the goddess of insanity) appear in a similar way in the air above the roof, and while Iris flies away, Lyssa descends into the dwelling of Hercules (down behind the *proskenion*) in order to derange the hero's mind." (Mantzius).

"In the BELLEREPHON the hero rode up to heaven on the winged steed Pegasus; and in the ANDROMEDA Perseus flew down through the air to the foot of the cliff where the heroine was chained. The *mechane* is also parodied in many places by Aristophanes. In the CLOUDS, Socrates is seen hanging in a basket in mid-air, and studying astronomy. Iris, in the BIRDS, comes floating down from the sky in such an irregular and eccentric fashion that Peisthetaerus has the greatest difficulty in bringing her to a standstill. In a fragment of the DAEDALUS the actor who is going to ascend entreats the man in charge of the machinery to give him warning, before he begins to haul up the rope, by exclaiming 'Hail, light of the sun.' The ascent of Trygaeus upon a beetle in the PEACE was intended as a parody upon the BELLEREPHON of Euripides. The speech of Trygaeus, in the course of his aerial journey, consists of a ludicrous mixture of phrases from the BELLEREPHON, shouts to the beetle to keep his head straight, and terrified appeals to the stage-manager to look after the security of the pulley." (Haigh).

11. "The ekkyklema was probably invented towards the middle of the fifth century, about the time when the actor's booth was first converted into a regular back-scene. It is used twice in the ORESTEIA. In the AGAMEMNON, after the murder has been committed, the platform rolls out, and reveals the person of Clytaemnestra, standing over the dead bodies of Agamemnon and Cassandra. In the CHOEPHORI there is a parallel scene. Orestes is brought into view standing beside the bodies of Aegisthus and Clytaemnestra, and pointing to the net in which his father had been entangled and slaughtered many years ago. He is seized with frenzy, descends upon the ekkyklema, and hastens away to the temple of Apollo at Delphi. The platform is then withdrawn into the palace. During the rest of the century there are many instances of the use of the ekkyklema in tragedy. In the AJAX the interior of the tent is exposed to view by this contrivance; and at the end of the ANTIGONE the body of Eurydice is exhibited, lying beside the altar at which she has stabbed herself. In the HIPPOLYTUS, after the suicide of Phaedra, her dead body is displayed upon the ekkyklema, and Theseus takes from it the letter in which she makes her charge against Hippolytus. In the ELECTRA of Sophocles the door is thrown open at the command of Aegisthus, and the platform rolls out and exhibits Orestes and Pylades

standing beside the corpse of Clytemnaestra, which is covered with a cloth. Aegisthus himself removes the cloth, and then Orestes and Pylades descend to the stage, and the platform is drawn back again. In the HECUBA the sons of Polymestor, who have been slaughtered inside the tent, are made visible to the spectators by means of the ekkyklema. In the HERCULES FURENS Hercules is exhibited lying prostrate between the bodies of his wife and children, with his face covered up, and his limbs chained to the broken column which he had thrown down in his frenzy. Amphitryon then comes out of the palace, and loosens his chains. Later on Theseus arrives, and uncovers his face and helps him to rise. He then descends to the stage, and the ekkyklema is rolled back into the palace. . . . The ekkyklema is also occasionally used in Comedy. . . . The device is also used in the CLOUDS to show the inside of the phrontisterion. The disciples of Socrates are seen hard at work on their studies, with globes, diagrams, black-boards, and other scholastic materials round about them." (Haigh).

"In the ACHARNIANS Dicaeopolis goes to the house of Euripides to borrow a tragic costume. Euripides, however, is just composing poetry, and does not want to come out of the house. So Dicaeopolis knocks at his door. . . .

D. Euripides, Euripides, come down,
If ever you came down in all your life!
'Tis I, 'tis Dicaeopolis from Chollidae.
E. I'm not at leisure to come down.
D. Perhaps—
But here's the scene-shifter can wheel you round.

"So Euripides is 'wheeled round,' and—as we gather from the subsequent conversation—appears in a reclining attitude surrounded by the costumes of his most pitiable heroes, and among these he makes his servants choose one for Dicaeopolis. . . .

"In THE MAD HERCULES the chorus finds itself alone on the stage, while Hercules in his castle is attacked by the goddess of insanity, and kills his own children in his rage; the chorus is ignorant of what has happened till a messenger relates it; but after the news has been delivered, Hercules appears before the eyes of the chorus—and of the spectators—as he lies after his furious rage, asleep and bound, near the dead bodies of his sons." (Mantzius).

12. "The Middle Ages were not purists about anachronisms, and what was good enough for an English bishop was good enough for Aeneas and Caiophas. The hands of the craftsmen who acted were discreetly cased in the gloves without which no ceremonial occasion was complete, and sometimes, at least, vizors and masks were worn. But, as a rule, the stage setting left a good deal to the imagination." (E. K. Chambers: *The Medieval Stage*).

"Happily the twelfth-century Mystery play of ADAM gives us some additional information. The disposition for the houses is still determined by the structure of the church. To the east stands the crucifix, to the left Heaven, and to the right Hell. This, at least, we may presume from the directions in the text. . . . The Paradise, we learn

'Is to be placed on a raised spot; curtains and silk cloths are to be hung about it at such a height that persons in Paradise are visible from the shoulders. Fragrant flowers and leaves are scattered there; in it are divers trees with hanging fruit so as to give the impression of a most lovely place. . . .'

"Of Hell we learn that

'Certain other devils point at them as they come, and seize them and bear them to Hell; and in Hell they shall make a great smoke arise, and they shall shout to each other in Hell in jubilation, and clash their pots and kettles, so as to be heard without.'

"Anachronistic as the drama regularly was in main outline, little details had to be scrupulously exact. There must be the bladder of blood and the sheephooks and the instruments of torture. The effect of Christ's crucifixion could not be complete unless the actor himself suffered. M. le curé, one Nicolle, of Metz, took the part of Jesus in 1437, and he 'would have died on the rood-tree, for he fainted and was like to have died had he not been rescued.'" (Nicoll).

The generally conventional effect of medieval drama was offset by a "sweeping away" of the spectators, by means of the effect of light, color, sound and incense. The liturgical drama was an extension of the church service itself, which was already highly developed in its sensory appeal. The solemnity of the religious service, taking place in a beautifully ornamented building amid shadowy space, lighted candles, glittering altars and vestments, music and singing, was transferred to the Church theatre. The dramatic spectacles were addressed to the people, at that time almost entirely illiterate, in order to strengthen the Catholic faith.

It is interesting that the Church drama, like the drama of ancient Greece, also had its burlesque form. The "Feast of Fools" was a kind of safety-valve for the jealousy which existed between the major and the minor clergy. It consisted of a burlesque of religious services and religious dramas, in which the parishioners also took part. The Fools' burlesque, technically considered, tore down all the subtle sensual impressions which the regular Church drama was at pains to create. According to Chambers, the Feast of Fools

"was an ebullition of the lout beneath the cassock. . . . It took place in the churches, and culminated in a burlesque of sacred services, with a mock bishop. There was feasting and dancing, with ribald songs to Church tunes; masks and women's dresses were worn by some participants; rubber and old shoes were burnt as incense; cowbells were used for music; each part of the Mass ended in a bray with the congregation responding in hee-haws."

13. ". . . no attempts are made to call forth illusion or to produce

on the feelings, by decorations, lighting, etc., those effects which form an essential part of the pleasure of European playgoers . . . the stage consists of a platform four or five feet high, at the back of the hall. It is framed with red drapery, and at the sides are closed boxes for spectators. A front curtain is unknown, nor are there 'wings' or any other decorations. The background is a canvas partition, which, according to very ancient custom, has two doors, one serving only as entrance, the other only as exit. . . . The orchestra is placed in sight of the public between the doors on the stage; it is composed of flute and clarinet players, but its chief ingredient is drummers and kettle-drummers. It is the chief task of this orchestra, whenever a sentence calls for particular attention, to underline it with a deafening accompaniment on their noisy instruments.

"A wood, for instance, is represented by tying a green branch to a chair-back. The apparently difficult problem of conducting an army to some remote province is solved in the following very simple and unmistakable way: the leader takes a whip in one hand and a bridle in the other, and gallops around the stage accompanied by loud music from the band; at last he informs the spectators that he has arrived at his destination. The passing from one room to another is expressed by making a movement which indicates the opening of a door, and lifting a leg as if crossing a threshold. A wall surrounding a town is represented either by a piece of calico held up by two coolies, or, in a more decorative but less comprehensible fashion, by three or four supers lying down one on the top of another in a corner of the stage. . . ." (Mantzius).

"An understood convention is the coloring in face-painting (the faces are often made-up until they are to all practical purposes masks); a whitened face denotes a wicked person, a red face is honest, a gold face heavenly, a streaked face belongs to a robber, and so on. A bride wears a red veil, deceased ancestors wear black veils or else strips of paper hanging from their right ears, a sick person wears an opaque yellow veil. Corrupt officials wear round hats." (Cheney).

"*Che-chi* is a cart. It is depicted by two flags upon which there are painted wheels. Two servants hold the flags on either side of the rider who may either stand quietly or move about . . . in the old drama the taking of food was never presented realistically. Eating was usually depicted through a song or through several tunes on a flute. . . . More interesting are the cases where the meanings are multifarious, where one and the same object, depending upon its use, may have more than one meaning. Such, for instance, are a table, a chair and a broom made of horsehair. 'A table or *Cho-Tzu,* more than any other object, can depict all sorts of things: sometimes it is an inn, sometimes it is a dining table, a courtroom or an altar.' A table is used when it is necessary to show that a man is climbing a mountain or jumping over a fence. When it is turned sideways (*Tao-I*) it symbolizes a man sitting either on a cliff or on the ground in an uncomfortable position. When a woman is climbing a mountain she gets up on a table. Similarly several chairs put together represent a bed." (Sergei Eisenstein: *The Enchanter from the Pear Garden*).

According to Cecilia S. L. Zung's *Secrets of the Chinese Drama* (which contains perhaps the most detailed account of Chinese stage usage so far published), every costume, makeup, gesture and property used on the Chinese stage is classified and named. There are twenty classified ways in which an actor may laugh or smile. Miss Zung lists twenty sleeve movements, nineteen movements of the hand, four of the arm, sixteen of the foot, six of the leg, two of the wrist, seven movements performed with a pheasant-feather headdress—all of these having their separate nomenclature. Symbolic actions include the following: "A bundle about the size of a head wrapped in a red cloth (sometimes with a beard if an old man) indicates a decapitated head. Any character decapitated runs quickly off the stage and the property-man produces the head if called for. . . . The poor are represented as living in caves, the entrance of which is very low, hence there is a special method for entering and leaving such an abode." To portray getting aboard a boat "The actor jumps forward and while resting on the floor his body sways gracefully back and forth, in harmony with the up and down movements in the knees, as if to balance himself on the unsteady boat. Then he picks up the oars, placed on one side of the stage. . . . If an actor comes on stage through 'Hsia-ch'ang-mên' (the exit curtain) with an oar in his hand, it usually means that he is already on the boat and is welcoming some passengers. In this case, he holds out the oar . . . toward those who enter through the 'Shang-ch'ang-mên' (the entrance curtain)."

14. Simonson's thesis that Greek stage form was, like all others, an attempt at illusion, is refuted at every turn by the type of evidence given by Haigh:

". . . in the groupings of actors and chorus in a Greek theatre there could be none of that realistic imitation of life which is sometimes seen on the modern stage.

"To produce an impression by scenic means would have been alien to the taste of the Athenians of the fifth century. . . . The long scene in the rear was so far decorated as to form a pleasing background, and to show off the persons of the actors to advantage. But no attempt was made to produce a realistic landscape, or to convey the idea of depth and distance.

"The representation of scenery on the periaktoi was probably of the simple and symbolic character which marked Greek stage scenery in general; a rock would stand for a mountain district, a waved blue line and a dolphin for the sea, a river god perhaps, holding a vessel of water, for a river.

"Several mechanical contrivances are mentioned in connexion with

Opening Night of Molière's Le Malade Imaginaire (1673)

the Greek stage. The most peculiar of these, and the one most alien to all our modern notions of stage illusions is the ekkyklema. . . . Such devices as the ekkyklema and periaktoi would never have been tolerated by them (the Athenians), if their aim had been to produce an illusion by the accurate imitation of real objects."

With regard to the mask Haigh states "There was a total disregard for realism and fidelity to nature." As to costumes "The nature of the tragic actor's dress was sufficient in itself to make a realistic type of acting impossible."

15. For a performance of Cardinal Bibbiena's CALANDRA settings were provided which were described by Castiglione as ". . . laid in a very fine city, with streets, palaces, churches, and towers, all in relief and looking as if they were real, the effect being completed by the admirable paintings in scientific perspective."

At Ferrara in a revival of the MENAECHMI of Plautus (1486) the scenery according to a contemporary account contained a ship which "had ten persons in it and was fitted with oars and a sail in a most realistic manner." (*The Stage Is Set*).

REFERENCES

Allardyce Nicoll: *The Development of the Theatre.* Harcourt, Brace.

A. E. Haigh: *The Attic Theatre.* Clarendon Press.

Lee Simonson: *The Stage Is Set.* Harcourt, Brace.

Karl Mantzius: *A History of Theatrical Art.* Duckworth, London, 1903.

E. K. Chambers: *The Medieval Stage.* Oxford University Press, New York, 1903.

Sheldon Cheney: *The Theatre.* Tudor Publishing Company.

Sergei Eisenstein: *The Enchanter from the Pear Garden. Theatre Arts.* October, 1935.

Cecilia S. L. Zung: *Secrets of the Chinese Drama.* Kelly & Walsh, Ltd., Hong Kong, 1937.

Josiah Condor. From Huntly Carter: *The Theatre of Max Reinhardt.* Mitchell Kennerley, New York, 1924.

John Mason Brown: *The Art of Playgoing.* W. W. Norton & Company.

Constantin Stanislavsky: *My Life in Art.* Little, Brown & Company.

3

SUNSET OF SPLENDOR

PERFECTLY NATURAL

The curtain rises on the Press Room of the Criminal Courts Building, Chicago: a chamber set aside by the City Fathers for the use of journalists and their friends.

It is a bare, disordered room, peopled by newspaper men in need of shaves, pants pressing and small change. Hither reporters are drawn by an irresistible lure, the privilege of telephoning free.

There are seven telephones in the place, communicating with the seven newspapers of Chicago.

All are free.

Here is the rendezvous of some of the most able and amiable bums in the newspaper business; here they meet to gossip, play cards, sleep off jags and date up waitresses between such murders, fires, riots and other public events as concern them.

The furniture is of the simplest; two tables, an assortment of chairs, spittoons, a water cooler, etc.—two dollars' worth of dubious firewood, all told.

There is one elegant item, however; a huge, ornate black walnut desk, the former property of Mayor Fred A. Busse, deceased about 1904. It now belongs to Roy Bensinger, feature writer for the Chicago Tribune and a fanatic on the subject of hygiene.

Despite Mr. Bensinger's views, his desk is the repository for soiled linen, old sandwiches, empty bottles and other items shed by his colleagues.

The two tables serve as telephone desks, gaming boards and (in a pinch) as lits d'amour. . . .[1]

We playgoers have gathered before the curtain of Ben Hecht and Charles MacArthur's THE FRONT PAGE. Now as the curtain goes up we are suddenly thrust into this smoke-filled room of a group of Chicago police reporters. We have returned to the pre-Newspaper Guild era. We hear the jangling of telephone bells. We spy upon the raucous existence of a bygone race of journalists, who carry on their crap games as if they had no idea that their hideaway has been transported through the air to a stage platform. One wall of their room has been removed. They are exposed to our gaze as if they were an ant colony in a glass box. . . .

Or perhaps we have gone to a movie instead. The credit lines at the beginning of the picture dissolve away, and a scene fades in. A row of crude house-fronts baking in the noonday sun; a strip of wooden sidewalk; a dirt road, with a stage coach pulling up before the Red Dog Hotel in a cloud of alkali dust, flea-bitten dogs yipping at the heels of the coach horses. . . .

We are no longer inside a picture theatre in Times Square, New York or in Muncie, Indiana. Instead we seem to have been transported to the town of Red Dog, Arizona, in the year 1894. We are there, in the desert town, prowling around like ghosts of the future. No one sees us. The inhabitants carry on their lives all unsuspecting that a movie audience is paying them a visit. They do not dream that some of the most intimate details of their lives are open to our inspection, that their very smiles and frowns are carried close for us to see.

This curious state of affairs does not seem at all curious to us, the audience. It seems perfectly natural for the theatre to be like that. Even the scene designers who planned the stage setting or the movie "location," even the actors who live their parts in these settings see nothing remarkable about it. (Unless, perhaps, they are white-haired veterans who can recall, somewhat dimly, a different relationship.)

But the theatre has not always been as "natural" as that. There was a time, not very long ago in history, when it was something else. For practical purposes you can name the very day on which our current form of theatre began. It was March 30, 1887.

This date, which marks the sunrise of modern theatre, is also notable for another reason. It witnessed not only a sunrise but a sunset. With this date one of theatre's most cherished ideals comes to an end. The Baroque ideal of theatrical *splendor* goes down forever, having outlived its usefulness.

Our own theatre did not merely *follow* the Baroque. It superceded the Baroque after a clash of philosophies, just as the Baroque had supplanted its own predecessor, the church drama, after a similar conflict of thought. We shall not fully understand our contemporary theatre unless we know why and how it differed from Baroque tradition.

Let us catch a last glimpse of that passing splendor.

"KINGS ARE IMMORTAL"

The year is 1673. Elkanah Settle's current hit, THE EMPRESS OF MOROCCO, is holding forth at the Duke of York's Theatre in Dorset Garden, London. It is a new production in a new theatre. For this playhouse—designed by the famous architect Christopher Wren for the equally famous dramatist and theatre manager William D'Avenant—has opened only two years before. Mr. Betterton, the leading actor and stage director of the Duke's Theatre, had journeyed to Paris, by order of King Charles himself, to make note of all the French improvements in scenes and machines which might be incorporated in the new stage. A pity indeed that Sir William did not live to see the building he had planned so carefully!

As to the play, it is a spectacular work by a young author; and it has already aroused the jealousy of the older dramatic poet John Dryden. Between ourselves, Dryden has been wrong to circulate a pamphlet against Settle. This attempt to dispose of a young rival by means of slurs and slanders is in no wise the best of taste and is more likely to harm Dryden himself. It looks as if THE EMPRESS will have a record run—a whole month! On the other hand it is not a profound work, and will never rank with Dryden's pieces for immortality. And surely Mister Settle had no right, in the first place to sneer at Dryden in his Prologue!

It is after three o'clock of a July day as our boat scrapes the dock below the Dorset Garden theatre. Our boatman shoves off again as we clamber up the wooden stairs to the street above. The flag is flying high over the theatre. King and court are attending the play today, and the seats have been filled ever since noon. We push through the crowd of idlers, gawkers, pickpockets and ordinary people who have come to stare at the gentry. Musketeers posted outside keep off those who might otherwise force their way in to join their betters. Fortunately no one stops us. We have sent footmen to hold our seats, since none are reserved. Or shall we say places, rather than seats? For we are to be in the pit, where there are long, green-upholstered benches instead of chairs. We drop our brass tokens in the doorman's cashbox and enter a playhouse whose style is modernism in Restoration England. Today we should call it the style of the late Baroque.

The Duke's Theatre constitutes one-half of the public theatres of London, the other half being the Theatre Royal in Drury Lane. The audiences of Shakespeare's day have dwindled to the handful of courtiers, officials and hangers-on who surround the newly restored throne of the Stuarts. There may be a few fans outside of London's two playhouses, but the Puritans and the general population are boycotting the stage, which they consider the favorite haunt of Old Nick.

Mere bigotry does not explain their abhorrence. The past quarter century had seen events which shook England's foundations and divided the population into warring camps. By 1642 the increasing power of the English industrial and mercantile classes became voiced in Parliament; and Parliament had decided that the feudal despotism of Charles I was out of date. In the civil war which followed, Parliament had the support not only of the wealthy merchants, manufacturers and bankers, but the growing city populations, the artisans and independent yeomen.

The Parliamentary army was under command of the redoubtable Oliver Cromwell. It was one of the most remarkable armies in history, with extreme democratic tendencies which passed beyond the desires either of the King or of Parliament. Cromwell handled this dangerous situation with sagacity and ruthlessness, first smashing the revolutionary influence of the Levellers which dominated the army, and then bringing Charles I to the execution block. The Puritan military dictatorship which he set up—known as the Protectorate—endured to his death in 1658. Two years later Charles II was called back from exile to a kingship shorn of autocratic power.

The new King remained unpopular with most of the nation. It was rightly suspected that he was hand in glove with the "Popish" circles so dreaded by the mass of the English people. The political intrigues of the court were matched only by the scandal of court life. "A sad, vicious, negligent Court," as Pepys noted in his famous diary. Cynicism and venality hid themselves under a sophistication which the King and his retinue had acquired during a not too painful sojourn in France, Italy and Spain. And the theatres, opened for the first time since the onset of the civil wars, combined the

From Vitruvius (Venice, 1566)

Classicism

Ancestor of Baroque

opulence of Louis XIV's playhouses with a license that would have surprised even the unmoral Elizabethans. . . .

The appearance of the theatre in which we are taking our seats seems rather more familiar than the historical background we have just recalled. The picture-frame of the proscenium, or "frontispiece," the boxes garlanded in gilt plaster and circling the auditorium, are all like those of the average theatre into which we go today. As we grow accustomed to the gaudy taffeta and brocade costumes of our neighbors, and to the hubbub—for the Second Music of the overture has just finished, and the audience is again exchanging loud witticisms across the auditorium—we begin to see the place as a smaller-scale opera house. It is horseshoe-shaped, the ends of the horseshoe curving toward the stage. Two tiers of boxes and a gallery line the interior; the second row of boxes even extends over the deep stage apron on either side of the proscenium.

This outthrust stage apron is cut off from the audience by a line of "floats" burning behind metal shields. (The floats consist of a long wick floating on corks in an oil-filled trough.) Right and left, the four entrance doors opening on the apron are ornamented with gilt pillars. High over the proscenium with its plush curtains hangs a heavy gilt cornice, at its center two cherubs and the crest of the Duke of York. On either side of the cherubs, caryatids representing Thalia and Melpomene support the ceiling of the musicians' gallery, which is enclosed by casement windows. The finest work of the master-craftsman Grinling Gibbons has gone into the design and carving of the ornaments.

The stage is artificially lit, but the afternoon sun, discreetly muffled by curtains, slants across the audience. We can look far up to the "paradise" of the commoners in their shilling seats. But the rest of the gathering is a select one indeed, from King Charles and his Queen to the pretty courtesans—the "fireships" in the cant of that day—for whom the playhouse is a proper anchorage. Since it is now the fashion for royalty to go regularly to the public theatres, the principal box, with its carving of Apollo, has been set aside for Their Majesties.

The royal presence does not seem to have subdued the manners of the playgoers to any great degree. But it has evoked a more lavish display than usual of jewels, feathers, ribbons, ruffles, gold and silver lace. The ladies in their puffed and slashed sleeves, their Vandyke collars, their crested headdresses *à la Fontanges,* their face-patches in the shape of little diamonds, crescents or flowers, are no more than a match for their gallants. These gentlemen, from their curled perukes to their high heels, are as vain and quarrelsome as barnyard cocks. They flutter their lace handkerchiefs delicately, but they are also ready to loll over the benches, to bellow out oaths, take swigs from a bottle and lay hold of their rapiers even during a performance. The seating arrangement of the playhouse permits them to display the prestige of their ancestry, the amount of their wealth and their standing with His Majesty.

A play is a social event of the first magnitude in that charmed circle. One goes to gape and goggle, to be gaped at in turn; and woe to the courtier whose seat shows a decline in fortune!

Eight years before, the pestilence had reduced London to a lazar-house, with people dying by the tens of thousands; but the theatres, temporarily closed, had reopened while the last of the dead were still being carried away in carts piled high with bodies. The following year a terrible fire had devastated half the city, but the playhouses opened again immediately. Not only the show, but the social comedy must go on!

The ladies whisper behind their fans or hide their faces in modish black "vizard" masks, pretending to ward off some of the none too delicate compliments of their sparks. Some of milords of high degree, their faces as rouged and plastered as any of the ladies', have taken privileged positions close to the stage apron. Here in their Fop's Corner they preen their curled periwigs or—if fireships and performance both prove dull—they deal a hand or two of cards. Did not Charles frown on the custom, they would as heretofore carry on their pranks on the stage itself, the better to embarrass the performers.

Fortunately the actors are likewise privileged members of this élite. The leading women, especially, have no poor opinion of themselves. If so disposed they will hold the rise of the curtain even though the King himself fret at the delay. It is only a few years since boy actors taking women's parts have been replaced by actresses, and in no time at all the women players have become the scandal of the kingdom. The feminine members of the audience nudge each other: two of Charles' dear delights are here today. The pert Nell Gwynn, and Mary Knight, Nell's neighbor in Pall Mall, had both been in the company of the Theatre Royal until they attracted the favor of the King.

Those who prefer to be charmed by virtue can admire the qualities of Mrs. Betterton, our leading lady, who is as gifted an actress as she is devoted a wife. La belle Betterton is being carefully invested in her costume as Empress—a garment with a foundation of twenty-four yards of gold brocade. Four wardrobe women are required, and the delay is not surprising considering that their mistress will eventually have on as many yards of material and pounds of gold and silver lace as she can carry without collapse.

Such elegance is worth waiting for. She will wear the latest mode from Paris, barbaric empress though she be. The sceneries are laid in Morocco, some of them in prisons and deserts, but she will be smartly dressed in each. 'Tis said, indeed, that so fine a costume tragedy has not been seen in the Duke's company since HERACLIUS. Greek and Roman plays are becoming to Mrs. Betterton, don't you think? Did you see her as Ianthe in THE SIEGE OF RHODES? So fetching in her big scene with the ancient Greek generals—carried off her new lace bodice and farthingale with such an air! They were a sensation at Fontainbleau that spring—the styles, not the generals.

The musicians are opening their windows above the stage—it is time for the Curtain Tune. The orchestra of twelve violins is augmented by harpsicals, theorboes, bass viols, "recorders," trumpets and a kettle drum. The curtains are looping up, and our neighbors begin to abate their noise a trifle. Really, something should be done to hush the bold-eyed sluts who sell oranges, and themselves—at the tops of their voices—to the gentlemen in the boxes. . . . And now, from one of the entrance doors of the forestage, enters the allegorical figure of the Prologue (female), attended by Cupid and Mars. She recites her verses sonorously at the footlights, curtsies toward the King as she nears the end of her greeting:

> We'll then presume, you are the Author's Friends,
> And tho' you miss your dear delights, you may
> Be to the Poet kind, and Clap the Play . . .
>
> And therefore, Sir, to you we humbly bend. [*To the King*
> Yet from your Constancy we need not fear;
> To all fair Nymphs you keep an open Ear.

As the lady of the Prologue curtseys low and with sweeping train exits through the opposite door of the forestage portals, she is followed by her attendants and the fulsome applause of the assembly. The painted scene behind her opens in the middle and slides off on either side, revealing what is supposed to be the interior of a Moroccan prison. It is a pretty scene, greeted with admiration. We visitors from the future observe this setting with rather tempered enthusiasm, although there is no denying its quaint charm.

Our first impression is of old-time vaudeville scenery, badly underlit. The stage floor, which slopes up from the footlights to the rear wall, is covered with a ground-cloth of green baize, temporarily buttoned down.[2] A row of six parallel side-wings (each wing made of canvas stretched over a wooden frame) stands on either side of the stage. The two rows diminish in size, converging toward each other as they recede from the audience, until a painted backdrop closes in the rear. Two additional wings downstage, known as shutters, can be brought together in the center to mask the changes of scene. Candles in tin sconces have been nailed to the backs of all these frames (in fine disregard of fire hazard), to illuminate the far end of the stage.

The stage is extremely deep, fully as deep as the auditorium. Half of the boxes do not see the backdrop at all; but what of that if the occupants can see each other? Besides not much acting is carried on at that depth. All the important action takes place at the very edge of the forestage, where the candle flames at every moment threaten to set fire to beribboned breeches and sweeping trains.

The dungeon of the Moroccan Emperor seems to be curiously like that of the Conciergerie in France; and indeed the design has been closely adapted from one of Vigarani's settings at the Paris Salle des Machines. The Duke's Theatre cannot boast of as many resources as its French counterpart, but it leaves its London competitor, the Theatre Royal, far behind in devising spectacles. That fully explains why the management of the Royal is forever casting innuendoes about the "odious and meretricious splendor" on the stage of the Duke's.[3] Indeed, Mr. Thomas Duffet is now preparing for the Theatre Royal a new piece, entitled THE EMPRESS OF MOROCCO, A FARCE, for no other purpose but to decry the success of Mr. Settle and to turn public opinion against his play.

The splendor of the scenery which stands before us is almost entirely painted. Each of the side-wings has been painted in conventional Baroque style to represent pillars made of great stone blocks, while the effect of an underground vault thus obtained is completed in the backdrop, which represents a stone wall pierced by barred windows. A row of framed arches overhead is painted like stone vaulting. The setting may be a prison, but it is wide open between all the wings on either side; while two magnificent chandeliers, most un-prisonlike, hang overhead to illuminate the actors.

To our Naturalistically-trained eyes the total effect is very unlifelike. But nobody else at this performance is trying to look at it with Naturalistic eyesight. Only a psychopath could believe he is looking at an illusion of life when he is obviously looking at rows of painted flats, arranged in a rigidly formal style. This arrangement of flats is a flimsy architecture conventionally painted —an architecture which, as Gregor remarks, is "incapable of sustaining any load." The stage with all its decorations is nothing more than a gracious room lined with curious panels.[4]

As we watch, the stage picture is completed by the actors, who enter from the prosenium doors. First comes the Prince of Morocco, Muly Labas, in chains, attended by his guards. He advances to the footlights, and there, striking a noble pose, he addresses the audience in stately Alexandrine verse. His wrists are shackled but the chains are long enough not to interfere with his ample gestures as he thinks out loud for the benefit of the public.

His imperial father, a ferocious old potentate, has sent him to prison because he has dared to fall in love with Morena, daughter of the enemy prince Taffalet. Such is the sad history he imparts to us. His soliloquy finished, he is joined forthwith by Morena herself, also in chains. The lovers mingle their sighs. And now there comes upon the scene the sorrowful Queen Mother, her sweeping train managed by a little Negro page.[5] No one could surmise at this instant that this regal figure, this grief-stricken beauty, is actually a super-Lady Macbeth, a demoniac murderess and adulteress capable of exclaiming later in the play,

> Let those, whom pious Conscience awes, forebear,
> And stop at Crimes because they Vengeance fear.
> My deeds above their reach and power aspire,
> My bosom holds more Rage, than all Hell Fire.

In these exalted dramas, says Dubech, nothing less than the fate of kingdoms suffices for a plot; and usurpation and treason are the mainsprings of the action:

It is not the character of the *dramatis personae* which saves these plays. The authors have never attempted to diagnose the souls of their people. Five or six sentiments, very simple but overexcited, are the rule; we are a long way from the diversity of the Elizabethans. All the stage characters resemble each other in the dramas of D'Avenant as

THE EMPRESS OF MOROCCO (1673)

From the first printed text

in those of Congreve. The heroes are of the blood royal. A subtle etiquette, codified by Rymer, establishes the rights of precedence in rank, religion and nationality; an infidel may never assassinate a Christian, nor a commoner slay a prince of the blood. The sympathetic characters are always young and beautiful, faithful, desperately in love. . . . The heroine is of an immovable constancy, generally enamoured; but sometimes she is an unfeeling beauty, a great princess who rebels against the commands of love; while the heroes are swept away by their passion at first sight and forever. These grand leading rôles feel themselves superior to destiny, they surrender only to love, defying in long tirades the earth, the heavens and common sense. The traitors, numerous and sinister, are disarmingly naïve compared with Iago. Criminals they are, and criminals they remain, out of motives lacking in originality: frustrated ambition, unhappy passions. They do not reform, and die with an insult on their lips, or else go mad.

It need not surprise us that a monarch whose debonair ancestor was deprived of his head by the usurper Cromwell should want to see treason receive its just deserts, at least on the stage.

Before being harrowed by the tigerish maneuvers of the Empress Laula, we are to have a respite of two eye-filling scenes, one of them an interlude or *intermedio*. Even as Laula leaves the dungeon in sinister converse with Crimalhaz, the shutters in the rear of the stage click together, removing the prison wall from sight. The arches overhead go up into the flies, revealing "sky borders," scenery painted to represent clouds. It appears that the method of shifting the scenery is like peeling cards off a card deck. The side-wings of the prison setting are drawn off, revealing others which show the entrance gates of a harbor.

The curtain remains up, the chandeliers illuminate the scene; the change of setting is accompanied musically by a shift of the orchestra to the wind and percussion instruments. Now the shutters reopen, sliding off to the sides. The prison backdrop has gone up on rollers, and there is revealed instead, to the prolonged applause of the audience, and to the sound of trumpets and the discharging of guns, a "Prospect of a large River, with a glorious Fleet of Ships, supposed to be the Navy of Muly Hamet, commander of the forces of Morocco." It is none other than Muly Labas who is being saluted as Emperor. The old Emperor has died, pardoning the lovers with his last breath. The son who was so unjustly imprisoned will now ascend the throne.

This picture is impressive not only as a tableau: it is filled with motion. In the foreground a rowboat is putting toward shore, while in the distance caravels under full sail ride the waves, which rise and fall. In the sky a natural sun seems to blaze over the heavens. (The rowboat is a cut-out setpiece, behind which the actors stand plying their oars. Back of the boat a cloth is stretched, painted to resemble the sea and diligently shaken by the stagehands in the wings on either side. The still more distant waves are papier-mâché, built like augur-shaped rollers and turned by a handle offstage. The ships are cut-out pieces heaved from below by men stationed behind the waves. The sun is a glare of light projected on the backdrop by a lantern.) With this scenic aid, the homage of the fleet to the new ruler becomes an impressive tableau animated by a doll-like life.

In the Interlude which follows, the ceremonies are continued:

> A State is presented, the King, Queen and Marianne seated, Muly Hamet, Abdelcador, and Attendants, a Moorish Dance is presented by Moors in several Habits. . . .

The Moorish men, their faces blackened like Negroes, with turbans like dunce-caps on their heads, prance about a feathery palm tree, shaking tambourines. Their women, in feathered headdresses more properly worn by American Indians, join in a statelier saraband.

Is it possible, we wonder, that the production can maintain this level of gaudy display all the way through? There are at least a dozen scenes to come! But there is no let-down either in the machinations of Laula and her paramour, Crimalhaz, or in the scenic effects which accompany them. To be sure some of the palace scenes have made their appearance in previous shows on this stage (for the management cannot afford to create an entirely new series of backgrounds for each production); and the connoisseurs in the audience assure their neighbors that the settings by Stephenson are inferior to those of the Italian, Bibbiena, whose stupendous vistas, angular perspectives and overpowering detail of ornament are the pride of the continental theatre. But on the whole the scenes follow upon each other with cumulative effect: palaces and more prisons, a hailstorm, a thunderstorm manufactured somehow in a heavy wooden mustard-bowl, and firework lightning (while the floats are lowered).

The storm is followed by a rainbow. A desert scene is disclosed. The emissaries of Crimalhaz lie in ambush, discharging their muskets upon Muly Hamet; but he overpowers them single-handed, crying

Dye Slaves and may this desart raise a brood
Of unknown Monsters from your venom'd Blood!

At the camp of the Queen Mother a masque is performed. Lycopodium fire, Bengal lights, fireworks and smoke (the stench partly overcome by rose water) rise from in back of the stage. The papier-mâché heads of frightful monsters emerge from behind cleft rocks; winged demons crawl out of trapdoors while others fly aloft on scaffolds masked by painted clouds. Under cover of this frightful costume-party the wicked Dowager plans to kidnap the Young Queen, who, in the guise of Eurydice, is to be handed over to Orpheus, to be spirited away to the underworld. Unknown to all, however, the King is also present, ready to confound this horrid plan.

Here a Dance is perform'd, by several infernal spirits, who ascend from under the Stage; the Dance ended, the King offers to Snatch the Young Queen from the Company, who instantly draws her Dagger, and stabs him.

As the King, dying, removes his mask, the Young Queen faints in horror.

The busy stagehands come forward and carry off the King's body on their shoulders, leaving us to the fifth, and final, act. Crimalhaz has succeeded to the throne. At his side stands the Queen Mother, Laula, and before him, attended by guards, is Morena, the Young Queen, accused of all the heinous crimes which have taken place since the curtain rose. The moment of Laula's triumph seems to have arrived. But the thrice-perfidious Crimalhaz has conceived a passion for the Young Queen, and it is not Morena but Laula whom the guards suddenly arrest at his order. The remaining events follow with terrifying swiftness. Apparently overcome by remorse, the Queen Mother kneels before her young rival:

Fair Innocence, I for your Pardon sue,
T'a condemned Traytor, but a Mother too:
Let her repenting sighs her griefs impart;
Who thus—offers her tears—and thus—thy Heart
[*Stabs the Young Queen*
Die Rival—and die Traytor—
[*Runs to stab Crimalhaz, but being stopt by the Guards, Stabs her self.*

The Young Queen is dead, and Laula is dying also, just as Muly Hamet and his attendants, with drawn swords and to the sound of trumpets, break in avengingly upon the scene.

There remains only the final picture for the shutters to disclose:

In the torture-chamber of a ruined castle the naked bodies of Crimalhaz and a few of his friends hang spiked upon a wall of steel hooks and curved knives, while Abdelcador, Muly Hamet's faithful friend, orates the moral:

> See the reward of Treason; death's the thing
> Distinguishes th' usurper from the King.
> Kings are immortal, and from life remove,
> From their lower Thrones to wear new Crowns above:
> But Heaven for him has scarce that bliss in store:
> When an usurper dies he reigns no more.

Subdued momentarily by this cruel scene, the audience presently breaks into tumultuous applause, bravos and huzzahs. "So perish all enemies of our King Charles!" roars someone in the assembly, and the cry is echoed and re-echoed through the house as His Majesty graciously acknowledges the sentiment. As the torrent of talk rises and opinions on the play are loudly exchanged, the charming lady of the Prologue reappears in front of the shutters, prepared now, with a sly curtsey, to give the Epilogue:

> Have we not seen (*Oh loves almighty Powers!*)
> A Wench with Tallow-Looks and Winter-Face,
> Continue one Mans Favorite seven years space?
> Some ravishing Knack i' th' sport and some brisk motion,
> Keeps the gilt Coach and the gallants Devotion.
> Be to this toy thus kind, and you will raise
> Much better Fancies to write better Plays.

The curtain falls. The members of the audience file out into the late afternoon as servants make a lane for them through the crowd. While the younger coxcombs push into the greenroom backstage to pick up the actresses, the wits and witlings return to the city by boat or climb into their coaches and sedan chairs to be carried to Will Unwin's coffee house, which serves as their Hotel Algonquin. There they will perform a solemn inquest on

Settle's tragedy. We, too, go over our impressions of the performance.

THE EMPRESS OF MOROCCO, with its rhymed speeches, its song and dance interludes, its painted picture settings, seems to us to have all the earmarks of opera rather than of tragic drama. Except that even in an opera we should be unlikely to see a tragedy of barbaric Morocco acted out in a chic Parisian wardrobe. Muly Labas, "son to the Emperor of Morocco," wears a gold crown while in jail in irons, and is otherwise a London gentleman in frilled lace, full-buttoned wig and petticoat breeches. Even if he occasionally wears a pseudo-oriental turban and carries a scimitar, sartorially considered he is really a figure from a Chinoiserie. Equally fantastic is the wicked Empress, in *commode* headdress and flowing streamers, stomacher and overskirt. Their garments, gleaming with pastel pinks, turquoise blues and chalky gold, blend in the suave candle light with the gold tones of the settings.

Pastel in its color, dim in lighting, at times softly accented by violins and viols, at times stirred by trumpet, drum and pistol-shots, its unreal characters mincing to the footlights where they declaim conventional sentiments in conventional rhymed couplets, this performance is like a fanciful gold mirror in which the playgoers see themselves idealized in thoughts and behavior.[6]

These fashionable heroes, these high-flown sentiments penned by court dramatists, is the court's opinion of itself. Surely it is not the wool merchant's idea of the court party, nor yet the artisan's, yeoman's nor Puritan's idea of the court!

So tiny a minority attended the theatre that between 1682 and 1695 a single playhouse served all of London. Dramatic works often did not earn enough money to pay for the candles used for lighting. Yet, in spite of its very limited audiences, the Baroque theatre everywhere in Europe found means to remain important. "Academies were created whose function it was to endorse and honor those authors who conformed, and to resist all apostates; and special theatres were subventioned, made the official homes of classic drama, and often given monopolies on legitimate tragedy-and-comedy production." (Cheney).

The cry of art for art's sake had yet to be uttered in the theatre. The Baroque plays were animated by the notion that the world circled about kings who sat enthroned by divine right. (Still it was also made clear that, ideally, kings must prove equal to their responsibilities or risk disaster, in spite of divine protection. This was a subsidiary idea which afterwards became Shakespeare's main theme.) The fact that the stage action took place in mythical kingdoms hardly tempered the effect of these dramas on the feuds which raged about the throne.

The other activities of Elkanah Settle, Gentleman, furnish an interesting sidelight on his writings. He was, of course, a hanger-on at court. He had the hardihood, just the same, to align himself for a while against the Duke of York, whose company had produced his EMPRESS OF MOROCCO.

Some time before 1679 he entered actively into political warfare as the literary supporter of the Earl of Shaftesbury, leader of the Whig party. Shaftesbury was sponsor for the Bill of Exclusion, which was aimed to keep the Duke of York from succession to the throne. As usual, this political maneuvering behind scenes had unexpected consequences "out front." A certain Titus Oates came forward and implicated the Duke of York in an alleged Popish plot to recover England to the Catholic Church. There was a widespread public fear of Roman agents, and Shaftesbury took care to inflame it further by means of Pope-burning ceremonies and other dramatic devices.

Settle wrote the script for the first of these anti-Roman pageants. In 1680 he turned out a play called FATAL LOVE, in which nuns and nunneries were held up to derision. This was followed by his FEMALE PRELATE, a scurrilous anti-Catholic fantasy on the fabled Pope Joan. The man-hunt of Catholics was now in full cry. In 1685 Oates was tried and sentenced as a perjurer, and the wave of persecution abated, having exhausted itself in a slaughter of Jesuits and other innocent Catholics. By then Settle had prudently deserted the Whigs and joined the Tories.

PANORAMA

Can we doubt that the Baroque method of production, which seems peculiar to us today, spelled eternal theatre to its coterie of playgoers?

Yet it, too, had had its beginnings and would have an end. It grew out of definite advances as well as limitations in thought. We shall have a better insight into our own stage practice if we review, briefly, a little of the theatre's history in relation to the general history of ideas.

What is more fascinating than the story of theatre's irregular and hesitating advance toward a knowledge of the world? To follow this story with attention is to bring ourselves face to face with the stage people and audiences of bygone times, with all their generous, forward-looking thoughts, all their passionate hopes, all their narrow assumptions and dark bigotry.

The ancient Athenian drama, so far away in time, seems much closer to us when we appreciate the meaning of that first great step away from the dramatic frenzy of the primitives. Discipline and logic helped to shape every part of that ancient stage form.

This discipline was mirrored in the formal rules with which the dramatic ceremony was conducted, the formal actions, costumes and settings. It was present in the dramatic poem, which was fundamentally rational in its approach to character and environment. The religious nature of this theatre was still evident, even in its architecture: the chorus-ground of the Attic theatre, surrounded by a bowl of seats and fronted by the scene-building (*skene*), crystallized the ritual of Dionysus, just as the scripts of the Attic poets continued to deal with the principles of Greek faith. But there was already a far-advanced technology, a superb order in the construction of these amphitheatres. The Attic theatre was still tribal and religious; yet it was capable of the highest flights of poetry and philosophy. It recognized eternal values and was still capable of dealing with matters of the keenest political moment in the Athenian city-state.

But the same theatre was handicapped by the limitations of its thought, which tended to end investigation at the borders of its polytheistic beliefs. The formal dialogue, characters, actions, setting and costumes (including masks) all enforced this taboo—not, of course, deliberately, but as a matter of long-established custom. When the study made by the dramatist threatened to go beyond the accepted views of his time he was unable to follow it further. (For that a later morality was necessary.) He could only end his quest abruptly, often by means of the *deus ex machina*.

These limitations are not mentioned here in order to discredit the Greek drama, whose achievements stand out as among the most wonderful in dramatic history. They are intended to remind the reader that no stage form, new or old, can rise, complete and perfect, above the imperfect thought of its own times.

The same rule applies to another important religious theatre —that of medieval Europe. The liturgical theatre addressed itself to an audience more barbaric, in some ways, than that of ancient Greece. In the centuries that followed the fall of the Roman Empire, disorder and darkness settled upon Europe—a long night ruled by sword and fire. Whatever order or hope prevailed were supplied by the Catholic Church, and in this work of redemption the Church drama proved vitally important. It is possible that the liturgical plays attracted the largest popular audiences known before the advent of motion pictures and radio.

This type of theatre, whose script form was derived from the chanting of the Mass, whose settings reproduced the Stations of the Cross, attempted, perhaps for the first time, that artistic synthesis later proposed by Richard Wagner. It gathered into one unified impression the dramatic symbols of Christian faith, together with the appeal of color, texture, music, dim lighting, and incense, which had already made their appearance in the cathedrals.

But this drama also had its limitations. If the Church was the only light of hope during so many centuries, one reason was its unwillingness to concede that enlightenment might come from other quarters as well. There were Popes like Clement IV, patron of the great friar, Roger Bacon, whose tolerance and statesmanship shine out across seven hundred years; but in general the Church insisted that all secular learning must adorn theology. This view applied also to the Church drama, which limited itself to the Christ story and the stories of the saints, ignoring the realm of nature and of the individual soul. When, in spite of these precautions, the performances became increasingly secular (being given in the popular tongue instead of in Latin, and by guildsmen instead of priests), they were formally banned.

It was not until the Italian Renaissance that theatre definitely outgrew its religious origins. The mercantile city-states of Italy had risen to power at the expense of the Church, whose strength was in decline. The iconography of the Church was forced to bow to a new secular art fostered by Italian merchant princes. This new art, neo-pagan, was modeled on the fragments of Greek and Roman civilization which scholars were digging up from the ground or patiently translating from forgotten manuscripts. Thus the glories of the city governments of Athens and Rome were bequeathed to Florence, Venice, Genoa and the new Rome.

Classicism may be said to date its formal installation in the theatre from the year 1584. In that year there opened (at Vicenza) the Teatro Olimpico, a playhouse that was like a diminutive Roman amphitheatre with straight walls and a roof. The plans for this theatre had come from the writings of the Roman architect Vitruvius. Aristotle's comments on drama, brought back to light, also helped to give outline to a new theatre which cut itself off completely from liturgical forms.

Perhaps this resurrected art seemed too cold, too pure at first. It was soon decked out in all the exotic ornaments which the trading ships of Venice and Genoa carried home from Asia, Africa and the Indies. Classicism in the theatre wore as a sparkling overdress the glamor of opera, ballet and triumphal procession. Artists no less gifted than Leonardo da Vinci designed its court tableaus, fêtes and *triunfos*. Composers like Monteverdi, Cavalli and Scarlatti launched its new musical form, opera.

The Renaissance, which saw the beginnings of modern science, also saw the first picture stage (at the Teatro Farnese, built about 1618), the introduction of artificial indoor lighting, the development of stage mechanics and the organization of professional acting troupes. Spectacular landscape and seascape effects reached the stage, in proof of a new kind of interest in nature, as well as of a knowledge of geography and history. Settings designed in perspective came into use—one of the results of the newly mastered science of optical perspective.

Of all the arts and crafts which graced the courts of the merchant princes of Italy, theatre, perhaps, outdazzled all the rest. The Italian courts faded in splendor as Spain, Portugal, France, Holland and England in turn began to dominate the trade routes of the world. But the luster of the new stage did not fade. Instead it shone even more brilliantly at the newer autocratic courts of western Europe. In the seventeenth and eighteenth centuries, in the hands of such talented designers as Pozzo, Piranesi and the numerous members of the Bibiena family, the neo-classic stage reached the heights of florid scenic form known to us in the Baroque style.

This cultivation of splendor was not limited to stage settings. Baroque production was classicism adapted to the palace ballroom; but so well adapted as to create a polished style in every branch of stagecraft. In the later French Renaissance, at the behest of exalted rulers like Louis XIV and of regal courtesans like Mme. de Pompadour, its form became strikingly voluptuous and ornate. Its splendor reflected the image of court society at its zenith. It expressed the social ideal of absolute monarchies—rigidly stratified, icy in wit, with an elaborate punctilio of manners that no plebeian or parvenu could hope to master.

Joseph Gregor, in the *Monumenta Scenica,* has expressed his wonder at

> . . . the marvelous cohesion, the embracing of all subjects, which really distinguishes the style of Louis XIV from and above the whole history of art. The ornament filled with esprit and passion . . . has in this epoch penetrated what is serious and important, as completely as the smallest and most obvious detail. Pictures as much as furniture, the interior of churches as much as the theatre, the functions of state which involve the lives of thousands as much as the latchet of a shoe, everything is covered with the heavy radiance of brocade. . . . The universal significance of the theatre is more complete than in any domain of the Baroque world, but it has abandoned the great allegory which saw in birth and death, marriage and coronation, the cause of theatrical opportunity; here it has descended into the smallest detail. . . . Costume has acquired, if this peculiar phrase may be admitted, the importance of a metaphysical uniform. Nothing is allowed to interfere with the slender, hard and peculiarly pretty outlines of the Louis XIV figurine, and every action, like man himself, is clothed in it: a hunt is not a hunt, but becomes at once an act of Heracles and a bed is not a bed, but the scene of the unhappy Cleopatra.

Thus the classic tradition, originally invoked as revolutionary, becomes rigidly codified and pedantic. This process applied to the script as well as to the other elements of production. The views of Aristotle were reinterpreted as ironclad laws of drama. It was asserted in the name of the great Ionian philosopher that the action of a play must be confined to twenty-four hours, that there must be only one consistent action, which must transpire in one locale.[7] These "Three Unities" fastened an iron mould on the writing of plays. Along with heroic themes and dialogue in Alexandrine verse they became the cornerstone of dramatic art.

The long history of neo-classic drama marked a signal advance in stage production. Its drawbacks were just as apparent. Grandeur and spectacle for its own sake, empty rhetoric, a venal commercialism, the prettified picture-frame stage, all became exaggerated as the neo-classic theatre entered its Baroque period. While lacking the fervor of the Church drama it made up this deficiency with a veritable mountain of symbols taken from classic (to a lesser extent, Christian) sources. This symbolism served not so much to make sense as to lend a recondite luster to this autocratic stage.

In sum, we find the theatre of the Renaissance-Baroque capable of expressing the widening of thought under the stimulus of expanding science and commerce. We find it, at the same time, reflecting all the pomposity, the grandiloquent fawning, the deft chicanery and narrow minds of a society of courtiers.

The court theatres of the Renaissance, it should be noted, were accompanied and supplemented by the popular, open-air theatres of the Commedia dell' Arte. While the Baroque, with its limited, snobbish audiences, belonged to the aristocracy, the Commedia reflected the views of the lower middle classes, artisans and town dwellers.

The Commedia had that gift of satire which has so often distinguished those dramatic forms which have sprung spontaneously from the people. A mobile playhouse, which set up its acting platform in the Italian market places, it was renowned for the verve of its acting. It liberated the actor for the first time from confining classic stage rules, allowing him to portray character as he saw fit, in terms of his own craft.

The actors of the vulgar Italian comedies became the teachers of Europe. They were the natural antidote to the stilted posing of the court theatres. More than that, they gave a new dimension to the drama in general, adding a great crew of scapegrace characters to the heroes of Corneille and Racine. Without the Commedia there could have been no Molière. Yet it must also be stated that if the Commedia was the father of modern comedy and farce, it was also the father of modern hokum. To arouse not thoughtful, but witless laughter, was one of the chosen specialties of this ancestor of today's second-rate stage and movie comedy.

Interesting and even important as the Commedia might be, it could only influence, not change, the tradition of neo-classic theatre. The Baroque represented the full development of a theatre centuries old. Its splendor had reached its peak at the very time that it was losing its original power of inquiry and suppleness of thought. A tradition so deeply rooted was not going to be replaced in short order. Centuries more were to pass before that would happen, and the impetus would have to come from a source powerful enough to bring to the stage human values greater than those recognized by the rigid code of the Baroque.

SHAKESPEARE, LIBERATOR

The immortality of Shakespeare has been attested for so long that we have all but forgotten the mortal origin of Shakespeare's genius. We celebrate him as a poet whose Olympian vision swept far beyond his own time and embraced the "unchanging" nature of man. We smile at the childishly crude settings which served the Swan of Avon for his plays.

Perhaps, though, we ought to smile at ourselves a little for romanticizing Shakespeare and his stage in a way that does credit to neither. That great poet wrote for the stage and audience of his day. His stage was excellent and so was his audience. To say that he rose above his time to the realm of eternal thought may sound beautiful, but it is not far from being an insult to Shakespeare and the Elizabethans. The best thought of Shakespeare's day was not perfect, but it was very good thought. Let us not lead slumming parties into Elizabethan England or Aeschylean Greece! When we speak of "eternal thought" we set up, all too often, our contemporary beliefs as the standards of eternity.

If we turn our attention to the Shakespeare of the acting platform rather than the Shakespeare of the pen, we shall be rewarded by a more practically inspiring picture than is current today. For Shakespeare was one of the greatest *liberators* of the drama, and his stage was a landmark in the development of scenic form.

Shakespeare's popular stage, supported by the London merchant class, the more liberal nobility and a growing urban population, might be called the first specifically middle class stage in history. That in itself is not so important as the type of middle class it served. Both the dramatist and his audience lived in spacious days. The Papacy and its ally, the Spanish Empire, both proved incapable of withstanding the rising power of England. English ships ruled the seas, finding whole continents open to conquest. The Humanist enlightenment which had dawned in Italy was now penetrating to northern Europe, and England became its new citadel, raising a generation of explorers, warriors, statesmen, scientists, artists, artisans and sturdy yeomen who matched the best that the Italian Renaissance had produced.

The Elizabethan dramatists spoke the thoughts, not of torpidly sentimental playgoers, but of an audience that was high-mettled, venturesome and democratic. Shakespeare was no plodding conformist but, as Gassner says, "a man of the world" who was in close contact with the notables of the English government; he was capable of dealing with court intrigues, and was acquainted with the important political issues of his times. He was not the kind whose genius seeks an ivory tower. If it is true that his views corresponded to the "man in the street," it is also true that the Elizabethan "man in the street" held views corresponding to Shakespeare's.

It was the stage technique of Shakespeare which fully measured up to, and overtopped, the ritualism of the Baroque. It was his stage which furnished the motive power which, in the end, swept classicism out of the playhouses of Europe. Even Voltaire, critical as he was of the Baroque theatre, was never able to grasp the full meaning of a dramatic genius so different from the tradition of the court stage. For Voltaire Shakespeare was a magnificent barbarian; yet the French dramatist, sitting before Shakespearean revivals in London, heard in his thoughts the challenging trumpet call of the Globe Theatre.[8] And until the days of Victor Hugo those who rebelled against the hardened conventions of classic theatre rallied under the banner of Will Shakespeare.

It is surely unnecessary here to analyze the technical qualities of Shakespeare's scripts. They have been painstakingly examined by scholars of every generation, who have underlined their utter freedom from the Three Unities, their richness of metaphor, the vigor of their melodrama, their unrivaled portrayal of character, their virile poetry, their bold juxtaposition of the sublime and the ridiculous, their masterly handling of suspense and climax. Here begins the technique of modern dramaturgy, with the dramatist freed from all shackles and permitted to mirror the world with his own individual talent. The plays of Shakespeare set an all-time standard in dealing with the most complex issues of political and social events, individual character and the qualities of environment.

Something needs to be added, however, concerning the Shakespearean ideals of staging. Shakespeare was emphatically not a "formalist" in the sense that he deliberately sought a conventionalized style. There is evidence, on the contrary, that he looked to illusory, emotional staging as the natural form of drama. He saw theatre as "a dream of passion," not as dead ceremony.

The Prologue of HENRY V furnishes us with a rich exposition of the ideals of Naturalistic staging and of the necessary work of the mind which must accompany it. Shakespeare says he would prefer real princes to do the acting, the warlike Henry himself to play the leading rôle. But since this is not possible, and since there is only an unworthy scaffold on which to attempt so great an object, the spectators must piece out the imperfections of the stage, divide one man into a thousand parts, deck out kings with their thoughts, see imaginary horses and perform other mental feats, including the fitting of many years' time into an hour glass.[9]

In Shakespeare's lifetime, perspective settings elaborately painted, of the type in use in Italy, were regularly used in English court masques. Italian painters had found employment at the court of Henry VIII; and the first English treatise on architecture, by John Shute, appearing in 1563, acknowledged its debt to the great Italian scene designer Sebastiano Serlio. The Italian settings represented the furthest development of Naturalism so far; yet Shakespeare gives us no inkling that he preferred them to the resources of the Globe Theatre.

Like every stage technique that ever existed, Shakespeare's method was a mixture of the illusory and the formal. It was, nevertheless, overwhelmingly formal. The outthrust stage platform, where visible scene shifters placed chairs, beds and tables; where night scenes took place in full sunlight, darkness being indicated only by the speeches or by the burning of candles or torches; the entrances and exits through doors which were part of the stage architecture—all this was even more formal, less illusory, than the similar conventions of the Baroque. The fact is that the true center of Shakespeare's stage technique must be looked for in his *dynamic use of space.* Compared with the limited functionalism of the classic and neo-classic stage, the dynamics of Shakespeare's scaffolding were very extraordinary. The amount and type of scenic space available to the actor on his stage have scarcely been equaled since. John C. Adams gives a picture of this not so unworthy scaffold which goes far to explain how the forty-two scenes of ANTONY AND CLEOPATRA could have been presented:

> The Elizabethan playhouse matched the resources of all but the most intricate modern stages in terms of levels, multiple settings, capacity for continuous flow of action and unexpected display, plasticity of scene and actor, use of traps and machines, and a permanent structure designed to show with unfeigned realism those domestic interior and exterior scenes which have predominated in the drama since the Middle Ages. . . . In a modern "dramatic" theatre the production rarely employs a set with a playing space of as much as 30 x 34 feet, or a total of 1020 square feet. The Elizabethan playhouse, on the other hand, had constantly available not only the outer stage—which in size was quite the equal of the modern—but also some six other stages, bringing the total acting area to approximately 1800 square feet.
>
> The modern theatregoer faces a proscenium rarely opened more than 34 x 24 feet, a frame which marks off, therefore, only a part of the smallest wall of the auditorium. Beyond the visible stage setting is, of course, the much larger but invisible stage-house needed to bring within the frame—following the Italian tradition—a variety of scenes. By contrast, the Elizabethan theatregoer faced not this narrowing proscenium but a dynamic stage of intercommunicating levels, comparable in cubic content to the whole unseen stage-house of the modern theatre. As a result, what he saw bulked larger in his vision; changes of place and scene were presented with greater "theatrical" logic; and the action which tended to advance toward the spectator, created an impact upon all his senses which the modern theatre of illusion cannot match.

The Elizabethan stage structure in its own way measured up to the demands of a forward-moving, vigorous drama. It was the physical counterpart of an intensely dynamic philosophy of theatre. This theatre moved in the direction of Naturalism, but it did not have the hallucinatory Naturalism which is the ideal of today. Story, suspense, sound, the pageantry of motion and color, were at the service of a statement, not the self-sufficient object of dramatic art. The Shakespearean stage was a product of its era at the same time that it forecast the long journey toward the picture-frame Naturalism of the present. Thus it stood at the crossroads of the slowly disintegrating Baroque and the slowly integrating Naturalistic form.

Most impressive is its independence of classic models, its eagerness to see the world anew with its own eyes. It was drenched in a new kind of poetic observation, based on the experience which had been brought to men by an astonishing development of science, commerce and exploration. Its physical equipment, the playhouse and settings, were not derived from the Greek or Roman auditorium but from the English inn-yards and bear pits, and from the mansion and wagon stages of the Morality plays. Its settings seized only upon stage space; yet the poet's insight brought human environment to the stage in words, with a richness never known before. Nature as revealed in the plays of Shakespeare accompanies the history of man in a way scarcely known to classicism. The liberating power of the Elizabethan dramatic form, from playscript to setting, established a new tradition, a major change in dramatic form. It closed Part I of dramatic history, that of the antique world, and opened Part II, that of the modern world.

The greatness of this dramatic form must not blind us to its shortcomings. Just as the Greek theatre could not see beyond polytheism and the rule of fate; just as the Church theatre saw all knowledge as designed to enhance the already accepted views of theology; so Shakespeare did not, and could not have been expected to, foresee modern democracy. His ideal seems to have been the enlightened rule of a constitutional monarchy. He held the common man at a low value, and would have been astounded at the suggestion that the worker, the farmer or the tradesman can also be the object of serious and sympathetic drama. Nor was Shakespeare free of all the vulgar prejudices and superstitions of his times. These contradictions, as Walt Whitman once noted, must be taken into account if we wish to make use of the treasures of the Elizabethan stage.[10]

History shows that there is some value in this reminder. When the time eventually came for the Baroque to be replaced, a new tradition, Romanticism, moved to the task under the inspiration of Shakespeare. If the Romantic movement was not as brilliant as it might have been, one reason was its seeming inability to tell the difference between Shakespeare's virtues and his faults.

Nevertheless Baroque theatre did, finally, pass away; and it was the Shakespearean tradition which helped to end it in the playhouses. By then the Baroque had long since been deprived of the court audiences to whom it owed its origin.

Between the middle of the eighteenth century and the middle of the nineteenth a drastic change came over men's activities. The long reign of feudalism came to its bitter end, and was given the *coup de grâce* by the French revolution. Its place was taken by mercantile capitalism, which swiftly expanded production and world commerce to undreamt-of proportions. For the first time since the liturgical drama of the Middle Ages and the theatres of Shakespeare and Lope de Vega, something like a popular theatre-audience emerged. The number of European playhouses tripled and quadrupled. Aristocratic audiences gave way to audiences of well-to-do commoners. Yet, through all this period the Baroque theatre continued unchanged except for an artistic hardening of the arteries. It even survived the French revolution, settling deeper and deeper into a mould of routine. Its technique, perfect of its kind, was strong enough to resist the pounding of time.

But a change was inevitable. At the beginning of the nineteenth century, *Romanticism* entered the aging body of the Baroque, hastening its decay.

HIERRO

What was the Romantic theatre? Like other dramatic formulas before and since, it was a complex of thought, with strengths and weaknesses which it was later to pass on to its successors.

The roots of Romanticism lie in Gothic rather than in Greek culture.

The Italian Renaissance had turned to the art of ancient Greece for inspiration in its struggles with ecclesiastic authority. In a like manner the newer age of industry sought out traditions opposed to the neo-classic art of the feudal world.

These traditions it found mainly in western and northern Europe, in such imaginative works as the Arthurian legends, the sagas of the Teutonic nations, the stories of Roland, Tristan and Iseult, Robert the Devil, Robin Hood, the Nibelungen, Faust and Hamlet. The precise quality of these stories and legends remains unclear. Certain marked characteristics, however, have been singled out:

> The absence of central plot, and the prolongation rather than evolution of the story; the intermixture of the supernatural; the presence and indeed prominence of love-affairs; the juxtaposition of tragic and almost farcical incident; the variety of adventures arranged rather in the fashion of a panorama than otherwise. . . .
>
> Prominent above everything is the world-old motive of the quest; which, world-old as it is, here acquires a predominance that it has never held before or since. (Saintsbury: *Romance*).

In addition Walter Pater in *The Renaissance* calls attention to the presence of nostalgia, grief, and rich subjective experience in the Gothic works of art as compared with the repose and objectivity of the Greek artistic works.

The era of neo-Gothic renaissance is usually known as the *Sturm und Drang* (Storm and Stress) period. It is believed to have originated in Germany with J. G. Herder (1744–1803) as its founder. At any rate it was this philosopher who strongly influenced Goethe, whose historic drama GÖTZ VON BERLICHINGEN, (1771) may be said to have inaugurated the Romantic age in the theatre. Written when its author was only twenty-two, this play was really unhistoric: Götz, who had in fact been an unscrupulous robber-knight, became a mouthpiece for the author's sentiments of justice and freedom. The poet's liberal views were further revealed in his novel *The Sorrows of Werther* (1774), described by the critic August Wilhelm Schlegel as "a declaration of the rights of feeling in opposition to the tyranny of social relations."

Goethe's position was that of moral insurgency rather than of social or political rebellion. He denounced the French revolution on the ground that it meant the abrogation of law and order. He even wrote two plays, DER GROSS-COPHTA (1792) and DER BÜRGERGENERAL (1793), as polemics against it. In the end, having launched Romanticism, Goethe tempered his views with a return to classicism, with the assertion, in fact, that "Classicism is health; Romanticism is disease."

We can hardly overrate the importance for our own times of

the ideals of Romanticism as conceived by Goethe and his fellow-dramatists Schiller and Lessing. The Storm and Stress literary movement of the liberal German middle class dreaded the fierce realities of the French revolution. Still in its own way it learned from that impact. It asserted the right of individual rebellion: no social organization, no national state, must presume to dictate to the individual conscience.

For the first time there arose the conception of the individual as a social unit. At the same time that individual was seen as a living and feeling unit, whose aims are in *conflict* with those of society as a whole.[11] Individual psychology takes the center of the stage, while the direction of society itself recedes into the background. This theme of the individual at war with society—in a compound of one thimbleful to a gallon of water—is the theme of present-day Broadway and Hollywood.

When Napoleon had suppressed the French revolution and had in turn met his own finish at Waterloo, the time came for Romanticism to be transferred to France. This ceremony was performed by the reactionary, egotistical statesman and novelist François de Chateaubriand (1768–1848), whose writings created the mental climate in which French Romanticism could flourish.

Among the French attacks on the Baroque the most famous, perhaps, was an essay by Stendhal, *Racine et Shakespeare*, published in 1823. Stendhal maintained that changed social conditions had outmoded the Baroque. From the point of view of technique, he questioned not only the Unities but the continual use of Alexandrine verse.

Essays like Stendhal's became a lever for prying loose the political control which the government of Napoleon I had established over the French theatre. A rigid dramatic censorship was in force. The dramatic repertory of the nation was divided among a small number of subservient theatres. The Comédie-Française had the exclusive right to perform the classics, while comic opera was assigned to another theatre, vaudeville to another, and melodrama to still another.

This regimentation of the French theatres was not popular. Resistance against it grew on all sides. This political struggle had its technical side as well. Soon after Waterloo the first French play in the new Romantic style received a hearing. It was Casimir Delavigne's VÊPRES SICILIENNES (1819). The new movement took its full stride, however, with the publication of Victor Hugo's unproduced play, CROMWELL (1827). In his famous preface to this play Hugo launched into a violent attack upon classicism. One phrase of his, "The object of modern art is not beauty but life"—came to have a significance for the future in a way which Hugo himself could not have foreseen.

By 1830 the clamor of the public had penetrated into the classic halls of the Comédie-Française, which accepted for production Victor Hugo's melodrama HERNANI. It was freely rumored that the motives of the Comédie's directors were something less than generous. It was said, indeed, that they accepted the play the better to sabotage it and thereby to discredit the whole Romantic school. Feelings were certainly running high.

Nor did the general temperature subside when the play went into rehearsal. The acting company, headed by the famous Mlle. Mars, did not feel at home with the new viewpoint of the script. She and others of the troupe became mutinous. But the young dramatist (he was not yet thirty) advanced undismayed to the fray. A threat to find another leading lady subdued Mlle. Mars and brought the company back to its work. Learning that the Comédie's *chef de claque* was a partisan of the classic school—and therefore likely to lead the applause at the wrong moments, or possibly not at all—Hugo prepared for that emergency. He had received a block of seats in the lower floor and second gallery. These seats he distributed to the young intellectuals of the new school, taking care to scrawl on each ticket the single word *hierro*. The word means iron in Spanish. It seems to have been all the instruction necessary.

Among those who arrived in the spirit of *hierro* that opening night were Théophile Gautier, Balzac, Berlioz, Mérimée and Achille Devéria. They took their seats early, a wild-looking crew in Spanish mantles and broad-brimmed hats. They sang songs and feasted on *petits pains*, sweet chocolate and garlic-flavored sausages. One imagines the contrast with the Comédie's regular public of dignitaries in *habit noir* and white shirt fronts who filed in later!

With this preparation an easy victory was scored over the champions of classicism. The publishing rights to the play were sold backstage before the final curtain. On the following nights the classicists, recovering from their surprise, returned to the battle.

TOWARD REALISM

Zola

Theatre + science

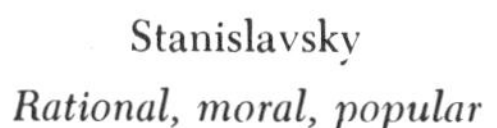

Stanislavsky

Rational, moral, popular

Hugo

"Not beauty but life"

Belasco

Singing birds and the agony of Mme. Butterfly

From
My Life in Art

Hissing mingled with cheers. But HERNANI, a huge success, ran for thirty-eight solid performances.

Romanticism had triumphed overwhelmingly. Hugo and his colleagues dominated the French playhouses for the next thirteen years, until the crushing failure of Hugo's LES BURGRAVES in 1843.

"CARNAGE AND VAUDEVILLE"

Romanticism proved capable of demoralizing the Baroque form. At the same time it did not have the vigor to develop a new form of its own. The disintegration of the theatre continued.

In the arts, disintegration begins when weaker artists imitate, within ever-narrowing compass, the work of their predecessors. Only creative talent has the power to carve images out of reality. In creating his images the true artist invents at the same time the technical instrument with which to carry out his work. His imitator sees only the instrument, not the purpose for which it was invented. The talent of an imitator consists in using new techniques to restate old clichés.

The idealism of Goethe which captured the theatre of the early nineteenth century looked upon the world as a valley of trial through which the soul must pass on its way to perfection. At the same time Goethe combined this viewpoint with an insight into the laws of nature and a real curiosity about the soul's temporary lodgings here below. His inquiring mind probed into the natural world as well as into the world of the spirit. "If you want to reach the infinite," he said, "traverse the finite to all sides."

But the Romantic after-followers of Goethe could not maintain the idealistic movement at this high level. Even in Schiller, his great contemporary, there is a noticeable cheapening and sentimentalization of the idealistic viewpoint. Philosophic idealism relies upon the intuition of gifted individuals. When these individuals go, the validity of their method departs with them. With less gifted people the realm of the spirit shrinks amazingly; the human soul becomes a collection of bathetic sentiments, while solid nature, on the other hand, becomes etherealized into nostalgic moods. The individual independence which Goethe had proclaimed became with his followers "a fetish of self-expression." In the words of Gassner (*Masters of the Drama*):

The revolt against a society hedged about by conventions led to an idealization of man as a being whose primal right was to coddle his emotions and realize his individuality privately. Santayana has noted that "the zest of Romanticism consists in taking what you know is an independent and ancient world as if it were material for your private emotions."

It is curious that while the individual soul was the first interest of the Romantics, their ability to create fully rounded, individualized stage characters fell distinctly below that of religious writers like those of ancient Athens, or of political writers like Shakespeare. Although, in the Romantic plays, the human spirit transcends all natural laws, it is also curious that they lack the serenity that ought to go with that conviction. Instead there is a characteristically morbid, tremulous or hectic tone in the Romantic dramas.

From Goethe onward, the Romantics drew upon Shakespeare as their greatest source of inspiration. But Shakespeare must be absolved from responsibility for the fustian dramatic products of the later Romantics. The playwriting ancestor of the later Romantics was rather Lope de Vega, who stated very candidly, "When I set out to write a play I lock up all the rules under ten keys, and banish Plautus and Terence from my study, lest they cry out against me, as truth is accustomed to do even from dumb books. For I write in the style of those who seek the applause of the public, whom it is but just to humor in their folly, since it is they who pay for it."

Lope did not find dramatic writing a very arduous task. It has been estimated by some authorities that he wrote a total of 1,800 plays and dramatic sketches. More conservative figures place his total output at 470 *comedias* and 50 *autos sacramentales* (religious masques). "Deft, clever, fast-flowing, with the most skilful mechanical articulation yet known to the world stage" (Cheney), his plays set a standard which the later Romantics lowered to the very ground. Lope's popular appeal, but not his fire or his powers of observation, characterize the work of people like Schröder, Iffland, Kotzebue, Tieck, Kleist and Werner, in Germany; Knowles and Bulwer-Lytton in England; Augier, Dumas or Dumas, *fils,* in France; Mrs. Mowatt or Boucicault in the United States.

These Romantic playwrights accomplished the feat of reducing the infinite complexity of life to patterns of good and bad behavior as portrayed in melodramatic action and rotomontade speech. Saints are contrasted with villains. High-minded deeds, carried out breathlessly in picturesque settings, reached heights of "melodrama, carnage and vaudeville," as Dubech puts it. Periods of history were dealt with, not for illumination, as with Shakespeare, but for their local color. The Middle Ages were especially popular: to be *moyenageux* was to have all the Romantic virtues. With the whole world of drama thus reduced to a stereotype, it is no wonder that plays were easy to write. Prosper Mérimée, one of the most facile of the French Romantics, summed up this kind of drama in a few words:

> Pan, pan, pan. The three raps. Curtain rises. Smile, suffer, weep, kill. He is killed, she is dead. Finis. (Dubech).

By 1887 this low form of dramaturgy ruled the stages of France and, incidentally, of Europe. At the time Antoine began work the French stage was in the hands of "an illustrious trinity: Augier, Dumas, Sardou, who for the past twenty years reigned not only at the Comédie-Française but everywhere else." Said one of the well-known managers of that period: "One year Dumas, one year Sardou, a third Augier, that's all I need."

But the disintegration of the script was only part of the disintegration of production in general. In the later years of Romanticism the Baroque style became a caricature of itself. Theatre auditoriums, their orchestras and galleries vastly enlarged to accommodate a new middle class public, fairly dripped gilt festoons. The proscenium was a picture-frame outlined in gilded plaster weighing many tons. Middle class actors strutted, struck noble poses, went into tirades, whispered "asides" to the galleries in imitation of long-forgotten aristocrats.

Leverton describes the American acting of the period as "a pyrotechnical use of the voice and body." Writing in the Brooklyn *Eagle* of 1846, Walt Whitman speaks of the earlier Romantic acting as

> . . . the loud mouthed ranting style—the tearing of everything to shivers—which is so much the ambition of some of our players, particularly the younger ones. . . . They take every occasion . . . to try the extremest strength of their lungs. . . . If they have to enact passion, they do so by all kinds of unnatural and violent jerks, swings, screw-

ing of the nerves of the face, rolling of the eyes, and so on. . . . They never let a part of their dialogue which falls into the imperative mood —the mood for exhorting, commanding, or permitting—pass by without the loudest explosion of sound and the most distorted gesture.

Mantzius pictures the German Romantic actor as "a strange being,"

. . . with long, wild hair, black if possible, framing a pale, emaciated face; deep, melancholy eyes under dark, contracted brows, and a bitter, sorrowful smile on his quivering lips; his form shrouded in a long Roman cloak, moving among his fellow men now with ostentatious, gloomy remoteness, now with hollow, rather scornful mirth.

The image, no doubt, of "the individual at war with society," the new kind of citizen sprung from the imagination of Goethe.

SUNSET

Like Baroque plays and acting, Baroque scene design, with an unaccustomed burden of sentimentalism thrown upon it, sagged under the strain. Formalism disappeared from the setting. Not splendor, but sentiment was wanted—preferably mournful sentiment. The clipped hedges of Baroque gardens must give place to desolate mountain crags. Perspectives of Baroque palaces must be replaced by sad ruins, by gloomy corridors in dank castles. The reign of man's reason over nature, as the Encyclopedists once saw it, was succeeded by the Romantics' lugubrious vision of the forces of nature overwhelming the works of man and gnawing at his soul.

The physical appearance of the Baroque setting also underwent changes. The side wings, once so prominent a feature, were pushed to the extreme limits of either side of the stage. The stage itself had become shallower and wider. The Baroque backdrop had been small, serving only to close in the vista presented by the side wings. Now it dominated the stage. Scene flats, arranged in the shape of a back wall and side walls, came into use for interiors. These walls continued to have a painted canvas quality, and part of the furniture of the room was often painted on them.

The vital secret of the older setting, the fact that it was really a flimsy architecture formally painted, was lost on the scene designers of the new period. These designers were, first and foremost, landscape painters of the school of Delacroix or Géricault. Scenic artists such as William Capon, J. R. Planché and Loutherbourg in England; Cicéri, Gué, Justin Leys, Dumay, Gosse, Ruggiery in France; Simon Quaglio, Karl Friedrich Schinkel, Karl Blechen, Fr. Jaeger, Josef Hoffmann, Von Mayer, De Pian in Germany and Austria; Gonzales, Gonzago, Roller, Ivanov and Fiodorov in Russia; John Watson, E. La Moss, Tomkins & Pitt, H. L. Reed, T. C. Bartholemew and George Curtis in the United States, looked upon the stage setting as nothing more than an ambitious easel painting—an oversize salon picture in the gilt frame of the proscenium.

In this flood of painted scenery there were examples, such as those of Goethe's designer, Friedrich Schinkel, whose combination of exoticism and "antiquarianism" command respect. By the 1870's, however, scene design had struck bottom, remaining there for several decades. In proportion as its dramatic significance disappeared, it began to thrive as a business enterprise. In Germany commercial scenic studios carried on a prosperous business in exporting scenery. Elsewhere, as in the United States, exterior or interior settings could be ordered locally by number from a catalogue. Even today a sizeable amount of Broadway work, dated in technique, continues to be turned out by hack commercial firms.

It should be observed that the tradition of painted scenery (scenery in which the painting quality predominates) is a rather restricted one in stage history. It accompanies the Baroque from start to finish, but for all that it remains subordinate to the Baroque scenic scheme of wing-and-backdrop setting; that is to say, it is only an element added to the flimsy architectural splendor of that type of setting. The "painter's stage" is, strictly, only of the Romantic period. Just before and shortly after the first World War painted scenery had a revival in France and Russia, especially for opera and ballet, as in the work of Anisfeld, Bakst, Golovin, Gontcharova, Soudekin, Léger, Picasso, Dufy, Laurencin and others. Indeed the painter's tradition still remains strongly noticeable in France.

The Romantic painter when he entered the theatre could not do much to cure the deterioration which had set in in the Baroque scenic method. The new tendencies, strongly illusory, did not mix well with the remnants of the old conventional technique.

In 1808 Wilhelm Schlegel complained: "Our system of decoration . . . has several unavoidable defects . . . the disproportion of the player when he appears in the background against objects diminished in perspective; the unfavorable lighting from below and behind; the contrast between the painted and the actual lights and shades; the impossibility of narrowing the stage at pleasure, so that the inside of a palace and a hut have the same length and breadth. The errors which may be avoided are want of simplicity and of great and reposeful masses; the overloading of the scene with superfluous and distracting objects, either because the painter is desirous of showing off his strength in perspective or because he does not know how otherwise to fill up the space; an architecture full of mannerism, often altogether unconnected, nay, even at variance with, possibility, colored in a motley manner which resembles no species of stone in the world. (*The Stage Is Set*).

Sixty or more years later these contradictions had grown worse rather than better. In 1870 Duke Georg of Saxe-Meiningen had to warn his actors not to lean against painted scenery. If the player acted freely and naturally he was likely to shake the setting and spoil the illusory picture. If he took care not to touch the scenery, his acting became constricted. Still later the same observation was made by Stanislavsky. By then such a state of decrepitude had been reached as can be described only in the Russian director's own words:

In the other theatres of the time the problems of scenery were solved in a very simple manner. There was a backdrop and four or five wings in arched form. On these were painted a palace hall with entrances, passages, open and closed terraces, a seascape, and so on. In the middle there was the smooth, dirty theatrical floor and enough chairs to seat the dramatis personae, no more. In the spaces between the wings one could see the whole world behind the scenes, a crowd of stage hands, extras, wig makers, and tailors who were promenading and eyeing the stage. If a door were necessary, it would be placed between the wings. It was not taken into consideration that a hole remained above the door. Let imagination add the piece of wall that was lacking. When it was necessary a street with a tremendous perspective of disappearing houses and a tremendous square with painted fountains and monuments was smeared on the backdrop and four wings. Actors who stood near the backdrop seemed to stand much higher than the perspective point of the disappearing houses. The dirty floor of the stage was naked, giving the actors full opportunity to stand in the middle of the stage near the prompter's box, which, as is well known, always attracts the servants of Melpomene.

It was the period of the reign of the luxurious theatrical pavilion, *Empire* or *Rococo,* painted on canvas. Canvas doors with the cloth shivering when they were closed or opened, and opening and closing of themselves in most cases, especially with the entrance of the stars, who would begin their acting by bowing in appreciation of the ovation with which the public met them.

The question of *mis en scène* and the planning of action on the stage was also solved in a very simple manner in those days. The usual *mis en scène* and scheme of properties, established once and for all for each and every play, was as follows: on the right a sofa, on the left a table and two chairs. One scene of the play would take place near the sofa, the next near the table with the two chairs, the third in the middle of the stage near the prompter's box; then again near the sofa, the table and the prompter's box. A painted red cloth with golden and tremendous tassels, also painted, was supposed to represent rich velvet material and real golden tassels. This had a bent corner beyond which one could see a landscape with mountains, valleys, rivers, seas, cities, villages, forests, parks, fountains and all the other attributes of poesy, prettiness and luxury. Ushers in red waistcoats with gold buttons, in uniforms with epaulets, ran all around the auditorium, making it impossible for the actors to play and for the spectators to hear or understand what was taking place on the stage. The orchestra, unnecessary for any purposes of the play itself, and living its own peculiar intimate musical life in the presence of the audience, was in the most prominent place before the stage and interfered with the actors, the spectators and the performance. Polkas and castanets in the intermissions, the exits of actors with applause, the sudden and unexpected return of heroes who had just died on the stage, endless curtain calls in the intermissions or at the end of the performance—all these ridiculous habits of the time were the changeless accompaniments of each performance.

Without having abolished the Baroque formalities, the Romantics had deprived them of their last shred of meaning. The Romantic movement lacked the strength to supplant with a new form the Baroque tradition which it had derided on the opening night of HERNANI. A curious thing had happened: the conventional splendor of court theatricals had become the outer dress of a drama more and more subjective and psychological. The type of drama whose thesis was the divine right of kings still gave form to a drama whose thesis was the divine right of the individual conscience.

The age of theatrical splendor was going down in a Romantic twilight. Very soon it would shine no more.

NOTES

1. Verbatim from the stage directions of THE FRONT PAGE, by Ben Hecht and Charles MacArthur (1928).

2. This green baize covering evidently remained as a tradition in the following century. "It is well known that on the eighteenth-century stage, when a theatrical death was imminent, two stage attendants walked on and solemnly spread a green carpet on which the hero, heroine or villain, as the case might be, could die in comfort without too much damage to his clothes." (Eleanore Boswell: *The Restoration Court Stage*).

3. No less a poet than John Dryden put this jealousy into words—in his Prologue given at the opening of the new Theatre Royal in 1674:

" 'Twere Folly now a stately Pile to raise,
To build a Play-house, while you throw down Plays;
Whilst Scenes, Machines and empty *Opera's* reign,
And for the Pencil you the Pen disdain; . . .
I would not prophesie our Houses Fate;
But while vain Shows and Scenes you over-rate,
'Tis to be feared—
That, as a Fire the former House o'erthrew,
Machines and Tempests will destroy the new."
(From Montague Summers: *The Restoration Theatre*).

4. The discovery of the laws of perspective by the artists of the Italian Renaissance provided a new instrument for grasping reality and bringing it to the stage. Using the science of perspective, Baldassare Peruzzi designed Cardinal Bibiena's play CALANDRE at Urbino in 1513. Vasari described the streets, palaces and other buildings in the scene as being "so perfectly presented that they did not look like things feigned, but are as the living reality." (Nicoll: *The Development of the Theatre*). It is evident that the ability to create an illusion was a great merit in the eyes of Renaissance audiences. This is an excellent example of the *beginnings* of the illusory system of stage production.

On this basis Simonson declares, "The Renaissance invented a complete illusion: painted perspective. Every theatre had its feints and tricks, but the illusions achieved were a fragmentary imitation of nature. At best no more than a part of the stage could be transformed. The laws of perspective proved to be the greatest stage trick of all." (*The Stage Is Set*).

This seems to the present writer an excessive conclusion. We are not justified in any belief that perspective on Renaissance stages offered a complete illusion, as our contemporary theatres do. The amount of illusion created by perspective remained only one part of what was, in general, an extremely conventional style. Nor may we read history backwards and imply that the scenic artists of the Renaissance really wanted the complete Naturalistic illusion that we have today, and would eagerly have dropped their own method of production in favor of the Broadway method. The perspective scenery of the Renaissance and Baroque playhouses was part of a form of staging which included both conventional and illusory elements. It answered the specific purposes of theatre in its own times. In addition to perspective settings, there were operatic conventions of acting, which were far from illusory. These conventions were not makeshift; they were an indispensable part of a ceremony in the theatre of that day.

5. In the *Spectator* of April 18, 1711, Joseph Addison has something to say about this custom. His critical essay on tragic costume begins with the statement, "The Dresses and Decorations of the Stage have their place in raising the Aristotelean Terror and Pity in the Audience, hence these adjuncts must neither be neglected nor disesteemed." His comments on the long-trained tragic gown, besides giving a picture of the stage of his time, indicate that few people in the audience were as troubled as he over the prevailing lack of Naturalism:

". . . a Princess generally receives her Grandeur from those additional incumbrances that fall into her Tail; I mean the broad sweeping Train that follows her in all her Motions, and finds constant Employment for a Boy who stands behind her to open and spread it to Advantage. I do not know how others are affected at this Sight, but I must confess, my Eyes are wholly taken up with the Page's Part; and as for the Queen, I am not so attentive to any thing she speaks, as to the right adjusting of her Train, lest it should chance to trip up her Heels or incommode her, as she walks to and fro upon the Stage. It is, in my Opinion, a very odd Spectacle, to see a Queen venting her Passions in a disordered Motion, and a little Boy taking Care all the while that they do not ruffle the Tail of her Gown. The Parts that the two Persons act on the Stage at the same Time, are very different; the Princess is afraid lest she should incur the Displeasure of the King her Father, or lose the Hero her Lover, whilst her Attendant is only concerned lest she should entangle her Feet in her Petticoat." (From Summers: *The Restoration Theatre*).

6. For his reconstructed performance of Settle's EMPRESS OF MOROCCO at the Duke's Theatre the author has pieced out extant information with details from other productions of the period, in the public theatres or at court performances. (No plan remains of the interior of the old Dorset Garden theatre as designed by Wren.) The members of the audience are conjectural. Both the Prologue and the Epilogue are derived from later performances of the same play given in 1698.

7. According to Lawson it was Lodovico Castelvetro, writing in 1570, who first formulated the "rule" of the Triple Unities, attributing such a rule to Aristotle.

8. Voltaire had a whimsical admiration for Shakespeare, whom he considered a barbarian but a natural genius, as is evident in the following dry commentary on HAMLET:

"It is a gross and barbarous piece, and would never be borne by the lowest rabble in France or Italy. . . . The grave-diggers . . . sing ballads worthy of their professions and their manners; at the same time throwing out the bones and skulls of the dead upon the stage. . . . In the first scene . . . the guard says: 'Not a mouse stirring!' Yes, sir, a soldier might make such an answer when in barracks; but not upon the stage, before the first persons of distinction, who express themselves nobly, and before whom everyone should express himself in like manner. . . . Imagine to yourselves, gentlemen, Louis XIV in the gallery at Versailles, surrounded by a brilliant court; and a ragged blackguard making his way through the crowd of heroes, lofty personages and beauties composing the court, to propose their discarding Corneille, Racine and Molière, for a merry Andrew, that cuts jokes and is a good tumbler. . . ." (From *Letters Concerning the English Nation, by Mons. de Voltaire.*).

9. PROLOGUE

(*Enter* CHORUS.)

CHOR. O for a Muse of fire, that would ascend
The brightest heaven of invention,
A kingdom for a stage, princes to act
And monarchs to behold the swelling scene!
Then should the warlike Harry, like himself,
Assume the port of Mars; and at his heels,
Leash'd in like hounds, should famine, sword and fire
Crouch for employment. But pardon, gentles all,
The flat unraised spirits that have dared
On this unworthy scaffold to bring forth
So great an object: can this cockpit hold
The vasty fields of France? or may we cram
Within this wooden O the very casques
That did affright the air at Agincourt?
O, pardon! since a crooked figure may
Attest in little place a million;
And let us, ciphers to this great accompt,
On your imaginary forces work.
Suppose within the girdle of these walls
Are now confined two mighty monarchies,
Whose high upreared and abutting fronts
The perilous narrow ocean parts asunder:
Piece out our imperfections with your thoughts;
Into a thousand parts divide one man,
And make imaginary puissance;

Think, when we talk of horses, that you see them
Printing their proud hoofs i' the receiving earth;
For 'tis your thoughts that now must deck our kings,
Carry them here and there; jumping o'er times,
Turning the accomplishment of many years
Into an hour glass: for the which supply,
Admit me Chorus to this history;
Who prologue-like your humble patience pray,
Gently to hear, kindly to judge, our play.
[*Exit.*

10. Whitman observed that Shakespeare "stands entirely for the mighty esthetic sceptres of the past, not for the spiritual and democratic, the sceptres of the future." Because "the low characters, mechanics, even loyal henchmen—all in themselves nothing—serve as capital foils to the aristocracy," Whitman could not bring himself to praise the Shakespearean comedies. "The comedies are altogether non-acceptable to America and Democracy." (Whitman: *A Thought on Shakespeare.* From *The American Theatre as Seen by Its Critics.*) From 1846 to 1848 Whitman functioned as editor, and incidentally dramatic critic, of the Brooklyn *Daily Eagle,* until discharged for his uncompromising stand against the extension of slavery into the new western states.

We have not far to go to understand Whitman's comments on Shakespeare. The great-hearted Quaker could not share Shakespeare's cynicism about the common man. In JULIUS CAESAR, Casca speaks of "the rabblement" that "shouted, and clapped their chapped hands, and threw up their sweaty nightcaps, and uttered such a deal of stinking breath." In CORIOLANUS the people are "rats" and "fragments"; Menenius tells the Tribunes scathingly,

You have made good work,
You and your apron-men; you that stood so much
Upon the voice of occupation and
The breath of garlic-eaters!

When Whitman speaks of "even loyal henchmen" serving as "foils to the aristocracy," he must have had in mind some such character as the First Servant of Cornwall in KING LEAR. This plebeian, with a better sense of *noblesse oblige* than his master, wounds Cornwall fatally after pleading in vain against the torture of Gloucester.

11. When the Romantics, maintaining the freedom of the individual conscience, stood upon the tradition of the Gothic tales, they were on firm ground. Walter Pater, in his revealing study of the Gothic influence upon the Italian Renaissance, emphasizes this element of rebellious idealism:

"One of the strongest characteristics of that outbreak of the reason and the imagination, of that assertion of the liberty of the heart, in the middle age, which I have termed a medieval Renaissance, was its antinomianism, its spirit of rebellion and revolt against the moral and religious ideas of the time. In their search after the pleasures of the senses and imagination, in their care for beauty, in their worship of the body, people were impelled beyond the bounds of the Christian ideal; and their love became sometimes a strange idolatry, a strange rival religion. It was the return of that ancient Venus, not dead, but only hidden for a time in the caves of the Venusberg, of those old pagan gods still going to and fro on the earth, under all sorts of disguises. And this element of the middle age, for the most part ignored by those writers who have treated it pre-eminently as the 'Age of Faith' —this rebellious and antinomian element, the recognition of which has made the delineation of the middle age by the writers of the Romantic school in France, by Victor Hugo for instance in *Notre-Dame de Paris,* so suggestive and exciting—is found alike in the history of Abelard and the legend of Tannhäuser. More and more, as we come to mark changes and distinctions of temper in what is often in one all-embracing confusion called the middle age, that rebellion, that sinister claim for liberty of heart and thought, comes to the surface. The Albigensian movement, connected so strangely with the history of Provençal poetry, is deeply tinged with it. A touch of it makes the Franciscan order, with its poetry, its mysticism, its 'illumination,' from the point of view of religious authority, justly suspect. It influences the thoughts of those obscure prophetical writers, like Joachim of Flora, strange dreamers in a world of flowery rhetoric of that third and final dispensation of a 'spirit of freedom,' in which law shall have passed away. Of this spirit *Aucassin and Nicolette* contains perhaps the most famous expression: it is the answer Aucassin gives when he is threatened with the pains of hell, if he makes Nicolette his mistress. A creature wholly of affection and the senses, he sees on the way to paradise only a feeble and worn-out company of aged priests, 'clinging day and night to the chapel altars,' barefoot or in patched sandals. With or even without Nicolette, 'his sweet mistress whom he so much loves,' he, for his part, is ready to start on the way to hell, along with 'the good scholars,' as he says, and the actors, and the fine horsemen dead in battle, and the men of fashion, and 'the fair courteous ladies who had two or three chevaliers a piece beside their own true lords,' all gay with music, in their gold, and silver, and beautiful furs—'the vair and the grey.' "

REFERENCES

Ben Hecht and Charles MacArthur: *The Front Page.* Covici-Friede, New York, 1928.

Passages from the Diary of Samuel Pepys. The Modern Library, 1921.

Eleanore Boswell: *The Restoration Court Stage.* Harvard University Press, Cambridge, 1932.
Joseph Gregor: *Wiener Szenische Kunst.* Wiener Drucke, Vienna, 1923.
Allardyce Nicoll: *The Development of the Theatre.* Harcourt, Brace.
Lee Simonson: *The Stage Is Set.* Harcourt, Brace & Company.
Montague Summers: *The Restoration Theatre.* Macmillan, New York, 1934.
Lucien Dubech: *Histoire générale illustrée du théâtre.* Vol. 3, Librairie de France, Paris, 1931.
Sheldon Cheney: *The Theatre.* Tudor Publishing Company.
Joseph Gregor: *Monumenta Scenica.* 11th Portfolio, National Library and R. Piper and Company, Vienna and Munich, 1925–1930.
John Gassner: *Masters of the Drama.* Random House, New York, 1940.
Letters Concerning the English Nation, by Mons. de Voltaire. Peter Davis, London, 1926.
John C. Adams: *Shakespeare's Stage. Theatre Arts.* October, 1936.
Walt Whitman. From Montrose Moses and John Mason Brown: *The American Theatre as Seen by Its Critics.* W. W. Norton & Company, New York, 1934.
George Edward Bateman Saintsbury: *Romance. Encyclopaedia Britannica.* 1937.
Walter Pater: *The Renaissance.* Macmillan, London, 1873.
Johann Wolfgang von Goethe. From Gassner: *Masters of the Drama.* Random House.
Lope de Vega. From Cheney: *The Theatre.* Tudor Publishing Company.
Prosper Mérimée. From Dubech: *Ibid.*
André Antoine: *Mes souvenirs sur le Théâtre-Libre.* Fayard & Cie., Paris. 12me édition.
Garrett H. Leverton: *The Production of Later Nineteenth Century American Drama.* Teachers College, Columbia University, New York, 1936.
Karl Mantzius: *A History of Theatrical Art.* Vol. 6, Duckworth.
August Wilhelm Schlegel. From Barrett H. Clark: *European Theories of the Drama.* Appleton, New York, 1929.
Constantin Stanislavsky: *My Life in Art.* Little, Brown & Company.

4

THEATRE IS LIFE ITSELF

ZOLA

COULD anyone imagine a more perfect picture of sick theatre than the Baroque dramatic style in its last Romantic stages? In the 1880's the great playhouses of Europe were still producing in the style inherited from the age of Louis XIV. But the clock of drama had run down.

It was clear to the more vigorous minds of the period that the creative forces of the theatre were being destroyed. No one saw this more plainly than a certain Frenchman whose writings and other activities were a continual annoyance to the stuffy-minded of his generation. The honor of sweeping away the pretensions of the old theatre and of outlining a plan of action for a new one fell to the energetic and intrepid Émile Zola.

In 1881 Zola, then in the full tide of success as a novelist, issued a famous collection of essays under the title *Le naturalisme au théâtre*. These and his earlier preface to his play THÉRÈSE RAQUIN (1873) exposed "the decayed scaffoldings of the drama of yesterday."

We must cast aside fables of every sort, and delve into the living drama of the twofold life of the character and its environment, bereft of every nursery tale, historical trapping, and the usual conventional stupidities. The decayed scaffoldings of the drama of yesterday will fall of their own accord. We must clear the ground. The well-known receipts for the tying and untying of an intrigue have served their time; now we must seek a simple and broad picture of men and things, such as Molière might write. Outside of a few scenic conventions, all that is now known as the "science of the theatre" is merely a heap of clever tricks, a narrow tradition that serves to cramp the drama, a ready-made code of language and hackneyed situations, all known and planned out beforehand, which every original worker will scorn to use. (Clark).

The old theatre was "the last fortress of conventionality." Zola raged at the case-hardened conventions which prevented a living portrayal of modern human activity. Stage conventions must be destroyed. To be replaced by what? "By science!" thundered Zola. "The experimental and scientific spirit of the century will enter the domain of drama." Science alone will save the theatre.

Science in the theatre! One imagines some of the comments on this suggestion. Doesn't Zola know that science is the very antithesis of art? Isn't he aware that the cold, dry pedestrianism of science is at the very opposite pole of the flashing inspiration which is art? The very notion of mixing the two is abhorrent. As the English poet Shelley put it: "To analyze a work of art into its elements is as useless as throwing a violet into a crucible." Science is not even a fit subject for drama. Who ever heard of a play about a scientist?

Zola might have replied that more than one violet has been thrown into a crucible by modern scientists, with benefit to the world. A play about a scientist happens to be one of the oldest in history—the PROMETHEUS BOUND, by Aeschylus, written about 465 B.C. Prometheus, who defied the gods, bringing fire to men so that men could become godlike—was not this Titan the dramatic symbol of the whole future of science? And the FAUST of Goethe (the DOCTOR FAUSTUS of Marlowe), another of the world's greatest stage figures—is he not a scientist, a man who is ready to forego hope of the hereafter for an accurate knowledge of the material world? Shelley himself found in the scientific laboratory the same joyous inspiration which other poets found only in "unspoiled nature." In his play PROMETHEUS UNBOUND, written in 1819, he prophesied that the liberation of Prometheus will mean the liberation of man himself.[1]

Some of the world's greatest artists had combined in themselves the talents of both artist and scientist. Leonardo da Vinci, writer and designer of court masques, was at one and the same time a leading artist and scientist of the Italian Renaissance. One of the world's greatest painters, he had written in his *Treatise on Painting*,

> Those who became enamoured of the practice of the art, without having previously applied to the diligent study of the scientific part of it, may be compared to mariners, who put to sea in a ship without

rudder or compass, and therefore cannot be certain of arriving at the wished-for port.

Goethe, dramatic poet of German Romanticism, occupied himself with practical scientific experiment, wrote papers in botany and physics, incorporated into his poetic imagery the results of his investigations. Was there anything surprising about this? Not at all. The same incisive observation which these men gave to science they also gave to their artistic work; it was precisely this clear vision which gave value to their works of the imagination.

But Zola was not satisfied with mere argument. He formulated in detail what he expected of a new theatre. He kept a keen eye on developments in the French playhouses. The time came when the forces for which he was searching appeared as though in reply to his wishes. *Naturalism* came to the stage on a spring evening in 1887. It was no coincidence that Zola's story, JACQUES DAMOUR, was the successful performance on that occasion.

THE UGLY DUCKLING

March 30, 1887. We have arrived in Paris in a fine drizzle, and are looking for the theatre where a momentous opening night is about to take place. Useless to ask the hooded and cloaked policeman under the gas-flare of the street lamp. He would direct us to one of the famous State-subsidized or private playhouses—the Comédie-Française, the Odéon, the Gymnase, the Vaudeville or the Porte-Saint-Martin. Our quest lies elsewhere. We must get into a *fiacre* for the long ride over cobblestoned, winding streets to the Butte Montmartre.

At the Place Pigalle, having gone by the street market, splashing through puddles of water, our cab halts for a moment. The coachman reins in his nag, squinting around vainly for a street sign. We go on again and turn the corner at a lighted wine shop, into a narrow, tortuous alley that goes up steeply from the street. The alley, dimly lit, runs between the high, dirty walls of neighboring buildings to a flight of steps at the far end. Number 37, Passage de l'Elysée des Beaux-Arts, the high-sounding address for which we have been searching, is scarcely more than a hole in the wall.

The playhouse at this address is a little wooden hall with a platform at one end. Enough restaurant chairs can be placed there to seat 343 people. Paintings, framed and unframed, litter the walls; a settee is pushed against the wall near the fireplace, a table or two, an old sideboard, are wedged into a corner, a long ladder extends to an attic door near the ceiling. These are the furnishings of the Cercle Gaulois, one of those little dramatic clubs so typical of the period. The young people of the eighties—and the older ones as well—are going in for dramatic societies, amateur performances and charades as we today go in for dancing.

The little theatre into which we have come is the handiwork of a retired army officer known to his flock of young people as Père Krauss. This kindly, rather timid old gentleman built everything in the hall with his own hands, even the scenery and many of the properties. He himself is working the curtain tonight.

But it is not Papa Krauss who is presenting tonight's bill, which is scheduled for a run of exactly one evening. Krauss is an admirer of the big theatres and of the popular dramatists like Eugène Scribe. Tonight's plays have not been written by any of the commercial "Boulevard" dramatists. Furthermore, they have been directed by a relative newcomer at the Cercle Gaulois, a young man named André Antoine, whose ambitions and notions are proving more and more distressing to the old amateur.

Like a hen that has hatched a duckling, Krauss cannot help feeling that Antoine is a sensational character. The *pièce de résistance* of Antoine's bill is a playlet, JACQUES DAMOUR, dramatized by one Léon Hennique from a story by none other than that famous —not to say notorious—man of letters, Émile Zola. Only a couple of evenings before, Zola himself had come to a rehearsal—that same reformer who was later to earn the ill will of just such conservative soldiers as Père Krauss. And Zola had been pleased. He had even drawn young Antoine under a gas jet to take a good look at him and then said, "It's fine, very fine, eh, Hennique? We'll come again tomorrow."

And now the little playhouse is in for it. A program that smells badly of all the new, sensational tendencies that are in the air! The plays scheduled are MADEMOISELLE POMME, by Duranty and Alexis; UN PRÉFET, by Byl; LA COCARDE, by Vidal; and finally JACQUES DAMOUR. . . . What a tornado of energy that Antoine is! He even got *Figaro* to publish an announcement of the play, and some of the metropolitan critics have come down here for the evening.

Who is this André Antoine? In the future it will be said, "M. Antoine is thirty years of French theatre history." On this evening, however, he is still an obscure office clerk at the Paris Gas Company, where he puts in some twelve to fourteen hours a day. Nobody was more surprised than Antoine himself when he became, overnight, a focus of attention in the European theatre.

Born in Limoges, Antoine, eldest of four children, had very early been brought to Paris, where he witnessed as a boy the siege of the capital by the Prussians, and the even more terrible events of the Commune. At the age of twelve he was earning his living as a delivery boy while reading Dumas, George Sand and Eugène Sue in his spare hours. Later a job as a bookseller's clerk enabled him to flirt with the theatre in the evening. Antoine's interest in theatre had been as fervent, and as uncritical, as Krauss's. At eighteen he made his bow in the professional theatre—as a member of the *claque* of the Comédie-Française. From there he worked his way upward (further downward being hardly possible) to a job as an extra. He even found an hour here and there to attend classes at a local school of recitation known rather expansively as the Gymnase de la Parole.

By 1876, while employed by the Gas Company, Antoine had mustered up the courage to take the entrance examination for the Conservatoire. Having no private recommendations, as he later explained, he was emphatically turned down. This put an end, for a time, to his dreams of advancement in the theatre. He put his dramatic ambitions behind him when he went off to his army service in Tunisia. It was not until he returned to Paris and his clerical duties that the theatre called him once more.

The way was not made easy for this son of the people. Fortunately he had the strength to make his own path. Antoine was broad-shouldered, stooping, with small, wide-set blue eyes and an obstinate jaw. Add to this an ungainly, brusk manner, gruff speech, and you have a picture of bulldog tenacity. You must know, further, that he had no business instinct—the sort of man who, as Dubech remarks, would sell his shirt to put a good show on the stage.

It was Arthur Byl, a budding dramatist impressed by the quality of Antoine's acting at the Cercle Gaulois, who suggested that it was time to try out some original plays instead of Krauss's usual repertoire. Byl and his friend Jules Vidal offered to contribute the first two plays to this venture. Antoine jumped at the chance, with no notion at all where it was to lead him. He said afterwards, "I had not the least intention of becoming a professional actor or director, and I should certainly have laughed if anyone had predicted that we were going to revolutionize dramatic art."

This is a significant statement. As on more than one occasion hereafter, the theatre of the modern age made its wishes known, it made progress, through the agency of men who only half-guessed their mission. Antoine, about whom the new conception of Naturalism would revolve, did not set out to achieve Naturalism in the theatre; in fact during most of his life he objected to being identified with the Naturalist technique. But it was enough that he was honest, that he loved theatre and was a man of amazing energy. Such a man, like Shaw's latter-day *Don Juan,* cannot escape his fate; the healthy theatre seeks him as a woman seeks a husband—if only to make his life a burden.

Antoine was going to get his full share of difficulties. They began at once when old Krauss and the more conservative members of the Cercle Gaulois refused to lend the name or resources of the society to the new plan. The old gentleman did not care to encourage an upstart in his own club, while the others wanted none of Zola's notoriety. Krauss would not even permit any rehearsals in his theatre. Finally he was persuaded to rent the hall for the one evening of the performance, at what seemed the huge sum of one hundred francs. Antoine accepted the difficulties as they arose. He had been doing some extra copying at home for the Gas Company; by the end of the month he expected to have the sum required. It was necessary to put the opening date off to the end of March, when his salary would be forthcoming.

In the meanwhile a name had to be found for the new theatre. Byl suggested the name Théâtre-Libre, which was adopted. The problem of finding a rehearsal hall was more difficult to solve. Since the members of the troupe worked at their trades by day, they could rehearse only at night. At last Antoine found a little billiard room behind a wine shop, whose owner permitted its use in return for a minimum number of drinks to be ordered by the players. As the director could not expect his actors to meet this expense, he took it upon himself to raise the amount nightly, even if it meant going without some of his meals. The billiard table, "truly the largest I ever saw," as Antoine declared, swallowed up most of the acting area, leaving only the space along the walls. Fortunately at the last moment Krauss's heart softened enough to let the company continue its rehearsals at the Cercle.

Another problem appeared. Antoine disclosed that he had a standard in stage settings. The main item of the bill, JACQUES DAMOUR, called for a view of living-quarters in the rear of a butcher shop. Unable to hire the furniture which he thought suitable, Antoine was in a quandary until a couple of days before the opening night. Then his mother made the supreme sacrifice, letting him borrow all the dining-room furniture, the table and chairs. It was impossible to get permission from the Gas Company to transfer that furniture during the day—Antoine's superior was already knitting his brows at the publicity which the young clerk was getting in the newspapers. At five o'clock with the help of a rented pushcart he began the moving job personally, trundling the family furniture over the Boulevard Rocheouart, the Rue du Delta and up the steep alley to the little theatre, where he deposited it before the amazed eyes of Père Krauss.

RETURN TO LIFE

Such is the background of the inauspicious opening night we have traveled through space and time to attend. The little hall is filled to the doors. Even some of the press critics have come. Drawn by the magic name of Zola, they have "passed up" the opening of Gaston Serpette's LA GAMINE DE PARIS and amused themselves by making this journey to the hinterlands. . . . And the performance begins disastrously.

Our dramatist friend Byl had written an introductory poem which is a little involved and which lauds the master of Naturalism, Zola. Henry Burguet, who is to recite the poem, comes out front without the manuscript, which he has mislaid; the prompter has evidently been mislaid also, for he is not in his box. Seized with stage fright the amateur player stumbles through the first few lines, chokes and hurries from the stage. "It's starting fine," says Antoine, dourly, who then notices that the chair for the second play is missing! He is obliged to rush out, makeup and all, to the nearest second-hand dealer to buy one. But the chair does not save LA COCARDE from a cool reception. Alexis' MADEMOISELLE POMME has already gone by "unnoticed," in Antoine's words. As for Byl's PRÉFET, it is actually hissed.

With the rise of the curtain on JACQUES DAMOUR, the evening, which has seemed irretrievably lost, is turned into a great triumph. Antoine plays Jacques, a Communard who disappeared many years before and who now returns as if from the grave. The man's wife has remarried, and Jacques is no longer wanted. Fiercely the man who has come back out of the past demands that his life be restored to him.

As we sit there we forget that we are in close-packed, uncomfortable chairs in an amateur dramatic club in Montmartre. Jacques' tragic predicament begins to have its own existence in the factual world. We are no longer looking at some fledgling actors on a makeshift stage. Instead we have stumbled into the backroom of a Paris butcher shop. The people before us are vivid Parisian types, who go on about their daily activities unaware that they have been transplanted to a stage for us to gaze at. The furniture around them (thanks to Antoine's long-suffering mother) also looks as if it had been in long contact with daily life instead of having been carried in from the property-studio.

As for the French Enoch Arden, it is not Antoine playing him, but Jacques Damour, the man himself. Jacques' bearing gives no hint that he ever heard of such a thing as theatre. He does not see an audience which is close enough to reach out and seize his jacket; he even plays whole scenes with his back turned. The playlet comes to an end, with the first husband beaten by fate but asked to sit down to supper. The curtain closes in an uproar, cheers, applause, a stamping of feet that shakes the rickety building, to the alarm of Père Krauss. . . .

Antoine awakes next day to find himself famous. Those critics who had come to the performance rave as if they have found a treasure in the backyards of Montmartre. Antoine himself is singled out as a remarkable actor. Porel, director of the Odéon, who had turned down the Hennique adaptation of Zola's story, now begs for it for his theatre. And almost unanimously, to Antoine's displeasure, the press terms the new producing group a Naturalistic theatre.

To be called a Naturalist in the Paris theatre of the seventies is like being called a Red in the New York theatre of today. It is a term not meant to be endearing. Antoine, whose name, like Stanislavsky's, is now synonymous with Naturalism, was to spend the rest of his life trying to peel this label off his back. Both these men insisted that they wanted only good theatre, good theatre without tags.[2]

Antoine made plans for a complete season of plays in the autumn following his first bill. Subscriptions failed to materialize in any large quantity, and in the meantime Krauss definitely made up his mind that the Cercle Gaulois could not continue to house the new venture. Just the same the Théâtre-Libre began its first complete season in the following October, in a little playhouse in the Rue de la Gaîté, Montparnasse. Here it managed to hold out for seven years—a long life for an independent theatre.

So dramatic Naturalism began—only dimly conceived by its parent, who did not hesitate to repudiate his offspring as soon as it was born. Today the tradition of dramatic Naturalism prevails in most of the world's great theatres and cinemas. Its birth was attended by controversy, its existence has been marked by continuous dissent.

What were its original principles? We can learn more about them from the grandfather of Naturalism, Zola, than from its father, Antoine.

NO MORE FORMULAS

In his preface to THÉRÈSE RAQUIN Zola invented a new formula, namely that there must be no more formulas. It was his desire, he said,

> . . . to bring the theatre into closer relation with the great movement toward truth and experimental science which has since the last century been on the increase in every manifestation of the human intellect. The movement was started by the new methods of science; thence, Naturalism revolutionized criticism and history, in submitting man and his works to a system of precise analysis. . . . There should no longer be any school, no more formulas, no standards of any sort; there is only life itself, an immense field where each may study and create as he likes.

Zola's views were brilliantly provocative, but hardly accurate. He was, temperamentally, a polemicist, of the kind who seem always to find the most irritating way to state a case. In his enthusiasm for putting an end to the Romantic tradition he jumped to some rash conclusions. Besides he was himself too much a product of the Romantic era.

He had been impressed by the researches of the physiologist Claude Bernard, whose *Introduction to Experimental Medicine* he was always quoting. Bernard's special study lay in the field of what is now called biochemistry, his work antedating that of Pavlov. This research, carried on in experiments on living animals, sought to find the relationship between the nervous system, nutrition and secretions. Bernard's experiments contributed to the theory of adaptation in physiology, a theory as important in its field as that of the conservation of energy in the field of physics.

If Bernard, by means of impartial investigation, could lay bare the sources of "animal passions," why could not a dramatist, in the interests of society, make an objective study of human emotions? The soul must be dissected scientifically, insisted Zola. Did not that great pessimistic philosopher of Naturalism, Hippolyte Taine (1828–1893), once write, "Vice and virtue are products like sugar and vitriol."? Just so did Zola declare, "A like determinism will govern the stones of the roadway and the brain of man."

But Zola was not justified in transferring mechanically to human behavior the Darwinian observations on animals and plants. Neither Bernard nor any other genuine man of science would have made such an assumption, and in fact Bernard himself repudiated the thesis of his literary disciple.[3]

Zola may have had the ideal of cool detachment and objective observation, but in practice, powerful figure as he was, he limped far behind his ideal. Thus his best play, THÉRÈSE RAQUIN, ran counter in many ways to his own expressed theories. GERMINAL, his novel about miners, when made into a film in 1914 under the same title, shocked Europe with its brutal "realism" and was not allowed to play in Tsarist Russia. Yet Zola was one of those writers who make their excursions into the world rather gingerly. Like the "documentary" novels of Flaubert and the Goncourts, his writings are filled with errors of fact. If we weigh carefully his ideas on staging we begin to see why the reformed theatre of Naturalism was bound to take an erratic course.

Zola understood scientific procedure as little as he did true deduction. To *reproduce* something vividly meant the same thing to him, it would seem, as to grasp nature in terms of science. "A fragment of existence" was what he wanted on the stage—or, as the Naturalistic playwright Jean Jullien later described it, "a slice of life." The decrepit Baroque theatre was a hodge-podge of ridiculous conventions. Ergo, to build a living theatre, it is necessary to get rid of all conventions. How was life to be brought to the stage? By bringing an *exact reproduction* of life to the stage.

"I am waiting," declared Zola, "until the evolution accomplished in the novel takes place on the stage; until they return to the source of science and modern arts, to the study of nature, to the anatomy of man, to the painting of life, in an exact reproduction, more original and powerful than anyone has so far placed upon the boards."

One hundred years before, Denis Diderot, that Encyclopedist who was also a playwright, had cried "Back to nature!" Zola was right in tracing the descent of Naturalism through that revolutionary figure. The war against neo-classic conventions, a struggle assumed in the theatre by the Romantics, was now passing to new fighters, those of the Naturalistic school. And when Zola speaks of "the evolution accomplished in the novel," he is referring to that powerful literary advance led by Stendhal and Balzac which already dominated French literature.

Zola was not destined to measure up to these literary giants of Naturalism who preceded him; and in the theatre he was not fated to equal Henrik Ibsen, who had already written A DOLL'S HOUSE (1879). To Zola, however, must go the credit for defining a new goal for theatre, for explicitly demanding the end of the Baroque form and for calling new techniques into being. He alone of the post-Romantic innovators had the singleness of purpose—perhaps the word temerity might be more correct—to call science to the theatre, to accept wholeheartedly the designation of "Naturalist." Since his day the term Naturalist has always been tagged upon unwilling people.

ROSSERIE

It is of interest that in the province of dramaturgy the Naturalists set themselves against Scribe's well-made play. Zola's dislike of the well-made play amounted to a passion (in spite of the fact that THÉRÈSE RAQUIN, his best drama, was well-knit and contained exposition, climax and dénouement in the most approved

Scribe style). Scribe, although he wrote in the Romantic period, was essentially a classicist who set great store by rules of construction. Zola had no use for Scribe. He insisted (quite wrongly) that the foremost French dramatist of the nineteenth century was Alfred de Musset, for the reason, evidently, that Musset simply ignored the technique of the closely-knit play.

Naturalistic theory favored loose construction, so much so that some of the Naturalistic dramas were little more than a succession of tableaus. The Naturalists feared that the well-made play has no compunctions about distorting characters and situations in order to fit these into arbitrary plots. As afterwards proved, it was a fear with some foundation.[4]

It would be incorrect to suppose that the Naturalistic plays of Antoine's theatre established a wholly new tradition. There had been important forerunners, among them HENRIETTE MARÉCHAL (1865), by the Goncourts; LA RÉVOLTE (1870), by Villiers de l'Isle-Adam; Daudet's L'ARLÉSIENNE (1872). But the Théâtre-Libre became the rallying-place of all those dramatists who differed with the tradition of the Baroque-Romantic.

Edmond de Goncourt gave his prestige in support of Antoine's theatre, as did Henry Becque, that harsh and gloomy dramatic genius whose masterpiece, LES CORBEAUX, was finally put on at the Comédie-Française (1882) after being refused for five years by one playhouse after another, and after a bitter controversy between Becque and the Comédie officials. The Théâtre-Libre itself brought forward three dramatists who were later internationally famous: François de Curel, Georges de Porto-Riche and Eugène Brieux.

The plentiful admixture of sordidness which characterized THÉRÈSE RAQUIN and LES CORBEAUX was not lacking in the plays of many of the Théâtre-Libre dramatists, who looked to Zola and Becque for inspiration. Jean Jullien's SÉRÉNADE, put on during Antoine's first season, was the archetype of the *rosse* plays with which Antoine's playhouse became identified. The term *rosse* may be roughly translated as "crass," but it has been more accurately defined by the critic Filon as "a sort of vicious ingenuousness, the state of soul of people who never had any moral sense and who live in impurity and injustice, like a fish in water." (Waxman). The description is an apt one for SÉRÉNADE, which is summed up by Waxman as "a blatantly cynical and crude picture of a quadrangle . . . in which a mother and daughter are mistresses of a family tutor who is finally accepted as a son-in-law by a complacent father."

Prostitution recurred often as a theme of the Théâtre-Libre dramas. (Following the production of LE FIN DE LUCIE PELLEGRIN in 1888, the conservative journals suggested a fumigation of the playhouse, while the leading lady publicly apologized for having taken the rôle.) Another play of this genre was Ancey's LA DUPE (1891); its "hero," a pauper, wife-beater and embezzler, morally destroys his wife, who is bound to him by a sexual mania. Some of the other themes of Antoine's repertory were equally lacking in charm. August Linert's CONTE DE NOËL, in which "an adulterous child is killed and its body thrown to the pigs on Christmas Eve to the sound of Christmas carols," proved too much even for the strong stomachs of the Théâtre-Libre audiences.

Today we should consider plays of this sort more appropriate for rougher nights at the Grand Guignol. They were responsible for much of the antagonism which the Naturalistic form aroused.

THÉRÈSE RAQUIN, the prototype of these plays, had been hissed off the stage, precisely because Zola had carried out the task which he set himself:

> Given a strong man and an unsatisfied woman, to seek in them the beast, to see nothing but the beast, to throw them into a violent drama and note scrupulously the sensations and acts of these creatures. . . . I have simply done on two living bodies the work which surgeons do on corpses. (Gassner).

Even Sarcey, who was inclined to look tolerantly on the Naturalistic trend in the drama, murmured, "This fellow Zola makes me a little sick."

In justice to Antoine and his dramatists, however, it must be made clear that they were not peddlers of pornography or sensationalism. In an age of revolt against wornout elegance and smug sentiments, they went to the opposite extreme. They portrayed the seamy side of existence in exaggerated fashion—far too often with a mere cynical acceptance of what they saw or thought they saw. Practically all the Naturalistic dramas, at the Théâtre-Libre and afterwards, were plays of social criticism, or at least of humanitarian mood. They struck a note which was conspicuously lacking in the plays of the Baroque or Romantic repertory. In the older plays nobility was frequently contrasted with baseness, but there was no hint that baseness was something implicit in the very structure of society. Antoine's dramatists usually began with the premise that sordidness, stupidity and hypocrisy are the dominant forces of the world.

However "crass" these plays might have been, some of them approached reality boldly. Brieux' DAMAGED GOODS (1902) is an example. Almost forty years before a film like DR. EHRLICH'S MAGIC BULLET (1940) became possible, Brieux tore away the veil of secrecy that surrounded the "social diseases." The play was denounced and censored but it left its mark on the public conscience just the same. Herman Heijermans, the Dutch dramatist whose one-act play AHASVÈRE was produced by Antoine in 1893, later on, in THE GOOD HOPE (1900), made a startling disclosure of the way in which greedy shipowners sent their men off to death in rotten ships. As a direct consequence of Heijermans' play new maritime laws were adopted in Holland.[5]

Among these earlier Naturalistic plays THE GOOD HOPE remains notable for its powerful delineation of character. Most of the others were more secure in their theses than in their characterization, which was inclined to be thin. Their quality at its best is exemplified today in the plays of Lillian Hellman. The obnoxious little Mary Tilford of THE CHILDREN'S HOUR (1934), and the equally unpleasant Regina Giddens of THE LITTLE FOXES (1939), are plausible characters, yet they have malice, rather than blood, in their veins.

THE ACTOR "LIVES THE PART"

Antoine, in spite of the natural handicap of a weak voice, showed unusual powers as an actor. This part of his talent received recognition at once. As an actor he set for his theatre a standard very different from that of the Romantic players who regularly singed their pants on the gas flame of the footlights. George Moore, who saw him in Ibsen's GHOSTS, has left his word-picture:

> Antoine, identifying himself with the simple truth sought by Ibsen, by voice and gesture, casts upon the scene so terrible a light, so strange an air of truth, that the drama seemed to be passing not before our eyes, but deep in our hearts in a way we never felt before.

With Antoine ended the stage conventions of "elocutionary" acting which required that an actor must always speak facing the audience, that he must rise from his seat and go downstage to deliver his monologue. But this change was more than the substitution of a new set of gestures. It was intended to be a very denial of theatre. The actor was not playing a part: he *was* the part, he *lived* the part. In describing his own feelings while playing Oswald in GHOSTS, Antoine makes this point very clear:

> I experienced a sensation hitherto unknown to me, the almost complete loss of my own personality. From the beginning of the second act, I remembered nothing, neither the public, nor the effect of the performance, and when the curtain fell, I found myself shuddering, enervated, incapable of pulling myself together for some moments. (Waxman).

"In our art you must live the part every moment that you are playing it," Stanislavsky said later. The ideal of the new actor must be to "creep into the skin and body" of the character he portrays. The Russian actor-director also gives a vivid impression of an actor's sensations while "living the part." In this case it is the rôle of Doctor Stockman in Ibsen's AN ENEMY OF THE PEOPLE:

> I was wrathful in the play at the people that I had loved once, while I looked at them through the eyes of Stockman's soul. I sincerely sympathized with Stockman and understood his feelings when his eyes saw the rotten souls of the men who had once been his friends. I feared in those moments—for Stockman or for myself—I don't remember. I felt and understood that with each succeeding scene I became more and more lonely, and when, at the end of the performance I at last stood alone, the final sentence of the play "He is the strongest who stands alone" seemed to beg for utterance by its own power.

How does the actor accomplish the magical feat of "creeping into the skin and body" of a character not his own? The modern theatre is indebted to Stanislavsky for a detailed analysis of this technique, which is practiced, more or less consciously, in the Naturalistic and Symbolist theatres. This analysis not only reveals the steps whereby an actor finds an identification with his rôle, but offers a practical training to the actor in his task.

The most important point in the Stanislavsky "system," as it is generally known, is the actor's duty of finding an "inner justification" for any action which he performs. For example, it is not sufficient for an actor playing an old man to mimic the behavior of an old man; the actor must look within himself for an emotional or imaginative sensation which approximates the state of mind of an old man. An actor who plays the rôle of a murderer may find an

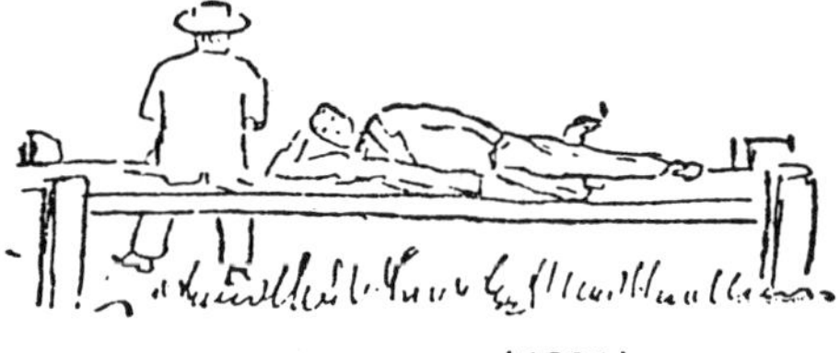

THE SEAGULL (1896)

Drawing by Constantin Stanislavsky

inner justification for the quality of his rôle by recalling a time when he killed a fly or committed some more atrocious act.

In this system, also, there is a specific method for relating the actor's rôle to the play. The play is analyzed for its main action, and each character is then assigned a subsidiary action. The subsidiary action is in turn broken down into "adjustments," or minor variations of action from scene to scene or from one moment to another.[6]

Drawing by Stanislavsky for THE SEAGULL

In rehearsal or during study the actor must perform definite exercises. These include "sense memory," the purpose of which is to heighten the physical sensitivity of the actor, and which may take the form of sewing with an imaginary needle or opening an imaginary jackknife. In "affective memory" exercises the actor learns to enrich his rôle by evoking memories of previous mental states which parallel the state of mind called for in the rôle. He also does "improvisations," in which he imagines or carries out acts which he does not perform in the play, but which his character may have performed elsewhere. The script may require that we meet a character for the first time as he comes from the deathbed of his child; under the Stanislavsky system the actor who has this particular rôle may very likely act out, as training, the whole deathbed scene.

EXACT REPRODUCTION

Naturalism required its own kind of stage setting. The audience must be made to forget that it is looking at décor. The setting must be the very place of the dramatic action itself, as if you walked into it off the street, as if it had grown there.

It was no coincidence that the furniture for JACQUES DAMOUR, on the Théâtre-Libre's first bill, was transplanted to the stage straight from the Antoines' dining room. Zola, who had definite ideas about the stage setting, again took his cue from Taine, who believed in the importance of "little, significant facts." Waxman relates that "The only praiseworthy element that Zóla could find in Sardou, for several decades the dramatic god of the Paris boulevard theatres, was his stage-setting, which was meticulously exact in every detail, and his realistic handling of crowds." When Zola's L'ASSOMMOIR was produced in play form (1879), the author saw to it that there was a truly vivid likeness of a barroom on the stage. He praised the *mis en scène* highly: "All my ideas are there in that exact reproduction of life. The men who enter, who leave, who drink seated at the tables or standing at the bar, transport us to a genuine drinking-shop." (Dubech).

Zola objected to the use of footlights because they cast an unnatural kind of illumination on the scene. This particular aversion was shared by August Strindberg, whose MADEMOISELLE JULIE was produced at the Théâtre-Libre (1893). Strindberg abominated the practice, then current, of painting furniture and kitchen utensils on the walls of stage rooms. The Swedish author's dynamic ideas on scenery are evident in his proposal that the straight back wall be done away with. A diagonal back wall, he thought, would help make stage action more lifelike. His suggestion might still be heeded by Symbolist designers today.[7]

If Sardou had plausible scenery for his plays, it was Naturalistic only by comparison with that of most Paris theatres, where stock settings made of flimsy painted flats and drops were the rule. A few pieces of furniture brought as if at random from the property rooms were scattered around the bare stage floor, supplemented at times with furniture painted on the walls. The stage floor itself sloped up toward the back wall and was cut through from front to back with slots running parallel to the footlights. Wooden posts known as *masts* worked in these slots. The posts were fixed into rolling chassis under the stage, only the masts themselves appearing above the stage floor. To these masts the scenery was lashed. Gas lighting had replaced the bland glow of candles; its brighter illumination showed up cruelly the flapping canvas wings, the tawdry, wrinkled backdrops.

Not only furniture but whole settings were taken out of the storehouse to serve again for a new production. When the Odéon presented a genre piece by Ancey called GRAND'MÈRE (1890), it gave the play a vast salon as a setting. It was the same setting, Antoine observed, which had completely smothered an act of RENÉE MAUPERIN. It was, no doubt, a cream-and-gold salon, and a handsome one. The public was used to it and after all (it was supposed) the public was there to applaud the actors, not to criticize the backgrounds. Antoine, however, saw that the acting problem could not be separated from that of the setting:

> The characters . . . of GRAND'MÈRE are people like ourselves; they live, not in vast halls having the dimensions of cathedrals, but in interiors like ours, around their fireplaces, under the lamp, around the table—and not at all, as in the classic repertory, in front of the prompter's box.

Antoine, without a prosperous clientèle or State subsidy, always up to his ears in debt, insisted on constructing new, carefully detailed settings for each of his productions.[8] To those who thought this obviously foolish, he replied

> I know the objections you may make—the stage setting is secondary. Yes, perhaps, in the plays of the classic repertory. . . . In modern works written in the spirit of truth and naturalism in which the theory of environment and the influence of external things has taken so large a part, is not the setting a natural part of the work? . . . Is it not a sort of exposition of the subject? (Miller).

THE DARWINIAN STAGE SETTING

Antoine was not the first to see more than a decorative importance in the setting. Goethe and Wagner had considered carefully its effect on an audience. Victor Hugo, leading spirit of the Romantics in France, saw a necessary relationship of the scenery to the play. A champion of local color in his scripts, he required it visually in the setting:

> The place where this or that catastrophe occurred becomes a terrible and inseparable witness thereof; and the absence of silent characters of this sort would make the greatest scenes of history incomplete in the drama. (*Preface to Cromwell*).

The Russian Romantics of later years may have been as indifferent to authentic costume as Stanislavsky declares, but in the west it was the Romantics who made the innovation of historically accurate costuming. Both the actor Talma and the actress Mlle. Mars are credited with making careful research into history when creating their costumes. Dumas' LA REINE MARGOT, with which he opened the Théâtre-Historique (1847), reproduced historic locale and costume so convincingly that "the spectator was carried away into the sixteenth century." (Moynet). By the early years of the nineteenth century the English Romantic directors John Philip Kemble, Edmund Kean and David Garrick had already established the principle of historic and geographic documentation for stage scenery.

In 1823 J. R. Planché, under Kemble's management, made a sensation when he put on Shakespeare's KING JOHN in costumes as historically accurate as "antiquarian" research could make them. Authenticity of settings and costumes were an established principle in the ensuing presentations of Macready, Charles Kean, Beerbohm Tree and Henry Irving. Historians were consulted for accurate data. In a preface to his production of THE WINTER'S TALE (1856) Kean admitted his worry over the non-existent seacoast of Bohemia: "I have therefore followed the suggestion of Sir Thomas Hanmer, in his annotations on Shakespeare, by the substitution of Bithynia."

But the director who most impressed Antoine and Stanislavsky in his handling scenic production was Duke Georg of Saxe-

Meiningen. Meiningen was the director of the court theatre of a little-known German state; but his genius made his acting troupe the admiration of Europe. By the time Antoine arrived Meiningen had already shown that stage production is not a mere accumulation of theatrical effects but an art whose elements must be deftly woven together with the most painstaking attention to detail. A scene designer as well as a director, Duke Georg went into production only after making drawings of whole scenes showing the actors in the proposed settings. The most devoted collective work

From *Die Meininger*

DIE HERMANNSCHLACHT (1875)

Drawing by the Duke of Meiningen

on the part of the acting company and its technicians was required to bring these penciled scenes to the stage effectively.

Meiningen seems to have visualized his productions as if each factor played its part like an instrument in an orchestra. Not only was the setting carefully related to the actor; every detail of costume or property was considered as part of a total impression. Sound effects were shrewdly used to heighten the emotional effect of the drama. In Schiller's FIESKO, as produced in Berlin in 1875, there was a whole gamut of sounds: alarm bells in the night; weapons pounding against wooden doors, the splintering of heavy gates; explosions; the clash of swords fading into the distance. Light was used in varying intensities, in the form of candle-light, moonlight, sunshine. Antoine, who encountered the Meiningen troupe in Brussels the year after the opening of the Théâtre-Libre, was so impressed that he sent home a long letter describing his reactions. He seems to have been especially struck by the "epic naïveté" of a lighting effect that he witnessed: a shaft of light which comes through a window, striking an old man at the moment of death.[9]

Antoine, however, saw the problem of the setting as involving more than local color or a necessary pictorial relationship to the actor. For him it had a still more vital meaning. By "the theory of environment" he meant quite evidently the belief that environment has an important influence on human behavior. It was a conception new to the theatre, even though Darwin had expressed it many years before in his monumental *Origin of Species.* Under Antoine's tutelage *the setting as environment* in this Darwinian sense came to the theatre for the first time.

No longer was the setting to be merely "appropriate," or an "added splendor," or picturesque background. It must have an individual character and history. It must be as genuinely observed, as significantly real, as the actor. It must loom up before the spectator with the same vividness, solid, palpable, substantial, as if plucked from the stream of life itself.

How was this to be done? Antoine had several sources of inspiration besides Meiningen. Zola, for instance, who insisted on the "exact reproduction" of environment. Zola was a close friend of Paul Cézanne, that anti-Romantic painter whose genius would some day change the world's eyesight. The Impressionists, Pissaro, Sisley, Monet, Degas, Renoir, Van Gogh, were already shocking the public out of its old complacency. But it was especially the Barbizon school and the art of such masters as Courbet and Manet whose approach to nature matched Antoine's scenic style. In that era, too, the work of the camera still seemed to be a miracle of "realism." (Louis Daguerre, co-inventor with Nièpce, of the photographic camera, had begun his career as a scene designer.)[10] Antoine's setting seized upon environment photographically, *in toto,* the whole body of environment with all its details, relevant or irrelevant. The more facsimile detail, the better.

For Fernand Icre's one-act drama LES BOUCHERS (1888) Antoine hung up on the stage real carcasses of beef; for Giovanni Verga's CHEVALERIE RUSTIQUE, on the same bill, he supplied, to the delight of the audience, a fountain with real water in the setting of a little Sicilian village. The council of war which occurs in the third act of Léon Hennique's LA MORT DU DUC D'ENGHIEN, as presented later in the same year, was illuminated only by lanterns on the table, "an effect so new and unexpected that everyone talked of it." On the other hand, in Catulle Mendès' LA REINE FIAMETTE (1889), when Antoine came onstage with a large sword which he handled like a walking stick, he was severely criticized, even though, as he insisted, it was "a detail absolutely exact and copied from a number of engravings and portraits of the period." Curel's FOSSILES (1892), although it all took place in the same salon, received three different settings showing different views of the same room, as if the room were turning on itself.

For Antoine crowds and mobs were crowds and mobs, not a few "supers." Broadway today considers a play with a cast of eighty to be a very large show. In J. H. Rosny's NELL HORN (1891) Antoine by his own account made use of almost five hundred extras! About the same number was employed for the Goncourts' LA PATRIE EN DANGER (1889). Antoine describes a rehearsal of the latter play:

> There was a startling effect of *mis en scène* in the third act, in the city hall of Verdun. I used again the method of the DUC D'ENGHIEN, overhead lighting, with the lamps making visible the swarming mob. Truly, at that moment it was altogether beautiful and I felt some pride in watching its effect on the face of [Edmond de Goncourt]. Into that small setting I allowed almost five hundred extras to filter in gently through a single door. They seeped in like a tide, ending by submerging everything from the furniture to the stage characters. In the shadow, with streaks of light falling here and there on the swarming crowd, the effect was extraordinary. (*Mes Souvenirs sur le Théâtre-Libre*).

Gerhart Hauptmann's THE WEAVERS (1893), put on during Antoine's next-to-last season at the Théâtre-Libre, was perhaps the peak of this theatre's creative life. The director brought to the stage the cramped sheds of the workers, crowded and darkened by the looms. The production had an unheard-of vividness that brought the audience to its feet. Antoine wrote of it:

> Here in our theatre, contrary to what I expected, this play of revolt rang first of all as a cry of despair and of misery; from act to act the

rapt audience never ceased applauding. It is the masterpiece of a social theatre which is rough-hewing itself, and Jaurès,[11] filled with enthusiasm, has told me that such a play accomplishes more than all campaigns and political discussions.

Moreover, as I feel strongly that it is one of the last plays which I am putting on and that the end of my efforts begins to appear on the horizon, I have consecrated to it all that I have left of force, of resources and of energy, and I can say that the interpretation has been admirable. Gémier, as Father Baumert, has revealed himself as what I have known him to be for a long time, a great actor, and Arquillière has been splendid. [Antoine himself was Hilse.] All the second act with the chant of the weavers, which serves as *leitmotiv*, and the cannonading, which rumbles continually off stage, has made a prodigious effect. In the fourth, in the storming of the manufacturer's house, the effect of terror was so intense that everyone in the orchestra stood up. The last scene, with the death of old Hilse during the fusillade and the uproar of the crowd, ended in the midst of applause. (Miller).

DOCUMENTED ENVIRONMENT

Scenic Naturalism as developed by Antoine characterized most of the productions of the Moscow Art Theatre. The scrupulous care with which this theatre *documented* its settings was evident in its very first play, Alexei Tolstoy's TSAR FYODOR (1898). After the libraries of Moscow were exhausted in the search for data on the times of Tsar Fyodor, Stanislavsky, Mme. Stanislavsky, the designer Simov, a costume designer and several of the actors obtained the use of a private railroad car, with which they visited ancient towns gathering "atmosphere" and buying up genuine period costumes and properties.

In producing Maxim Gorky's LOWER DEPTHS (1902), members of the troupe prepared by visiting the underground hideouts of the Khitrov Market, headquarters of thieves and outcasts:

It was necessary to enter into the spiritual springs of Gorky himself, just as we had done in the case of Chekhov, and find the current of the action in the soul of the writer. . . . We arranged an expedition, in which many of the actors in the play, Nemirovich-Danchenko and I, took part. Under the leadership of the writer Giliarevsky, a connoisseur of the life of tramps, who always helped them with money and advice, we went by night to the Khitrov Market. . . . It was hard to get permission from the secret organizations of the Khitrov Market. A large theft had taken place that night and the entire Market was in a state of siege. Patrols of armed gunmen were stationed in various places. They would stop us in the endless underground passages, demanding to see our passes. . . . In the very centre of the underground labyrinth was the local university and the intelligentsia of the Market. . . . The excursion to the Khitrov Market, more than any discussion or analysis of the play, awoke my fantasy and my creative mood. . . . Everything received a real basis and took its proper place. Making the sketches and the *mis en scène,* or showing the actors any of the scenes, I was guided by living memories, and not by invention or guesswork. (*My Life in Art*).

Similarly the production of Tolstoy's POWER OF DARKNESS in the same year required a visit to the distant province of Tula, where actors and scenic artists made a close study of the local architecture, furnishings, costumes and festivals. Two old peasants, a man and a woman, were brought back to Moscow as consultants, to make sure that there would be strict fidelity in the interpretation of peasant life. Of these two, the woman seems to have been invaluable in making the production an authentic picture of provincial Russia. Stanislavsky wrote: "It was she who showed for the first time on the stage the real Russian village in all its spiritual darkness and power."

Plays with foreign backgrounds received the same careful documentation. For JULIUS CAESAR (1903), illustrations and properties were fetched from Rome. This production reconstructed a whole section of the Imperial City, complete with shops and houses clinging to the hillside:

The construction of the floor and the motives for the scenery of the first act were brought from Rome by Simov and Nemirovich-Danchenko. We were able to make use of the great trap in the stage in creating the impression of a street disappearing under a hill. In its depth the effect of a moving crowd was created in the same manner as the movement of the armies, and a whole cross-section of the life of ancient Rome was shown on the stage. Rows of stores stretched from the forestage into the trap and were lost in the movement of the crowd. Merchants stood in front of them, calling in the buyers; here and there was seen the shop of an armorer where swords, shields and armor were in the process of forging, and in the necessary places the ringing of the hammers in the shop covered the talk of the crowd. The street passed along the whole width of the stage and disappeared in the wings, while on the right an alley with a typical Italian stairway poured into it from the hills. In this way the citizens moved towards each other, up and down and along the stage, and their movements on meeting created a garish and lifelike picture of Roman street life. At the point where the street rose from the trap to the stage, was the shop of a barber, where Roman patricians met and engaged in conversation, as we do in our clubs. Above the shop on a typical flat roof there was a little garden with a bench. From there the people's tribunes delivered their speeches, stopping the mob which crowded the forestage for the time being.[12] (*My Life in Art*).

A study of Stanislavsky's notebook (*Regiebuch* would be a more exact term) for Chekhov's THE SEAGULL reveals the difference between the Naturalistic scenic method and that of the

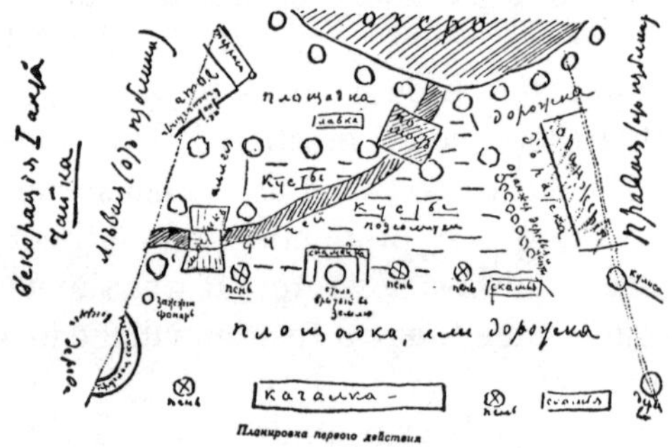

THE SEAGULL

Drawing by Stanislavsky

Baroque. For the Baroque director or designer the setting was a formal arrangement of painted side wings and backdrop. For Stanislavsky the setting was first of all the environment of human beings. The notebook contains Stanislavsky's own ground plans for the play. These drawings are impossible to transfer to the stage. They are maps of the Sorin estate: the park of birch trees, the house with its veranda, the lawn, the path, the lake, a little stream with wooden bridges. Only after he understood the whole geography of the neighborhood could the director approach intelligently the work of designing the stage setting. On the stage this new, Naturalistic setting did not add up to a formal structure on a platform. It was an illusion of the Sorin estate, complete with depth, atmosphere, earth and sky.

THE FOURTH WALL

One additional principle of the Naturalists should be recorded. Antoine and other Naturalistic directors after him knew that the stage could maintain its facsimile illusion of the life only if the audience were held spellbound. A restless mood in the audience would destroy it. This iridescent image of life could not for a moment survive the boisterousness of past audiences—the roaring, heel-kicking "bleachers" of the Attic plays, Shakespeare's boorish groundlings, the rowdy stews of Lope de Vega's corral theatres, the mob that crowded the Hôtel de Bourgogne. The theatre has always been that sort of unruly place: people of "breeding," young "bloods" who chattered and tripped up the actors had sat on Shakespeare's own stage. And on the sides of the Baroque stage too, until Voltaire drove them off for good.[13]

In Antoine's day theatre audiences had not reformed their ways very much. No small part of his difficulties was with his audiences, who entered the doors of the Théâtre-Libre unawed by the fact that it was a temple of dramatic art. They smoked, shouted wisecracks, howled and slammed seats and doors when displeased. During NELL HORN the sight of the great mob on the stage for some unexplained reason put the audience in an uproar of catcalls and "pleasantries." This tumult ceased only after three hundred of the extras, at Antoine's signal, let loose such a storm of noise that the audience was left fatigued, stupefied and *hors de combat.*

It was one of these encounters with his own public which finally decided Antoine to give up the Théâtre-Libre. Marcel Luguet's LE MISSIONNAIRE (1894) had as one of its characters a commentator in the audience. Antoine, who had the rôle of the commentator, was exposed to the antics of the playgoers. During the hubbub someone, with a gesture which Antoine considered "extremely symbolic," hit him in the face with a handful of sous.

We may well believe that Jean Jullien, who was both a dramatist and a spokesman for the Théâtre-Libre, echoed the views of the director when he proclaimed: "The public must lose for a moment the feeling of its presence in a theatre, and for that I believe it is necessary, as soon as the curtain rises, to have complete darkness in the auditorium. The stage picture will stand out with greater vividness, the spectator will remain attentive, will no longer dare to chat, and will become almost intelligent. . . ."

The same belief is mirrored in Strindberg's preface to MADEMOISELLE JULIE. The Swedish dramatist explains that he no longer divides his plays into acts because

> I have come to fear that our decreasing capacity for illusion might be unfavorably effected by intermissions during which the spectator would have time to reflect and get away from the suggestive influence of the author-hypnotist.

Nor must the spell be broken through a direct contact of actor and audience. Antoine's dread of forestage acting has already been described. Julien continues: "If the actor must always follow carefully the impressions of the audience, he must conceal the fact, must play as if he were at home, taking no heed of the emotions he excites, of approval or disapproval; the front of the stage must be a fourth wall, transparent for the public, opaque for the player. . . ."

Thus the theatre curtain becomes the "fourth wall" of the stage setting. It is a new task for the curtain. The stage curtain has a history which goes back to the Romans, who, on good evidence, used a type of curtain which dropped down into a slot in the ground in front of their open-air stage. By the late seventeenth century the curtain had become indispensable. Now, without changing its appearance any further, it entered on a new phase of its history.

It was no longer a mere device to hide the shifting of scenery. It became the portal of a magic world of illusion, a world whose compelling truth seemed to vie with life itself. It sealed the opening of a lighted peep-box; and when the curtain rose, the contemplative spectator peered into that lighted box with the absorption of one who looks at images in his own mind. His imagination soared up and away from the seats of the theatre. The new dramatic magic caused the stage platform to vanish. You might almost say it caused the theatre building itself to disappear from the mind of the playgoer as he sat there entranced.

FORTY SOUS

The technique of Naturalism contained too much truth to be ignored. Naturalistic scripts began to reach the other Paris stages.

From Le Théâtre

L'ASSOMMOIR. Revival at the Théâtre de la Porte-St.-Martin (1900)

Zola: "All my ideas are there in that exact reproduction of life."

There they failed as often as not, until other managers woke up to the fact that Naturalism was a matter not only of scripts but of a whole new production method. In a short time Antoine's views on acting and scene design began to penetrate to the more conservative stages. His actors also arrived there. Indeed the Théâtre-Libre encountered the usual difficulty of successful new theatre movements—its talent was constantly being drawn off by the larger playhouses.

In 1906 André Antoine was called to manage the Odéon as sole director of that State-subsidized theatre—an event which may be said to mark officially the triumph of a new order in the European theatre. Official recognition of the Naturalistic stage method was a belated sequel to its public recognition. By 1893 it had already been established, in script form at least, in the work of dramatists like Ibsen, Strindberg, Wedekind, Hauptmann, Tolstoy, Shaw, Becque, Zola, Curel, Brieux and Porto-Riche.

It has been intimated that the progress of Naturalism was not altogether a triumphal parade. Antoine, a young unknown, almost immediately found influential friends (including the critic Francisque Sarcey) when he began his work. But he had more than his fill of discouragement as well. Among the partisans of Romanticism, many who had once derided the classicists with the cry, "Your Racine is a scoundrel, Messieurs!" treated the new style with the same sort of ridicule.

Naturalism, it should be remembered, was obliged to make its first appearance in an obscure playhouse under the baton of an unknown director. In getting started, the new technique at first showed the usual tendency of pioneers to cause annoyance. The Théâtre-Libre *rosse* dramas were perhaps the worst offenders. But it was not alone the Naturalistic plays which met with dislike; the whole Naturalistic style was held to be a fad that would disappear one fine evening. The hack dramatist Georges Ohnet called the Théâtre-Libre company a set of "errand boys," while the gifted classic theorist Brunetière hated Naturalism so fiercely that he considered Zola a personal enemy. Sarah Bernhardt, whom the ambitious young director tried to interest in his project "because she holds in her hands a public ready to follow her wherever she wishes," replied with nothing more than a gracious smile.

Like so many experimental groups which followed it, the

Théâtre-Libre eventually broke down under financial strain. Antoine's troupe consisted of young middle class people as well as some proletarians who gave their time after working hours, rehearsing at night. Mademoiselle Barny, for instance, who created almost seventy rôles, was a dressmaker. In THE POWER OF DARKNESS (1888) the cast, which received high praise from the critics, included "two clerks, an architect, a chemist, a traveling salesman, a wine-merchant, a manufacturer, a dressmaker, a bookbinder, and a post-office employee." With such amateurs Antoine, between 1887 and 1890, produced 125 new acts, while in the same length of time the Comédie-Française and the Odéon, receiving, together, about one million francs in subsidies, produced 25 acts and 67 acts respectively.

This young director had embarked on his career with forty sous in his pocket. After he resigned from the Gas Company he went through a period in which he had to depend on friends for a square meal, in spite of his overnight rise to fame. At the beginning of the Théâtre-Libre's last foreign tour, its director was afraid that the company's baggage would be impounded to pay the debts of the manager who had signed them up; he ran around Paris all night like a crazy man, trying to raise some money. In September 1894 the story of his theatre comes to an end in Italy, where the company was left stranded. Antoine found in his pocket about the same amount with which he began:

> Here finishes the Odyssey of the Théâtre-Libre. Starting seven years ago in my attic room in the Rue Dunquerque with forty sous in my pocket, to go and rehearse our first show at the little wine shop in the Rue des Abbesses, I find myself in Rome with about the same sum, surrounded by some fifteen comrades as badly off as myself, with a hundred thousand francs in debts awaiting me in Paris, without knowing what to do next day. (*Mes Souvenirs sur le Théâtre-Libre*).

In spite of financial failure the tide was with Antoine's "slice of life" technique. The reforms which he proposed were long overdue; they could no longer be held back. His example aired out and purified the French stage. The Romantic theatre of declamation, of "vehicles" and stellar rôles, of bathos and vaudeville, of perfunctory rehearsals and shoddy production, was left behind—not, indeed, entirely, but as a standard of theatre. The way was opened for a new reform which might hope to measure—as the faded Baroque conventions could not—the tumultuous, perplexing life which science and industry had created in the course of two centuries.

BACKGROUNDS OF NATURALISM

We have tried to show that the historic forms of drama did not emerge full-grown and perfect at stated intervals of history; that, on the contrary, each arose slowly and haltingly, containing in itself all the limitations of the general thought of its era.

We may now ask, "What are the backgrounds of thought of the Naturalistic form? What made its coming inevitable? What kind of audiences gave it welcome?" And, most interesting of all such questions, perhaps, "Why that emphasis on science?"

Let us begin by answering the last question, for it gives us the clue to the others. To do so we must go back, for a few moments, to the days when Baroque theatre, the theatre of feudal autocracy, still played to its select audiences.

In the year 1687 a deeply religious Englishman who had been studying the movements of the "celestial bodies," published his observations in a book. This book, the *Principia* of Sir Isaac Newton, affirmed on the basis of mathematical proof that the solar system obeys the laws of mechanics.

It was not the first scientific book ever written. But it contained the most inclusive formula which science had so far presented to the world. Newton's deductions gripped men's minds with a force hardly understandable today. It looked as if the riddle of the universe were solved, and as if the key of life had been found. All knowledge seemed within reach; one need only apply the simple laws of physical mechanics to all known phenomena, including man. As Whitehead relates, "It was as if the heavens were being opened, on a set plan."

So it seemed, indeed, to the French Encyclopedists who stood at the forefront in the battle against the feudal order. Feudalism was buttressed in its authority by a host of powerful supernatural beliefs. It was necessary only to direct the new weapon forged by science against these ancient ramparts in order to crumble them to dust.

This belief did not work out so simply in practice. Just the same it proved to have a tremendous liberating force. No field was barred any longer to scientific investigation. No academic theory, however impressive, could stand without verification by accurate test. No authority which rested upon the "divine right" of kings for its sanction could long endure in that new atmosphere of thought.

We may recollect that it was not until a long time after the French revolution that the Baroque dramatic form was challenged in its turn. The new playgoers were no longer a court audience but the wealthier members of the middle class—the class that had overthrown the nobility. Romanticism—the doctrine of the divine right of the individual soul—was the dramatic form sponsored by this new audience. The drama's center of interest was no longer the heroic deeds of rulers but the study of individual will and conscience.

But no sooner did history solve one great problem than it presented another. The nineteenth century was a period of overturn in the methods of science and industry. Handicrafts were succeeded by mass production in power-driven factories. Technological improvements, especially in the second half of the century, added momentum to the process. This industrial revolution created a new class of people—the modern proletariat, a huge working population existing usually on the narrowest of margins. In addition there was a smaller but still very numerous class of professional people and tradesmen with a status not very much more secure than that of the workers. Social reorganization could not keep pace with these events, which moved swiftly, leaving behind them a widespread distress which no amount of soul-searching could dissolve.

As might have been foreseen, the workers organized to demand social reforms. The strength of the organized working class began to be felt. Protests, collective demands, strikes and revolts, the rise of trade unions and of the socialist political parties, alarmed the leaders of industry. Police suppression answered these movements. In 1848 a strong working class movement in Germany was put down. In 1870 the workers of Paris for a few months actually seized political power, losing it again under fire of the troops of Versailles.

These events deeply affected the thoughts of men. It became necessary to revise the Romantic doctrine of the individual soul.

This doctrine had once seemed adequate; it was no longer adequate in the face of the very material difficulties which time had brought on. In the theatre, some seventeen years after the episode of the Paris Commune, a new formula was ready to appear. Its adherents, like Antoine, came mostly from the ranks of labor or the less wealthy sections of the middle class. At the same time theatre audiences widened to receive a great influx of white-collar and lower class playgoers.

Like all other dramatic formulas, Naturalism was made up of inconsistent elements. Its general direction, however, was apparent. It had an extroverted approach to reality. It turned its back on Spanish palaces, dashing heroes and sinister villains in black capes. Instead it walked into everyday living rooms, the cottages of laborers, the police courts and brothels of the sadly real world. In the same way it forewent the high moral discussions of a Schiller or Goethe and began to agitate for specific social reforms.

An objective study of life—such was the ideal of men like Zola, Ibsen, Hauptmann, Strindberg and Shaw. Naturalism did not usually rise to cosmic heights. That was not its purpose. Instead it tried to seize life in its very hands, to dissect it with the curiosity of a surgeon. To change life for the better, you must know life. When the Naturalists invoked the aid of science they followed in the footsteps of Diderot.

We have already called attention to some of the flaws of the Naturalistic method. Although it gave its allegiance to science, its scientific method was based on the naïve doctrine of simple materialism—a doctrine better suited to the days of Newton than to the nineteenth century.

Naturalism succeeded rather in taking snapshots of life than in explaining life scientifically. It seemed to think that a vivid impression of life was an explanation of it. Its philosophy was too often that of mere cynicism: "Here is life as it is, full of meanness." It had a way of uncovering cesspools without getting very much further in its investigations. In 1900 this sordidness was "realism." It is no longer realism today—not because every cesspool has been cleaned out, but because we know that sordidness in itself does not explain or clarify anything.

Yet it is impossible not to respect this valiant effort to come to grips with reality, this honest attempt to be of service to an audience. In setting up, for the first time, a scientific goal for theatre, the Naturalists made a suggestion which may yet have important meaning for the future. And in their fight against stage convention they were animated by the desire to rid the stage of all burdensome laws that still remained. They demanded for the playwright, actor and designer a complete and unconditional freedom.

ACROSS FRONTIERS

It was not long before the inspiration of Antoine's method spread beyond the borders of France. The German and Russian theatres of the Romantic decadence had been subsisting on a warmed-over French repertory of plays by Augier, Dumas, *fils*, Sardou, Scribe, Ohnet, Erkmann-Chatrien. The international reign of these playwrights was virtually undisputed, even though Ibsen had already appeared over the horizon. (The Meiningen Players had staged THE PRETENDERS as early as 1876 in Berlin.) Two years after the opening of the Théâtre-Libre its Berlin counterpart, the Freie Bühne, opened with a production of Ibsen's GHOSTS, with Otto Brahm as director. As in France this opening signalized a new era on stage.

The Freie Bühne closed after its second season, but not before introducing a powerful new dramatist, Gerhart Hauptmann, whose BEFORE SUNRISE (1889) constituted its second bill. Hauptmann's play was an almost typical example of *rosserie;* but the background of socialist thought from which it emerged gave it a new dimension in the theatre of that time. BEFORE SUNRISE was acted before an excited audience divided into factions which alternately applauded and hissed the performance.

Loth, the socialist hero of the play, and the representative of the views of the youthful Hauptmann, was a new character. Socialist-minded critics greeted his appearance with enthusiasm.

> For the first time a man walked over the German stage, who openly and frankly gave as his view of the whole existing society that it with all its furnishings was dedicated to destruction. . . . No critic of society like Ibsen, who scourged its morals to elevate them without shaking society to its foundations, was speaking here to the very pillars of this society, but a citizen of the future who had lost faith in the existing order and expected no more of it but who perceived in secret

strength the upholders of a new structure. (Edgar Steiger: *Das Werden des neuen Dramas*).

The place vacated by the Freie Bühne was immediately occupied by the Freie Volksbühne, organized by Bruno Wille, Julius Türk and Wilhelm Bölsche. All three were active members of the German Social-Democratic Party, and their theatre was dedicated to the dual purpose of advancing the Party program and of building a truthful theatre, one capable of seeing "life as it is, not as it is not" (Brahm). Like its predecessor it gave its performances on Sunday afternoons to a membership audience which, by 1908, numbered twelve thousand. Its productions, which began with Ibsen's PILLARS OF SOCIETY (1890), included the plays of Schiller, Hebbel, Otto Ludwig, Ibsen, Anzengruber, Zola, Gogol, Pissemsky, Fulda, Sudermann, Hauptmann and Halbe.

By a curious circumstance the organizer of this theatre, Wille, came to organize a rival society shortly afterwards. The Berlin police, who found the Freie Volksbühne distasteful, looked for some excuse to wreck the undertaking. They resorted to the device of barring women from the theatre, on the ground that the performances were political meetings. (German women at that time did not have the right of political assemblage.) At the ensuing court trial Wille successfully maintained that a distinction must be made between socialist propaganda and the artistic expression of the socialist viewpoint. Although Wille won in court through this argument, he lost with the members of his own society, who repudiated his arguments as being non-socialist and even voted him out of the directorate.

With the assistance of Maximilian Harden, Hartleben, Emil Lessing, Victor Hollander and the brothers Kampfmeyer, Wille founded the Neue Freie Volksbühne. The new organization began its career in November, 1892, with Goethe's FAUST. Its membership grew rapidly, especially after it produced Hauptmann's THE WEAVERS, whose performance in the regular theatres had been interdicted by the police. In 1914 Wille's group was carrying on repertoire at its own theatre as well as Sunday afternoon shows at a dozen other theatres—the plays involved including those of Schnitzler, Strindberg, Wedekind, Wilde, Ibsen, Shaw and Tolstoy. Its audience membership had risen to fifty thousand.

Police enmity, which figures so largely in the history of the German Naturalistic groups, was unsuccessful in halting the progress of the new movement. As early as 1894 Otto Brahm had gone on to the directorship of the Deutsches Theatre, and within the playhouses themselves Naturalism went steadily forward.

In England, as in Germany, it was Ibsen's plays which proved the opening wedge for the coming of Naturalism in the theatre. PILLARS OF SOCIETY was put on at the Gaiety Theatre, London, as early as 1880, in a translation by William Archer. Agitation for bringing the English theatre "into some sort of relation with contemporary culture," as Bernard Shaw phrased it, was supported by such able writers as Matthew Arnold, Percy Fitzgerald, Clement Scott, William Archer, Shaw, and George Moore. Archer made it his particular task to champion Ibsen, while Moore, who had been watching Antoine's progress at first hand, called for the founding of an English Théâtre-Libre.

In 1891 the Independent Theatre was organized, under the direction of J. T. Grein, a young Hollander living in London. With the sum of £80 in hand, Grein proceeded to put on Ibsen's GHOSTS at the Royalty Theatre, before a distinguished audience. The drama was greeted with something less than well-bred politeness by genteel reviewers and polite society.[14]

The Independent Theatre managed to last out the uproar, going ahead with THÉRÈSE RAQUIN as its second bill, and again meeting with hostility from the same quarters. English dramatists were sorely needed by the new theatre. George Moore, on a bet (made by a disgruntled playwright whose drama Moore had reviewed), turned out what was perhaps the first class-war play in English history, THE STRIKE AT ARLINGFORD (1906).[15]

It was not Moore, however, but another critic whose aid to the Independent Theatre made the name of that organization forever illustrious in stage history. Encouraged by the Independent's controversial career, George Bernard Shaw, who had been dabbling in play-writing for some years past, dug up one of his neglected manuscripts, gave it a general overhauling and turned it over to the new theatre. WIDOWERS' HOUSES opened in 1892 amid the cheers of socialists and liberals and the gibes of conservatives.

The Independent Theatre had only one prosperous year (in 1894), and closed in 1897; but it definitely launched the new era of Naturalism in England. Two years after its departure it was replaced by the Stage Society, which was initiated by Frederick Whelen, and which numbered among its Council of Management, at different times, Sidney Colvin, J. M. Barrie, Gilbert Murray, Mr. and Mrs. George Bernard Shaw, Harley Granville-Barker, Edith Craig, St. John Hankin, Ashley Dukes and W. L. George. In 1899, when the Stage Society opened its career with Shaw's YOU NEVER CAN TELL, it was clear that the Romantic theatre had come to the end of its road in England.

It was neither in German nor English theatres, however, that the technique of Naturalism was to attain its full development. It was in a new playhouse in far-off Russia.

NATURALISM IN MOSCOW

On a day in early summer in 1897 in a certain Moscow restaurant called the Slavic Bazaar two young men met in a conference which has since become legendary. One of the conferees was a member of the nobility—Vladimir Ivanovich Nemirovich-Danchenko, stage director at the school of the Moscow Philharmonic Society. His play THE PRICE OF LIFE had, two years before, shared the Griboyedov Prize with THE SEAGULL, the play of another young dramatist named Anton Chekhov.

The other member of the conference, which lasted eighteen hours without interruption, was Constantin Stanislavsky, son of a wealthy merchant and director of the semi-professional acting troupe known as the Society of Art and Literature. Theatre was a passion in Stanislavsky's family. He had begun his stage career at the age of two by playing in amateur theatricals at home.

These two men, the patrician Nemirovich-Danchenko and the tall, handsome and gracious Stanislavsky, agreed that the time had come to found a theatre given over, with almost religious devotion, to the quest for truth. To this ideal they pledged a reformed technique in production and self-discipline in the acting company which they proposed to create.

That summer a new troupe known as the Moscow Art Theatre, with a membership carefully chosen by the two directors, went into intensive rehearsal in a barn in Pushkino, about ten miles from the city. Returning to Moscow in the fall the company took over an old beer-garden, the Hermitage, on Karetny Row. It was a place which Stanislavsky described as "in a terrible state, dirty, dusty, ill-constructed, unheated, with the smell of beer and some sort of acid." Not an auspicious beginning for the company which was destined to lead a whole epoch of theatre in Russian history! Hasty repairs put the place into some kind of order, and on October 14, 1898, the Moscow Art Theatre successfully launched its first performance, Alexei Tolstoy's historic drama TSAR FYODOR.

The other plays of the Art Theatre's first season were THE MERCHANT OF VENICE, THE MISTRESS OF THE INN, GRETA'S JOY, ANTIGONE, HEDDA GABLER, and, finally, a play by an author whose name was to be forever linked with that of the Moscow Art Theatre—THE SEAGULL, by Anton Chekhov. THE SEAGULL was the choice of Nemirovich-Danchenko. It is interesting to recall that Danchenko experienced some difficulty in "selling" it to the others of the company.

> THE SEAGULL has qualities which thirty years ago might well have affrighted a director—slightness of plot, when Russian audiences had a taste for the exaggeration of French and German farces, a theme raised little above every day existence, yet subtle in emotion, with half moods of doubt, of wistfulness, of baffling and unexplained suffering, and of a groping for joy. Added to this are a dialogue of a peculiar key broken yet lyrical, constant slight movement of people on the stage, subdued tones almost without contrast. Finally, the previous history of THE SEAGULL was an alarming one, for it had been a failure on the St. Petersburg stage. The playwright, ill and discouraged, was in such a condition that Nemirovich-Danchenko and his other friends realized that a second failure might easily kill him. The Art Theatre was forced, as it had not been in its other productions, to seek for inward emotion, the springs of character, living speech, and a shadowing forth of contemporary life. Producers and company rose to the challenge. The triumph, a great one, connected Chekhov and the Art Theatre inseparably in the minds of the public. (Miller).

Chekhov was in fact brought into the "family circle" of the Art Theatre. The close relationship of playwright and acting company proved very fruitful. The delicate overtones and undertones which Chekhov added to Naturalistic writing called for new standards in scene design and acting as well; and the Art Theatre was equal to the challenge.[16] At the same time the dramatist found inspiration in the members of the troupe (beginning, of course, with the actress Olga Knipper, whom he married). The actor Artem, famous for his characterizations of old men, became Chekhov's model for Chebutikin in THE THREE SISTERS (1900) and for Firs in THE CHERRY ORCHARD (1904). In the latter play it was the comedian Moskvin whose antics suggested the character of Epikhodov.

In Maxim Gorky the Art Theatre discovered its second great writing talent. Like Chekhov a Naturalist, Gorky brought to his plays, SMALL PEOPLE (1902), THE LOWER DEPTHS (1902) and CHILDREN OF THE SUN (1905), glimpses of a more somber reality existing side by side with the nostalgic life of Chekhov's gentlefolk. Gorky reported the milieu of the Russian proletariat and of the misfits of the cities and villages, a world of dire misery in which revolution was already gathering its forces.

After forty years of theatrical experience, during which it survived even the change from the Tsarist to the Soviet regime, the Moscow Art Theatre shows no signs of closing its career. Its ideal of ensemble acting remains unimpaired after all these years, and its disciplined and seasoned company is continually replenished by younger actors.

The Art Theatre in the course of its history has founded a number of subsidiary groups, or studios, some of which have since become theatres in their own right. Among these were the First Studio, under the direction of Leopold Sulerjitsky, which is now the Second Moscow Art Theatre; the Musical Studio directed by Nemirovich-Danchenko; and the Third Studio, under the direction of Eugene Vakhtangov, which became the Vakhtangov Theatre.

NATURALISM CROSSES THE ATLANTIC

Early in 1879 Zola's L'ASSOMOIR, produced in New York by John Daly at the Olympic Theatre with Ada Rehan in the cast, failed completely. This did not deter a younger director, working at that time at the Baldwin Theatre, San Francisco, from making his own version of the play and bringing it to the stage that same year. The San Francisco version, as directed by David Belasco, with Rose Coghlan in the lead, ran for a successful two weeks. The link thus made between Belasco and Zola was no mere whim of fate. Both men were on the road to a new standard in the theatre.

Zola's *rosse* play was described unsympathetically by Augustin Daly, who had seen the original production at the Paris Ambigu-Comique:

L'ASSOMMOIR is a disgusting piece,—one prolonged sigh from first to last, over the miseries of the poor, with a dialogue culled from the lowest slang and tritest claptrap. . . . The only novelty in it was in the *lavoir* scene, where two washwomen (the heroine and her rival) throw pails of warm water (actually) over each other and stand dripping before the audience.

The young Californian, however, approached Zola's play with no such distaste. Belasco's story of his rehearsal of the play forecasts his own rôle as America's leading Naturalistic director:

I remember I had an even more disagreeable passage with Lillian Andrews (who had been brought in to play *Big Virginie*) than that at my first meeting with Miss Coghlan. The Washhouse Scene was a hard one—you couldn't fool with it; the only way to make it go was to *do* it!—and at the dress rehearsal Miss Andrews refused point-blank to go through it as it was to be done at night. Both she and Miss Coghlan were under dressed with close-fitting rubber suits to keep them dry; but, even so, it was no fun to be drenched with hot soapy water, and I was sorry for them. But, of course, the scene had to be properly and fully rehearsed, and the upshot was I had to tell Miss Andrews she must do her business as directed or leave the company. And, after a grand row, we had the scene as it was to be at night. She and Coghlan and everybody concerned were in such tempers by the time I finished reading the riot act, that everything was marvellously realistic; I doubt whether it was ever quite so well done at a public performance! [17] (William Winter: *The Life of David Belasco*).

David Belasco was born in 1853 in San Francisco. He carried on his early dramatic work in that city, at times trouping through California and across the United States. By 1882 he had drifted to New York, where Bronson Howard's YOUNG MRS. WINTHROP was produced under his management at the Madison Square Theatre. Beginning 1893 with his first great success, THE GIRL I LEFT BEHIND ME (by Belasco and Franklyn Fyles), he won a national reputation for colorful plays produced with meticulous Naturalism. THE GIRL I LEFT BEHIND ME was a melodrama of the American Indian Wars, which were at that time claiming public attention. Its story concerned a Montana army post. Its swift action included a siege by the Indians, who are dispersed at the last harrowing moment by relief troops. The last touch was frankly borrowed from Boucicault's JESSIE BROWN, OR THE RELIEF OF LUCKNOW (1858).

The same Romantic atmosphere in Naturalistic guise invested the presentation, at the Herald Square Theatre, of THE HEART OF MARYLAND (1895), written and directed by Belasco. The play contained such scenic elements as "an old Colonial mansion, deep-bowered among ancient, blooming lilac bushes," suggestions of the movement of large bodies of troops, "the red glare and dun smoke-pall of conflagration." For two hundred consecutive nights Mrs. Leslie Carter swung from the clapper of a church bell to keep the bell from tolling curfew.

In the Belasco production of Francis Powers' THE FIRST BORN, at the Manhattan Theatre (1897), the Chinatown quarter of San Francisco was reproduced almost to its smells.

> The play is in two acts. In the first, Chinatown is shown in the bright light and bustle of a busy noonday and against that setting is displayed the sudden bereavement and afflicting anguish of the father. In the second, an alley-end in the same district is shown, with a glimpse of contiguous gambling hells and opium dens, under the darkening shadows of evening. There the inexorable avenger lounges, leaning against a door post—apparently an idler smoking his evening pipe and talking with a Chinese girl who leans from a window; in fact, vigilantly observant of *Man Low Yek*, visible within a shop, and intent on slaying him. The alley grows dark and becomes deserted. The neighboring houses are illumined. The chink of money and the bickering chatter of unseen gamblers are heard. A police officer saunters by and disappears. *Man Low Yek* comes forth from his shop, closing it after him. Then, suddenly, as he passes, *Wang*, with fearful celerity, leaps upon him wielding a hatchet, strikes him down, drags the dead body into convenient concealment, and is back again at his former loitering place, outwardly placid, before the fire in his pipe has had time to become extinguished. . . . The spectator seems to behold two veritable segments of Chinatown life. (Winter).

Short and stocky, dark-eyed, with a smooth oval face and a benign manner, Belasco was affectionately known as "the Governor." He had the personal distinction of the old-fashioned actor-manager, a dignity which he accentuated by means of a professional costume, which included the suggestion of a clerical collar and bib. He became a veritable legend in his own lifetime. By 1907 he was successful enough to build his own theatre, the Stuyvesant (since renamed the Belasco), in New York. In the American theatre by the time of the first World War, "Belascoism" was sweeping everything before it.

Belascoism may be considered a specific American form of Naturalism for a variety of reasons, not all of them excellent by later standards. The meticulous regard for detail, the attention to "little, significant facts," to which Taine alluded and which Antoine brought to the stage, was certainly in the American method; Antoine's passion for the verities of life was not to be found there. We have already seen that Antoine, Zola, and the other builders of Naturalism were by no means free of the Romantic background from which they emerged. It is impossible not to see in Belasco the return of that cycle which would bring back Naturalism to the bathos of Romanticism from which it had once emerged.

Belasco's career was not lacking in expeditions into *rosserie,* as for instance in his presentation of Eugene Walter's THE EASIEST WAY (1908); but such productions were not in the same class with Antoine's attacks on smug propriety. Belasco's melodramas had an admixture of sweetness and light in a blend to which, it is likely, he had a unique claim. If any social criticism remained, it was reduced to a whisper.

To borrow a phrase for the occasion from Joseph Wood Krutch, these plays had "excellence in their kind" even if their ideas were not fresh. During this period, as during most of the years up to the financial crisis of 1929, new evaluations were at a discount in the American theatre.

Belasco's activities coincided with America's Gilded Age. It was a soothing era for the audiences that could afford to go to the theatre. The settlement and unification of the American states from coast to coast was now accomplished. "Manifest Destiny" was carrying the stars and stripes into imperialistic adventures, and the Spanish-American War only whetted the appetite for further conquests abroad. Industry boomed and profits mounted staggeringly. To be sure the American Federation of Labor was also advancing. The midwest farmers grew strong politically under the banner of Populism; in the far west the I.W.W. gained a foothold; there were some shocking class-war battles at the Chicago Haymarket and at Homestead. These ominous signs, however, did not disturb too much the serenity of the theatregoers of that period. For them all roads lay open. It was no time for soul-searching. Red-blooded, two-fisted entertainment satisfied these audiences best of all.

Belasco used an idiom newer than that of his Romantic predecessors. The acting was believable in comparison with nature; the settings were infinitely more lifelike than in the past. But underneath both the Romantic stereotype was there for any alert observer to see. By the time Naturalism received its American expression at the hands of Belasco, it was no longer a life-storming technique. It was no longer necessary to pioneer in it, either. The standing of Naturalism was no longer in doubt; enthusiastic audiences were greeting it the world over. Nevertheless a struggle involving the new style took place even in the United States. After a hard-fought battle between Belasco and the Theatrical Syndicate, which complained that the new manager was "spoiling the public," the last obstacles in the way of American Naturalism were eliminated.[18]

BELASCO LOOKS AT ENVIRONMENT

The stage settings of Belasco acquired a unique, and not undeserved fame. It was not only that they set a high standard of execution at a time when careless, slipshod settings were the rule. They contained a good deal of the lyricism which underlay his melodramas. It was this lyricism which gave life and distinction to scripts otherwise hackneyed. Belasco had an eye to the poetry of American environment—even though he was no Whitman—and he could bring that environment convincingly to the stage.

At the same time there was little, in his scenery, of environment in the Darwinian sense—that goal at which Zola and Antoine had aimed. It was not meaning, but *effect* that was important. Belasco maintained that

> . . . the great thing, the essential thing, for a producer is to create *Illusion* and *Effect*. The supreme object in all my work has been to get near to nature; to make my atmosphere as *real* as possible, when I am dealing with a drama or a comedy of life. In mounting a fantastic play there is but one thing to do, and that is to be as fantastic as possible. And so, in a realist play to be as realistic as possible. . . . When I set a scene

representing a Child's Restaurant how can I expect to hold the *attention* of my audience unless I show them a scene that *looks* real? They see it, recognize it, accept it and then, if the actors do their part, the audience forgets that it isn't looking into a real place. (Winter).

But in fact, in the American Naturalistic technique, environment is only partially real. The treatment of the environment is basically Romantic in the style of Meiningen, existing only as a picturesque obligato to dramatic action. This is all the more curious since hardly anywhere else in the world has the rôle of environment been more striking than in its effect upon the character of the American people. One might have expected to see, on American stages, the Naturalistic setting at its highest point of vitality. One might have expected it to show, in a luminous manner, the relation between environment and character. If it had done this it might have been a full and triumphant vindication of the scenic approach which Antoine described.

Just what Belasco supplied can best be inferred by recalling some of his famed scenic effects. In TIGER ROSE (1917), a log cabin was shown in a forest of the Canadian Northwest; the stage was covered with pine-needles upon which the actors trod, wafting the scent into the auditorium. In the second act of the same play there was a rainstorm so convincing in its effect that at the end of the act spectators, going to the lobby, were astounded to find that it was not raining outside the theatre.

In MADAME BUTTERFLY (1900) the deserted Japanese wife, Cho-Cho-San, knelt before the paper panes of the *shoji,* keeping vigil as the scene, over an actual timing of fourteen minutes, changed from dusk to dawn. The fascination of this scene was due in a large degree to its lighting.

When, at evening, the forlorn *Butterfly* . . . sees the warship to which *Pinkerton* is attached entering the harbor of Higashi she believes that her "husband" will immediately repair to their abode and she becomes almost delirious with joy. She prepares for his reception, attiring herself and their little child in fine array and decking the house with flowers and lighted lanterns. Then, with the child and a servant maid, she takes station at a window, to give him welcome—and there she waits and watches through the night, until the morning breaks. The lapse of time was, in the performance, skilfully and impressively denoted,—the shades of evening darkening into night; stars becoming visible, then brilliant, then fading from view; the lighted lanterns one

Museum of Modern Art

Lumière's boy with the hose (1895)
"You feel indefinably awestruck."

TOWARD FILM REALISM

POTEMKIN (1926)
Mass grief, mass anger

.Y. Public Library Picture Collection

by one flickering out; the gray light of dawn revealing the servant and the child prone upon the floor sunk in slumber, with the deserted mother standing over them pale and wan, still gazing fixedly down the vacant road, while the rosy glow of sunrise grew into the full light of day and the sweet sound of the waking songs of birds floated in from a flowering grove of cherry trees. (Winter).

For THE GIRL OF THE GOLDEN WEST, which opened at the Belasco Theatre, Pittsburgh, in 1905, Belasco used an orchestra of popular instruments including the concertina, the banjo and the "bones" of oldtime minstrels. The play began with what is today a characteristic "pan down" of cinema technique: at first a romantic picture of Cloudy Mountain by moonlight, with the Girl's cabin perched on the mountainside; then a winding path leading down to a view of the town, ending outside the Polka, the Girl's saloon. In the stage directions,

The cheerful glow of kerosene lamps, the rattle of poker chips and an occasional "whoop," show that life in the Polka is in full swing. The strains of "Dooda Day" are heard from within, the singer accompanying himself on the concertina.

During a blackout the scene is shifted to the interior of the saloon, where the first and third acts take place. The production is still more famous for the second-act poker game, which takes place in the Girl's cabin while a snowstorm rages outside. The storm effect has been described graphically by William Winter:

Nothing of the kind which I have ever seen in the theatre has fully equalled in verisimilitude the blizzard on Cloudy Mountain as depicted by Belasco in the Second Act of this fine melodrama—such a bitter and cruel storm of wind-driven snow and ice as he had often suffered under in the strolling days of his nomadic youth. When the scene, the interior of the *Girl's* log-cabin, was disclosed the spectators perceived, dimly, through windows at the back, a far vista of rugged, snow-clad mountains which gradually faded from vision as the fall of snow increased and the casements became obscured by sleet. Then, throughout the progress of the action, intensifying the sense of desolation, dread, and terror, the audience heard the wild moaning and shrill whistle of the gale, and at moments, as the tempest rose to a climax of fury, could see the fine-powdered snow driven in tiny sprays and eddies through every crevice of the walls and the very fabric of the cabin quiver and rock beneath the impact of terrific blasts of wind,—long-shrieking down the mountain sides before they struck,—while in every fitful pause was audible the sharp click-click-click of freezing snow driving on wall and window. . . . [The] operation of the necessary mechanical contrivances required a force of thirty-two trained artisans,—a sort of mechanical orchestra. . . .

In these productions what interested the director primarily was the emotional appeal of the scent of pine needles, not the law of existence which the forest lays down to its people; the technical trick of the rainstorm, not the change in environment (restricted space, and so on) created by the rain; the exoticism and virtuoso lighting occasioned by Cho-Cho-San's mood, not the surprising moral rigidity of the Japanese environment, whose materials are so fragile. The human dread of a raging blizzard is used (in somewhat irrelevant fashion) in order to deepen our concern over the outcome of a poker game, rather than to show how the untamed elements driving over western ranges have shaped the course of western life.

It should be remembered on the other hand that these effects have a certain validity in proportion as they do realize the power of environment. The storm, whether wholly relevant or not, is impressive because it describes with truth the violence of which such environment is capable. The indifference of nature to the fate of human beings is nowhere better given than in the contrast of lovely sunrise and singing birds with the suicidal agony of Madame Butterfly. On the whole, Belasco's scenic imagery while inclined to be superficial, was not lacking in a poetic pessimism of its own.

"CAME THE DAWN"

Such was the form in which Naturalism crystallized on the American stage. But this was not the whole extent of Belasco's influence. Belasco Naturalism has been perpetuated in still wider fashion through the American motion picture.

Let us note that the American cinema was coming out of its swaddling clothes at the very time when Belascoism was the standard of American dramatic art. The record indicates that Belasco Naturalism appeared on the scene in time to affect the whole future of the motion picture.

In 1895, scarcely a decade after the founding of the Théâtre-Libre, some of the first motion pictures in the world—a number of "shorts" produced by Lumière—were on view in Paris. The Russian dramatist Maxim Gorky, who eventually saw these films, wrote a review of them. It is worth while resurrecting a fragment of his impressions:

> The cinematograph is a moving photograph. A beam of electric light is projected on a large screen, mounted in a dark room. And a photograph appears on the cloth screen. . . . We see a street in Paris. The picture shows carriages, children, pedestrians, frozen into immobility, trees covered with leaves. All of these are still. The general background is the gray tone of an engraving; all objects and figures seem to be 1/10 of their natural size.
>
> And suddenly there is a sound somewhere, the picture shivers, you don't believe your eyes.
>
> The carriages are moving straight at you, the pedestrians are walking, the children are playing with a dog, the leaves are fluttering on the trees, and bicyclists roll along. . . .
>
> And suddenly it disappears. Your eyes see a plain piece of white cloth in a wide black frame, and it seems as if nothing had been there. You feel that you have imagined something that you had just seen with your own eyes—and that's all. You feel indefinably awestruck.

Among other items on the same film program was a sequence in which a boy played a prank on a gardener by stepping on a rubber hose; and an idyl of domestic life—a young mother watching her husband feed their baby. Gorky seems to feel that these "moving photographs" are almost terrifying transcripts from life. He adds: "I am convinced that they will soon, very soon, be replaced by pictures in a genre more suited to the 'Concert Parisien' and the demands of the fair." Science had delivered to the coming century an elemental dramatic force—a new instrument which approached life with an astounding precision. It seemed to Gorky that this powerful dramatic medium would not be allowed to transcribe reality without a restraining hand laid on its shoulder.

The motion picture camera's ability to seize life struck awe into the hearts of its first spectators. That primitive power required a harness. A definite technique had to intervene in the cinema before Will H. Hayes could declare (in a speech at Harvard University in 1927):

> It [the film] has clothed the empty existence of far-off hamlets with joy; it has lifted listless laboring folk till they have walked the

peaks of romance and adventure as if they were the pavements of their own main street.

Once Antoine had learned from photography. Now came the turn of motion picture photography to learn from Belasco. In 1918 Victor Freeburg in *The Art of Photoplay Making* pointed out that "deep reality and convincingness result when a setting is used as environment instead of a mere background for the action." But this observation only proved that American cinema producers had already learned how to substitute background for environment. It was Belasco who taught them. Writing in 1912, Robert Grau exclaimed,

> I would like to pay a little tribute to the master mind whose province it is to stage the photoplays for the Thanhouser Company, particularly the film, NOT GUILTY, in which the particular attention to detail raised the production almost to the state of art. . . . it is just such perfection in detail that has given David Belasco his great fame, and it is indeed consoling to know that the producers of photoplays are aspiring to reach great heights in such matters.

The Naturalism of Hollywood is the very apotheosis of Belasco's "came the dawn" technique.

"Oh my mountains! Oh my California—my Sierras!" cries the Girl of the Golden West as the rising sun gilds the mountain peaks.

Today the American cinema enters a new phase, in which the camera begins to descend from "the peaks of romance and adventure" and is trained once more upon the activities of the vital American people and the panorama of American environment. Such pictures as THE GRAPES OF WRATH will stand as a monument to the beginning of this new era.

But meanwhile Belascoism is still with us. You will find the Belasco touch in the next Hollywood picture you go to see; and you may well ask yourself what Hollywood could have done without it.

Out of the virtues and faults which Antoine, Zola, Brahm, Stanislavsky and their followers built the Naturalistic form in defiance of an already established style, there has been created a gigantic theatrical enterprise. Antoine and Zola may once have been considered impractical theorists; but their invention is today the chief asset of a billion-dollar industry.

NOTES

1. "Shelley's attitude to science was at the opposite pole to that of Wordsworth. He loved it, and is never tired of expressing in poetry the thoughts which it suggests. It symbolizes to him joy, and peace, and illumination. What the hills were to the youth of Wordsworth, a chemical laboratory was to Shelley. . . . [In] the fourth act of PROMETHEUS UNBOUND . . . the Earth and the Moon converse together in the language of accurate science. Physical experiments guide his imagery." (Whitehead: *Science and the Modern World*).

2. "Antoine maintained, from first to last, that the Théâtre-Libre was not exclusively a Naturalist theatre, and a careful examination of his programmes will dispel the current notion that he was Zola's tool. Antoine was producing plays that were refused elsewhere, and these plays were, for the most part, of the ultra-realist type." (Waxman).

3. Bernard, it is worth noting, did not hesitate to make unwarranted assumptions about the field of literature. He considered that a literary work is a spontaneous creation having nothing in common with scientific phenomena.

4. Compare the views of Epic theatre on the well-made play: Chapter IX, p. 413; also Chapter IX, Note 12.

5. Plays of social criticism of course did not begin with the Naturalists. From Goethe onward, the Romantics called for the reform of those agencies that oppressed the human soul. The tradition remained even with some of the later Romantics. The younger Dumas declared "If I can exercise some influence over society and require the law-maker to revise the law, I shall have done more than my part as a poet. I shall have done my duty as a man." (From Sobel: *The Theatre Handbook*).

6. The Stanislavsky system in practice can be followed in the acting of the Group Theatre, which has long experimented with the system. In directing Odets' ROCKET TO THE MOON (1938), Harold Clurman conceived the main action of the play as "finding love." Eleanor Lynn, who had the role of Cleo Singer in the play, had the subsidiary action of "finding love" under her given circumstances. In order to find love Cleo was accustomed to make herself agreeable even under trying circumstances, to flirt, to lie, to make up in imaginary love what she lacked in reality, and so on. The way in which she behaved varied from moment to moment, sometimes drastically, but always with the same objective. These variations are the "adjustments." Thus when the wife of her lover, Dr. Stark, was on the stage, Cleo had to "make an adjustment" by *masking* her action of looking for love; and a further adjustment by seeking the love even of Mrs. Stark.

In Odets' GOLDEN BOY (1937), Frances Farmer, who played Lorna

Moon, had the action, or "spine," of "helping others." The instinct for helping other people was conceived as basic to her rôle. Her adjustments, of course, varied greatly in her relations with the other characters, altering drastically—but not changing—in the case of the gangster Fuseli.

7. The ground plan of the large majority of Broadway settings is basically that of a rectangular box with the long wall parallel to the footlights. Such a plan, often symmetrical as well, tends to be static and unrelated to the movements of the actors.

8. ". . . the meticulous artist in Antoine forced him to maintain a ruinously expensive workshop where special scenery for each play was made, in spite of the fact that his contract with the Menus-Plaisirs gave him the right to use the scenery of that theatre." (Waxman).

9. Lee Simonson, who has done full justice to Meiningen in *The Stage Is Set,* thus reconstructs a scene from the Duke's production of Kleist's HERMANNSCHLACHT (Berlin, 1875):

"In the opening scene . . . the invading Roman legionaries enter a primitive German village. At royal theatres elsewhere it was the rule to send twenty or thirty supers, bright as tin Caesars, marching with the precision of Prussians on parade against a landscape back-drop. At Meiningen the invaders debouched through a narrow lane that barely allowed them to pass four abreast. Their bronze armour was dulled to a brown black as if by months of campaigning. They entered down stage and disappeared up stage into the alley behind the house-fronts. What the audience saw most of the time was not a succession of faces but the somber repetition of the backs of bucklers and helmets; the total effect was that of an almost impersonal, a relentless military machine."

10. With another designer, Bouton, Daguerre put on near Vauxhall a series of tableaus which he called a "Diorama." For the Ambigu-Comique, according to Moynet (*L'Envers du théâtre*), Daguerre designed a moonlight effect in which "the clouds in motion alternately obscured and disclosed the stars, while actors, trees and houses threw their shadows over each other and on the ground. This décor was so successful and so obliterated the play that no one any longer even remembers the title of the play."

11. Jean Jaurès, socialist deputy and idol of proletarian and liberal France. He was assassinated on the eve of the first World War, in 1914.

12. Compare this production of CAESAR with that of the Mercury Theatre, New York, 1937. Chapter VII, pp. 281–282.

13. "The stage gallants . . . often directly interfered with the performers. On one occasion, for instance, Peg Woffington played the entire part of Cordelia clasped round the waist by an over-amorous seat-holder. Mrs. Cibber, too, in the tomb scene in ROMEO AND JULIET fre-

quently thrilled the audience to enthusiasm—including the hundred or so who were with her in the tomb." (Stephen Tait: *English Theatre Riots*).

14. In his *Quintessence of Ibsenism* Shaw lists some of the phrases used by contemporary reviewers following the first night of GHOSTS: "revolting obscenity," "the world of the lugubrious," "the malodorous Ibsen," "a loathsome sore unbandaged," and so on. In New York William Winter called Ibsen's plays "flaccid, insipid, tainted, obfuscated and nauseous." Clearly Winter preferred the Belasco, rather than the Ibsen, version of Naturalism.

15. A much earlier strike play appeared in the United States: Dion Boucicault's THE LONG STRIKE, OR THE MEN OF MANCHESTER, at the Boston Theatre, 1870.

16. Stanislavsky in *My Life in Art* gives an amusing account of the stories which appeared in the press concerning the new Naturalistic mode of production which his troupe was using in rehearsals:

"There appeared clever writers who chose us to be the victims of their irony and witticisms. They affirmed for the sake of laughter that we were breeding mosquitoes, flies, crickets and other insects, so that for the sake of realism we might crush some on our foreheads and others on the walls, and force the crickets to chirp in order to create an atmosphere of truth to life on the stage."

He adds that such ridicule helped materially to win an audience for the theatre, more so than praise would have done.

17. Another interesting example of Belasco's directing is given by George Middleton, who worked with him in adapting Brieux's L'AVOCAT, produced in New York as THE ACCUSED (1925), at the Belasco Theatre:

"Too strict an adherence to the stark economy of the stage directions in the French script evoked the lesson Belasco gave me. 'You don't dramatize each situation enough, George,' he used to say. The curtain rose on the second act, with the audience knowing the lawyer had worked all night preparing his defense on a murder charge brought against the woman he loved. . . . I had followed the French script, telling Sothern merely to walk up and down to express his agitation. Belasco rushed to the stage. He clapped his hands for 'Matty,' his amazing assistant, who could have produced in a few minutes, if suddenly asked, a live elephant from his property room. Authentic French law books began suddenly to appear. Large strips of paper were torn up dramatically and hectically placed between the pages to mark citations the lawyer had discovered. Cushions were thrown upon the floor and a myriad of crumpled paper scattered about, to reveal his mental confusion. A lamp was left lighted in the early sunlight, a curtain half opened, and the French window widened to catch the morning air. And, as a crowning touch, the head cushion on the couch was pushed in to indicate where his head had rested in his futile efforts to relax.

'This is how the room should look. Anyone can see now what he had been through,' Belasco said." (New York *Times*, October 23, 1938).

18. When Belasco first came to New York the American stage was in the hands of actor-managers like Augustin Daly, Lester Wallack, John T. Ford, Samuel Colville, Dion Boucicault, J. H. McVicker, R. M. Hooley, Henry E. Abbey, Montgomery Field, and A. M. Palmer. Within a very short time, however, most of these managers had died and some of the great star actors who had dominated the stage—such as Joseph Jefferson, Edwin Booth, Ada Rehan and Mary Anderson—had passed out of the picture. By then, the veteran critic William Winter declared bitterly, the theater no longer belonged to "actors and men truly comprehensive of, and sympathetic with, actors . . . that institution had passed almost entirely into the hands of the so-called 'business man.'"

Winter reserved his greatest antagonism for Charles Frohman, whose policy in the theatre, alleged to have been stated by Frohman himself, was: "I keep a department store." Frohman was said to be the guiding spirit of the Theatrical Syndicate, a firm which included Al. Hayman, S. F. Nixon, J. Fred. Zimmerman, Marc Klaw and A. E. Erlanger. The Theatrical Syndicate was accused of being a booking-monopoly, and of having a controlling interest in all the "first class" playhouses of the United States. According to Belasco's court testimony, when he asked for bookings for his successful production of THE AUCTIONEER (1901), starring David Warfield, Erlanger demanded fifty percent of the proceeds.

As related by Belasco, Erlanger declared that "if I refused his terms he would compel me to go into the streets and blacken my face to earn a living. He said that I spoiled the public instead of compelling them to take what the Trust chose to give, and that a man with ideals in the theatrical business wound up with a benefit within three years." (A "benefit" is a special performance of a play given to raise money for a deserving case of charity.)

This litigation spelled eventual doom for the Syndicate. In 1904–05 the Syndicate received another blow when Belasco entered into an alliance with the brothers Sam, Lee and Jacob Shubert, who had started a competitive chain of independent theatres, rounding up all the "second rate" playhouses which the Syndicate had overlooked. It should be added that after all the linen had been publicly washed, Belasco made his peace with the Theatrical Syndicate and even formed a partnership with Frohman.

REFERENCES

Émile Zola: *Preface to Thérèse Raquin.* From Barrett H. Clark: *European Theories of the Drama.* Appleton.

Alfred North Whitehead: *Science and the Modern World.* Macmillan, New York, 1929.

André Antoine: *Mes souvenirs sur le Théâtre-Libre.* Fayard & Cie.
Samuel Montefiore Waxman: *Antoine and the Théâtre-Libre.* Harvard University Press, Cambridge, 1926. Reprinted by permission of the President and Fellows of Harvard College.
August Filon. From Waxman: *Ibid.*
Émile Zola. From Gassner: *Masters of the Drama.* Random House.
Bernard Sobel: *The Theatre Handbook.* Crown Publishers, New York, 1940.
George Moore: *Impressions and Opinions.* From Miller: *The Independent Theatre in Europe.* Long & Smith.
Constantin Stanislavsky: *My Life in Art.* Little, Brown & Company.
Émile Zola. From Dubech: *Histoire générale illustrée du théâtre.* Librairie de France.
Victor Hugo: *Preface to Cromwell.* From Clark: *Ibid.*
M. J. Moynet: *L'Enverse du théâtre.* Librairie Hachette, Paris, 1873.
Charles Kean. From Allardyce Nicoll: *The Development of the Theatre.* Harcourt, Brace & Company.
Lee Simonson: *The Stage Is Set.* Harcourt, Brace & Company.
André Antoine. From Miller: *Ibid.*
Stephen Tait: *English Theatre Riots. Theatre Arts,* February, 1940.
August Strindberg. From Waxman: *Ibid.*
Jean Jullien. From Miller: *Ibid.*
Edgar Steiger: *Das Werden des neuen Dramas.* From Miller: *Ibid.*
George Bernard Shaw: *The Quintessence of Ibsenism.* B. R. Tucker, Boston, 1891.
Joseph Wood Krutch: *The American Drama Since 1918.* Random House.
Augustin Daly. From William Winter: *The Life of David Belasco.* Vol. 1. Jefferson Winter.
William Winter: *Ibid.,* Vol. 1 and Vol. 2.
David Belasco. From Winter: *Ibid.,* Vol. 1.
David Belasco: *Six Plays.* Little, Brown & Company, Boston, 1929.
Gorky on the Films. New Theatre and Film. March, 1937.
Victor Freeburg: *The Art of Photoplay Making.* Macmillan, New York, 1918.
Robert Grau: *The Stage in the Twentieth Century.* Broadway Publishing Company, New York, 1912.

5

LETTER AND SPIRIT

PASSING OF NATURALISM

BY 1914 Belasco Naturalism reigned almost unchallenged in the American theatre and cinema. Its eternal enthronement seemed assured.

That Naturalism will reign forever in the motion pictures seems to be taken for granted, at least by movie reviewers. But even the layman knows now that on the Broadway stage the career of Naturalism is over as a creative force. Almost without warning Belascoism lost its prestige. It was replaced by another dramatic form which set out with a different goal in mind.

Like other dramatic formulas before and since, the style which succeeded Naturalism was a mixture of elements experimentally brought together. Only this time the elements were so varied, the mixtures so ingenious and the experimenting so consciously undertaken, that it was not easy to find a name to cover all the aspects of the new form. Contemporary writers were hard-pressed to find an expressive name. "The New Stagecraft," "Presentational Staging," "The Plastic Stage," "Expressionism," "The Theatre Theatrical," were only a few of the terms which came into use. It will be best, perhaps, to take *The New Stagecraft* as the most comprehensive of these terms.

The confusion in names gives some idea of the diversity of the theatrical movement which took command of the world's stages soon after the first Great War. It is possible, nevertheless, to recognize three distinct currents within this movement. These will be denoted as Symbolism, Neo-Romanticism and Theatricalism.

Each of these will be considered separately. At the same time it should be kept in mind that they are not independent of each other but are closely interrelated. Taken together they are the forces which advanced into the future while Naturalism retreated into the past.

FAUST IN SYMBOLS

The passing of Naturalism in the American theatre was rather less sudden than appears at first glance. Naturalism had already been left behind in Europe.

Sunday May 17, 1908 was a red-letter day for the intellectual and fashionable world of Munich. The calendar marked the opening, that evening, of the new Munich Artists' Theatre, a project sponsored by His Highness Prince Rupprecht of Bavaria, carried out under the direction of the architect Max Littman, the designer Fritz Erler and the critic Georg Fuchs. The Bavarian capital in those days was a leisurely and gracious city. Its new playhouse had been given a leafy setting in the Ausstellungs Park, through which the playgoers sauntered. Torches lined the avenue under the trees, the flares merging softly with the twilight. The playhouse itself echoed that festive spirit, consciously "modern" yet with a note of Hellenic repose.

Only the rustle of programs disturbed the restfulness of the interior as the audience took its seats. The walls gleamed with the sheen of panels and inlaid wood. No gilt festoons, no murals of Nymphs dragging the car of Thespis were on display. Instead of a horseshoe of boxes, *de rigueur* in theatres elsewhere, there was a single row of booths in the rear. In front of the paneled proscenium a ledge of forestage swept in an arc close to the front seats. Behind this forestage the portals on either side receded far enough to contain, each of them, a severely designed door surmounted by a balcony window. The stage area between the portals was raised a step above the "apron"; in turn the remaining stage depth was several steps higher than the portal area, so that the stage as a whole seemed built in terraces.

As the house lights dimmed, a glow of electric light sprang up from the recessed footlights, from behind the portals, and below the upper frame of the proscenium opening. Shafts of light, their sources discreetly hidden, outlined the portal opening. Noiselessly the curtain rose on the first *Symbolist* production of Goethe's FAUST.

We may be sure that Herr Fuchs, who is now commonly regarded as the founder of the Munich Künstlertheater, found joy in that gathering of people of degree. It was, indeed, his contention that the theatre must in future dedicate itself to such an "élite" if it wished to progress. For him the theatre was "the temple of a festival community" of players and audience. In those years Fuchs was a slim and fair-haired young man of forty, with a rather humorless expression which was not softened by his pince-nez and mustache à la Wilhelm II. The idea for the new playhouse is believed to have originated with Littmann, one of Germany's greatest theatre architects. It matured with the help of the gifted scene designer Fritz Erler. Fuchs was its philosopher, historian and propagandist.

It is likely that Fuchs was a more consistent theorist in matters of drama than in other matters. In 1908 his political views were of a sort to find distinct favor with Bavarian nobility. In 1919, *per contra,* he presented to the communist government of Bavaria a memorandum calling for the socialization of the film industry. It seems that he afterwards lent his support to a scheme to separate Bavaria from the German Republic. Influential monarchist politicians were in the background; they remained there when Fuchs was arrested. The German social-democratic government sentenced him to twelve years in prison. He served six years, during which time the memory of the opening night of the Künstlertheater must have been a consolation.

Perhaps on that May evening many of Herr Fuchs' guests imagined that they were going to see something even more photographically explicit, even more solidly reproduced, than anything Otto Brahm had so far brought to the German stage. If so, they were due for a surprise. It may be there were others who expected an even more grandiose display of *mise en scène* than at the FAUST revivals at the Weimar Theatre—acres of painted backdrops, a Mephisto capering nimbly in a fluttering Spanish cloak, a Gretchen even more doll-like. These, too, were going to be disappointed.

First surprise was the fact that the stage itself was scarcely twenty-six feet deep, the merest shelf compared with the capacious depths of older theatres. Surprise number two: the whole stage area proved mobile: it contracted, opened up, became higher, lower. Behind the proscenium-thickness, at either side of the stage, stood huge square inner portals capable of sliding noiselessly onstage and off, connected overhead by a bridge that masked a battery of light-projectors. In the rear, instead of painted backdrops, four differently colored cycloramas rolled across when needed, at the touch of an electric button.

Surprising beyond belief, the scenery. Not so much scenery as a kaleidoscope made up of simple prisms. These combined almost inexhaustibly to form suggestions of locale. In the rear, a platform, in neutral gray, which is sometimes raised, sometimes lowered, which becomes a wall, a road, a horizon. The inner portals, colored faintly like gray stone walls, approach each other or recede, indicating streets, rooms, garden walls. The niche that forms Faust's study becomes Margaret's bedroom; the tavern, with minor changes, turns into a prison. A few properties are brought on and off; the shifts take no longer than ten seconds apiece. Each time the gray prismatic shapes reassemble under the modulated light and color, which pours from the lighting instruments as if under the hand of a master musician. The production has a scenic unity which moulds the play from opening to final curtain.

Prologue: the frame of the stage is opened wide, like a window upon the universe of space. As if on a limitless horizon stand the three Archangels: male, youthful figures awesome in size. They are corseted in metal; their arms are outstretched, holding their great swords; their bronze wings open like gates toward the endless yellow space. In the foreground Mephistopheles crouches in his russet scholar's gown. We hear music, the song of the spheres, the chant of angels, ever more distinct. God's voice speaks, out of the depths. Mephistopheles replies with head averted. A sound like a hollow groan—night swallows the Spirit of Darkness.

Faust's study: a niche in a bare, massive wall. Beyond, dimly visible, a narrow Gothic window. A desk, an armchair; only those properties which are indispensable. The Demon appears. We hear only his voice; but the walls of the study turn crimson, as if blood were seeping through them, the silhouette of Faust becomes a deep purple. These impassioned colors seem to reveal to us a soul torn with loneliness and fearful torment. . . . Now the cathedral. Shadows. In the foreground the vestibule of a basilica. The depths of the stage swallow the crowds of worshippers. Candles flicker far off. Margaret, not blonde, but brunette, leans against a pillar, cringing, while an accusing voice from on high sends daggers into her soul. In the pauses, trumpets and the choral of the *Dies Irae*. . . . The prison cell: a long wall, in the center a barred door. Stairs descend into this cold space, into this place of outer darkness. We know that the final scene of the tragedy has been reached. . . .[1]

Where is the characteristic stonemasonry of the Middle Ages? We have forgotten all about it, we do not care whether it is here or not. Where are the authentic costumes of medieval Germany? The costumes of this production are not vouched for by Viollet-le-Duc or Racinet; in their subdued color, their posteresque simplicity, they have nothing in common with the Faustean operatic tradition. Where is the startling Naturalistic imitation of day and night in the stage lighting? We see instead shafts of illumination, pools of shadow, light joyous or sorrowful, stained through with colors which seize upon our emotions. . . . No, nothing is authentic, nothing is solidly "real" or indubitably historic.

The designer, Fritz Erler, makes clear that he is after something entirely different. Of what use are authentic costumes, facsimile streets and fields, when all this environment is not really environment at all? It is *the realm of the soul* which must be portrayed, not the minutiae of facts concerning the Middle Ages. When Faust wanders through the desolation of the mountains with the Demon at his heels, Erler does not try to say whether these mountains are in Bavaria or Saxony. He does not stop to give us their geological composition. "I attach no importance to the fact that the scene takes place in front of a glacier. Let them show me rocks, wooded mountains, if they please. . . . What difference does it make? What matters is that the 'wandering in the wasteland' be made clear, that it be contrasted with the scene which follows: Margaret at the spinning wheel."

Fuchs is even more iconoclastic. Let the audience know that theatre is something better than life, that it is an insight into life. The theatre is not a vulgar peep-show. No longer must the audience watch costumed actors moving inside a gilt picture-frame. The dramatic action goes half-way to meet its public. The actors work far out on that ledge of forestage, so that their bodies loom up in relief against the setting behind them. This "relief stage" will replace existing stages. "The whole Talma world of cardboard, wire, canvas and tinsel is ripe for its fall."

"POETIC TRUTH"

In New York seven years later it was the Belasco world which was ripe for its fall.

In 1915 a Broadway audience at Wallack's Theatre applauded a stage production which was not at all in the immediate tradition of Belascoism. The play on this occasion was THE MAN WHO MARRIED A DUMB WIFE, a one-act comedy by Anatole France, produced by Granville-Barker, who was then directing for the Stage Society of New York. This playlet, it is interesting to note, was only a curtain-raiser for Shaw's ANDROCLES AND THE LION. But history has chosen to remember the curtain-raiser rather than the main course of that evening's dramatic fare. Anatole France's comedy, under the auspices of an independent producing company, set a new production standard.

As in Munich the change was heralded in the work of the scenic artist. Laid in the Middle Ages, the little play might have been subjected to a treatment featuring Gothic masonry, tapestries, gargoyles, stained glass, pointed arches, trefoils and crenelations. Its designer, a young man named Robert Edmond Jones, chose to take a different course. The play was a comedy. He symbolized its comic spirit in primary colors, light frame construction and an almost Japanese architectural style: square open windows, a light wooden balcony supported on stilts. The costumes, scissored out of richly colored felt cloth, had the stiffness of medieval woodcuts. What could be further from the traditional gray and grim Gothic than this poetic conception?

The Symbolist designer's approach to his work has been described by no one more eloquently than Jones himself:

> A good scene should be, not a picture, but an image. . . . Everything that is actual must undergo a strange metamorphosis, a kind of sea-change, before it can become truth in the theatre. There is a curious mystery in this. You will remember the quotation from HAMLET—
>
> My father!—methinks I see my father.
> O where, my lord?
> *In my mind's eye, Horatio.*
>
> Stage-designing should be addressed to this eye of the mind. There is an outer eye that observes, and there is an inner eye that sees. . . .

The designer must always be on his guard against being too explicit. A good scene, I repeat, is not a picture. It is something seen, but it is something conveyed as well; a feeling, an evocation. Plato says somewhere: It is beauty I seek, not beautiful things. That is what I mean. A setting is not just a beautiful thing, a collection of beautiful things. It is a presence, a mood, a symphonic accompaniment to the drama, a great wind fanning the drama to flame. It echoes, it enhances, it animates. It is an expectancy, a boreboding, a tension. It says nothing, but it gives everything.

Historical accuracy, a pedantic reverence, were furthest from Jones's thought. His was a response distinctly emotional and highly personal. His individuality impressed itself on the production. He took the play into his own deft hands, designing and painting every detail, draping and pinning the costumes on the actors.

Jones might have served to typify the awakening of the American theatre to a new cosmopolitanism. Born in 1887 on a New Hampshire farm, Jones was still a rawboned and callow youngster when he came to Harvard. As an undergraduate he revealed a gift for "smashing" dramatic effects in designing the settings and costumes of the university shows. It was a gift which did not take him very far after commencement. When he came to New York he slept, for a time, on park benches—an experience which served to temper some of his native lyrical enthusiasm. Never a radical politically, he drifted into the company of insurgents, both artistic and political (including the famous John Reed) who crowded the salon of Mabel Dodge. They helped send him off to Europe for further study.

In Berlin, Jones, on a student's pass, watched Max Reinhardt conduct rehearsals. To the American it was as if the portals of a new world of theatre were swung open. A scenic Renaissance was under way in Europe; it was the opportunity of a lifetime. It must have been agony later on when Jones was refused admission to the school of Gordon Craig, an artist whom the American designer resembles in temperament and whom he has never ceased to admire. But the period abroad was well spent just the same. When in 1914 Jones returned, hiding his youth under a leonine beard, a new era was about to begin in the American theatre.

The Barker-Jones production was not America's first glimpse of Symbolist theatre, any more than the Künstlertheater's FAUST was the first Symbolist presentation in Europe. Both remain out-

From Drawings for the Theatre

THE MAN WHO MARRIED A DUMB WIFE (1915). Design by Robert Edmond Jones

History remembers a curtain-raiser

standing, however, for the attention they drew, and for their subsequent effect upon staging. In the United States a year or two earlier the Viennese designer Joseph Urban had begun the work of restyling the opera; Granville-Barker had imported English productions by men of the new school, such as Norman Wilkinson and Albert Rutherston; and Winthrop Ames had brought over Max Reinhardt's production of SUMURÛN. Yet it is likely that this production by Jones, more starkly lyrical than anything in Reinhardt, fastened the Symbolist method more securely upon America than the imported work of Reinhardt himself.

In subsequent years the name of Reinhardt became a synonym of theatrical progress for dozens of pioneering "little theatres" in the United States, along with the names of Edward Gordon Craig and Adolphe Appia. Max Reinhardt has been described by Cheney as "the great popularizer, the great practical advocate of the newer ideas." It may have been Reinhardt in particular who struck the imagination of Americans, but in fact all through Europe a passionate reconstruction of dramatic style was going on.

Designers like Ludvig Sievert, Knut Strom, Rochus Gliese, Emil Pirchan, Hans Strobach, Emil Löffler, Hans Poelzig, Caspar Neher; directors like Fuchs, Leopold Jessner, Jürgen Fehling, Gustav Gründgens; technicians like Adolphe Linnebach, were arriving in Germany. There were the Austrian designers Oskar Strnad and Alfred Roller; the Hungarian Ladislas Medgyes; the Dane Svend Gade; the French designers Déthomas, Drésa, Léger, Picasso, Barbey; the French directors Jacques Copeau, Louis Jouvet, Fermin Gémier, Gaston Baty. In England, in addition to Barker, the directors Macdermott, Barry Jackson, William Poel. (To Poel, who founded the Elizabethan Stage Society in 1895, goes the credit for the rediscovery of Shakespeare's stage form.) In Czechoslovakia there were the designers Hilar, Heythum and Čapek; in Sweden the designers Grunewald and Dardel, the director Per Lindberg. In Russia directors like Alexander Tairov, Vsevelod Meyerhold; designers like Bakst, Benois, Exeter, Egerov, Vesnin, Federovsky, Gontcharova, Golovin, Soudekin, Shestakov. . . . These were but a few of the men and women who, at the very time when Belasco was making the American stage safe for Naturalism, were rising in revolt against the tradition of the Théâtre-Libre.

Once again an incoming dramatic movement issued manifestos and assaulted the Old Order. "Not realism but style!" demanded Gordon Craig. "Max Reinhardt fought against Naturalism," wrote Moussinac. Maurice Denis looked for "the triumph of the emotion of beauty over the lie of Naturalism." Hildebrand asserted "The condition of dramatic life is *poetic truth* and not *reality.*" "The theatre will be what it should be: an excuse for dreams," announced Quillard.

"INNER TRUTH"

The tide of criticism rose, and Naturalism lost its defenders. Suddenly it appeared that no one, with the possible exceptions of Zola and Belasco, had been completely "sold" on it.

As far back as 1890, when preparing Ibsen's THE WILD DUCK, Antoine declared, "Just as I was the first to open my doors wide to the Naturalist drama, so I shall open them wide also to Symbolist drama, provided it is drama."

Antoine may have represented Zola's ideals in scientific staging, but he never shared Zola's formal philosophy of science in the theatre. And from first to last, Antoine confessed his embarrassment at being labeled a Naturalist. When the critic Bauer told him, in 1889, "If it wishes to continue to prosper, the Théâtre-Libre will be Naturalistic or it will not be at all," Antoine indignantly replied "I do not at all agree with this opinion. I think that a too strict formula will be death. . . ." Indeed, on the very first bill of his theatre there had been a "scientific prologue" in the form of a poem by André Byl, which had made Antoine squirm. The verses implied that the new theatre was dedicated to Naturalism; they conjured up a vision in which the four plays on the program were represented as animals in a zoo attended by Zola as keeper. "Not genial," Antoine noted in his diary; but he had to leave the verses on the program because Byl had worked so hard for the new theatre. If some of Antoine's settings approached the acme of the Naturalistic style, some of them did nothing of the sort. Thus, for Maurice Vaucaire's UN BEAU SOIR (1891) he employed as designer Henri Rivière, "the artist of the Chinese shadows of the Chat-Noir." (Miller).

Stanislavsky was just as emphatic. "Those who think that we

sought for Naturalism on the stage are mistaken. We never leaned towards such a principle. Always, then as well as now, we sought for inner truth, for the truth of feeling and experience, but as spiritual technique was only in its embryo stage among the actors of our company, we, because of necessity and helplessness, and against our desires, fell now and then into an outward and coarse Naturalism." The Moscow Art Theatre can name many productions in support of this statement, among them Ostrovsky's THE SNOW MAIDEN (1900); Andreyev's THE LIFE OF MAN (1907); Hamsun's THE DRAMA OF LIFE (1907); Maeterlinck's THE BLUE BIRD (1908); the Gordon Craig version of HAMLET (1911). In plays like these the Art Theatre not only sought for the inner value of the surface fact: it departed altogether from literalism.

Even in the more literal method—it would be more correct to say, precisely in the literal method—Stanislavsky had occasion to see, more than once, that the stage remains the stage; that Naturalism, fundamentally, is not only unattainable but even injurious.

The old village woman whom the Art Theatre brought back to Moscow as consultant on the *milieu* of THE POWER OF DARKNESS gave Stanislavsky a lesson which staggered him. It happened that the actress playing Matryona fell ill during rehearsals, and the villager was pressed into service to take her place. (The old woman had already learned the texts of all the rôles without the aid of the prompter.) The impression she created on the stage was so overpowering that it ruined the ensemble of one of the best professional casts in Europe.

When she gave Anisya the powder with which the latter was to poison her husband, when she put her crooked hand in her bosom, seeking there for the little package of poison, and then quietly, in a business-like way, as if not understanding the depth of her villainy, explained to Anisya how to poison a man gradually and secretly, the cold sweat broke out on our foreheads. . . . [She] interpreted the inner and outer contents of Tolstoy's tragedy so fully, truthfully, and in such bright colors, she justified each of our Naturalistic details of production to such an extent that she became unreplaceable to us. But when she left the stage and the regular actors of the company were on, their spiritual and physical imitation betrayed them. . . . We made a final trial. We did not let her come on, but made her sing in the wings. But even this was dangerous for the actors. Then we made a phonograph record of her voice, and her song provided a background for the action without breaking up our ensemble. (*My Life in Art*).

Therewith one of the greatest stage directors of modern history was confronted with the question which the farmer asked himself in Aesop's cynical fable of *The Clown and the Countryman:* How can the truth seem false? This was something which Stanislavsky could not answer with any satisfaction. Yet it was just this question which the new generation of theatre workers insisted upon asking. Naturalism, they contended, for all its devotion to authentic fact, is no more convincingly real than a stuffed parrot or a wax dummy. The most vividly counterfeited reality, even reality itself, is somehow wrong on the stage.

Said Georg Fuchs:

> There are spectators who are like children. Give them a doll which is too perfect an imitation and their imagination has nothing left to invent. The doll with its gross realism has shattered their little world of fantasy, and they do not know what to do with a useless plaything.

In the United States Arthur Hopkins called attention to the paradox that the upshot of the realistic effort is further to emphasize the unreality of the whole attempt, setting, play and all.

The dramatist Nikolas Evreinov added a note of irony to the discussion.

> The only logical solution, of course, is that proposed cynically by the Russian dramatist Evreinov. In effect his thesis is as follows. If you wish realism, if you do hold this philosophy, for heaven's sake be reasonable. Never let a play be acted in English or in Russian the characters of which are supposed to be Swedes or Germans. Never employ a careful reproduction of a fourteenth-century oak table, always purchase an original specimen. Don't bother about the audience; be logical and build up that fourth wall . . . our logical application of the realistic theory has resulted in a familiar *reductio ad absurdum.*

Soon the failings of Naturalism were made clear to everyone inside and outside the theatre. Naturalism was drowning in the morass of its own petty truths. The method sponsored by Zola had lost its way; it had become the letter without the spirit. All its carefully verified facts revealed only that it no longer contained a central meaning.

DUALISM

As usual we must go outside the theatre in order to comprehend more fully what was happening inside.

What was the reason why theatre people began to find fault with the extroverted, scientific-minded style of Naturalism? Why did they choose this particular time to point out its defects? We have seen that Naturalism was far from accurate scientifically. Why did not its critics correct these mistakes in scientific fashion? Why, instead, did they propose a method that was the reverse of objective?

We get a hint of the answer if we remember how mixed in thought all previous dramatic styles had been. None of these styles were completely objective. All were, in fact, typically compounded of objective and subjective thinking. As it was with dramatic thought, so it was with general thought.

Man's thinking has not developed harmoniously from primitive subjectivism to scientific enlightenment. The development has been uneven and irregular. Philosophically speaking, the development has been *dualist* in character. That is, thought has developed along both subjective and objective lines. These two categories have continued on down the centuries, into our own era. The average man of today lives with, and uses, both. He may often be aware of the inconsistency, but he accepts it as inevitable. In everyday life, therefore, this inconsistency is reconciled.

But it never becomes entirely reconciled in the more exact fields of thought—in art, science or philosophy. Instead the two currents of thought become more and more contradictory. A kind of intense rivalry develops, and any move made by one line of thought is quickly checkmated by the other.

We know that science, the modern expansion of objective thought, had much to contend with in making headway. Still, from the time of Newton onward it made immense strides. By the middle of the nineteenth century, science, so long ignored and even persecuted, seemed ready to control the destinies of mankind. This new prestige of science was one of the important factors in the appearance of Naturalism in the theatre.

But it turned out that the victory of science was by no means assured as yet. Subjectivism yielded ground, but remained opposed.

It had reason to take heart again as the further progress of science itself began to throw doubts on scientific premises. The latter half of the nineteenth century was remarkable for the crumbling away of a whole superstructure of scientific thought. All those theories which had been built upon Newtonian science and which envisioned a mechanical world, proved inadequate. Simple mechanical causation could no longer explain the latest discoveries of chemistry, biology, astronomy or even physics itself.

The result was confusion. "The nineteenth century," says Whitehead, "has been a perplexed century, in a sense which is not true of any of its predecessors in the modern period." The way was now wide open for subjective thought to reassert itself.

New subjective philosophies arose. Some of them, like the dialectic idealism of Hegel, were brilliant contributions. Others were almost purely mystical or anti-rational. Unlike the earlier subjective systems, most of the newer philosophies accepted as valid the more practical discoveries of science; but they denied that scientific thinking can explain the world.

These new introspective systems of thought were fundamentally *idealistic.* (The term "idealistic" as used in philosophy has nothing to do with the idea of aspiring toward perfection. It describes the belief that there is no objective reality made up of material things; that *ideas* alone are real.) Idealistic philosophy denied that any adequate deductions can be made from "brute facts." Attacking science on its own ground, it demanded laboratory proof of the basic axioms of science. Since axioms are, by definition, not subject to proof, science for a time could make no reply.

Interestingly enough, it was at this very time that a new science began, to which subjective philosophy attached much importance. This was the science of *psychology.* Although it was inclined to distrust the other sciences, idealist thought hoped that the systematic study of the human mind might reveal the truths of existence.

Such were the conflicting philosophic trends at the time Naturalism took root. Scarcely was the Naturalistic form established at the Théâtre-Libre, when subjective idealism also appeared on the stage, insisting that "poetic truth and not reality" must be the object of drama.

What describes the dramatic form which the idealist philosophy wished to substitute in place of Naturalism?

SYNTHESIS

The New Stagecraft covered a wide range of technique. We have already named three separate tendencies. All were part of the broad anti-Naturalistic movement, and many artists worked in all three styles, many critics argued for all three viewpoints. Most extreme of the new tendencies was Theatricalism, most moderate was the Symbolist method, with an indeterminate middle ground between the two. In the present chapter we are concerned with the more moderate wing of the movement, which today dominates the practice of the American stage.

The memorable production of FAUST which has been sketched here was the work of the Munich Artists' Theatre inaugurated 1907, and with the participation of Fuchs, Littmann, Benno Becker, and the designers Oscar Graf, Fritz Erler, Ernst Stern, Hans Beatus Wieland. The Künstlertheater, however, was bringing to fruition the work of a little Paris theatre which lasted only two years and whose contribution to stage history has all but been obliterated.

On January 17, 1891, Antoine noted in his diary:

> A committee of poets has been formed to create a *Théâtre d'Art* which will presently give, at the Salle Montparnasse, plays by Pierre Quillard, Rachilde, and Stéphane Mallarmé. It is a good thing, for the Théâtre-Libre is not enough; other groups are becoming necessary to play certain works which we cannot present. I don't see any competition there, but a complement in the evolution which is going ahead with increasing speed.

Thus the Théâtre d'Art came into existence only four years after the founding of the Théâtre-Libre. Paul Fort, who called himself "Prince of Poets," seems to have been its organizer. Fort envisioned a type of playhouse where, in the words of Quillard, the spectator "will abandon himself completely to the will of the poet and will see visions terrible and charming, lands of deception into which none but he can penetrate." With the encouragement of the Symbolist poets Mallarmé, Verlaine, Henry de Regnier, Jean Moreas, Verhaeren, Alfred Vallette and others of their circle, Fort kept his playhouse going for two years, striking a spark from which others afterwards kindled their torches. In 1893 Lugne-Poë took over the directorship for the remaining year, renaming the playhouse the Théâtre de l'Oeuvre and producing Shelley's THE CENCI, the FAUSTUS of Marlowe and Verlaine's LES UNS ET LES AUTRES.

Scenic reform had an important place in the new program. If we begin by analyzing the scenic theories of Symbolism, it will prepare us for an understanding of the aims of this style—a style which differed sharply in many ways with Naturalism yet has come to exist side by side with it.

Komisarjevsky writes: "According to the French Symbolists, the scenery had to be a pure ornamental fiction and had one function only—to complete, by means of analogies between the colors and the shapes of the décor and the spoken line, the esthetic illusion created by the poetry of the play." Fuchs, according to the same commentator, "was against Naturalism, but he was also against detached-from-life symbolism and estheticism. His main idea, which actually belonged to Goethe, was to combine in the scenic work 'the talents of the landscape painter and of the architect.'" Fuchs' designers "were not so much scenic painters as 'space artists.'" Their task, according to Fuchs, "was to think concretely (*sachlich*) in three dimensions so as to be able to subject the decorative and pictorial elements to the dramatic substance of the theatre."

By 1921 Kenneth Macgowan, in *The Theatre of Tomorrow*, had condensed the scenic philosophy of the Symbolists into four main principles. These were: simplification of effect and of means; a proper relationship of actor to background; suggestion, as when a single candlestick serves to give the whole quality of the Baroque period for LA TOSCA; and synthesis, "a complex and rhythmic fusion of setting, lights, actors and play."

WAGNER

The artistic ideals of the Symbolists had their origin in the theories of Richard Wagner, who propounded them half a century before. It was Wagner who surmised that the unified productions of the Meiningen troupe were but a first step toward an almost disembodied musical art of production. It was Wagner who first revealed the possibilities of the "synthesis of music, chant and color." (Carter). The scenic principles of this great Romantic, principles which were in their time disturbingly radical, underlie conservative Broadway and Hollywood practice today.

Indeed the artistic tradition of Richard Wagner is now so orthodox that the stormy career of Wagner the man has been well-nigh forgotten. He was born in Leipzig in 1813, the ostensible son of a police-court clerk. It is believed that he was really the son of the actor and dramatist Ludwig Geyer, who afterwards became his stepfather. At twenty he entered upon a wretched career as a conductor of small opera companies in Würzburg, Magdeburg and elsewhere. He was self-taught as a musician, and his musical views were as non-conformist as his views in politics.

The place and year of his birth were those of the battle of Leipzig, which liberated the German states from the yoke of Napoleon. Wagner's career seems to have developed inevitably from this background. The tyranny of Napoleon had been attended in part by liberal ideas derived from the French revolution. After the French invader was expelled, the rulers of the German petty states tried to get rid of the new ideas as well. The attempt was stoutly resisted by the German people. In this struggle with despotism at home the intellectuals also ranged themselves against the princes. Beginning in 1830 Wagner threw himself into the turmoil of his day. As he related it afterwards:

> Now came the revolution of July (1830). With one bound I became a revolutionist, and adopted the opinion that every man with any aspiration should devote himself to politics. I enjoyed nothing but association with political literati; I even began an overture dealing with political themes. . . . I soon came to my senses, however. (Burlingame).

But Wagner did not "come to his senses" quite as soon as he afterwards liked to believe. In fact his political heresy went on unabated for at least twenty years. He took an active part in the events which led to the uprising in Dresden in 1849. When the insurrectionary movement was suppressed in Germany and Austria he fled abroad, remaining in exile until 1869. Some of his finest work was done during this period, when bitter persecution was visited upon him for his independent political and artistic beliefs. At last all was forgiven and he came back to the court of Bavaria and the favor of the eighteen-year-old King Ludwig II.

He returned with a large amount of mental baggage, most of it militantly nationalist in character. It was a curious assortment: anti-classical, anti-industrial and anti-Semitic (the last despite the fact that there is reason to believe Wagner himself was Jewish). Wagner shared with Nietzsche an exaltation of Germanism and of the primitive Nordic heroes. Like Nietzsche he had no use for a meek Christ or for "the common herd."

In his musical dramas he gave idealized life to a pagan world of supermen, dragons, amazons and giants. These figures could exist only in a misty region of dreams, with the help of the emotional persuasion induced by an overpowering type of music. It is evident why, on the stage, the Wagnerian operas require suggestion, symbolism, vagueness of outline, posteresque light and shadow and, most of all, an impenetrable blending, "a complex and rhythmic fusion of setting, lights, actors and play." Wagner himself saw this clearly, and strove for a lyrical synthesis with the help of his designers Max Brückner and Christian Jank. We shall see later that when the Baireuth Opera House was built under his direction, it was specially designed to make dream worlds possible on the stage.

THE PLASTIC STAGE

Let us note into what rarefied air we have ascended during our study of the Symbolist theatre. We seem to be dealing with utterly abstract principles of technique. We are far removed from the opinions of a Zola, an Antoine or a Stanislavsky, whose manner of thought is a constant glancing back and forth from the stage to life outside the theatre. Today we are a long way even from Wagner, whose operatic fables were a deliberate embodiment of his political beliefs. Here our glance never once strays from the stage. This narrowed interest is the source of both the strength and the weakness of Symbolism in production.

In insisting on the priority of the actor in the scene, the Symbolists undoubtedly had a "case" against Naturalism. If, as the Naturalists themselves insisted, the relation of human character to its environment must be made clear, it follows that the actor must be singled out in the scene. The player cannot remain part of the kind of stage picture in which human shapes have no more significance than the shapes of furniture. It is impossible in that case to give the actor the attention he deserves from us. He is lost in accidental shadows; his ill-considered costume disguises his appearance, distorts his movements. Properties, unexpectedly and without the intention of the director, get in his way. His face and gestures are indistinct. The color of a wall, the pattern of a tablecloth, the erratic, chance composition of other objects, compel our attention more than the action or words of the player.

The stage area cannot be a mere collection of shapes in which the actor knocks around. The spatial functions of the setting must be understood and related to his movements. This relationship cannot be fully realized so long as the stage is viewed as a picture. It becomes possible only when the stage is seen in terms of sculpture or architecture.

Hence the Symbolists came forward with the new principle of the *plastic stage*. The plastic stage setting is a shaped (sculptural or architectonic) structure. The Symbolists saw it as recessive and *static* in quality while complementing the emphasized, *dynamic* figure of the actor. "The scenic illusion lies in the living presence of the actor," Appia declared. Fritz Erler explained, "My point of departure was, before everything, to render clear and distinct the figure of the stage character."

Logically considered, the formula of the plastic stage is a sentence of death passed upon the old stage picture. The technique of the stage picture had been built up, little by little, through all the centuries since the Italian Renaissance. From now on, if the stage continued to look like a picture, it was only incidentally; its real form was sculptural, "plastic." We shall see, however, that while the Theatricalists took a strict anti-pictorial attitude toward the setting, the more moderate Symbolists did not.

APPIA

The invention of the plastic stage is closely linked with the invention, in the same period, of electric stage lighting.

The first recorded use of electric lighting on the stage dates from 1846, when an arc light was used at the Paris Opera to give the illusion of a natural sun in the sky. In Rossini's opera MOSES (1860), also produced at the Paris Opera House, the first floodlight and follow spot made their stage debut. For some time electrical equipment continued in use for special effects of rainbows, lightning and so on, in conjunction with gas lighting systems. An interesting example of this combination is given by Max Grube, stage manager of the Meiningen troupe. In the Meiningen production of JULIUS CAESAR (Berlin, 1874), the wraith of Caesar in a crimson robe stood well-nigh invisible in front of the crimson tent of Brutus, until the face of the ghost was startlingly revealed in the rays of an electric spotlight. . . . In 1882, as a result of systematic research carried on at the Paris Opera, a fully electrified stage lighting system was shown in Munich at the International Electro-Technical Exhibition. About twenty years had to elapse, however, before gas lighting disappeared from the world's stages.

The introduction of electric lighting in the theatre was followed by the development of a large variety of lighting units, dimmer systems, color filters, and special "effect" machines. It became possible to project whole "backdrops," images in light (the Linnebach projector). In connection with the lighting-system devised by Fortuny, there was developed in Germany the so-called *Kuppelhorizant,* or plaster-dome. This is a dome-shaped rear wall faced with a granular surface of plaster; it simulates infinite space when flooded with light, and is in some ways superior to cloth cycloramas. Some idea of the revolution in scenic technology caused by electric light can be gathered from the fact that every one of the special optical effects which the Baroque theatre obtained with paint are now possible by means of light.[2]

This amazing new scenic element was shaped by Symbolist designers. The esthetics of electric stage lighting found their first expression in a book by a Symbolist. In 1895 there appeared *La Mise en scène du drame Wagnérien,* an essay by Adolphe Appia, accompanied by eighteen of the author's scene designs for Wagner's operas. It was followed in 1899 by another slender volume, *Die Musik und die Inszenierung* (Music and Staging), in a German translation from the original French of the same author.

Appia, one of the most important figures of the New Stagecraft, was born in 1862, the son of a Geneva physician. He lacked interest in medicine as a career; instead he gave himself passionately to music—a love which endured his lifetime. While studying in Germany he visited Baireuth, where he saw how practical difficulties all but ruined the staging of lyric drama. It seemed to him that the methods at Baireuth, in spite of the hopes which Wagner had pinned on them, were uninspired and unmusical. In setting forth his own views he found it necessary to make sketches for settings; from then on he worked principally as a scenic artist.

Like Gordon Craig, he rarely designed for the professional theatres, being content with less than a dozen productions in the whole of his career. These included Byron's MANFRED, with music by Schumann, produced in Paris in 1903; Glück's ORPHEUS, at the Dalcroze Institute, Hellerau (1913); a spectacle, LA FÊTE DE JUIN, in Geneva (1914); TRISTAN AND ISOLDE at the Scala Theatre, Milan, with Toscanini conducting (1923); THE RHEINGOLD and THE VALKYRIE at the Basel Stadttheater (1924). Appia's hermit-like seclusion within a medieval château on Lake Geneva was not due to Olympian aloofness but to an unusually reticent, sensitive and kindly personality. The designer-musician with the white Shavian beard and glowing dark eyes was a legendary Great Unknown at the time of his death in 1928.

Appia's work was an immediate extension of Wagner's in the field of the stage setting. Proceeding from the ideal of Wagner, "the projection of music into visible scenic form," Appia devoted himself to showing, in sketches, models and light-plots, how this could be carried out on the stage. Symbolist technique owes much to Appia's conception of the stage as a cubic volume of space in which there takes place a continuous functioning of light. The setting upon which this light plays is thought of as a single plastic unit, regardless of the number of its details. Appia showed also that two kinds of lighting are necessary: a general illumination (furnished on most American stages today by the so-called X-ray group of first border lights) and accentuation (spotlights and other types of projectors).

No doubt Appia's researches were guided in part by the experience of architecture and sculpture, both of which have understood since antiquity the rôle of light and shadow in defining form. In addition the school of Impressionist painting (Cézanne, Monet, Manet, Renoir, Pissaro, Seurat, Sisley) was then making its epochal investigation of the nature of light. Appia's light-plot for the staging of TRISTAN AND ISOLDE shows what he meant by the assertion that dramatic light is the light that casts shadows. Note the precision with which the nuances of light are set down:

> The walls of the castle, which bound the setting at stage left as well as upstage and from there extend towards stage right must surround Tristan as a screen might surround a sick person. The scenery down stage right must seem to indicate the end of this screen, so that it seems almost as though one had removed part of the screen to enable the audience to see the stage. The two ends of this screen leave a wide view of the sky and are connected with the stage floor by a bounding wall.
>
> . . . The high point, from which Kurwenal can watch the horizon, must be incorporated in the wall at the right side of the stage, but downstage so that it does not obviously break the unity of line and at the same time keeps Kurwenal throughout as an expressive silhouette. . . . In order that Tristan may be illuminated by the natural play of light, he is placed opposite the open sky and surrounded with as few accessories as possible. . . . On p. 215 [of the score] the growing light begins to play around Tristan's feet. On p. 218 it reaches his belt, on p. 221 it grazes his face, on p. 223 he is entirely immersed in light; p. 225 the light spills over his immediate surroundings. . . . Beginning p. 236 the light is the color of the sunset. But this rapidly dims during the singing of pp. 238–242; the animated scene (pp. 245–248) plays in relative darkness, so that the details are no longer recognizable; in contrast the foreground is bathed in blood red light which continues to grow in intensity.

The sensitivity of modern stage lighting is matched by no other element in stage production except the actor himself. An idea of the rôle played by modern lighting may be inferred from the example of Gaston Baty's staging of MADAME BOVARY at the Théâtre Montparnasse, Paris, 1936. (The example is taken at random.) The opening scene at the inn is aglow with old-fashioned lamps. There is a lamp on the table at right. Two others stand on a low chest at the rear. Through the blue haze in the window at back, street lamps are visible; and the lights of a carriage are added when the Bovarys arrive. In scene 4, the Homais' salon, a background curtain of brown and gold brocade, sparkles like dim stars as Emma sits in a reverie. The friends of Emma's girlhood, who are a sort of chorus, occupy boxes on either side of the auditorium. The boxes are draped in gauze, through which the chorus is revealed a dim pink light. Scene 6: The Bovarys' living room. Emma's young admirer leaves. An organgrinder is heard outside, while a terrible sorrow fills the room; as Emma sinks down in her chair the light in the window darkens, the yellow walls are overcast by a faint blue.

Although "lighting for mood" was known to Renaissance designers like Leone de Somi, the range and delicacy made possible by electric light has brought stage lighting to a new standard of perfection. Its emotional possibilities have made it especially useful to the Symbolists. The New York stage has developed specialists in this field, whose contributions to production deserve to be recognized and appraised. Examples are Feder's lighting for the Orson Welles presentation of Marlowe's DR. FAUSTUS (1936); that of Moe Hack for George Sklar's LIFE AND DEATH OF AN AMERICAN (1939); and of Michael Gordon for Robert Ardrey's THUNDER ROCK (1939).

It is difficult to recapture today the impression which electric light made upon theatre workers and audience alike when it first appeared. Some of the pristine joy of the theatre at its discovery can still be experienced, however, at a performance of Maeterlinck's THE BLUE BIRD at the Moscow Art Theatre. Produced in 1908, it is still in the repertory of that company after more than thirty years. The production remains unsurpassed in its use of trick lighting effects. The cottage of the children loses all reality as the Fairy Bérylune waves her wand: the cottage becomes a revolving wheel of sparkling golden light, in which the furniture waltzes. In the Palace of Night Tyltyl opens the door of war: red light glares, a Goliath in armor dances to the rattling of chains. The little boy opens the last door: we see vivid azure space filled with the darting of a thousand birds. It is curious that all this trickery does not ring false. Its tricks are childishly magical; the production has an eternal freshness.

CRAIG

If the name of Adolphe Appia is associated with Symbolist lighting, that of Edward Gordon Craig, English designer and director, is linked with the Symbolist doctrine that every stage production must be a highly integrated esthetic system planned by a single mind. The mantle of Wagner has been large enough to cover both Appia and Craig.

The ecstatic talent of Gordon Craig flows from a personality that is eternally boyish, idealistic and exuberant. The passage of years, and a pince-nez, have not altogether hidden the earlier Craig of the tossing blond mane and almost feminine features. (Craig resembles his actress-mother, Ellen Terry, whom he idolized.) Isadora Duncan met him when he had a studio in Berlin on top of a high building. She recalls in *My Life* that the studio has a "black, waxed floor with rose leaves, artificial rose leaves, strewn all over it," even though it lacked the most ordinary furniture. Like Isadora, Craig was penniless, but rich in dreams. She adds, "He was one of the few people I ever met who was in a state of exaltation from morning to night. . . . An ordinary walk through the streets with him was like a promenade in Thebes of Ancient Egypt with a superior High Priest." Most of Craig's portraits give a misleading impression of fragility; he is unusually tall and sufficiently robust.

Although born to the theatre (in 1872), he rebelled early in his career against the practices of the existing theatre. His first seven years on the stage—as an actor in Sir Henry Irving's company and as an independent London director—convinced him that he had no future in England. In 1913 Craig exiled himself to Florence, where, under the patronage of Lord Howard de Walden, he established his School for the Art of the Theatre in a beautiful outdoor playhouse, the Arena Goldoni. Robed in spotless white he officiated, like a master of the Renaissance, over the students who came to those cloistered halls from all parts of the world.

Craig's magazine, *The Mask* (published in Florence), and his books, beginning with *The Art of the Theatre* (1905), have had a great vogue, especially in the United States. Less workmanlike than Appia, diffuse, extravagant and self-contradictory in much of his writings, Craig sums up in his own work the inconsistencies of the Symbolist school of thought. Theatre for the sake of theatre, theatre as an art governed by laws unrelated—even opposed—to the workaday world, is the viewpoint, either implied or stated, underlying all his sketches and written essays.

Craig is in fact an ardent champion of ivory towers, from whose heights he engages the enemy with some of the recklessness of a James McNeill Whistler. Craig's definition of theatre as given in his first book was timely and sound, as far as it went. It was not new, of course, but it encountered opposition just the same:

DESIGNERS OF A NEW THEATRE

N.Y. Public Library Theatre Collection

N.Y. Public Library Theatre Collection

Appia

Light in cubic volume

Craig

The rock and the mist

Geddes

America looks industrial and scientific

Léon de Vos photo

R.K.O.

Jones

Theatre is revelation

> . . . the Art of the Theatre is neither acting nor the play, it is not scene nor dance, but it consists of all the elements of which these things are composed: action, which is the very spirit of acting; words, which are the body of the play; line and color, which are the very heart of the scene; rhythm, which is the very essence of dance.

The theatre in its totality as an artistic instrument; the theatre as a composite art with laws of its own—to this formal program Craig swears his allegiance. In his defense of that program and his lifelong battle for an adequate dramatic method, he has shown an integrity which must be taken into account in weighing his shortcomings.

Having asserted the artistic unity of stage production, Craig went on to a more dubious conclusion: each stage production must be the work of a single mind.

> *Playgoer:* I understand, then, that you would allow no one to rule on the stage except the stage-manager? *
>
> *Stage Director:* The nature of the work permits nothing else.

Some of the implications of this "master mind" formula of stage production will be discussed later on. In this, as in many other declarations, Craig's reasoning was not without its flaws.

The emphasis which the Symbolists laid upon *simplicity* was likewise dictated by the need for reform, and was just as open to error.

The Symbolists could point to a very obvious defect in the Naturalistic style. "Do not bring on the stage your carcass of reality," they might have said. "Do not exhibit there your vanloads of bricabrac, your butcher shops with real meat, your restaurant walls of cement and tile, your streets paved with real cobblestones. These collections of materials do not tell us the nature of the world; rather they confess your inability to define the nature of the world. If you really wish to give us an illusion of life, you must seize upon the essence of life. Forget the body; give us the soul."

And the Symbolists showed, on the stage, how the soul of environment is separated from its body. You do this by bringing forward only some significant detail of the whole environment, by using a part as a symbol for the whole.

A single cathedral pillar, as Erler proved, can convey the

* The English term "stage manager" corresponds to the American "director."

architecture of a huge basilica; it can even represent the Catholic Church. In Arthur Hopkins' production of RICHARD III (1919) the entire list of scenes as designed by Jones was represented by a section of the Tower of London. This central piece of scenery remained continuously on the stage, supplemented from time to time by various properties. In Reinhardt's production of MUCH ADO ABOUT NOTHING (1912) the Italian Baroque was re-created by means of crystal chandeliers and Venetian mirrors. The project of Norman Bel Geddes for KING LEAR concretized ancient Britain in the form of a dolmen. The period of the onset of the American economic crisis was summed up by Mordecai Gorelik, for Paul and Claire Sifton's *1931—*, in the steel doors of a warehouse. For the Vienna Burgtheater's production of ROMEO AND JULIET (1937) Emil Pirchan symbolized the era of the Pre-Renaissance by means of "columns exaggeratedly slender, pilasters supporting looped swags; veils, laces, the glowing color of blossoms. . . . The Franciscan peace of the frescos of Giotto broods over Lorenzo's cell and garden. . . . The hostile families wear strongly contrasting colors: black and gray for the Montague family; yellow for the Capulets; the Prince and his retainers are in red."

STYLIZATION

Heretofore we have been concerned with the term *style,* which we have used as a synonym for the technical form of staging. We have taken pains to show that style, in this sense, is the expression of theatre at different periods of the world's history. Thus the style of the Attic theatre, with its outdoor amphitheatre, its chorus and masked players, is different from the style of the Baroque, with its ballroom-auditoriums, its chamber-music, mincing actors and wing-and-backdrop settings.

We now come upon the term *Stylization,* used for the first time in the theatre by the Symbolists. How does Stylization differ from style?

The Symbolists contended that style was a matter not only of broad historic periods, but of each individual play. Every play must be regarded as a unique phenomenon, for which a unique style of production must be found. To stylize a play meant to invent for the play an individual style or idiom.

Naturalism was almost unaware of the fact that every play requires its own individual manner of statement. It did not even see clearly that different genres must be approached differently. The staging of a farce requires settings, costumes, properties and lighting altogether different in quality from those used in staging a tragedy. Comedy must be handled differently from farce, and in turn the various types of comedy or farce must be handled differently from each other. The farce of Mack Sennett is not the same as the farce of Beatrice Lillie. The comedy of George Kelly's THE TORCH BEARERS differs in quality from the comedy of George S. Kaufman and Moss Hart's THE MAN WHO CAME TO DINNER.

The task of stylizing a play is an important one for the designer. We have seen that the Symbolist designer works by selecting one aspect of an environment to symbolize the whole environment. The furrowed fields of the American midwest; the narrow, aspiring walls of a lighthouse; the massive strength of a pyramid; the glitter of the Baroque; the decrepit lines of the Art Nouveau —such qualities exist in certain environments. The qualities are there because history has put them there. To describe a particular environment the designer selects one of its qualities. He tries to choose the attribute which is most characteristic, most salient.

But now he takes another step. Having discovered the necessary quality, he is not content to let it symbolize the environment from which it came. Instead he turns it into a dominating idea, *a stylistic law* which governs the whole scenic production. The fact that the locale is a lighthouse is almost forgotten, while the lines of aspiration dominate the scene; the Baroque period of history recedes from attention, while the scene glitters with mirrors, tinsel and gilded curlicues.

For the Reinhardt production of THE MIRACLE in New York (1924), Norman Bel Geddes based some of his costume designs upon the forms of gold and jeweled reliquaries; others were derived from the quality of medieval hunting tapestries. For Granville-Barker's presentation of TWELFTH NIGHT (1912), Norman Wilkinson's designs had the style of Maxfield Parrish's illustrations for *Mother Goose*. Natalia Goncharova's trees and buildings in her design for COQ D'OR (1914) were painted in the style of Russian peasant toys. For the production of Katharine Cornell's ROMEO AND JULIET (1934), Jo Mielziner made his scene and costume designs in the stiff, quaint and oversimplified manner of Giotto's frescos.

But we have not yet reached the limits of Stylization. By degrees the use of the symbol becomes even more extreme. In the beginning the symbol was discovered as an historic attribute of a locale. Now it begins to dominate the environment arbitrarily, at the will of the designer. The metaphor becomes an entity in itself. The environment exists for the sake of the metaphor.

Thus we may find in the Gothic arch (if we fetch rather far) the symbol of a dull-pointed, murderous dagger; we may find, as Shakespeare chose to present it, that the background of Macbeth's career contained superhuman elements. On the other hand neither the Naturalists nor Shakespeare could have conceived the Stylization with which MACBETH was produced by Arthur Hopkins and Robert Edmond Jones in New York in 1921. Central feature of the Jones-Hopkins production was a trio of enormous masks far above a practically empty stage. The masks represented the masked spiritual influences which, according to Jones, dominate the characters of MACBETH. Even the environment was supposed to be "projected" by the supernatural powers denoted by the masks. The castle of Inverness, for example, resembled a group of arches leaning at an angle to the stage floor. At the height of Macbeth's career these arches or shields seemed to advance in military formation. Toward the end, however, there remained only a single arch, which slanted as though about to fall.

The use of stage levels similarly stylized for HENRY IV is described by Lee Mitchell:

> These vertical qualities of the main plot suggested the employment of levels. Broadly, we must begin with the King high up on his throne, bring Hotspur in the succeeding scenes gradually upward (reaching the height during the stirring speech to his troops), play the last scenes over an up-and-down maze of levels, concluding with the triumphant King on the highest possible point of the stage.

In these examples environment is no longer represented by a symbol. It would be more correct to say that environment is *reduced* to a symbol. Environment is no longer brought to the stage; instead it merely furnishes scenic elements, such as arches and levels, for a production.

THE STYLIZED SCRIPT

It must be admitted that stylized settings are not easy to explain to a layman. It is easier to explain what happens in the case of the stylized playscript. For Stylization is not limited to scenery and costumes. It takes place also in the Symbolist writings of the dramatists Ibsen, Strindberg, Dunsany, Synge, Yeats, Maeterlinck, D'Annunzio, Pirandello, Molnar, Ostrovsky, Evreinov, Andreyev, and the Yiddish Hassidists Hirschbein, Ansky, Gordin, Pinsky. Among American dramatists we may list Eugene O'Neill, Maxwell Anderson, Paul Green, Martin Flavin, Philip Barry, John Howard Lawson, Clifford Odets, Irwin Shaw, William Saroyan. Many of these playwrights alternate between Naturalistic and stylized writing. Philip Barry, for instance, writes drawing-room comedies, as in PARIS BOUND (1927), HOLIDAY (1928), THE PHILADELPHIA STORY (1939), along with Symbolist pieces such as WHITE WINGS (1926), HOTEL UNIVERSE (1930), HERE COME THE CLOWNS (1938). In these Symbolist works the objective causes of conflict are pushed into the background, while the conflict in the play takes place in terms of symbols.

It is interesting that such masters of dramatic Naturalism as Strindberg, Hauptmann and Ibsen were also the innovators of Symbolist dramaturgy. The man who wrote MADEMOISELLE JULIE also wrote THE DREAM PLAYS. The writer of THE WEAVERS also penned THE ASSUMPTION OF HANNELE, SCHLUCK AND JAU, and THE SUNKEN BELL. Ibsen, who could create the archetype of the Naturalistic play in A DOLL'S HOUSE (1879), also wrote the archetype of the Symbolist play in PEER GYNT (1867). Ostrovsky, one of the great forerunners of Naturalism, author of THE STORM, also wrote the delicate Symbolist fantasy of THE SNOW MAIDEN.

This paradox is explained in part by the limitations of Naturalism which we have already noted. It is not surprising that many of the most gifted Naturalistic playwrights turned to a different form when they wished to show life at its fullest. In this alternative technique, life, documented and certified, became only a *symbol* of some deeper significance which the dramatist wished to make clear. The Symbolist play is really an allegory in which the immediate dramatic action must be reinterpreted on a higher (or at least different) plane of philosophy or metaphysics. No great importance should be attached to the story in the foreground, which is a kind of charade permitting us to guess at a greater meaning.

For example the immediate story of Eugene O'Neill's MOURNING BECOMES ELECTRA (1931) is a record of crass jealousies and murders; but this crude melodrama is not at all the point of the ELECTRA trilogy. The author has interpolated moral values which far exceed the immediate issues of the story. Or, as Krutch puts it:

> Obviously O'Neill is moved by the conviction that this debasement of a story of passion and crime to the police court level is not inevitable; that there remains to us depths and dignities which could lift it into a different realm if they were properly exploited.

Moreover, in examining plays of this type we are almost always struck by the fact that their stories fail to make complete sense. Frequently there is no apparent logic in the events, while the characters remain improbable and even baffling. An interpretation becomes urgently necessary. The interpretation is sometimes given by the dramatist in veiled words; but often it is lacking altogether.

In Philip Barry's HERE COME THE CLOWNS all the stage characters were non-human. They were embodiments of good and evil. The action of the play was irrational also. It was a kind of "dumb show" symbolizing the struggle between God and Lucifer. In THE TIME OF YOUR LIFE (1940), William Saroyan used an identical technique. The bar-flies, prostitutes and other hangers-on of an alleged San Francisco saloon were not real people, and their behavior cannot be fully explained on the basis of human motives. They were in fact involved in a parable intended to prove the undisputed fact that good will is more attractive than malevolence. Fortunately for Saroyan his play had plot development and suspense—qualities too often lacking in scripts which do not adhere to the laws of logic.

The most important single reason for the failure of the Group Theatre's production of Clifford Odets' NIGHT MUSIC (1940) was the obscure, allegorical nature of the script. According to Harold Clurman, the director,

> The play stems from the basic sentiment that people nowadays are affected by a sense of insecurity . . . and whether they know it or not

they are in search of a home, of something real, secure, dependable in a slippery, shadowy, noisy and nervous world. . . . On the whole, the play tends to present this deeply serious pursuit in a light vein—wistful, tender, pathetic and sometimes in a combination of the delicately charming and farcical.

To some extent the director made this clear in the style of the production, but the story itself, the odd love affair of a wild Greek-American boy from Brockton, Mass. and a gentle girl from Philadelphia, never really found a plausible explanation.

John Howard Lawson, in spite of the fact that most of his own dramatic work is in parable style, has made a valuable analysis of PEER GYNT, the first important Symbolist play of the modern theatre:

. . . Peer goes out into the world, testing reality in a series of picaresque adventures. But what Peer seeks is "to be wafted dryshod down the stream of time, wholly, solely, as oneself." Like Goethe's Faust, Peer gains all the wonders of the world; he becomes rich and finances wars. Then he decides that "my business life is a finished chapter; my love-sports too are a cast-off garment." So it might be a good idea to "study past ages and time's voracity." He asks the Sphinx for its riddle; in answer Professor Begriffenfeldt, a German philosopher, pops up from behind the Sphinx; the professor is "an exceedingly gifted man; almost all that he says is beyond comprehension." Begriffenfeldt leads him to the club of wise men in Cairo, which turns out to be a madhouse. The professor whispers to Peer dramatically: "The Absolute Reason departed this life at eleven last night." The professor shows him the assembly of lunatics: "It's here, Sir, that one is oneself with a vengeance; oneself and nothing whatever besides. Each one shuts himself up in a barrel of self, in the self-fermentation he dives to the bottom—and with the self-bung he seals it hermetically, and seasons the staves in the well of self."

. . . But in the end Peer must face *himself;* on the barren heath there are voices around him: "We are thoughts; you should have thought us. . . . We should have soared up like clangorous voices. . . . We are a watchword; you should have proclaimed us. . . . We are songs; you should have sung us. . . . We are tears unshed forever." He meets the Button-Moulder with a box of tools and a casting-ladle; the Button-Moulder tells him he must be melted up, return to the casting-ladle, "be merged in the mass." Peer refuses to be deprived of himself, but the Moulder is amused: "Bless me, my dear Peer, there is surely no need to get so wrought up about trifles like this. Yourself you have never been at all."

. . . Peer returns to the home he had left and to the woman who has been waiting; he asks Solveig if she can tell him where he has been "with his destiny's seal on his brow?" She answers: "In my faith, in my hope, in my love." He clings to her as both mother and wife; he hides his face against her, as she sings, "The boy has been lying close to my heart all the life-day long. He is weary now!"

According to Lawson, "This is a new idea of escape; the woman-symbol typifies the life-force; man finds salvation at his own hearthstone." More explicitly the meaning of this elaborate fable seems to be that egoism is a sterile way of life.

But it is noteworthy that in most of his later plays Ibsen found it possible to make the same point, with even greater lucidity and force, in a Naturalistic technique. What advantage is there in presenting truths in an elaborately roundabout manner?

The answer, according to Maurice Maeterlinck, Symbolist playwright *par excellence,* is that all real significance is "inward." "The true tragic element of life begins only at the moment when so-called adventures, sorrows and dangers have disappeared. . . . Indeed when I go to the theatre I feel as though I were spending a few hours with my ancestors, who conceived life as something that was primitive, arid and brutal."

For Maeterlinck all the adventures and encounters of life are mere symbols for the invisible states of the soul. His assertion has impressed others, including Allardyce Nicoll, who wrote that "this, probably, is the most important piece of creative criticism on the drama that has appeared for the last century." And Leonid Andreyev, approaching the technical work of the stage in the same mood, asked, "Is action, in the sense of movements and visual achievements on the stage, necessary to the theatre?"

Such are the extreme lengths to which the supposedly moderate Symbolists were ready to go in disputing the here-and-now materialism of the Naturalists. Fortunately in playwriting as in scene design the Symbolists did not put their theories completely into practice. Else Andreyev might have put an end to theatre altogether.

REINHARDT

In actual practice Stylization led, not to the theatrical Nirvana of Andreyev but to the commercially successful productions

TOWARD SYNTHESIS

N. Y. Public Library Picture Collection

Wagner

A mystic gulf to divide the real from the ideal

From Die Meininger

Saxe-Meiningen

Not an accumulation but an art

Reinhardt

Intimacy at a circus

From Theatre Arts

Hopkins

Thought from emotion versus emotion from thought

From Theatre Arts

of Max Reinhardt, whose fame is known today to millions who never heard of Adolphe Appia, Max Littmann or Paul Fort.

The small, sturdy and amazingly energetic Max Reinhardt was born in Baden, near Vienna, in 1873. At nineteen he began playing old men's parts in the Salzburg Stadttheater. Here the Naturalistic director Otto Brahm found him. Brahm took him to Berlin, where between 1900 and 1901 he made a name for himself with a dramatic cabaret called Schall und Rauch, attached to the Kleines Theater. He was soon promoted to direct the Neues Theater, to which was added the Deutsches Theater in 1904 and the Kammerspielhaus in 1906. For three years beginning 1915 he managed the Volksbühne. In 1924 he was once more in command of the Deutsches Theater, along with the Kammerspielhaus and the new Komödie Theater. At the same time he took charge of the Josefstadt Theater in Vienna—by remote control, apparently—and conducted the Salzburg Festspielhaus each summer.

Beginning with his first production at the Kammerspiele, GHOSTS (1906), Reinhardt placed strong emphasis on the work of the scenic artist. As designed by Edward Munch, GHOSTS had a sensational last scene in which the hanging lamp over the table cast phantom-like shadows of mother and son on the walls.

The pictorial quality of another of Reinhardt's early productions, THE WINTER'S TALE (1906), has been praised by Josza Savits:

> Almost all the scenes in Sicily were played in a perfectly simple yet impressive decoration—a mere suggestion, without any disturbing detail, of a lofty hall in Bohemia. On the other hand, a delightful scene was designed, for all the world like a page from a child's picture book. The grass was bright green velvet, spangled with conventional flowers. A blossoming fruit-tree shadowed a toy cottage; and in the background some quaint masts and pennons showed the proximity of the sea. The whole effect was charmingly fantastic and admirably in keeping with the action of the scene.

At the Deutsches Theater, from 1904 on, Reinhardt proved himself a master of Stylization, which he afterwards developed to its utmost in his "circus" productions and his enormous spectacles at the Grosses Schauspielhaus, Berlin. It was his eclecticism which brought back to life, with popular approval, all the historic techniques of the theatre. The major dramatic styles of the

Attic stage, the Passion Play, the Japanese playhouses, served as Stylizations of OEDIPUS, EVERYMAN, THE MIRACLE, SUMURÛN.

These dramatic forms, which had once answered the needs of historic periods, now passed in review as the scenic motifs of Symbolist pageants. Reinhardt opened to Europe a coffer of *beaux jeux;* and the number of his stratagems was matched only by the number of his productions. In his hands the distinctly "precious" Symbolist movement took on an astonishing box-office appeal. He was the master showman of the new theatre. His methods continued their conquering march right on to the United States, where his name became a household word.

SYMBOLISM OVER BROADWAY

The departure of Belascoism from American stages was as swift as it was unexpected. At the close of the War in 1918 America was ready for a new era of sophisticated liberal theatre. The United States had come out of the War as a world power of the first rank. The holocaust had beggared Europe but inaugurated a "boom" period in America. A large, prospering, cosmopolitan-minded audience now came to the theatre, prepared for the most modern drama which the world had to offer.

Many crude "Victorian" taboos had been sloughed off in the interim, and life looked a little saner. Yet, in spite of ever-growing prosperity, there was an uneasy feeling that there might be a dark side to this bright picture. At any rate, few American dramatists were entirely optimistic, while many of the more serious ones were almost morbidly attuned to undertones of frustration and despair in the country at large. Eugene O'Neill, Paul Green, Sidney Howard, Elmer Rice, Arthur Richman, John Howard Lawson, consistently struck a note of pessimism. Of such writers only Lawson seemed buoyant enough to deal with the conflicts which the future had in store.

The others were satisfied to mirror their own thoughts in stage characters with a rather elaborate "inner life" but with few constructive ideas. As Krutch says, these dramatists

> . . . were compelled to be primarily playwrights in the sense that whatever relative interest or novelty or power they may have possessed was largely dependent upon their ability to carry on from the point where

the exponent of new ideas leaves off, upon their ability to vivify such ideas in terms of situation and character, to explore their meanings in terms of specific human lives.

The fact was that the post-War American audiences, essentially middle and upper class, were inclined to agree with Maeterlinck. Only the conflicts of the inner life seemed really worthy to be portrayed on the stage. The crass issues of the Naturalistic drama were outmoded, even in Belasco's Romanticized form. The theatre must look for eternal values in those more lofty regions where serenity merges with art. The problem facing the playwright was not to pose new questions but to restate accepted beliefs in the best possible technique, in the most interesting way. This is the background of the contention by Krutch that "a critical discussion of the recent American drama is most fruitful when it is a discussion, not in terms of 'ideas,' but in terms of imagination and literary form."

For the playwrights the exploration of technique in the Symbolist style was aided by the development, in the same period, of the doctrines of Sigmund Freud. A whole new psychoanalytic stage literature arose, and even scene design and acting were greatly affected. It became possible to speak of the "inferiority complex" of a dramatic hero, his "father complex" and "compensating mechanism." A red signal lamp portrayed sadism and a departing train symbolized the "father-imago." [3]

For the search for adequate form was not at all limited to the playwright but was true of all departments of the re-energized American theatre. Experiment was in the air. The dynamic, post-War experimental theatres of Russia and Germany were filling Europe with their clamor and finding an echo in America.

The public welcomed the new theatrical movement not only on Broadway but throughout the country, where hundreds of "little theatres" led an artistic rebellion against the stereotypes of the older Naturalistic theatres. These community and college playhouses devoted themselves ardently to the cause of the New Stagecraft. Individual groups became famous: the Wharf Theatre of Provincetown, Mass., which afterwards moved to New York and became the Provincetown Playhouse; the Neighborhood Playhouse and Washington Square Players, of New York; the Boston Toy Theatre; the Hedgerow Theatre of Rose Valley, Pa., under the direction of Jasper Deeter; the Chicago Little Theatre, managed by Maurice Brown; the Carolina Playmakers, of Chapel Hill, N.C., under Frederick A. Koch; the Dallas Little Theatre, Texas; the Cleveland Playhouse, directed by Frederic McConnell; the Pasadena Community Playhouse, organized by Gilmor Brown. In New York the Washington Square Players, managed with exceptional shrewdness, became a powerful, sophisticated

Drawing by Lucie R. Sayler

Wharf Theatre, Provincetown

From *The Provincetown,* by Helen Deutsch and Stella Hanau

commercial producing firm, the Theatre Guild, whose productions of George Bernard Shaw, O'Neill, Molnar and others carried the Symbolist attack to the front line of Broadway itself.

As in Europe, it was the designer even more than the playwright or director who led the advance toward the Symbolist form. Within a decade of Jones's designs for THE MAN WHO MARRIED A DUMB WIFE, a whole corps of new designers found places on Broadway: Aline Bernstein, Watson Barratt, Claude Bragdon, Henry Dreyfus, Norman Bel Geddes, Mordecai Gorelik, Frederick Jones, Jo Mielziner, Donald Oenslager, Rollo Peters, Livingston Platt, James Reynolds, Herman Rosse, Lee Simonson (famous scenic artist of the Theatre Guild), Raymond Sovey, Woodman Thompson, Cleon Throckmorton (designer of the early plays of

O'Neill), and John Wenger. These were followed in later years by many more: Boris Aronson, Herbert Andrews, Howard Bay, Stewart Chaney, Manuel Essman, Lawrence Goldwasser, Albert Johnson, Nat Karson, Arch Lauterer, Vincente Minelli, John Root, Irene Sharaff, Sointu Syrjala, Robert Van Rosen, Walter Walden.

These artists knew how to obtain a necessary unity of line and color. Their settings—to use a phrase much in vogue—"caught the spirit" of time and place with a few symbolic details. Their work had emotional atmosphere and was as rich in color and bare of detail as their predecessors' had been crude in color and cluttered with odds and ends. With comparatively simple means they obtained a degree of convincing illusion which their predecessors could not. And many of them could, and did, raise the symbol to the level of Stylization in the manner of Reinhardt.

In scene design, at least, Broadway cannot complain of lack of talent. American settings will bear comparison with those of any other theatre in the world. Some of its finest examples have that gleam of true poetry which so often flashes from the American stage. From a craft point of view, also, our designers have a command of ingenious, light-weight scene construction which is probably unrivaled.

These new designers were immediately joined by directors and actors for whom the object of production was no longer primarily to bring "life itself" to the stage, but to create style, atmosphere, pace, dramatic intensity. A few directors like George Abbott or George S. Kaufman have specialized in a breathless dramatic pace which gives an impression of dramatic rise even where there is little plot development to build on. Some, like Robert Lewis, Robert Milton or Benno Schneider, have an aptitude for style. Herman Shumlin is one of the few who have retained a strong interest in character. The main objective of the majority of the new directors, including Maurice Brown, Harold Clurman, Jed Harris, Arthur Hopkins, James Light, Guthrie McClintic, Worthington Minor, Philip Moeller, Lee Strasberg, Margaret Webster, has been the creation of dramatic mood and atmosphere. In this field the American theatre is especially indebted to Arthur Hopkins, James Light and Philip Moeller for their pioneer work.

In the province of acting the emphasis shifted almost imperceptibly away from the delineation of character. It moved toward a rather different thing: the projection of personalities. The actor became less interested in investigating character. The actor sought the "mood and atmosphere" of the personage, so to speak, rather than his motives. In the United States, Naturalistic acting had never been taken as seriously as it was by Antoine, Brahm or Stanislavsky. The Romantic style had persisted even through the Belasco period, and it needed only a slight retouching to serve the Symbolist era. Purified of its crass posing, its elaborate gestures held in restraint, the tradition of the Baroque-Romantic entered on a new lease of life. The reformed style became the standard of hundreds of gifted players, including George Abbott, Ethel, John and Lionel Barrymore, Katharine Cornell, Ina Claire, Eddie Dowling, Lynn Fontanne, Ruth Gordon, Helen Hayes, Walter Huston, Alfred Lunt, Burgess Meredith.

In Symbolist acting on the "legitimate" stage the personality of the actor could be felt distinctly back of the stage character, although not to the same degree as in the Baroque or Romantic periods. In film acting, on the other hand, the Baroque-Romantic ideal was still intact. It was even strongly emphasized. The rôle became a transparent screen for the projection of the "star"; the glamor of the film character was frankly that of the player himself.

In the twenties, representative actors, designers, directors and playwrights of the Symbolist style were already the acknowledged leaders of the American stage. By the thirties this stage belonged completely to the Symbolists; its future was in the hands of stage people who had begun their careers as rebels against the accepted theatre of their day. The new viewpoint was installed in all the posts of authority. The conquest was complete.

Another decade has passed. To all appearances the American theatre still remains firmly in the same hands. In this theatre the Symbolist point of view in production is no longer challenged. Even when a new, social-minded left wing came into existence on Broadway it disagreed only with the "message" of the Symbolist playwrights. It did not challenge the general mode of production, and did not even inquire into the accepted form of the script. Does this prove that Symbolism is the perfect stage method? Will Symbolism reign from now on for the rest of theatrical history?

There is no ground for such a belief.

Whether or not the axioms of the Symbolist method have been questioned in the United States, the years have already tarnished the luster of this form of theatre. Its assumptions no longer seem self-evident. New methods have arisen abroad, and even in the United States the time approaches when the worth of the Symbolist formula may have to be tested.

NOTES

1. The present account of the Munich Artists' Theatre production of FAUST is based largely on the following press reviews in Georg Fuchs' *Die Revolution des Theaters:*

William Ritter: *Chronique des Arts,* May 20, 1908.

Dr. Jos. Popp: *Kölnische Volkszeitung,* June 14, 1908.

Robert Brussel: *Figaro,* August 20, 1908.

2. See Kranich: *Das Bühnentechnik der Gegenwart.* Volume 1, Diagram p. 240.

3. "Liliom, literally translated from the Hungarian, means Lily, which is a synonym for a tough. . . .

"In the fourth scene we come upon an embankment, in the center a red and white signal flag. Here the conflict raging within Liliom is symbolized. The red deed to be committed and the white state of inertia he has been in during his unemployment. A red signal lamp gleams, portraying his sadism. In an earlier scene one of his admirers presents him with a red carnation and later we shall see red appearing in his punishment. Liliom and Ficsur watch the vanishing train. Liliom is fascinated by the snorting engine. "When you stand there at night it snorts past you and sits down," he remarks. . . .

"The engine which snorts and rattles and spits down and goes 'to Vienna and farther,' represents his father, who came and was responsible for Liliom and went away, spat down on Liliom and his cast-off mother. Then society took over the father's attitude and ever since has been spitting down and looking down on Liliom and then on their way. 'Swell people'—who 'read newspapers'—'and smoke cigars' and 'inhale the smoke.' . . . Here we get the beginning of Liliom's great feeling of inferiority; an inferiority which led to a compensating mechanism —his sadism. The speeding train symbolism is overdetermined. It also represents the possibility of flight from the situations which he could not face." (Stragnell: *A Psychopathological Study of Franz Molnar's Liliom*).

REFERENCES

Georg Fuchs: *Die Revolution des Theaters.* Georg Müller, Munich, 1909.

Fritz Erler. From Jacques Rouché: *L'Art théâtrale moderne.* Bloud & Gay, Paris, 1924.

Georg Fuchs. From Walter Grohmann: *Das Münchner Künstlertheater in der Bewegung der Szenen und Theaterreform.* Selbstverlag der Gesellschaft für Theatergeschichte, Berlin, 1935.

Robert Edmond Jones: *Art in the Theatre. Yale Review.* October, 1927.

Sheldon Cheney: *Stage Decoration.* The John Day Company, New York, 1928.

Léon Moussinac: *La décoration théâtrale.* F. Rieder & Cie., Paris, 1922.

Denis, Hildebrand, Quillard. From Moussinac: *Ibid.*

Antoine. From Waxman: *Antoine and the Théâtre-Libre.* Harvard University Press.

Constantin Stanislavsky: *My Life in Art.* Little, Brown & Company.

Arthur Hopkins: *How's Your Second Act?* Samuel French, New York, 1931.

Nikolai Evreinov. From Allardyce Nicoll: *The Development of the Theatre.* Harcourt, Brace & Company.

Alfred North Whitehead: *Science and the Modern World.* Macmillan.

Theodore Komisarjevsky and Lee Simonson: *Settings and Costumes of the Modern Stage.* The Studio Publications, New York, 1933.

Huntly Carter: *The Theatre of Max Reinhardt.* F. & C. Palmer, London, 1914.

Richard Wagner. From *The Art Life and Theories of Richard Wagner.* Selected by Edward L. Burlingame. Henry Holt & Company, New York, 1889.

Friedrich Kranich: *Das Bühnentechnik der Gegenwart.* Vol. 1. R. Oldenbourg, Munich and Berlin, 1929–1933.

Lee Simonson: *The Stage Is Set.* Harcourt, Brace & Company.

Appia's Directions for the Staging of Tristan and Isolde. Translated by Lee Simonson. *Theatre Workshop,* April–July, 1937.

Isadora Duncan: *My Life.* Garden City Publishing Company, Garden City, New York, 1927.

Erward Gordon Craig: *On the Art of the Theatre.* Browne's Bookstore, Chicago.

Emil Pirchan in *Die Stunde,* Vienna, December 4, 1936.

Lee Mitchell: *The Space Stage Defined. Theatre Arts,* July, 1936.

Joseph Wood Krutch: *The American Drama Since 1918.* Random House.

The Conductor Speaks. Harold Clurman in the New York *Times,* March 3, 1940.

John Howard Lawson: *The Theory and Technique of Playwriting.* G. P. Putnam's Sons.

Maurice Maeterlinck: *The Treasures of the Humble.* From Lawson: *Ibid.*
Allardyce Nicoll. From Lawson: *Ibid.*
Jasza Savits. From Huntly Carter: *Ibid.*
Gregory Stragnell: *A Psychopathological Study of Franz Molnar's Liliom. Psychoanalytic Review,* January, 1922.

6

THEATRE IS STYLE

THE DREAM OF BONAMY DOBRÉE

About a decade ago, at the height of the Symbolist movement in the drama, there appeared an engaging little book called *Timotheus, The Future of the Theatre.* Its author, Bonamy Dobrée, an English dramatic historian, speculated on the probable form of the theatre in the year 2100 A. D. *Timotheus* is a witty forecast, serious in its wit. Its prophecies continue to have a compelling interest for us.

The play which Dobrée attends in that future year is known as a *clutch,* meaning that all its verses, dialogue, sequences and settings have been created by one individual, the *fairfusser.* The theatre building, a "huge, hyperboloid pit," has a luminous domed ceiling. This ceiling is the stage. The theatre seats, resembling dentists' or barbers' chairs, are slanted far back with a rest for the head, enabling the audience to gaze comfortably upward at the ceiling-stage.

As the *clutch* begins this stage becomes cloudy with obscure human figures, some of gigantic size. The story or thesis of the play seems to be obscure also. The atmosphere of the theatre pulsates rhythmically, musical voices float everywhere. The playgoer sinks into a dreamlike trance suffused with a sort of perfume combined with overwhelming emotions. Thus entranced our playgoer runs a gamut of sensations from nightmare terror to triumphant joy. He remembers little more until he finds himself on the outer landing of the theatre, waiting for an air-taxi after the performance.

Later on our author is permitted to view the mechanism of this theatre. He learns something about the perfumes, which were "led along each row of seats by what I had taken for hot-water pipes." It seems that these scents were of certain emotion-producing gases which had been refined from the poison gas originally used in the World War of 1914–1918. It was thus possible to pipe to the spectators "gases which brought about sorrow, fear, joy, shame, the love of glory or of animals, and indeed any emotion, all without the least risk of harm. . . . The combined result was that almost any feeling, and any required degree of that feeling, could be produced by the fairfusser, and this the government found of the greatest use at times of political or European crisis, when wars were to be declared or averted, or any controversial measures passed."

Indeed, upon coming away from the performance already described, Dobrée found that the theatregoers had been led into a mood combined of generosity and self-sacrifice; with the result that large numbers of them flew straight from the theatre to subscribe for loans to the government, whose finances were in a critical state.

Some shrewd observation on staging exists in this little fantasy. Has its author followed the methods of Symbolism to their logical conclusion? The trancelike reverie, the nebulous images, the contemplative audience drugged into a sensual stupor, the whole performance consisting of propaganda under a cloak of art for art's sake—is this the future toward which our contemporary theatre is moving?

"BEAUTY IS TRUTH, TRUTH BEAUTY"

It was Richard Wagner who maintained that the production of opera requires a type of stage illusion in which all the factors of theatre are perfectly blended. Wagner asked for "a voluptuous mingling of all forms of art, under whose spell men would reach an emotional union." (Carter).

Wagner's thesis was strongly dominated by musical feeling. It referred to opera and not to drama; and Wagner's gifted follower, Adolphe Appia, on applying the idea, at first dealt only with opera. Later on Appia approached the plays of Shakespeare and Claudel with the technique of synthesis. Gordon Craig even designed Ibsen's ROSMERSHOLM (1906) on that basis. Finally Max

Reinhardt boldly applied to all fields of the theatre the principle of a harmonious, emotional synthesis of the arts of dramaturgy, acting, design and music.

However forward-looking Wagner may have been in his scenic theories, on stage his productions at best looked like those of Meiningen. If he had lived until the Symbolist period he would have seen the fruition of his hopes. He had asked for a unity of dramatic elements, an esthetic harmony of composition on the stage. This esthetic unity the Symbolists provided.

When Craig, reacting against the doctrine of the Naturalists, used the slogan "Not realism, but style," it was on the correct assumption that "life itself" cannot be brought directly into the theatre but must be recast and reinterpreted for stage use. The Symbolists attacked craft problems, a number of which they solved. While they were thus occupied, what became of the purpose of theatre itself?

The Symbolist method, like all other stage methods, is a way of dealing with life. But careful study reveals that it is a way of dealing rather hesitantly with life.

If we begin with Craig's phrase "Not realism, but style," we are struck by the fact that it contains an implied *contrast* between realism and dramatic style. Is it the merest accident that Craig used this particular combination of words? Is it the merest chance that he did not say, for example, "*Both* realism and style"?

Of course Gordon Craig in a way was simply hurling insults at the Naturalistic theatre. Extreme formulations are not unusual in the early days of any new theatre movement. Still it is significant that in practice no less than in theory Symbolism has not been conspicuously anxious to meet life head on.

Not that the Symbolists wished deliberately to shut their eyes to the chaos of life around the harmonious stage technique which they were building. They were undoubtedly troubled by the contrast. They wished to influence life, and they had their own views on how this was to be done. In Craig's opinion,

> The duty of the theatre (both as art and institution) is to awaken more calmness and more wisdom in mankind by the inspiration exhaling from its beauty.
>
> The artist must never lend his art, with its terrible power of appeal,

toward the destruction of that just Balance which it is the aim of mankind to create and preserve. (Dickinson).

Surely this is a just and noble aim? What better service can the theatre give than to awaken greater calm, greater wisdom? The need for both grows with each instant. In the fever-racked world of today that "just Balance" of which Craig speaks has become crucially necessary.

In the (comparatively) idyllic days before the first World War it was much easier to remain calm. Life and the stage could both be viewed with a tranquil mind. In 1910 the aims of Reinhardt in the theatre were capable of being described in exalted terms:

> . . . the theatre must be liberated and given an artistic, noble and pure purpose. This art form will not have a schematic kind of organization: it will be built up so as to address itself to the senses of the spectator, without tiring him. . . . We must study the grand forms and contours which envelop everything, the flowing line of the pre-Raphaelites; creations of ornament, contrasts of light and shadow, brightness of color. . . . (Rouché).

This was four years before the guns began to speak on the western front. The theatre had set itself a great ideal. Would the ideal be maintained in practice? How would it measure up to its task? Would Reinhardt, for instance, be greeted in later years with the same sense of exaltation?

In 1929 the German critic Ihering saw Reinhardt in a quite different light:

> When Max Reinhardt, at the beginning of the century, returned to the classics, what prospects were before us? Did Reinhardt offer us a new relation to the souls of these classics? Was the basis of drama to be opened to discussion? Reinhardt and his period offered only a new relation to the mechanics of production.
>
> . . . Otto Brahm had an insight into the content of drama; he tried to express it in the form of Naturalism. There his attempt ended; he did not go on to a critical analysis of the classics. Max Reinhardt in his turn looked upon this classic legacy with the eyes of a Romantic actor of the nineties. He saw the colors, the tonalities, the atmosphere. He fed himself full on sound effects, nuances, artistic delicacies. (*Reinhardt, Jessner, Piscator*).

"THE PROUD FRAGILITY OF DREAMS"

It was Reinhardt who taught the Symbolist theatre. He taught it not so much style as that more peculiar thing, Stylization. How to turn THE MIRACLE into a Passion play; how to translate THE WINTER'S TALE into a child's picture book. In the American theatre, especially, he found an apt pupil. But at the very time when Reinhardt Stylization was leaving its impression on the United States it was losing ground at home.

For the Naturalists the theatre was not "beauty." For the Symbolists it is. This "gilding of the theatre," as Ihering has phrased it, precipitated an issue in Germany after the first World War, with the celebrated director as its center.

The showmanship of Reinhardt had left no dramatic medium untouched, from circus arenas and revolving stages to luxurious playhouses and the bare boards of the Elizabethan platform. It was he who proved that, properly beautified, even the classics of drama could attract large metropolitan audiences. It was something, after all, to show that Goethe, Schiller, Shakespeare and Molière were people of dramatic taste, wit and color! Everyone was pleased except those recalcitrants for whom the classics still had meaning as a guide to life.

American Symbolists have not had to feel the irony of critics like Alfred Kerr of the *Berliner Tageblatt* or Herbert Ihering of the *Berliner Börsenkurier*. These middle class reviewers, for whom the classics were a sacred trust, were roused to harsh words over some of the failings of Symbolism. Reinhardt, as leader of the German Symbolists, was Ihering's *bête noir*. The production of OEDIPUS which made so great a stir elsewhere only caused this critic to note that "when Reinhardt's chorus let loose, several housemaids fainted."

But of course it was not at Reinhardt alone that such shafts were directed. Ihering was deeply wounded by the superficial Stylizations which became the mode. Karlheinz Martin's production of GÖTZ VON BERLICHINGEN seemed to him "a Wild West show." What reason had the director Fritz Hall to dress FAUST in a dinner jacket and silk hat? What valid excuse had the director Hans Hilpert to clothe THE MERRY WIVES OF WINDSOR in Biedermeyer costume? What justified the banality of "witty" settings in Karl Walser's direction of AS YOU LIKE IT? Why did the Berlin production of O'Neill's THE EMPEROR JONES become nothing more than an exercise in stage lighting?

Again and again Ihering returned to the charge against Stylization. "What is this costume and perruque folderol which Jessner unpacked from the moth closet?" he asked after seeing this director's staging of Goethe's EGMONT (1928). When Karlheinz Martin put on Grillparzer's MEDEA (1923), the terror of the play was characterized as "more in the pose (Medea with the dagger), in the crashing scenery (the burning of the palace), than in the passion of the poetic image." The stylized dramatic writings of Toller and Andreyev were received just as coldly: "The drama of HINCKEMANN, who is deprived of his sex, is as dishonest as the drama of SCHWEIGER, who is deprived of moral certainty. Crudeness takes the place of strength, mechanical construction replaces suspense . . ." Of HE WHO GETS SLAPPED he observed, "Shakespeare never made his fools the central figures of drama. He wrote HAMLET. Andreyev wrote something that might properly be called 'THE PRINCE AS COURT FOOL.'" (*Aktuelle Dramaturgie*).

"Es gab keine Tradition, nur Verbrauch," he declared, in summary. Nothing was added to the creative tradition of the past; on the contrary, the achievements of the past were consumed, the tradition was used up.

It would be a mistake to look upon these comments as the jibes of some morose, irresponsible critic. They represented the views of a substantial, conservative press. We Americans find criticism like Ihering's too savage. On the other hand we did not lose a million and a half dead in the World War, we did not have to listen to machine guns spitting out civil war in our streets.

Once the Symbolist theatre had issued its manifestoes against Naturalism. Now Symbolism was rudely challenged in its turn. There was an agony of spirit in Germany which spared nothing that was faulty in Symbolist practice. Such middle class liberals as Ihering and Kerr grew up in a spirit of reverence for the great dramatic works of the past. Schiller, Goethe, Shakespeare, were mountain peaks of ordered thought; and this kind of thought was disappearing from sight as chaos engulfed the German Republic. The German middle class audience, for whom thoughtful drama was not only a necessity but a passion, went to see serious plays even in the darkest meatless and heatless days. They went there looking for enlightenment. In exchange for its hard-earned money this public all too often received an *Ersatz* of bright theatrical ideas—gauze sprinkled with tinsel.

Perhaps in many cases it was really a rare and delicate fabric that was spread before the audience in those days. There must have been times when it was truly a fabric woven of star dust, "the loftiest expression of the eternal in man." (Appia). Its fragility was "the proud fragility of dreams." (Yeats). But life was asking savage questions that required immediate answers. The dream of beauty was neither an immediate nor informative reply. Life might find it hard to pry open the hermetically sealed doors of the Symbolist theatre, but it had no difficulty in pounding its hammer blows on the mortal men and women who made up theatre audiences. . . . Under such pressure the time comes when theatre customers turn regretfully away, leaving the dream-fabrics on the counter.

It cannot be denied that symbolism is a legitimate way of conveying ideas. Our thought-processes are carried on by its means; it is the very substance of thought. In this respect Gordon Craig was perfectly correct when he wrote that "it is only by means of symbols that life becomes possible for us":

> The letters of the alphabet are symbols, used daily by sociable races. The numerals are symbols, and chemistry and mathematics employ them. All the coins of the world are symbols, and business men rely upon them. The crown and the sceptre of the kings and the tiara of the popes are symbols. The work of poets and painters, of architects and sculptors, are full of symbolism: Chinese, Egyptian, Greek, Roman, and the modern artists since the time of Constantine have understood and valued the symbol. Music only became intelligent through the employment of symbols, and is symbolic in its very essence. All forms of salutation and leave-taking are symbolic and employ symbols, and the last act of affection rendered to the dead is to erect a symbol over them.
>
> I think there is no one who should quarrel with Symbolism—nor fear it.

But granted that this is so, we are only at the beginning of a problem. Decidedly there can be questions over the relevance, clarity, truth and artistic caliber of the symbols which we choose.

We are under the necessity for asking such questions about

the symbols which Craig himself likes to use: the grandeur (of a particular sort) which he applies to his scene designs; the huge but nebulous architecture which reduces players to the size of insects; the immense sweep of light and shadow which nevertheless does not reveal the form of environment.

MIST

Since the question of the stage setting occupies so large a part of Symbolist thought, we may ask: what did the Symbolist designers do with the effect of environment upon human character?

The word environment is rarely met with in the vocabularies of Edward Gordon Craig, Adolphe Appia or any of the other designers, directors and theorists of the Symbolist school. Their concern was not with environment but with the stage setting. They evolved the plastic stage, relating actor to setting.

They did not, however, relate character to environment. They saw the actor as a dynamic figure related to a static, sculptural background. For them the setting was essentially static—a neutral surrounding in which the human figure moved with entire free will. They looked in the setting not for the stubbornness of things but for the immaterial, disembodied spirit of things. Of all the functions of environment little remained but its "psychology," —that is to say, its supposed emotional effect upon the beholder.

Craig has revealed in detail how he works as a designer:

> Come now, we take MACBETH. We know the play well. In what kind of place is that play laid? How does it look, first of all to our mind's eye, secondly to our eye?
>
> I see two things. I see a lofty and steep rock, and I see the moist cloud which envelops the head of this rock. That is to say, a place for fierce and warlike men to inhabit, a place for phantoms to nest in. Ultimately this moisture will destroy the rock; ultimately these spirits will destroy the men. . . .
>
> But you ask me what form this rock shall take and what colour? What are the lines which are the lofty lines, and which are to be seen in any lofty cliff? Go to them, glance but a moment at them; now quickly set them down on your paper; *the lines and their direction,* never mind the cliff. . . .
>
> You ask about the colours? What are the colours that Shakespeare has indicated for us? Do not first look at Nature, but look in the play

of the poet. Two; one for the rock, the man; one for the mist, the spirit. Now, quickly, take and accept this statement from me. Touch not a single other colour, but only these two colours through your whole progress of designing your scene and your costumes, yet forget not that each colour contains many variations. If you are timid for a moment and mistrust yourself or what I tell, when the scene is finished you will not see with your eye the effect you have seen with your mind's eye. . . .

It is this lack of courage, lack of faith in the value which lies in limitation and in proportion which is the undoing of all the good ideas which are born in the minds of the scene designers. They wish to make twenty statements at once. They wish to tell us not only of that lofty crag and the mist which clings to it; they wish to tell you of the moss of the Highlands and of the particular rain which descends in the month of August. They cannot resist showing that they know the form of the ferns of Scotland, and that their archaeological research has been thorough in all matters relating to the castles of Glamis and Cawdor. And so in their attempt to tell us these many facts, they tell us nothing; all is confusion:

> Most sacrilegious murder hath broke ope
> The Lord's anointed temple, and stole thence
> The life o' the building.
>
> (*On the Art of the Theatre*).

What is visible to the eye is not important; one must give it only a momentary glance. What is important are the values seen by the inner eye: rock and mist, and the rock is seen so vaguely that it is just as nebulous as the mist. We gather that Craig feels the rock and the mist are important because they are timeless, eternal. How important are they, in fact, to the story of MACBETH? In 1936 the American Federal Theatre produced a so-called Negro MACBETH whose locale was made, quite arbitrarily, an island in the West Indies. It cannot be said that this was a first-class inspiration, but the story of MACBETH still held, even in the absence of the mist and the rock.

Indeed, Craig may almost be accused of temporizing with his mist and his rock. It is possible to reduce environment to something even vaguer. In the Jones-Hopkins production of MACBETH in 1921 the structure of a feudal society, the environment which precipitated the tragedy, becomes a trio of baleful masks radiating a mystic light upon the predestined murderer of Banquo. The fortress-architecture of a medieval Scottish castle is turned into a crazily-slanted arch. These scenic properties, it is felt, hold all that is necessary to show of the environment of the tragedy. They are its essence, its very soul. In order for us to understand fully the background of MACBETH, the background must be obliterated; the environment must be disembodied, its physical presence must not impinge on the stage characters.

Jones remains to this day the most uncompromising of the American Symbolist designers. He has retained consistently the same attitude as Craig, for whom Hamlet is "a soul placed in a cold and infinite space," rather than a living and breathing prince caught in the meshes of palace intrigue.

Why is it that the Symbolist designers, searching for the essence of an environment, so often discover that it is not something clear, bright, sharply defined or very detailed, but rather something simple, semi-invisible, shadowy and amorphous, a thing of gauze and muted spotlights?

> Ship's rigging, ragged artificial flowers and painted masonry, are only the earthbound relics of former productions of this opera [TRISTAN AND ISOLDE]. The scenes themselves are in the past and timeless: the deck of Tristan's ship, Mark's castle in Cornwall and Tristan's ancient manor in Brittany. They were once definite places, but in the theatre they must be only "visible manifestations" of Wagner's dramatic music. Let these scenes be bounded by high folds of transparent gauze, and as each act begins, let gauze curtains draw off to reveal some actual indication of scene. (Donald Oenslager: *Scenery Then and Now*).

When Adolphe Appia wished to design a forest as a stage setting it was not the forest as environment that was his first thought. For him the forest was "atmosphere"—not the trees and the leaves, but a thought in the mind. "We must no longer try to create the illusion of a forest, but instead the illusion of a man in the atmosphere of a forest." For the famous American Symbolist designer, Donald Oenslager, the artist's first task is not to explain environment but to create visions on the stage. "The twentieth century stage designer can paint with light; invention has made him a fellow of infinite jest, of most excellent fancy able, like Prospero, to create in a moment the baseless fabric of a vision."

In May 1937 the German designer Traugott Müller, working in Nazi Berlin with Jürgen Fehling (who once directed the left-wing production MASSE MENSCH), hit an all-time record in the use of gauze and mist. Craig may have dreamt of "a cold and infinite space" in which to set HAMLET, but it was Müller who managed, in the case of RICHARD III, to dissolve environment completely in actual practice.

> Significant and notable is the stationary set, designed by Traugott Müller . . . a boxed-in scene of transparent milky material, of which the sides, top and floor converge toward the 120-foot-deep back. Entrances and exits are by way of barely noticeable slits and two subterranean stairs in the extreme rear. The ceiling is crossed by heavy beams, sparingly draped in black rope over which, for outdoor scenes, threatening clouds are lowered. That and a few props, such as stones, bars, fences, chairs, a severe throne, etc., indicate the change of scenery, together with unusually effective network scrims for interiors, often three in succession, with their divergent openings, so as to make all entrances angular, besides being visible from afar.

What is it that makes an environment live, what makes it a dramatic factor in the lives of human beings? What has given it its special form, color, texture and weight? How does it operate? Is it the result of handicraft labor, or has it been manufactured by machines? Or is it merely untouched raw material? Has it a simple or complex structure? Can it be understood with the naked eye, or are special instruments like the microscope or the X-ray necessary?

None of these questions, fundamentally, interest the Symbolist designer. His purpose, avowed or implicit, is to withdraw attention from the objective qualities of environment. Instead he presents it in terms of a vague and attenuated symbol. How does he arrive at this symbol? Chiefly by trusting his own intuition. The true artist, he feels, understands environment instinctively. His intuition tells him when he has chosen a valid symbol. The symbol must be true because he is inwardly convinced that it is true.

But it can be shown that a sense of inner conviction is no proof of the truth of that conviction. The faith of Mohammed, held fervently by millions of people, strikes non-Mohammedans as a grievous error in judgment. Many of the beliefs to which we were utterly devoted at fourteen seem to us rather puerile at forty. In the same way beliefs which we once thought extremely definite often strike us later on as having been quite vague after all.

Lacking comparison with reality, how can we tell which of our beliefs are sound and which are foolish? Relying only on an inner sense of certainty, can we really tell which of our ideas are noble, which are trivial?

Many of the Symbolist "revelations" turn out to be nothing more than restatements of old theatrical clichés. Others may be based on pseudo-scientific notions, stale adages, even crude superstitions. This is an ever-present danger in the Symbolist method of work. That danger becomes even more evident if we examine Symbolist playscripts.

THE IRRELEVANT SYMBOL

It is safe to prophesy that next season's plays will include at least one drama based on the idea of reincarnation. This problem, which was a rather urgent one in the period of Tut-Ankh-Amen (14th century B. C.), turns up regularly on Broadway in plays which vary in talent from THE LADDER to I HAVE BEEN HERE BEFORE. Such plays attempt to revive an ancient conjecture for which there happens to be no basis in fact. Whether the attempt is made with the finesse of a paving machine as in THE LADDER (1926) or in well-constructed Romantic style as in BERKELEY SQUARE (1928), it will not be taken too seriously by the more sophisticated public or the more responsible reviewers.

Yet in the course of almost any theatre season we are asked to take quite seriously many conjectures which are just as stale. All too often such clichés become the backbone of Symbolist dramas, sometimes for no better reason than that the dramatists have not troubled to look for any fresh idea.

Why, after all, should playwrights exert themselves to arrive at a mature statement? It is not expected of them. Their first duty, by current standards of criticism, is not to sponsor constructive ideas, but to essay their craftsmanship upon no matter what ideas, "to vivify such ideas in terms of situation and character, to explore their meanings in specific human lives," as Krutch says. From this point of view it hardly seems to matter whether the idea with which the playwright begins is as dead as King Tut. It is only necessary that he "explore" it, taking its truth for granted.

If it is all right to proceed from stale ideas, need it astonish us to learn that some of the ideas which pass muster in our theatre are very stale indeed? Or that many of them have little basis in common sense?

Most of the current dramatic output falls into three main idea-patterns, each as feeble as the next. The notion that Love Solves All Difficulties amounts to a Broadway and Hollywood *deus ex machina;* it serves almost every dramatist from Maxwell Anderson to the most obscure writer of screen stories. The notion that Self-denial Solves All Difficulties runs it a close second. Third, a more recent contribution from the left, is the notion that Class Consciousness is quite enough, in itself, to Solve All Difficulties. The truth is, of course, that these supposed solutions solve little, and are usually the beginning of even greater difficulties.

Yet pretentious dramas are reared on these frail foundations. Critics scent out an unutterable grandeur, sometimes, in plays whose quality of effective thinking matches that of an average schoolchild. By way of exception Krutch has made a devastating onslaught on the weakness of thought in the writing of Philip Barry, using HOTEL UNIVERSE as an example:

> Every incident loses its outlines because every incident is swathed in layer after layer of fuzzy verbiage about Life, Death, the Great Beyond, and the fact (announced by a mysterious white cock given to apparently untimely crowings) that "somewhere it is always dawn." The dramatis personae are supposed to represent the intellectual as well as the social élite, but they indulge in the most appalling mystical chitchat and are responsible for a stream of discourse upon the surface of which float fragments of mangled Einstein together with all sorts of spongy, half-digested or completely indigestible bits which seem to be the remains of a meal formerly made upon some of the more repulsive varieties of New Thought. Such ideas pass current in Greenwich Village salons when dusk and cocktails have combined to elevate the spirits and depress the judgment, but they are not taken seriously by captains of finance and other authentic bigwigs, unless the upper classes have degenerated further than even the most earnest satirists maintain.

Offhand it is a little hard to explain why Krutch is so ready to give Philip Barry a spanking while he remains impressed at the intellectual clarity of Eugene O'Neill and S. N. Behrman. By the same rather extreme standard Behrman also elevates the spirit and depresses the judgment; while of O'Neill it might even be said that he sometimes depresses both the spirit and the judgment.

It is only fair to point out that a dramatist may think more clearly in terms of his characters and situations than in terms of his formal philosophy. Fortunately for both dramatist and public, this happens quite often. But why should confused thinking be encouraged? Especially when it has the most harmful consequences in practice? Does unclear thought help a dramatist to grow to his full stature? Isn't it more likely that it mars and stultifies the work of dramatists who are otherwise unusually talented?

It is very possible that "third-act trouble," the ailment which afflicts so many playwrights of the Symbolist school, is traceable to the Symbolist inability, or unwillingness, to follow out the implications of the problem set forth in the preceding acts. The action ceases while the dramatist goes on "exploring." In the third act he is generally found exploring the cloudy regions of metaphysics while his characters remain far below in the landscape where we originally met them.

This phenomenon has been noted by John Howard Lawson, who describes it as a tendency to substitute *recognition* for *action*. That is to say, the Symbolist playwright is inclined to finish the play at the moment when his protagonist recognizes more or less fully the issues with which he is faced. After that, real plot development stops.

For example, in Sidney Howard's THEY KNEW WHAT THEY WANTED (1924), Joe is torn between love for Amy and loyalty to Amy's husband, Tony. The climax is reached when Amy becomes pregnant with Joe's child. From this point on the play hurries to a conclusion in which Joe sacrifices his own happiness to the comparative contentment of Amy and Tony. This conclusion makes a hash out of the believable characters whom Sidney Howard had brought to life. The same kind of arbitrary conclusion, in the form of abnegation, occurs in the example given by Lawson from Sherwood's THE PETRIFIED FOREST (1935). The frustrated intellectual, Squier, whose life is supposedly finished, falls in love with Gabby; but this love gives him only the "strength" to commit suicide.

To follow out the full consequences of their own plots would require more objectivity on the part of both dramatists. Instead they merely *repeated* the pattern which they had laid down, intensifying the situation but not developing the theme. Lawson observes:

> Ibsen avoided preparation, beginning his plays at a crisis, illuminating the past in the course of the action. This retrospective method has now been carried to a further extreme; the crisis is diluted, and the backward looking or expository material is emphasized. . . . The modern play often consists of elaborate preparation for a crisis which fails to take place.

The hesitation, or inability, of certain American playwrights to deal fully with life has been further shown by Eleanor Flexner. In Maxwell Anderson's SATURDAY'S CHILDREN a young wife, Bobby Halevy, is revolted by the dullness of a poor middle class marriage, with its pettiness and its nagging. She runs away to a boarding house, where she rediscovers romance when her husband steals in to visit her. A remarkably anti-climactic finish to a real problem!

In the same author's WINTERSET the boy Mio, who sets out to avenge his father, is eloquently presented, only to be completely erased when Mio conceives a self-sacrificing love for the sister of the man who had murdered his father.

Miss Flexner writes, apropos of another of Anderson's plays:

> Two things strike us in THE MASQUE OF KINGS. One is Anderson's fondness for introducing love into his plots as a crucially decisive factor. With incurable romanticism, love—disillusioned or betrayed or triumphant—tips the scales in NIGHT OVER TAOS, in VALLEY FORGE, in WINTERSET, and in THE MASQUE OF KINGS. That is to say, it alters what would otherwise be the normal development of the plot.

There are occasions when a dramatic pattern is not only irrelevant to its theme but becomes an elaborate structure which quite overshadows the theme. The baffling quality of Saroyan's THE TIME OF YOUR LIFE results from a mechanism of this kind. In the opinion of Richard Watts, critic of the New York *Herald-Tribune* (January 6, 1940), "Mr. Saroyan's love for the human races gives his play a curious sweetness, while his hearty gift for laughter provides it with a saving saltiness." In actual structure the play's "love for the human race" is more apparent than real, for the human race is not involved in the doings of THE TIME OF YOUR LIFE. Its characters are wraiths, resurrected and sentimentalized stage types from the Commedia dell' Arte or from bygone American burlesque shows. They carry on fascinating vaudeville turns instead of human activities.

THE TIME OF YOUR LIFE is contrived, however, in a way to make us think its gossamer people must be taken seriously; we must find their erratic movements somehow representative of our own real lives. The play's overtones are also meant to be serious: there are allusions to crime, prostitution, vice-squads, strikes, intolerance, depravity, and all the heartbreaks which fall to the lot of the average citizen. After magically eluding every issue which these topics might be expected to bring up, the dramatist manages to imply a vague moral verdict—quite as if he had actually set up and investigated a dramatic conflict.

Equally interesting structurally is Robert Sherwood's THERE SHALL BE NO NIGHT (1940). Although this play takes up the complex political issues of the Soviet invasion of Finland, it begins with a psychological premise. This premise is set forth in the radio speech of Dr. Valkonen, pictured by the dramatist as just having been awarded the Nobel prize. Dr. Valkonen declares that wars are the result of an insanity which is spreading among the human race; that wars will cease only when a new light dawns in the minds of men. But this new consciousness can be won only through pain.

Had the playwright gone on seriously to develop the theme that wars are caused by psychology, he would have had to defend that viewpoint against the testimony of anthropology, psychopathology, economic science and plain history. It would have been necessary, as well, to prove that "there is no coming to consciousness without pain,"—a statement for which Jung is quoted as authority. (Jung notwithstanding, there seems to be no basis for the rather sadistic idea that consciousness is necessarily painful. It is a normal process which can be painful, painless or joyous, depending on circumstances.) All of this, however, is not developed but assumed.

Even so, the playwright might be permitted this assumption if it afterwards resulted in an explanation of the "new consciousness," which Dr. Valkonen presumably finds when he joins the war. But that, too, is left obscure. If Sherwood had in mind any revelation other than the familiar slogan of a "war to end wars," it remains unstated. Instead the play in its main outlines falls into desultory, pseudo-scientific talk, while the action itself becomes an agitational appeal to meet force with force. To the extent that THERE SHALL BE NO NIGHT is propagandist, it can only be accepted or rejected, according to the emotional convictions of the playgoer. To the extent that it is meant to be an inquiry into the ills of the modern world, it does not make the revelation which Dr. Valkonen's speech led us to expect.

It may be taken for granted that Sherwood's play is animated by the highest motives, whether or not it proves that Soviet Russia is a cat's-paw for Hitler Germany. But the play would have had more dramatic caliber if its author had relied less on an abstract pattern of good versus evil and more on the specific events of the Finnish tragedy. He might, for example, have found more drama in the story of Finland itself. In his opening act he has tied up that country so closely with the U.S. through intermarriage that one almost expects to find it on a road map between Illinois and Wisconsin. Actually Finland has had a typically somber European history of a kind that—let us fervently hope—our own country may be spared.

O'NEILL

The case of Eugene O'Neill, greatest of the American Symbolist playwrights, is even more striking, all the more since O'Neill has been an innovator scenically as well as in his writings. O'Neill's whole career has been built on the conception that tragedy is due to an inherited weakness of the will. This "weakness of the will" is not explained further, but is looked upon as a kind of entity in itself, the modern equivalent of the ancient Greek Fate. O'Neill is avowedly in debt to the Attic "explanation" of tragedy: "The Greek dream in tragedy is the noblest ever!" (Quinn).

In our own age, in which millions of men and their families are thrown into tragic situations because of unemployment, it would seem that the conception "weakness of the will" requires a more careful analysis than this great humanitarian playwright has ever given it. But in fact many students of O'Neill have understood that his ability to create character and situation in general far transcends the ready-made pattern of his philosophy.

At the same time it is important to notice that this fault in O'Neill's work is a very real fault, one which limits and distorts his genius as a dramatist.

In ANNA CHRISTIE (1920), Greek Fate enters disguised as "old davil sea," which is made to blame for the troubles of the stage characters. Heijermans in a like situation in THE GOOD HOPE puts the blame on the unprincipled owners of ships. Miss Flexner has shown that O'Neill always blames some unknown, sinister Fate rather than some more corporeal agency (which he does not even consider).

This tendency is still more noticeable in the GLENCAIRN plays. In THE LONG VOYAGE HOME (1921), just as the sailor Swede is about to sail for home he is shanghaied aboard a ship bound for ports beyond the Cape of Good Hope. We are asked to conclude that this is the work of an ironic and capricious Fate rather than the result of a well-organized predatory racket. The squalor of sailors' lives is presumed to be an eternal and inevitable phenomenon, and sailors themselves are represented as extremely simple-minded. The environment and the characters in this play are both falsified, unwittingly of course, to make them fit the dramatist's arbitrary pattern.

Was O'Neill justified in taking this peculiar sort of "poetic license"? For some people at least, Heijermans' sober and unromantic play, which incidentally led to reforms in the Dutch maritime laws, remains to this day fully as dramatic, moving and *poetic* as any of the sea plays of O'Neill.

Fate dominates the story of THE EMPEROR JONES (1920), in which the Negro monarch of a West Indian island is hounded to death by his own fears. Most of the action is purely retrospective, and the impressive self-confidence of Jones is undermined by racial memories and a bad personal conscience. It has not generally been noticed that the Jones of the opening scene is incompatible with the Jones of the later scenes. There is no attempt to prove through analysis of character that a bold and ruthless man can be changed overnight into a craven one. Instead we are shown flashbacks of Negro history and of the life of Jones himself; we are told that each time these thoughts occur to Jones they haunt his mind and break down his will. We are not told *why* Jones, unlike other hardened adventurers, is troubled by such thoughts.

There is a tom-tom accompaniment to the play. In the original production by the Provincetown Players this sound, which began at the beat of the normal human heart, rose in tempo and volume "until it filled the tiny Provincetown theatre with an ocean of clamorous sound and lifted the hearers out of their seats." (Flexner). Sound has a powerful affective value in the theatre. In this case it helped greatly to distract attention from a number of flaws in the script, including the alleged psychology of "racial memories," a conjecture by Jung which has so far not been established by the valid methods of science.

The pattern of JONES is repeated in THE HAIRY APE (1922), with the powerful Yank going to pieces just as illogically. The poor thinking of the dramatist is again camouflaged by means of an assault on the senses of the spectator. In this case the most effective scene is that of the stokehole, with its noise, glaring furnaces, frightful heat and piercing whistles. The tough stoker, Yank, is also undermined—not by racial memories—but by the contempt and loathing of a society woman, Mildred. Why the crude and brutal Yank should be more sensitive to snobbery than a college junior is not explained. The whole action is transferred to a plane of Symbolist writing in which the dramatist imposes any pattern he likes.

Miss Flexner asks, "Just what does all this mean? Symbolism, even fantasy, must have some sort of logic. What is the significance of Yank's spiritual collapse because of a petty insult? Why do the I.W.W. reject him? Why the insane episode in the Zoo?"

The answer is that the dramatist had no clear statement to make. He had only a vivid emotion. He created pictures corresponding to his subjective state, trusting to his own feeling of inner certainty that they would make sense. If they do not make sense to Miss Flexner, so much the worse for Miss Flexner! Krutch also realizes this when he considers O'Neill's intentions:

> It seems plain . . . that the history of his development is the history of a persistent, sometimes fumbling attempt to objectify his emotions, accompanied by a persistent hope that this or that opening

suggested by some current intellectual fashion would provide the opportunity for which he felt the need.

With the Fifth Avenue scene of THE HAIRY APE begins O'Neill's preoccupation with masks in the drama. The mask finds a conspicuous place in the story of THE GREAT GOD BROWN (1926). O'Neill explains:

> Brown has always envied the creative force in Dion which he himself lacks. When he steals Dion's mask of Mephistopheles he thinks he is gaining the power to live creatively while in reality he is only stealing that creative power made self-destructive by complete frustration. This devil of mocking doubt makes short work of him. It enters him, rending him apart, torturing him and transfiguring him until he is even forced to wear a mask of his success, William A. Brown, before the world, as well as Dion's mask toward life and children. . . . Dion's mask of Pan which he puts on as a boy is not only a defense against the world for the super-sensitive painter-poet underneath it but also an integral part of his character as the artist. The world is not only blind to the man beneath it but also sneers at and condemns the Pan-mask it sees.

A close study of this play, which contrasts the self-torturing, creative temperament with the uncreative, placid one, shows that every understandable shade of thought in it could have been made clear—if not clearer—without the use of masks. (Granted, in the first place, that creative temperaments necessarily torture their owners. This happens to be a simple, unproved assumption. It is equally an assumption that unimaginative people are placid and do not torture themselves mentally.) Not being satisfied with understandable nuances, the playwright expanded his characters until they became abstract symbols, until even their relationship became an abstract symbol—the theft of the mask.

What added value did the dramatist gain? None. The mask in this play symbolizes Fate in the form of a self-destructive will. It is the pattern which O'Neill borrowed from the Attic theatre, and we need not be surprised that he uses the distinctive property of the Attic theatre. To force this mask on a modern play in such a manner is an act of violence. It may be true that in THE GREAT GOD BROWN the dramatist tries to present a picture of the modern man's painful dualism of mind. This complex theme is not clarified when the writer is almost as bewildered as his own characters or when he chooses a technique which leads to confusion worse confounded.

For LAZARUS LAUGHED (1926), O'Neill requires a chorus wearing forty-nine different kinds of masks. The idea is evidently derived from Pollux' account of the Greek stage, but it serves no discoverable purpose. This spectacle, with its neo-Greek form, is one of the very few optimistic pieces of O'Neill. He proclaims,

> Man's loneliness is but his fear of life! Lonely no more! Millions of laughing stars there are around me! And laughing dust, born once of woman on this earth, now free to dance!

For a moment the dramatist almost shakes off his familiar bogy of Aeschylean fate. It is impossible to miss the note of exultation. The rare, warming smile of O'Neill flashes, and we wait breathlessly to share the news that has induced his mood. What has the playwright seen from where he stands? What has he to tell his millions of fellow Americans whose frustrations have haunted him? We ask in vain. We must expect nothing more than his mood. His optimism cannot be used or even made rational. In the realm of ideas it amounts to a combination of Zarathustra and Pollyanna.

From here on most of O'Neill's dramas become distressingly grandiose and vague. Greek Fate does duty once more in STRANGE INTERLUDE (1928), this time as the "life stream" which links parent to child and child to grandchild. The continuity of life is seen as an ultimate value transcending the lives of individuals—"Our lives are merely strange dark interludes in the electrical display of God the Father!" This lofty conception, however, is only a tincture of Darwinian thought, with some of O'Neill's own notions of Freudism thrown in. The pattern of STRANGE INTERLUDE compares in sterility only with that of DYNAMO (1929), in which a dynamo becomes a religious and sexual symbol. In both plays the characters speak and behave portentously, but the portent never materializes into any discovery.

Miss Flexner believes that MOURNING BECOMES ELECTRA (1931) is O'Neill's masterpiece, while Krutch maintains that it is this century's best tragedy in English. ELECTRA represents its author at his best and worst. Its pattern, that of the Aeschylean family curse, is frankly borrowed from Greek tragedy. But it was a conception which was fading even in the ancient world. In the words of A. E. Haigh, it "no longer held a prominent place in the moral ideas of the post-Aeschylean poets." Krutch does not attempt to prove the validity of the idea for modern audiences, but indicates that the real object of the play is to show that

> . . . human beings are great and terrible creatures when they are in the grip of great passions and that they afford a spectacle not only absorbing but also and at once horrible and cleansing. Once such stories have been adequately reclaimed for us in the only way in which it is possible to reclaim them; once they have been retold in terms we can understand, we cease to be concerned chiefly with the terms and again lose ourselves in amazement at the height and depth of human passions, the grandeur and meanness of human deeds.

But Charmion von Wiegand, in a study of O'Neill, finds that

> More normal alternatives of action were open to all the characters than the one they chose of murder and blood, or which their author chose for them, in mechanical imitation of the Attic pattern.

Irrational people overwhelmed by their passions are undoubtedly a horrible spectacle, but scarcely a cleansing one. When so much of their passions happens to be flagrantly sexual, as in the O'Neill ELECTRA, they may even become morbidly fascinating. These characters in whom one sexual neurosis leads to another, who take the law into their own hands, who live in mouldering mansions shut off from human contact—what do they mean to us as the author presents them? Are they really any more than the shadows of the original Electra, Clytaemnestra and Agamemnon? George Bernard Shaw has described O'Neill as a "banshee Shakespeare" (Krutch), and in this case at least the celebrated ire of G.B.S. is understandable. It may not be improper to add that in Clifford Odets' far less massive AWAKE AND SING (1935) we get a real insight into family neuroses, and this in spite of the fact that Odets' play is a homely picture of life in a Bronx tenement.

It seems likely that in the future O'Neill's fame will rest less upon his elaborately mystical efforts than upon the more Naturalistic ones like DESIRE UNDER THE ELMS (1924), whose stern, hard-bitten characters are logically related to their New England soil. The action of this play develops inevitably; it grows in true dramatic fashion; its roots are in American life rather than in a ready-made poetic pattern. Here the dramatic poet speaks intelligibly, eloquently, to his American audience.

INVENTING HUMAN PSYCHOLOGY

O'Neill's later plays by his own admission depend on Freudian psychology. But O'Neill feels no responsibility even to Freud, and he invents his own brand of psychology whenever he pleases. The right to invent human psychology has long been one of the privileges of the dramatic poet, even though the poet does not claim to be a scientist. Psychology, as it happens, is one of the fields of study in which most of us feel we are expert without any particular training. It is more likely, however, that most of us are working with rags and tatters of the little that is known about human psychology. Any "psychology" which corresponds to the superstitions which have already been spread abroad will usually be accepted as authentic. TOBACCO ROAD (1933) had the distinction of introducing the tenant farmer and his troubles to a national audience. Rather less happily it fastened on the southern poor white all those clichés which Broadway and Hollywood had already stamped upon the southern Negro.

In the stream of films which Hollywood puts out each year there is a certain percentage with a "race psychology" of a type that can only be described as libelous. Italians and other Latins are represented as "greasy" and criminal-minded; Negroes are servile and superstitious; Irish are bellicose; Jews are opportunists; native races of all kinds are pictured as sub-human. Such pictures are quite indifferent to the fact that science refutes them at every turn, just as they are indifferent to the racial antagonisms which they spread among the American people year after year.

But psychological clichés do not occur only at this low level of theatre. They can be found in the more "elevated" regions of dramatic writing, as for example in the plays of Luigi Pirandello.

Pirandello's influence, which dominates post-War Italian drama, is to be found in the work of Rosso di San Secondo (THE SLEEPING BEAUTY, 1919); Luigi Chiarelli (THE MASK AND THE FACE, 1916); Gugliemo Zorzi (THE VEIN OF GOLD, 1919); Fausto Maria Martini (CIRCLES UNDER THE EYES, 1921); Alessandro de

20th Century-Fox
THE GRAPES OF WRATH (1940): *Closeup of an American Exodus*

CLOSEUPS

Technology versus romance

Stefani (WHAT YOU DON'T EXPECT, 1921). According to the fascist Italian critic Silvio D'Amico,

> . . . the theme recurring in all these authors is basically the same: bewilderment; fluctuation of the individual consciousness; the eternal problem of knowledge presenting itself again without a possible solution; and the dreadful shifting of the values of life, under which one sobs and chuckles in turn. (Dickinson).

The truth is that the plays of Pirandello, which pass current as revelations of the human spirit, are based on a cheap formula of solipsism, which has long been discredited as valid philosophical reasoning. Pirandello's formula is elaborately "psychological." It assumes the existence of secondary and tertiary personalities and other alterations of the ego—hypotheses which science has approached with the utmost caution. As a medium for fantasy this formula might serve (as in Ansky's THE DYBBUK) to grasp some phase of life. With Pirandello, however, bewilderment over the identity of one's self or of others becomes the whole purpose of the drama, in order to question the very existence of reality. D'Amico makes this quite clear in the case of Pirandello's EACH IN HIS OWN WAY:

> In CIASCUNO A SUO MODO, after having reduced reality to illusion, he denies even the relative stability of that illusion; he destroys it even as an illusion; he shows its dizzy appearance and disappearance—like a man who is left with a fist full of flies in his hand. But all that does not make him happy.

For some people this may represent the furthest reaches of psychological drama. Others may consider it about as strenuous as a pillow fight without half the fun.

For the progressive dramatist of today there is a kind of submerged reef of danger in such stale dramatic patterns; and it matters little whether these clichés have been left over from Romanticism, Naturalism or Symbolism.

SYMBOLISM OVER HOLLYWOOD

One form of cliché as practiced by Hollywood has already been mentioned. But the American cinema is by now famous for its stock patterns; the merest layman knows that life as described in the average movie is not real life. The movies long ago made the discovery that all human experience could be interpreted on the principle of Boy Meets Girl. In the overwhelming majority of Hollywood offerings the plot reduces itself to the simple idea of Glamor Boy meeting Glamor Girl in front of Glamor Setting. We need not bewail too long the past results of such a dull formula. The pity is that on a number of occasions when Hollywood had the courage (and good business sense) to try something better, the work was stultified because an outdated and irrelevant pattern was used.

Warner Brothers' JUÁREZ (1939), directed by William Dieterle, is an example. The picture's intention is clear: to prove, by a comparison of democracy and dictatorship, that democracy is superior. The story deals with Napoleon III's attempt to foist upon the Mexican people, led by President Juárez, an absolute monarch in the person of Maximilian von Hapsburg. The choice of this particular story is a good one, because dictatorship is given a chance to show itself in attractive colors, only to be revealed later in all its ugliness.

Maximilian was an idealist as well as a charming, cultivated gentleman. Juárez was an uncouth, plain-spoken man, an Indian Lincoln. This premise being given, the further development of the film would seem to be clear: to get behind both personalities to the causes they represented. What was Maximilian trying to do in Mexico? Who were the people behind him, and what did they want? Why did the Mexican nation refuse to accept this hand-picked European emperor?

We never really learn. In one sequence Porfirio Díaz, Juárez' aide, who has been captured by the French, is visited in prison by Maximilian. The emperor talks convincingly of his good intentions. Díaz, released, recounts this talk to Juárez. "He is like you, Señor Juárez, he wants to help the people of Mexico. . . . He says there is only a word, democracy, between him and you."

JUÁREZ: What does that word democracy mean, Porfirio?

DÍAZ: It means liberty, of course. A man can say what he thinks, worship as he believes. It means equal opportunity for all.

JUÁREZ: But Maximilano offers us all this without democracy. Then what is it that he is withholding? It is rule over ourselves. In a democracy no one rules himself into slavery; that is why democracy is the fountain-head of all liberty. To put one's fate into the hands of an individual, no matter how superior he may be, is to betray all liberty.

This answer profoundly impresses Díaz in the film. But we might ask ourselves why it was that afterwards the same Porfirio Díaz, as president of the Republic of Mexico, saw fit to rule the country for thirty-four years as an iron-handed dictator. He praised democracy in the abstract, but in practice he was guided by more material considerations.

In the same way the rather abstract debate over definitions acquires vividness and dramatic force in proportion as we understand the interests which were at stake. The Mexican people did not take up arms over a definition. Maximilian's government did *not* offer to defend the constitution; it did not offer "liberty for a man to say what he thinks." It did not really offer a man the right to "worship as he believes." It certainly did not offer equal opportunity.

Maximilian was a figurehead for the rapacious Napoleon III, whose object was to plunder Mexico while returning its people to colonial peonage. Juárez' government, besides being formally a democracy, was administered in the interests of the Mexican population. Maximilian's government, in spite of the emperor's formal declarations, was one of force and violence against the people. The fact that the emperor was personally charming was nothing but an accident.

It is true that Maximilian was not satisfied to be a puppet, and that he even made some overtures toward the Mexican liberals. But it is also certain that if he ever got out of hand his clique of supporters would have removed him from the scene very swiftly.

All this remains vague in the film. The emperor is usually seen surrounded by a brilliant court. Only the short, almost unexplained sequence of the cabinet meeting brings us face to face with Maximilian's crowd of greedy *hacendados*, politicians and militarists. We get only the dimmest notion of the quality of the Mexican people who support Juárez. There are plenty of mobs but no Mexican people. In this particular Dieterle might well have learned something from Eisenstein, whose peons in THUNDER OVER MEXICO (1933) are something different from the sullen extras of JUÁREZ.

No, the contrast in JUÁREZ is not between democracy and dictatorship. It is between the personality of Maximilian and that of Juárez—glamor versus menace—and Juárez comes off a bad second. Why, in that case, should any honest person prefer the ugly, grim and wooden little Juárez to someone as gracious and handsome as Maximilian?

It may be objected that, after all, JUÁREZ does not claim to be history; it is only a film story derived from historic materials. And there, precisely, is the point. The pattern of JUÁREZ has not been taken from history but from the movie storerooms. A fresh pattern, derived from history itself, would have made an even greater, an even more exciting and incidentally more profitable film.

If JUÁREZ began as history and settled into a studio cliché, the Selznick film GONE WITH THE WIND set its course for romance and on the way encountered history. It must have been in the cards that some day there would be a Boy Meets Girl picture big enough to astound the neighboring planets. Now that the drums of ballyhoo are subsiding, perhaps a little analysis will be permitted, even in the case of a superspecial reputed to have cost four million dollars and to have grossed over thirteen million in its first year.

The story of GONE WITH THE WIND took place in the days of the old South. The crinoline hoops, magnolia trees and pillared porticoes were all familiar properties. Although the Tara and Twelve Oak estates seemed to cover all Georgia and the Wilkes homestead was as large as the Coliseum, we could accept them as fitting background for the leviathan romance of Scarlett O'Hara. What really mattered was the drama of Vivien Leigh, Clark Gable and Leslie Howard.

As it turned out, however, the drama of history began to steal the show. (This became quite evident in the latter half of the picture, when the war years faded away and Leigh and Gable were left to carry on their romance alone.) The one really poignant element of the story—Scarlett's infatuation for the colorless Ashley Wilkes—was comparatively lost in the pageant of Technicolor. At the same time the story of Civil War and Reconstruction grew in importance. However, this was not a complete misfortune. Perhaps we could learn why Father Abraham and his

Union army wanted to ruin the deep South atmosphere of ringing banjos and mint juleps.

To the likely surprise of the producers, who were merely incorporating history into their story (with a little sawing and hacking at history here and there), some unromantic questions came up. Negro intellectuals objected that the film was sympathetic in its portrayal of "handkerchief heads," or servile Negroes, while it presented all others as "uppity." What jarred them most was the Reconstruction sequence, in which the freedmen were represented as carpetbagging and walking Atlanta with leering insolence until they were "shown their place" by vigilantes.

GONE WITH THE WIND attempted no such glorification of the Ku Klux Klan as did Griffith's BIRTH OF A NATION (1915), against which the National Association of Colored People conducted a boycott. But the odor of Ku Kluxism, never very fragrant, hung over that particular sequence in the new picture. Race-conscious Negroes maintained hotly that Emancipation did not turn their forebears into criminals; and that the Klan was a device used by the former slaveholders to block all the reforms that had been wrested from them after a costly civil war. Why was this old wound being reopened at a time when America needs a unified citizenry?

Here was one embarrassing result of art-for-entertainment's sake. If it forgets that screen productions are intended for audiences, even a film as expertly charted as GONE WITH THE WIND may run into unforeseen reactions.

LEFT-WING SYMBOLISM

It is rather surprising to find that the Symbolist form has a strong hold on the more left-wing writers in the American theatre. These dramatists seem to have been impressed with the allegorical tradition of Ibsen's PEER GYNT, Strindberg's DREAM PLAYS and the writings of O'Neill.

But the allegorical method is a subjective one more than usually open to error.

Even the most Naturalistic play is itself a complex allegory. To extract symbols from symbols does not tend to give added clarity. Elmer Rice's AMERICAN LANDSCAPE (1938), a political allegory, falls into this group, as do most of the plays of John Howard Lawson, including PROCESSIONAL (1925), SUCCESS STORY (1932) and MARCHING SONG (1937). Other examples are Archibald MacLeish's PANIC (1935), Paul Green's JOHNNY JOHNSON (1936), Clifford Odets' PARADISE LOST (1935). Among foreign equivalents of these plays there are Auden and Isherwood's ASCENT OF F 6 (1937), Bertolt Brecht's ROUND HEADS AND PEAKED HEADS (1936).

Plays of this type have a common tendency to substitute lyricism for the clash of drama; instead of suspense and climax they have a poetic mood of growing intensity. The issues of the play are not clearly seen or clearly developed. By the third act the line of the play is usually derailed, the resultant confusion being hidden in a burst of rhapsodic poetry.

This does not mean that the allegoric method is unfit for use. Many examples of successful allegories could also be given, including the R.U.R. (1922) and INSECT COMEDY (1921) of Karel and Josef Čapek; Irwin Shaw's BURY THE DEAD (1936); Marc Blitzstein's THE CRADLE WILL ROCK (1937). But in general it is a treacherous method. It fairly invites poor thinking, since it tends to use an arbitrary poetic pattern instead of a dramatic pattern found in the material itself.

Clifford Odets is perhaps the most gifted of American lyrical dramatists—a fact which accounts for several of his failures. Odets has never been able to strike a balance between his amazing intuitive grasp of the American scene and the oversimplified pattern into which he forces his materials.

Even his most popular work, GOLDEN BOY (1938), betrays the fact that it is an allegory not completely related to its ostensible subject matter, the life of the prize ring. Joe Bonaparte is really the symbolic figure of an idealist in boxing gloves. He is a symbol in the fighting-trunks of a ring champion, and only the author's intuitive feeling for character makes this symbol credible. This intuition, however, is unable to carry the play to a logical and believable finish in terms of ring environment. Odets' idealistic hero commits suicide; whether Joe Bonaparte would do so is less certain.

Up to now the Group Theatre has shared with its representative dramatist the same tendency to think in terms of poetic aspiration rather than of dramatic development. The Group, like Odets, makes use of patterns whose relevance it generally takes for granted. A surprisingly large number of the Group plays are built around the formula "For what is a man profited, if he shall gain the whole world, and lose his own soul?" Among the plays cut to this pattern were Lawson's SUCCESS STORY and GENTLEWOMAN; Sidney Kingsley's MEN IN WHITE; Odets' AWAKE AND SING, PARADISE LOST and GOLDEN BOY; Melvin Levy's GOLD EAGLE GUY; Piscator's CASE OF CLYDE GRIFFITHS; Paul Green's JOHNNY JOHNSON; William Saroyan's MY HEART'S IN THE HIGHLANDS; Robert Ardrey's THUNDER ROCK.

This theme was more important up to the time of the economic crisis of 1929 than it is now. The Group Theatre, as it happens, put on its first production in 1931. The Group's lower middle class audiences scarcely need the advice not to gain the whole world. Most of this audience is concerned with holding on to jobs or meager professional clientèles or keeping their small businesses from going bankrupt. The Group needs a new general metaphor, one better suited to the depression years in which it lives.

SYMBOLIZED CLASSICS

What does the dramatic work of the past mean to us today?

The patterns used by the Attic poets came from the life and thought of their times. It would be absurd to say that they have no relevance whatever to the life of today. But they can be adapted to modern use only with the greatest caution. It cannot be merely *assumed* that they fit the present day. We may profitably make comparisons between the past and the present; but we have no right to ignore the difference between past and present.

To compare the behavior of an Athenian of 440 B. C. with that of a New Yorker of 1940 A. D. we must first of all seek out and understand all the *differences* between them. We will throw no light either on past or present if we go by the facile premise that "human nature does not change." The "human nature" of the spectators who witnessed the première of Sophocles' OEDIPUS REX may have been the same as ours. But to us, as Gilbert Murray says, parricide and incest are "moral offenses capable of being rationally judged or even excused as unintentional." For ancient audiences these offenses were "monstrous and inhuman pollutions, the last limit of imaginable horror."

We have discussed the Reinhardt Stylization method of reviving the past. The strength of this method lies in its search for historic metaphors—such as the genuine conventions of the Baroque for a production of FIGARO. Its weakness lies in its readiness to accept the metaphor as an end in itself, as the object of production. The meaning of FIGARO'S WEDDING (1784) is not in the fact that it is exaggerated in action and speech and full of curlicued scenery. The significance of this play lies in Beaumarchais' making mince pie out of the debilitated aristocracy of his time. To unearth past metaphors is not enough; we must understand the society which used the metaphor, or we understand very little.

The opposite approach, of course, is to translate the classics into the modern idiom. Donald Oenslager devotes his book *Scenery Then and Now* to just this method in putting the classics to work in the modern theatre:

> From the theatre of Greece to the theatre of O'Neill I have selected certain plays which both allow for modern production and enable me to bring to life the theatre of these great epochs as I see them in terms of our own theatre.

In Oenslager's designs the Birds in Aristophanes' comedy become a race of aviators, the setting is a Cubist edifice in structural steel. Plautus' CASINA is viewed in terms of the painted backdrops of a modern burlesque show. HAMLET is designed in Symbolist style *à l'outrance,* as if the actors walked under water:

> Hamlet dwells in a dual world, the everyday world of external events which is the life of the Court, and the haunted, brooding world of the imagination which is the inner world of an avenging Prince, who drifts down endless corridors of dark, fir-bordered streams. . . . It is the conflict of these two worlds that unbalances his mind and goads him on to indecisive action and helpless frustration.
>
> The way he distorts the external world through the eyes of his own inner world of the imagination must determine the nature and the appearance of the scenes. Just as he sees the events of the Court in the curving mirror of his own brooding conjectures, so the scenes which he inhabits must appear as indefinite embodiments of his own inner preoccupations. The members of the Court must seem to be resolved into dewy shadows of this "too, too solid flesh" and cloaked in veiled frag-

ments of reality. . . . For all the Castle Scenes bare, chalky walls are pierced with tall tragic doors—always three, whose depth beyond is as black as Hamlet's sable suit. They must be high, very high, to admit his anguish and his spirit. Only flashes of red, the red of blood, livens the scenes—washed over walls, or splotched on characters' clothing. (*Scenery Then and Now*).

Just what is accomplished by this method? Some of us who had never heard of Aristophanes or Plautus, or thought of their classic works as probably very boring, would learn that these plays really belong on a stage. This is a good beginning. But in itself it is only a bright idea. That bright idea in turn becomes soporific after one scene if the plays themselves do not speak to us *of the past.* For they can tell us nothing about the present except by way of the past!

Some years ago the acme of obviousness was reached in productions of modern-dress Shakespeare and Molière which had nothing to recommend them except the "novelty" of their being in contemporary dress. Reviewing such productions in Germany Ihering remarked, "The actor no longer lights a cigarette in the plays of Ibsen and Wedekind, but he smokes when he plays in Molière." He quoted the opinion of the composer Igor Stravinsky that the way to re-create classic dramas is "to *cool* them; to bring them closer by making them more distant." (Herbert Ihering: *Reinhardt, Jessner, Piscator*).

Both Stravinsky and Ihering would probably be startled to learn that in this opinion they are at one with Karl Marx and Friedrich Engels. The hard-headed founders of Marxism seem to have followed the dramatic writings of their period with keen interest but with no great hope. Their disappointment was based mostly on the way in which the dramatists of the time sentimentalized reality, especially the reality of bygone periods. Marx described the music festivals at Baireuth as the "fools' festival of the State musician Wagner." THE NIBELUNGEN struck him as a sensational cheapening of the nature of prehistoric society.

George Lukas gives the following summary of Marx' and Engels' suggestions on how to approach the artistic work of the past:

[Their opinion] is especially destructive of the attempts to bring ancient times and their creative efforts at closer range by introducing contemporary conceptions, problems and conflicts into those periods. It is only when we understand the periods of the past as they actually were, that we are able to comprehend them as integral elements of our own period. Only by this can they be brought at closer range, and never by means of a decadent apologetic substitute, by a superficial dressing up of the old with contemporary trimmings.

CYNICISM AND HYSTERIA

It is clear by now that Symbolists like Appia and Craig, O'Neill and Pirandello used, not symbolism in general, but a type of symbolism congenial to themselves. Their particular choice of symbols, the quality of their metaphors, links them directly to the Romantics.

There has been a certain degree of development in the type of metaphor which the Symbolists have used. O'Neill's middle period made use of symbols considerably more vehement than those of his earlier and later periods. And the later dramatists and designers of the Symbolist school brought forward metaphors which have not been altogether palatable to the immediate followers of Appia and Craig.

The later period of Symbolism may be labeled for convenience the *Neo-Romantic* period. This Neo-Romantic period may in turn be subdivided into three important sections: Dadaism, Expressionism and Surrealism. The type of symbols used by the Dadaists and Expressionists has been explosive rather than tranquilly beautiful. That of the Surrealists has featured incongruity rather than grandeur. The qualities of cynicism and hysteria pervade all three.

To surprise, to wound, above all to make a mockery of hitherto accepted artistic values, was the purpose of Dadaism during its brief reign. André Breton, spokesman for the French Dadaist painters Duchamp, Picabia, Tzara and others, wrote, "The main thing is to disturb the ceremony." The Philistine must not only be disgusted, he must be terrorized. The adherents of Dada "spat in the eyes of the world."

Dada—the word is derived from the French for "hobby-horse"—made its first appearance at Zurich in 1916, with manifestoes by Tristan Tzara and Richard Hülsenbeck. Its subsequent activities were marked by "desperate amusement," including the suicides of some of its devotees. Julien Levy recounts some of the curious doings of that cult:

> Ribemont-Dessaignes wrote, "What is beautiful? What is ugly? What is great, strong, weak? What is Carpentier, Renan, Foch? Don't know. What am I? Don't know. Don't know, don't know, don't know." In Cologne . . . Max Ernst was involved in a Dada Exhibition which created such a scandal that it had to be closed by the police. "In order to enter the Gallery one had to pass through a public lavatory. Inside the public was provided with hatchets with which, if they wanted to, they could attack the objects and paintings exhibited.

Some time during 1919 the Dadaists conducted a soirée at which five people dressed in stovepipes performed a dance entitled *Noir Cacadou* and flowers were laid at the feet of a dummy. Dadaist theatrical work was apparently confined mostly to private entertainments of this sort. However in 1928 New York had a brief view of dramatic Dada at the Provincetown Playhouse, where E. E. Cummings' HIM swung dizzily through twenty-one scenes of repartee. The environment of New York City and other places turned like a revolving door, and the stage was filled with such personages as Me, Him, the three Weirds, Mussolini, a Blonde Gonzesse, and Six Hundred Pounds of Passionate Pulchritude. Six years later there was a production of Gertrude Stein's FOUR SAINTS IN THREE ACTS, an opera with music by Virgil Thomson. The opera contained fifteen saints, cellophane scenery and four (not three) acts. It was dismissed by Burns Mantle with the description, "Colored cast against a cellophane setting representing visionary Spain. Libretto incomprehensible." (Sobel).

The Dadaist group in Berlin, which afterwards proved to be the cradle of Epic theatre, included William Herzfelde, John Heartfield, Erwin Piscator, Bertolt Brecht, George Grosz. At Sunday morning performances open contempt was shown for the audience. The stage manager, coming to the footlights, yelled to the box-office treasurer, "Is the money in the safe? Then let the show begin."

The Dadaist movement does not seem to have lasted long enough to carry out any memorable productions in the French or German theatres. Its influence continued, however, in the work of such artists as George Grosz, who was associated with Piscator in the production of THE GOOD SOLDIER SCHWEIK (1928). For the final scene of this play Grosz designed a line of piteous soldiers, foul, mouldering and streaked with blood. One man carried his own head, another carried under one arm his own leg, like a ham. This appalling tableau was voluntarily omitted before the show opened.

In Germany, at any rate, it was not Dadaism but *Expressionism* which took center stage after the War. Just what Expressionism meant was rather puzzling to its reviewers at the time, and in fact is not entirely clear to this day. For some writers, like Macgowan, it represented almost any new trend except the attenuated Naturalism of the more conservative Symbolists. Macgowan's definition, for instance, included Cubism, Vorticism, and even Futurism and Post-Impressionism in some instances.

It may be doubted whether Expressionism ever had anything to do with genuine Cubism. The scenery of the Expressionist-Theatricalist film THE CABINET OF DOCTOR CALIGARI used the geometric patterns familiar in Cubist work; no doubt it also derived a certain strangeness from the Cubist method of breaking familiar space into unfamiliar planes and prisms. But its insane distortions really have little to do with Cubist painting, which is a painstaking study of the functions of space. Stage Expressionism owes less to the painting of Cézanne, Braque, Léger or Picasso (in his Cubist period) than it does to the fantastic painters like Klee, Ernst, Chirico, Chagall, Grosz or the primitives and the insane.

Both Macgowan and Cheney have asserted that one of the technical aims of Expressionism in the theatre was the attempt to leave the picture-frame stage in favor of the stage platform. Their belief seems justified, especially since no definite line can be drawn dividing the activity of the Expressionists from that of the Theatricalists. The insurgency which was so marked a feature of Expressionism applied not only to playscript and settings but to the form of the stage itself. But on the whole the distinguishing feature of Expressionism would seem to lie elsewhere—in a symbolism notable for the vehemence of its symbols.

Vehemence more than any logical thesis is the key to the plays of Georg Kaiser, Expressionism's best-known playwright. Typical is his trilogy of plays written between 1918 and 1920: THE CORAL, GAS I and GAS II.

In GAS I the liberal son of a billionaire helps to reorganize society on a cooperative basis. The profit system is eliminated, and social democracy is established. Although this begins to look like the millennium, for no evident reason the gas machines on which the new culture depends start to go wrong. The Billionaire's Son and an Engineer watch the gages of a gas generator just before the terrible explosion:

ENGINEER: It works out—and does not work out. We have reached the limit—works out and does not work out. Figures fail us—works out—yet does not work out. The thing sums itself up, then turns against us—works out and does not work out! . . .
WORKMAN: Report from Shed Eight— Central— White cat burst . . . Chase away the cat— Shoo! Shoo! Smash her jaws— Shoo! Shoo!— Bury her eyes—they flame— . . . Report from Central—the white cat has—exploded! (*He collapses and lies prone.*)
BILLIONAIRE'S SON: (*Goes to him.*)
WORKMAN: (*Gropes with his hand.*)
BILLIONAIRE'S SON: (*Takes his hand.*)
WORKMAN (*With a cry*): Mother! . . . (*dies*).
BILLIONAIRE'S SON: (*Bending low above him*) O man! O mankind!

In GAS II the country is invaded. The Billionaire's Son is a pacifist, but the Engineer preaches war against the invader, against whom a new, inconceivably powerful gas bomb can be used. When the masses side with the Engineer the Billionaire's Son hurls the bomb at his own people, putting an end to civilization.

The explosion in GAS I symbolizes the fact that the new system has broken down. "Not because of faulty organization, but because industrialism itself is evil, destroying the human soul and enslaving man to the machines." (Steinhauer). That *industrialism itself is evil* is self-evident to Kaiser; at least he makes no attempt to prove his assumption. The behavior of the Billionaire's Son in GAS II defies rational explanation. If we are asked to take seriously the pacifism or humanitarianism of this character, how can we justify his going to pieces in a fit of pique?

This confused picture of the martyrdom of man acquires, by means of the playwright's terse, hectic style, a seeming unity. Kaiser's dialogue, like some of Toller's, has aptly been called "telegraphic." In the original German such "unnecessary" parts of speech as articles, prepositions, adjectives and adverbs are omitted. Huntly Carter and Herman George Scheffauer, among others, have tried to explain this use of clipped dialogue:

> Huntly Carter . . . writes, "Expressionism is simply expression taking the form of a new technique for the purpose of giving the most intense effect—say a one hundred percent effect—to the species of drama that expressed pre-war and war-time insurrectionary tendencies. Dramatists found it necessary to put a punch into their plays, to make them violently aggressive, in order to arouse the playgoers into active sympathy with their insurrectionary ideas." Scheffauer considers the central idea of expressionism "direct action in art—the forthright naked impulse, delivered without intermediaries, straight from the imagination to the outer world—like a child from the womb." (Miller).

Kaiser liked to think of himself as an "apostle of energy." To his mind, "Energy is the driving force of the world. Without energy there is nothing. Sentiment, pity, romance are only the refuge of the weak, who must inevitably go down. The unfortunate are hindrances. Go out into the world and see what men really are. They are brutal, self-seeking, egotistical, heartless, energetic. It is only through will power that injustice and stupidity can be done away with." (Clark).

Like his plays, Kaiser's philosophy reflects the dualism of thought which pervaded the whole Expressionist movement. On the one hand there is the Nietzschean attempt to be hard-boiled; on the other there is a tender, romantic love for humanity. Expressionist playwriting has even been called *O Mensch Dramatik* (O mankind drama) after the well-known line in the gas explosion scene.

Although the German Expressionists attracted worldwide attention after the War, the movement dates from 1910, when a small group led by Herwarth Walden dedicated its theatre, the Stormbühne, to "Expressionist drama in Expressionist style." It produced at special matinées the plays of Walden, August Stramm, Lothar Schreyer, Herman Essig, Oskar Kokoschka and Kurt Schwitters.

The disaster of the War and the disillusionment which followed offered fertile ground for the growth of the Expressionist technique in the theatre. Directors like Leopold Jessner, Jürgen Fehling and, in particular, Reinhardt,[1] were attracted by it. New groups, such as The Dramatic Will and Young Germany, embraced the Expressionist ideal, as did a dozen or more of Germany's leading post-War dramatists. The plays of Sorge, Hasenclever, von Unrüh, Reinhard Goering, Werfel, Kaiser, Stramm, Toller and Arnold Zweig had in common a vehemence born of social indignation. It was an understandable reaction to the complacency with which Europe had been turned into a shambles. Unlike the Dadaists the Expressionists felt they had a duty toward their audiences.

It would be too much to expect, of course, that the new movement would agree on a united viewpoint. There were in fact two distinct lines of thought, represented by the Expressionists proper and the Activists. The former carried on the Romantic lyricism of Wagner, the Romantic philosophy of Nietzsche. Appalled by the complexity of modern life, they looked back with nostalgia to the past, echoing Herder's cry to the Middle Ages,

> Give us in some respects your devotion and your superstition, your darkness and your ignorance, your disorder and rude manners, and take from us our light and disbelief, our enervated coldness and subtlety, our philosophic debility and human wretchedness. (Steinhauer: *Das Deutsche Drama*).

The more realistic-minded section, the Activists, were not inclined to sigh after an idealized past which never existed. They tried, instead, to find some constructive way out of the dilemma which faced them and their audiences.

> The Activists remained faithful to the traditions of the *Aufklarung* and the French Revolution. They believed, like the Naturalists before them, that the immediate need of mankind was a rationally ordered society based on the Christian ideal of social justice. A few of them identified themselves with one of the left-wing political parties; but most of the Activists remained free from any political affiliation. They did not believe in class conflicts or proletarian dictatorships. (Steinhauer).

Expressionism was historically a movement of insurgent liberals, with standards of abstract justice and a message of good will, but without a clearly defined program. In practice the Expressionist longing for "a rationally ordered society based on the Christian ideal of social justice" meant a return to the ideals of the primitive Christian community. This could not be incorporated in the platform of any German political party, since it was unworkable under conditions of mass industry.

The Expressionists felt, also, that man is enslaved to the machine; and that the only solution to this slavery is to abolish industry and return to agriculture. This idea, too, was unworkable. The social-democratic German government tolerated the Expressionists and even encouraged them, considering their social doctrines harmless. The other German workers' party, the communist, was more critical, maintaining that no constructive return can be made to a primitive society, and that the proposal to abolish industry is destructive and defeatist.

Few Expressionist dramas were on a political plane. Fritz von Unruh's OFFICERS (1911) and A FAMILY (1917) both exposed militarism, while Reinhard Goering's SEA BATTLE (1918) anticipated the German naval revolts. The rest can aptly be described as "Messianic" rather than political:

> I will take the world on my shoulders
> And bear it sunward with a hymn of praise.

These lines from Reinhardt Sorge's THE BEGGAR disclose the spirit of Expressionism better, perhaps, than any formal description.

We have already spoken of the "telegraphic" dialogue in which this spirit found expression. The "oblique," seemingly irrelevant speeches used by Chekhov and Wedekind also attracted the Expressionists. With writers like Kaiser the callous overtones of this kind of dialogue became intensified to a point of nightmare unreality.

The hysterical symbolism of the Expressionists was often drawn from Freudian psychoanalysis. The poetic and scenic imagery was supposed to be on the level of subconscious thought as in dreams. On the other hand some playwrights like Paul Kornfeld called the whole science of psychology "spurious," insisting that it tells nothing about man's real nature. They wrote instead in terms of "myths" and of abstract qualities, as in the old Morality plays. Characters labeled "The Poet," "The Man in Gray," even "X," "Y" and "Z" were brought to the stage.

Acting ceased almost completely to be "psychological" in the

Stanislavsky manner, returning in some degree to the Baroque declamatory style. Kornfeld urged the actor to spread his arms boldly before the audience, to speak as he would not in real life. To be ashamed to "act" was a betrayal of theatre. Unlike the Baroque, however, the new acting was often speeded up to a prodigious tempo. Movements were jittery and gestures unpredictable, delivery jerky and shrill. Cheney says the Expressionists "claimed the right to violate, deform and reshape outward nature just as far as such violence furthered emotional expressiveness." (*Stage Decoration*).

In scene design there developed an hysterical view of environment. Leaning walls, doors and windows at impossible angles, writhing trees in human shape, gave an unearthly aspect to the once familiar world. In Max Slevogt's design for Mozart's DON GIOVANNI at the Dresden Staatstheater (1924), a Baroque palace seems kneaded out of dough. The setting of C. T. Pilartz for the throne-room in Hamsun's QUEEN TAMARA (Vereinigte Stadttheater, Cologne, 1924), is constructed in diagonal prisms, while the thrones have forked and jagged outlines. In Fritz Schaefler's settings for MUCH ADO ABOUT NOTHING (Residenz Theater, Munich), the stage is filled with huge, grotesque flower-shapes leaning at all angles. Ernst Stern's design for DIE WUPPER (1919) shows a mass of houses like crumpled cardboard. In MORN TO MIDNIGHT (1916) the stage directions of Georg Kaiser read, "The wind shakes the branches of a tree and the snow clings to it, forming the shape of a skeleton."

Transferred to the United States the Expressionistic mode found itself considerably toned down. Kaufman and Connelly's BEGGAR ON HORSEBACK (1924), one of the first American essays in this style, contained a Naturalistic prologue and epilogue; the bulk of the play, which was supposed to be a dream, was presented Expressionistically. The dream passes through the mind of a young composer, Neil McRae, who sees in fantasy what the consequences will be if he marries Gladys Cady, daughter of a big business man. The rites of the fantasied wedding are incongruously jumbled with the act of grabbing a train. Finding his in-laws unbearable, McRae murders them all. He is tried in a court where the judge, witnesses and everyone else are the same Cady family, which has come back to torment him. He is found guilty and sentenced to turn out popular songs for the Cady Consolidated Art Factory for the rest of his life. Fortunately he wakes up from this dream.

The comparatively gentle satire of the script may be inferred from the dialogue which ensues when Neil tries to borrow a pencil in Cady's office:

MISS HEY: Of course you've filled out a requisition?
NEIL: No—I haven't. A piece of paper, isn't it?
(*She hands him a tremendous sheet of paper. It is about twenty inches by thirty inches.*)
What *I* want is a pencil. There's a place for that to be put in, I suppose?
MISS HEY (*Wearily*): Yes—where it says "The undersigned wishes a pencil to do some work with." How old are you?
NEIL: Thirty-two.
MISS HEY (*Taking the paper away*): That's the wrong form.
(*She gives him another—a blue one this time*).

This musicomedy variation of Expressionism was more poignantly used in THE MOON IS A GONG (1926) by John Dos Passos. Its long list of characters, almost as fantastic as Cummings', included two Cousins with an Arrow Collar Face, three Young Men with a Cold Cream Face, a He-Intellectual, a She-Intellectual, five Tea-drinkers, and the like. In the opening scenes the elegant figure of Death in a dress suit meets a girl on the stairway of a prim New England home.

The adolescent hero of John Howard Lawson's Expressionist play ROGER BLOOMER (1923), looks for a job and has to pass through a labyrinth of offices until he reaches the inner sanctum of the boss. The play winds up with a nightmare ballet of the "sex complexes" and "death complexes" which haunt young Roger Bloomer. In Elmer Rice's THE ADDING MACHINE (1923) the hero is a bookkeeper named Mr. Zero, whose friends are named Mr. and Mrs. One, Mr. and Mrs. Two, and so on. Mrs. Zero has a scene in which she reproaches her husband in a monologue which is almost as long as Mrs. Bloom's in Joyce's *Ulysses.* Fired after twenty-five years' drudgery, Mr. Zero kills his employer while the offices spins around on a turntable and printed numbers and spots of blood are projected on the walls.

PARANOIA

The hysterical trend in Symbolism is carried still further by *Surrealism,* which asserts the artistic priority of insanity.

The term *Surrélaisme* seems to have been coined by the writer Guillaume Appolinaire in 1917. The actual founder of the movement was André Breton, who, in 1924, when he issued the first Manifesto of Surrealism, was an ex-medical student given to wearing green glasses and a green suit. The Manifesto defined the new form as "pure psychic automatism, by which it is intended to express, verbally, in writing or by any other means, the real process of thought. It is thought's dictation, all exercise of reason and every esthetic or moral preoccupation being absent." (Barr).

According to the Surrealists, anything resembling deliberate procedure in art spells artistic death. Real creativeness is entirely subjective, unpremeditated and inspired. The greatest artist is he who does not choose a subject, but rather he who is chosen by it. The ideal way to produce work is "automatically," as in the automatic writing supposedly done by spiritualist mediums. Did not Socrates say that there is no invention in the poet until he is out of his senses? [2]

Surrealism finds its symbols in the poems and paintings of children and the insane, the scrawls "doodles," which nervous people execute upon telephone pads, the antics of asylum inmates, the dreams of psychopaths and the vain and fugitive images which lurk in the dark corners of the normal mind.

Late in 1939, in New York, the Monte Carlo Ballet staged a number called BACCHANALE, conceived and designed by the Surrealist artist Salvador Dali. Dali, who paints pictures of limp watches hanging from trees, and who likes to give public lectures in a diving suit and helmet, called his ballet a "paranoiac performance." Centered rather casually around the mad King Ludwig II of Bavaria, Wagner's patron, the action was based on the Venusberg scene from TANNHÄUSER. It made use of Wagner's music also. The ballet took place before a backdrop on which was painted a huge swan made of cracked plaster with a classical pediment on its neck. Ludwig, chased by Death in the form of an umbrella, fell dead surrounded by a ring of umbrellas. In the interim there were dances by fauns with bushes as well as horns growing out of their heads. *Prima ballerina* was a dreamlike albino Venus in white tights.

In the field of motion pictures Jean Cocteau's privately filmed BLOOD OF THE POET had preceded Dali by seven years (Paris, 1932). The Cocteau film, while inexplicable, was shot through with strangely assorted elements of Naturalism and of feverish mental pictures, and ranged emotionally from tranquillity to anguish. Childhood memories of a snowball fight were mingled with classic sculptures. One notable scene showed a child floating against a ceiling to the continuous tinkling of little bells.

Since Surrealism is a method of insane production *per se*, it is obviously useless to dispose of it by calling it insane. The movement is not as crazy as it at times affects to be. Its theorists take care to provide it with a tradition as old and distinguished as that of any of the saner styles; and in justifying its point of view it has put itself on record (somewhat confusedly to be sure) both esthetically and politically. It describes itself as anti-Naturalistic and Neo-Romantic. These designations are quite correct. In demanding that insanity be accepted as equal or superior to sanity, Surrealism carries on the Goethean tradition of individual subjective freedom in an objectively hostile world.

Surrealism is, indeed, Romanticism pushed to the logical limit of unreason. It differs from previous Neo-Romantic techniques in the fact that it is not so naïvely anti-materialist. Instead of denying the material world, instead of reducing reality to fogs and vapors, it accepts the materials of reality while profoundly distorting those materials. To that extent it is more subtle than earlier Romantic forms. It understands better the functioning of the disturbed mind. Herbert Read, one of its spokesmen, explains:

> In dialectic terms we claim that there is a continual state of opposition and interaction between the world of objective fact—the sensational and social world of active and economic existence—and the world of subjective fantasy. This opposition creates a state of disquietude.

Politically the movement has conflicting tendencies. Its line of thought can be traced back to the manifesto of the *Futurist Synthetic Theatre* (1915) given out by the future fascist *raisonneur* F. T. Marinetti, and others:

For example, it is stupid to represent upon the stage a struggle between two persons, always carried on with order, logic and clarity; while in our experience we find almost exclusively fragments of disputes which our activity as modern men has permitted us to witness for but a moment in the street car, in a café, at a station, and which have remained filmed (cinematografati) upon our minds as dynamic, fragmentary symphonies of gestures, words, sounds and light.

There is nothing in the tenor of this manifesto which fascism would find uncongenial today. Still, according to Read, Surrealism "is rooted in opposition to the capitalist system on all fronts." It likes to associate itself with the names of those poets, such as Wordsworth, Coleridge, Blake, Byron, Shelley and Keats, who in their youth were the objects of Philistine displeasure or police attention. It considers that it employs "Marxian dialectics" in the field of the arts. In 1925 the movement announced its formal adherence to communism. The Communist International, however, seems to have remained unperturbed.[3]

In juxtaposing waking life and dream images the Surrealists evidently feel that they are pursuing dialectic thought. But in spite of its political talk Surrealism is even more obscure and less social-minded than Expressionism (although it is not without its own right and left wings). Its choice of symbols—trivial, perverse and decrepit—does not appear to fit in so well with a program of struggle or with the "revolutionary optimism" that Marxists believe in.

It is certainly a little difficult to picture Einstein or Pudovkin in agreement with Dali that the future of the movies lies in the direction of a "paralyzing fantasy." As Dali sees it,

. . . the cinema can only develop in the direction of "wireless imagination" and "paralyzing fantasy"—the very prey and food of the immense "famine of illusion" of the public and the masses in general. Reduced to idiocy by the material progress of a mechanical civilization, the public and the masses demand urgently the illogical and tumultuous images of their own desires and their own dreams. It is for this reason that today these crowds press hungrily around surrealism's rescue table, digging their nails into the living flesh of morsels of dreams which we offer them that we may "save their fantasy" and proclaim the "rights of man's madness." Thus do we try to keep them from sinking forever into that thick leaden sea which is the every-day vulgarity and stupidity of the so-called "realist" world. (*Surrealism in Hollywood*).

Lest this same leaden sea should engulf Shakespeare, the Surrealists endorse the belief that HAMLET is a thoroughgoing illusion. This thesis, quoting Professor J. Dover Wilson, makes the point that HAMLET is simply a mysterious work without ulterior purpose.

> In fine, we were never intended to reach the heart of the mystery. That it has a heart is an illusion; Hamlet is an illusion. The secret that lies behind it all is not Hamlet's, but Shakespeare's; the technical devices he employs to create this supreme illusion of a great and mysterious character, who is at once mad and the sanest of geniuses, at once a procrastinator and a vigorous man of action, at once a miserable failure and the most adorable of heroes. The character of Hamlet, like the appearance of his successive impersonators on the stage, is a matter of "make-up." (*What Happens in Hamlet*).

If Professor Wilson had in fact succeeded only in proving Hamlet to be an imaginary character, he would have made a weighty contribution to the obvious. But Wilson's book, as delightful as it is scholarly, is a closely reasoned study of one of the greatest masterpieces of the drama, and the paragraph in question is intended to illuminate the working methods of Shakespeare, not to establish HAMLET as a piece of Surrealist automatic writing.

The Neo-Romantic trend in drama, which began with Goethe, who proclaimed the rights of man's conscience, now ends with Dali, who proclaims "the rights of man's madness." We may ponder the question whether this represents a triumphant development of Romanticism. At a time when alertness, lucid thought and open eyes are needed as never before in history, the sleepwalking troubadours of Surrealism come on the scene. As we shall see eventually, there is a reason why obscurantism begins to blossom at this time.

IRONY

Stripped of its sensationalism, the Surrealist form has possibilities as an ironic technique. It has already been tried in this way in some of the progressive theatres of Europe and the United States.

Kjeld Abell's musicomedy THE MELODY THAT WAS LOST, produced originally at the Riddersal, Copenhagen (1936), had as its theme the ennui of the middle class. Its style was a Surrealist juxtaposition of all the clichés of middle class comedy with new and flippant comment. Thus it arrived at a happy ending, but only after it aired out, to the satisfaction of the public, the whole question of happy endings. Scenically the show combined the trappings of a Shubert musical with the grotesque fantasies of a Dali or a Joan Miro:

> A bouquet, bridal gown and silk hat drift across the stage. Mendelssohn's "Wedding March" floats raucously out to the audience, a stereoptikon from the rear of the stage repeatedly flashes pictures of second-rate honeymoon resorts while a toilworn waiter drags a dinner table in and out. "I am Aurora," explains a chambermaid with the wings of an angel, who dusts off the morning sun just as the alarm clock rings and the curtain goes up on the Larsons' little two-room apartment. . . . (*Man in a White Collar*).

In this play, as designed by Abell himself, the trivial and melancholy symbols contributed by Surrealism were deftly employed in characterizing the environment of a Danish bourgeois family.

The musicomedy HEAVEN AND EARTH, produced in 1936 by the V & W Theatre, Prague (an anti-fascist theatre wiped out by the German annexation of Czechoslovakia), remade Fletcher's THE SPANISH CURATE in a fashion influenced by Surrealism. Jupiter, coming to earth to escape his nagging spouse Juno, is so beset with bureaucrats and racketeers that he concludes the earth is as bad as Olympus. The writing parodied the Baroque style. Voskovec and Werich, the comedian-managers of the theatre, played, as was their custom, in clown-white makeup. Olympus consisted of some pseudo-classic Chirico clouds. The ancient temple which Jupiter comes to inspect has been turned into a veritable pigsty by its two priests; it is represented in a Surrealist setting consisting of both the exterior and interior of the temple. Ionic pillars ornament the classic façade, which is enlivened with strings of dried corncobs, a beehive and bundles of rags; the columns, about to fall to pieces, are tied together with wire and twine. The interior consists of a single crumbling wall from which the wallpaper is peeling off in shreds; it has a hole in the middle for the tin flue of a coal stove. When Jupiter is annoyed, rain, bricks and plaster spatter down in front of this setting.

For the Group Theatre's experimental production of Irwin Shaw's THE QUIET CITY (1939) as designed by Gorelik, beside the permanent background of large plaques representing skyscrapers, there was a projection-screen which hung over the stage. Photographs of New York faded in and out on this screen in counterpoint to the action going on below.

For the Federal Theatre production of George Sklar's LIFE AND DEATH OF AN AMERICAN (1939), Howard Bay designed a series of Surrealist backdrops which depicted in mournful, decrepit and surprising symbols some of the typical backgrounds of American life over a thirty-year period. Most impressive of these fine images was one showing the feudal pattern of modern industry—a bare hill with a factory on top and scarecrow houses of workers scattered all the way down.

In the same season William Saroyan's cryptic MY HEART'S IN THE HIGHLANDS was clarified—though not completely—in a Group Theatre production directed by Robert Lewis, with Herbert Andrews as designer and Paul Bowles as composer of the musical score. According to Saroyan this whimsical allegory was intended to prove that anyone can become successful if he is sufficiently determined. What Lewis saw in it was more in line with the comment by Eleanor Flexner, "Saroyan seems to be saying that this is a hard world for a poet, particularly a bad poet." With the help of picture-book settings and properties, acting that was childlike in mood, and music which combined the quacking of ducks and the chirping of crickets with overtones of a calliope, the fable became delightfully capricious.

A descent into Naturalism would have been fatal. It would have brought up embarrassing questions. (How is it that the Poet's little boy, who lives on a handful of grapes a day, shows no signs of undernourishment?) By the same token the inability of the play to stand more robust treatment must be ascribed to its not very robust grasp of a serious problem. It may be a beautiful parable to affirm that man can live on the good will of his neighbors alone, but anyone who actually tries it will soon lose the good will of his neighbors, and the parable will prove inadequate. The case of MY HEART'S IN THE HIGHLANDS is an example of the possibilities and pitfalls of Symbolism in the theatre. The Saroyan play found a childlike production in which there was a faint hint of irony, but it also represented a distortion of truth.

From the examples just cited it would appear that Surrealist symbols used in an ironic manner and with a scrupulous regard for truth, have constructive value. Used as "automatic," instinctive patterns they are at least as unreliable as any of the Symbolist techniques that preceded Surrealism.

HYPNOSIS

Is it only another coincidence that the Symbolist theatre, which in practice has made such a poor choice of symbols, lays so much emphasis on the heightening of emotion in the theatre? Its theorists take for granted that the whole object of drama is to sweep audiences away emotionally. Appia concentrates light on the actor because the actor is the focus of emotion, "and it is this emotion that we have come to seek." Cheney, in *Stage Decoration*, speaks of "the far more important requisite of creating atmosphere, of slyly putting the audience into the spirit of the action, of intensifying quietly the intended emotion." Terry Ramsaye, the movie historian, asserts that cinema art and industry "are laboring alike, and by very like steps, for one and the same service—the pleasant titillation of the five senses of the human animal and that sixth product of those five factors which is euphemistically called the soul." What Ramsaye puts so bluntly has been said more gracefully by Pirandello:

> The eye and the ear are the most aesthetic of the senses, and they should become united in a single artistic delight, the beauty of which is felt by the heart so that the subconscious mind is moved and influenced by novel images that may be either as terrible as nightmares or mysterious as dreams; sometimes soothing and sometimes alarming according to the rhythm of the music.

According to this view an emotional conquest of the audience is attained by appealing to the "unconscious mind" of the audience. The "unconscious" is held to be the larger, emotional and suggestible personality of the spectator as contrasted with the prosaic, practical and comparatively narrow personality of the spectator as he commonly appears. Such a belief rests partly on the Romantic tradition and partly on the writings of Freud in psychopathology.

In 1918 the celebrated producer and director Arthur Hopkins wrote in his brochure, *How's Your Second Act?*, that the director must capture the unconscious mind of the playgoer. "The emotional reaction must be secured first," he declared. The director must imitate the hypnotist and "still the conscious mind . . . by giving the audience no reason to think about it, by presenting every phrase so unobtrusively, so free from confusing gesture, movement and emphasis, that all passing action seems inevitable, so that we are never challenged or consciously asked why. This whole treatment begins with the manuscript, continues through the designing of the settings, and follows carefully every actor's movement and inflection. If, throughout, this attitude of easy flow can be maintained, the complete illusionment of the audience is inevitable."

John Mason Brown indicates that a theatre audience must have a state of mind which consists, as Coleridge said, of a "remission of judgment" concerning what it sees before it. "This 'suspension of disbelief' by the audience is the foundation upon which the gossamer structure of all theatrical illusion is reared." Still more directly, George Jean Nathan once affirmed, "The whole object of theatre is to hypnotize and captivate the spectator and auditor by various shifts and stratagems."

In the course of a Symbolist performance every stimulus of color, movement, light and sound is directed upon the spectator in order to wear down his power of resistance, to win him over to a belief which may or may not have genuine merit. This is why Reinhardt felt that the theatre must be built up "so as to address itself to the senses of the spectator, without tiring him." This is the reason for the emphasis on the "grand forms," the "contours," the light and color. The audience must be snared, charmed, entranced.

So far has this theory gone that it ignores, even resents, the suggestion that logical, responsible and factual proof is as necessary in the theatre as in a court of law.

But the stage is a responsible public institution. It is true, of course, that the stage usually deals with matters of personal experience rather than with more abstract facts. Just the same it remains answerable for any statement or impression which it makes.

Symbolist theory has borrowed a good deal from the writings

of Freud and his school. But Freudian psychoanalysis is overloaded with speculation, much of which has been repudiated in recent years. It remains to be seen how much of this clinical phraseology is warranted on the stage.

Certainly the theatre's use of the word "hypnotism" has not been very accurate. Little is actually known about hypnotism, but few theatre people have shown the caution of Professor Clark L. Hull, of Yale, who conducted a series of experiments in hypnosis. Professor Hull arrived at the conclusion that at the present time a serious program of investigation of hypnosis would "court scientific disaster." On the basis of their studies Hull and another investigator, Estabrooks, agree that the mind appears to change very little under hypnosis.[4]

The Symbolist thesis is that production must build up an emotional rapport between actors and audience (in the sense that the actors are to enlist the heedless sympathy of the audience); and that the audience must suspend its more critical judgment. By now this view of production has spread so widely and been so little challenged that we have almost forgotten that it is only an opinion.

Those who maintain it should prove their case. Meanwhile we have every reason to go on believing that a playgoer is a complete, rational as well as emotional personality in the theatre as out of it; and that his normal inclination is to attend the theatre with all his senses and critical faculties in use instead of checking some of them at the door.

It is rational to believe that the healthy playgoer is always on his guard against spurious dramatic patterns, even when they are accompanied by a strong appeal to his prejudices. A healthy playgoer forms his own judgment about the metaphors which the production has chosen. He can tell a hawk from a handsaw. He knows a trivial metaphor from a noble one. He knows the difference between a symbol which is packed with observation and experience, and one which is large and "simple" only because it is pretentious and lacking in observation and experience.

A healthy playgoer is not awed by the fearsome word "psychology." Whatever merits psychology may have (it is still far from an exact science) it should not be made into a reason for honoring all kinds of conjectures. Every hack journalist and radio speaker sees life in terms of "psychology": the economic crisis is due to "lack of confidence"; the rise of the C.I.O. is due to "mob psychology"; wars are due to the "fight instinct." Speculations of this kind are produced by the yard, often out of whole cloth. If this tendency is running away with the press and radio, that may be all the more reason why it should not run away with the stage.

PSYCHOLOGY ON STAGE

By now the reader must have been struck by the enormous emphasis which the Symbolist theatre puts on "psychology."

The systematic study of the human mind emerged as one of the important products of nineteenth-century thought. Although it was quickly labeled a science, the controlled clinical work done in that field to this day is as nothing compared with the amount of "psychological" conjectures that have accumulated. Subjective thinking, which looked with suspicion on most other sciences, seized eagerly on this one. Idealist philosophers hoped, from the first, to use psychology as a kind of buffer state between the domain of science and the more indefinite realms of idealist thought.

The idealist-minded felt they could show that the practical discoveries of science were subject to a higher metaphysical interpretation. Reality as known to science must be considered only as a complement to the private world of sensation which exists in individual minds.[5] This private world has its own laws, which are charted by psychology, the science of the mind.

Although psychology looms so large in the Symbolist theatre, it should not be forgotten that the Naturalists also attached importance to it. Did not Taine himself, the ancestor of Naturalism, announce that "History is a problem in psychology"? It was clear to Antoine, for example, that environment had a psychology of its own, which could be shown in the setting. There was also the psychology of the audience to be considered. The theatregoer had to be made as introspective as possible, so as to give his full attention to the action which transpired before him.

But then as now the content of psychology was so vague as to leave room for conflicting interpretations. Zola was sure that the actions of men and women could be explained in terms of their psychology; one had only to observe this psychology closely enough. But just what was the content of human psychology? Here there was less agreement. For the idealists the human mind was the scene of moral warfare between abstract good and evil. The more thoroughgoing adherents of Naturalism believed there was no such war; that the human psyche is beset by specific, not abstract, problems.

If it was so inexact a science, what was to prevent anyone from turning "psychology" into anything he pleased? Nothing prevented it then, and nothing prevents it now.

In today's theatre "psychology" tends to crowd out every other science necessary for the investigation of human life and environment. Few of our dramatists know any other method of analysis. The psychological method is held to be the most truthful, the most penetrating, the only dramatically valid method. Yet this "method" is so undetermined that each playwright feels he can invent his own version of human psychology on the spur of the moment.

Overtones of profundity and nobility accompany the use of the psychological method. Yet quite often the particular psychologies which dramatists invent rest on the merest assumptions or superstitions: primeval guilt, reincarnation, racial theories, death-wishes, incest-wishes. To these psychological systems all the findings of the sciences, all the precision of the technologies, are subordinated.

The "survival of the fittest" psychology is gravely accepted on the stage although there is no proof that it can be applied to social relationships. The Mendelian Law stands no chance against the "sins of the fathers" psychology. Slanderous racial psychologies are invented and imposed upon stage Irishmen, Jews, Negroes, Scandinavians or Chinese. Economics are trodden underfoot by both right and left wing playwrights who have psychological stories to tell.

How much science is there in the psychological approach to dramatic writing? It is a matter of individual guesswork. Chekhov, for instance, was a keen and honest observer. When he first brought his plays to the Moscow Art Theatre, that producing company, already familiar with various brands of psychology, was dubious about Chekhov's variety. Only continued experience with the texts proved to them that the psychology of Chekhov's characters was more accurately and objectively recorded than that of many other dramatists'.

The Naturalists maintained that the stage setting also has psychology. They meant by this that environment, like human beings, has a character due to its history, and that it is this character which impresses the beholder. Today the Symbolists talk even more about the psychology of the setting,[6] but it is evident that the Symbolists have a rather different emphasis. The physical quality of the setting, which was so typical of Naturalistic staging, tends to disappear in the Symbolist style. Instead the Symbolist designer looks for the essence, or soul of the environment, which seems to be always nebulous. There is a passage in William Butler Yeats' *The Shadowy Waters* (1900) which might well serve to explain the psychology of the psychological designer:

> Could we but give us wholly to the dreams
> And get into their world that to the sense
> Is shadow, and not linger wretchedly
> Among substantial things.

In practice the Symbolist psychology of environment is too often the negation of environment, its attenuation into dreamlike mists or even into virtuoso essays in composition, color and lighting.

This reduction of environment to atmosphere in the setting is the counterpart of the reduction of human actions to "psychology" in the playscript. Both represent, much too frequently, a lack of real interest in life. Both are part of a theatre which finds analysis wearisome. Neatly packaged in "psychology" and wrapped in dreams, this tired concept of life can be sold daily to millions of theatregoers and movie fans. As George Jean Nathan has observed in his *Materia Critica,* "The goods in the American theatrical emotion market are stable products, each clearly labeled, capped and trade-marked." The life which so puzzles the playgoer outside the walls of the playhouse is here harmonized into an esthetic unity, "hypnotizing" him into lack of thought.

Who can deny the commercial success of this kind of drama? An immense audience buys it. An audience of men and women who do not find what they need in life and who therefore take refuge in the inner world which Goethe discovered for them, and which Wagner helped to bring into illusory existence on the stage. Constant visits to this low form of theatre keep the illusion going, until the taste of millions of playgoers is undermined.

It is easy to bring out the standard alibi about "giving the public what it wants." The public too often looks for shoddy because it is accustomed to nothing else. After all, the public did not invent the Symbolist theatre. There are others more directly responsible than the public. For instance, the directors.

Even more than a technique of dramatists, designers or actors, Symbolist drama is a medium for directors. It is a movement initiated and still led by régisseurs. We have many expert, theatre-minded directors in our theatre today. They are stage generals who remain cool and collected in the very thick of dress rehearsal, when stars sulk, designers tear up blueprints and producers tear their hair. Yet we could well stand a few others less artistically expert and a little more awake to the full cruelty and tenderness of the world in which we live.

"FORMALISTIC EXERCISES"

In March 1937 there occurred in Soviet Russia an interesting episode in the life of theatre. It attracted widespread attention not only locally but in all foreign countries. After a flurry of news items it was forgotten. But the story is worth digging up again.

It concerns the film BEZHIN MEADOW, on which Sergei Eisenstein had been working for two years, and which was suddenly halted by the Central Administration of the Photo-Cinema Industry. Neither the past contributions of Eisenstein nor his world renown saved him from a stinging rebuke. An article in *Pravda* by Boris Shumiatsky, at that time head of the Soviet film industry, charged him with relying on his own "scholastic profundities" rather than upon living experience. With the unlimited resources afforded him, he had produced only "harmful formalistic exercises."

The film was supposed to deal with the struggle in a farming village between two classes of peasants during the period of collectivization. Eisenstein saw these circumstances as an elemental war between good and evil; in his film the peasants became Biblical figures, saintly or demoniac. It was this metaphor which caused the reprimand.

The *Pravda* article insisted that Eisenstein's attention "was centered in the main not on the presentation of people typical of our epoch, not on providing real insight into the process of the socialist reconstruction of our village economy, but on a metaphor concerning the centrifugal character of unleashed elemental forces."

To illustrate this point, Shumiatsky cites a scene which Eisenstein significantly entitled "Smashing the Church." A highly stylized, almost mystical depiction of peasants, in a frenzy of destruction, tearing down icons, breaking altar vessels, swaying rhythmically to the broken tune of a revolutionary marching song. . . . "Yes, he presents in this scene a veritable bacchanalia of destruction; and the collective farmers as vandals! Needless to say . . . these scenes do not in any way reflect the real processes in the reconstruction of the life and social forms in the Soviet villages in the years of collectivization. Depicting the Soviet village, Eisenstein never gave a thought to actuality. . . . Eisenstein even hit upon the clever idea of portraying the chief of the political department as a man with an immobile face, enormous beard and the conduct of a biblical saint. The Young Pioneer's father, a kulak tool and a bitter class enemy, instead of being endowed with the features of the real enemy, appears like a mythological Pan stepped out of paintings of the Symbolist Vrubel." (Kunitz).

A conference of studio managers, directors, camera men and other film people was called in Moscow to discuss the Eisenstein case and related matters. It was one of those sessions of self-criticism which the Soviets seem to value highly. Eisenstein, according to the news report, admitted that he had acquired a swelled head which interfered with his work, and BEZHIN MEADOW was abandoned.

The film director had relied upon psychology in choosing his metaphor. Was psychology the only science which applied to the task in hand? Was it not essential to know something of economics, of agriculture, of history, of the technology of farm implements, possibly of housing and the administration of Tsarist and Soviet law? Was psychology important enough to outweigh all of these?

"CRISIS OF SUBJECTIVISM"

The Symbolist theatre has brought on its own crisis—what Ihering terms a "crisis of subjectivism." The philosophy of Naturalism led to a number of mistakes. The Symbolist form in some ways has fared worse. If Naturalism halted at half-truths, Symbolism has, without knowing it, opened the gates wide for a retreat from truth.

The Symbolists had the idea of the synthesis of theatrical elements in production. But their interest was narrowly technical. What the production meant in terms of thought was much less important. The Symbolists proposed to represent life by means of symbols. But they were not on guard in the matter of the symbols they admitted. Symbolism remained poor in its ability to judge between insipid meanings and vital ones; between confusion and clarity.

Nowhere was this more apparent than in the playscript. The Symbolist script carried mystical, non-rational overtones. It was the medium adapted to those playwrights who believed that life's conflicts cannot be explained in rational terms but only cryptically in terms of some indefinable standard of values. It is not strange that it has led to so much vagueness and confused thought.

The Symbolist designers invented the plastic stage, a highly important invention. They emphasized the actor, an indispensable emphasis. But the way was left open for plastic stages that were merely plastic stages; for unified lighting that was merely unified lighting. In the search for perfect technique, the reason for the technique was forgotten.

The Symbolists perfected their form with the help of new stage technologies such as electric lighting. But the Symbolist artistic form, which shaped these materials, was never in turn shaped by its materials. It never really acquired that craft wisdom which comes from insight into the structure of the materials used by the craftsman. The Symbolist form (following the example of the Naturalistic one) chose to deny that it employed any technology at all. The stage picture was supposed to be a shining, disembodied thought, "the baseless fabric of a vision" which had reached the stage without benefit of any such agency as a counterweight system.

The Symbolists emphasized the need for discipline of personnel, for the responsibility of executive officers. A dramatic production, like all undertakings in which more than one person is involved, requires such discipline and such leadership. The theatre has of course never lacked executives. In fact Gordon Craig, who is most insistent in demanding autocratic rule in the theatre, began his career under Sir Henry Irving, an actor-manager of the old school. Craig must have been aware of the authority which such a manager can exercise.

On the other hand, if a production is the synthesis of many arts, it is also the synthesis of many talents. The greater the director, the better he knows that he holds his authority in trust for his colleagues. It will tax all his skill as an artist and a human being to weld all these separate talents together. Unfortunately Craig's thesis that stage productions must be the work of a single mind does not help to make this point clear. It has served as a mandate for despotic directors rather than as a reminder of the heavy responsibility which falls upon directors who are conscientious.[7]

Finally the Symbolists have placed a tremendous weight upon the already overburdened science of psychology. Who can rightfully object to the development of this science? It is certain that the human mind has a specific way of working; and it is extremely important that we learn what this way is. This does not justify the improvisation of all kinds of "psychologies," nor the explanation of everything in terms of psychology alone, nor the importation of all kinds of banalities under the guise of psychology.

The Symbolist movement as a whole has shown a squeamish distaste for the less pleasant aspects of reality. It has tried to substitute a spurious esthetic harmony in place of a thorough knowledge of people and events. It has tried to substitute love of beauty for love of life.

Must we believe that Symbolism is the final and perfect conception of theatre? Will theatre continue along its present lines until, in 2100 A. D., it resorts to lethal gases to put its customers into a streamlined trance? Already the playgoer is asked to check his reasoning powers at the door. A calculated assault is made on his emotions and prejudices. He is not permitted to think logically for an instant. What he sees on the stage does not, apparently, matter very much; it is important only that it be a story whipped up in excitement or bathed in a dreamlike nostalgia.

Dramatic forms have changed before, however. We may reasonably expect the Symbolist form to change. As we shall see later, there are other theories of production which require an alert, thoughtful and critical attitude on the part of the spectator.

Whatever the Symbolist form has contributed (and it has contributed a good deal), it has not yet given a final answer to the question "How shall an audience be convinced?" In the interests of theatre audiences and of theatre itself, that answer must remain open for discussion.

NOTES

1. "Between December, 1917, and 1920, Reinhardt produced for Das Junge Deutschland the most prominent group of the advance guard in Berlin, plays of the new mood; DER BETTLER (THE BEGGAR) by Reinhard Sorge; SEESCHLACHT (A SEA BATTLE) by Reinhard Goering; DER SOHN (THE SON) by Walter Hasenclever; DER BESUCH AUS DEM ELYSIUM (THE VISITOR FROM ELYSIUM) by Franz Werfel; KAIN (CAIN) by Friedrich Koffka; EIN GESCHLECHT (ONE FAMILY) by Fritz von Unruh; DER STURTZ DES APOSTELS PAULUS (THE FALL OF THE APOSTLE PAUL) by Rolf Lauckner; DIE WUPPER (THE WUPPERS) by Elsa Lasker-Schüler; DER BRENNENDE DORNBUSCH (THE BURNING BRIAR BUSH) by Oscar Kokoschka; DIE SENDUNG SEMAELS (SEMAEL'S MISSION) by Arnold Zweig. In addition Reinhardt gave plays by several of these playwrights and other dramatic revolutionaries upon his public stages. In the list are Georg Kaiser's DIE KORALLE (THE CORAL), DER BRAND IM OPERNHAUS (THE FIRE IN THE OPERA HOUSE), VON MORGENS BIS MITTERNACHTS (FROM MORN TO MIDNIGHT) and EUROPA (EUROPE); Reinhard Goering's DER ERSTE (THE FIRST ONE); Paul Kornfeld's HIMMEL UND HÖLLE (HEAVEN AND HELL); Walter Hasenclever's JENSEITS (BEYOND); and August Stramm's KRÄFTE (POWERS)." (Miller: *The Independent Theatre in Europe*).

2. "For all good poets, epic as well as lyric, compose their beautiful poems not by art, but because they are inspired and possessed. And as the Corybantian revellers when they dance are not in their right mind when they are composing their beautiful strains; but when falling under the power of music and metre they are inspired and possessed; like Bacchic maidens who draw milk and honey from the rivers when

they are under the influence of Dionysus but not when they are in their right mind. And the soul of the lyric poet does the same, as they themselves say; for they tell us that they bring songs from honeyed fountains, culling them out of the gardens and dells of the Muses; they, like the bees, winging their way from flower to flower. And this is true. For the poet is a light and winged and holy thing, and there is no invention in him until he has been inspired and is out of his senses, and the mind is no longer in him: when he has not attained to this state, he is powerless and unable to utter his oracles!" —Socrates. (From Herbert Read: *Surrealism*).

3. The Second International Conference of Revolutionary Writers, assembled at Kharkov, U.S.S.R., in 1931, considered, among other matters, a schism which had arisen among the French Surrealist writers. This quarrel had ended in the expulsion of certain "reactionary elements" from the Surrealist movement. Commending the expulsion, the conference adopted the following statement (in the course of a resolution on the proletarian literature of France): "This process encourages the hope that the better part of the present group of Surrealists, continuing its theory of 'the decomposition of the bourgeoisie by intensifying its internal contradictions' and correcting the flagrant errors contained in its 'Second Manifesto of Super-realism,' will finally find its way to the real proletarian ideology." (*Literature of the World Revolution,* 1931, Special Number).

4. G. H. Estabrooks: *What Science Knows About Hypnotism.*

"Despite the widespread and longstanding belief to the contrary, the author is convinced that no phenomenon whatever can be produced in hypnosis that cannot be produced to a lesser degree by suggestions given in the normal waking condition." (Clark L. Hull: *Hypnosis and Suggestibility*).

5. See John Howard Lawson's *Theory and Technique of Playwriting* for a valuable study of the effects of this philosophy on dramatic writing.

6. "Incidentally, designers must be skilful psychologists, Oenslager points out. . . . Psychological scenery, if one can use such a phrase, is what Mrs. Bernstein is wont to create." (Norris Houghton: *The Designer Sets the Stage*).

7. Gordon Craig's idea of discipline is amplified in the advice he once gave to English designers: "What you ought to do to begin with, is to get together and form yourselves into a properly organized body. . . . I suggest that you get a book of the rules of the Fascist Party, and without slavishly copying them in all their ways, copy them in their rules which seem to you practical to your idea and helpful to yourselves, especially those dealing on discipline." (*To the English Designers of Sceneries and Costumes*).

The idea that designers might perhaps organize themselves on the basis of democratic trade union discipline (as in the United States) did not occur to Craig; he probably never heard of such a thing. Compare with the Soviet views on discipline, as given by the Russian director B. E. Zakhava in *Principles of Directing, Theatre Workshop,* April–July, 1937.

REFERENCES

Huntly Carter: *The Theatre of Max Reinhardt.* F. & C. Palmer, London.

Edward Gordon Craig. From Thomas H. Dickinson: *The Theatre in a Changing Europe.* Henry Holt & Company, New York, 1937.

Jacques Rouché: *L'Art théâtrale moderne.* Bloud & Gay, Paris.

Herbert Ihering: *Reinhardt, Jessner, Piscator oder Klassikertod.* Ernst Rowohlt Verlag, Berlin, 1929.

Herbert Ihering: *Aktuelle Dramaturgie.* Verlag der Schmiede, Berlin (no date).

Edward Gordon Craig: *On the Art of the Theatre.* Browne's Bookstore, Chicago.

Donald Oenslager: *Scenery Then and Now.* W. W. Norton & Company, New York, 1936.

Claire Trask: *Richard III Adorns a Berlin Stage.* New York *Times,* May 30, 1937.

Joseph Wood Krutch: *The American Drama Since 1918.* Random House.

John Howard Lawson: *Theory and Technique of Playwriting.* G. P. Putnam's Sons.

Eleanor Flexner: *American Playwrights 1918–1938.* Simon & Shuster, New York, 1938.

Eugene O'Neill. From Arthur Hobson Quinn: *History of the American Drama.* F. S. Crofts, New York, 1936.

Eugene O'Neill: *Nine Plays.* Random House, New York, 1932.

A. E. Haigh: *The Attic Theatre.* Clarendon Press, Oxford.

Charmion von Wiegand: *The Quest of Eugene O'Neill. New Theatre.* September, 1935.

Silvio D'Amico. From Thomas H. Dickinson: *Ibid.*

George Lukas: *Marx and Engels on Problems of Dramaturgy. International Theatre.* No. 2, 1934.

Julien Levy: *Surrealism.* Black Sun Press, New York, 1936.

Burns Mantle. From *The Theatre Handbook,* edited by Bernard Sobel. Crown Publishers, New York, 1940.

Georg Kaiser: GAS I. From S. Marion Tucker: *Twenty-Five Modern Plays.* Harper & Brothers, New York, 1931.

H. Steinhauer: *Das Deutsche Drama, 1880–1933.* Vol. 2. W. W. Norton & Company, 1938.

Carter, Scheffauer. From Miller: *The Independent Theatre in Europe.* Long & Smith.

Georg Kaiser. From Barrett H. Clark: *New Trends in the Theatre in Germany. The Forum.* November, 1924.

Johann Gottfried Herder. From H. Steinhauer: *Ibid.*

Sheldon Cheney: *Stage Decoration.* The John Day Company.

George S. Kaufman and Marc Connelly: *Beggar on Horseback.* Boni & Liveright, New York, 1924.

Alfred H. Barr, Jr.: *Fantastic Art, Dada, Surrealism.* Museum of Modern Art, New York, 1936.

Herbert Read: *Surrealism.* Harcourt, Brace & Company, New York, 1936.

F. T. Marinetti: *The Futurist Synthetic Theatre* (1915).

Salvador Dali: *Surrealism in Hollywood. Harper's Bazaar.* June, 1937.

J. Dover Wilson: *What Happens in Hamlet.* Cambridge University Press.

Mordecai Gorelik: *Man in a White Collar. Theatre Arts.* November, 1936.

Eleanor Flexner in *TAC.* May, 1939.

Adolphe Appia: *Die Musik und die Inszenierung.* F. Bruckmann, Munich, 1899.

Terry Ramsaye: *A Million and One Nights.* Vol. 1. Simon & Schuster, New York, 1926.

Luigi Pirandello. From Allardyce Nicoll: *Film and Theatre.* Thomas Y. Crowell Company, New York, 1933.

Arthur Hopkins: *How's Your Second Act?* Samuel French.

John Mason Brown: *The Art of Playgoing.* W. W. Norton & Company.

George Jean Nathan: *Materia Critica.* Alfred A. Knopf, New York, 1924.

Clark L. Hull: *Hypnosis and Suggestibility.* D. Appleton-Century Company, New York, 1933.

G. H. Estabrooks: *What Science Knows About Hypnotism. Scientific American.* March, 1936.

Sir William Dampier: *A History of Science.* Macmillan.

Norris Houghton: *The Designer Sets the Stage. Theatre Arts.* November, 1936, January, 1937.

William Butler Yeats: *The Shadowy Waters.* Dodd, Mead & Company, New York, 1921.

Boris Shumiatsky. From Joshua Kunitz: *Formalist Defects Scrap New Eisenstein Film. Moscow News.* March 31, 1937.

Edward Gordon Craig: *To the English Designers of Sceneries and Costumes. Design in the Theatre.* The Studio, London, 1927.

B. E. Zakhava: *Principles of Directing. Theatre Workshop.* April–July, 1937.

7

THEATRICAL THEATRE

ART AND THE PEOPLE

On what used to be Bülowplatz in Berlin there stands a beautiful theatre building of gray stone. Its colonnaded façade is in the posterized classic style which was the fashion in German architecture just before the first Great War. High up above the row of stone figures over its portals are inscribed the words

DIE KUNST DEM VOLKE

meaning "Art for the People." At the moment this book is written the building is known as the Theatre am Horst Wessel Platz. It has been renamed officially after Horst Wessel, patron saint of the Nazi movement. When it first opened its doors—in January 1916, with a production of Goethe's GÖTZ VON BERLICHINGEN—its name was the Volksbühne, or People's Theatre.

The interior of this playhouse, an auditorium seating two thousand, is lined with polished mahogany of a rich and somber color. A square mahogany frame shapes the proscenium with its great draw-curtains. Back of the proscenium is an adjustable portal, arranged, like that of the Munich Artists' Theatre, so as to narrow the stage opening for more intimate plays. A revolving platform working on elevators occupies the center of the stage area. Back of it the stage wall curves outward and overhead, forming a concrete half-dome faced with roughened plaster to receive the illumination of a Fortuny lighting system. Light striking the curving wall is refracted until it gives the effect of unending space; or images may be projected on to the dome as on a screen. Behind the wall stretches a large area of scene docks, wardrobes and workrooms.

Designed by the architect Oskar Kaufmann, this building was made possible by the combined memberships—about thirty thousand people—of the Freie Bühne and the Neue Freie Bühne, audience groups affiliated with the Socialist Party of Germany. These organizations represented an important sector of the Socialist Party's cultural work among the German masses. Both groups, as their names implied, could trace their origin to the Naturalistic inspiration of Antoine's Théâtre-Libre. In spite of this genealogy, or perhaps as a consequence of it, the stage of the Volksbühne in September 1921 saw the opening night of a production which was to become one of the landmarks of a different style. The play was MASSE MENSCH (MAN AND THE MASSES), written by Ernst Toller, directed by Jürgen Fehling and designed by Hans Strohbach.[1]

Toller, slight, shy and poetically handsome, was not the type one pictures as the center of angry events. Born in 1893 in Posen, he was studying at Grenoble when the World War broke out. He came home at once to defend the Fatherland. Thirteen months at the front proved disillusioning, but it did not turn the young soldier into a cynic. Toller's whole life consisted of the championing of ideals; his was an idealism which became ever more saddened and brooding, yet was not, until the very end, without a newer hope when an old one failed. From the trenches he was invalided home, where he became involved in a strike of Munich munitions workers, a strike called in protest against the imperialist War.

He was arrested and sent to prison for several months for this activity, but emerged in time to join the November (1918) revolution which broke out in Munich under the leadership of returned soldiers and workers. A short-lived Soviet State of Bavaria was set up, and Toller was elected its Commissar of Education. The revolt was harshly suppressed. Toller, middle class liberal and pacifist, was miscast in a revolutionary rôle. He found himself completely out of his depth, and had in fact repudiated his part in the insurrection at the time he was arrested. Nevertheless he was sent back to jail, this time for five years. It was in Niederschönenfeld Prison that he wrote three of his most impressive plays: THE MACHINE WRECKERS, HINCKEMANN and MASSE

Theatre Arts

MASSE MENSCH (1921). Design by Hans Strohbach
Revolution translated into theatre

TOWARD A THEATRICAL STAGE

THE DIVINE COMEDY. Model by Norman Bel Geddes (1921)
The amphitheatre becomes the stage

Bruguière photo

MENSCH. With the advent of Hitlerism Toller fled to America. Here, in the midst of his work for the victims of the fascist terror in Spain, despair overcame him and he died by his own hands in 1939.

MAN AND THE MASSES

In the black days of defeat in Germany, MASSE MENSCH gave voice to the anguish of a whole nation. Yet its grim, stormy poetry seems to hold an inner flame—that flame to which the dramatist refers in his dedication of the play:

Gebärerin des neuen Schwingens.
Gebärerin der neuen Völkerkreise.
Rot leuchtet das Jahrhundert.
Blutige Schuldfanale.
Die Erde kreutzigt sich.

On stage the stark beauty of the script was superbly matched by the production.

The front curtains draw apart revealing the full height of the proscenium. Three people stand before the great shadowy inner curtain: *The Woman*, Sonia, in a dark, long-sleeved dress; two men in the simple clothes of workers. These are the leaders of the workers' executive board. They are faced with a heavy responsibility: a strike vote must be taken in the morning. The workmen exchange final instructions, depart into the shadows as a new character steps forward. A modern classic figure in an overcoat and bowler hat. It is *The Man,* Sonia's husband, a government official. He warns her.

THE MAN: . . . this is treason
To the State!
THE WOMAN: Your State makes war,
Your State betrays the people,
Your State robs, stifles and oppresses
The disinherited,
The people.

The short scene is ended. The action has been as restrained as Attic tragedy. The speeches have rung like metal. The stage, bare of furniture, seems to enclose the players in abstract space. Only the human shapes stand out—now caught, now lost, by the spotlights overhead. Most memorable of these light-sculptured figures is that of Sonia Irene L., whose restraint of voice and gesture have a poignancy almost unbearable.

The scene ends, the lights dim abruptly on the forestage. The dark curtains in back are withdrawn, revealing a great staircase, simply designed, which seems to fill the whole stage. It stands there as if hewn out of rock. Beyond it is a dim infinity of space. The scene is the first of the *dream interludes;* for the action of the play takes place in what its author called "dream pictures" and "visionary abstracts of reality." An element of cartoon humor is added to the sternness of the previous scene. Perched on a fantastically high stool the Man, who is now a ledger clerk, writes swiftly as Bankers and Brokers call out their offers. They are bidding for war contracts.

VOICE: Munitions factories
Are offered
At one fifty.
VOICE: Liquid-fire-thrower Trust
On offer.
VOICE: War-prayerbook Limited
On offer.

A new enterprise is launched: soldiers' brothels, to be known as War Convalescents' Homes, Ltd. In high silk hats the Bankers foxtrot. The music is like the jingling of coins. The lights fade. . . .

The lights rise again on the huge stairs. The vista of infinity is gone, blotted out by dark draperies. The stairs hold a chorus of men and women in blue denim, standing in formation. The decision to call a general strike is before them. They do not hesitate; the vote to strike is unanimous. Then the *Nameless One,* counselor of "violence," appears from their midst.

THE NAMELESS: . . .
Whoever stands across our path,
Be trodden down!
Masses are deeds!

Torn by her indecision the Woman dares not contradict him as the masses echo "Deeds!"

Again a dream interlude. We hear a song of evil, the chant of the outcasts of society—criminals, prostitutes, beggars. The Nameless One, his movements as swift as a bolt of lightning, is suddenly in the middle of the crowd. A concertina is in his hands. Wildly he leads the dancing of the mob. Spotlights, ever-changing in color, turn, flickering, over this scene from Hades.

A transition through darkness to the massed workers on the stairs. The revolt is not going well. Workers, like antique messengers of doom, run down the steps shouting news of strategic positions lost. The workers' battalions have been cut down by grenades and poison gas in front of the railway station. The post office, captured, is lost again. So run the reports. Fear begins to paralyze the crowd, packed now at one side of the great stairs. Shots echo offstage. From the stricken mass, thinly at first, then in full chorus, rises a song of defiance, *The Marseillaise.* It is broken by a crash of machine-gun fire. The rearmost curtains loop up, disclosing an officer in a steel helmet. At his order, a soldier arrests the woman.

Another dream replaces this reality. The Woman crouches imprisoned in a birdcage beside which stands a Warder. Shadows of men circle around her in gigantic silhouettes thrown on the cyclorama. These are the ghosts of workers killed in the revolt. Their voices echo from a distance accusingly: why had she not opposed the counsel of the Nameless One? She does not know how to answer: she has not been more, or less, guilty than anyone else. Who is to blame for these killings? No one? Everyone? Or the Being who made such things possible? But God is in everyone, including one's self. . . . Do these reflections liberate the tortured mind of the prisoner? At any rate the shadows vanish. The Warder opens the door of the cage.

The lights seem to stab the last scene out of the darkness of the stage. They reveal a prison cot, and the Woman. She speaks her thoughts aloud.

THE WOMAN: O way through fields of ripened wheat
In August days . . .
Rambles over winter mountains . . .
O little cricket in the hush of noon . . .
O world. . . .

The Man appears. Their dialogue is short. She considers him as guilty—or as blameless—as herself.

> Give me your hand, my brother. . . .
> You, too, are my brother. . . .

The Man is gone, and the Nameless One has replaced him. "Two guards are bribed," the Nameless One informs her. The third, outside the door, must be struck down. Her freedom for the jailer's death. Will she consent?

She refuses. The Nameless One vanishes. The Officer appears and bids her follow. The stage remains empty for a moment, then two female Prisoners glide in to steal bread and trinkets. There is a harsh volley offstage. The second Prisoner sobs: "Sister, why do we do such things?" The final curtains close.

Those accustomed to Naturalist or even Symbolist staging might well rub their eyes with bewilderment at this production. A play of a great many scenes, almost completely without furniture or properties. Lighting like nothing in reality, consisting only of evanescent shafts of light. Scarcely a hint of locale; an abstract stairway dominates the play. Troops fire into an assembly of people; we see only a lifted curtain, a steel-helmeted soldier. Streets, slums, a union hall, a prison, are supposed to pass before our eyes; there is only an occasional property to denote them. The actors do not personify human beings; they clothe moral principles in human shapes by means of gesture, voice and costume. Above all, that impression of fathomless dark space in which flashes of light look for and reveal transient shapes and actions constricted and severe. . .

The meaning of the script is blurred and confused. An affirmation of idealism. A protest against a so-called civilization which depraves and murders human beings. God and men are in turn accused and pardoned. A condemnation of violence under any circumstances. The individual soul as against the class viewpoint. We encounter all these themes, none of them embodied in characters more concrete than those of Morality plays. But the script and the production are unified by a single outburst of passion revealed in terms of the stage.

In Toller's autobiography we can trace this almost disembodied story back to the real circumstances from which it was derived. The original of Sonia Irene L. was Frau Sonia Lerch, wife of a professor at the University of Munich, who disowned her when she joined the insurrection of the working class. Her deep love for her husband caused her to return home, where she was seized by the police. In Stadelheim Prison she wept for three days without pause; she refused all consolation and finally hanged herself in her cell.

In much the same frame of mind Toller wrote out the first draft of his play at Niederschönenfeld in two and a half days. (It was not finished until more than a year later.) The performance at the Volksbühne is usually described as an example of Expressionism. There are many reasons why such a description is justified. It is even more correct, however, to say that it bridged the gap between the technique of Expressionism and that of *Theatricalism.* The production as a whole brings us closer to the formalized, "presentational" type of staging which we must now consider.

It may be of interest to record that MASSE MENSCH derived its use of "searchlight" technique from an earlier production, Reinhardt Johannes Sorge's THE BEGGAR (1912). It is interesting, too, that the director Jürgen Fehling, who on this occasion staged the singing of *The Marseillaise,* proved later that he could serve German fascism equally well—as director of the State Theatre under Vice-Führer Göring.[2]

CAESAR WITHOUT SCENERY

New York City, sixteen years later. In a side street that is just off Broadway but seems remote from it, we come upon a small playhouse with a Rococo auditorium and a shallow stage. A newly painted signboard informs us that this is the Mercury Theatre. Until now it had been the Comedy, but the atmosphere here has not been very gay. The productions which have found shelter in this playhouse lately have not been overburdened with cash. Now it had become a haven for a troupe of players who had bravely left their "relief" jobs on the Federal Theatre Project to follow their leaders, John Houseman and Orson Welles, into the hazards of commercial production. On November 1, 1937, the Mercury raised the curtain on its version of Shakespeare's JULIUS

CAESAR. Next morning the young, cherub-faced director, Orson Welles, was on the high road to the Martian Wars, Campbell's Playhouse and a movie career.

The curtain of the Mercury production went up and stayed up to the end of the show. The whole depth of the stage was revealed, to the brick walls, which were painted a deep red. The stage floor consisted of a platform painted the same color; it jutted out far into the audience in front and fell away in a series of invisible steps toward the back. Stage walls and floor were only faintly visible in a shrouding darkness.

Scene after scene passed, with no hint of a setting. No street, no palaces, no forum, no senate, no market place; no chairs, no tables. Only for Marc Antony's oration two properties were brought on: a rostrum, and a coffin containing Caesar's body. Conspirators in present-day American hats and overcoats, or in military dress reminiscent of Italian fascist uniforms, swirled out of the darkness, picked out by the ever-shifting beams of light. Scenes followed each other with staccato speed, to the accompaniment of footsteps racing over the resounding platforms, with now and then an interlude of curious music vibrating through stage and auditorium like the shudder of doom.

The Mercury production's empty-appearing stage at once earned for CAESAR the name "no-scenery play." By a coincidence two other stage hits of that season merited and received that title. One of them was Marc Blitzstein's THE CRADLE WILL ROCK—also put on by the Mercury; the other was Thornton Wilder's OUR TOWN, produced by Jed Harris.[3]

Dramatic critics seemed to think that a new technique had arrived on Broadway. It was not the first time, however, that plays had appeared on Broadway with a minimum of scenery or with stage walls showing.[4] Of the three productions, OUR TOWN was the only one which apparently started out with a new type of staging in mind. In the case of JULIUS CAESAR the Mercury's lack of funds seems to have been the motive prior to any conscious aim at a new style, while the scenic form of THE CRADLE WILL ROCK was a complete accident. (THE CRADLE, originally placed in rehearsal by the Federal Theatre, had been put on without scenery or costumes by the actors themselves after the Federal Theatre disowned it.)

The term "no-scenery" is of course misleading. It is physically impossible to do away with the stage setting, since actors cannot move in a scenic vacuum. The setting may consist only of the bare walls of the stage; and this quality may be as helpful or as harmful as any other quality. The plays under discussion used considerable scenery in the way of platforms and lighting apparatus, not to mention the solid brick walls of the stage and the festoons of steam radiators. In CAESAR one of the most effective scenes employed a speaker's stand for Antony's oration; and it could be argued that the later scenes of the same play lost heavily because they lacked the scenic means to convey Brutus' defeat in war.

Yet, taken together, the "no-scenery" productions awoke public interest.[5] Broadway audiences, long accustomed to Symbolist picture settings, acclaimed a method of production which did away with these settings. The average playgoer saw actors move through stage space unhindered by scene flats, and there was something about that fact which gave him a sense of long-forgotten freedom.

Broadway has a short memory. Not many of the critics or laymen who hailed this trio of plays as the beginning of an era seemed aware that the "no-scenery" phenomenon was not altogether new. They were looking upon a temporary revolt against illusory staging. But the original uprising had taken place almost two decades before on a wider front, not only in Europe but in the United States.

"STUDY THE STAGE"

The struggle against Naturalism had been fought and, it was supposed, won. It had been won, presumably, by the Symbolists. But time passed, and a curious fact became evident to many people in the theatre. Instead of putting an end to Naturalism the Symbolists had only revealed their own Naturalistic turn of mind.

What was the difference whether you reconstructed Mrs. Alonzo Smith's parlor on the stage to the last cracks in the plaster (as the Naturalists did), or whether you reconstructed the same room with the poetic and austere "atmosphere" of the Symbolists? In each case you were still trying to persuade your audience that it is not in a theatre but is looking into the very home of Mrs.

Smith. What was Symbolism at bottom but an *attenuated Naturalism?* What was it but Naturalism of a thinner, prettier and less cluttered sort?

It was true that Naturalism had not been very selective. That was one of the faults which Symbolism had overcome. But was that the essential and basic fault of Naturalism? No. The great fallacy of Naturalism was its belief that it could bring to the stage a convincing illusion of life. And the Symbolists never really challenged that belief.

They did not challenge Zola's premise that a lifelike quality must be the aim of scenic art. They did not conceive of a type of scenery which did not belong inside the gilt picture frame of the proscenium. Their real aim was only to perfect that very illusion which the Naturalists believed in. And in that aim the Symbolists had succeeded.

They succeeded in making the illusion of life more convincing. But even if complete conviction could be attained, what then? Is it really the theatre's business to create an illusion of life? Is it not rather the theatre's business to affect its audiences significantly? The fact that something lifelike has been brought to the stage is no evidence, in itself, that anything significant has been brought there. Perhaps Symbolist staging, instead of giving Naturalism its death-blow, had succeeded only in giving it a new lease of life.

But Symbolism, it should be recalled, was only one part of the New Stagecraft. The Symbolists were content with their cautious program of improvement. That program did not satisfy the more daring directors, actors and designers. Lifelike quality, the idea of replica in any form, must be repudiated. Naturalism in its new guise must be fought down all over again.

In which direction must the theatre go now? The Naturalists of the nineteenth century had banished stage conventions. Well, then, these conventions must be restored. Theatre is theatre, not a slice of life. "Back to theatricalism!" became the war cry.

Manifestoes appeared once more. Or perhaps it would be more correct to say that nearly the entire following of the New Stagecraft went back to its original manifestoes, threatening at any moment to go off the deep end into out-and-out Theatricalism.

In 1909 Georg Fuchs had written:

. . . drama must be understood in terms of the materials in which it is made manifest. The term *theatre* consists of the totality of these materials. This is what we mean when we demand that the drama become once more theatrical.

Two years later Gordon Craig added:

Avoid the so-called "naturalistic" in movement as well as in scene and costume. The naturalistic stepped in on the Stage because the artificial had grown finicking, insipid; but do not forget that there is such a thing as *noble* artificiality.

In the twenties, with the Theatricalist advance far under way in Europe, American authorities like Kenneth Macgowan, Robert Edmond Jones, Sheldon Cheney and Oliver Sayler, back from journeys abroad, recommended the new form to the American theatre in the most glowing terms. Kenneth Macgowan in 1921 foretold the final eclipse of the "peep-hole" stage. In 1928 Sheldon Cheney in prophetic mood declared in his *Stage Decoration,*

I have come to the firm belief that ultimately the theatre will abandon almost entirely the realistic mode, will develop a stage almost as far from the current proscenium-frame peep-hole affair as were the Greek and Elizabethan platforms. . . .

Had they thought of it, the Theatricalists might have invoked at least one great name from the past. About 1775 Johann Wolfgang von Goethe, in his essay *On Dramatic Form* advised that,

He who would work for the stage should, moreover, study the stage, the effects of scenography, of lights and rouge and other coloring matter, of glazed linen and spangles. He should leave nature in her proper place, and take careful heed not to have recourse to anything but what may be performed by children with puppets upon boards and lathes, together with sheets of cardboard and linen.

DRAMA ON THE FORESTAGE

Thus the manager of the Weimar Theatre anticipated the formulations of Fuchs and Craig by one hundred and twenty-five years. More than that, he brought up a question which long afterwards became a center of controversy in the era of Theatricalism. His question had to do with the forestage, or "apron"—that part of the stage which extends out toward the audience beyond the proscenium (the picture frame) of the stage proper.

By the 1920's the forestage, where it existed at all, was to be found only in abbreviated form in contemporary theatres. Yet this little space became, with good reason, a battleground of dramatic theory.

Goethe raised a practical question in a practical manner—by including an emphasized forestage in the plans of the theatre at Weimar. For Goethe, Shakespeare was a tremendous aid in the struggle against Baroque classicism. But Goethe was an old man before he finally understood that Shakespeare's writings were an organic part of the whole manner of Elizabethan staging.

Shakespeare, he realized, had not written for a picture-frame stage, but for a platform stage, a type of playing space which thrusts the players and their actions far into the center of its audiences. A performance on this type of stage is something different from a performance on a recessed, curtained picture stage. Goethe and his architect, Carl Friedrich Schinkel, tried to bring back the direct actor-audience relationship which the Elizabethan theatre had enjoyed.

Goethe's innovation claims a place in history. It started a counter-movement when the current was flowing ever more swiftly in the direction of illusory staging. It set forth the issues of a problem which has yet to be settled.

The stage aprons in our Broadway theatres are a relic, the last remaining strip of conventional ground in the illusory theatre. From the time of the Attic *orkestra,* the dancing ring in which the chorus was stationed, until the middle of the seventeenth century, the stage was thrust into the audience, carrying the actor into direct contact with the spectator. Even Shakespeare's scaffold had been more forestage than stage.

By the end of the Italian Renaissance, however, there was a marked change. In 1584 the prototype of the modern stage building arrived—the Olympic Theatre, at Vicenza, Italy, designed by Palladio. An indoor playhouse, it was a miniature, roofed-over edition of the ancient Roman amphitheatre, with a semicircular auditorium, a balcony, and a stage platform set within an elaborate architectural façade.

By 1618 or 1619 the first playhouse of our current type had

come into existence—the Farnese Theatre at Parma, Italy. Here the sculptured Roman façade of the stage was turned into a typical proscenium frame. The whole stage was recessed behind this frame, which accommodated a great tapestried curtain. It is true that the orchestra floor in this theatre could still be used as additional playing space. But the stage itself had acquired a *picture* quality. With rise of curtain the play was revealed as essentially a picture framed by the proscenium. The spatial direction of this

From Burlingame

Wagner's Baireuth Theatre (1876)

dramatic picture was *inward,* into the stage depth. This direction was emphasized by the use of scenery painted in a perspective which stretched to the horizon of the backdrop.

Clearly, scenic form was undergoing a revolution. The front curtain was turning into an indispensable part of a performance. The forestage receded. Actors and audience were sharply separated at the boundary of the footlights. This separation in time strongly affected the quality of performance. More and more the audience became passive, introspective. At the same time the players, and in fact the whole scenic world, acquired an independent existence on the other side of the curtain.

There is a vital difference between the kind of performance in which an obviously visible platform brings audience and players together for a theatrical ceremony, and the kind inaugurated in Italy, in which the theatregoer sits relaxed in his seat, contemplating the lighted picture before him as if he were musing upon an image in his own mind. The first is the archetype of conventional technique; the second is the archetype of illusory technique.

A "mystic gulf" or abyss, as Richard Wagner called it, had opened between the life of the stage and the life of its audiences. The stage had become a peep-box, magically lit, where elaborate dreams like Wagner's could be glimpsed only through the pathos of distance. The technical requirements of Wagner were just the opposite of Goethe's; Wagner wanted the separation of stage and audience made all the greater by sinking a pit for the musicians just in front of the stage. In 1876 his views on staging were incorporated in the newly opened Baireuth Opera House, built from the plans of Gustav Semper.

Wagner has explained why he was so taken with the idea of a space between auditorium and stage:

> My requiring the concealment of the orchestra soon led the eminent and ingenious architect whom it was my privilege first to consult with upon the subject, to conceive the idea of a vacant space between the proscenium and the first row of seats. This we called the "mystic gulf," since it would seem to divide the real from the ideal; and the architect placed in front of it a second and wider proscenium, the effect of which was intended to be a wonderful illumination to the senses, the stage appearing to be more distant from the spectators than it really was, owing to the difference between its width and that of the second proscenium. Thus, though the spectator would see what took place on the stage, with all the directness of actual proximity, he would imagine that a considerable space intervened. From this would result another illusion, viz., that the dramatic personages would seem to be magnified into superhuman proportions.
>
> The result of this contrivance might of itself suffice to show how admirably this new relation between the spectator and the scenic tableau works. On taking his seat, the spectator straightway finds that he is in a "Theatron" indeed; i. e. simply a place where one may witness a spectacle, and witness it straight before his eyes. Between himself and the spectacle there stands nothing that is clearly perceptible; only between the two prosceniums the skill of the architect has produced a certain indefinable effect of distance, which causes the tableau to retreat from the spectator, as in a dream; meanwhile, the music, as it comes forth like a spirit voice from the "mystic gulf," or like the vapor rising from the sacred bosom of Earth beneath the tripod of the Pythia,

induces in him that spiritualized state of clairvoyance wherein the scenic representation becomes the perfect image of real life. (Burlingame).

Antoine a little later might set himself apart from such cloudy visions and demand a sharp focus upon existing reality; but Antoine no less than Wagner needed the protection of a picture frame. In spite of Goethe's experiment the stage apron continued to shrink.

It was not until the beginning of the present century that a reaction set in against the framed-in picture stage. The Munich Artists' Theatre, built in 1908 on Theatricalist principles, with a shelf-like stage brought close to the audience, was perhaps the first conventional-style theatre building of the modern era. Here a notable step was taken toward the reunion of stage and auditorium.[6]

For Erler, Littmann and other Theatricalists the architectural union of playing and seating areas became a major item in a bill of reform. The arena of a dramatic performance is not only the stage; it is the stage plus the auditorium. The picture stage is nothing but a relic of Italian opera. The gilded proscenium frame must vanish. In its place we must put the platform stage known to Shakespeare and Molière, re-establishing that intimacy, that unity of player and spectator, which alone can give freshness to the drama. A bridge must be flung across the mystic gulf of Wagner.

The so-called relief stage used by Fuchs threw his actors into sharp focus against a shallow stage setting. The Munich Artists' Theatre settings were as a rule so slight in depth that they appeared two-dimensional and therefore deliberately un-Natural. The Munich designers provided either screen-like flats or painted curtains hanging in folds behind the acting area. When Naturalism could not otherwise be avoided it was negated by means of a very severe, simple handling of the scene design.

In 1921 Macgowan reported that more than a dozen German playhouses had incorporated some means of tying together stage and auditorium along the lines of the Künstlertheater. These included the Court Theatre, Stuttgart, built from the same plans, and the Schiller Theatre in Charlottenburg. At Hellerau, near Dresden, Heinrich Tessenow designed for the Dalcroze School of Eurhythmics an oblong hall of the starkest simplicity. The stage area was the floor of the hall itself, in front of a steep incline of seats. The lighting of the hall, as arranged by Alexander von Saltzmann, merged imperceptibly with that of the stage. Colored light, ever-changing, suffused the walls—an idea which has since been adopted by the American movie palaces.

Similar innovations appeared in other countries. Jacques Copeau's Théâtre du Vieux Colombier, in Paris, continued the architecture of the auditorium up to and upon the stage platform,

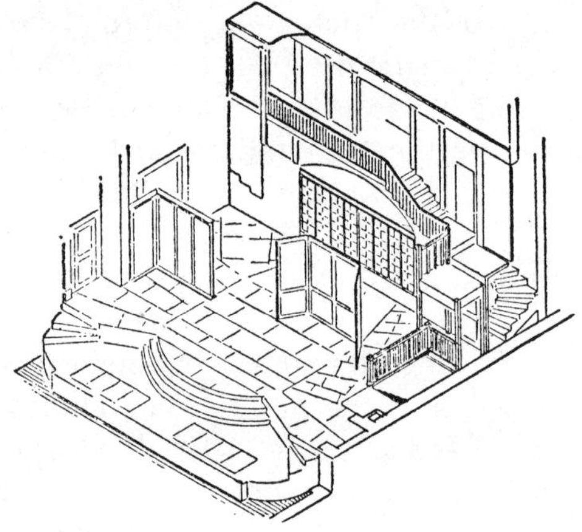

From *Theatre Arts*

THE BROTHERS KARAMAZOV at Copeau's Théâtre du Vieux-Colombier

Basis of the setting is the architecture of the stage itself

which was joined to the hall by three broad sections of steps. Copeau used the formal architecture of this stage as the basis for all his settings, with minor changes such as the addition of properties or draperies, the insertion of doors and windows. A like scheme was used for the Marais Theatre in Brussels designed under the supervision of Copeau's gifted pupil Louis Jouvet. In 1925 A. and G. Perret and A. Granet erected for the Exposition of Graphic Arts, Paris, a theatre oddly Japanese in its treatment; it had a forestage with three inner stages opening upon it. In Vienna after the War Max Reinhardt and Alfred Roller turned a palace ballroom, the Redoutensaal, into a theatre by placing a stage platform at one end and backing it with a Baroque screen.

PRESENTATIONAL

The return to stage conventions affected not only stage platforms but settings and acting as well. If Naturalist and Symbolist productions had tried to "represent" places and characters, the Theatricalist ideal was to "present" them directly to the audience, bringing them in on the stage platform as on a tray. Some notable Theatricalist productions had already been carried out by Appia and Craig, and these were followed by even more striking examples in Germany, and in Russia both before and after the revolution.

In 1911 Craig, through the good offices of Isadora Duncan, was invited to design a production of HAMLET for the Moscow Art Theatre. He worked out a combination of screens, abstract and towering. It was a noble experiment, not without its ridiculous side. The Art Theatre spared no pains to give the designer what he asked for in labor and materials. Apparently Craig, ready enough with brush and pen, proved unequal to the mechanical side of his work, and even absented himself from Moscow during most of the crucial weeks of preparation.

In spite of everything the production and Craig's designs for it made theatre history. Stanislavsky has given a fascinating report of the project:

> Having no faith, just like me, in the usual theatrical methods and means of production, in wings, flies and flat scenery, Craig refused to have anything to do with them, and turned to the use of simple convex screens which could be placed on the stage in endless combinations. They hinted at architectural forms, corners, niches, streets, alleys, halls, towers, and so on. These hints were aided by the imagination of the spectator, who in this manner became one of the active creators of the production. . . . Craig's ideas of Hamlet displayed themselves in a monumentality, in a largess of measure, in a generality and simplicity of decorative production. The divine right, the power, the despotism of the King, the luxury of court life were treated by Craig in a color of gold that approached naïveté. For this he chose simple gilt paper very much like that used to decorate Christmas trees, and pasted it all on the screens used in the court scenes of the play. He was also very fond of smooth, cheap brocade, in which the golden color always preserves the imprint of childish naïveté. . . . Having told us of all his dreams and plans of production, Craig left for Italy, and Sulerjitsky and I

began to fulfil the ideas of the chief stage director and initiator of the production [Craig]. This moment saw the beginning of our tortures. . . . The great screens could not stand up well and would fall. If a single screen fell, all the others followed it.

At the final rehearsal, just as the audience was entering the theatre the screens fell, breaking frames and tearing canvas all over the stage. The curtain, which Craig had intended to keep unused throughout the performance, had to be lowered and used all through the performance to cover scene shifts.

In 1913, at the Dalcroze School which we have described, Appia brought to the stage his version of Claudel's TIDINGS BROUGHT TO MARY. The settings followed the sketches he had made for THE VALKYRIE in 1895. It had become possible, in the interim, to create on the stage that cubic volume of illumination which must have seemed only a fantastic notion eighteen years before.

A casual glance today may find nothing of great interest in the TIDINGS setting. It consisted of a central platform reached by stairways on either side. Smaller platforms stood upon the large one, below which a kind of crypt appeared, in the rear, six square columns towered up out of sight. The total effect was still that of a picture setting; yet the tendency to break up the stage picture is already foreshadowed in this scheme composed of abstract prisms, and in the starkly Cubist handling of stage space.

Appia's manner of handling space may be traced in the work of later directors such as Leopold Jessner. As director of the State Theatre, Berlin, between 1919 and 1925, Jessner proved himself a master of stage space, using consistently the idea of platforms and stairs to enable his actors to move through a cubic area. For WILHELM TELL (1919) the stage was terraced back in planes suggesting mountain country, and scene shifts were effected by a few changes in properties and lighting. Such productions as RICHARD III (1921) or Grabbe's NAPOLEON (1922) were played almost entirely on stairways, the so-called *Jessner-treppen.*

Wedekind's MARQUIS OF KEITH, as directed by Jessner, contained two levels. The lower level, designed as a Naturalistic room, belonged to the middle class characters; the upper level was backed by a wall like a white screen, with invisible, automatically-opened doors through which the other, demented characters

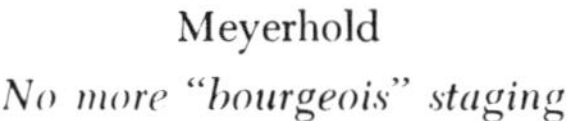

Meyerhold
No more "bourgeois" staging

Tairov
"The stage is a keyboard."

TOWARD A THEATRICAL STAGE

ON BOARD (1927) by Prince William of Sweden, at the Royal Dramatic Theatre, Stockholm. Setting by Jon-And

Plausibly Naturalistic, the setting shows the influence of Theatricalism and Constructivism

darted in and out. The rattle of drums was substituted for the sound of bells, champagne glasses were pointed pieces of wood.

Into the many scenes of NAPOLEON, as designed by Cesar Klein, Jessner crowded a whole tornado of history. Mobile platforms with fragments of environment displayed on them—a throne at the head of a regal stairway, the heights of a battlefield,—all loomed up before a translucent cyclorama. Upon this cyclorama designs were projected (from in back) with the aid of a new type of projection lantern invented by Adolpf Linnebach. Romantically stormy sky pictures were thus wrought in light; but these remnants of picture-staging were keyed to the presentational quality of the production as a whole. The violent mood of the staging, reflected in the abrupt, sudden gestures and shouted lines of the actors, broke through the old passive relationship of players and audience.

Some memorable examples of the "direct," presentational way of staging were furnished by Max Reinhardt at the Grosses Schauspielhaus, Berlin, just before the first War. The value of direct contact between players and audience had been made clear to Reinhardt at the very beginning of his career when he managed the cabaret Schall und Rauch. The principle of intimacy between stage and auditorium remained with him even when he took command of the Grosses Schauspielhaus, a reconstructed circus building in which a great stage was combined with a central arena.

Such spectacles as OEDIPUS (1910), SUMURÛN (1910), THE MIRACLE (1911) and DANTON'S DEATH (1916) took place partly on the stage, partly in the arena of this circus building. SUMURÛN employed runways similar to the "flower paths" of the Japanese stage. For THE MIRACLE the whole interior of the playhouse was redesigned as a cathedral. The stage contained a façade of Gothic architecture pierced by windows of stained glass. Religious processions moved down the aisles of the theatre.

For the Berlin production of OEDIPUS (produced originally at Munich, 1906), Reinhardt erected on his stage a palace-front of great columns approached by a broad stairway from the arena, in which hundreds of extras represented an angry populace rather than an antique chorus. The nearness of actors to audience was quite literal, since players' entrances and exits were made from the orchestra and even from the balconies, whence their voices, at the very elbows of the spectators, swept toward the action on the stage. Huntly Carter has given an account of Reinhardt's production of the same play in London (1912) which is worth quoting here:

As at Berlin and Frankfurt, the whole of the interior of the theatre was made to serve the "scene," the entire proscenium was fitted with a black screen representing the front of the palace of Oedipus. The center of this screen was occupied by high, impressive brass doors, on either side of which were three massive black columns supporting a grim portico. The orchestra well was covered by a black platform, with a piece projecting from the center upon which the altar was placed. On either side of this "apron" flights of steps led to the arena, or ball-floor of the theatre. This floor formed a lower stage, and was built up in order to enable the spectator to realise that he was participating in the scene before him. In pursuit of the intimacy idea, a space was cleared in front of the stage by removing rows of stalls, for the chorus and crowd to act in and mix with the spectators. The front row of the stalls was, in fact, in touch with the outer fringe of the crowd, while all the players made their entrances and exits through the audience at various points of the arena.

The scene was lit from all points of the theatre according to the new methods, whereby coloured limes [calcium-lights] are thrown on neutral surfaces, and the desired effects obtained by mixing the coloured rays as they fall on each object. The principal aim of the lighting was, however, to keep a blinding white light beating upon the palace, and to break it up with vivid bits of colour. The general conception of colour was black and white, great masses of white, sometimes tinted with yellow, moving against the dense blue background which occasionally deepened to violet.

Perhaps the most artistic effect was that attained by the crowd and Oedipus. Oedipus stood on the rostrum calm and self-possessed. Beneath him surged the infuriated mob, with outstretched arms, swelling up to him like a sea of angry emotions, and returning thence to the Leader of the Chorus in response to his call. There on one side Oedipus stood like an intellectual pinnacle islanded in the billowing ocean of human beings; and there on the other side the Leader stood like the Spirit of the Infinite swayed to and fro by elemental passions.

Some of Reinhardt's less radical productions also contained Theatricalist features. Typical was this director's use of the revolving stage, in which the turntable platform was emphasized instead of hidden. Often a number of settings were placed on the turntable simultaneously, the transition from one locale to another being made by revolving the stage in full view of the audience.

In a MIDSUMMER NIGHT'S DREAM a whole forest was erected on the revolving stage of the Deutsches Theater. Two hills, with a bridge arching the valley between them, were likewise built upon the revolving stage for Kleist's PENTHESILEA (1911). FAUST (1909) held eight scenes on the turntable, with two more settings on upper floors, making ten scenes in all. For OTHELLO (1910) five major scenes were pre-set. These included canals in Venice, landing stages, streets, a harbor, canal bridges, the Senate, and so on. The players walked from one locale to another as the stage platform revolved. Much the same plan was used for THE MERCHANT OF VENICE (1905).

In these productions, aside from the "direct" use of the revolving stage, the technique remained illusory, as in the opening scene of OTHELLO, in which two gondolas collided and swords flashed in the light of torches.

TAIROV

Under the heading of Theatricalism we have been considering a number of examples which at first glance seem to have little in common. In reality they are united by at least two features.

First of these characteristics in the frankly artificial "scenography" which interested Goethe—a recognition of the stage as platform rather than as picture, a tendency to "leave nature in her proper place," subordinating the illusory elements to a scheme that is largely conventional. The technique of MASSE MENSCH shows this trend quite clearly. It can be seen, however, even in such a production as NAPOLEON, in which all the outward rules of the illusory stage picture are observed, while all the inner rules are broken. A cyclorama upon which designs are obviously projected in lantern slides; scenery composed of platforms and steps, upon which fragments of locale are placed; dialogue shouted at the audience—all these seem in contradiction to the whole spirit of the illusory stage picture.

The second feature is a shift in emphasis from the *walls* of the setting to the *floor* of the setting. This is an important technical distinction. For the designer of picture scenery, the setting is a picture which surrounds the actors. Hence its quality remains

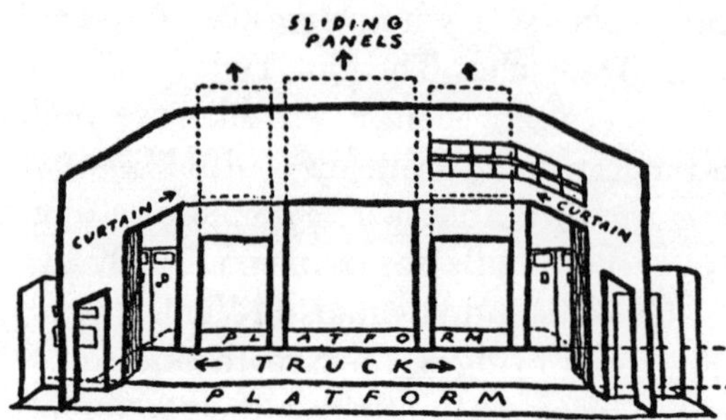

General plan of setting

Three platforms run parallel to footlights. Two are stationary, the third slides between them. Right and left stage walls have openings closed by draw-curtains. Three openings in rear wall are closed by panels sliding vertically. This structure, with varnished blue walls, white curtains and black linoleum floor, suggests a hospital. Scene changes consist only of changes in properties and small flats, set in place on offstage section of truck while onstage section is in use.

Act I, Sc. 1. Staff Library

R. and L. panels, rear, are open, giving a view of corridor upstage. Downstage portals and half-open curtains, L., reveal additional corridors. Actors cross front and back of bookcase.

Act I, Sc. 4. Interne's Room

A three-fold flat, indicating walls of room, contains a window, R., and a door, L. Remainder of stage represents hallways outside room. Simultaneous action in corridor at portal, L.

THE SEMI-PERMANENT SETTING

From *Theatre Arts*

Act II, Sc. 1. Board Room

Left panel, rear, is open and backed by a two-fold flat containing large swinging doors. Both curtains closed. Elaborate modernistic filing cabinet encloses the area where the board meets.

Act II, Sc. 3. A Corridor

Rear panels closed. Opened curtains help the suggestion of a long hospital corridor. Center, a desk and medicine cabinet. Left, a telephone table.

Act II, Sc. 4. Operating Room

Both curtains closed. Anaesthesia room is offstage through portal, R. All rear panels are open, disclosing operating room and autoclaves. Area downstage, L., is localized as scrub-room.

Designs by Mordecai Gorelik for Sidney Kingsley's MEN IN WHITE (1933)

From *Theatre Arts*

fundamentally the same as that of a backdrop. The ground plan of the picture setting, as is clear from most current Broadway examples, is a simple box shape. There is a long line across the back, parallel with the footlights, with lines perpendicular to it at stage right and stage left. This box-like floor plan serves for both interiors and exteriors.

The Theatricalist designer has a different problem. He must treat the setting as a component part of the action. The setting does not surround the actors. It deals with the actors. Hence the floor plan of the setting becomes very important. When the area of the stage is broken up by means of platforms, steps, ramps, partitions or barriers of any kind (including articles of furniture deliberately placed there for that purpose), the actor is vitally affected. The actor's movements become defined for him by the spatial arrangement of the setting. Where steps are placed in his path he must ascend; where an area is restricted by visible (or even invisible) partitions or other barriers, the actor's movements are restricted. Conversely, in order to carry out certain movements which may be necessary, the actor must call upon the designer for differentiated playing areas, for steps and levels, for oblique walls, for railings or partitions.

The Theatricalist setting, instead of surrounding the actor, functions throughout the same cubic space in which the actor moves.

This Theatricalist principle of *stage space* has increased steadily in importance. The principle is a highly technical one. Among the more understandable explanations is one given by Alexander Tairov, founder and director of the Moscow Kamerny Theatre.

"The stage," Tairov said, "is the instrument on which the actor plays, is a keyboard with the help of which the actor and the régisseur build up the scenic action so as to convey the meaning of it to the audience as effectively as possible." He declared further that all scenic constructions must be designed on the principle of *rhythm.*

Why rhythm? The Russian Theatricalists looked for inspiration to such anti-Naturalistic theatre styles as the circus and the ballet. In the ballet, which the Russian imperialist theatres had brought to a high point of excellence, Tairov discovered an important Theatricalist principle. The true basis of movement in acting cannot be a servile imitation of life, but must be a series, a symphony, of movements. Upon this rhythm he based his conception of the setting as well:

> Suppose we are given the task of depicting on the stage the descent to earth of the Madonna. How must the stage be arranged in order to give an intense impression of this descent? Obviously such an impression is not possible on the even level of the stage floor. This level must be broken up and made to consist of a number of levels of varying height; these, taken together, must form something like an endless stairway down which the Madonna steps toward earth.
>
> But how shall this stairway be constructed, how shall we create the relationship that must exist among these levels?
>
> The solution depends entirely upon the rhythmic intention of the director.
>
> If the spectator is to receive the impression that she is drifting down, scarcely touching the ground with her feet; if the descent is to have a solemnly liturgical quality, the steps and platforms must be so constructed that their dimensions will have a constant relationship throughout; their rhythmic relationship should be expressed in terms of 1 to 4 or 1 to 8, so that the movements of the actress may in turn acquire a regular and flowing rhythm.
>
> On the other hand let us imagine that we wish to impart to the stage the quality of a stormy, passionate Bacchanal in honor of Dionysus. We must then break up the stage level in such a manner that the steps and platforms are united by manifold and varied rhythms. By this means the Bacchic gestures and satyr-like leaps on the stage acquire a complex rhythmic extravagance which evokes from the spectator the proper impression of a Bacchic action.

In Tairov's so-called neo-Realistic period just before and after the Russian revolution he carried out a number of productions illustrating this thesis: Claudel's TIDINGS BROUGHT TO MARY (1920); ROMEO AND JULIET (1921); Racine's PHAEDRE (1922). Most clean-cut scenically was the PHAEDRE, as designed for him by Alexander Vesnin. Here the stage space was broken—one might almost say smashed and splintered—in Cubist style, into crystalline forms. At the same time the design retained such classic elements as simple round columns. The costumes and makeup were similarly treated, in strongly emphasized but abstract high lights and shadows. The acting, according to Huntly Carter, was a rhythmic harmony of "Yoga practices and circus acrobatics."

Tairov's idea of the actor's task is perhaps best defined in his statement: "As there is a *corps de ballet,* so there should be a *corps de théâtre.*"

GROTESQUE

Closely allied to Tairov's work was that of the Habima Theatre. This Jewish troupe, which plays only in Hebrew, has had a romantic history. Its leaders, Nochum Zemach, Menachem Gnessin and others, came originally from small playhouses scattered as widely apart as Warsaw and Palestine. Bialostok, in Poland, seems to be its accredited birthplace. By 1917 the Habima had emerged as one of the leading dramatic groups fostered by the Zionist movement. In Russian Poland and Russia itself such groups wandered through the hinterlands, always on the alert for the Tsarist police. Since the actors in these strolling companies expressed Jewish aspirations, they were regarded with less than pleasure by the Tsarist government, and their performances were in fact illegal.

Nevertheless some of the Habima's leading members were able to establish themselves in Moscow at the beginning of the first European War. After the Soviet revolution the troupe was legally recognized by the Bolsheviks. The Hebrew players were befriended by Lunacharsky, Gorky, Stanislavsky and other important figures in the Soviet theatre. (Gorky in particular often attended their plays, which seem to have moved him deeply.) In 1918 the Habima became one of the four studios of the Moscow Art Theatre, with the Armenian director Eugene Vakhtangov in charge. Curiously this intensely Jewish theatre owes its professional training to two "Gentiles," Stanislavsky and his pupil Vakhtangov.

Between 1918 and 1924 in Moscow the Habima produced six important bills, among them David Pinsky's THE ETERNAL JEW; Ansky's THE DYBBUK and Leivik's THE GOLEM. In common with other dramatic companies during the civil war period the troupe endured great privation. For a time its members foraged in neighboring villages in a desperate hunt for food.

The new government passed laws for the protection of Jewish culture and against anti-Semitism. It encouraged the Habima troupe and even provided it with living quarters and a theatre in

Toward Hysteria: CALIGARI (1919)

The scenery writhes, the action has spasms

Toward Irony: LIFE AND DEATH OF AN AMERICAN (1939)

Design by Howard Bay

Industry in terms of Surrealism

Moscow. Differences arose, however, between the Habima and the more radical wing of its Jewish audiences. For these audiences, as for the government, Jewish culture was a step in winning over the Jewish population to communist ideals. The Bolshevik policy in this respect was contained in the phrase, "National in form, socialist in content." The Habima devoted itself to a content of Jewish nationalism. In 1928, after a long tour abroad, the group decided to make its home in Tel-Aviv, Palestine.

The Habima's best known and perhaps most representative production, THE DYBBUK (1918), was directed by Vakhtangov, then mortally ill. (THE DYBBUK was in fact the last play which this very gifted director took in hand.) The settings were designed by Nathan Altman; Joel Engel wrote the music, and Lashchilin was in charge of the dances. Scenically the play took full advantage of the eerie atmosphere of demoniac possession. Prismatic walls, warped stairways, chairs and tables slanting toward the audience, spotlights hidden in strategic corners of the stage setting, all created a bizarre, unearthly technique which occupied a middle ground between Expressionism and Theatricalism.

Under the direction of Alexis Granovsky another important company, the Moscow State Jewish Theatre, began work in 1919, performing in Yiddish. Between 1919 and 1922 this troupe put on three notable productions in the same grotesque Theatricalist form: 200,000 by Sholom Aleichem; Abraham Goldfaden's THE SORCERESS, and Karl Gutzkow's URIEL ACOSTA. Granovsky's desingers, Altman, Isaac Rabinovich and Marc Chagal, borrowed from the Cubists in order to create fabulous, macabre scene constructions on the stage.

The musical comedy 200,000 had a setting which represented a Jewish town in a Cubist, non-illusory manner, by means of spars, beams and crazily-leaning triangular walls. THE SORCERESS (1922) pushed this technique still further, adding ladders and a variety of platforms, upon which the actors in heavily greased and puttied Cubist makeup performed with the agility of acrobats. Even weirder was the same theatre's production, in 1923, of A NIGHT IN THE OLD MARKET PLACE, by I. L. Peretz, with settings by R. Falk. A market place in an old Jewish town was indicated by means of a beggar's patchwork of decaying medieval walls, steps and balconies, with a huge papier-mâché hand of God suspended overhead. The theme of the production—a satire on Jewish superstitions—was further emphasized in the horrible, corpse-like makeups and costumes of the players, whose acting resembled a *danse macabre*.

In 1919 a technique of the sort used by the Habima and the Jewish State Theatre was introduced to an international audience via the UFA motion picture THE CABINET OF DOCTOR CALIGARI (story by Karl Mayer and Hans Janowitz; directed by Robert Wiene; settings by Hermann Warm, Walter Riemann and Walter Rohrig). This picture affected to relate a madman's fantasy as seen in his own mind. The basic action is the kidnapping of a young woman by a somnambulist in the power of a sinister charlatan, Doctor Caligari. The action moves in spasms, while the unnatural scenery writhes in tortured lines or is broken into creased, angular planes.

The grotesque form which we have considered in these examples derives from the Jewish cultural tradition known as Hassidism. At the end of the seventeenth century there arose in the ghettos of eastern Europe under stress of persecution a fervent mysticism which preached the doctrine of unbroken communion between God and man. Its tenets further included pantheism and an emotional interpretation of the apocryphal book known as the Kabbala. Worship became ecstatic, and music, dancing and even drinking were brought into the synagogue.

Hassidic doctrine supported the idea that release of the spirit could be found only in one's own soul as distinct from the observation of rabbinical laws. It was therefore considered heretical by the orthodox rabbis, who, in Russia, sought the aid of the Tsar's police in suppressing the new religious movement. They did not succeed. Hassidism fostered a rebirth of the literary and graphic arts among the Jews, in a vein of melancholy and quaint lyric fantasy.

The work of the Habima was permeated with a religious lyricism. Chain-Nachmon Bialik, one of its dramatists, speaks glowingly of that "genuine ecstacy . . . which dissolves everything that falls into it and turns even slag into gold. . . . The words give forth light and joy as upon the day when they were issued on Mount Sinai." During the preparation of THE DYBBUK so intense was the state of mind of the company that Bialik exclaimed, "We were torches of fire burning so for three months, and it is really surprising that we weren't all burnt to ashes. . . ."

In Russia by 1930 the grotesque form seemed to have reached the end of its career. It was obviously unsuited to deal with problems of scientific or industrial reconstruction, and had long been under fire of the Soviet press for that reason.

MEYERHOLD

Of the many renowned European directors who interested themselves in Theatricalism (and the list would include every important name from Antoine and Stanislavsky onward), the Russian Vsevolod Meyerhold must be considered the Theatricalist director *par excellence.* Meyerhold's viewpoint in the theatre may be gathered from a characteristic statement like the following, in which he gives his impression of seventeenth-century theatre:

> On the extreme west . . . in France and Italy, Spain and England, and on the extreme east in Japan, within the limits of one epoch (the second half of the sixteenth and the whole of the seventeenth century), the theatre resounds with the tambourines of pure theatricality. . . . The academic theatre of the Renaissance, unable to make use of the greatly extended forestage, removed the actor to a respectable distance from the public. . . . Molière is the first of the masters of the stage of the era of Louis XIV to bring the action forward from the back and the middle of the stage to the forestage, to the very edge of it. (Sayler).

Quick, spidery, rather tall, with a prow of a nose and a shock of unruly hair, Meyerhold is the physical embodiment of restlessness. Yet his background (in spite of a grandmother who was a French comedienne) was placid enough. He was born in the provincial town of Penza, near Saratov, of a very rich mercantile family of German origin. A year's study of law convinced young Meyerhold that he had a more lasting passion for theatre, and he enrolled at the Philharmonic School in Moscow as a student of Nemirovich-Danchenko. Without waiting to finish his studies he joined the Moscow Art Theatre at its inception. He proved himself a brilliant actor. A secure career awaited him as one of the luminaries of the Art Theatre. But within four or five years he had decided that there was a fundamental defect in the method of Stanislavsky, and that it was necessary to push onward.

Stanislavsky directed as if an audience did not exist; but for Meyerhold the audience was the focus of dramatic art. With his usual liberality Stanislavsky placed the younger man in charge of an experimental studio in 1905, in the hope that something of value might result. The new studio was deep in its rehearsals of Maeterlinck's DEATH OF TINTAGEL when the political storm which had so long been brewing in Russia burst forth in the 1905 revolution, putting an end to the studio work and pushing Meyerhold into the agitated streets of Moscow. The production was never resumed.

By 1910, however, the young director was already far out on a career of bold experiment destined to make even the work of Reinhardt tame by comparison. Style in production, a groping toward direct contact with his audiences, was his objective from the start. In association with the actress Kommissarjevskaya he put on shows like THE LIFE OF MAN, by Andreyev (1906), which brought praise from a small following of intellectuals and derision from others. The Andreyev play was staged in an auditorium lined with gray drapery, with only one source of light. Properties were exaggerated in design; the actors' makeups were mask-like and sculptural in quality.

In 1908, after a break with Kommissarjevskaya, who felt that his experiments were wrecking her theatre, Meyerhold produced in Minsk a version of BALAGANCHIK in which screens were used, in Japanese fashion, instead of scenery. The author was introduced in the course of the action, which took place in the orchestra; the lights remained on in the auditorium throughout the play.

For his staging of Molière's DON JUAN at the Alexandrinsky Theatre in St. Petersburg (1910), he removed the proscenium and front curtain of the stage (an effect he had already tried out in 1906 for Ibsen's GHOSTS), bringing the actors as far as possible out on the forestage.

With the curtain removed that it might not create even a momentary coldness between actors and spectators, with auditorium lights blazing to intensify the excitement and gaiety, but paling before the hundreds of wax candles in great chandeliers upon the stage, moved the splendid creatures of the age of Molière and Louis XIV, the personifications of luxury and extravagance. That these magnificent courtiers might never be required to tax their delicate strength, little negro servants flitted about moving a chair, retrieving a handkerchief, or tying the ribbon of a shoe. They also scattered perfumes that the audience might breathe luxury as well as behold it, rang a tiny silver bell to reassemble the spectators, and made necessary announcements. (Miller).

For Blok's THE UNKNOWN (1914), with which he undertook the use of Constructivist forms, he employed also "eccentric accessories, jugglers, Chinese boys throwing oranges among the audience, quaint things and human figures . . . interwoven in a fantastic manner." (Carter). By the outbreak of the Soviet revolution he had introduced gymnastic training for actors, resurrected the pantomime tradition of the Commedia dell' Arte, tried out improvisation in performance.

The year 1918 found him on the communist side of the revolution. He was pressed into service in organizing the People's Commissariat for Education. That same year he was caught and imprisoned by the Whites at Novorussik. When released he joined the Red Army. This time he was given the work of sending out dramatic troupes to spread propaganda.

But Meyerhold was a man of the theatre and not a politician. It is probable that these new activities affected his dramatic imagination more than they did his political convictions. At any rate they resulted in a new phase of dramatic work, which we shall examine later.

"PURE THEATRICALITY"

With the productions of Meyerhold we are at the furthest reaches of Theatricalism in which a dramatic story is still retained.

Like the Post-Impressionist painters Braque, Picasso, Gleizes, Metzinger, Gris or Léger, who made clear that painting consists of paint applied upon a square of canvas, the Theatricalists established once for all that the stage is an acting platform onto which "life" is brought only through translation into stage values.

A great many of the canvases of the "Modernistic" school of painting are sheer technical exercises, not even abstractions from reality. In the same way we encounter stage productions now and then which can be classified only as purely technical experiments.

The exploration of the stage as a volume of cubic space was

the motive behind the TRIADIC BALLET of Oscar Schlemmer, produced at the Stuttgart Landestheater in 1922, with the dancers Albert Bürger and Elsa Hötsel. The stage was conceived as a cube; the dancers, in rigidly geometric costume, were space-objects, geometric automata functioning within the stage space. Schlemmer's experiments were continued later at the famous Bauhaus School at Dessau, under the general direction of Walter Gropius, Kandinsky, Moholy-Nagy and Paul Klee.

A like use of the stage had been proposed, with a good deal of italics, by Enrico Prampolini, director of the Teatro Magnetico, Rome. His purpose seems to have been more ambitious than Schlemmer's. Lacking more concrete explanation of this purpose, we must be content to let it remain in his own words:

> From painting, *sceno-synthesis,* to plastic, *sceno-plastic,* from this to the architecture of plastic planes in movement, sceno-dynamic. From the traditional three-dimensional scene to the creation of *polydimensional scenic-space,* from the human actor to the new scenic personality of space, the actor, from this to the *polyexpressive magnetic theatre;* which I see already outlined architectonically in the center of a valley of spiral terraces, *dynamic hills* on which rise bold constructions of *polydimensional scenic-space, center* of irradiation of the futuristic atmospheric scenery.

THE AMERICAN THEATRE THEATRICAL

Symbolism took a relatively firm hold on the American theatre. Theatricalism did not. Nevertheless a number of Theatricalist productions were carried out in the United States.

For the Arts and Crafts Playhouse, Detroit, beginning about 1917, Sam Hume used Gordon Craig's screen idea as an inspiration for an "adaptable setting" consisting of mobile units such as screens, pylons, stairs, arches and draperies. For Masefield's Japanese drama THE FAITHFUL, as produced by the Theatre Guild (1919), Lee Simonson used very effectively a background of Japanese screens.

A transition from Symbolism to Theatricalism occurs in the Aubrey Beardsley black-and-white designs used by Raymond Johnson for Cloyd Head's GROTESQUES (1916), as produced by Maurice Brown at the Chicago Little Theatre. Eva LeGallienne's production of ALICE IN WONDERLAND at the Civic Repertory Theatre (1933), as designed by Irene Sharaff, used black-and-white adaptations of Tenniel's pictures; the pictures were painted on a "panorama" behind the actors.

The Hassidist grotesque style has been cultivated in New York by two Jewish theatres: the Yiddish Art Theatre under the direction of Maurice Schwartz and the more radical Artef Theatre directed by Benno Schneider. For Maurice Schwartz and other managers Boris Aronson designed many interesting productions in this style, including Ansky's DAY AND NIGHT (1923) for Unser Theater; Sholem Alekhim's STEMPENU THE FIDDLER (1926) and Goldfaden's THE TENTH COMMANDMENT (1926) for the Yiddish Art Theatre. For the latter company Mordecai Gorelik set Gordin's GOD, MAN AND DEVIL in the same tradition.

Most of the settings of the Artef have been designed by Moi Solotaroff, who is at his best in productions like Resnick's RECRUITS (1934), in which the Hassidist inspiration is satirized in its own terms. The Artef's director, Benno Schneider, has made colorful use of the same form, as in RECRUITS, or in Kulback's THE OUTLAW (1937). The limitation of this technique becomes apparent, however, when applied to such dramas as Gorky's YEGOR BULITCHEV (1933) and DOSTIGAYEV (1935) or Ornitz's HAUNCH, PAUNCH AND JOWL (1936). In these Artef presentations the development of the content was hampered instead of aided by the grotesque method.

Examples of Meyerhold Constructivism were brought to these shores in Louis Lozowick's designs for Kaiser's GAS, produced by the Goodman Memorial Theatre, Chicago (1926); in Woodman Thompson's settings for the Actors' Theatre production of McEvoy's comedy GOD LOVES US (1926); in Donald Oenslager's setting for Farragoh's PINWHEEL (1927), at the Neighborhood Playhouse; and in Mordecai Gorelik's setting for a farce by John Howard Lawson, LOUDSPEAKER, produced by the New Playwrights' Theatre (1927).

We have already described the Jones-Hopkins production of MACBETH in 1921, with its bold attempt at anti-Naturalism.[7] Among unrealized scenic projects which captured attention during the twenties were Jones's plans for staging Shelley's tragedy, THE CENCI, on a platform erected in the center of the audience. The same designer's sketches, made as long before as 1911, for

Maeterlinck's THE SEVEN PRINCESSES, proposed the use of Gothic architecture in skeletonized form.

The sketches and models worked out by Norman Bel Geddes in 1921 as a project for an outdoor spectacle of THE DIVINE COMEDY (based on Dante's poem) show a scheme of a terraced amphitheatre crowned with great structures shaped like wings. The grandeur of this conception remains unequaled in the American theatre; it is unfortunate that it has never been put into execution.

In the next few years following his work on the DIVINE COMEDY, Geddes experimented with space-stages consisting mainly of unadorned geometric platforms, as in ARABESQUE (1925), by Cloyd Head and Eunice Tietjens; Mercedes d'Acosta's JOAN OF ARC, produced in Paris in the same year; LYSISTRATA, an adaptation from THE TROJAN WOMEN, in 1930; and HAMLET (1931). For Irwin Shaw's short-lived SIEGE (1937), Geddes employed a large turntable in the Reinhardt manner. The setting was a Spanish fortress which revolved as the actors walked from the ramparts to the tunnels inside.

Small and solid, like Reinhardt, Geddes is a powerhouse of energy. More than that, however, he is a gifted artist, whose Theatricalist turn of mind has been conditioned by an awareness of industrial and scientific America. His work as an industrial designer has received proper recognition (especially in the case of the General Motors' *Futurama* which he designed and executed for the New York World's Fair of 1939–1940). On the whole the significance of his work has not dawned fully on our theatre, which is inclined to be over-lyrical. When the theatre turns to a new mood its scenic artists will find that Geddes has preceded them.

A Theatricalist excursion into a distinctly American vernacular was the production, by the Theatre Guild, of Lawson's PROCESSIONAL (1924), with designs by Gorelik. The garish backdrops of the cheap burlesque stage were the scenic inspiration for this cartoon fantasy, which related the events of a mine strike in terms of jazz. Miners, soldiers, the Ku Klux Klan, an agitator, a Man in a Silk Hat, a reporter, took part in a furious merry-go-round, proving Lawson's thesis that "the Twentieth Century is exciting to the point of chaos." While the general outline of the play was as confused as its characters, it was carried along by its

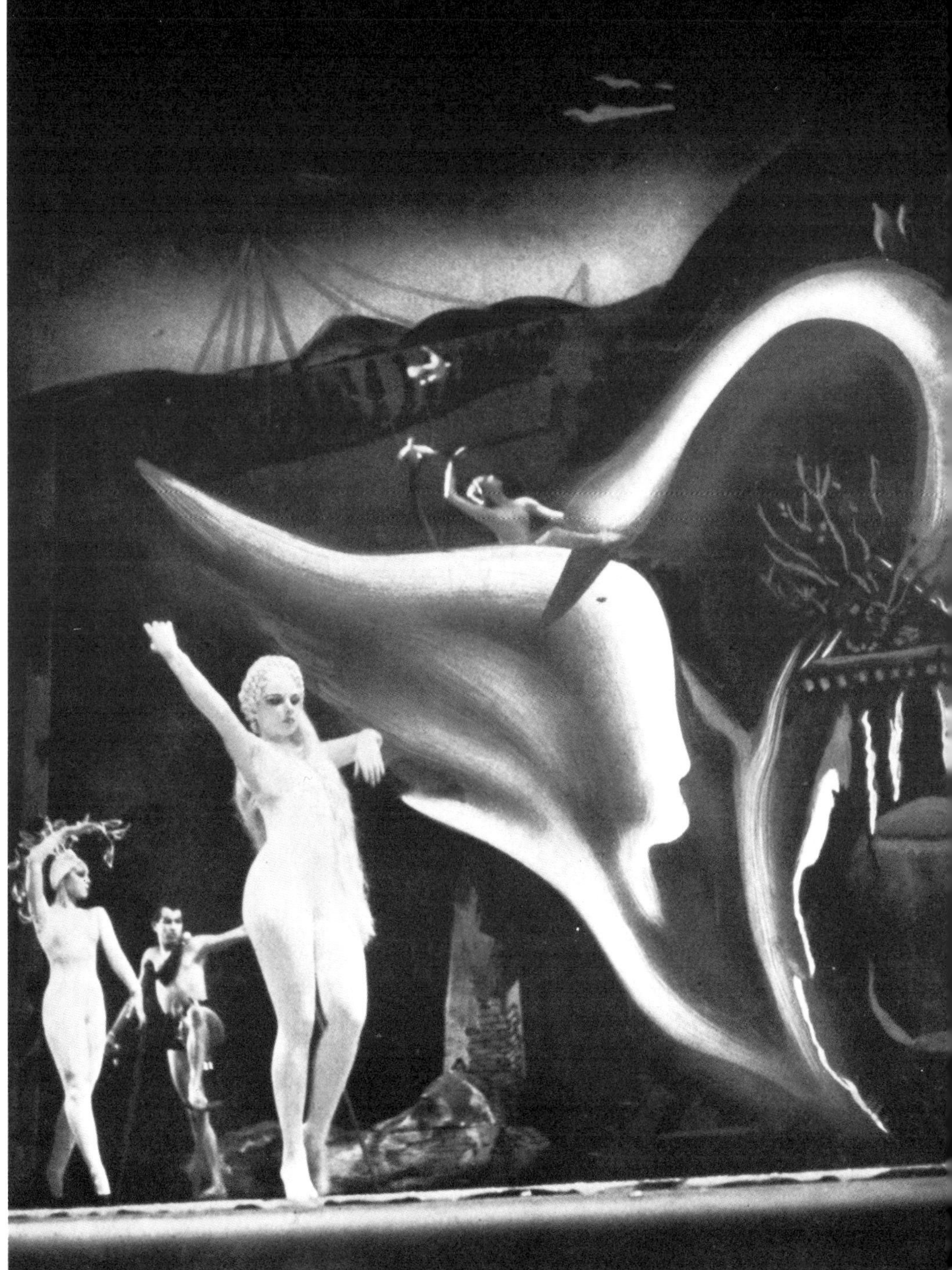

Henle-Black Star

Dali's BACCHANALE (1939)

Paranoiac performance

surging poetry. High point was a dance of the Ku Klux, to moaning jazz music. Led by the King Kleagle smoking a big cigar, the goblins intoned "Halleluiah!" while their leader roared

> Clean up the dirty foreigners, make 'em kiss the flag!
> Skin the Jews, lynch the niggers, make 'em kiss the flag!

There were a few other essays in the Theatricalist style in the twenties and later. But the tendency did not take root. Instead a slow process of deterioration began in the Symbolist technique which was already in use. In the twenties there was a good deal of talk about Stylization on Broadway; by the late thirties Theatricalism had been relegated to the field of revues and light musicals, while Symbolist work in the drama had returned in a large measure to Naturalism.

In 1940 such examples of Theatricalist design as Mielziner's settings for Rice's TWO ON AN ISLAND or Gorelik's settings for Odets' NIGHT MUSIC were no longer part of a line of advance in the American theatre. Albert Johnson, Nat Karson, Sointu Syrjala and Raoul Pène du Bois were among those who showed Theatricalist influence in the field of musical comedy and revue design. Howard Bay, Arch Lauterer and Herbert Andrews were among the younger artists in the field of drama who showed the same influence. But in general a certain amount of simplification, agreeable color schemes, tasteful furnishings and pleasant lighting were almost all that remained to tell the story of the hard-fought struggle to pass beyond the Naturalism of Belasco. American scene design was losing the lessons it had learned in the school of Robert Edmond Jones. Few of that school had Jones's restless, poetic spirit; fewer still seemed destined to create new schools of their own.

STYLE WITHOUT STATEMENT

Craig had demanded "Not realism but style." The style of the Symbolist wing of the New Stagecraft had turned out to be only a thin Naturalism. It was the Theatricalist section which caught style in bushel baskets. Did this achievement of the Theatricalists do away with the contradictions which we noted in the Symbolist theatre? It did not.

Instead of examining reality the Symbolists moved away from it into a region of abstract art. The Theatricalists lived in an atmosphere not very different. Theatricalism in its own way was an undoubted advance. At a time when our stages were devoted almost exclusively to illusory stage pictures—whether Naturalistic or Symbolist—the new form broadened our concepts of stage technique by reminding us of the traditional method of platform-staging. It brought back some of the lost vigor and imaginative power of earlier stage methods. It resumed direct contact with theatre audiences. Yet it, too, was inclined to see the art of the theatre as something sufficient unto itself.

The greater vitality of Theatricalism resulted sometimes in productions of genius, but also in productions that were nothing but fads, excrescences, displays of dazzling mediocrity. Who can foretell the products of a stage technique which owes no allegiance to reality? For one such presentation as Orson Welles' CAESAR there may be far too many like Orson Welles' FAUSTUS (1937), in which Marlowe's classic was turned into a sleight-of-hand performance.

While the American theatre was receding from the high-water marks of experiment, the Theatricalist style was arriving at an impasse in Europe. Having carried out its mission of smashing the stage picture and bringing back to life the traditions of conventional staging, having produced directors of great personal resource, it showed only too clearly how limited was its program. It could not go on reiterating that theatre must be theatre; it could not continue to make a full evening out of yet another clever theatrical idea.

Living theatre outran the program of Theatricalism—because living theatre must return to the duty of clarifying life. The patterns of the circus and the ballet, however novel on the dramatic stage, cannot forever replace an attempt at a philosophy. Especially at a time when an adequate philosophy is needed as never before.

That part of Theatricalist tradition which confined itself to trivia could go on for a while longer putting eccentricities on the stage. The part which represented the more serious side of Theatricalism was left in midair. It had perfected its method of saying something, but had no philosophy on which to base a statement.

A new philosophy appeared—one which few people of the older theatre could have foreseen.

It made its appearance on the stages of Soviet Russia. It proclaimed in so many words that theatre is a weapon, and the stage is a battleground of class war.

NOTES

1. MASSE MENSCH was produced in New York (1924) by the Theatre Guild under the title MAN AND THE MASSES.

2. See Chapter VI, p. 223.

3. See Chapter IX, p. 407.

4. For example, Paul and Claire Sifton's THE BELT (New Playwrights Theatre, 1927), See Chapter VIII, p. 342 for an account of productions in which Meyerhold showed the bare walls of the stage.

5. Just what the "no-scenery" plays meant artistically was not clear from the reviews in the newspapers. Most reviewers welcomed the phenomenon on the ground that it was a return to "simplicity." Brooks Atkinson in the New York *Times* (November 28, 1937) declared that it permitted the audience to concentrate on the actors and the play. There was considerable dissent, however. Robert Benchley, of the *New Yorker,* found the style of OUR TOWN pretentious and unintelligible. According to Eugene Burr, of *Billboard* (November 20, 1937), the director of CAESAR "completely buried the play in its lack of scenery." As against this, John Anderson, of the New York *Journal-American* (November 12, 1937), contended that one of the chief assets of the Welles CAESAR was its scenic effectiveness, an opinion in which *Stage Magazine* concurred (June, 1938).

Some further insight was provided in Thornton Wilder's explanation of the scenic method of OUR TOWN: "I tried to restore significance to the small details of life by removing scenery. . . . When the theatre pretends to give the real thing in canvas and wood and metal it loses some of the realer thing which is its true business." (New York *Times,* February 13, 1938). About the same time Hallie Flanagan, national director of the Federal Theatre, urged in a memorandum that the "no-scenery" type of production be used for Federal Theatre work: "Just as architecture today stresses function, and emphasizes rather than conceals, so the stage should stress the fact that it is a stage." (*Theatre Workshop,* April–June, 1938).

6. See Chapter V, p. 175.
7. See Chapter V, p. 200, Chapter VI, pp. 222–223.

REFERENCES

Ernst Toller: *Seven Plays.* J. Lane, London, 1935.

Georg Fuchs: *Die Revolution des Theaters.* Georg Müller, Munich, 1909.

Edward Gordon Craig: *On the Art of the Theatre.* Browne's Bookstore, Chicago.

Sheldon Cheney: *Stage Decoration.* The John Day Company.

Goethe. From Clark: *European Theories of the Drama.* Appleton.

Richard Wagner. From Burlingame: *The Art Life and Theories of Richard Wagner.* Henry Holt & Company.

Constantin Stanislavsky: *My Life in Art.* Little, Brown & Company.

Huntly Carter: *The Theatre of Max Reinhardt.* Mitchell Kennerley.

Alexander Tairov. From *The Moscow Kamerny Theatre.* Intourist, 1936.

Alexander Tairov: *Das Entfesselte Theater.* Gustav Kiepenheuer, Potsdam, 1927.

Huntly Carter: *The New Theatre and Cinema of Soviet Russia.* International Publishers, New York, 1925.

Ch. N. Bialik. From *Habimah.* Bamah, Palestine, 1937.

Vsevolod Meyerhold. From Oliver Sayler: *The Russian Theatre.* Brentano's, New York, 1922.

Miller: *The Independent Theatre in Europe.* Long & Smith. (This quotation is a summary of Meyerhold's own account as given in Oliver Sayler's *The Russian Theatre.* Brentano's.)

Enrico Prampolini: *La Scenografia Futurista* (1915).

John Howard Lawson: *Processional.* Thomas Seltzer, New York, 1925.

8

THEATRE FOR AUDIENCES

OLD WINE IN NEW BOTTLES

On a winter evening in 1926 Muscovite theatregoers, wrapped in fur coats salvaged from the days before the revolution, or bundled up to the ears in old sweaters and jackets, hurried over the icy streets to Triumph Square to attend a historical opening night. The play they were going to see was the comedy REVISOR (THE INSPECTOR GENERAL), whose author was the tragic humorist Nikolai Gogol. The play had been presented for the first time in 1836. Tonight it was due to be performed in a manner which its author could not have anticipated. Yet it is likely that Gogol, that melancholy poet whose short career ended in fanatical repentance, would not have withheld his approval from the kind of life, both eccentric and brilliant, which was imparted to his comedy by the Soviet director, Vsevolod Meyerhold.

Ten years earlier there had taken place in Russia a bewildering upheaval. The despotic rule of the Tsars, corrupt and inefficient, kept alive only by a system of terror, was finally overthrown. From an empire steeped in Tsarist darkness Russia was being turned as if overnight into a laboratory for socialism—for that theory of science and government hitherto considered the vision of Utopians. An experiment was beginning whose outcome was going to arouse the most furious debate in human history.

The whole face of Russia was changing. Factories were springing up on steppes where cattle had grazed. Tractors, reapers and binders rattled through peasant villages that had seen no agricultural machines more complex than an iron plow. Habits of mind that had seemed forever sanctified were everywhere being cast off; the old order of thought had departed. Why was one of the best-known playhouses in Soviet Moscow reviving a farce-comedy written almost a century before?

The script was, substantially, the same. The performance was something very different. Why the script could continue to be the same, why the production should be different, is worth study.

THE TSAR LAUGHED

In 1836, at the time England was waking to the industrial revolution, Russia was enjoying the deep slumber of feudalism. Or, to put the metaphor more correctly, the feudal nobility of Russia and their little group of retainers were enjoying it; the rest of that enormous country was living in serfdom and black political reaction. Gogol when he wrote REVISOR did not believe that this state of affairs was due to the mournful Russian soul. Rather he was convinced that the mournful Russian soul was the result of an arrangement which enabled the nobility and their bureaucratic satraps to devour the countryside like ravenous crows. In REVISOR he painted a picture of the little bureaucratic Caesars which set the whole world laughing. Even the Tsar saw the play and laughed.

The central figure of REVISOR is Khlestakov, an indigent young government clerk who is wandering footloose through the provinces, accompanied by his rascally servant Ossip. When the play opens, the two are lodged in a shabby tavern of a provincial town. Having no money they make demands on the tavern-keeper, using lordly airs in place of coin. Their arrogance impresses the innkeeper. It impresses still more two of the local gentry, named Dobchinsky and Bobchinsky. It alarms the Postmaster, who has opened a sealed official letter and learned that a Government Inspector is about to descend on the town to search out grafters.

"This young man gets everything gratis, he refuses to pay a kopek," Dobchinsky and Bobchinsky relate. "He must be the Inspector General in disguise." These terrible apprehensions are brought to the Mayor, who hastily summons his council. Two steps are decided upon: there must be a temporary political housecleaning; and the Inspector General must be "appeased."

Both decisions are catastrophic. The mere hint of reform on the part of the Mayor brings delegations of citizens and petitioners with importunate demands. At the same time Khlestakov, having smelled out the situation, begins to reap a golden harvest. He pockets bribes, tells tall stories, makes the most arrogant demands and pursues the chicken-brained wife and daughter of the Mayor with his attentions. Finally he blunders into becoming engaged to the daughter. Fortunately for Khlestakov, Ossip, who is

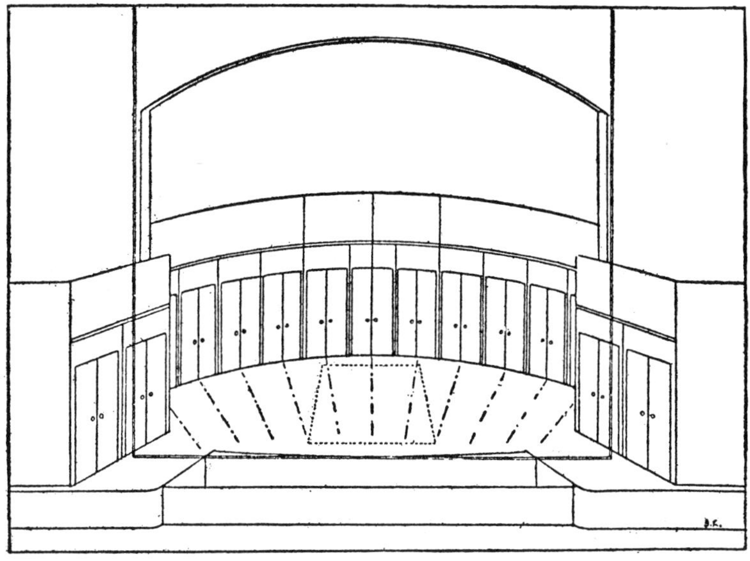

REVISOR (1926) General plan of setting

a man of foresight, hastily packs their belongings, and the two vanish from the province and from the play.

Not yet aware of this the local bigwigs gather for the engagement feast. Our hero does not appear; instead comes the Postmaster in great agitation with the news that he has opened and read a letter sent by Khlestakov to a friend. The town has been honoring an impostor! Reeling from this blow, the company receives the *coup de grâce* when the breathless Dobchinsky rushes in with the most dreadful tidings of all: the real Inspector General has arrived!

MEYERHOLD VERSUS STANISLAVSKY

Into every line of his play Gogol, himself a government clerk, put his contempt for his grafting superiors. On the other hand he did not try, in the play itself, to analyze the reason for this corruption. Neither did he suggest any remedy other than the threat of supervision by a less corruptible Inspector General. Gogol, who undoubtedly had strong feelings about grafters, had no intention of throwing himself into the struggle which was going on between the feudal masters of the country and the country's inhabitants. In his day, as in Chekhov's many years afterwards, men of letters were content to dip only their fingers in the raging stream of political struggle.

In a letter to his friend Suvorin (reactionary editor of *Novoye Vremya*) Chekhov once wrote, "The artist must be not the judge of his characters and their conversation, but merely an impartial witness." [1] Chekhov's views on this point were fully shared by Stanislavsky. The director's opinion occurs in a very revealing passage in his autobiography, *My Life in Art*. On its first visit to St. Petersburg, in 1900, the Art Theatre had scheduled its production of Ibsen's AN ENEMY OF THE PEOPLE. It so happened that the massacre in Kazansky Square took place on the very day of the opening. In Stanislavsky's words:

> The average run of spectators that night was from the intelligentsia, the professors and learned men of Petrograd. . . . Thanks to the sad events of the day the auditorium was very excited and answered even the slightest hints about liberty in every word of Stockman's protest. . . . The atmosphere in the theatre was such that we expected arrests at any minute and a stop to the performance. Censors, who sat at all the performances of THE ENEMY OF THE PEOPLE and saw to it that I, who played Doctor Stockman, should use only the censored text, and raised trouble over every syllable that was not admitted by the censorship, were on this evening even more watchful than on other occasions. . . . In the last act of the play . . . Stockman says to his wife:
>
> "One must never put on a new coat when one goes out to fight for freedom and truth."
>
> The spectators in the theatre connected this sentence with the massacre in Kazansky Square, where more than one new coat must have been torn in the name of freedom and truth. Unexpectedly my words aroused such a pandemonium that it was necessary to stop the performance, into which a real mob scene was interpolated by impromptu.

There had taken place the unification of the actor and the spectators who took on themselves the rôle of the chief actor in the theatre, that same mob action of which so much is said by the theoreticians of art. . . . From that evening many attempts were made to drag our Theatre into politics, but we, who knew the true nature of the Theatre, understood that the boards of our stage could never become a platform for the spread of propaganda, for the simple reason that the very least utilitarian purpose or tendency, brought into the realm of pure art, kills art instantly.

Stanislavsky minces no words. He wants no propaganda in the theatre. Also he indicates that the technical basis of the propaganda theatre is the unification of actor and spectator—"that mob action of which much is said by the theoreticians of art."

As he writes his memoirs Stanislavsky momentarily forgets that he was once an outstanding "theoretician" of the Russian theatre. In 1905 he himself encouraged Meyerhold to devote a studio of the Art Theatre to experiment with that direct contact of actor and playgoer which he now calls "mob action." He even forgets his own inaugural speech at the first rehearsal in Pushkino:

Bear in mind that we are striving to bring light into the dark lives of the poorer classes, to give them a few moments of aesthetic pleasure amid the gloom that envelops them. We are striving to create the first rational and moral popular theatre, and it is to this high aim that we are devoting our lives.

Perhaps to Stanislavsky the intention to "bring light into the dark lives of the poorer classes" may have meant something different from propaganda, but neither the Tsarist police nor the Tsarist censor looked upon it as anything else. The government kept a hostile eye on the Art Theatre's presentations. Stanislavsky himself has described the censorship of Ibsen's AN ENEMY OF THE PEOPLE (1900) and the attempted suppression of Gorky's SMALL PEOPLE (1902), when mounted gendarmes surrounded the playhouse.

Certainly the St. Petersburg audience and the imperial censor looked upon the Art Theatre's performance of AN ENEMY OF THE PEOPLE as propaganda, whether Stanislavsky disclaimed the intention or not. Disclaim it or not, Stanislavsky's truth-seeking theatre was accepted as propagandist by the Bolshevik regime, which invited him to put on plays like THE CHERRY ORCHARD before audiences of workers, soldiers and peasants. Work-calloused hands applauded Chekhov's dramas on the simple assumption that these plays showed convincingly how unfit to rule had been the masters of Russia. The Moscow Art Theatre found a distinguished place under a government committed, in no uncertain terms, to the principle *Theatre is a Weapon!*

After the Soviet revolution, which abolished private ownership of public institutions, the Moscow Art Theatre ceased to be a private enterprise. It assumed a State function—that of educating its playgoers in the aims of the new government. This was true of the other playhouses also. A statement by P. A. Markov, dramatic critic of *Izvestia* and director of the literary department of the Moscow Art Theatre since 1925, may be regarded as summarizing the new relationship officially:

> Under the conditions of the second Five-Year Plan the theatre has been assigned the task of transforming the individual, and bringing up citizens of the socialist State.

So that, to understand fully such a production as Meyerhold's REVISOR, we must also take account of its agitational use.

The court society of Tsar Nicholas I found REVISOR highly diverting. Bureaucratic corruption had been nurtured by feudalism and had returned to plague it. The Russian communists, who received this bureaucracy as an heirloom, also found the play amusing. Their amusement, however, was rather less genial; they were faced with the job of tearing this bureaucracy out of Russian life root and branch. To make Gogol's REVISOR a weapon for this purpose was the task set himself by Meyerhold, who had joined the Communist Party before 1918.

We need not be surprised, therefore, if Meyerhold's direction emphasized everything which Stanislavsky dismissed as "mob action."

In his Theatricalist period Meyerhold had already devoted himself to non-illusory staging and direct contact with his audiences. In the words of Huntly Carter, "Meyerhold had learned that for Stanislavsky the audience did not exist. . . . He discovered the audience, and his discovery took him from the center of the stage to the center of the auditorium." It became a veritable mania with him to seize audience attention. Some of the technical devices he used for that purpose are on record:

> A chair is shot up through the floor, beds actually fly, walls run . . . real automobiles and motorcycles run down the aisles, up over the orchestra rail and then among the populace upon the stage!
>
> There are no lights upon the stage. Two projectors, one from each side of the orchestra, next to the stage, throw light upon each actor in rotation as he plays, or upon the decorations, properties, etc., wherever the accent of the plot falls at that particular moment. . . . Movie captions, slogans . . . appear across the stage when they fit in with the action. As the act ends, the stage gets dark–finish. There is no curtain. . . . Sometimes, if the occasion warrants, an actor comes forward to where our footlights usually are, and shoots into the orchestra with his revolver, shouting "Entre'acte!"–"Intermission!" (*The Miracle of Meyerhold*).

In the Theatricalist era Meyerhold had insisted on audience-contact for purely formal reasons. Now it became a matter of seizing the audience forensically—by the lapels, so to speak. With Meyerhold "direct staging" ceased to be an esthetic idea and became a political policy.

But the fact that he was making a political statement did not release Meyerhold from the need for making this statement with artistry. Propaganda must be artistic to be convincing. The propagandist REVISOR, which Moscow saw for the first time in that converted music hall with its battered Baroque interior, fascinated the Bolsheviks in the audience just as it delighted the coat-tailed and ermine-wrapped carriage trade customers who saw it afterwards during its tour of western Europe. Let us examine it for ourselves.

SOVIET GOGOL

There is no front curtain; the permanent setting of REVISOR is already on the stage as the playgoers come in. It is a great semicircle of polished mahogany doors—fifteen doors in all—gleaming under the stage worklights and in the reflected light of the auditorium. The house lights fade. A trumpet call, as in Shakespeare's time, warns that the play is beginning. In the dimness of the stage the center panels of the curved mahogany screen are shoved aside. Stagehands visible in the worklights offstage convey toward the front a platform behind which the screen closes once more. The acting lights come up. The platform stands out boldly in the middle of the stage before the mahogany screen.

On the platform, whose floor pitches up toward the back, stands a round, solid oak table, an Empire armchair, half a dozen wooden seats. The chairs are occupied by the Mayor and his staff of officials, whose lace jabots and glittering orders fail to conceal their heavy wits. A partition, made up of three small classic columns and a drapery of green brocade, closes in the rear of the acting space.

We are permitted only a few moments to get the drift of the Mayor's report—crafty, incompetent and worried all at the same time—yet not lacking in the pretentious oratory of the period. One of the mahogany doors flies open and Dobchinsky and Bobchinsky tumble in together in their haste to squawk out their remarkable story. As the Russians say, they are in socialist competition with their news, chasing each other around the table until Dob, or maybe Bob, plants himself right under the Mayor's nose. "The Inspector General is already here, incognito!" The Mayor leaps into action. He claps his hands for the attendants. A bronze basin in which the Mayor must dip his fingers. An atomizer to perfume him. His fur coat, his tall hat, his staff. . . . The light is fading, the screen opens in back, the platform rolls upstage under cover of music. In the dimness hurrying stagehands push forward a tall structure.

The screen closes, the lights go up. The structure is a curved staircase leading to a platform. Wedged under the stairs is a Russian stove (a *petchka*), with a shabby couch huddled close to it for warmth; next to it are two worn stools, a little table. In front of the veneered screen, which fills the stage with a suave richness, stands this vignette of a dismal hostelry: the creaking, dusty stairs, the almost heatless stove in a remote, forgotten province. This is where Khlestakov and Ossip have deigned to lodge. Ossip, sly, agile and insolent, having tried unsuccessfully to seduce the chambermaid, stretches himself lazily on the couch. He sings. A whistle repeats the melody. The door at the head of the stairway opens and Khlestakov makes a grand entry down the stairs.

The little adventurer is a curious specimen: thin, with a dead-pan face; his horn-rimmed glasses and black cutaway give him the air of an elegant, pedantic jackdaw. Two pretzels hang in his lapel like a boutonniere. His whistling stops as he discovers Ossip on the bed. He tosses Ossip the pretzels, demands, "Why can't you scare up anything to eat, you lout?" They summon the hotel waiter, whom they terrorize into bringing an alleged chicken soup—lukewarm water with a chicken feather floating in it. Indignantly they chase the waiter up the stairs. In his haste the servant leaves his pots and pans on the landing.

Dobchinsky appears, an agitated herald as usual. Ossip and Khlestakov soon smell out what has happened. Khlestakov, the

The inn scene, REVISOR

clerk, has been mistaken for a high government official. He is not one to overlook an opportunity. Dismissing the others he retires to the couch under the stairs.

The scene develops like a levée at the court of Louis XIV. The Mayor himself has arrived. In his luxurious fur coat which reaches to his feet he tiptoes to the edge of the balcony, inquires for the mysterious stranger in the most dulcet of accents. Khlestakov answers with hauteur from under the stairs. The august visitor descends, assures the clerk anxiously that the whole city is at his disposal. Dismissed, he makes his way backwards up to the door. The little clerk is jubilant.

Suddenly Bobchinsky breaks in. He has come late, he has missed snooping into this important interview. Profusely apologetic, obnoxiously nosy, he starts down the stairway, falls over one of the waiter's stewpans, which goes banging down the stairs. He follows it in a cataclysmic somersault, headlong toward the audience. When he is about to touch bottom a trapdoor opens; he flies on out of sight, pursued by the deafening clatter of pots and pans. The stage lights blot out. The house lights come on for the act intermission.

We understand now that the curved screen of mahogany panels encloses nothing but beautiful stage space; it is like a sounding board for the players, throwing their gestures and voices back at the audience. The stage action itself, in most of the en-

REVISOR: *exostra*

suing scenes, is carried forward on the small trucks which are like the *exostra* of Greek tragedy.

Our first glimpse of the Mayor's home begins with a platform covered with a deep Persian rug. Like the other platforms it slopes up, seeming to pitch its contents toward the audience. Flickering candles stand on the gilt side-table. A sofa upholstered in apricot satin, a heavy mahogany wardrobe at the rear of the platform, conjure up for us the long-departed Biedermeier interior with its rose-colored light and its waltz music coming sedately from offstage. Khlestakov is in the pretty lap of luxury; he conducts himself stiffly but his cat's eyes gleam, he can see a future that is promising indeed.

In the scene that follows he is far along on the road of high living. It is the only scene without a platform. The curved line of doors suggests a street; the stage light is cold and spotty. Mahogany balusters close in the front of the scene on either side, reinforcing the street idea. Worried bureaucrats, citizens in beards and long overcoats, turn restlessly in and out of doors. The crowd awaits the Inspector General. Murmurs, shouts, the great man is coming! Here he is now—Khlestakov in the Mayor's big fur coat. He staggers, almost falls, regains his feet with an acrobatic dexterity.

He is dead drunk, as he informs the audience confidentially! That pedantic primness has not deserted him; instead he has added to it the roar of authority. . . . And now it is indoors, presumably, because an armchair has been brought on. Two gendarmes stand at attention before the center door, where Khlestakov is to enter. He reels in through a different door, drops into the chair. One of the town's officials hurries to his side to introduce (and intervene for) all the petty racketeers, who are coming to grease the palm of the Inspector General. Heads peer in fearfully from all of the fifteen doors. One after another the suppliants are brought into the dread presence and leave their cash behind them. The parade goes on, the high official murmurs to the Inspector. . . . The Inspector is snoring in a drunken sleep.

The vignettes of action on the central platforms follow each other like movie closeups. The raked floor of the platforms throws every detail of the scene as if into the middle of the auditorium. Before these incisive episodes which surprise and agitate the audience, within hearing of dialogue which bites like acid into the Biedermeier atmosphere on stage, no spectator can relax in his seat. No spectator can look on with the tolerant indulgence of a bystander, as if he were smiling at an abstract harlequinade. That curved and polished mahogany surface seems to cut off the mind's attempted retreat into stage depth. The audience is shaken, prodded and taunted into alertness. The playgoers are awake, a battle of wits goes on between them and the director; with each new scene they vow not to be caught napping next time.

We are at the last scene, and the director has outwitted us all the way. The truck for the scene has been rolled into place.

It represents the salon of the Mayor's mansion. There is a great crowd, come for the engagement party; but the crowd is all on that rather small platform in the middle of the stage.

The ladies in crinoline, the gentlemen in their high cravats, are wedged into seats in front of an openwork screen of silver Baroque. A kind of twittering goes on, a birdlike chatter accompanied by fluttering fans. Restiveness grows on this crowd perched so formally on its seats. Will the distinguished bridegroom-to-be never arrive? The Mayor's lady is already preparing herself for a fashionable swoon. It is growing darker on the stage. At last, voices! The inevitable Dobchinsky rolls in, shrieking. The Postmaster follows him, panting hard. He has opened a letter! (Quite illegally, as usual!) The letter is from Khlestakov! He can't believe his eyes. Read it! Candles! Candles!

Servants rush on. Lighted candles appear in the hands of the company, wavering with more and more agitation as the Mayor reads out loud the contents of that accursed letter.

"They took me for an Inspector General, I'm having a great time. The officials in this town—what a crew! The Mayor is asinine, I'm carrying on with his wife. . . . The Postmaster drinks, the School Superintendent reeks of onions, the Judge is *mauvais ton* . . ."

Exclamations, snorts of indignation, thin shouts of rage. Now comes a new messenger of evil. Bobchinsky, with a *new letter* which is passed tremblingly from hand to hand. An official letter to the Mayor, a missive on parchment with dangling ribbons and red and blue seals. The Mayor opens it with shaking fingers. As he reads there is a terrible outcry, as though from fifty stuck pigs. Candles go out, the stage lights follow after; for the first time a curtain descends, but it is not really a curtain. The front lights coming on show us it is a huge white placard on which is printed in black letters the contents of the official document:

HIS EXCELLENCY THE IMPERIAL INSPECTOR GENERAL JUST ARRIVED REQUESTS YOUR IMMEDIATE ATTENDANCE.

In front of this curtain the fashionables are now waltzing in a kind of agony, to some of Grieg's most unearthly passages.

REVISOR (1926) by Gogol and Meyerhold
No spectator can relax in his seat

CLASSICS, ECONOMICALLY DETERMINED

Socialist Shakespeare: KING LEAR (1935) at the Jewish State Theatre. Setting by Alexander Tishler

Quickly the lights go down, the curtain goes up, and the lights, returning, show us the company once more in a final tableau. Strewn about the stage in contortions in all their finery lie—no longer the characters—but a crowd of gaping papier-mâché dummies.

How is this production to be classified? That assault on the spectator, that macabre masquerade, is Theatricalist. Sensationally so. It even calls forth criticism from people like Radek, Bukharin and Litvinov. They object that the social meaning of Gogol's play has been butchered to make a Roman holiday for the tricks of Meyerhold. At this rather short historical distance their criticism does not seem quite justified. The director has undoubtedly brought with him from the Theatricalist period some of Theatricalism's bad habits. But the fabulous visit to the past, that mad vision of a society of politicians, bootlickers and rascals, that agitational projection of the story to the audience, have all gone past the limits of Theatricalism. They are in movement toward a new conception of dramatic form.

FLASHBACK

But the Soviet theatre as a whole was already on its way in a direction of its own. We have considered Meyerhold's production first, because its style shows so clearly the transition from Theatricalism to the principle of *Socialist Realism.* That same year a Soviet film became the first of a new tradition of motion pictures. The picture was THE BATTLESHIP POTEMKIN, produced by Goskino, directed by Sergei Eisenstein with Alexandrov as assistant director and Tisse as cameraman.

What made the film important? Our explanation must begin with a quick glance at cinema history.

By 1919 Hollywood, aided by war conditions, had taken control of the world cinema market and inaugurated the era of mass film production. We may remember Gorky's skepticism about the future of "moving photographs." He questioned whether the cinema would be allowed to glance very long at life. His skepticism was justified. The movie studio product which flooded the world market after the War was a standardized article of sale. While Naturalistic in appearance it was actually a carefully worked-out recipe containing romance, a mild seasoning of sex, a good deal more of prudery, melodrama, super-patriotism and glamorous personalities. The whole made up an internationally famous brand of sedative.

Beginning with Lumière's short untitled films—like that of the boy with the hose (1896)—the film camera had worked in extroverted style. This style had continued with Porter's THE GREAT TRAIN ROBBERY (1903), the Wild West "horse operas," Griffith's and Bitzer's experiments with fadeouts, irising, closeups and panning, Ince's objective approach to reality, as in his depiction of city slums in THE ITALIAN (1914).

Almost immediately, however, the introverted movie style also began its development with Méliès and Zecca, originators of the trick film, and Cohl, first of the cartoon animators. By the outbreak of the War the studio picture was firmly established—subjective and Romantic in content, with a veneer of Belasco Naturalism. The search for living character and Darwinian environment seemed practically over.

In Griffith's BROKEN BLOSSOMS (1919) the fuzzy soft-focus lens reigned supreme. The same process that had been at work in the "legitimate" theatre, reducing environment to a symbolic mist, had fastened on the cinema. From now on such extroverted pictures as von Stroheim's GREED (1924) would have to make their way against the inertia of the whole vast motion picture setup.

> The film that Metro later cut and released as GREED, Stroheim filmed from beginning to end without a single studio set. He insisted on filming every scene of the picture against its original backgrounds, and went to the streets, the sewers, the mines, the desert, the theatre-lobby, the dental parlor, the saloon, that were actually or resembled Frank Norris's locales—knocked out walls for cameras and lights, bought street-corners and ran up expenses that far exceeded the reproductions of FOOLISH WIVES. (Leyda).

In Europe the same general recession from reality was under way. By 1920 the great German studio, UFA, had likewise abandoned the objective viewpoint. Lubitsch received orders to forget the contemporary scene and to concentrate on the distant past—not in the spirit of historic inquiry, but in a hunt for exoticism. In such films as MADAME DUBARRY, SUMURÛN, ANNE

BOLEYN, Lubitsch and his designer, ·Kurt Richter, established a parallel to the stage work of Reinhardt. The prospect of history was used only to "lend enchantment to the view." By then, such probing European films as Pabst's JOYLESS STREET (1925) and SECRETS OF THE SOUL (1927), also had the tide against them.

At the same time Theatricalism made its appearance in the European cinema with its first, and best, effort, THE CABINET OF DOCTOR CALIGARI (UFA, 1919, featuring Werner Kraus and Conrad Veidt). CALIGARI was followed by the much weaker GOLEM (1920), SIEGFRIED (1923), METROPOLIS (1926). METROPOLIS, an allegory of industrial civilization, was a typical ingrown studio product, showing little grasp of its subject in its settings, which ranged from mistily romantic slums to Aubrey Beardsley palaces.

As in the case of the stage, certain important advances in technique contrasted with the general retreat from reality. There was a notable development in film technique. The movies were cutting the apron strings which tied them to the stage and growing up as an independent form of theatre. Still all the new technical resources of the film—montage, optical printing, fast and slow motion—were no longer devoted to examining life but to camera tricks, novelties, the suave manipulation of screen stories, the glorifying of vapid personalities.

But the eye of the camera is an objective instrument. Its fundamental nature cannot be changed by any amount of cliché handling. Any new approach which gives it the chance to go back and look at life will find it eagerly ready to work. POTEMKIN gave it this opportunity. POTEMKIN was conceived on the basis of the most outspoken propaganda. It was militantly partisan, fully in accord with the slogan "Theatre is a weapon in the class struggle." How could such a theme and viewpoint enable the motion picture camera to take a real view of life?

Is it not possible to maintain that the doctrine of social criticism, as used by the Naturalists, is itself a ready-made pattern in the theatre? Is it not possible to maintain even more strongly that the doctrine of class criticism, as used by the Soviet theatre, is an especially rigid cliché? Merely to announce that "Theatre is a weapon" would appear to serve notice that no holds are barred; that all kinds of lies and distortions will be pressed into service.

Soviet critics believed they had the answer to these questions. In their view, theatre was not only a Soviet weapon; it was the weapon of the enemy as well. In theory there is nothing at all to prevent either side from using every slander at its disposal. Soviet criticism contended that all this was natural and inevitable. What it questioned was the claim that theatre is an impartial art which takes no sides in class struggle. This claim it considered purely academic.

In establishing a policy on motion pictures the Bolsheviks had not the least doubt that all films are propaganda, whether or not they are art. They insisted that the products of Hollywood have a special way of looking at the world—not an ideal artistic way uncolored by any bias. They asserted flatly that the overwhelming majority of Hollywood films are capitalist in philosophy; and that these films have an ingenious technique which presents capitalist opinions in a favorable light.

The movies are an immensely powerful agent of propaganda. Did not Thomas A. Edison, one of the fathers of cinema, make the statement, "Whoever controls the motion picture industry controls the most powerful medium over the people"? In the bourgeois countries, said the Bolsheviks, the cinema is in the hands of the capitalist class. In the Soviet Union it would be otherwise. Clearly that was Lenin's policy in the matter, as reported by Lunarcharsky:

> Lenin told me many times that among the instruments of art and education, the cinema can and must have the greatest significance for the State. It is a powerful weapon of scientific knowledge and the most effective agitation. (Carter).

We now arrive at a rather different question. If it takes as an axiom that theatre is propaganda, why should Soviet policy insist, as it does, that stage and film must face toward reality?

Because the Bolsheviks, in accordance with the findings of Marx and Lenin, insisted that life itself supports their views, whereas it does not support the assertions of the enemy. We may propagate all kinds of doctrines, but not all of them will correspond to the facts. Lenin said, "Facts are stubborn things." Soviet opinion held that the facts were on its side. This was not very new: most of us are convinced that the facts are on our side—whatever our side may be. But the Soviet did risk turning to documented science and history for confirmation.

From the beginning the Soviet film industry had made up its mind that the viewpoint of the working classes must be expressed with decision and with a technique suited to its message. At the close of the civil wars the Soviet cinema began to review Russian history in order to bring out forgotten facts and events proving the heroism of Russian workers and peasants. It was especially interested in bringing back into daylight those records which had embarrassed the imperial government and which had been allowed to gather dust in official archives. In the story of the Tsarist cruiser *Prince Potemkin,* whose crew mutinied during the 1905 uprising, it found a subject suited to its purpose. The film was in fact produced to celebrate the twentieth anniversary of the 1905 revolt.

POTEMKIN

POTEMKIN opens with a sudden shot of the battleship, which is approaching Cape Tentra, near Odessa, shortly before daybreak. The camera begins an inspection of the ship. From the upper decks it peers into the dark interior, where the sailors, naked to the waist in their swinging hammocks, are sleeping fitfully. Here the camera lingers. A petty officer, obviously on bad terms with the men, has thrashed a young sailor. The smouldering hostility of the crew finds expression in the bitter comment of Sailor Vakulinchuk. We catch a glimpse of this man's face—proletarian, bronzed and work-hardened. . . . Now the camera climbs upward as the day's routine begins. We are alongside Lieutenant-Commander Geilinovsky on the quarterdeck. Expressionless, he looks down on a milling crowd of sailors just below him. . . .

The tempo of transition has been incredibly rapid, with a pulsating rhythm of light and shadow. It is a proper introduction, for the entire film has a jerky, abrupt sequence reminiscent of the earliest days of motion pictures. It has, also, the same emphasis on physical action. As Meyerhold tore away the introspection of his audience, so Eisenstein disposes at once of the whole atmosphere of nostalgic yearning which is the pervading atmosphere of so many Hollywood films.

THE MEAT IS WORMY! [2]

A knot of men in angry discussion blocks the gangway outside the cook-house. The sailors are gathered around the quarters of beef that hang in front of the galley door. Officer Smirnov, the ship's doctor, a little, pompous man with a beard, inspects a slab of meat through his pince-nez. The meat looms up before the camera; we see it is infested with white grubs. The officer shrugs his shoulders.

FLIES' EGGS. JUST WASH THEM OFF WITH SALT WATER.

The camera follows the Lieutenant-Commander down the ladder. The sun is overhead, casting the barred shadows of rigging and gratings. Along the gangways the men move through light and shadow as if through the spokes of a wheel. The officer steps into the messroom. He sees the mess tables, hung on cords, swinging back and forth. The place is deserted; the men are refusing their food. They are drifting out toward the decks, meeting each other at the canteen, hunching their shoulders when an officer passes.

THE FORWARD TURRET–

The bugle blows assembly. Tensely the men find their places in formation—two lines facing one another in the bow of the ship. There, also, the officers are drawn up. Formidable in gold lace, Commander Golikov comes up from the hatchway. His eyes seem to flash Jovian lightning; his forked beard lifts in the breeze. Unhurriedly he surveys the scene. Then a command rasps out. "Those who are satisfied with the food, advance one pace!" The line of officers steps forward; a few men follow. The long ranks remain motionless.

Evidently the men need a lesson. The next order follows. "Call out the marine guard!"

From the bridge the camera watches the entrance of the

marines, led by their officer. A spasm of fear goes through the ranks. Grimly one of the sailors turns his head, whispers to the man beside him, "The forward turret." The whisper goes down the line. Without orders, as with one accord, the crew breaks ranks.

All except a handful, far forward, who have hesitated too long, and find themselves isolated. In a desperate attempt to escape they make for the admiral's hatchway. The fists and guns of the officers drive them back. These men must pay with their lives as an example to the rest. A huge tarpaulin is brought out and thrown over them. While their comrades stand by, powerless, the marines lift their guns.

READY! . . . AT THE SAILCLOTH! . . . AIM!

The camera darts away up forward, it seems to waver in front of the flapping Imperial ensign, the Tsarist crest below. It returns, as if unwillingly as the command comes:

FIRE!

For a fraction of an instant the marines hesitate. Despair forces Vakulinchuk to cry out—

BROTHERS, DON'T SHOOT!

The cry seems to ring through centuries of time. Hesitantly the guns begin to drop back to the deck. The marines have not fired. The old discipline vanishes into thin air. The officers scatter, the men in pursuit.

The gun-racks are emptied as squads arm themselves. Officers are caught and beaten. The doctor is heaved over the side; his pince-nez, caught on a rigging, swings complacently.

But the Lieutenant-Commander has managed to find a gun. Whatever the consequences, he is determined to bring down the leader of the mutiny. Vakulinchuk, trapped, starts overside, drops with a bullet in his head. A looped cable stops his fall. He clings to the heavy cable in a deathly stupor. We get a last view of him alive—the form of a tired workman. The sailors, now in possession of the boat, discover their leader just as he drops off again into the water. A dozen of the crew jump in after him, but they can save only his body. He who led them is the first victim of official vengeance.

THE PEOPLE OF ODESSA.

The crew must present its case to the city of Odessa at once. In the late afternoon a steam launch with the body of Vakulinchuk makes its way shoreward. The tempo slows down to less than normal as the launch glides through the rising mist. Spars of shipping appear; freighters at their docks; rows of mechanical cranes. The sun is going down. . . . In the morning the people of Odessa come to pay tribute to the dead. A whole population seems to move over the long causeway, over the flying bridges. On the beach the seaman's body lies under a rude canvas tent. Through the flaps of the tent we see people passing—workmen, toilworn women, children. A bourgeois woman in white, holding a white sunshade, stares in curiously.

Mass grief, mass anger. "We must stand by the crew of the *Prince Potemkin!*" Speakers—workmen, women, intellectuals—rise vehemently to put the mass emotion into words. . . . On board the cruiser the white-clad sailors are assembled in one huge gathering from upper deck to crow's nest. A civilian worker addresses them from the captain's bridge, pledging the sympathy of the people of Odessa. . . . Like swift birds, sailboats loaded with provisions make toward the cruiser. Geese, loaves of bread, are handed up to the men. On the shore the population watches intently, cheering the sailboats.

THE COSSACKS

Suddenly, as we look down the long stone stairway that leads to the sea, a platoon of Cossacks passes under the camera. Their guns, with bayonets fixed, are held before them. A line of military boots descends the steps methodically.

The crowd is scattering in a terrible panic. The Cossacks are firing. People scream silently and fall. A young woman, shrieking, leans over the body of a little boy. The steps, the line of military boots. The young woman with the boy in her arms, carrying him insanely up the steps toward the Cossacks. She slumps

DIRECTORS OF A NEW CINEMA

Kornman, 20th Century-Fox

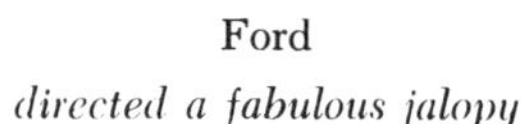

Ford
directed a fabulous jalopy

Griffith
For movies, movie technique

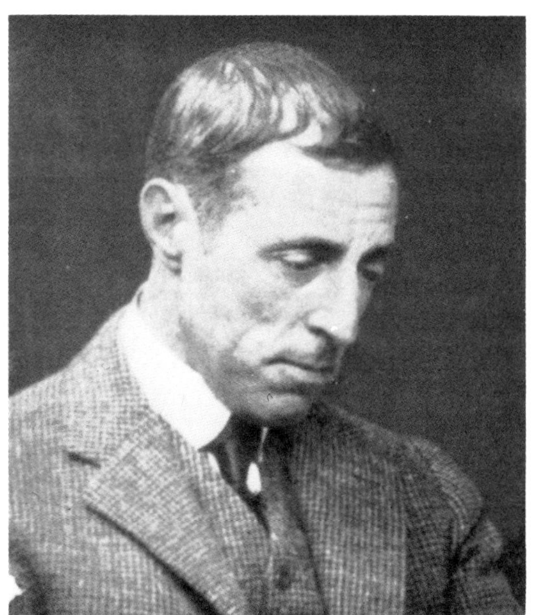

Museum of Modern Art

Artkino

Eisenstein
Leonardo da Vinci, Marx, Lenin and Freud were his gods

Columbia

Capra
directed Mr. Deeds, Mr. Smith, Mr. Doe

down, the two bodies lie together. Again the steps. A young mother, distraught, trying to turn the carriage containing her baby. She is struck, and falls. Unattended, the baby carriage rolls backward down the stairs. Its wheels bump from step to step. Huddled figures lie along its path. Miraculously it continues its backward descent. . . .

The *Potemkin* in the harbor is lifting its turret guns, turning them toward the stairs. Its guns are firing. The screen seems to whirl from stairs to terrified figures, to the soldiers, to the marble sculptures reeling under explosion. A stone lion pricks up his ears, raises his head with astonishment.

ALL AGAINST ONE

Night. Those of the *Potemkin's* crew who are off duty try to sleep. But the camera prowls over the boat. In the offing is the Tsarist fleet; the warships are approaching, ready to blow the *Potemkin* out of the water. But the cruiser is humming with activity. The decks are cleared. Steam rises in the boilers. The first rays of morning find the gunners at their stations. Sailors are moving heavy shells out of the munitions chambers, guiding them along conveyor-lines to the guns. And the Tsar's battleships line the horizon. Is this to be the end of the armored cruiser *Potemkin?* Her signal flags spell out the appeal: "Join us!" Her gunners stand rigid at their posts. A broadside? Or—?

The fleet is drawing back. "They are letting us through!" Astonishment gives way to a delirium of relief. Cheer, throw caps in the air, crowd to the rails as the *Potemkin* makes for the open sea!

BROTHERS, THEY ARE LETTING US PASS! [3]

THE MOVIES LOOK AT LIFE

Has this film of Eisenstein's used a "realistic" technique? We have already explained that the word "realism" indicates a *direction,* a movement toward objective reality. It has no immediate technical meaning. The word Naturalism has. POTEMKIN used Naturalistic elements. It was made up mostly of Naturalistic "frames," or individual shots. Some of these were of an old Tsarist battleship which was pressed into service. The scenery on which most of the action took place was a wooden construction built over the water, a replica, in Naturalistic style, of the decks and superstructure of the old *Potemkin.* Few of the actors were professional. The sailors of POTEMKIN were men of the Soviet navy. The Odessa character-types had actually been picked up in that city. Yet the film's total effect was something different from the Naturalism known to Belasco and Hollywood.

For those accustomed to Hollywood Naturalism its films seemed "photographically real." It might be that the average movie was not very profound, but as far as its dramatic technique went, that technique was "life itself." The Symbolists had objected that Naturalism was not selective. It now became clear, however, that Naturalism was selective almost unconsciously. Belasco used a technique of Naturalism, but somehow he managed to select Romantic elements. In the same way Hollywood's "lifelike" technique was not always like life.

Just how lifelike were the smooth faces that went through dramatic conflicts, or even the supposed passing of forty years, without showing a sign of care? How close to life were the studio settings, devoid of function, which served with equal neatness for film tragedy or comedy, and which turned even hall bedrooms and prisons into palaces of dreams? How lifelike was the shimmering, diffused lighting which reflected people and events about as substantially as a soap bubble?

These questions persisted, and they could be applied for many years afterwards, not only to cinema musicomedies and romances, but even to films of heavy industry and war. The latter themes were attempted by the American cinema in such pictures as BLACK FURY (Warners, 1935), whose story was of a strike in the coal-pits; THE PLOW AND THE STARS (RKO-Radio, 1937)[4] and THE INFORMER (RKO-Radio, 1935), both concerned with the Dublin Rebellion; THREE COMRADES (MGM, 1938), set in post-War Germany; BLOCKADE (Walter Wanger, 1938), dealing with the Spanish Civil War. The action of these films took place in a proletarian milieu, but they contained only "glamorous" middle class characters or bohemian types disguised as proletarians. The settings as a rule remained hazy, dreamy backgrounds.

What gave POTEMKIN such a semblance of vivid reality? A

great deal of its force came from its subject matter, which had the ring of authentic history as compared with the carpentered plots and distortions of history which have characterized so many Hollywood shows and not a few other Soviet productions. But POTEMKIN also showed a new type of observation on the part of the director and his co-workers. It related human beings to their environment in a way which Antoine had understood but which the cinema had forgotten.

Since the object of Hollywood technique is usually to "put over" the personalities of screen stars, environment becomes reduced to flattering backgrounds. Such conceptions as men living among machines, the functioning of a sea-going fortress, the discipline of a naval crew, the action of a whole population—all these require a type of observation not often permitted to Hollywood directors. Eisenstein reached into objective reality, taking from it elements which clarify, not elements which disguise and distort.

In 1926 Eisenstein was still in his twenties, a heavy-set youngster with a mop of curly hair and a chubby, serious face. Leonardo da Vinci, Marx, Lenin and Freud were his gods. Beginning as an architect, he had tinkered with the theatre even before the revolution, had later managed the Proletcult Theatre, tried Futurist painting and become identified with the sophisticated LEF group of intellectuals which included Meyerhold, the dramatist Tretiakov and the poet Mayakovsky.

He had developed a theory of the mass-hero play. His films must contain stories only of masses or groups of people in action —the individual hero was purely incidental. This was a doctrinaire idea, later amended. But it was certainly a break with the idea of glamorous personalities; and it was typical of his deliberate, reasoning mind. He considered himself "a scientific engineer whose field happened to be cinema." (Freeman).

Eisenstein's manner of thought may strike some people as almost inhumanely precise. Yet his camera-eye was human to an extent never known before. The young director understood, even more profoundly than Griffith, who had preceded him, that the human eye sees things not in a mechanical manner but in a series of miraculously swift impressions. It is these impressions, rather than the tricks of the studio, which interest Eisenstein, Pudovkin,

Dovchenko, Pabst, Stroheim, Renoir, Ford, Milestone, and other non-stereotyped film directors.

The eye never sees anything squarely before it except by the merest chance. It views everything at an angle, sideways, from above or from below. It never sees anything without a profound impression of texture and weight. It does not see disembodied environment made of mist, but decides at once whether something is made of wood, steel or paper. The camera eye of a talented director acts like a human eye, which is not a mechanical recorder of images but an instrument sensitively linked with a brain. It weighs and estimates, emphasizes or understates, changes its tempo at each instant. This fact, and not cleverness in finding "unusual" shots, explains POTEMKIN.

POTEMKIN was propaganda, but it swept away mountains of studio rubbish. As Meyerhold reached back to the Commedia, so Eisenstein went back to the outwardly directed camera of early cinema. He had the will to look at people and things with open eyes.

Fortunately for the art of the motion picture there are many capable directors today, even in Hollywood, who have the courage to look at life. There are men with a zest for the people and events of the real world. Give someone like John Ford a chance, and with a cameraman like Gregg Toland he will create for you an unforgettable vision of America as it really is—with its splendid, indomitable people, its long roads, its plains and streams, its moods of anxiety and hope. How many contrived allegories can compare with the story of that forlorn, careening jalopy in THE GRAPES OF WRATH? How many "inner" Symbolist dramas have the shock of that unendurable ride into the transient camp?

Because Ford looked outwardly he also saw inwardly. And so Ma Joad's old straw bonnet, the desert mirrored in the windshield, the sand drifting across the concrete roads—all these outward things stir us inwardly.

THEATRES OF SOCIALISM

In 1934 the Soviet theatre, after a series of conferences and in line with decisions already made by artists' and writers' organizations, fixed upon the term *Socialist Realism* as describing the style which it considered best suited to its audiences and theatre workers.

What is the definition of this term? For the first time in history a political word is prefixed to the description of a stage form. Is there anything valid about such a combination?

It is well known that Soviet theatre and the political views of the Soviet State are inseparable. Outside Russia it is supposed that this relationship consists quite simply of theatre people taking orders from political commissars. The actual situation, which developed historically, is rather complex; it is the result of a balance of forces in the theatre and out of it.

One of Tsarist Russia's unwilling bequests to the Soviets was a small number of theatres (two hundred and fifty in the whole empire, seven of them in Moscow). But they were theatres of unusual talent. They ranged all the way from the imperial theatres and operas of St. Petersburg and Moscow, through the private opera of Mamontov and the self-exiled Ballet Russe of Diaghilev, to the liberal Moscow Art Theatre and the radically experimental studios of Meyerhold and Tairov. (In addition Moscow and St. Petersburg regularly welcomed the best players and productions of the western capitals.) The brilliance of the Russian productions were renowned throughout Europe. Their scenic richness was well represented in what was perhaps the last imperial production in Russia—Lermontov's MASQUERADE, presented by Meyerhold in Theatricalist style at the Alexandrinsky Theatre, Petrograd, on the eve of the February revolution.[5]

These theatres were by no means agreed as to what constitutes the ideal technique of production. There were many views on the subject. Two dominant—and divergent—tendencies could be noted, however: the school of Naturalism as exemplified by Stanislavsky and that of Theatricalism led by Meyerhold. The November revolution only accentuated these differences.

The struggle over creative method in the Soviet theatre has not been waged in a teacup. If the aim of this theatre is "the task of transforming the individual, and bringing up citizens of the socialist State," just how is this to be accomplished on an actual stage? It is not easy to work out a Five-Year Plan for factory production; and it is even more difficult to lay a creative course for dramatic production.

Confusion was inevitable at first. Immediately after the victory of the Soviets, some proletarian theorists demanded the destruction of both the imperial and liberal theatres and their dramatic forms, on the ground that they were relics of the old regime, "citadels of reactionary thought." Others, imbued with the spirit of Cromwell's Ironsides, wanted an end to the whole institution of theatre.

The question whether the existing theatres should be "liquidated" continued to be fought over for a period of ten years. Many of the older dramatic companies remained covertly or passively hostile to the new regime. Others, in the Theatricalist tradition of Andreyev and Evreinov, limited themselves to "revolutionary" experiments in dramatic form. These experiments were as a rule no more than excrescences of Theatricalism, which was already going sterile. The fact that the experimenters spoke in favor of the revolution did not lessen the skepticism of the Bolshevik Party leaders.

> The left wing of the Russian theatre which soon formed and rallied to the slogans of the proletarian revolution appreciated the revolution in a very general way and accepted it only casually. This left wing immediately began the destruction of the old theatrical forms. They thought that the whole evil was in old forms. Like Trepliev, a character of a young decadent writer described by Chekhov in his play THE SEAGULL, the lefts incessantly cried, "We want new forms, we need new forms; either we procure them or we decline to use the old ones any longer."

Litovsky, from whom this paragraph is taken, insists that the destruction of old forms and the creation of new ones was merely "the reflection of petit-bourgeois romanticism." We get a clue to this writer's impatience when we consider the productions which were put on during the years immediately following the revolution. Most of these were extravagantly lyrical, like Mayakovsky's OPERA BOUFFE (1918), a Meyerhold production which pictured not only a Soviet revolution, but insurrection throughout the world, even "a cosmic revolution of the universe." The play had a Morality form and shifted in scene from earth to hell and paradise. Dana describes the author as the "amazing, bronze-throated, tub-thumping Futurist poet who used to shout his verses over the heads of the workers massed in the Red Square." Dana goes on to report:

> Even when one of these early plays tried to deal with the actual Bolshevik revolution itself, there was a tendency to allegorize this in the same way. For example, on November 7, 1920, at the third anniversary of the Russian Revolution, a great pageant called THE STORMING OF THE WINTER PALACE was enacted by some 8,000 persons on the very spot where that momentous historic event had actually taken place three years earlier. Part of the action, to be sure, was a more or less realistic reproduction of the attack on the Winter Palace itself. Yet, under the guidance of the all-too-imaginative Evreinov, the major part of the performance took place on two artificially built-up stages: a White Stage on the right and a Red Stage on the left and on a connecting bridge where the struggle took place symbolizing, as though in a sort of political mystery, the struggle between Left and Right, between Reds and Whites. Out of the darkness thousands of voices were heard crying "Lenin! Lenin!", the Cruiser *Aurora* was heard firing its cannon from the river Neva, rockets shot up, and to the sounds of the "Internationale," in which 100,000 in the audience joined, a gigantic red flag was raised.

In the next few years there was a rash of dramatic productions, operas and even ballets which extolled imaginary revolutions in an allegorical manner. In 1923 Germany was pictured as a scene of mutiny; the next year several plays speculated on revolt in the United States. In 1926, with Meyerhold's direction of Tretiakov's ROAR CHINA! the revolutionary spirit went on to the Far East. In the ballet THE RED POPPY (Bolshoi Theatre, 1927), "a red poppy given by the captain of a Soviet ship to a Chinese dancing girl became a symbol of the spread of the Russian Revolution to the East and above all to China." The lighting effects of this spectacle included a huge poppy which shone forth when the Chinese Revolution broke out, while "lights resembling red poppies showered through the whole theatre." Revolt did not stop at China. In one play it even spread to a nearby planet:

> Not satisfied by representing on the stage revolution running over the surface of the earth, the early Soviet playwrights liked to imagine the revolution as spreading out into the universe, reaching to the planet Mars, for example. The very popular story of *Aelita,* written by Alexei Tolstoy in 1924, was turned into a play, a film, and even a musical comedy. It represented a Soviet engineer and a Red soldier, shooting

to Mars in a rocket, and, aided by the Princess Aelita, starting a revolt of the oppressed workers on the Red Planet.

Today, says Dana, the Soviet playwrights are inclined to smile when they recall these productions. At that time the government leaders must have found some of the dramas pretty trying. Lenin, in the midst of affairs of state, took time to warn against purely formal experiment in the theatre, and the warning remained pertinent for a long time to come. By 1927 the program of converting the older theatres to new uses had carried the day, due largely to the influence of Lenin and of Anatoli Lunacharsky, the first Commissar of Education.

Lunacharsky, himself a dramatist, recognized in the older theatres a precious heritage of culture, to be adopted (after critical examination) to the needs of the present and future. To call this dramatic culture reactionary and throw it away would be as senseless as throwing away all "bourgeois" machinery and starting Soviet industry from scratch.

It was not an easy matter, however, for Lunacharsky to prove the correctness of his viewpoint in practice. The former Tsarist and liberal theatres could not at once re-evaluate their traditions. They were criticized as being burdened with mysticism, faddism, preciosity, and—what was equally bad in the eyes of the new regime—a viewpoint of art for art's sake. Nevertheless the government, for a time, took no official action; it had learned not to rush into a field in which it had little experience. There was a period of NEP [6] theatres during which private ownership of certain playhouses were permitted temporarily, and which proved a dismal one for dramatic art. But even the State-subsidized theatres had difficulties.

The country was engaged in a herculean task of reconstruction after the war, the revolution, civil war and foreign intervention. The theatres were requested to do their part of this job. To offer relaxation was not enough. They were asked to explain life in the particular way that Marx saw it, in material terms and with a revolutionary outlook. It was a new experience for the older theatres.

The Moscow Art Theatre, playing now to audiences of workers, peasants and former middle class, was agreeably impressed by the high level of appreciation shown by these audiences. At the same time it was clear that the repertory of the Art Theatre had become outdated, being far removed from the life and experience of the new playgoers. The Kamerny Theatre of Tairov had to begin learning how to put its Theatricalist language to the use of social statements. Meyerhold, whose iconoclastic qualities had put him at the forefront of theatre in civil war times, was finding himself out of step in the period of reconstruction. Eugene Vakhtangov, young director of the Moscow Art Theatre's Third Studio, was at this time the only prominent theatrical leader who seemed to be making progress toward a synthesis of the methods already in use. Unfortunately his efforts were cut short by his premature death in 1922.

Evidently the hope of transforming a brilliant, talented bourgeois theatre into a socialist theatre that might equal or surpass it in talent was not going to be realized all at once. It was to be expected that the revolutionary government would try to hasten the process. Shortly after the events of November 1917 it had appointed a commission, headed by Kel, to supervise theatrical activity. This commission, according to Huntly Carter, distinguished itself unpleasantly by banning many of the insurgent plays of the Naturalistic theatre, including those of Chekhov, Tolstoy and Dostoevsky. It also lent its encouragement to the extreme Theatricalists at the expense of the more conservative techniques.

By 1921 the government had come to the conclusion that the future of the theatre lay in the hands of the theatre-workers themselves. The government, through the medium of the Communist Party, could scold, point out blunders, coax or praise, but its desires had to wait upon the comparatively slow unfolding of the dramatic medium itself. A new commission composed entirely of theatre people, and including both Stanislavsky and Meyerhold, replaced the older one. From then on the Soviet theatre would have to work out its own salvation, with every technique given a score of years in which to sink or swim. The work of the Soviet theatres has since been coordinated in the Dramatic Section of All-Union Committee on Art, whose policy remains one of alert neutrality toward existing techniques.

SOVIET DIRECTORS

What has been the artistic history of the Soviet playhouses in their quest for Socialist Realism? These theatres have been adequately supported by the government in their search, have made achievements and been encouraged; have produced expensive failures and been rebuked.

The victory of the Soviets was the signal for the liberation of many "extremist" dramatic tendencies which had previously known the displeasure of the academies. The school of Russian Constructivist sculptors (Tatlin, Gabo, Pevsner and others) at first took the lead in this revolt of the arts. Constructivism had commenced in embryo about 1912, and had been ridiculed by Tsarist esthetic criticism on general principles. It was not surprising that with Tsarism gone, this extreme form of sculpture sprang into favor. It was not surprising, either, that Meyerhold found use for it on the stage. His way of using it, however, differed in some measure from its original purpose.

Constructivist sculpture looks like pieces of plane surface or materials (wood, celluloid, glass, rubber) fastened together in strange intersections or related to each other by strips of glass or lines of wire. But in fact this sculpture is not intended to look like anything; it is strictly non-representational. Its relationships are those of texture, balance and planes, in almost scientific precision.

In his war on the "bourgeois" form of the drama (which meant to him all types of illusory staging), Meyerhold saw a real inspiration in Constructivism. It was a non-representational plastic art, yet it offered unusual possibilities to the actor. In exploiting this new sculptural form Meyerhold, as usual, stopped at no half-way measures. The front curtains of his theatre were ripped out, the stage lights were exposed, the "sky drops" or cycloramas were torn aside, revealing the bare walls of the stage. In front of the brick walls actors dressed in overalls played Crommelynck, Verhaeren and Ostrovsky on Constructivist platforms whose function was not to supply any illusion of locale but merely to give the players new ways of moving through stage space.

Scaffolds of drama in a literal sense, these structures resembled bricklayers' catwalks or Coney Island scenic railways.

Useless to look for a forest in THE FOREST of Ostrovsky; ladders, skeletonic forms, a trapeze, fill the stage. In the center, suspended from the flies, hangs a spiral wooden ramp, the abstract equivalent of a winding country road. For THE COMMANDER OF THE SECOND ARMY, by Selvinsky (1929), the stage setting was mostly a semicircular wall of pine panels, a long, curving flight of steps and some wooden screens. The locale of ROAR CHINA (1926) was

Constructivism

Setting by Alexander Vesnin for THE MAN WHO WAS THURSDAY (1923)

a battleship; but on stage it was scarcely more than lathes and scaffolding. If it dimly resembled a ship it was only because the captain's bridge and the gangways were needed by the action.

On such stages there was no room for the introspective playing of Stanislavsky. Nor was there room for any quality of nostalgic atmosphere. This was "direct staging," with a vengeance. DAWN (1920), a Symbolist play by the Belgian poet Verhaeren, in the words of the Soviet critic Mologin, became

. . . a militant spectacle, imbued with topical themes by means of the introduction of direct reports from the front of the Civil War into the action of the play. At one of these performances a telegram from Comrade Smilga reporting the capture of Perekop was read from the stage.

Meyerhold was not the only director to work with Constructivism. The technique was very popular. Several of Tairov's best-known productions were in Constructivist style (although rather less skeletonic and abstract than the Meyerhold version). Three of Eugene O'Neill's dramas were put on at Tairov's theatre in Constructivist settings: THE HAIRY APE (1926); DESIRE UNDER THE ELMS (1926) and ALL GOD'S CHILLUN GOT WINGS (1929). The Tairov production of THE MAN WHO WAS THURSDAY (1923), adapted from the novel by G. K. Chesterton, was in the early, distinctly amusement-park Constructivist form. His version of Sophie Treadwell's MACHINAL (1933), much richer in quality, included huge shutters reminiscent of New York skyscrapers. Among many interesting variations of the Constructivist form was the production, by the Theatre of the Revolution, of Pogodin's MY FRIEND (1932), in which mobile platforms were combined with photo-mural panels used as shutters.

Even more than Theatricalist plays, the Constructivist productions of Meyerhold and his colleagues banished illusion completely from the stage and returned to convention. The theatre went back to its ancient tradition at the behest of flaming revolutionaries.

An ardent lover of music, Meyerhold even put that abstract art to functional use. He used it in positive fashion to set the style of a play, in the manner of Reinhardt stylization. Some of his productions have been described by Volkov as musical variations on the themes of the authors. His production by Griboyedov's WOE TO WIT (1928) is an excellent example of this type, with its half Romantic, half Constructivist style, whose lines seem dominated by a musical idea. This director also used music as *counterpoint,* or even as dissonance, to the rhythm of the action, in a way which has become characteristic of Soviet presentations. (These, by the way, seem never to be given without music of some sort.)

Music is especially valuable in making difficult transitions from Naturalism into fantasy, permitting the actor to change his style midway. To cite one instance: Simonov, who plays the thief Kostya in the Vakhtangov Theatre's production of Pogodin's ARISTOCRATS (1935), has a serious piece of business during which he steals a cigarette case. He then goes into a grotesque dance of triumph, out of key with Naturalism. The transition is covered merely by the theatre orchestra.

The acting of Meyerhold's troupe, needless to say, was not in the direction of inward studies of character. In older theatres the actors on stage spent most of the performance sitting in parlor chairs. Meyerhold's theatre had no use for such sedentary acting. To negotiate the Constructivist ramps and platforms an actor needed gymnastic, almost acrobatic training. By 1922 Meyerhold had instituted for his players a series of gymnastic exercises which he labeled *bio-mechanics*. Its purpose was to vivify the whole body of the actor, giving decision, grace and authority to the actor's movements. It was based partly on the Taylor system of regulated gesture for workers in mass industry; also partly on the biological study of the muscular and nervous system. Carter explains that

> *Bio-mechanics* is really the application of the construction or mechanical theory to the actor. It assumes that the actor is a rather wonderful engine composed of many engines. The new problem of the theatre is how to get this engine in full motion, with all its parts—muscles, sinews, tendons, representing flexible piston rods, cylinders, etc.—working at their full capacity and, moreover, conveying their proper meaning according to the message sent by the brain along the spinal cord and the great system of nerves. The principles of bio-mechanics were first applied by Meyerhold in his Studio theatre. The system to which they belong is an outcome of the study of the Italian comedians of the Commedia dell' Arte period. They became systematically applied by him in the R.S.F.S.R. theatre in Petrograd from 1918 to 1922.

The imprint of the ballet tradition is notable in this insistence on a well-controlled body, just as it is in Tairov's "rhythmic" method and in the "plasticity" which Vakhtangov demanded.

The legacy of Vakhtangov may be seen in his production of Gozzi's PRINCESS TURANDOT (1921), which is still in the repertory of the theatre which bears his name. Its quality is that of gay, ironic clowning in harlequinade style. The setting by Nivinsky is Cubist, strongly influenced, however, by Baroque form. There is a kind of centrifugal movement in the design.

Before TURANDOT begins, the whole cast in evening dress lines up before the curtain, introducing itself to the audience. Each actor then costumes himself onstage with the help of a few scraps of silk material which he holds. In a moment, turbans. sashes, wigs and draped garments have been twisted out of these scraps and applied over the formal dress. Dominos are freely used. The settings are shifted by costumed property-men and property-women, in imitation of Oriental staging. In addition the story itself is parodied in *entre'acts* during which the stagehands burlesque the action in ballet numbers.

Today the production seems superficially an example of Theatricalist art for art's sake. Viewed historically it presents a quite different picture. It was put on during the civil war and interventionist period, when hunger stalked the Soviet Union and the people went about in rags, exhausted, dying of typhus by the tens of thousands. This was the appalling background against which TURANDOT, with its lightest of irony, appeared. It was an affirmation of human optimism in the face of starvation, suffering and death.

The original sketches by Nivinsky, which are still in the archives of the theatre, show how the production-idea developed. At first Vakhtangov thought of showing a house in ruins, with a huge window in back, through which one saw the ragged, hurrying crowds of Moscow. The joyous production was to be played literally against that somber picture. The early costume sketches show old army coats worn by the actors under the oriental costuming. Evidently it was realized later that the idea was too literal.

The distinctions which can be drawn between the aim of Vakhtangov and those of his fellow directors at that period, may seem over-fine, but they were not lacking in significance for the future.

Stanislavsky's viewpoint may be summed up as "We show life as it is." "The artist looks at life" might well have described Tairov's approach. Meyerhold, Vakhtangov and the later directors have all been propagandists in a direct sense. Yet each has had his own approach. Thus Meyerhold was essentially the man of the revolutionary and civil war period, an iconoclast, a restless destroyer of mouldy tradition. Vakhtangov was the man of reconstruction, the temperate planner, the workman carefully estimating his materials. Where Meyerhold said, "We must show our scorn," Vakhtangov said, "We must show our attitude."

Even in the details of acting we can note different shades of thought. Meyerhold's actors were trained to physical vigor and decisive movement. Vakhtangov, seeking the same physical aliveness and control, saw the body of the actor as an instrument under conscious command; the rôles must be played with this instrument, and with a certain sense of detachment. While Meyerhold's acting technique derives from the Commedia, Vakhtangov's recalls the acting philosophy of the oriental theatre.

Youngest of the internationally known directors today is Nikolai Okhlopkov. His work is indebted to Meyerhold, yet is strikingly individual while showing a more carefully considered approach. In the period from 1932 to 1936 at the Realistic Theatre, Moscow, he attacked an old problem with new determination and ingenuity. It was the question of direct audience contact: how to abolish the proscenium, how to bring the stage into the audience. Okhlopkov quite literally carried his stage into the center of a hall where no proscenium stage existed, varying the shape of his central stage platform from one bill to the next, along with the seating arrangement around it.[7]

To Norris Houghton Okhlopkov gave a revealing description of the effect he had in mind in founding his theatre:

> One day during the Civil War I stood on a railway station platform. From one direction a troop train drew in and stopped. In a moment another troop train arrived from the opposite direction and halted across the platform. Soldiers poured out to refill their tea-kettles, buy a bun, or stretch their legs. Near me one man alighted. From the other train came another soldier. They saw each other, ran forward and embraced, unable to speak for emotion. They were old comrades, dearest friends, whom the war had separated. There on a station platform, as one went one way and the other another, they met for a moment, clasped hands, and parted. In that instant I knew that that was what I wanted my theatre to be—a meeting where two dear friends experience an emotional union, in which for that moment all the rest of the world may be forgotten. Ever since I have worked for that. In my the-

atre, actor and spectator must clasp hands in fraternity. On my stage, when the mother cries, a dozen in the audience must be ready to spring forward to dry her tears. (*Moscow Rehearsals*).

The return to human values as compared with the unrelieved propagandist agitation of Meyerhold is very noticeable. Okhlopkov has combined this emotional method with Theatricalism in in a number of experimental plays. In his staging of THE IRON FLOOD by Serafimovich (1934), the stage was built in the shape of hill with three foothills rising from among the seats of the auditorium; the Red partisans pitched their tents alongside the chairs of the spectators. In MOTHER (1932) a central platform was surrounded by a ledge which went around all sides of the auditorium. The players, far from being distant visions, were at one's elbow, not merely as an artistic novelty but as actors absorbed in episodes furiously played. When an illegal printing press is raided by Tsarist police in the course of the play the impression is: "A rush of soldiers to the scene. Heavy boots stamp about. The creaking of leather, clank of accoutrement, the smell of gun-oil, sweat and tobacco." (Karnot). For the Realistic Theatre's staging of Pogodin's ARISTOCRATS (1934) there were two connecting stages within the auditorium; stagehands, masked and costumed, sprinkled paper snow, held telephones for stage characters to use.

The influence of Japanese scenic methods is very pronounced in these examples. The Japanese theatre with its "flower paths," or acting ledges, its family cubicles in place of orchestra seats with a fixed direction, has an auditorium that is literally "directionless." The audience does not necessarily face the stage proper but may turn freely in any direction, while the dramatic ceremony dominates the hall.

ENVIRONMENT IN MOTION

By now it must be clear that the director has an important place in the Soviet theatre. This is equally true of the scene designer. Indeed the Soviet stage owes much of its prestige to the exceptional talent of its designers.[8]

We have already referred to the scenic period of Constructivism. This period has long since been left behind. Yet its influence remains in almost every type of Soviet scenery. It is an important contributing factor in the rather astounding quality of current Russian design. The ability of Soviet design to surprise the spectator is due to a bold approach to environment. The designer does not take environment for granted, but catches it in the dynamic process of change. He sees *environment in motion.*

In Griboyedov's WOE TO WIT, as designed for Meyerhold by Shestakov, stairways fly into space, doors stand up without walls, windows fade in and out. Yet the setting does not seem implausible. The reason is that it does not attempt to reproduce a room; strictly speaking it does not even symbolize a whole room by means of parts of one. It is really a *stage apparatus* whose elements have been derived from the Empire style of interiors. Because every element used is so truly of the period, so vividly related to the actors, each chair, each door, each spindle of the stairway seems to live and speak.

The lyricism of the designer Isaac Rabinovich relies upon an exceptional grasp of stage space. His settings for LYSISTRATA (1923) and CARMENCITA AND THE SOLDIER (1924), already known in the United States, have the quality of flying through the cubic volume of the stage. His designs for EUGENE ONEGIN, at the Bolshoi Opera, in Moscow, have this spaciousness in an unusual degree. The duel scene fills the whole volume of the stage with Tchaikovsky's music, the grief of winter and the distress of a sensitive individual at war with society. The palace scene re-creates the Tsarist Empire with a romantic, musical lavishness which the imperial designers themselves could not attain in the older theatres.

So that even in "grand" opera, considered since Wagner's day to be a world set apart from mortal concerns, we find scenery which, at its best, is an illuminated section of human environment. It is conceived not as an inert surrounding but as a place which acts upon human character and upon which human character in turn exerts an influence. Sometimes this section of environment may be so alive on the stage that it seems to be only poised in its place. This is often literally true, for many of the new settings actually move in the middle of a scene.

The setting as a dynamic stage apparatus is typified in V. F. Rindin's designs for Vishnevsky's THE OPTIMISTIC TRAGEDY (1933), at the Kamerny Theatre.

Basic mechanism of Rindin's setting is the *raked stage,* a device much favored by Soviet designers. Meyerhold's use of raked *exostra* platforms has already been mentioned. The raked stage is merely a stage floor which is not level but slopes up from the proscenium to the back wall at a noticeable pitch. The inclined plane of the floor seems to project the action more vividly to the audience; it discloses the floor plan, which is the most important dimension of stage space, and it permits of unique "camera angles." Examples of its use also occur in Akimov's designs for Schiller's LOVE AND INTRIGUE (Vakhtangov Theatre, 1930) and in the designs by Rabinovich for Slavin's INTERVENTION (1933) at the same theatre. In the latter production it contributes greatly to the remarkable café scene of the second act.

Controversy still goes on about the origin of the raked stage. Meyerhold is believed to have used it for a studio production about 1915. Tairov used it for THAMIRA OF THE CITHER in 1916. Although it looks somewhat startling to audiences accustomed to level stages, it does not endanger the actor. The raked stage is not a new device but the revival of an old one. The traditional stage, in fact, was pitched at a steep angle from the time of the Baroque until quite recently. It was inevitable that Theatricalists like Tairov and Meyerhold would rediscover it in the course of their research into past conventional forms.

In THE OPTIMISTIC TRAGEDY the slanted stage is combined with a central pit in the stage itself. (The pit was derived from the idea of a shell crater.) This combination is made mobile besides. It is a mechanism so well geared to the play that it serves equally as a shell-hole, as trenches, as a battleship, as a prison camp. The ever-moving environment and the lights which play upon it are combined with a cyclorama which does not imitate a sky but is a luminous changing background. During the battle scenes the stage turns eccentrically, adding a savage impetus to the action. The platform is also used as the deck of a ship which is leaving port; as the platform turns slowly away from its moorings it divides the men on board from the women on the dock.

In INTERVENTION Rabinovich manages a difficult shift from the side of a French transport in Odessa harbor to a scene on the long stairway which Eisenstein made famous. The transition is made in a style reminiscent of the movies: the ship at the end of the scene divides in half, each half sliding offstage so that the stairway is revealed.

Sometimes the designer finds important values in the texture of materials. An interesting example is the setting by Goncharov and Popov for MTSISLAV THE BRAVE (1932) at the Theatre of the Red Army, Moscow. The scene is an armored train, but the setting itself is sculpture in twisted iron and steel. The life of the play seems to pound against the riveted steel walls of the car; the armored train and the partisans who defend its slotted windows are an indissoluble interplay of human bodies, steel framing and sheet iron.

Not all these scenic mechanisms are ponderous in feeling. The great uptilted silver disk used for LOVE AND INTRIGUE has all of Akimov's sophisticated elegance. Tishler and Falk manage to "gear" their designs without losing the quality of whimsical grotesque. The same can be said of the *bravura* humor of Williams, who adroitly combines painted and functional elements. Shtoffer, designing for Okhlopkov's Realistic Theatre, solved unusual problems with a particularly delicate handling of mobile forms.

MACHINE FOR THEATRE

If these designers have contributed the principle of dynamic environment, they have also contributed some technical solutions of an unusual character.

Their particular use of the semi-permanent setting tends to alter the whole character of this type of setting. It was the New Stagecraft which discovered the advantages of the semi-permanent setting, which is a technical method of making quick shifts without the use of elaborate revolving, sinking or sliding stages. A general plan is decided upon in the setting which allows of an architectural frame that occupies most of the stage area; changes from scene to scene consist only of minor shifts of furniture, drapery, panels, doors and windows.

With the Theatricalists the permanent section was usually a formal structure designed to link together separate scenes as though inside a neutral frame. In the hands of the modern Russian designers this device became a veritable *machine for theatre.*

The setting is looked upon as a dramatic mechanism which functions throughout the period of the performance. It receives its form and movement from the total meaning of the play. Each locale of the drama becomes a separate part of the scenic machine. In this way a scenic structure is arrived at which is not content with being neutral but which has an active relationship to the play as a whole. At the same time it functions in special ways for the separate scenes. Huntly Carter describes this effect very well when he says of Rabinovich's design for THE SORCERESS that "The model of the scene had the appearance of a scientific toy which can be taken to pieces and put together in different forms."

To design a semi-permanent setting which is a dramatic mechanism requires selectivity of a high order, since it involves a philosophy of the whole play. The New Stagecraft proved that it is possible to unite philosophically locales which are far apart geographically and historically, as for instance in Lee Simonson's designs for O'Neill's MARCO MILLIONS (Theatre Guild, New York, 1927). The Russian designers discard unessential detail even more drastically than do the Symbolists. Ceilings, for example, are nearly always absent in their designs. The Russians explain laconically that the dramatist does not write about ceilings and the actors do not walk on them.

A curved screen surrounding a succession of small platforms is the "machine" of REVISOR. A mobile platform with its circular pit is the mechanism of THE OPTIMISTIC TRAGEDY. A silver desk is the essential "machine" of LOVE AND INTRIGUE. The central mechanism of Rindin's designs for THE UNKNOWN SOLDIERS (Kamerny Theatre, 1932) is a gun-turret. The design by Lutze for BREAD, by Kirshon (State Dramatic Theatre, Leningrad, 1930), shows a country village dominated by a church steeple; parts of the village, including interiors, work on two small turntables. Favorsky's setting for TWELFTH NIGHT as produced by the Second Moscow Art Theatre (1935), consists throughout of a platform with a number of Renaissance arches built upon it and surrounded by a draped curtain on which is pictured an Italian town.

The new scenic art is particularly sensitive to the value of the discoveries made by the lens of the motion-picture camera. Instead of taking its axis parallel to the footlights, the dynamic stage setting is designed from the start as if viewed from an oblique camera angle. (An innovation that would have pleased Gustav Strindberg!)[9] Akimov, among others, has experimented with designs in aerial perspective, as in his setting for Verneuil's MY CRIME (1936), for the Leningrad Theatre of Comedy.

Movie technique has also had an effect on stage lighting. Soviet lighting methods are in general Theatricalist in the sense that they are only incidentally Naturalistic; they function actively throughout the performance. The light is often irised or shaped. In the prologue to Tairov's production of THE EGYPTIAN NIGHTS (1935) a red light, keystone-shaped, rises, disclosing the face of the Sphinx. In INTERVENTION the battle scenes are illuminated by the flash of searchlights, while many of the other scenes "fade in." The pharmacy scene of this play opens with red and green macabre highlights and the sound of a storm—we see afterwards that the red and green are reflections from bottles and retorts. It is an interesting development that the cinema, which once sat at the feet of stage technique, has reached the point at which it is in turn teaching the stage.

To sum up, present-day scenic art in Russia appears to find room for both illusory and non-illusory methods. Certain aspects of it that seem quite new exist side by side with practices inherited from the past. It has adopted from the Theatricalists the breaking-up of the stage level, the accommodation of the setting to the full physical action of the performer, the thrust of the scenery toward the audience. The Constructivist influence is felt in a careful selection of textures and in the way the setting functions as *machine for theatre.* The heritage of Naturalism and Symbolism is visible in the facsimile quality of the fragments of locale and of the stage properties. This illusory quality is often used as part of a non-illusory scenic scheme. That is to say, the immediate surroundings of the actor on stage are Naturalistic or Symbolist, while the scenic plan or structure as a whole is often quite arbitrarily formalized.

In one respect, however, Soviet design contrasts sharply with that of the Symbolists. The Soviet designer does not look for the "eternal essence" of environment. He sees it not as timeless, but as dynamically changing, something which may be one thing today and another tomorrow. He thinks of the setting not as a picture of an abstract mood, but as something intimately related to the physical movement of the actor. For the "proletarian" artist, environment is something that may be moved, carried, dug or lifted, rather than a phrase found in legal documents or a row of figures in a bookkeeper's ledger. In view of the many physical changes that have taken place in Russia—as one result of the transition from agriculture to industry—this viewpoint of the designer is understandable.

SOVIET SCRIPTS

If we have dealt first with Soviet directors and designers rather than with dramatists, one reason is that the playwrights have so far contributed less to new technique (as distinct from new content) than the other workers in this theatre. Most of them continue to write in the fairly Naturalistic style known to Broadway and Hollywood.

Soviet dramaturgy has been distinctly underrated abroad. Possibly this has been due less to its conservatism in form than to its anti-capitalist viewpoint, which is of course unpalatable to most foreign critics. It is also likely that the extroverted character of modern Russian drama contributes to that low estimate. American critics accustomed to a highly subjective inner content in playwriting are inclined to put Soviet authors in a class with Boucicault, James A. Herne and Bronson Howard. The Soviets have their share of hack writers, even as Broadway, and they seem to be just as good at flag-waving and tear-jerking. They also have writers like Bulgakov, Afinogenov, Katayev, Kirshon, Vishnevsky and Pogodin, whose command of character and situation compares favorably with the craftsmanship of serious dramatists anywhere.

H. W. L. Dana, in his *Handbook on Soviet Drama,* notes that, of the new Russian writers—poets, novelists and dramatists—the dramatists have developed most slowly. This has frequently been the case in other countries and periods as well. Soviet playwrights, on the whole, have shown a pronounced conservatism as regards new forms of theatre. We have already alluded to the period in which no small amount of animosity was aroused over the experiments in mere form (without content) which some of the older dramatic companies carried on. In the eyes of the Bolsheviks this activity amounted to nothing more than sabotage.

Whether willful or not, it must have had a high nuisance value. Lenin, who was said to have had an almost inhuman patience, exploded one day at the suggestion of certain formalists that those who did not understand them were "barbarians":

> I, however, make bold to declare myself a "barbarian." I cannot consider the productions of expressionism, cubism and the other "isms" as the highest manifestation of artistic genius. I do not understand them. I do not derive any pleasure from them. . . . Art belongs to the people. . . . It should be comprehensible to these masses and loved by them. (Zetkin: *Recollections of Lenin*).

Evidently the Soviet theatre lived through an intensive experience with experimental form. No theatre has done more experimenting. At the same time the Soviet theatre also burned its fingers on the problem, and the lesson seems to have struck home with the dramatists especially. Perhaps they remember not only with a smile, but ruefully, that early period of fevered lyricism when they indited mystical and allegorical plays of revolution.

At any rate when the civil wars ended, about 1921, the "Mayakovsky period" of rapturous drama also came to a close. Revolution continued to be the central theme, but the playwrights now began to analyze the phenomenon in more prosaic, more reasoned terms. Such plays as Lunacharsky's OLIVER CROMWELL (1921); Globa's WAT TYLER (1922); Glebov's ZAGMUK (1925), were part of a cycle which investigated the course of revolts ever since the days of ancient Babylon—a study of "the evolution of revolution."

By 1925 the revolutionary history of Russia itself had begun to reach the stage in a new rush of plays. These included Kamensky's STENKA RAZIN (1919) and the same author's EMELIAN PUGACHEV (1925); several plays concerning the Decembrist "palace revolt," including Kozyrov's THE DECEMBRISTS (1921); Kugel's NICHOLAS I AND THE DECEMBRISTS (1925); and IN THE YEAR 1881 by Venkstern (1925). THE YEAR 1825, by Shapovalenko (1924), probed into the circumstances of the assassination of Alexander II.

The twentieth anniversary of the 1905 revolt was commemorated not only by the film POTEMKIN but by a number of stage plays as well. Two years later the tenth anniversary of the Soviet revolution of 1917 ushered in a large number of plays dealing with that struggle. Ivanov's ARMORED TRAIN 14–69 appeared at this time; so did Bulgakov's THE DAYS OF THE TURBINS and Glebov's POWER.

These cycles of historic drama brought to the stage for the first time an evaluation of history from the viewpoint of the Russian proletariat. They were plays concerned with violent and bloody events. But the time had now come for plays of a different type. The first Five-Year Plan of reconstruction, adapted in 1928, opened the way to dramas of peacetime. The playwrights began to deal with basic reconstruction problems, among them the necessity for modernizing agriculture. Dramas on this theme included A WINDOW ON THE VILLAGE (1928), by Akulshin; Kirshon's BREAD (1930). Plays also dealt with the growth of large-scale industry; Gladkov's CEMENT (1926) was followed by Kirshon's THE RAILS ARE HUMMING (1928); Bykov's BLACK GOLD (1928); Nikitkin's LINE OF FIRE (1931); and two well-known dramas by Pogodin, THE POEM ABOUT AN AXE (1931) and MY FRIEND (1932). The dramatists were taking part actively and systematically in the drive to bring Russia into the twentieth century.

Still another field awaited the efforts of the playwright. The change to a new type of government had affected not only the economic life of the country but the lives of individuals also. The World War, the revolution, the civil wars, intervention, the battle inside the Communist Party itself, had left behind them human as well as economic wreckage. It became the duty of the dramatist to understand these misfits—the criminals, the incorrigibles, the wild children, the remnants of the middle class, the richer peasants (*kulaks*), who remained for a long time hostile to the new order. At the same time the dramatists sought out the new, constructive types who were emerging—the younger generation of Soviet intellectuals, engineers, scientists, explorers, not to mention the young men and women of the new era.

Among the large number of such plays there is space to name only a few: Kirshon and Uspensky's RUST (1926); Faiko's THE MAN WITH THE PORTFOLIO (1928); Katayev's SQUARING THE CIRCLE (1928); Mayakovsky's THE BEDBUG (1929); FEAR, by Afinogenov (1931); Gorky's YEGOR BULITCHEV (1932) and his DOSTIGAYEV

(1933). From 1932 on, a tone of distinctly greater cheerfulness and optimism is to be felt in this category of plays. Examples are Mikitenko's THE GIRLS OF OUR COUNTRY (1933); Katayev's THE PATH OF FLOWERS (1934); Pogodin's ARISTOCRATS (1935); Korneichuk's PLATON KRECHET (1935); Afinogenov's DALEKOYE (REMOTE) (1935).

The themes of dramaturgy on Soviet stages were closely paralleled by those of Soviet film. It should be kept in mind, in addition, that alongside of the purely Soviet plays which have been described there has been a showing of the world's classics on an unprecedented scale. These have included pre-Soviet Russian masterpieces and plays from all languages and all periods, including those of modern British and American authors.

To the extent that Soviet scripts have tended more and more to base themselves upon an interest in objective events rather than upon inner experiences, their content may be accurately called Socialist *Realistic*. Whether this phrase also describes their *form* is questionable. It might be more accurate, perhaps, to describe their form as Socialist Naturalism or Socialist Romanticism.

On the other hand there is reason to believe that new types of writing are also bound to develop in the Russian theatre. Its dramatists have the advantage of handling very fresh material—a material which will, more and more, demand new techniques in order to find clear interpretation. Even more decisive is the quality of the audiences for whom these playwrights do their work. The composition of Soviet audiences is something new in theatre history. They are "class conscious" proletarians and peasants, none of whom deal with life at arm's length. They have the wisdom which comes of nearness to life. Neither "bright ideas" nor stereotyped patterns can hope to outlast the judgment of such audiences. It is worth while recalling the impression they made on Stanislavsky when he met them for the first time:

> With the coming of the Revolution many classes of society passed through our Theatre—there was the period of soldiers, of deputies from all the ends of Russia, of children and young people, and last, of workingmen and peasants. They were spectators in the best sense of the word; they came into our Theatre not through accident but with trembling and the expectation of something important, something they had never experienced before. (*My Life in Art*).

SOCIALIST REALISMS

In this short survey of Soviet stage theories and practices we have tried to see how many of them can be classified under the heading of a new style in the theatre—the style designated as Socialist Realism. The answer cannot be given with assurance. Socialist Realism must still be regarded as the search for a technique rather than the technique itself. (To a degree this is true of any of the other forms we have considered. All of them were experiments rather than clearly defined formulas.) The name Socialist Realism indicates that the new dramatic metaphor is being sought in outer reality, not in inward certainty. But as yet there is no well-integrated technique to which the name can be applied.

It is not even clear whether conventional or illusory staging is to be the method of Soviet drama. The practice today seems to be a mixture of both, with the illusory dominant but with the conventional side strongly emphasized. Not long ago the celebrated Soviet designer Nikolai Akimov made the following analysis:

> Notwithstanding the enormous number of methods, systems and manners practised, we may sort the Soviet theatre designers into two large groups: the "illusionists" and the "constructivists." . . .
>
> The illusionary method considers the stage as a frame enclosing an undefined depth in which the designer presents a desired illusion of space. This method, while permitting any degree of conventionality in the action upon the stage, denies realistic stage space. For artists employing this method, the stage-box is a necessary prerequisite.
>
> The second method, conditionally called "constructivism," considers the stage as a known quantity of space, the dimensions of which are in no way hidden from the audience. Upon this space are erected, or placed, certain objects that help the actor in movement, and serve also to emphasize the realistic dimensions of the stage platform—but never with any purpose of illusion. Only indirect representation is thus achieved. These artists do not require the stage box. On the contrary, they strive to enter the auditorium itself, a tendency brilliantly furthered in Okhlopkov's Realistic Theatre, notably in his ARISTOCRATS.
>
> Naturally the literate designer of either tendency must master the same ABCs: how to build a stage platform adaptable to all requirements, how to use materials, and the fundamentals of architectural knowledge. Neither a weakness for painted canvas, nor, on the other hand, a weakness for varnished surfaces of wood—not even the degree of mechanization of the production—can positively catalogue a designer.

A naturalistic detail in a construction or a conventional technique applied by an "illusionist" mixes up all the labels. The only exact token is the use made of stage space. As soon as the visual dimensions of the stage begin to surpass all possible reality of stage space, we may know that we are dealing with illusionary scenery.

It would be absurd to declare one of these methods to be law, and outlaw the other from the contemporary theatre. Both methods derive from solid historical traditions, and both were born of real theatre demands, and naturally, both must and will develop further.

Like many other designers, I used both methods in my work—until one day when I found that I had become a firm and conscious adherent of illusionary scenery and, consequently, an ardent defender of the stage-box.

From all that we have been considering it is evident that in its relationship to the theatre the Soviet regime has no simple job on its hands. What it expects of the theatre is clear enough. How it expects to get it is less obvious. We have seen that, shortly after the revolution, it fought down the idea that the older theatres should be destroyed. For a while after that it permitted the Constructivists and other Theatricalists to gain the upper hand. This in spite of the resolution adopted in 1927 by the Soviet All-Union Theatrical Conference:

> Nowhere in the administration of the politics of the theatre shall any one tendency, any one style or genre, be given ascendancy. We must not harbor the desire to subordinate the various trends of the theatre to the service of any single idea, however valuable, because that would mean the destruction of other ideas. Only through mutual competition, and through the play of reciprocal influence, is it possible to maintain a vitality that will arrest the attention of the public.

Eventually the resolution was carried out when, in 1932, the Communist Party itself broke up cliquism in the arts. Today the Soviet theatre continues to give its support to experiment, always with the reservation that experiment does not become the self-sufficient purpose of theatre. It is convinced that the technique known as Socialist Realism will be a synthesis of the most valuable elements in previously known techniques. The official attitude is that the way is open for any style to prove its mettle.

On the other hand this state of affairs does not reflect a drifting policy. There is obviously far too much at stake in the outcome for a theatre which looks upon all drama as a weapon. The new regime expects its purpose to be mirrored in the theatre; in turn the theatre, by clarifying the new society in its own way, exerts an influence on the regime. It is a program which requires "Policy turned into image, and image into policy." (*Contemporary Soviet Playwrights*). The image must not be distorted, but clarified. The government supports the theatre, giving it some latitude, apparently, for expensive mistakes; but it also demands that the theatre take itself seriously as a cultural force.

Meyerhold was under fire as early as 1928 for producing eccentricities unrelated to the life of his audiences. A similar rebuke was given the Jewish theatres for their continued preoccupation with grotesque forms. In 1934 Meyerhold received another warning. Two years later the opera LADY MACBETH OF MTSENK, by Shostakovich, was hauled over the coals for its "formalist trickery" and "coarse naturalism." It was declared to be a cheap attempt at originality combined with vulgarity. (According to *Pravda,** "The merchant's double bed is the center of the production. In this bed all problems are solved." Theatres abroad continued to look upon LADY MACBETH OF MTENSK as art.)

This particular case inaugurated a vigorous housecleaning. It was followed by the banning from the stage of Bedny's opera BOGATYRY (1936), which Tairov had produced, and which *Pravda* called "an attempt to glorify the bandits of Kievan Russia as real revolutionary elements." ** At the dramatic discussions held in Moscow that year there was a general admission of formalist mistakes by Meyerhold, Tairov, Okhlopkov and others.

Nevertheless by the following year the issue had become even sharper. Tairov put on a new version of Gorky's CHILDREN OF THE SUN (1937). Gorky had written this play in order to satirize those intellectuals who had no contact with life. Tairov, it was alleged, had cut out the satire. The magazine *Soviet Art* declared that the director seemed unable to realize the basic reason for his mistakes and that he had antagonized his acting company; it then hauled over the coals not only the acting company but the government Committee on Art.† The fact that Tairov had spent three years rehearsing a pretentious Theatricalist failure,

* January 28, 1936.
** November 14, 1936.
† *Soviet Art,* May 17, 1937.

THE EGYPTIAN NIGHTS (1935), did not help matters. The Kamerny Theatre was reorganized, incorporating the Realistic Theatre; Tairov was continued as director, with Okhlopkov as his assistant.

The case of Eisenstein's BEZHIN MEADOW has already been described. Meyerhold's difficulties came to a head following the dress rehearsal of his production of ONE LIFE (1938), a version by Gabrilovich of Ostrovsky's HOW THE STEEL WAS TEMPERED. The new production was described in the bluntest terms as "alien to Soviet art and to the Soviet spectator." [10] Meyerhold had in fact been steadily losing his audiences, while some of his best actors had drifted away to other companies. He was removed as head of his theatre, work was suspended on the new playhouse which was to have borne his name, and his actors were assigned to other playhouses.[11]

As a result of these events alarming reports spread abroad concerning a "liquidation" of Soviet art and a "purge" of Soviet artists. In fact nothing much happened. Shostakovich went on to write the musical scores of a large number of films including the MAXIM trilogy (beginning 1935), THE GREAT CITIZEN (1938) and FRIENDS (1938). His Fifth Symphony, put on in Leningrad in 1937, was highly praised. Meyerhold became director of the Stanislavsky Opera Theatre. Okhlopkov later went into movie work, acting with distinction a leading rôle in the film ALEXANDER NEVSKY (1938), with which Eisenstein scored a success both at home and abroad. Apparently directors and dramatists are not shot for artistic reasons, even by Soviet commissars. Conversely the prestige of the dramatists Afinogenov and Kirshon did not save them from disgrace when they became involved, as communists, in the factional warfare inside their party.

ON PROPAGANDA

It is no easy task to evaluate the work of the Soviet theatre in terms of its contribution to stage form. A theatre which was estimated to have put on 7,000 new productions in 1939, giving 235,400 performances for an audience of 77,000,000 in that year,* a theatre with large numbers of training schools, studios and dramatic museums—such a theatre is a huge phenomenon. It is a

* Figures are quoted from H. W. L. Dana in *Soviet Russia Today*, July, 1940.

theatre capable of large-scale achievements and experiments, as well as large-scale mistakes. In this theatre tendencies of iconoclastic radicalism exist side by side with genuine conservatism; but these two tendencies do not temper or nullify one another necessarily. They often cause a conflict which can only be solved "dialectically," according to the Russians.

This is the Russian way of maintaining that the technique of the future, which they call the technique of Socialist Realism, will not be a compromise including the methods already known, but will be a distinctly new method using the current practices in new and unexpected ways. There are strong and weak points both in the traditional approach and in the newer tendencies. Some aspects of both have already been left behind. Other features seem to continue as time goes on.

In the Soviet view, the first and most important thing that has come to stay is the principle of propaganda. But even this cannot be put down as a brand new principle. In fact it is not new at all; the theatre has been an instrument of social agitation practically since its beginning, and many of the greatest dramatists of history, from Aeschylus to Shaw, have taken part in social controversies both in their plays and out of them.

It is true that in the sixties of the last century Gustav Freytag maintained,

> If a poet would completely degrade his art, and turn to account . . . the social perversions of real life, the despotism of the rich, the torments of the oppressed . . . by such a work he would probably excite the sympathy of the audience to a high degree, but at the end of the play, this sympathy would sink into painful discord. . . . The muse of art is no sister of mercy.

This, however, was an extremist opinion in its own day. Only a few years before, Harriet Beecher Stowe's propaganda novel UNCLE TOM'S CABIN reached the boards of the American stage. The pro-slavery New York *Herald* denounced the production as an insult to the South and a reflection on what it called "the delicate institution of slavery." [12] The play was bitterly attacked and defended in many other publications because of its abolitionist point of view. Nobody thought of suggesting that it had no business on the stage because it was propaganda, not art.

In a way, Soviet drama may be said to have simplified matters for itself by adopting from the start the simple premise that drama is propaganda, and sticking to it through thick and thin, even though it had to find a place for art in that formula. We in the United States, used to dividing drama into separate categories of art and propaganda, find it harder to classify plays of either type.

Robert E. Sherwood's THERE SHALL BE NO NIGHT is a case in point. For Brooks Atkinson, distinguished New York *Times* critic, this play belongs on the plane of art. In a valuable discussion of the relation of the propaganda play to art, Mr. Atkinson once observed,

> Although an artist may well be inspired by a particular cause, his capacity for understanding carries him beyond causes, parties, creeds or local characteristics into the vast chaotic tragedy of the human race. (New York *Times,* January 12, 1936).

Specifically, Mr. Atkinson was defending Maxwell Anderson's WINTERSET against certain left-wing critics. These critics had objected to the fact that Anderson did not blame anything but "the stars in their courses" for the outcome of the Sacco-Vanzetti case. It must be inferred, therefore, that the *Times* critic found in Sherwood's play the same impersonal serenity that marked WINTERSET.

On the other hand Raymond Clapper, seasoned political commentator of the New York *Herald-Tribune,* did not see that Mr. Sherwood was blaming the stars overhead for the invasion of Finland. The dramatist was specifically accusing the Soviets and Nazi Germany. For Mr. Clapper, not a dramatic critic but a member of the audience, THERE SHALL BE NO NIGHT was not an example of "the vast chaotic tragedy of the human race," but "a rank inflammatory job, pleading for intervention, sneering at our reluctance to go in." [13]

Propaganda ceases to be propaganda, it has been said, as soon as it becomes art. Perhaps it also ceases to be propaganda when it coincides with our own beliefs. The radical Soviet critics see nothing inartistic about agitational communist plays, but look upon plays like WINTERSET as "bourgeois" propaganda. Conservative critics see the left-wing plays of Odets as propagandist, but are inclined to view THERE SHALL BE NO NIGHT as pure artistry. As it happens, the pattern of the Sherwood play closely resembles—Christmas tree scene and all—the pattern of the popular Soviet drama THE DAYS OF THE TURBINS, by Bulgakov, in which a foreground of civilized family life is imposed upon a background of militant propaganda.

The Soviet theatre, it has been noted, takes pride in the fact that it is propagandist. But even in the case of the Soviets it is necessary to approach the definition of propaganda with some care. The propaganda of the modern Russian drama has a particular object—namely, *class criticism*. Class criticism—the criticism of one social class by another—happens to be very ancient, since the lower strata of society have been weighed by upper class writers, and found wanting, since time immemorial. What is comparatively new about Soviet propaganda is the fact that the tables are turned: the "upper" class is now being weighed by the "lower," and found wanting. This represents a distinct change from the more general, impersonal *social criticism* of the Naturalist era.

Yet even Soviet critics admit that class criticism as practiced by the proletariat is much older than the Soviet theatre—more than half a century of working class literature has contained that point of view. And criticism of the rulers by the ruled occurred in many plays put on before, during and after the French and the American revolutions. It can even be traced in the Fools' Festivals of the Middle Ages, which served the lower Catholic clergy as a means of lampooning their superiors. The buffoonery of the Commedia dell' Arte, was directed against smug middle class types, as well as against the Spanish rulers of Naples. Some of the very earliest Greek comedies did not hesitate to ridicule the gods, to show Hercules drunk or Apollo out on a limb.

It is, of course, the capitalist class which is the butt of Soviet criticism and satire. Some of our own commentators apparently believe that no one would want to write or go to plays which attack capitalism except under compulsion. It is only wishful thinking, however, to suppose that Soviet playwrights write such plays only under duress, or that the population is herded in to see these plays against its will. There was a time shortly after the revolution when a definite amount of covert hostility against the Bol-

Okhlopkov's MOTHER (1932). Setting by Jacob Shtoffer
Tsarist emblems, Japanese flower paths, proletarian actors

AUDITORIUM THEATRE

THE START (1932) at Okhlopkov's Realistic Theatre. Setting by Shtoffer

sheviks still existed in the Russian theatres, but that is no longer true. Plenty of differences remain, as in other theatres, but the question of capitalism versus communism is not one of them. Neither dramatists nor audiences have any attachment to the capitalist viewpoint. There already exists a second generation of theatre people who have been reared from childhood in the doctrines of communism, and who therefore see it as the natural way of life. In this sense Soviet drama is not propagandist as regards its own audiences and theatre workers, however propagandist it appears to the world outside.

MARXISM ON STAGE

It should be noted that there is one feature of Soviet dramatic propaganda which happens to be a great deal broader in some ways than anti-capitalist satire. It is an aspect which is not anti-capitalist at all, as a matter of fact. It consists of propaganda for the age of science and machines.

The Soviet views on science are taken from the philosophy of Karl Marx. Marxism as an economic philosophy has received wide attention. It is less well known that Marx worked out a general philosophy, known as *dialectical materialism,* in which he tried to reconcile objective and subjective thought into a single system of reasoning. Some of the doctrines of this system have a broad interest of their own apart from their relation to Marxian economics.

Briefly, dialectical materialism maintains that an objective, physical world exists prior to any ideas that we may have about it. At the same time, our knowledge of that world changes as we deal with it. Our knowledge grows not through sheer speculation but through experience with the objective world. Our practice is guided by theory and imagination, but on the other hand, theory and imagination are guided by, and verified through, practice. This new materialism, unlike the "simple" materialism which preceded it, denies that life is constructed on a simple mechanical model. Life is a matter not only of mechanics and physics, but of chemistry, biology, sociology, economics, and many other relationships, some of them very complex. Life is in constant process of change, so that the beliefs of today may be amended tomorrow. This does not mean that we cannot really know the world. It means only that our grasp of nature's laws becomes more exact from day to day. As regards the value of science, Marxian materialism seems to be in full accord with those who believe that the scientific age and the machine mean the liberation, not the enslavement, of human beings.

Nothing impresses foreign observers more than the confidence which the Soviet has in the future of machines. Much of the scenic form of its theatres is derived from the machine, and all of its plays are serene in their acceptance of science and machinery. In Soviet philosophy, this does not mean that the new Russia "worships" the machine or has a "mechanical" view of human life. It means only that the machine is not considered something artificial and alien to the human spirit, but something which is a natural and wholesome extension of that spirit. It is a mistake to blame science and machinery for the chaos which has resulted from the fact that they are not properly geared to the social needs of today.

This optimism is in the sharpest contrast with the views of the Expressionists, for example. Like Ned Ludd in Toller's THE MACHINE-WRECKERS, the Expressionists looked upon the machine itself as basically evil.

The artistic fear of machines evokes some curious assertions in Russia. Is it not true, ask the Marxists, that certain people who feel that a man with a hoe is a poetic sight find no poetry in a man with a tractor? Such people are at home in the age of handicrafts but not in the age of mass production. It is not really machinery that frightens them, but the size and complexity of the machinery. The modern factory machine is very often, even typically, larger than the human being. (This phenomenon, by the way, is described in Marx's *Capital.*) A hammer can be gripped in the hand; a hydraulic press cannot. . . .

It is characteristic of Soviet theatre that it looks upon stage form not as a kind of esthetic envelope for stage productions but as something having a highly important social propaganda of its own. "Style is not surface; style is world-outlook," declares Zavadsky, one of the directors of the Vakhtangov Theatre. Characteristic also, is the Soviet belief that a new stage form must be fought for, in a fight that is waged along the whole line of dramatic production. It may well be that the script holds the most important position in this war; but no sector can be considered unimportant.

If we wish to understand fully the Soviet theorists' point of view we must understand their corollary to the principle that a new form must be fought for. With their usual hard Marxian logic they reason that this fight takes place concretely in the course of specific productions. Since every production is the combined result of the personalities at work on it, it represents a balance of forces, a balance of the viewpoints of the personnel. It is asserted that each person who takes part in a dramatic production brings to it his whole class background and sympathies, which may or may not be the same as his neighbor's.

In the Marxian philosophy the clashes which nearly always take place in the course of any stage production (in Russia or elsewhere) are not merely the result of "temperament"; they have a more deep-seated reason, being due to the conflict of class viewpoints as expressed in personal behavior, social outlook and dramatic philosophy. The putting on of a dramatic production is a class war in miniature:

> In such upsurges and vacillations in the creativeness of the theatre lies a phase of theatrical life, concealed at times from the audience, but acutely felt by theatre workers. Theatre work is affected unevenly according to the artists participating. At times the influence of the regisseur may be stronger, other times that of the actor, artist, or musician. Aware that each of the artists, who works in this complex art, performs his particular creative, class-ideological part, we find, within the theatre, an intense class struggle—a crossing and clashing of different class interests. A historian of the theatre will doubtless make the most interesting and important discoveries along this road. The reciprocal and inseparable influences of playwriting on the theatre and of the theatre on playwriting, for the mutual development of each art, are necessary for the presentation of the new class-ideological contents. (Gvozdev).

This frank recognition of the human equation in production, as the Russians view it, seems to be among the reasons why their theatres go in for group discussion. Creative discussion is supposed to help clarify misunderstandings and to establish a common ground for all concerned.

Let us suppose that a Soviet dramatic company wishes to put

on HAMLET—one of the favorite plays of the Soviet repertory. It will make this decision only when it is sure that it has something of vital importance to convey to its audiences. It may wish to show that Hamlet was a man of the new Humanist era, a brilliant student at Wittenberg, who is obliged to cut short his schooling to return to the provincially feudal court of Denmark. The feudal nobility live by the simple code of the sword, whereas Hamlet has room in his soul for all the introspection, all the scientific curiosity, of a man of our own times. The wit and courage with which Hamlet faces his problems, the particular group of circumstances which defeat him, can be an education and inspiration for Soviet audiences, who are convinced that as a nation they are building a new society.

If this idea appears sound, it is then explained to the assembled company, and questions and suggestions are invited. The actor who is to play Hamlet realizes that his rôle needs those elements which show the prince as a scholar, a Humanist, the equivalent of a cultured man of our own day. To this he adds the more detailed characteristics of a barbed wit, manliness, touches of delicacy and playfulness, and so on. In the same way the designer understands that his settings can best serve the play if they emphasize the rude strength of feudal architecture, if his costumes faithfully resurrect some of the boorishness of the nobility of feudal times—in order that the contrast with Hamlet becomes clear.

Indeed it is not necessary to believe in class war in order to outline a rational plan of production. Why trust to diverse inspirations which may or may not belong together when they are finally assembled on the stage? Because a hitch in movie rehearsals can be completely ruinous, Hollywood has learned to make clear the artistic "line," the "yangle" of its productions before putting them into work. There is a certain amount of democracy in this Hollywood procedure. Broadway productions too often take on the form of a fairly benevolent dictatorship by the producer. The producer in turn tends to proceed on "hunches," so that it is not unusual for everything to go at cross purposes at the most crucial times. More than one production per season is taken apart and made all over again before it finally opens.

ROMANTIC RENAISSANCE

By 1940 those Soviet theatre people who favored the technique of conventionalism were getting rather the worst of the "class-ideological" controversy. The field was open for both tendencies, and Naturalism was as much suspect as the various brands of formalism. In practice, however, Socialist Realism was beginning to look more and more like Socialist Romanticism. Such Romantic productions as the Moscow Second Art Theatre's PICKWICK CLUB (1934), the Vakhtangov Theatre's HUMAN COMEDY (1934) and MUCH ADO ABOUT NOTHING (1936), the Moscow Art Theatre's ANNA KARENINA (1937), or the Eisenstein film ALEXANDER NEVSKY (1938) had become typical.

In the 1939–1940 season there was a vogue of Wagnerian concerts. This was set down by some commentators abroad as part of a "communazi" alliance. But in fact the operas of Wagner, which Marx and Engels so detested, had long been in the repertory of Soviet playhouses along with other classical works of the world theatre. (In this case, at any rate, some of the Soviet theatres have not been as Marxian as Marx!) If the popularity of Wagner had shown an increase, it was for the same reason that the other Romantic productions had come into favor. All were part of a trend in which color, glamor, a growing optimism, began to take precedence over the depiction of class struggle.

In 1936 the Soviet government had announced that class society was finally eliminated within its borders; that is to say, there was no longer a middle, upper or lower stratum, that there was only one category of Soviet citizens, neither upper nor lower. The civil war period was now a memory, the period of reconstruction was safely launched. For the first time since the revolution the nation as a whole felt itself prepared for whatever the troublous future might bring. It is against this background that the Romantic Soviet period has developed. It is a period which is trying to combine the somber Marxian conception of class war with the subjective technique of Romantic Naturalism. The result has been a kind of renaissance of Romanticism. Soviet critics insist that it is a Romanticism purified of decadence, one which has the spiritual power which animated Goethe with hope for the future.

The present Soviet interest in Romanticism may remind us of one side of the Soviet theatre which is too often forgotten—its conservatism. The Russians seem to be as devoted to all that is old in stage tradition as they are to all that is new. In this sense the significant thing about the revolution in their theatre is less

Lear and the Fool

Drawing by Alexander Tishler

the *change* in viewpoint, radical as that is, than the *widening* of viewpoint to include new and old in one continuous survey.

This paradox can be noted in many of the day-to-day activities of the modern Russian theatre. The classics of the world stage have been on the boards ever since the revolution.[14] Each theatre has its archives. Mementoes of performances dating back to the Middle Ages are treasured. New productions of Shakespeare, Ostrovsky, Molière or Shaw are accompanied by museum exhibitions in the lobby, and the public crowds around to compare the

Vakhtangov Theatre production of MUCH ADO ABOUT NOTHING with Shakespearean sketches by Gordon Craig or the Duke of Meiningen. The Russians are "sold" on theatre as an instrument of propaganda, and they are just as sold on "the art of the theatre" as envisioned by Richard Wagner and Edward Gordon Craig.

Still, interesting as the new Romantic trend may be, we may wonder whether it has the right to call itself Socialist Realism. There is nothing like the glow of optimism and faith in the future; but a rather more incisive approach would seem to be needed in the complex and highly explosive times into which the whole world—including the Soviets—has moved.

But there is not much reason to assume that the present tendency will last indefinitely. In the past, Soviet theatre has gone through distinct epochs, each of which has culminated in an abrupt change in policy after having served a particular period. The line of development just now favors the Romantic Naturalists. We have tried to infer the reasons. Among these may be the quite simple fact that the Naturalists have made fewer mistakes, to date, than their opponents the formalists.

Tomorrow it might be the turn of Romantic Naturalism to be critically examined. In the spring of 1939 *Pravda* published two articles which contained some significant passages:

> There is no need to color, smooth over or idealize life in the Soviet Union today nor the great historical past of the Russian people. . . . Consequently the public is very severe in its criticism of writers whose works depict virtuous, super-courageous, 100%-perfect characters. . . . Such an oversimplified picture of reality quite fails of its purpose and has no educational effect, for it blots out the complexity of real life. . . . The scene in the film ALEXANDER NEVSKY, for instance, where Vasili Buslai, the Russian warrior, beats down dozens of mailed knights with nothing more formidable than a wagon tongue was justly strictured, while the second part of PETER I was felt to give a too-idealized picture of Peter. (Dubrovsky).

THEATRE FOR AUDIENCES

We believe enough data has been given to show that it is necessary to keep an open mind about the innovations which the Soviet theatre has brought forward. Lenin, Lunacharsky and other communist leaders felt that the Soviet regime would never be justified in a wholesale condemnation of the "bourgeois" dramatic culture which this regime inherited; and even the most hostile among us might be wise to return this obviously sincere compliment.

We are not compelled to share the political or social beliefs of the Soviet Union or its playhouses in order to make use of many of the artistic ideas which the modern Russian theatres have advanced. *Environment in motion, machine for theatre,* the contrapuntal dramatic use of music, the quest for an adequate technique of the stage and screen, an optimistic view of the machine age, are among these new ideas. Like earlier techniques, that of Socialist Realism has points of merit which will remain part of the general heritage of theatre as long as theatre lasts.

Of such concepts perhaps the most striking is the belief that theatre exists to serve its audiences. With the deterioration of the Naturalistic style our theatres set foot on a road which has taken them steadily away from their audiences. The techniques of Symbolism, Expressionism, Dadaism, Surrealism and Theatricalism have pushed the thoughts of stage people further and further inward—upon their own activities, their own problems, themselves. New stage techniques were addressed to narrower and narrower circles of initiates, until the point was nearly reached at which stage people were talking only to themselves.

But of course it is true, isn't it, that the stage does not exist for the sake of its own technique? It does not exist for the sake of producers, dramatists, actors, designers or technicians. A healthy theatre exists first of all for its audiences. If a stage technique does not serve theatre audiences, it really does not function any longer, whatever else may be said for it. If the Soviet theatre has reminded us of this fact rather rudely, we may at least be grateful for the reminder.

NOTES

1. In her *Anton Chekhov, the Voice of Twilight Russia,* Princess Toumanova, who stresses the timidity of Chekhov, ascribes it to his background: he was descended from serfs and was the son of a hymn-singing provincial grocer, who taught him submission. Unlike the aristocratic Tolstoy, he never got into trouble with the Tsarist censor. Incidentally, Chekhov's plays annoyed Tolstoy, whose views on art were

both independent and unorthodox. That rugged oldster once told Chekhov, "I cannot bear Shakespeare, you know, but your plays are even worse. Shakespeare, for all that, takes the reader by the neck and leads him to a certain goal, and does not let him turn aside. And where is one to go with your heroes? From the sofa where they are lying to the closet and back."

2. The subtitles as given here have been adapted from those in the original scenario, by courtesy of Amkino. Some of the other original subtitles have been incorporated into the present description of the film.

3. The *Potemkin* was in fact permitted to go through. She sailed to the Rumanian port of Constantza, where her crew was interned. A few months later the crew of the *Potemkin* came back to Russia upon the Tsar's promise of a fair trial and consideration for their grievances. The promise was not kept. The leaders were shot and the rest were exiled to Siberia.

4. The film version of THE PLOUGH AND THE STARS, derived from the stage play of the same name by Sean O'Casey, was a strange mixture of subjective and objective techniques, with the former predominant. For those interested in dramatic form, the clash of these two techniques was more enthralling than the story itself.

The heroine, Nora Clitheroe (played by Barbara Stanwyck), was supposed to be a humane Irish proletarian girl who tries to keep her husband—a Republican leader—away from the struggle with the British. To the film producers this story must have seemed uncontroversial, humanitarian art. To Irish Republicans whose women-folk had fought shoulder to shoulder with them for Irish freedom, the film must have seemed controversial pro-British propaganda. Whether art or propaganda, the contrast of philosophies, if developed, would have made for powerful drama.

It was up to the film to make plausible the character of an idealist like Nora, who is caught in a terrible fix: her husband, her friends, are involved in savage war. This problem the movie failed to deal with. Nora became a wraith out of Maeterlinckian soul-drama, moving always in a haze which betrayed an excessive use of the diffusion disk. Supposedly this meant that she was "spiritual." Actually it meant that she had been plucked out of the environment of her own story and given an arbitrary saintliness. Since her character was never explained it seemed, on the basis of her behavior, to be petulant and treacherous.

The high point of incongruity was reached in the barricade scenes. Here we were allowed a glimpse of some Republican women, presented quite sympathetically as honest proletarians. Miss Stanwyck was shown nagging these women, whose faces were caught by the open lens while hers appeared in soft-focus. . . . Not only the people but the settings were given this confused treatment. For instance the clear, powerful photography of the attack on the Post Office was in startling contrast with the sequence of the man-hunt over dreamy roofs in the style of Walt Disney.

5. The February, 1917, revolution ended the reign of the Tsars and established a provisional (coalition) government under Kerensky. This gave way to the Soviet regime after a second wave of revolt in the following November (October in the old-style Russian calendar).

6. NEP: New Economic Policy. In 1921 the Soviet government, as a temporary post-war expedient, inaugurated a system of limited private enterprise. Since then the government has continuously withdrawn and restricted the NEP, which is now practically non-existent.

7. Productions in which the audience surrounds the stage have been attempted in the United States. Best known are the Penthouse Theatre plays directed by Glenn Hughes at Washington University, Seattle. In the summer of 1940 Jacob Weiser conducted an open-air theatre at Long Beach Stadium, New York, using a converted boxing-ring on which to stage such plays as MORNING STAR, by Sylvia Regan, and KISS THE BOYS GOODBYE, by Clare Boothe. Madison Square Garden, in New York City, has witnessed centrally-staged pageants given by the International Ladies Garment Workers Union, the Communist Party and other organizations.

8. Norris Houghton in *Moscow Rehearsals* asserts that "the Russian designer is primarily a painter and afterwards a man of the theatre." He implies, in addition, that scene design, while contributing to the excellence of the new theatre, is after all a minor factor.

Neither idea is correct. Houghton's description would properly apply to the Tsarist designer-painters like Bakst and Golovin. It does not apply to the modern designers, who as a rule are attached to dramatic companies and receive their training there. The contribution of the designers seems to be highly rated by the public and the critics. The foreign observer is struck by the large amount of comment and discussion devoted to scene design in the Soviet press.

I can find no factual basis for Houghton's assertion that because of "Russian temperament," "the *décor* of the Moscow stage is brave in conception, weak in execution." The temperament of Russian designers struck me as being singularly like that of American, Swedish, French, German or English scene designers. I may note, in passing, that Soviet design seemed to me often rather clumsy in sheer mechanical ingenuity. The settings are ponderously built, and there appeared to be a lack of special theatrical hardware. From this point of view most European designers have something to learn from the Americans. This, however, is not the point of Houghton's remark.

9. See Chapter IV, p. 138.

10. Committee on Arts of the Council of Peoples Commissars of the U.S.S.R. Moscow *Daily News*, January 8, 1938.

11. *Izvestia,* December 17 and 18, 1937; January 27, 1938.

Soviet Art, July 5, 1937; October 11, 1937; December 29, 1937.

For a discussion of the Meyerhold case in English see *Formalistic Stagnation* (Moscow *Daily News,* January 9, 1938), in which one of Meyerhold's former actors complains that the director never permitted his actors to work on their own parts. "Under such conditions all the initiative of the actor is killed. The actor becomes a tool in the hands of the producer." The famous Vakhtangov Theatre actor, B. V. Shchukin, in an open letter, also quoted, makes the following appeal to Meyerhold:

"You have lost your best actors, you have not produced a single performance that can move and appeal to the Soviet audience; and finally you have lost your audience. Your theatre is rightly called an unnecessary theatre, a theatre hostile to the people. What have you been left with, Vsevolod Emilyevich?"

12. The C. W. Taylor adaptation of UNCLE TOM'S CABIN (with a happy ending) was produced at the National Theatre, New York City, in 1853. It had a mild success, running two full weeks. In the same year (July 18), and at the same theatre, it was followed by George L. Aiken's version, which achieved the amazing run of over three hundred performances. It thus became the TOBACCO ROAD of its day. Its success was undeterred by denunciations like the following, printed in the New York *Herald* of September 3rd:

"Any such representation must be an insult to the South—an exaggerated mockery of Southern institutions—and calculated . . . to poison the minds of our youth with the pestilential principles of abolitionism. . . . The institution of Southern slavery is recognized and protected by the federal constitution, upon which this Union was established, and which holds it together. . . . And yet, here in this city—which owes its wealth, population, power, and prosperity, to the Union and the constitution, and this same institution of slavery, to a greater degree than any other city in the Union—here we have nightly represented, at a popular theatre, the most exaggerated enormities of Southern slavery, playing directly into the hands of the abolitionists and abolition kidnappers of slaves, and doing their work for them. What will our Southern friends think of all our professions of respect for their delicate institution of slavery? . . . Is this consistent with good faith, or honor, or the every day obligations of hospitality? No, it is not. . . . We would . . . advise all concerned to drop the play . . . at once and forever. The thing is in bad taste—it is not according to good faith to the constitution . . . and is calculated, if persisted in, to become a firebrand of the most dangerous character to the peace of the whole country." (From George C. D. Odell: *Annals of the New York Stage,* Volume 6.)

13. "The topic is a big one. . . . But Mr. Sherwood has admirably

created the atmosphere of a wholesome family, which is the basis of the play. Part of it is humorous; all of it is affectionate. The whole thing has the feeling of modern times. When the war begins Mr. Sherwood has more difficulty in revealing character from the inside rather than by external circumstances, and the play loses the direction of the splendid first act. But the events are too poignantly true to be resisted by the usual cant of criticism. In the last act Mr. Sherwood twice pulls the whole thing together with magnificent statements of what goes on in the mind of an enlightened man confronted with the destruction of his aspirations. . . . Although THERE SHALL BE NO NIGHT is uneven drama, it honors the theatre and the best parts of it speak for the truth with enkindling faith and passionate conviction."—Brooks Atkinson (New York *Times*, April 30, 1940).

"I am not a dramatic critic and I call attention to this play only because it may have a deep influence upon national feeling about the war. Sometimes plays are more potent than statesmen in stirring and directing the impulses of a people. This play, depicting the tragedy of Finland, seemed to me a rank, inflammatory job, pleading for intervention, sneering at our reluctance to go in. America, still hesitant to plunge into the burning ruins of Europe, was compared to Pontius Pilate, callous and cowardly, evading a responsibility. . . . Most of those who saw the play [in Washington, D.C.] were swept off their feet. Unfortunately the audiences were predominantly women who are suckers for emotional crusading of the kind which this play stimulates." —Raymond Clapper (New York *World-Telegram*, April 30, 1940).

14. Concerning the production of foreign stage classics in the U.S.S.R., Dana gives the following examples in *Soviet Russia Today* (July, 1940):

"THE DOG IN THE MANGER [by Lope de Vega] has been acted in no less than twenty-six theatres in the Soviet Union and is scheduled to be performed in twelve more. THE MISTRESS OF THE INN, written by the great Venetian dramatist of the 18th Century, Goldoni, has been acted in thirty theatres. Molière's TARTUFFE has been acted in twenty-four theatres, including a production rehearsed by Stanislavsky just before his death and produced by the Moscow Art Theatre last October. Balzac's THE STEPMOTHER has been acted in fifty-two theatres and is billed in eight more. Schiller's LOVE AND INTRIGUE has been performed in fifty different theatres during the last season.

"On April 23, 1939, the 375th anniversary of Shakespeare's birth was celebrated throughout the Soviet Union as it was nowhere else on earth. Two hundred and twelve theatres put on Shakespeare plays that night. During the last season OTHELLO has been acted in sixty-seven different theatres, and ROMEO AND JULIET in thirty, and during the present year, 1940, no less than sixty-nine productions of Shakespeare are planned."

REFERENCES

Letters of Anton Chekhov to His Family and Friends. Macmillan, New York, 1920.

Constantin Stanislavsky: *My Life in Art.* Little, Brown & Company.

Stanislavsky: Speech at Pushkino. From *USSR in Construction.* September, 1938.

Pavel A. Markov: *The Soviet Theatre.* Victor Gollancz, London, 1934.

Huntly Carter: *The New Theatre and Cinema of Soviet Russia.* International Publishers.

The Miracle of Meyerhold. Related by B. Tchemerinsky of the Habimah to Ella Barnett. New York *Times,* January 23, 1927.

Jay Leyda: *The Background of Film Reality* (unpublished).

Thomas A. Edison. From Jay Leyda and Peter Ellis: *A Guide to the Social Study of the Film. Theatre Workshop.* April–July, 1937.

Joseph Freeman: *An American Testament.* Farrar & Rinehart, New York, 1936.

O. Litovsky: *Sixteen Years of the Soviet Theatre.* From *The Theatre in the USSR.* Voks, Moscow. Vol. 6, 1934.

Henry W. L. Dana: *Notes on the Development of Soviet Drama.* From Dickinson: *The Theatre in a Changing Europe.* Henry Holt, New York, 1937.

Nikolai Mologin: *The Meyerhold State Theatre.* International Theatre Bulletin No. 2.

Nikolai Okhlopkov. From Norris Houghton: *Moscow Rehearsals.* Harcourt Brace & Company, New York, 1936.

E. Stephen Karnot: *Krasny Presny. New Theatre.* July–August, 1934.

Henry W. L. Dana: *Handbook on Soviet Drama.* American-Russian Institute, New York, 1938.

Clara Zetkin: *Recollections of Lenin.* From Moscow *Daily News.* January 9, 1938.

Nikolai Akimov: *The Designer in the Theatre. Theatre Arts.* September, 1936.

Contemporary Russian Soviet Playwrights. International Literature. No. 4, 1931.

Gustav Freytag. From Clark: *European Theories of the Drama.* Appleton.

George C. D. Odell: *Annals of the New York Stage.* Vol. 6. Columbia University Press, 1931.

Yuri Zavadsky: *Conversations With a Young Régisseur. Theatre Arts,* September, 1936.

E. E. Gvozdev: *Problems in the Study of the History of the Theatre. International Theatre.* August, 1935.

D. Dubrovsky: *Achievements and Drawbacks of Soviet Art Discussed.* Moscow *News,* May 15, 1939.

9

THEATRE IS A TRIBUNAL

"ABOVE THE BATTLE"

AFTER forty-odd years the staid and distinguished Theater-am-Nollendorfplatz in Berlin's run-down Western quarter, in 1927 underwent a change of name, becoming the Piscator Theatre. The Nollendorf had housed the plays of Schiller, Goethe and Hebbel; its Italian Baroque auditorium had echoed to white-gloved hands applauding classic revivals. What was it going to see now?

Erwin Piscator, who set up his office in the room where the Kaiser used to freshen his uniform before entering the imperial box, was no plodding, routine director. The productions which carried his imprint at the Nollendorf Theatre—HOPPLA, WE LIVE!, RASPUTIN, SCHWEIK—proved both dynamic and startling. Nor were they lacking in greatness of form. On a certain January evening in 1928, with the opening of Piscator's THE GOOD SOLDIER SCHWEIK, it seemed to many observers that another milestone had been passed on the road of world-theatre.

SCHWEIK was a dramatization of a great satirical novel of the first World War. The novel, of the same name, was written by the Czech journalist Jaroslav Haček, who died when the book was two-thirds finished; someone else had completed the story. SCHWEIK recounts the adventures of a Sancho-Panza type of peasant soldier, from the time he is conscripted until he has assimilated all the lessons which the War had to offer. During that momentous period Schweik seems to march on with a wooden head, but his eyes and ears are really wide open. To the delight of the audience he also keeps his mouth open; his wagging tongue leads him into trouble from which it constantly leads him out again.

A packed house, with the aisles filled, rocked the play in applause through the almost endless succession of its scenes. For the overwhelming majority of the audience the round-faced little Czech soldier served to measure the full insanity of the imperialist war of 1914–1918. On that evening, almost a decade after the most appalling slaughter in history, a theatre audience found means to view the Great War with Homeric laughter.

A new dramatic form made this possible. A form which was still in its early period of experiment, which seemed in many ways to deny the worth of some of the most striking achievements of the past, but which in other ways brought new values to the theatre's ancient tradition.

It was the almost paradoxical value of this form which explained the composition of the audience which sat before SCHWEIK. Not one assembly was there, but two: an audience in dress clothes, smart, worldly, aloof; and an audience of young radicals in *Schillerkragen*—sharp-witted, vociferous proletarians and lower middle class youngsters alert beyond their years to the signals of disaster which had already appeared in the Fatherland. Since the young people, most of them members of the Junge Volksbühne, were subscribers with the right to sit anywhere in the theatre at a uniform fee, there was an unaccustomed spectacle of dinner jackets mingling with ready-made suits. The elegant world was here because a Piscator production was a "must" event in art. The radicals considered it a political event. For both it was indispensable.

Both classes of theatregoers belonged to that exhausted, impoverished Weimar Republic which President Ebert (and afterwards President Hindenburg) tried to hold together by main force. In 1918 the iron-gray German armies had returned defeated and decimated. These troops had gone to war goose-stepping for the glory of the Kaiser and the Empire. They returned to take part in demonstrations demanding work and bread, in street fighting and the Spartacist revolts, proclaiming the end not only of the Kaiser but of the German profit system.

Torn economically and socially, Germany teetered wildly between Right and Left. In a land whose paper money eventually sold at nine billion marks to an American dollar, a "coalition" government of Centrists tried vainly to effect a coalition. It was much too late. The Fatherland was already headed for the abyss. Fascist gangs were roaming the streets, the gutter press was demanding the blood of "Jews and communists," Hitler and his troopers had already found warm sympathy in the hearts of German industrial rulers.

The government, led by men who hated communism and fascism with equal fervor, tried forcibly to end all opposition. It was easier, however, to put down the uprisings of despairing workers in Thuringia and the Ruhr than to deal effectively with the putschists of the Right. Kapp and Lüttwitz in Berlin, Hitler in Munich, had powerful friends to intercede for them. The illness was not to be cured in that fashion. Not peace but Nazism was the result.

All in all it was an instructive period, during which the issues at stake in Germany became defined with terrible clarity. Between the class-conscious rich, who looked to a fascist dictatorship for protection, and the class-conscious poor, who demanded release from the horrors of a bankrupt German economic system, was any middle ground possible?

"The middle ground is in the arts," was the opinion of the older generation of liberals, including some of the leading dramatic critics like Julius Bab. It was the opinion also of the directorate of the Volksbühne, who were trying in their accustomed way to keep the flag of culture flying amid the struggle. Undoubtedly this opinion was part of the faith of many Germans who had been taught from childhood that art is a consecrated activity "above the battle," that art is a temple where democracy reigns and where the muddy shoes of political strife are left outside the door.

But as time pressed forward and social difficulties became mountainous, the artists themselves were finding it impossible to remain above the battle. While the advance guard of art and literature, aware of the tragedy that was impending, cried out—to deaf ears—their warning against this somnolent "neutrality," the Nazis were already writing down the names of those artists who had the "insolent provocation" to make a stand for freedom of thought. The once treasured ideal of artistic neutrality was crumbling away.

Without waiting for permission from the more conservative theorists, the German theatre had gone on to its necessary work, associating itself with the great majority of the people in their fight for liberation. The working class led the way. At Leipzig in 1920 a great spectacle was put on by the Spartacist League. Searchlights illuminated a stage on which was represented the bacchanalian orgies of the rulers of Rome, slaves fainting under forced labor, the battles of gladiators, and the trial and execution of Spartacus, leader of the slave revolt.[1]

The influx of new audiences in the left sections of the theatre was prodigious. By 1930 the older Volksbühne numbered over half a million members, with groups in three hundred cities. The German Workers' Theatre League, established in 1919, sent dozens of "agitprop" troupes, composed of proletarian amateur actors, to the gathering places of the workers, in union halls, summer camps, strike headquarters.

Meanwhile the path toward a new dramatic technique—one which would be answerable to audiences rather than to abstract canons of art—had been opened as early as 1919 by the pioneer Karlheinz Martin with his theatre, Die Tribüne, in Charlottenburg, Berlin. The Tribüne's program read: "The urgent revolution of the theatre must start with a transformation of the stage. . . . We do not ask an audience, but a community, not a stage, but a pulpit."

Such were the groundswells of the movement which, between 1919 and 1932, brought into existence the stage form known as *Epic*. Epic arose on the premise that there can be no middle ground of artistic neutrality for a theatre whose very life is at stake. For Piscator—stage director, ex-soldier and anti-militarist—there was no middle ground between theatre which faced life and theatre which evaded life. For Bertolt Brecht—saturnine playwright, who had been a medical attendant in war hospitals—there was no middle ground. The Epic theatre, shaped in practice by Piscator, in theory by Brecht, called for a definition of the word art. Was it not conceivable that art might be one thing today, another tomorrow? They asked: Art for whom? For an audience of a fortunate few, or for an audience of the whole population?

THE GOOD SOLDIER

Before SCHWEIK Piscator had already established his position as a startling innovator. Perhaps the appearance of the SCHWEIK production as the curtain rose on it was at first glance unusually mild. Three thin portals spanned the depth of the stage—Baroque fashion—and were closed in with a translucent drop in the rear. Between the portals, and parallel with the footlights, were two treadmills (or "conveyors," as Piscator called them), whose combined widths formed the depth of the stage. That was all; and as

From *Hintergrund*

SCHWEIK (1928) Drawing by George Grosz for animated film

the stage darkened it was filled with the lilt of a Czech folksong played on a hurdy-gurdy.

But now the backdrop springs into life, turning into a large motion picture screen as the projector strikes it from the back. A black dot jumps to the blank screen; it races over the white brilliance with fantastic speed, leaving behind it lines as jagged and scratchy as barbed wire. Rapidly it traces in the distinctive style of the artist George Grosz, a mustachioed and puffy Austrian general. The hilt of a heavy sword appears in the general's right hand; his other hand clasps that of the neighboring figure, who emerges as a German field marshal, his aristocratic scowl half hidden by his *Pickelhaube* helmet. Between this bellicose pair the figure of a lawyer makes its appearance—severe, long-nosed, corpselike, holding legal briefs in one hand, a knout in the other. Finally an ignoble preacher is sketched out, balancing a cross on his bulbous nose.

The treadmill begins to work. From the left a little corner of a room trundles on by itself, a flea-bitten room as dog-eared as the cur in Schweik's lap. Schweik, in shirt-sleeves, puffs away at his tasseled pipe while his landlady, Frau Müller, sweeps the conveyor belt energetically. Frau Müller recalls some gossip. "It seems they murdered our Ferdinand!"

She means Ferdinand, Archduke of Austria. The news arouses Schweik to idle speculation. He wonders if the assassins wore dress suits and high hats for such distinguished quarry. Something like a fox-hunt, perhaps. "It's a great loss for Austria," thinks Schweik, as the corner of his room moves off and he rolls into his favorite pub, the Glass of Beer, almost as soon as the bar travels onstage. A new customer, Bredtschneider, is there already, trying to make conversation with Polivec, the owner. "You can't replace Ferdinand with just any damned fool," Schweik explains to Bredtschneider, who happens to be a police spy. Bredtschneider makes a mental note of this somewhat cryptic remark. Schweik will have to accompany Polivec, who has given no satisfactory reason for suddenly taking down the picture of the Emperor that hung over the bar. "The flies specked all over the Emperor!" Not half good enough! Ten years is what Polivec gets, while Schweik comes limping home from the police investigation to find his mobilization papers lying on the table.

They are in a big envelope with a double eagle and official seals; Frau Müller is excited. "Calm yourself, Frau Müller, I'm going to war. . . ." On the screen the invisible pen scratches furiously a hairy hand heaping gold coins upon a figure with the head of a phonograph. The figure types reams of propaganda: *Gott strafe England, Jeder Stoss ein Franzos,* while a fountain pen gives a military salute and screams *Hurra!* In a wheel chair propelled by Frau Müller, Schweik is on his way to medical inspection at the regional Army H.Q. "On to Belgrade!" he shouts, waving his crutches, while the streets of Prague flash by behind him in motion pictures. The Good Soldier is off on his adventures

In the wings Piscator, small, bright-eyed and sharp-nosed, shakes his head over the rumble of the "conveyor belt." It ought to have been more perfect, he thinks. Didn't the mechanicians swear that it would function as smoothly as a fine automobile? And some of the scenery and properties that speed in on the conveyor tumble down in the opening-night rush. But the audience is not as critical as the director. These episodes seem to have an added charm. The "conveyor belt" is intrinsically a comic idea; added to a story of a wandering soldier it is a device which penetrates to the heart of the action.

The construction of the play into its continuously flowing episodic character had been hardly less difficult than the construction of the treadmills. Before Piscator decided to use it, the novel had been turned into a play by Max Brod and Hans Reimann, who owned the rights of dramatization. When the director read their version his worst fears were realized: Haček's satire had become a musical comedy with a military background. Gasbarra, Leo Lania and Brecht were added to the council of war and the script began to change, racing against time. Some of the episodes, especially the ending, were not decided upon until the opening night. . . .

But we must return to Schweik. He and his fellow-recruits in grotesque underwear have been lining up for medical inspection, swapping hints, meanwhile, on how to keep out of the military draft. Malingering is hard to get away with. A consumptive soldier, no malingerer, is simply falling apart; but the doctors are callous to every kind of symptom, however alarming. And the army physician whose face, dueling scar and all, now fills the whole screen, has a reliable formula for handling all cases. "Physic and aspirin!" he roars, alternating this with "Stomach pump and quinine!" Schweik nevertheless assures the doctor that he has a severe case of rheumatism. So now our hero is on his way again, to start his army hitch in the guard house, where two soldiers, gigantically padded out, receive him.

Fortunately he does not stay in long. A certain Lieutenant Lukasch, who needs an orderly, acquires Schweik in a poker game. For the Lieutenant, war is only an avocation. His real profession is women. In a short time Schweik, following out the Lieutenant's whims, is involved in so many scandals that official punishment becomes necessary for appearance's sake. Lukasch and his orderly are dispatched to the front lines on the Serbian border. In the painted and cut-out train rushing past moving-picture scenery, Schweik is arrested for pulling the emergency cord without good reason. A grilling by the railway police ends in a stalemate. "Corporal, this halfwit must go on to Budweis to join his company. Take him to the ticket window and buy his fare." But neither Schweik nor the Corporal have money. "Then he can walk!" roars the officer in charge.

Thus Schweik is started on his famous march to Budweis, a march which is not as straight as the crow flies. For the direction in which our hero advances is not likely to get him to Budweis very fast, especially since a paper snow is beginning to fall. He meets sympathetic peasants, deserters. "Scenery from the right. A town appears. Policemen are seen through the map on the screen. Scenery from the left. A town. The map shows Schweik making a wide detour around the town."

Film: railroad tracks, signal lamps, signal posts, a watchman's shanty, gates at a crossing, and then the highway. On the left the lights of Tabor can be seen. The lights travel along for a stretch, keeping pace and shifting toward the middle, slip back into the distance, then disappear entirely as if behind a hill. In the background the night sky, against which a hilly, wooded landscape is silhouetted dimly. Fade into a map showing Budweis. The titles point out Schweik's direction. The following caption appears on the map (white print): "Xenophon, a general of ancient times, hastened across all of Asia Minor, without maps, and ended up God knows where. A continuous march in a straight line is called an anabasis. . . . Far away, somewhere north on the Gallic Sea, Caesar's legions, which had gotten there also without the aid of maps, decided to return to Rome by a route different from the one by which they came. Since then it has been said that all roads lead to Rome. It might just as easily be said that all roads lead to Budweis—something which Schweik fully believed. And the devil only knows how it happened that instead of going south to Budweis, Schweik marched in a straight line west. . . ." (*From the stage directions*).

In custody after many adventures, Schweik is pushed aboard an "army transport"—meaning an ancient freight car. He is being shipped to his outfit, under suspicion of attempting to desert. The freight car, which rumbles along on the treadmill without ever really getting anywhere, is nothing but a platform masked by a semi-transparent setpiece of a railroad car. It is adorned with chalk-scrawls and patriotic witticisms on the order of *Serbien, diesmal musst Du sterbien!* Schweik and two or three other hungry soldiers peer out of the open door; the rest of the *Kanonenfutter* in transit have been drawn by the scene designer. . . .

On a battlefield consisting of a couple of small mounds behind which Schweik and another soldier, Marek, are hiding, the saga approaches its end.

> SCHWEIK: I think we went the wrong way, the battle is over there.
> MAREK: I'll remember this war for weeks.
> SCHWEIK: There's plenty of good points to this war, don't forget. After the war there will be good crops around here . . . made out of us. They'll burn us, our ashes will be used for sifting sugar in the sugar factories. A war makes us useful to posterity. Our children will drink coffee with sugar sifted through our remains.

But Marek has taken himself elsewhere. "I'll do my duty for the Emperor to the end," adds Schweik. On the screen a Russian soldier is swimming in a pond. A bush rolls on with the Russian's uniform hanging on it. "A souvenir," thinks Schweik. He puts it on. A shot rings out, and a Hungarian patrol rushes on and seizes him in loud Hungarian tones. "What do you mean, prisoner?" Schweik demands, "I'm on our side. . . ." A shell bursts. Schweik falls. From the upper corner of the screen a procession of crosses starts toward the audience. As the crosses, growing nearer in perspective, reach the lower edge of the screen, a muslin drop, lowered downstage, catches them once more, bringing them still closer to the spectators. A rain of crosses falls upon this wry comedy as the lights begin to go up. . . .

PISCATOR

Tomorrow the more reactionary newspapers of Berlin will again thunder at this so-called "profanation" of art. Baiting Piscator, creating a to-do over each of his shows, had by now become a regular diversion not only in newspaper dramatic columns, but on front pages. Unflustered, Piscator expresses surprise at the lengths to which such art criticism can go even while it loudly proclaims that "art is above the battle." But it was not only his productions that were discussed. It was freely insinuated that he was an "outsider," a Bolshevik Jew and an alien Red.

In fact, however, Piscator, like Brecht, is of Lutheran stock and German to the core. Born 1893, at Marburg-an-der-Lahn, in Hessen-Nassau, Piscator is descended from the churchman Piscator who made a new translation of the Bible during the Reformation.

Like many of the other leaders of the present-day theatre, Piscator left his schoolroom opinions of life and theatre behind

From *Hintergrund*

SCHWEIK. "Look pleasant, please"

Drawing by George Grosz

the curtain of fire of the World War.[2] Returned from the trenches after three years' service, he made the acquaintance of the Berlin Dadaists, who were then annoying the stolid-minded with an art that professed to "debunk" all art. The period of Dadaism seems to have left a permanent mark upon Piscator and Brecht; but neither of them could remain satisfied with a program of nothing but cynicism. Piscator was beginning to learn that theatre owes a responsibility to its audiences.

In 1920 he opened, at Königsberg in East Prussia, his first important theatre, Tribunal. Although the Königsberg venture proved unsuccessful financially, he was sought out by the renowned Volksbühne, for which he served as head stage director between 1924 and 1927. Differences developed, however, between the young director and the Volksbühne management; these differences reached the proportions of a violent public controversy in which each side expressed itself fully.

Piscator was told that he had turned art into propaganda. In turn he charged that at a time when the Volksbühne subscribers, in the midst of life-and-death struggles, were looking to their theatre for guidance, the Volksbühne management was prudently limiting itself to "cultural" productions of FAUST and HAMLET which were devoid of all "culture," since they were scarcely more than displays of costume and elocution.

It was Ehm Welk's STORM OVER GOTHLAND (1926) which precipitated this crisis. For the managers of the Volksbühne, this was a play whose action belonged far back in the Middle Ages. Piscator accentuated the medieval atmosphere, but he brought to the production the most immediate significance for today, reinforcing the scenes on the stage with motion picture sequences showing in panorama the rebellion of the fishermen of Gothland. In the dissension that followed this successful production, the Volksbühne management was embarrassed to find even the conservative newspapers ranged on the side of Piscator. The younger minority of the subscribers took the same position as the newspapers. The Volksbühne and its chief director parted company. Piscator was once more left on his own, but this time he could count on a potential audience of the Junge Volksbühne, thirty thousand in all.

He had need of this audience when he established his theatre on Nollendorfplatz; it was both a moral and financial backbone for his enterprise. Yet it proved not enough. His productions over a ten-year period were on the whole unusually successful; but their expenses were hard to cover. Piscator had never hesitated to spend freely for experimental effects which he thought valuable. The situation was a precarious one; it could not continue indefinitely, especially when SCHWEIK was followed by two unsuccessful productions. Within three years of the

SCHWEIK production, financial pressure combined with the growing strength of reactionary political forces, succeeded in ending Piscator's work in Germany.

THE THEATRE LOOKS AT WAR

What distinguishes the viewpoint of Epic from that of previous styles in the theatre? At first glance the SCHWEIK production does not seem to define this viewpoint enough. It is only when we go deeper into the implications of the SCHWEIK production that a new trend becomes apparent.

As a start let us compare the script of SCHWEIK with those of two other famous plays, Anderson and Stallings' WHAT PRICE GLORY? (produced by Arthur Hopkins in 1924) and Sheriff's JOURNEY'S END (put on by Gilbert Miller in 1929). All three dramas were humanitarian, all three were reactions against the first World War (a war which stands indicted today as having been caused by commercial rivalries). Granted that such was the nature of the plays, their manner of execution may seem relatively unimportant. Practically speaking, however, there was a notable difference between the structure of SCHWEIK and that of the other two plays.

Analysis shows that WHAT PRICE GLORY? and JOURNEY'S END were only incidentally concerned with war. The dramatic action of WHAT PRICE GLORY? was that of a swashbuckling tale of adventure, a picaresque rivalry of two male characters. The scenes of war-suffering which occurred in the course of the story were independent of the main theme, to which they contributed a background of fear and excitement. Without appreciably damaging the story the main action could have been transferred to a peacetime barracks. Idyllic and exotic backgrounds could have been introduced just as appropriately. In fact they were so introduced in THE COCK-EYED WORLD (William Fox, 1929), a later movie sequel to the play, in which the rivalry of Captain Flagg and Sergeant Quirt continued with all its roughhousing against a background of banana palms. Similarly the central theme of JOURNEY'S END was the code of *noblesse oblige*, for which the circumstances of trench life were merely a convenient foil.

The irrelevance of the dramatic patterns of these two plays

to their ostensible themes is hard to disprove.[3] It is sometimes insisted, however, that this is just what made the plays effective. This *indirectness* has been commended by American dramatic critics of both right and left wings.* It is asserted that, even though the main action is not a direct indictment of the character of that war, yet the indictment is to be found indirectly, in the local color. The audience, taken unaware, is moved obliquely, perhaps even illogically, to an emotional reaction.

In the course of his illuminating study of the Anderson-Stallings play, Joseph Wood Krutch, perhaps unintentionally, makes this mechanism apparent. The *dramatis personae* of WHAT PRICE GLORY? have an attitude far removed from the "rationalized anti-militarism" of John Dos Passos' *Three Soldiers*, for instance. What passes before us on the stage is a kind of "anti-civilization," the brutal code of men at war. But neither in its personages nor in its own action does this play condemn unjust or useless wars. Flagg and Quirt simply accept the situation. "For all their ribald recklessness," says Krutch, "the combatants are so disciplined as to respond automatically to the call of 'duty.' " Flagg in particular is "heroically faithful to his job for no reason at all except that men must have something, however irrational, to believe in and serve." Even more interesting is the fact that the story builds up to an "emotional response" which it safely drains off, removing all the turbulent questions which have arisen in the minds of the audience. As Krutch puts it:

> What is more, this emotional response, or rather this set of emotional responses, could be made to yield a certain desperate exultation not wholly unjoyous, and the result was to achieve for the audience a clarification and a release. A channel had been provided for the discharge of confused emotions. Here was a pattern into which, without recourse to dead ideas, hitherto confused reactions could be arranged, a channel through which pent-up emotions could flow.

The device of a "desperate exultation not wholly unjoyous" has accompanied a large number of war plays and films. It may help to explain why audiences have been able to view the carnage of war in the theatre and yet go away with the idea that war is after all a rather exultant and not wholly unjoyous experience.

* American left-wing critics seem to disagree among themselves on that point.

This was not the sort of emotion that interested SCHWEIK. In fact SCHWEIK was not particularly interested in creating emotions on the subject of war. Piscator's production was an account of the way in which the War of 1914–1918 had been waged by the despotic empire of Austria-Hungary. In that war, Czechoslovakians like Schweik had been conscripted to defend an empire which they hated, and from which they eventually freed themselves. To dramatize that war as mere butchery might give an audience a rather gruesome emotional titillation, but would teach nothing.

By itself, hatred of war, as history has made very plain indeed, has nothing to do with the cause or cure of war. War did not suddenly fall out of the sky on the Austro-Hungarian empire. It was the inevitable result of the previous history of that regime. Nor was the Austrian war machine any more inspired than the creaking machinery of its peacetime politics. It was important to show, by careful consideration, that Austria carried on in wartime as it did in peacetime, but with even less regard for human values and even greater cruelty and stupidity.

From beginning to end Piscator's SCHWEIK was a clinical history of the Austrian war machine: the mechanics of war propaganda, police spying, mobilization, transportation, bombardment. The script, rather too hastily patched together, was vigorously supported by the other elements of production. Where the script did not make a necessary point, or did not make it sufficiently, the screen took up the work in a kind of jagged editorial comment. Conceiving the basic action as a perpetual motion of troops and machinery, the director staged the whole story on a double treadmill. It became the business of the actor Pallenberg, who portrayed Schweik, to register the effects of this process on the common soldier. Thus the whole picture of the war, with its efficiency and inefficiency, its cant, its bungling, class and national antagonisms, profiteering, bootlicking and pointless slaughter, became clear to the average spectator, as it had become clear to the more thoughtful of the men in the trenches.

"LOW SENTIMENTS"

As SCHWEIK was the outstanding popular success of Piscator's management at the Nollendorf Theatre, so THE THREE-PENNY

OPERA was the most successful, by far, of Brecht's productions at the Theatre-am-Schiffbauerdamm. THE THREE-PENNY OPERA (text and direction by Brecht, settings by Caspar Neher, music by Kurt Weill) opened in 1928. It ran for four hundred performances—a Berlin record for any production of serious intent—and was re-staged throughout Germany and Europe.

Like THE BEGGARS' OPERA, the English work from which it was adapted, Brecht's production won its popular success against an overwhelming tide of sentimental musical shows.[4] Raffish, sardonic, with a plaintively melodic score and stage settings of the barest functional type, THE THREE-PENNY OPERA offered little of the accepted patterns of comic opera. Its basic theme, to which it held remorselessly, was the connivance of criminals with the supposed guardians of law and order—not a lilac-scented idea or one to be hailed as an inspiration by those who specialize in musicomedy.

The plot of THE THREE-PENNY OPERA is substantially that of John Gay's THE BEGGARS' OPERA (1728), even though there is a vast difference in technique and detail between the two. Polly Peachum, the heroine, is the daughter of a remarkable character who had made a flourishing, highly moral business out of dealing in stolen goods. Polly has the ill-luck to fall in love with a desperado named Macheath, who is already married to the daughter of a prison Warden and is, besides, a notorious pimp. Peachum ultimately persuades his daughter to abandon Macheath. The connivance of Peachum and the Warden, together with the treacherous prostitutes, lands Macheath in jail, whence he is rescued by a Royal Messenger just in time for a happy ending. In Brecht's version Macheath is locked up twice; the first time he escapes by blackmailing the Warden.

Back of this meandering, derisive story there is an indignation so genuine that the commercial success of Brecht's OPERA becomes a real enigma. Who could guess the sales-value of a refrain such as this?

MACHEATH:
For how do people live? By hourly
Tormenting, stripping, assaulting, strangling, eating, other people.
Man lives only because he can so utterly
Forget that he is man.

If sentimental illusions were lacking in the text, they cannot be said to have been compensated for in the staging. The acting was close to the declamatory, lacking "psychological" nuances, and the actors went into their song numbers without graceful transition but rather with the obvious intention of bursting into song. The costumes, which elsewhere would have been smartly modern or exotically "period" (for the OPERA was purposely kept vague as to century), instead became a mixture of anything that suited the point to be made by the play; they tended to gravitate about the period of the nineties, but nothing from the eighteenth or twentieth centuries was barred in principle.

Scenically the great number of locales was resolved into a semi-permanent arrangement of a stage bare except for an elaborate pipe-organ at rear center and projection screens downstage right and left. (The reason why two screens were used was merely one of sight-lines; the screens carried identical projections.) The projections served either to carry subtitles or indications of locale. Thus the subtitle of Scene 2 was,

"DEEP IN THE HEART OF SOHO THE BANDIT MACHEATH CELEBRATES HIS MARRIAGE TO POLLY PEACHUM, DAUGHTER OF THE KING OF BEGGARS."

This legend was followed by a picture of the stable in which the wedding takes place. A few properties such as a large wire-mesh screen to represent the prison and a wooden carousel horse for the Messenger, completed the scenic effects. Ordinary white lighting revealed the actors; it was replaced by a more golden brilliance for the song numbers.

The author of THE THREE-PENNY OPERA is today one of the many distinguished creative workers who have been driven from the Fatherland. His plays, among them EDWARD II, MAN IS MAN, RISE AND FALL OF THE CITY OF MAHAGONNY, THE EXPEDIENT, and ST. JOAN OF THE STOCKYARDS, have been officially proscribed by the Nazi regime as possessing "low sentiments." Lean and frail, with an owlish face and an addiction to bad cigars, Brecht is that rare being, a scholar who has spent most of his life inside the theatre. Incidentally he is neither Jewish nor communist.

BRECHT

Bertolt Brecht was born at Augsburg, in Bavaria, in 1898. He prepared for a career in medicine and natural science, but eventually went on to dramatic writing. In 1922, at the height of the Expressionist period, he won the coveted Kleist Prize with his play DRUMS IN THE NIGHT, in which a war veteran returns from the trenches to find that the war profiteers have grabbed everything that makes life worth living. Critics hailed the play with relief as being solidly in the tradition of German classicism. They held to this opinion about Brecht's plays long after he had identified himself with the militant left-wing theatre.

The work of Brecht supplements and amplifies that of Piscator. It is upon the basis of Piscator's practice that Brecht, in his plays and critical writings, has worked toward a new evaluation of the stage. This evaluation is as provocative as it is sweeping. Although it is a product of left theatre, in some degree it cuts across political alignments, earning enthusiasm and hostility in both conservative and radical camps.

The earlier Brecht plays have a sarcastic imagery which is often at war with their purpose. And yet the larger purpose is always there, building up scene by scene an inexorable logic. Typical of the earlier dramas is MAN IS MAN (1927), whose atmosphere is a travesty on Rudyard Kipling. In the fabled tropical country of Kilkoa, a gentle native, Galy Gay, meets with three infantrymen of the British Imperial Army. The soldiers walk on stilts, they are padded to enormous proportions, their tunics smeared with blood and filth; each of them is a living arsenal of weapons. They are about to conduct a "defensive" border raid, and Galy Gay would come in handy as reinforcement. But this Rousseauan man is not open to persuasion on the glories of military life. It is therefore necessary to change his fundamental nature. Two of the soldiers, bent under an oilcloth with a gas mask hanging in front, rudely caricature an elephant; the third tricks Gay into auctioning off this regimental elephant. Thereupon Gay is accused of selling what he does not own; he is formally tried, convicted and sentenced to lose his identity. The sentence is carried out by means of hypnosis. A ceremony of rebirth takes place. Armed to the teeth, decked out with grenades, the timid native emerges transformed into a cog of the imperialist war machine.

DIE MASSNAHME (THE EXPEDIENT) is much less mystical in treatment. Its form is that of an oratorio; and it was in fact performed on a concert stage, with music by Hanns Eisler (1929). The writing is starkly classic, and the story, a modern parable, has great dramatic strength while retaining the tenacious reasoning which is Brecht's at his best. Four revolutionary organizers bring their report to the Control Commission of their Party. With one other, a younger man, they had been sent to do political work in Mukden. They have returned without him; they themselves had shot him and thrown his body into a lime-pit. Now they relate the circumstances, re-enacting, step by step, the tragedy of a young idealist whose compassion, not balanced by judgment, ruined the work and put his comrades in extreme danger. The four are exonerated and the oratorio ends in the solemn words of the chorale:

> Only when taught by reality can we
> Change reality.

In ROUND HEADS AND PEAKED HEADS, produced at the little theatre of the Riddersal, Copenhagen (1936), Brecht exposed the political meaning of the "race decrees" of the fascists. The agricultural land of Yahoo is threatened with a peasant insurrection following an "overproduction" crisis. When things look blackest for the rulers of the country, a saviour arrives, inspired with the idea of dividing the population into round-headed élite and peak-headed mongrels. The scheme works well enough to defeat the peasants, but in turn gives rise to political contradictions which do not augur well for the continued rule of the dictator. Unfortunately this allegory had more than its share of poorly chosen symbolism, including an accent on prostitution, which the dramatist uses too often to describe the venality of a corrupt social system. These failings were not strengthened by the production, which made use of grotesque makeup and cluttered scenery that lacked precision. On the other hand the play contained a notable figure; the peasant Callas is enormous, rude, hard-headed, muddled and crafty, but endowed with a rude majesty.

MOTHER (1932) derived from Gorky's novel, is a simpler account—the story of the political awakening of a Russian working class mother, who ultimately takes an active part in the movement to oust the Tsar. Staged in New York by the Theatre Union in 1935, MOTHER had as poor a reception as did the New York production of THE THREE-PENNY OPERA two years before. In the case of MOTHER the play ran counter to the whole "psychological" line of New York staging (whether in the right or left wing theatres). The cast attempted to put an inner life into characters which were not psychologically written. In adapting the script the Theatre Union tried to correct what it considered a lack of dramatic excitement in the play, by adding melodramatic scenes. Brecht ordered these new scenes taken out.

Scenically the play achieved, for some spectators, a functional elegance with simple means. A small revolving stage partitioned through the center stood just under a projection screen. At stage right were two grand pianos. The stage was illuminated by rows of visible spotlights. The beautiful chorales by Hanns Eisler were sung by the actors standing at stage right; from there they would, on occasion, go to the revolving stage to join the acting scenes. The projection screen was in constant use as an editorial commentary.[5]

Critical reception of MOTHER was more than usually confusing. It was, however, rather consistently patronizing. To a large extent the production itself was to blame, beginning with the script, which tried to build an abstract lecture around the humanly appealing central character of the Mother. For many people the screen was especially disturbing; it was resented as making obvious statements and detracting from the action on the stage. Faulty as it undoubtedly was, the artistry of the production was on the whole underestimated. Some even thought it pretentious, but in fact it was simple to the point of absurdity, as Richard Lockridge dryly observed:

> The point is, of course, that Pelagea Vlassova, the mother, started out by believing in God, the Czar and private property, and was gradually converted, chiefly by precept. It was all explained to her very carefully, and after she understood, she explained it, still very slowly and carefully, to the audience.

MOTHER may have alienated some with its subject matter, but its chief offense was undoubtedly its strange approach in script and stage form.

TRIPLE-A PLOWED UNDER (1936)
Loudspeakers, projections, statistics, riots

The Inductive Setting

TALES OF HOFFMANN (1928) at the State Opera, Berlin
Setting by László Moholy-Nagy

From The New Vision. *Courtesy W. W. Norton & Co.*

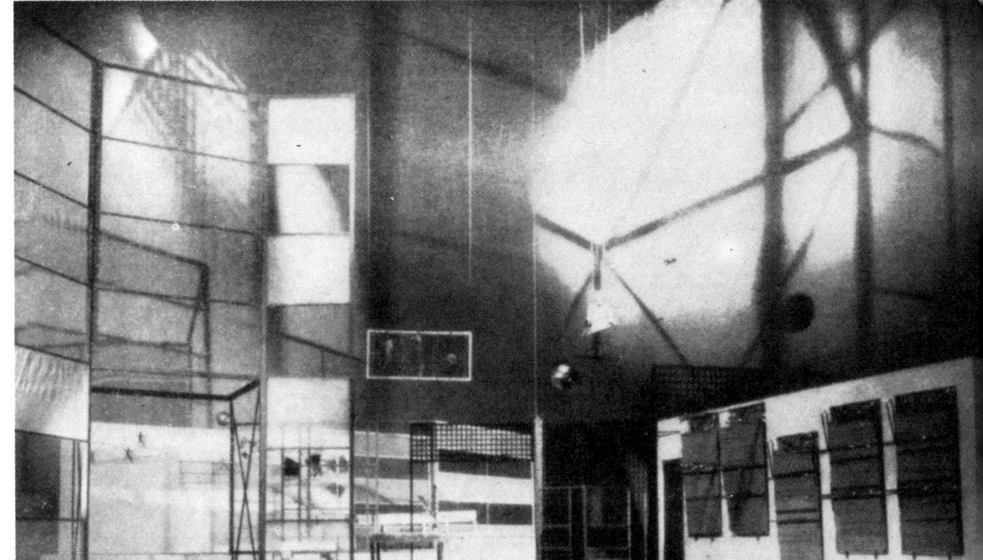

Yet only a few months later there opened on Broadway, successfully, the first example of American Epic production. The play was TRIPLE-A PLOWED UNDER, presented by the Living Newspaper unit of the Federal Theatre on March 14, 1936.

ENTER STATISTICS

In the fall of 1935 the newly instituted Federal Theatre went into action with a score of production units in New York City alone. Among these was a producing organization of a unique type—the Living Newspaper, created by Elmer Rice, headed by Morris Watson and sponsored by the national union of newspaper workers, the Newspaper Guild. The office of the Living Newspaper was that of an active newspaper or periodical rather than a theatre; it had an editor-in-chief, managing editor, city editor, reporters and a large staff of copyreaders and research men. The Living Newspaper proposed to bring journalism into the theatre: to dramatize the most important social and political issues of the day in terms not of romantic stories but of the documented facts themselves.

The first Living Newspaper production was a factual study of the invasion of Ethiopia by Italian imperialism. The production went as far as a private dress rehearsal. Suddenly it was banned by the State Department in Washington, a move which caused Elmer Rice, New York administrator of the Federal Theatre, to resign in protest against censorship. Meanwhile a special rehearsal of ETHIOPIA, given for the critics, had left a deep impression. The impression remained when the following production, TRIPLE-A PLOWED UNDER, came to the stage.

The conflict of opinion which attended the birth of America's first government-subsidized theatre did not spare TRIPLE-A any more than it did ETHIOPIA. Some of the cast of TRIPLE-A rebelled at appearing in it. On the opening night another attempt of sabotage was attempted from out front in the audience.[6] These harassing circumstances, plus the fact that the production dealt with abstract economics, were not a good augury. But TRIPLE-A proved hardy enough to survive all ill omens.

Written by the editorial staff of the Living Newspaper under the direction of Arthur Arent, TRIPLE-A PLOWED UNDER filled the stage of the Biltmore Theatre with twenty-six scenes, each of them based upon undisputed news accounts and published statements. The scenes, as designed by Hjalmer Hermanson, followed each other with staccato swiftness, to the flash of images projected on a picture screen, the counterpoint of music and the incisive comment of a loudspeaker. They traced the origin of the New Deal's Agricultural Adjustment Administration, its economic consequences, its invalidation by the United States Supreme Court and the new problems posed by this invalidation. Speeches, statistics and the re-enactment of large and small news events rolled up a dynamic account of a crisis in the economic life of the nation. Farm and city, a milk strike, a farm auction, stores and restaurants, a police station, a church, a wheat exchange, the Supreme Court, were among the locales depicted in this ever-spreading panorama.

WORKER: We starve.
FARMER: The wheat stands high in our fields.
FARMER'S WIFE: *Our* fields no longer.
WORKER'S DAUGHTER: Feed us.
FARMER'S FIRST SON: Pay us.
WORKER'S FAMILY: Feed us.
FARMER: The wheat is better destroyed. I say, burn it!
FARMER'S FAMILY: Burn it! Burn it!

(*Flame lights up, changing the sky from blue to red. Against the flames is silhouetted the picture of a farmer in shadow, holding a pitchfork. Farm and city families hold this tableau, all through speech of* GENERAL JOHNSON *over the Loudspeaker.*) . . .

. . . .

VOICE OF LIVING NEWSPAPER (*over Loudspeaker*): Washington, May 12th, 1933— the AAA becomes the law of the land. It is hereby declared to be the policy of Congress . . .

(*Spotlight on* SECRETARY WALLACE)

SECRETARY WALLACE (*picking up sentence*): . . . to increase the purchasing power of farmers. It is, by that token, farm relief, but also, by the same token, National Relief, for it is a well-known fact that millions of urban unemployed will have a better chance of going to work when farm purchasing power rises enough to buy the products of city factories. Let's help the farmer. . . . It is trying to subdue the habitual anarchy of a major American industry, and to establish organized control in the interest of not only the farmer but everybody else. . . The bill gives the Secretary of Agriculture the power to . . .

(*Lights fade on* WALLACE. *The projection of a map of the United States, showing acreage reduction, comes up on the scrim.*)

VOICE OVER LOUDSPEAKER (*staccato*): . . . Reduce acreage. The visible supply of wheat diminished from two hundred and twelve million bushels in 1932 to one hundred and twenty-four million bushels in 1934.

(*The projection changes to a number of little pigs in front of a number of large pigs, labeled "1933 production," the smaller pigs labeled "1934 production."*)

VOICE OF LOUDSPEAKER (*continuing*): To curtail production. Hog production was cut from sixty million in 1933 to thirty-seven million in 1935. . . .

The final tableau of the play, which depicted farmers and unemployed workers coming toward an understanding of their common needs, was regularly followed by loudspeaker broadcasts giving "spot news" of that very day or evening bearing upon the formation of a farmer-labor political alliance.

The dependence of the Living Newspaper style upon that of the Epic theatre has been denied by both Hallie Flanagan and Arthur Arent, who insist that it is a native technique.[7] The Living Newspaper has an American content and American idiom, but it is no more indigenous than any other theatre form the United States has ever had—which is none, with the exception of Indian dance ceremonies and, possibly, the minstrel show. The immediate ancestor of the Living Newspaper in this country was, beyond question, the March of Time radio program. And that was in turn preceded by the so-called agitprop plays of the American workers' theatres, which were inspired in some degree by the anti-fascist theatres of Germany.

WORKERS BUILD A THEATRE

Late in 1931, two years after the historic stock market collapse, at the time when America was taking its first shocking nose dive into the "depression," it was Mrs. Flanagan who called attention to the fact that a new theatre, one almost without precedent, was emerging. "The theatre being born in America today," she wrote, "is a theatre of workers. Its object is to create a national culture by and for the working class of America." What was this theatre like, and where was it going? Theatres which reflected the viewpoint of the working class, although scarce in the United States, were not new. What was new was the surprising fact that for the first time in history American workers took the problem of theatre into their own hands.

In New York, in 1926, a number of radical intellectuals formed a short-lived Workers' Drama League, whose most successful production was a satire adapted from the German—Karl Wittfogel's THE BIGGEST BOOB IN THE WORLD. The League lasted long enough to advance the idea of an American working class theatre.

The following year, encouraged by a sizeable endowment from the millionaire art patron Otto Kahn, five young playwrights —John Howard Lawson, Michael Gold, Francis Farragoh, Emjo Basshe and John Dos Passos—established the New Playwrights' Theatre. This theatre, frankly devoted to the defense of the underprivileged, lasted three ragged years. America was then enjoying all the fruits of "normalcy," and the New Playwrights awoke only a tepid response in the "bourgeoisie" and "proletariat" alike.

Yet their plays begin to acquire significance in retrospect, and they are worth recalling. Lawson's LOUDSPEAKER, a farce about politics, opened the first season. Later productions included EARTH, a story of Negro life, and THE CENTURIES, a chronicle of Jewish immigrants, both written by Basshe; Upton Sinclair's SINGING JAILBIRDS, dealing with the I.W.W.; Lawson's INTERNATIONAL, with its picture of world imperialism; and THE BELT, by Paul and Claire Sifton, which brought to the stage a glimpse of the conveyor-system in use in the large automobile factories.

The demise of the New Playwrights' Theatre brought to a close that era in which the leadership of workers' theatres lay in the hands of sympathetic intellectuals. From now on the impetus was to come from a new direction. It came originally from the amateur stages of foreign-language workers' groups in the United States. In 1929 there were in existence in this country many hundreds of dramatic clubs attached to foreign-born workers' organizations performing in German, Italian, Yiddish, Finnish, Russian, Ukrainian, Swedish, Lithuanian, Hungarian, Polish and half a dozen other languages. The social dramas of the Naturalistic theatre were kept alive on their stages at a time when they had begun to be forgotten on Broadway.

In most cases these amateur dramatic groups were totally cut off from the main stream of the American theatre, whose plays did not interest them and whose admission prices they could not afford. (In spite of this isolation, at least two such groups in New York had attained importance in their own spheres—the Artef, a Jewish workers' theatre, and the Ukrainian Dramatic Circle.) In most cases such club theatres sprang up or disappeared from week to week. Strangely enough the economic crisis, instead of destroying them, apparently steeled them to new conceptions of drama. Some of the more radical adopted the fighting slogan of the Soviet drama, "Theatre is a weapon," and proceeded to label themselves agitprop (agitation and propaganda) troupes. Yet the first group to inaugurate the new method was not Russian but German—the Prolet-Bühne, whose home was in the center of New York City's German working class population. Ben Blake gives us a snapshot of this amateur theatre at work:

> In the fall of 1930, word began to spread from mouth to mouth in radical circles of the New York labor movement of a German-speaking theatre group that gave exciting performances of a new, chanted type of play which the group called "agitprop" (agitation-and-propaganda) plays. No theatre housed them. They would turn up at labor meetings, rallies of the unemployed, and the like, give one or two of their agitprop plays on the stage if there was one, or on the speakers' platform, or even on the floor if there was no platform. This group, known as the Prolet-Bühne, staged plays and mass recitations with very little scenery and simple, symbolical costumes, deliberately calculated for mobility and adaptability to the playing environment. The plays themselves, like all the scripts of the early years, were crude in plot and characterization and full of revolutionary labor "clichés." Yet they had a hard-hitting directness of statement that would often strike off flaming sparks of emotion in the beholder. Satirical rhymed verse and powerful rhythmic refrains characterized most of their work. . . .
>
> "In Scottsboro,
> In Scottsboro,
> Murder stalks the streets,
> In Scottsboro,
> In Scottsboro,
> Death haunts the cells."

Almost simultaneously an English-speaking agitprop troupe made its appearance. This was the Workers' Laboratory Theatre, one of the cultural sections of the Workers' International Relief (an organization now extinct). These troupes and their repertory were closely patterned on similar German mobile stage units such as the Kolonne Links and Rotes Sprachrohr, as well as on the Blue Blouse troupes of Soviet Russia. Both the German and Russian prototypes dressed in blouses and overalls, grouped themselves on the platform or stage, chanting through megaphones in solo or mass voices. The scripts were terse and journalistic. The following lines from UNEMPLOYMENT, an early U.S. agitprop play, clearly anticipates in style both the March of Time and the Living Newspaper:

5 WORKER: Won't somebody give me a job?
1 WORKER: I am hungry, why can't I have food? I see lots of food in restaurants. I am cold, why can't I have a coat? I see many coats in clothing stores. . . .
CAPITALIST: There isn't anyone can have a better yacht than I. I've got to have the best little yacht in the world. . . .

The new agitational technique spread quickly across the country. Outstanding groups like the Blue Blouses of Chicago and of Los Angeles joined with those in New York and elsewhere to create the League of Workers' Theatres in 1932. They operated under great difficulties, rehearsing at night at workers' centers in rooms grudgingly spared them, since the centers are always overcrowded. In the larger cities even the most dirt-ridden factory lofts (unrented since the "crash") cost too much for working class pocketbooks. Membership dues, parties at the troupes' headquarters, helped pay expenses. Sometimes appeals to wealthier friends brought contributions, which rarely passed the $25 mark. Some of the young actors finally gave up a futile hunt for jobs; they pooled their meager resources, established living quarters and kitchens and gave all their time to dramatic production. Best known of these "shock troupes" was the Theatre of Action, of New York, which finally hit Broadway with its full-length play THE YOUNG GO FIRST (by Scudder, Martin and Friedman, 1935).

The cycle of growth of this earlier technique included three plays which received wide recognition. NEWSBOY (1934), produced by the Theatre of Action and directed by Alfred Saxe, used the *montage* method of the cinema—a kaleidoscope of movements, lights and voices. It pointed the moral that the "capitalist" press contains plenty of scandal but that it suppresses the news of workers' struggles.

Clifford Odets' WAITING FOR LEFTY (1935), originally put on by individual members of the Group Theatre for a special performance during a taxicab strike in New York, proved remarkably successful. The play opens on a bare stage. Men seated in a semicircle are presumed to be at a union meeting. While a strike is debated we are given flashbacks into the lives of some of the speakers. The action links the audience into the play, and rises to a crescendo as the strike vote is called. Irwin Shaw's BURY THE DEAD (1936), in the same staccato, journalistic style, projected a fantasy in which six dead soldiers refused to be buried but instead marched implacably against those responsible for their death.

As might be expected, plays of so controversial a nature aroused hostility in some quarters. WAITING FOR LEFTY in particular became an object of censorship in various parts of the country. By this time, however, the influence of the workers' plays was distinctly visible on Broadway (later even in Hollywood). The old alliance of workers' theatres had broadened until it included middle class and community theatres of many shades of political opinion. In 1935 the Workers' Theatre League gave place to the New Theatre League, which adopted a new program, liberal rather than radical. This called for "a mass development of the American theatre to its highest artistic and social level; for a theatre dedicated to the struggle against war, fascism and censorship." (Blake).

Another step forward in the almost biological process of growth from "social significance" to art was the opening, in 1933, of the Theatre Union, which leased Eva LeGallienne's former playhouse, the Civic Repertory on Fourteenth Street. The dramas produced by the Theatre Union—PEACE ON EARTH (1933) by Maltz and Sklar; STEVEDORE (1934) by Sklar and Peters; Wolf's SAILORS OF CATTARO (1934); BLACK PIT (1935) by Maltz; MOTHER (1935) by Brecht; Wolfson's BITTER STREAM (1936); and Lawson's MARCHING SONG (1937)—proclaimed it the natural successor of the New Playwrights. Unlike the New Playwrights, however, it arrived at a time of growing social antagonisms. The Theatre Union received no aid from wealthy patrons; on the other hand it attracted a large working class audience for the first time in the history of the American left-wing theatre. It managed, with the direst economy, to put on professional shows at very low admission fees. For a while it successfully built up a "benefit" audience of proletarian and middle class organizations, including labor unions and groups affiliated with the Socialist and Communist Parties. It even gave away free seats to the unemployed.

Like the New Playwrights and the Theatre Guild, the Theatre Union was ruled by a board of directors, with Miss Margaret Larkin in a position similar to that of Miss Theresa Helburn at the Guild. In one other respect the later group followed the New Playwrights' tradition. The Playwrights were convinced that they were the victims of hostile press criticism; they had even accused the metropolitan critics of conspiring against them in the depths of the Hotel Algonquin. The Theatre Union seemed almost as inclined to do battle in the same cause. It was elated because PEACE ON EARTH, which the critics had received lukewarmly, was kept running by appreciative audiences.

Few of the critics could reasonably be expected to enthuse over labor "ideology." It is likely, also, that the reviewers were more alert to flaws in protest plays than they normally were to the failings of more conformist dramas. Yet the same reviewers were genuinely proud of the Theatre Union's artistic achievements. STEVEDORE, the group's most successful show, was highly praised by them throughout its run. (They were not so kind to Brecht's MOTHER; but neither were many of the Theatre Union's own fans.) This desire to be fair—imperfect as it might be in its results—may still serve as an inspiration to our critics in the stormy days to come. After all it was not easy for the critics to maintain judicial calm in the case of dramas whose viewpoint was not soothing to most of them. Nor could the Theatre Union, in most instances, claim much interest on the score of brilliant technique. Its artistic contribution lay in enriching and deepening the earlier agitational plays, in bringing to the new content some of the stored-up experience of older theatre.

One of the most interesting developments in the field of labor theatre should now be described. Although the Labor Stage

I.L.G.W.U.

LABOR + STAGE

WAITING FOR LEFTY (1935)
"Too many cabs on the street"

Vandamm

musical revue PINS AND NEEDLES was not the first example of a left-wing revue, its record is a unique one.

The background of Labor Stage is the I.L.G.W.U.—the International Ladies Garment Workers Union. This union came into existence in 1900 as a result of "sweatshop" conditions in the garment industry, in which, according to the union, an "economic law of the jungle" prevailed. Public opinion was on the side of the garment workers when they successfully carried out two great strikes beginning 1909. Scarcely two years later the union lost many of its members among those 146 workers—men, women and children—who perished in the Triangle Shirtwaist Factory fire in New York.

Originally affiliated with the A.F. of L., the garment workers union has lately shifted to the C.I.O. and back again. It is today one of the most powerful labor unions in the United States, with a membership of almost a quarter of a million workers of the most diverse racial and national types. It carries on not only trade union work but a number of business and cultural activities, of which Labor Stage is one.

Fannia M. Cohn, secretary of the union's Educational Department, has written:

> The history of the labor movement is rich in social conflict; it is full of drama. The classic drama emphasized the conflict of the individual and nature; the background of the new drama is the social conflict—the struggle of the millions of disinherited, of the masses who are the backbone, the makers of our civilization, those working men and women who extract from the earth's core its natural resources, transform these into machines, factories, railroads, ocean steamers, skyscrapers—in a word, into fabulous wealth. . . .
>
> Of all arts, the drama makes the greatest appeal to man. It is the best medium for making people think, because it is a creative interpretation of their own experience. In a few hours it can enlighten and make the workers conscious of social and economic conditions which would require volumes to explain. . . . The labor movement should take advantage of this oldest of human arts, which is the most effective medium of teaching.

That this view is shared by a large section of American labor is evidenced by the vote of the A.F. of L. convention of 1935 to sponsor labor drama.[8] The I.L.G.W.U. took a momentous step in this direction; it "streamlined" the old Princess Theatre in New

York, converting it into Labor Stage, which opened in March, 1937 with John Wexley's STEEL. Labor Stage discovered it had a mine of dramatic talent among the 63 amateur dramatic groups belonging to the I.L.G.W.U. in 52 cities. PINS AND NEEDLES opened November 27, 1937, as a satirical revue presenting the workers' "slant" on current topics. With occasional changes in material and personnel it ran until June 22, 1940—a total of 1,105 performances, the Broadway record for any musical show.

The success of PINS AND NEEDLES is all the more interesting since its material was of the sort that Broadway would scarcely have considered suitable for a comic revue. Such numbers as CHAIN STORE DAISY, DEAR BEATRICE FAIRFAX, ONE BIG UNION FOR TWO, CALL IT UN-AMERICAN, LESSON IN ETIQUETTE, or SUNDAY IN THE PARK, managed to deal with poignant, even painful, matters, in a vein of good-natured foolery that was always witty and often hilarious. The freshness of the material was matched by the youthful verve of the amateur acting company composed of "paid-up" members of the I.L.G.W.U. The gaiety of Harold J. Rome's music and the lightness and swift pace of the direction by Charles Friedman, were additional reasons for the triumph of labor theatre in a field where few ever expected to find it.

Actually there was always a leaven of satiric humor in the viewpoint of workers' theatres. TILLY THE TOILER, OR VIRTUE REWARDED, as produced by the Brookwood Labor Players, is an example. Its young dramatist, William Titus, adapted ancient melodrama of the Boucicault vintage to the requirements of unionism, showing Tillie making the inevitable choice between Trade Union, the handsome hero, and Company Union, the poisonous villain. Titus, incidentally, was the author of SIT DOWN, a Living Newspaper account of the C.I.O.—General Motors conflict, as seen from the workers' angle. Titus' very promising career, like that of the actor-director John Lenthier, was abruptly ended on the battlefields of Spain, where both these young people gave their lives in defense of the Spanish republic.

THE CRADLE IS ROCKED

The same dramatic season which greeted PINS AND NEEDLES also welcomed the Mercury Theatre's production of Marc Blitzstein's "play in music," THE CRADLE WILL ROCK. (Incidentally Blitzstein's play had won the prize that year in a contest held by the New Theatre League.)

Archibald MacLeish has noted shrewdly the technique of THE CRADLE, which in its approach to the stage parallels the work of Brecht. (Its published edition is dedicated to Brecht.) Yet the form which THE CRADLE acquired on the stage was in some respects a complete accident.

This hauntingly funny account of a strike in an American steel town was placed in rehearsal in the Federal Theatre unit directed by John Houseman and Orson Welles. On the very night of the scheduled opening, with the audience assembled in front of Maxine Elliot's Theatre, the Federal Theatre administration took sudden fright at its own temerity and canceled the show. As MacLeish recounts the story,

> . . . when Welles and Houseman took over the play themselves, hired the Venice Theatre twenty blocks away, loaded an old piano on a truck and started off with their angry audience at their heels, they walked into the most exciting evening of theatre this New York generation has seen.
>
> In an unaired theatre, on a stage illuminated by a couple of dusty spots, with a cast scattered through the audience (where a ruling of Equity kept it), and to the music of an upright piano manipulated by the composer in his shirt sleeves, there occurred a miracle. . . . Upon that evening Mr. Welles built his Mercury production.

The script form of THE CRADLE is obviously indebted to THE THREE-PENNY OPERA. In its Federal Theatre phase it had elaborate settings designed by Welles. These settings it was obliged to leave behind when it went off in search of its own destiny. Its final form was substantially that of the opening night at the Venice Theatre, except that the actors were gathered together on the stage, where they sat on tiers of seats behind the small piano which stood downstage left. In this form it was even barer than the OPERA, since it had no properties whatever and hardly a suggestion of costume.

Meanwhile Epic tendencies could be discerned in a few other Broadway productions. Thornton Wilder's OUR TOWN (1938) had the distinction of telling a story that is the chronicle of an American town more than that of a romantic boy and girl. Sentimentalized as it was, it still retained something of the meaning of the *Spoon River Anthology*. It was also anti-illusory in its settings.[9] If the musicomedy I MARRIED AN ANGEL (1938) followed Piscator in using the treadmill method of SCHWEIK, in the same year another play with music, EVERYWHERE I ROAM, moved a good deal closer to Epic style in both script and production. Written by Arnold Sundgaard and rewritten by Marc Connelly, it outlined a history of the American economic structure. It suffered from the chief fault of the Epic style—diffuseness; and in addition it failed to integrate its facts with its romantic poetry.

Many more such examples could be cited in the United States and in Europe. They tend to show, not that there has been an imitation of Brecht and Piscator, but rather that many theatres and theatre workers are feeling the same impetus toward "documented" plays and non-illusory staging. In part this new impetus will be absorbed by the contemporary theatre, to re-emerge as mannerisms or "good ideas." Eventually, however, our contemporary theatre will have to find room somewhere for the analytical and precise qualities of this new trend in theatre.

It is not too much to say, perhaps, that the cradle of a possible new American theatre is being rocked in an arc between propagandist drama and the learning-play.

It is true that throughout history the stage has always been propagandist in some degree. But never before, perhaps, has there been such a call to direct action. This tendency appeared first in the radical and left wing of the theatre. The reasons for its emergence there are not far to seek. The world had spun into one of the most embattled periods of all time, with unemployment, and all its attendant ills, bearing down most heavily upon the laboring classes and the lower middle groups of professionals and small tradesmen. It was inevitable that these classes, comparatively inarticulate before, should begin to speak.

However, this new consciousness has not been confined to only one part of the American drama. Its effects can be traced through a decade of American playwriting, in plays that run the whole gamut of social and political opinion: Maltz and Sklar's MERRY-GO-ROUND (1932); Sklar and Peters' STEVEDORE (1934); Elmer Rice's WE THE PEOPLE (1933) and AMERICAN LANDSCAPE (1938); Kaufman and Ryskind's OF THEE I SING (1932); Wexley's

THEY SHALL NOT DIE (1934); Paul Green's HYMN TO THE RISING SUN (1936) and JOHNNY JOHNSON (1936); Albert Bein's LET FREEDOM RING (1935); John Haynes Holmes' IF THIS BE TREASON (1935); Irwin Shaw's BURY THE DEAD (1936); Sinclair Lewis's IT CAN'T HAPPEN HERE (1936); Sidney Howard's PATHS OF GLORY (1935) and THE GHOST OF YANKEE DOODLE (1938); Maxwell Anderson's VALLEY FORGE (1934); Lawson's MARCHING SONG (1937); Kaufman and Hart's THE AMERICAN WAY (1939); Sherwood's ABE LINCOLN IN ILLINOIS (1938) and THERE SHALL BE NO NIGHT (1940); Clare Boothe's MARGIN FOR ERROR (1939); S. N. Behrman's RAIN FROM HEAVEN (1934) and NO TIME FOR COMEDY (1939); Hemingway and Glazer's FIFTH COLUMN (1940); and literally dozens more.

It would be absurd to suppose that the left-wing propagandist theatre is directly responsible for the emergence of all these plays. But it is quite clear that when the more radical theatres first came forward with propagandist drama they were reacting, a little before the rest of our theatre, to the pressure of new times and new problems.

Still, if propagandist drama had this sort of value, its main fault was also glaringly evident. Rarely was a propaganda play capable of cleaving its way through the thick fog of dispute surrounding its particular theme. As a rule its verdict was arrived at before it judged the evidence, and it was considerably more intent on stating its views with eloquence rather than in proving its charges. The propagandist play's undeniable value in speaking to audiences on topical themes was a progressive step too often offset by a reversion to the theatre's everlasting illness—primitive hysteria.

Propagandist drama in the United States was moving in a straight line toward the realization that theatre is not a weapon unless it is something better than a weapon. In this realization the Epic theatre of Germany had preceded our own theatre.

TRIBUNAL

It has been made clear that the Epic theatre was, originally, a polemical form launched against the faults of the older theatre. The occasion of the original quarrel is past, but Epic has been slow to give up the caustic tone of its first pronouncements. Still it would be idle to imagine that when it returns to the amenities it will be ready to embrace illusory staging, emotionalism, symbolism, synthesis, the "well-made" play, or "psychological" staging.

And yet, with the possible exception of illusory staging, it is not really against any of these things. The Epic mode of reasoning in the theatre cannot be easily understood. Once understood it is not lightly disposed of. It is capable of producing real exasperation even in many who have maintained an open mind toward the theatre of the Soviets.

It may be asked, "How does it happen that a theatre which came originally out of the working class movement in Germany, can have an outlook in some ways quite different from that of the Soviet stage?" The answer is that the requirements of a new drama in various countries cannot be determined mechanically. The Epic theatre of Germany developed under auspices different from those of the Socialist-Realistic theatre of Russia. The Soviet theatre functions under communism. The German Epic theatre, on the other hand, functioned under capitalism. At that time German capitalism was desperately bankrupt as an institution; still it was inclined to be hostile to any theatre which did not look to the future with rose-colored spectacles. In the light of subsequent events in Germany, what doubt is there that the theatres of Brecht and Piscator spoke with foresight? The Epic theatre spoke clearly, emphatically and straight from the shoulder at a time when the older theatres were still unable to see the peril into which the culture of Germany was drifting.

From a technical point of view, therefore, it became a primary task of the Epic theatre to understand the artistic weakness of the older theatre. Thematically this was true also. Soviet drama stresses reconstruction. Epic devoted itself, by force of necessity, to disclosing the shaky foundations of the post-war German social structure, in the hope of fending off the calamity that has since come to pass.

According to Piscator, theatre is a *tribunal.* In the crisis in which the Fatherland found itself, the Epic theatre was squarely on the side of the German people as against their betrayers. It abstained, however, from justifying this partisanship on *moral* grounds. The theatre as a moral institution was an important concept of the French revolution as seen by Diderot, and of the Romantic movement as seen by Goethe. It was a concept which Epic regarded not as incorrect, but as outdated.

Epic theatre taught that the German people will inherit Germany. This will occur, however, not as a matter of justice, but as a result of the exigencies of history. The German common people will win not necessarily because moral right is on their side but because the truth is on their side. The executioners of the German people live in mortal fear of the truth, hence their ability to learn is limited in many ways. The people, however, can and will learn—not through mere indignation, but by harsh experience—to understand the processes whereby the modern world lives. The people will grow strong in proportion as they accept the facts of this world and reject the fallacies which confuse them—fallacies which have accumulated through the ages of human existence.

Hence it was the duty of Epic theatre to teach, and to teach scientifically, practically. Each production was meant to be an impartial tribunal where facts were investigated. The faults of the oppressed could no more be condoned than the faults of the oppressors. The young organizer in THE EXPEDIENT is well-intentioned but mistaken. Because he endangers the lives and missions of his co-workers, he must pay with his own life if necessary. But the audience, sitting before this drama and making its own thoughtful conclusions, will profit therefrom. The emotions of the oppressed do not of themselves constitute a weapon of liberation. Dramatic experience becomes a weapon only when it is tempered in the white heat of knowledge, which in the long run is always objective, *scientific* knowledge.

SCIENCE AND ARISTOTLE

This feature of Epic theatre, its supreme confidence in scientific method, is traceable in large part to certain conditions under which the Epic style arose—namely to the high degree of industrialization of Germany and to German specialization in scientific research. According to Sir William Dampier, "the systematic organization of research has been carried further in Germany than in any other country, and German compendiums and analyses of the world's work have been pre-eminent." Alfred North Whitehead, also speaking of a Germany still untouched by its present blight, declared:

> . . . the Germans explicitly realized the methods by which the deeper veins in the mine of science could be reached. . . . This discipline of knowledge applies beyond technology to pure science, and beyond science to general scholarship. It represents the change from amateurs to professionals.

It need not surprise us that the people of that theatre saw no reason why drama, like all other phenomena, should not be examined in the light of science.

In following their researches we may very well begin by asking where their usage of the word *Epic* comes from. It may be traced to Goethe, who borrowed it from Aristotle.[10] It distinguishes a type of drama which supersedes tragedy in that its canvas is the broad one of events rather than the narrower one of personal fate. In Goethe's words, "The epic poem represents above all things circumscribed activity; tragedy, circumscribed suffering. The epic poem gives us man working outside of and beyond himself: battles, wanderings, enterprises of all kinds which demand a certain sensuous breadth. Tragedy gives us man thrown in upon himself, and the actions of genuine tragedy therefore stand in need of but little space."

An identical usage of the terms exists in the American motion picture industry. An "epic" is a large-scale film in which the events, usually historical, take precedence over the "love interest."

It is evident from these definitions that an important question of emphasis is involved. Epic writing looks beyond personal comedy or tragedy to the relationships which are bigger than people. These sociological—sometimes even technological—relationships are the fundamental cause of comic or tragic events. Epic of course is not alone in looking upon these larger relationships as primary. Most stage techniques accept the philosophy that men and women, like the actors of HENRY V, are "ciphers" to a "great account." But Epic is prepared to take this view quite literally, and to urge that the "great account" receive principal attention.

Aristotle, who first differentiated between tragic and epic poetry, was also the first to define the purpose of tragedy as an emotional catharsis, or cleansing, of the spectator. All aspects of theatre which have this aim of an emotional cleansing are therefore denoted as "Aristotelian" by Brecht, to distinguish this tradition from the alternative, knowledge-seeking tradition which has also endured and developed through the ages. Brecht insists that the Aristotelian tradition is unhealthy, because an emotional catharsis of itself does not add one cubit to the stature of the person who undergoes it: catharsis in drama means something only when it accompanies an objective clarification in terms of practical knowledge gained.

It may be said in passing that Brecht's use of the term "Aristotelian" does not seem very apt. Aristotle himself called for a "*proper* purgation" of the emotions. Aristotle, like Brecht, would call inadequate any emotional cleansing unaccompanied by real thought. The point of the criticism, however, is fairly clear.[11]

Further according to Brecht and Piscator, drama in its weakened form tends to build up a meretricious system of suspense and climax having very often no logical relation to the themes with which it proposes to deal. Epic opinion, like that of Naturalism before it, has an almost morbid distrust of the keying up of emotion, whether that emotion be relevant or not.[12] Indeed Brecht has taken the position, which is certainly extreme, that suspense and climax in dramatic scenes should be avoided, that the development should be on a narrative basis, gaining dramatic power only by means of the cumulative effect of the total number of scenes.

The fundamental point at issue between "Aristotelian" and Epic writing has sometimes been described as the difference between emotional appeal and "cold, dry logic." This is a badly vulgarized statement. The idea that logic must be cold and dry is sheer fantasy. And certainly there is no guarantee that the finest logic will convince where such logic is against the interest of the person to whom it is addressed. Nor will the Epic dramatist himself guarantee to use perfect logic. (Unfortunately, like the rest of us, he often does not.) The point is not whether we wish to be emotional or logical. The point is whether we prefer to aim at being objective in the theatre or whether we insist that dramatic technique is essentially an appeal to prejudice as against the consideration of facts.

For Epic theory recognizes no such opposed categories as *emotional thought* and *logical thought.* It recognizes only clear and unclear thought, both of which are inseparable from emotion. Unclear thought when not caused by shock or injury may be due to ignorance, prejudice, apprehension, dishonesty, inexperience. To create a separate, emotional, "unconscious mind," in the manner of some of the more romantic followers of Freud, is both unnecessary and confusing.[13]

Thus the Epic style in effect changes the value of psychology in the drama. To give one example, it alters the meaning of Stanislavsky's views on character. It is true that the Russian director understood that people are conditioned by outer forces as well as by inner qualities; on assigning a rôle he would tell the actor, "Give this character his past." Still in practice the Stanislavsky system has a tendency to become introspective and even static. The reason, perhaps, is that the actor's adjustments are in terms of *thoughts* rather than in terms of *actions.* According to the Epic view, behavior can be understood best in terms of *tactics.* That is, feelings, thoughts and moods represent latent behavior; but tactics describes an active functioning of mind and body in relation to a goal.[14]

This does not mean, of course, that Epic stage characters shall be left without thoughts, moods, reflections, aspirations, peculiarities of behavior, vacillations. The importance of the individual personality cannot be denied. (Consider, for instance, the crucial importance of the personality of someone who is left to guard a dangerous prisoner.) Indeed, Epic points out that the "psychological dramatist" rarely succeeds in creating more than a cliché figure unless, like Chekhov, he sees with extraordinary clarity that his characters are reacting to a central dramatic situation which is bigger than they are.

RÔLES AND TACTICS

If this is what happens to the playscript from the Epic point of view, it need not surprise us if the other factors of production are treated just as drastically. To begin with, the idea of synthesis which the Symbolist theatre, ever since Wagner, has fought so hard to establish—the belief that the ideal production must be a suave blending of all its elements—is categorically challenged.

And in contrast to the fusion of the arts that has been attempted by our musical theatre—most ambitiously and confusedly in Wagnerian opera—the new synthesis is based on a "dissociation of elements." In the theatre with which we are familiar, a particular production is dominated entirely by one art; the other arts are subordinated, used merely to support it and unable, usually, to exist by themselves. In the epic theatre all the arts are considered of equal importance and are used as independent elements; their relative importance changes as the production demands. (Eva Goldbeck: *Principles of "Educational Theatre"*).

What is the reason for this opinion that the elements which Symbolism tried to fuse together shall instead be dissociated? Why shall each element be given autonomy? It is to keep clear thought from becoming muddled. Symbolist theatre, which is especially given to unclear thinking, tries to overcome that defect by means of sensual appeal. Examples are the tom-tom beats of THE EMPEROR JONES, the barrages of WHAT PRICE GLORY?, the offstage shouting and gunshots of MARCHING SONG.

These examples are simple sound effects. But the same purpose is served by the mood, atmosphere and rhythm of the play, beginning with their indication in the dramatist's script. Epic does not ask that these elements be banished from production: they may be urgently necessary. But they are essentially *by-products.* They are by-products of a dramatic situation. In staging A DOLL'S HOUSE, what matters is the explanation of Nora's mean place in her own home. A production which does not make this clear but which becomes instead a picture of a Norwegian Christmas or an orchestration of Ibsenian dialogue, may be an artistic achievement but is still inadequate drama.

Epic considers that the misuse of the audience's emotions is a warning symptom of decay in drama. It maintains further that *to fuse the technical elements into one emotional impression is the ideal way to increase this decay.* It contends that the audience's mind cannot be clarified if it is confronted at every moment with an overpowering emotional synthesis. So that the spectator may use his mind unhurriedly, calmly and with alertness, everything that might influence him insidiously must be removed. Each technical factor must be frankly and obviously used, frankly and obviously related to the other factors.

This is evidently a parallel to Epic's criticism of the well-made play; and it is likewise open to the charge of being much too extreme as formulated here. Yet an important element of criticism remains even if we refuse to believe that the fusion of dramatic elements is a bad thing. When too great an emphasis is placed on fusion, we are likely to overlook the quality of what is being fused. The wrong things may be splendidly fused to make a single, unified—and irrelevant—result. If we forget about fusion for a moment, our attention returns to the separate elements of playwriting, acting, design and so on. We may find that these have suffered from lack of criticism.

Consider the acting problem. When Katharine Cornell, for instance, in playing Shaw's ST. JOAN, practically becomes St. Joan before our eyes; when Helen Hayes becomes Queen Victoria, Epicists shrug their shoulders. They see little merit in the fact that the audience is grieving and rejoicing with these reincarnated figures. That, by itself, is not enough. What is important is that the audience learn something during this sequence of emotions. If the actress herself is undergoing an emotional experience, she cannot very well explain a situation to us. To use Brecht's expression, "She can only live the situation, not interpret it." Her own comment is lacking, and without this comment the rôle has no life.

But as a matter of fact this paradox is understood by Miss Cornell and Miss Hayes, and by good actors of all schools, even the Naturalistic. In stressing the point Epic merely calls attention once more to what is healthy in the actor's work.

It is not often realized that the traditional acting of the Orientals is even more subtle than occidental acting in its grasp of emotions. Chinese acting, for example, is based on emotions (in fact on emotions almost exclusively). Yet the actor himself is far removed from the emotions he portrays. The Chinese actor employs his voice and body as if they were musical instruments upon which he can sound the gamut of human emotions with philosophic insight.

The traditional Chinese theatre, like that of the ancient Greek, is religious in character. In the case of the Chinese theatre, the religion consists of ancestor-worship. The conduct of the ancestor is held up as an example for the descendant to follow. The metaphors of the Chinese stage, which are very ancient, have long since become ossified. In portraying a famous prince of the fourth century A. D. the Chinese actor does not propagandize the audience by creating a resurrected, emotionalized picture of the prince. The audience takes for granted the greatness of the prince. The audience is interested rather in the actor's ability to show greatness in the rôle itself, by delivering the long-accustomed lines and gestures of the rôle with superlative grace and power.

Only an actor who is a great master of his craft will be permitted by his audiences to change an iota of the traditional rôle. In the modern period Mei Lan-fang belongs in the category of those actors who have had sufficient authority to make changes in the traditional playing of their parts.

The characters who tread the Chinese stage are not ghosts from the past temporarily lodged in the body of some player. They are like the characters of our own Morality players—abstractions of human character, living homilies. They are Theatricalist conceptions, having undergone that sea-change of which Jones speaks. Only in this case it is the sea of time which has pressed what may once have been a furious primitive ritual into something as immovable as stratified rock. The same thing has happened to the acting and the settings. Hence the Chinese stage presents us with a classic example of a conventional form adapted to the purpose of teaching. The timeless nature of the Chinese stage conventions here are well adapted to the ancient, inflexible laws which this theatre has to teach.

Of course the actor of the western world must find his own conventions. And the way to find them, Epic believes, is not to *live* another character, but only to *mimic* another character. To believe that one can live a part, become someone else, is a form of superstition. One can only *understand* a character and, for the benefit of an audience, give an imitation of his actions along with an unspoken, illuminating comment. Brecht, commonly rumored to be lacking in human interest, has written some of the fullest and most rewarding rôles in modern drama—as for instance the peasant Callas in ROUND HEADS AND PEAKED HEADS, or the tremendously restrained leading part of GALILEO.

The tumultuous inner thoughts which are so typical of Odets' characters are not to be found in Brecht's people. For Odets the circumstances of people are in the background; in the foreground are their psychological tensions, which find expression in the fire of their dialogue. Thus ROCKET TO THE MOON proposed to show that under the conditions of contemporary life, the love of men and women is distorted and stultified. This is an original and valuable theme. But by the third act the dramatist had lost his hold on the outer circumstances which defined his characters. His gift for psychological nuances as expressed in dialogue could not help him out of this dilemma, and the audience could not understand the characters any longer.

In the best of Brecht's work all the responses of the characters, whether inner or outer, are related to the theme of the play as tactics primarily, rather than as mental attributes. The behavior of Galileo is one long, complex attempt to establish the Copernican theory. We follow his tactics and see that they are sometimes brilliantly effective, sometimes ill-advised; sometimes they are advanced with optimism, sometimes temporarily abandoned in despair.

SETTINGS AND SCIENCE

Even more than Epic acting the Epic stage setting is relentlessly anti-illusory. At first sight many of the settings which have been used in Epic plays seem akin to those of Meyerhold's Constructivist period. This is only because, strictly speaking, there is no stage picture intended in either. But there the resemblance ends. Among the designers who have worked on Epic productions are Caspar Neher, László Moholy-Nagy, George Grosz, John Heartfield, Traugott Müller, Teo Otto and Wolfgang Roth, in Germany; Antonín Heythum in Czechoslovakia; Svend Johansen in Denmark; Hjalmar Hermanson, Howard Bay and Mordecai Gorelik in the United States. It was the task of these designers, when preparing Epic plays, neither to make an exact reproduction of life nor to build up an atmospheric stage picture. Their business was to supply such fragments of environment as were needed to show the meaning of the play. These fragments might be isolated and simple (as in the case of MOTHER) or they might form an intricate mechanism (as in Piscator's MERCHANT OF BERLIN). This type of design has an infinitely greater variety of function than Constructivism, whose function is almost entirely spatial.

It was above all Piscator who shaped Epic scene design in its early stages. The demands which he placed upon the setting may be enumerated indefinitely: it must be part of the exposition of a play, it must be mobile, it must be non-psychological, non-pictorial, and so on. But all these requirements arise from a fundamental requirement—the setting must be utile. Whether Piscator had any "taste" at all was a moot question in his early productions. It was sufficient for him to hang up a wretched piece of canvas and throw a light on it. Did it serve its purpose? Excellent. "His scenery," observes Wadsworth, "was not meant to be a delight to the eye. It was a deliberate shock to the optic nerve." But a new road was being hacked out.

Piscator's settings were influenced by another consideration also. As director he found himself hampered by the outmoded Naturalistic or Symbolist scripts which were supplied him. These scripts, focussed upon individual psychology, could not give him the wide scope which he needed. It became necessary to widen the horizon of the environment by means of the stage setting. Typical of this procedure was the scene design for Gorky's LOWER DEPTHS (1926).

For Piscator the object of the production was to explain the concept *Lumpenproletariat* (rabble). Since this is scarcely the task which Gorky set himself in writing the play, some drastic changes were required in presenting it. Instead of viewing the actors as "fellow human beings," which would mean highlighting the actors and leaving the setting incidental and obscure, the director began by showing the place of the *Lumpenproletariat* in the social plan of a city. The curtain goes up on a slum district of a large city. A narrow twisting street winds among the crumbling buildings until it reaches the raked forestage, where dim, huddled figures lie in uneasy sleep. One hears them gasping for breath. From far off comes the whine of a street car. Morning is at hand, and as the street lights fade we begin to see workers, pale, yawning, off to work with lunch-pails in their hands.

These hurrying people are the proletarians. The figures in front continue to sleep. They do not work. They are not the working class, they are the outcasts of the working class and of other classes, the riffraff and the dregs, who live in twilight. Although it is growing brighter outside, a ceiling descends upon the scene and shuts out the sunlight. The recumbent figures begin to stir, a woman rises finally and lights a lamp. . . . In the fourth act the fight in the backyard becomes a scene of the upheaval of this outlawed class. A woman screams, the inhabitants crawl out of their holes, moving far toward the front of the stage; a cordon of police, their backs to the audience, drive these menacing wretches back to their homes, as though to keep them from reaching the audience.

Toller's HOPPLA, WE LIVE! (1927) is a fable of a man who comes out of a lunatic asylum for the first time in nine years, gets a look at the world and decides to hurry back to the asylum. Before he can get there he becomes enmeshed in the violent events which are going on around him, finds himself in prison and escapes from an insane world only by hanging himself. Piscator had hoped to receive from the dramatist "clear-cut dialogue, hard, gem-like, crystal-pure." Toller's writing, however, was that of "lyrical pathos." The production, in which stage action was combined with motion pictures, had in part to offset the quality of the script. HOPPLA was provided with a cinematic overture. Upon a great central screen there was flashed a newsreel review of the nine years of world events which had taken place before Karl Thomas' release from the asylum. Behind the large screen, which was translucent, there was another one, narrow and vertical, upon which additional images were projected in counterpoint to the larger screen.

As time went on Piscator deepened his interest in the possibilities of the motion picture as a means for broadening the scope of dramatic action on the stage. Refusing to accept the dictum that stage and cinema are mutually exclusive mediums like oil-painting and water-color, he proceeded to bring the two together.

RASPUTIN (1927) was characteristic of this phase of his work.

Schweik is arrested

The army doctor

Schweik retires

SCENES FROM SCHWEIK (1928)

From Das Politische Theater

Barracks

The treadmills, seen from the wings

It was an exposé of wartime European intrigue; the charlatan who ruled the Tsarist court gave the measure of incompetence of the people who ruled Europe during one of the grimmest periods in world history. For this "documentary play" which was put on almost a decade before New York's first Living Newspaper production, Piscator used three film projectors and two thousand meters of film. The stage setting was shaped like a segment of a globe which opened in sections and turned on a revolving platform. The globe itself formed one projection screen; another screen hung above it, while at one side of the stage a narrow filmic "calendar" kept marginal notes on the multitude of events, giving dates and footnotes.

A typical instance of the use of the film, the calendar, and the ordinary stage together was the passage setting forth the ancestry of the late Czar. First the normal film showed, one after another, the long row of Nicholas' imperial ancestors, while the calendar made appropriate, and illuminating remarks: "Died Suddenly"; "Died Insane"; "Committed Suicide," and the like, as each portrait appeared. And finally, out of the darkness of the back of the real stage, but overshadowed by the huge, ghost-like shadow of Rasputin, came forward the living Czar himself, now revealed as the last of a long line of monarchs, all degenerate or mad. (Wadsworth).

To give another instance: while the Tsarina, toward the end of the play, kneels imploring the ghost of Rasputin for advice, the revolutionary regiments are flashed upon the screen, marching on Tsarskoe Selo. At times captions were super-imposed on the film as it ran along. Over a shot of the Battle of the Somme the words: "Loss—a half million dead; Gain—three hundred square kilometers." The central screens permitted of a vast expansion of the action, as when the scope of military and naval operations was shown by means of three simultaneous battles.

It was even possible to give an effect of a character stepping directly off the screen onto the stage, the effect being produced by means of intervening scrim drops. Apparently Epic does not consider such an obvious piece of legerdemain to be "illusory," since no adult person in the audience remains unaware of the trick, or is "taken in" by it.

Most interesting, perhaps, of all Piscator's experiments with the setting, was the scenic arrangement of Leo Lania's COMPETI-

TION (1928). An oil field is discovered in Albania. The land is staked out and two international oil concerns begin a ruthless war for domination.

> On an empty stage—the bare field—from the smallest beginnings, there must develop like the movement of an avalanche this struggle over an accidentally discovered oil well. It is a play-construction which is carried out under the eyes of the spectator, and shows the whole technical process of oil production. The discovery of the well, the well-drilling, the construction of the oil derricks, and finally the commercial exploitation of the product—this story of oil, with its rivalries, graft, corruption, killings, revolution—must enroll before the spectator, involving him in this way in the whole machinery of petroleum-politics. (*Das Politische Theater*).

The play opens on a bare stage. Three travelers lie down to sleep. They discover the oil, hammer a crude stake into the stage floor. Now begins the sale of parts of the stage. Large signs go up as the rival companies fence off with barbed wire. The drillers arrive, followed by loads of lumber for the derricks, which are erected then and there. The stage is finally crowded with oil-derricks. . . .

The static setting is unknown to Piscator, to whom must go the credit for a conception of the setting which is completely and utterly mobile. His projected showing of Tolstoy's WAR AND PEACE, which he dramatized together with Alfred Neumann, contains some forty-five scenes, of which at least thirty are separate locales, and some of which are multiple settings of several rooms or of interiors combined with exteriors. Therewith a script for stage use becomes scarcely distinguishable from a motion picture script.

Under the direction of Piscator and Brecht the Epic stage setting presents an impression of an animated laboratory or factory filled with mobile scenic units (including, very often, a picture screen), which are brought into action in the course of a performance. These units, thus used functionally, are themselves often Theatricalist in quality: for Brecht's ROUND HEADS AND PEAKED HEADS, a full-size jointed paper horse, a collection of assorted shop signs (a golden pretzel, a silver opera hat, a barber's basin, a black cigar, red shoe and red glove), strung together; for SCHWEIK, cut-out cartoons of soldiers; for HOPPLA an X-ray film of a beating heart; for BANNERS (Piscator's production of the Alphonse Paquet drama of the Haymarkets Riot—1924) a veritable forest of flags for the last scene.

THE INDUCTIVE SETTING

The settings which have been described here have been typical of the Epic style up to now. However, their general appearance may not typify Epic scenery in the future. More basic is the fundamental scenic principle that every element of design must be handled in a non-illusory, utile manner. Light, for instance, acts only as light, to illuminate, to color; never to *imitate* sunlight, moonlight or a parlor lamp. Nothing is used for the sake of its own beauty or for "psychological" effect, but strictly for explanatory or utile purpose, as it might be used in the course of a lecture-demonstration.[15]

In design, therefore, the process of thought is purely *inductive*. The designer does not imagine a room for the characters, or a striking atmosphere. Instead he supplies all necessary properties, sections of doors or windows or steps, and arranges for these units to function with workmanlike precision. Of course beauty is not excluded, since the resultant arrangement may possess its own beauty of form, and since beauty and color in some or all of the properties may be specifically necessary.

It is the *function* which is essential. Hence Epic design, instead of reproducing the object (as in the Naturalistic method), or symbolizing it by means of a significant part (as do the Symbolists), represents the object by means of its function. In MOTHER the wall between two rooms was indicated by means of a small curtain hung from a metal rod; its only purpose was to mark off space. In the factory scene of the same play the factory was represented not so much by a photograph of the building as by the picture of the owner; the point of the scene was not that the workers were in a factory, but that the factory belonged to Mr. Sukhlinov and not to them. The shop signs of ROUND HEADS AND PEAKED HEADS represented not so much a market place as the anarchy of small business competition; these objects outshouted each other in calling their wares.

If scenic elements are used in this laboratory fashion, what is the difference between such usage and the handling of materials in an actual laboratory? Very little. The physics laboratory works in the same way as the Epic setting—by finding in the environment those functions which are useful for any given demonstration. This sort of functionalism, which is scientifically true on stage just as it is offstage—not a "theatrical truth," as the Theatricalists would have it, but a scientific truth applying with equal force on stage or off—is it not a step toward a new sort of convention?

An interesting speculation becomes possible here. We recall Stanislavsky's challenge to scenic artists after that humiliating experience in the palace garden in Kiev.[16] It was an experience that ate into his soul, casual as the occasion seemed to be. When will the designer be able to bring real life to the stage instead of faking life? The answer seems less distant once we begin to grasp environment in terms of sheer function. . . .

THE STEEL STAGE

It was inevitable that Piscator, like every important director before him, would give thought to the question of the whole theatre building and its stage. Compared with the cramped stages in New York, those of other cities are capacious. Yet the Berlin stages were not roomy or efficient enough when Piscator began work on mobile constructions such as the treadmills of SCHWEIK, the revolving globe of RASPUTIN or the mobile scaffolds of THE MERCHANT OF BERLIN. Nor was he satisfied with the way his elaborate constructions, such as the treadmill or the globe, turned out to be unwieldy and in some ways dangerous on the stage. Modern stages should be so planned and equipped as to permit large mobile settings to work with freedom and assurance. A stage-machine is what is needed, one which will work as smoothly as a typewriter or a good automobile.

Piscator has certainly not been alone in regarding the theatre-building of our day as "the outlived form of absolutism—the court playhouse." Its division into orchestra, parquet, boxes and balconies reflects the social strata of feudal society. Since Karl Lautenschlager in 1896 installed at Munich what is reputed to be the first revolving stage in the western world, there has been considerable progress made toward the ideal of a beautifully mechanized theatre; and some superbly equipped playhouses have been built, especially in Germany at the turn of the century and in Russia in recent years. It is noteworthy that the German mechanized revolving, sliding, sinking and swinging stages were put to use only in shifting the usual type of picture scenery. Even so they apparently overwhelmed many directors, who preferred to ignore these resources and to look for simpler methods of making scene-changes.[17]

Piscator on the contrary is one of the few directors who consider the modern stage insufficiently mechanized. Certainly few other directors have felt so at home with mechanized stages. His chief technician, Richter, has visualized, in place of present stages, steel and electric structures of ample size, "with mobile bridges, elevators, cranes, motors, great scene docks and moving platforms with which it would be possible to transport tons of weight to the stage in short order without human labor." (*Das Politische Theater*).[18]

Lest anyone get the notion that such a mechanism can be part only of some monstrous, steel Constructivism in which the human actor is a mere afterthought, it should be pointed out that there are very few stages indeed which have the mechanical precision and efficiency of an ordinary modern factory. Settings for the contemporary theatre may be spiritually designed, but you will always find stagehands wrestling with them under material conditions that are surprisingly primitive. The modern stage, especially in the United States, is badly in need of streamlining in every part of its technical equipment.

To give a single instance, a tremendous amount of work needs to be done in the stage control of sound. In spite of the development of "sound tables," sound recording and mixing, sound effects continue to be a thorn in the side of any production that requires them. "With respect to the auditory component of the show . . . we are still in a sub-primitive condition," declares Burris-Meyer, who is now engaged in research on this problem under the auspices of the Rockefeller Foundation. What this gap in the mechanism of the stage can mean to the dramatist is made plain in the letter by Eugene O'Neill on the production of DY-

NAMO.[19] Also under Rockefeller Foundation auspices, Hanns Eisler has undertaken three years of experiment in correlating music and cinema artistically.

A thoroughly dynamic viewpoint in the theatre is not permitted much development on stages which are fundamentally static. On present-day stages it is possible to build or install moving platforms, turntables and trucks of a crude type, but even these mean a big outlay of money. In New York the expense is usually met by the producing firm, not by the theatre. As a result experiment is greatly limited. Under such conditions what inducement is there to develop a theatre of *facts in movement*—a theatre not of static facts but of facts in conflict, facts in mounting progression?

According to Julius Bab, "Piscator overreached himself in his passion for machinery." It is probably true that the settings used by Piscator were too often diffuse instead of incisive in their levels, screens and properties. Too often the stereopticon, cartoon and loudspeaker comments stressed the obvious.

But Piscator has the great merit of taking modern environment seriously. He has tried to examine it, to make it functionally real, to show its indispensable rôle in the world of men. He knows that science and technology are the creators of modern environment, and that their aid is necessary in understanding the world they have created.

This is something which the "psychological" Symbolist theatre has yet to learn. Technology, in particular, does not exist for the contemporary theatre. Technology has supplied the stage with superb lighting and elaborate mechanical equipment. With these aids Symbolist staging tries its hardest to make us forget there is such a thing as technology, unless it is the "technology" of a "master-mind's" laboratory in horror melodramas. Even the movies, which owe their very origin to mechanical inventions, are almost as squeamish, as if machines were not a part of life but some strange hidden abnormality.

In spite of this taboo the value of the machine both as a subject of drama and as an element in stage form continues to make itself felt. The cinema, a form of theatre created by the machine, has grown so immensely that a degree of artistic interest in technological subjects has become necessary for business reasons, if not for artistic ones. Having originally taken over from the stage the technique of illusory production, lock, stock and barrel, the cinema in the end found this stage technique not entirely suited to its practical needs. A long process of trial and error and a prodigious waste of money was required to make the motion pictures understand a little of their own nature as a dramatic medium. And this process had to be repeated when the sound film took the place of silent pictures.

Motion picture directors, designers and camera men discovered the principles of the "frame," camera angles, panning, dissolving, filmic time, processing and editing. These techniques, now considered indispensable to the cinema, have also become part of the more general field of theatre. The "legitimate" stage is beginning to take lessons from its former pupil. The stage is also taking lessons from a still newer dramatic medium—the radio, even though radio has only begun to find its own path. This new theatre of the air is repeating the history of the cinema, beginning with stage technique and groping its way toward new forms better suited to its own needs. The newest medium of all, the electronic theatre known as television, faces technical problems still more complex than those of radio. For purely business reasons, if for no other, television must find a new style; it will have to push dead wood out of its way or it may be smothered.[20]

DUTIES FOR PLAYGOERS

On the whole the Epic style under the auspices of Piscator and Brecht would seem to resemble a resourceful lecture-demonstration rather than stage production as we have known it. It is in fact freely admitted that there is no sharp dividing line between Epic drama and a demonstration in a surgical or chemical auditorium. Epic plays have made use of lantern slides, placards and radio loudspeakers. For this reason the new form has been accused of being "didactic."

This reproach leaves it unabashed. It merely replies, "Why take it for granted that teaching must be as dull as it is in some of the stuffy classrooms we have today, where cut-and-dried information is crammed down the throats of apathetic students? Correct teaching must be dramatic in the best sense of the word."

It has been asserted, in objection to the Epic method, that "People don't want to think in the theatre." Not much proof of this assertion has been brought forward. People have a tendency to think all the time, even in the theatre—which is perhaps the reason why believers in emotive theatre, like Arthur Hopkins, have had to formulate plans to keep them from thinking.[21]

However, it can be successfully contended that people don't like to think *painful* thoughts. No one likes to go to the theatre just to be harrowed or shocked. There is indeed no reason why any rational person should go to the theatre for that purpose.

Many of the plays of Eugene O'Neill, for example, are lacerating and depressing, especially since they give no way out of the conditions which they describe. Audiences accept such plays only because the pictured sufferings are made unreal, immersed in a nostalgia which makes them painless. It can therefore be argued that a play which examines a painful state of affairs while offering at the same time a constructive way out is a truly "healing" play in the Aristotelian sense.

It is quite true that no dramatist or other theatre worker has the right to pain his audiences by explaining things in a dull, dry, pedantic manner, without dramatic interest. This responsibility rests upon the Epic dramatist and his co-workers in the same, or greater degree, as upon any of their predecessors.

On the other hand a responsibility rests upon the audience as well. If it is the responsibility of the theatre to teach, it is the responsibility of the audience to learn. This truth is too often forgotten in both the right and left wings of the contemporary theatre. The conservative producer goes by the principle that "The customer is always right." The radical one goes by the supposition that "The judgment of the masses is correct." Neither slogan ought to be accepted without question.

The Epic theatre, especially, is on guard against certain tendencies of its audiences. Brecht says: "The contemporary spectator is primitive. He only half listens, half sees. He has been conditioned to go to the theatre for a mild emotional jag. This spectator must be reconditioned." Piscator speaks of "the education of the audience even against its will."

It is certain that not only the "carriage trade" but a movie audience of millions has been corrupted to some extent by bad

Museum of Modern Art

THEY SHALL NOT DIE: The Courtroom in Dexter. Project by Gorelik (1934)

How not to design a Naturalistic play: Turn the setting into a mural on the theme of Justice. Use projected photos to show that a case is being tried in the streets of the U.S. as well as in the Dexter courtroom

stage and film productions. That fact cannot be left out of account in any realistic approach to the problems of modern theatre. However, the above comments by Brecht and Piscator represent Epic theory at its primmest. The popular response to Epic productions (crude as many of these productions have been so far) has been very satisfactory; and on a broader basis the response to documented or fact-seeking films has been heartening indeed. This is good evidence that most playgoers and moviegoers do not need to be greatly "reconditioned." On the contrary there is every reason to believe that the public will continue to show enthusiasm for plays which know how to teach brilliantly.

HOW NARROW IS EPIC?

Thanks to the work of the Living Newspaper, some of the possibilities of Epic production have received acknowledgment in the United States. John Mason Brown, among others, considers the Living Newspaper technique one of the most important contributions of the Federal Theatre:

> From the beginning it was clear that the most vital idea the Federal Theatre had as yet contributed to stagecraft as we have known it in this country lay in these dramatizations of current events which it was attempting to make. . . .
>
> That the Federal Theatre has brought these newspapers to a high state of development is a fact no one can deny who has seen POWER [a Living Newspaper production]. It is one of the most telling propagandist offerings our stage has produced. It is as skillful as it is forceful, and can boast the exciting virtue of having perfected a novel dramatic form. . . .
>
> Here is a performance which is part lecture and part history; which utilizes lantern slides, motion pictures and an amplifier to make its points; which resorts to vignetted playlets as well as to statistics; which is as broadly humorous in its stylized manner as it is indignant throughout; and which, though it has little or nothing to do with the theatre of entertainment as we ordinarily encounter it, it is none the less theatrically exciting even in its most irritatingly partisan moments.

Nevertheless it comes as a surprise to most people that Epic claims a wider field of interest than the fact-finding, statistical dramas of the Living Newspaper. Most commentators think of this new form of production as highly "special." They cannot visualize it apart from statistics, projections and radio voices.

But Epic does not require that the didactic quality of drama shall be projected in an obvious manner in speeches or lantern slides. (The lantern-slide era of Epic will sooner or later draw to a close.) The point on which it insists is that all good drama—or the best in any drama, good or bad is didactic; and that this is true not only of the playscript but of every element that goes into play production. This didactic quality, it maintains, is what makes all the difference between a cultural medium and a mere device for idling away time.

Furthermore the Epic style is not the property of Piscator or of Brecht, and it is evident that it will survive even their mistakes. It is earnestly iconoclastic, almost absurdly doctrinaire in some ways. This style took root in one of the most bitterly disputed periods of stage history. Much of its dogmatism is traceable to that fact. Some can be traced to a residue of mysticism and pedanticism in Brecht himself, and to Piscator's tendency to widen his themes rather than to narrow them down for the sake of more incisive analysis. A great deal more is due to the fact that the development of Epic in Germany was cut short by the Hitler regime, which put an end to creative drama. Epic has shown, however, that it can survive and grow even under conditions of exile.

It may be objected that, if it once be granted that all valuable drama is didactic, there is nothing really new about the Epic idea. Epic theory admits this. It does not claim to be an entirely new theory of drama sprung full-grown into being. It insists only that in every age the worth of drama has depended upon a penetrating observation of life; that a theatre which no longer sees objectively is ready to be scrapped. In the past the power of observation has often been a highly intuitive poetical gift, like that of a Molière or a Shakespeare. For the life of today one must bring to the theatre a different kind of beauty in observation: the deliberately experimental, unprejudiced and precise method of the scientific laboratory.

NEW WINE IN OLD BOTTLES

It is especially the life of today which is hard to fit into the framework of subjective drama. From the Epic point of view many potentially fine plays in the progressive and left-wing sections of the modern theatre have been stultified because they could not achieve an objective type of production.

THE FIFTH COLUMN (1940), as written by Ernest Hemingway and adapted by Benjamin Glazer, is an almost classic instance. The play's title reminds us that the term "fifth column" was originally used by General Mola to describe his fascist agents inside loyalist Madrid. The Spanish republic, obliged to deal with these secret enemies, organized a system of counter-espionage. . . . Here was a chance to throw light on a matter of real public importance. What was the war in Spain about? What were the links in the chain of Spain's betrayal, from the spies of Franco to the farcically named Non-Intervention Committee? Who saw to it that arms were denied to the Spanish republic at a time when a loyalist victory might have headed off the war plans of Hitler and Il Duce?

Had THE FIFTH COLUMN answered some of these questions it might have been an important and dramatic play. But if that was its intention it did not choose a very serviceable dramatic pattern. In the Hemingway-Glazer play the death-struggle in Spain between democracy and fascism became subordinate to a love story more appropriate to the Café du Dôme. The play bogged down somewhere between political propaganda and the kind of melodrama that is filled with spies, señoritas and shrieks in the night.

Some of the plays of Sidney Howard are even more interesting as examples. In such dramas as YELLOW JACK and PATHS OF GLORY Howard had shown an instinctive bent for Epic writing. Instinct was not enough, however, to help him carry out the work successfully. The plays themselves suffered, and in production most of the Epic quality was sifted out.

YELLOW JACK (1934) was a play new and fresh in many respects. Based upon one of the episodes in Paul de Kruif's *The Microbe Hunters,* it had as a springboard the story of man's winning battle against disease. An Epic dramatist might have developed the theme in terms of the nature of man and microbes, the tactics of each, the incidents, ludicrous or exciting, which arose out of these tactics in the case of yellow fever.[22] All this might have been done without sacrificing atmosphere, emotion, characterization or poetry. Conceived, however, in Symbolist style, Howard's script never took firm hold of the scientific theme—if, indeed, it was seriously interested in handling that theme in the first place—and wandered into a blind alley of personal anecdotes.

The scenic production of YELLOW JACK, to be relevant, might have made clear to us what a bacteria-laden atmosphere is like. The proximity of this kind of disease can be shown even spatially, by means of various restrictions of space, activities in space, and so on. To carry the suggestion even further, in Living Newspaper style, for instance, there might have been projections from time to time illustrating some of the technical discussions among the army doctors, so that the audience could follow that side of the story. It is now even possible to project living images of Yellow Jack,[23] the fever bug of whom the audience heard much, but apparently only as a local topic of conversation. The Broadway production used instead a classic arrangement of platforms derived from the ancient Greek tragedies. This gave a certain dignity to the play, but had little other significance.

PATHS OF GLORY (1935), which Howard dramatized from the novel by Humphrey Cobb, also had new possibilities but was handled in the more accustomed manner. There was a fine Epic quality about Cobb's novel, which told with dry humor how a tough and vain French general brought his troops to the verge of mutiny. Much of this quality passed into Howard's play. But the playwright wished to describe the French war machine as a kind of Greek Fate. The attempt to squeeze the story into this metaphor did not have happy results. Howard considered the privates and the general equally the pawns of Fate. But the death by firing squad of innocent men chosen by lot cannot be regarded in the same light as the fact that General Assolant had to forego his coveted decoration. The story hinged upon army politics; cast in a mould of Attic drama it gained a vague sort of nobility but lost its essential meaning. In production Arthur Hopkins emphasized the mystic side of the script by means of Symbolist settings (including the use of scrim drops), and by organ music to symbolize the sound of battle.

In 1936 the Group Theatre made an attempt to stage a play specifically written in Epic style—Piscator's adaptation of Dreiser's

An American Tragedy, under the play title of CASE OF CLYDE GRIFFITHS.

Young Griffiths, son of desperately poor parents, gets a job as foreman in the factory of his rich uncle. Carried away by dreams of marrying wealth, he rids himself of his factory-girl sweetheart, Roberta. He is brought to trial, found guilty of murder and electrocuted. The story is unusually poignant, lending itself to emotional emphasis. In his playscript, however, Piscator wished to deal not so much with the inner feelings of Clyde Griffiths as with the meaning of Clyde's attempt to vault from one economic class into another. After recounting in very direct fashion the episodes leading to the murder, Piscator uses the trial scenes to show almost statistically that tragedies like Clyde's are due less to the so-called "murderous instincts" of individuals than to the imperfections of our social order. (This was, of course, the point of Dreiser's novel as well.) But the rich world does not consider such proof as justification of the murderer, while the working class from which he came disowns Clyde as an unprincipled climber, an outcast from its ranks.

An infinite number of scenes and properties were called for in the script. To meet this problem the Group decided to use a permanent platform setting and no stage properties whatever. The actors merely went through the motions of closing doors, driving an automobile or working with machinery. A Speaker in the audience commented on the behavior of Clyde all through the play. In performance the lack of properties seemed an affectation, and the Speaker even more so. There was a general impression that the Speaker's comments were superfluous. The setting, lighted in shadowy Symbolist style, was a construction of platforms based on no particular idea except the necessity for getting the actors to all parts of the stage.

Piscator's own stage directions for this play called for a special forestage with pianos at either side. The stage itself was to be divided into two parts of three levels each. The parts represented the Rich World and the Poor World, with an elevator working in between.

An alternative suggestion by Gorelik was that the play be staged from start to finish as a veritable trial of Clyde Griffiths, with the audience sitting as jury. Stage and auditorium would be united by means of a formal structure resembling a courtroom but retaining the quality of a stage. The action would be the immediate and actual one of the trial itself rather than that of a nostalgic, make-believe story viewed beyond the proscenium. That is to say, it would not even be an imitation legal trial, but a kind of *stage trial* with an audience-jury, the audience seriously considering evidence rather than "making believe" that it is a jury.

In such a production the acting done without properties would become plausible re-enactments by witnesses. The Speaker in the auditorium would be in character as a sort of counsel for the defense. In the course of the trial he would, from scene to scene, sift out the faults of Clyde himself from the circumstances over which Clyde obviously had no control. In summing up at the end the Speaker would try to show that the number of factors for which Clyde could be held personally were far outweighed by those for which he could not be held responsible. On this basis the Speaker would move for the acquittal of the accused. Members of the audience would then offer their opinions, which would be taken into account by the Rich and the Poor on the stage in rendering judgment.

FILM EPICS AND EPIC FILMS

The stultification of Epic tendencies in American drama has not as a rule been remedied in the film versions of Broadway plays. Transferred to the films, Howard's YELLOW JACK (MGM, 1938) became further constricted in a story which gave equal emphasis to the romantic adventures of some American soldiers in Cuba. Sufficient examples have been given of the cinema's ability to "eat away" much that is vital or objective in new material. The American movies are still a stronghold of "Aristotelian" emotional drama. Yet, curiously enough, they also supply us with some fine examples of Epic technique.[24] Thus the cinema version of YELLOW JACK contains closeups showing the behavior of the malarial mosquito, while other films about science, such as PASTEUR (Warner Brothers, 1936) or DR. EHRLICH'S MAGIC BULLET (Warner Brothers, 1940), while still rather Romantic, have begun to give us some insight into the methods of medical research. Warner's ZOLA (1937) and Columbia's MR. SMITH GOES TO WASH-

INGTON (1939) both had illuminating sequences showing how public opinion is systematically influenced and directed.

But there are also fragmentary examples in many run-of-the-mill pictures. Around the familiar Hollywood triangle situations there are sometimes excellent portrayals of technical processes, such as the building and flying of an airship in DIRIGIBLE (Columbia, 1931); the navigation of a submarine in HELL BELOW (MGM, 1933); racketeering in PUBLIC ENEMY (Warner Brothers, 1931).

These factual, technological secondary themes are as fascinating, exciting and thought-provoking to the audience as the main love themes are callow and insipid. (Yet the notion continues in the film industry that Boy Meets Girl is the real dramatic interest.) Even in the realm of fantasy the exposition of a technical process may have great dramatic charm: in THE INVISIBLE MAN (Universal, 1933) the precautions used by the police to trap the invisible culprit are the "high spots" of the film. Indeed a little Epic applied to Hollywood's all-important theme of Boy Meets Girl might not be amiss. We might for once see something in the way of love which is a little maturer than the passions of high-school undergraduates.

Of recent American films perhaps THE GRAPES OF WRATH (Twentieth-Century Fox, 1940) has a claim to being Epic that rests on something more than publicity blurbs. The trek of the Joad family from the Oklahoma dust bowl to the fruitful valleys of California has stirred movie audiences profoundly. It would be incorrect to say that this picture is not propagandist; it is every bit as propagandist as UNCLE TOM'S CABIN or POTEMKIN. But one thing can be said about the Steinbeck film which was far less true of the play taken from Mrs. Stowe's novel. THE GRAPES OF WRATH has implemented its story with facts at every turn and developed its thesis with an almost merciless logic.

The facts of course can be called into question. (Philip Bancroft, a member of the executive committee of the Associated Farmers of California, calls the Joad story untrue and libelous; while Carey McWilliams, chief of the California Division of Immigration and Housing, declares it is a true picture of conditions in 1937, when Steinbeck made his studies for the book from which the movie was taken.)* But no Epic play or film can hope

* New York *Post*, March 8, 1940.

to present facts which will not be questioned, no matter how well supported the evidence may be. What is significant is the tendency to rely upon facts, to rely upon the objective logic of events rather than upon subjective emotion. This is one of the main reasons why the good or ill luck of an "Okie" family becomes, in this picture, something more than that. It is the story of a terrible defeat for American agriculture; it is the story of a painful setback in the unceasing struggle for democratic American ideals.

THE GRAPES OF WRATH is Epic in the broad sense that it approaches life in a mood of factual inquiry. Fortunately it is far from being alone in that category. In this broader sense there has been a veritable rebirth of cinema in recent years. In spite of every inducement to cheap propaganda, box-office formulas and experiments with "technique," a large number of films have appeared whose interest in life has not been hemmed in by national boundary lines or even by political ideologies. Not all of these films have carried out their aims completely, but many of them have already earned a secure place in the artistic history of the cinema.

In the years before they were officially denounced as *Kultur Bolschewismus,* films like THE LAST LAUGH, JOYLESS STREET, KAMERADSCHAFT, THE BLUE ANGEL, "M," THE CAPTAIN OF KÖPENIK, THE THREE-PENNY OPERA, MÄDCHEN IN UNIFORM, expressed that humanitarianism which represents the real views of the now enslaved German people.

Before it was overrun by Hitler's legions and betrayed by its own high officials, France gave us such important pictures as GRAND ILLUSION, À NOUS LA LIBERTÉ, HEART OF PARIS, CRIME ET CHÂTIMENT, POIL DE CAROTTE, BALLERINA, CARNET DE BAL, LA KERMESSE HÉROÏQUE, HARVEST, THE BAKER'S WIFE. The Führer may proclaim that France was a "decadent democracy"; but the testimony of these films does not bear him out. Rather they offer proof that the French people have all the means necessary to carry on a constructive life, and that they will bring their work to a triumphant conclusion after Hitler and his French imitators have gone the way of all plagues.

In Soviet films the realism of POTEMKIN has been perpetuated in films like MOTHER, TEN DAYS THAT SHOOK THE WORLD, THE ROAD

Brecht

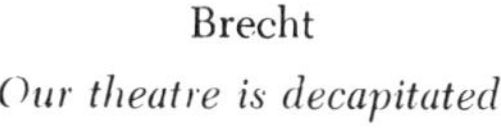

Our theatre is decapitated

Piscator

"I uttered the word 'actor' with shells bursting around me."

Brecht and Piscator: *They saw political forces unchained*

The anti-illusory setting: OUR TOWN (1938)

Vandamm-Theatre Arts

TO LIFE, THE MAXIM TRILOGY, CHAPAYEV, BALTIC DEPUTY, THE PEASANTS, PROFESSOR MAMLOCK.

Pictures like THE BARTERED BRIDE, SCHWEIK and JANOSIK are tributes to the always fanciful creative power of the Czechs.

Quite recently England has brought out many memorable films, among them PYGMALION, THE CITADEL, THIRTY-NINE STEPS, THE LADY VANISHES, SOUTH RIDING.

Most heartening of all, there has been a flood of Hollywood films which completely belie the assertion that our movie capitol dare not look a fact in the face. Europe cannot claim a better average than is represented in such pictures as FURY, PUBLIC ENEMY, MR. DEEDS GOES TO TOWN, ZOLA, PASTEUR, JUÁREZ, THEY WON'T FORGET, MR. SMITH GOES TO WASHINGTON, A MAN TO REMEMBER, DR. EHRLICH'S MAGIC BULLET, OF MICE AND MEN, MY SON, MY SON, THE GRAPES OF WRATH.

Finally there are the news films, educational, technical and documentary films in all countries, whose numbers and high standard are far beyond what most people imagine. The documentaries, especially, are growing in importance. We may pause to name a few from a long list. Flaherty's NANOOK, MOANA and MAN OF ARAN; Ivens' BORINAGE, SPANISH EARTH, FOUR HUNDRED MILLION; Grierson's DRIFTERS and NIGHT MAIL; Paul Rotha's SHIPYARD and TODAY WE LIVE; Cavalcanti's NORTH SEA; Kline's CRISIS and LIGHTS OUT IN EUROPE; THE WAVE, by Paul Strand, are among films dealing with material abroad. Among those concerned with American material are three by Pare Lorentz: THE PLOW THAT BROKE THE PLAINS, THE RIVER and THE FIGHT FOR LIFE; Frontier Films' THE PEOPLE OF THE CUMBERLANDS, Steiner and Van Dyke's THE CITY, Ivens' POWER AND THE LAND. The movie MARCH OF TIME has become a national institution, even though it too often sensationalizes its interpretation of facts. In 1940 the United Automobile Workers (C.I.O.) made history by turning out the first documentary ever filmed by organized labor's own cameras—UNITED ACTION, produced in association with Frontier Films.

SCIENCE AND THEATRE

We have tried to outline the development of the post-War German stage form known as Epic theatre; its origin as a propagandist medium opposed to the doctrine that art is "above the battle"; its head-on collision with the existing forms of theatre.

It will remain the historic merit of the Epic theatre of Germany that it was the first in modern times to subject "the art of the theatre" to the most searching examination.

Like the United States, Germany had for generations led a scientific and industrial life which was exacting, precise, systematic. In both countries the quality of theatrical life—sentimental and romantic—has been *in contrast* to the scientific genius of its people. Under conditions more crucial than those in America, Germany finally reacted against the outdated influence of the Romantic tradition. The reaction, when it came, was a severe one.

The experiences of the War, the long agony of the descent into fascism, drove the thinking people of Germany either to the blackest despair or to a new affirmation of loyalty to science. The short Expressionist period in the German playhouses after the War tried for the last time to assert that the individual will can rise superior to chaos. The even briefer Dadaist period was a mocking echo of chaos itself. For Piscator, Brecht and their colleagues, neither the idealism of the Expressionists nor the cynicism of the Dadaists was enough. Life had become a bloody mess indeed. Neither prayers nor mockery helped any longer in dealing with it. From now on the air must be cleared of passionate clamor. Analysis must take the place of assertion; the theatre must be brought closer to scientific truth.

The initial period of Epic theatre in Germany has undoubtedly been sectarian. But sectarian periods are the rule with new tendencies. They are the periods of incubation, when a new idea is engaged in establishing its own identity, marking itself apart from what it is not. Once this identity is established it takes up the much longer task of linking itself once more with tradition. The result is not a compromise, as some might imagine. The result is a tremendously broadened activity, informed by a new, vital principle.

Nothing is easier than to dismiss Epic theatre as a mere peculiarity or cult. The Epic style has proved capable of arousing violent reactions from many who like to believe that they have unbiased judgment. Brecht's "learning-plays" have been dismissed as pedantry. Piscator's animation of the stage has been regarded as no more than a holiday for stage mechanicians. Because Epic is constantly on guard against the misuse of emotion on the stage, it has been called stupidly anti-emotional.

Epic has sinned most by asserting flatly that the search for objective truth must replace all subjective, magical formulas. Such a challenge to the ancient magic of the theatre may seem almost blasphemous to some people. But science itself proceeds by a systematic questioning of all accepted opinions; and it may be that a theatre of the scientific era has a similar duty. Epic is not without some precedent in its attitude toward subjective thought. In his *History of Science* Sir William Dampier takes a similar position:

> In spite of the teaching of so many idealistic philosophers, it is impossible to deduce the nature of the external world by a priori mental processes. The observational and deductive methods of science are necessary.

Epic has insisted on the right of the theatre to express its views with an utter lack of mystical coloring. To some this may mean that it wishes to abolish all subjective feeling, inspiration and imagination. Actually it is less interested in questioning these things than in asking us to understand the full possibilities of objective study in our times. In the past half-century science has perfected instruments whose sensitivity surpasses that of the most inebriated poet.[25] Scientific conceptions of the world as embodied in the quantum theory or the theory of relativity were unknown not only to Horatio but to Shakespeare. Surely it is something like arrogance to insist that the modern world can be explained by artists who know nothing of science, and who do not even wish to know!

As a medium of discussion, Epic refused to carry on a debate in terms of moral issues. It took its own moral virtue for granted, perhaps, as we are all inclined to do. But it understood, just the same, that something else is required to give weight to its pleas. Both Piscator and Brecht are artists of the stage, not politicians. They saw tremendous political forces unchained, and they did indispensable pioneer work in trying to seize upon and interpret these forces for the benefit of stage audiences. Time has proven them correct in many of their fears concerning their country's future, but neither of them was a political expert, and in point of fact neither of them was able to satisfy any political party, whether fascist, socialist or communist. Today, in exile, both men are finished with the duty of trying to translate political meanings into artistic ones. Yet, with all these reservations, we must not overlook the essential contribution of their theatre. Epic wished to make itself a tribunal where "the facts in the case" might be determined with rigorous impartiality.

But if the Epic style, like science itself, made progress by systematically questioning every accepted rule, it eventually saw its connection with all truth-seeking theatres of the past.

None of the virtues claimed by Epic have been lacking in the best drama of the past. The honest observation of Sophocles, Lope de Vega, Corneille, Shaw, Galsworthy, Ibsen, O'Neill or Odets is Epic to the extent, precisely, that it corresponds to what really exists in the life around us. The great achievements of the dramatic past are all revelations of what exists. The theatre in future must continue to observe life if it is not to degenerate into fakery.

If Epic thought is valid, it may be leading the way back from the long detour taken by the theatre on its way to the goal which Zola envisioned. In that case at least one of the Naturalist principles of reform has been abandoned, or so drastically changed that it is hardly recognizable.

The exact reproduction of life is left behind. It gives way to the selection of functional elements necessary to make clear a given dramatic situation. The building-up of illusion is replaced by a precise, direct method in which illusion in the sense of replica has no place. The stage platform reappears. In this new sort of conventional drama the theatre's scaffold is changed to a laboratory work-table. Its settings are no more than tokens of environment, this time derived from the concepts of science. The scenic production is no longer fused with the other dramatic elements into a single, synthetic effect. Autonomous, working in harmony or in counterpoint with the other factors of production, it is more than ever before an indispensable, organic part of the meaning of a performance.

EPIC IN PRACTICE

In the spring of 1940 Carly Wharton and Martin Gabel made history by bringing to Broadway the first privately produced Living Newspaper—MEDICINE SHOW, written by Oscar Saul and H. R. Hays. Will the American stage find any further, wider use for the Epic form? Has this form any other practical work which it can do in our theatre?

Epic can render an immediate service by sharpening critical thought. One standard of criticism which Epic suggests has been so little applied lately that its renewed use should prove of value. It is the question, "How much basis in fact is there in this or that dramatic idea?" The answer may not tell us all there is to know about a particular play, stage-setting, costume or acting rôle; but it may tell us something else which is all too often left out of consideration.

We are not asked to accept Epic as a "pure form." Epic, like all other stage forms, is an experiment. In years to come, if it has any validity, it may become a highly integrated, distinctive style. (The present lantern-slide type is crude and transitory.) But Epic principles can, quite definitely, be applied to the other styles of theatre—Naturalism, for instance—as a means of clarifying and strengthening those other styles.

Let us imagine we are rehearsing a Naturalistic play. In the past Naturalism was not very selective. Often it was not factual. It is possible to overcome such errors if we recognize what is lacking. The analytical method of Epic enables us to do just that. We can take a play like A DOLL'S HOUSE and ask "What is the central process which is described here?" What are the tactics of Nora? What function of Nora's environment is it necessary to stress? What are we trying to teach our audience with this particular play of Ibsen's? What practical knowledge are we giving our audiences, who live in a period very different from the time of Ibsen?

When classics are revived, such questions always come up, in some degree at least. But usually we only pose the general problem: "How can we bring this classic up to date?" The more concrete questions remain vague. Epic enables us to ask pointed questions and ask them systematically, almost in the manner of a questionnaire.

This sort of approach to the classics is a constructive one. It may help bring back to life thousands of plays which now stand neglected on library shelves. And if it can help perfect old plays for use today, it can do the same for new plays. It begins to be possible to take a more concrete and incisive approach to the building of new plays.

We are a nation distinguished for very high standards of industrial organization, scientific progress, technological precision. Epic thought conceives of a theatre having the same standards. Perhaps, as one very practical measure, we can begin to dream of a type of theatre suited to industrial, scientific and technological America.

NOTES

1. Later the same group produced another mass spectacle, DER ARME KONRAD, in a "foreplay" and four pictures dealing with the uprisings of the Württemberg peasants in 1514. The action took place before a great staircase, at the head of which stood sculptured figures of a Knight, a Priest, and a Judge. These productions brought together fifty thousand spectators at each performance.

2. Piscator relates the following incident which occurred during the War:

"We pushed on. In the Ypres salient. The German army was in the midst of the celebrated spring offensive of 1915. For the first time poison gas was released. English and German corpses lay stinking under the comfortless gray heaven of Flanders. Our companies were decimated. We were to get reinforcements. On the way to the front lines we were mauled back and forth. As we moved forward once more we encountered the first barrage. An order to deploy and dig in. I lie there like the rest, my heart beating, trying to dig my spade into the ground as fast as the others. The others succeed; I do not. The corporal, swearing, creeps over to me.

'Come on, zum Donnerwetter!'

'I can't make it.'

He rails at me. 'What's your profession?'

'Actor.'

"At that moment, as I uttered the word 'actor,' with shells bursting around me, my profession seemed . . . so stupid, such a ridiculous caricature, so little related to . . . life and the world, that my fear of the oncoming shells was less than the shame I felt at my profession." (*Das Politische Theater*).

3. The irrelevance of Sheriff's story to the theme of war has been noted by George Jean Nathan:

"Nor can I persuade myself, with all the good will and respect in the world, to imagine a group of British soldiers, some of them already more than three years in the filth and fury of war, carefully refraining from even a trace of high profanity, conducting the bulk of their speech much after the punctilio of Pinero actors, treating the dugout in the light of a gentleman's club, disgustedly objecting to allusions to loose women, and condescending to masculinity in the rough only in desultory and somewhat abashed references to whiskey, cockroaches and French post-cards. Finally, may I add a bit of skepticism that men—whether English, American or what not—are generally in the habit of facing death, be they heroes or just ordinary soldiers, with such indifferent and carefree *prosits* as 'Cheerio' and 'Righto.'" (*Testament of a Critic*).

4. Gay's opera was a satire directed against the moralizing "tearful comedies" fashionable in his day. Its quality has been amusingly pictured by Dubech:

"It is a *ballad-opera*—dialogue interspersed with couplets set to well-known melodies, the most languorous songs accompanying the most risqué situations. . . . Gay satirizes his times in the style of Hogarth and Swift. . . . With an inexhaustible comic spirit he piles on his characters: bandits, thieves, receivers of stolen goods, wenches, jailers. This pretty crowd speaks with the lofty eloquence of sentimental heroes. *Macheath* and *Polly* sing a duet in the grand manner, three of four jades who have just delivered *Macheath* to the police bid each other adieu with deep curtsies. An irresistible comedy is born of these contradictions. The cynicism of the author is bitter and violent. . . . Gay wrote POLLY as a sequel to his OPERA. His second play was banned by the censor, but its success was tremendous, and all the ladies sang Polly's verses. However, after a temporary eclipse, tearful comedy resumed its sway."

5. As for example,

"Before scene one:

Title. THE LIFE OF THE REVOLUTIONIST PELAGEA VLASSOVA OF TVERSK.

Picture of the Mother.

Scene one:

Title. IN 1907 THE WORKERS OF THE CITY OF TVERSK LIVED UNDER CONDITIONS OF EXTREME HARDSHIP.

Picture of shopping list in large handwriting of an untutored person." (From Brecht: *Gesammelte Werke*, Vol. 2).

6. "During the rehearsals of TRIPLE-A PLOWED UNDER we had one night a rebellion of some of the actors who sent word by the stage man-

ager that they did not want to appear in this kind of performance. Philip Barber, director of New York, Morris Watson, Arthur Arent, Joe Losey and Gordon Graham, the directors, and I met with them after the rehearsal and listened to impassioned speeches explaining why this swift, pantomimic, factual document was not drama and why no New York audience would sit through it. They complained that there was no plot, no story, no chance to build up character, no public interest in the subject matter. 'Who in New York cares about the farmer, about wheat, about the price of bread and milk?'

". . . We argued that people today are interested in facts, as proved by the enormous increase in circulation of newspapers and news sheets and by the MARCH OF TIME (radio and motion picture dramatizations of the news of the day). We urged the actors to withhold judgment as to the effectiveness of the play until we added two powerful elements which were an intrinsic part of the plan, the music score and the light score. We ended with a mutual agreement: the actors were to give us all they had through the first performance; if the play failed we promised to drop all plans for future Living Newspapers. We then proceeded to screw our courage to the sticking point, and we had need of it, for the last days of the rehearsal were hectic. It was reported that an organization calling itself the World War Veterans threatened to close the show on the ground that it was unpatriotic. Rumor ran through the project that the curtain would never be allowed to rise, that the performers would be hauled off the stage and into patrol wagons. Opening night found the actors full of misgivings, the audience full of tension, and the lobby full of police.

"The danger point was a line by Earl Browder (secretary of the American Communist Party). . . . At this juncture an irate gentleman arose in the back of the house, and in stentorian tones started singing the *Star-Spangled Banner,* demanding that the audience join him. The police who had been warned by the Veteran's Association to be on guard against Communist activities evidently misunderstood the nature of the song and promptly ejected the gentleman. The play went on; not only on that night but through many succeeding months, not only in New York, but later in Chicago, San Francisco, Cleveland and Los Angeles." (Hallie Flanagan: *Introduction to Federal Theatre Plays*).

7. "Although it has occasional reference to the *Volksbühne* and the Blue Blouses, to Bragaglia and Meyerhold and Eisenstein, it is as American as Walt Disney, the MARCH OF TIME and the Congressional Record, to all of which institutions it is indebted." (Hallie Flanagan: *Federal Theatre Plays*).

"As a matter of fact, it was only about a year ago that I learned that there had ever been anything like a Living Newspaper before ours. . . . I find that the number of claimed birthplaces of this particular medium is exceeded only by the number of beds the Father of Our Country . . . is supposed to have slept in. These (birthplaces) range all the way from Soviet Russia, where the political form has been an institution for years, to Vassar College; from the Political Cabarets of the Left Bank cellar theatres to the al fresco Varieties put together by Chu Teh's propaganda divisions in Red China.

"These events certainly took place. Everybody says so. But, and here is the point, I never seem able to locate anybody who saw one. Nor have I ever seen the script of such a production. And so, while admitting the possibility of a whole avalanche of predecessors, I deny their influence. . . .

"What are the sources of this technique? As far as I know, there aren't any. At least if there are, we didn't know about them." (Arthur Arent: *The Technique of the Living Newspaper*).

It may be true that Mr. Arent never heard of any predecessor of the Living Newspaper at the time he began his work for it. It may also be true (but rather more peculiar) that he never encountered a single person who saw one of the productions—as for instance, the MARCH OF TIME—which preceded the Living Newspaper. Just the same, the technique in question did not spring into life full-grown from the forehead of Zeus.

8. "The struggle of Labor is a drama which is being played upon the stage of every industrial nation in the world! It is concerned with the lives and hopes of countless millions; it is the very stuff of which great drama is lived as well as acted. The growing use by Labor of the spoken drama to tell Labor's story is not new: it is the recovery of an ancient practice which dates back to Greek civilization and before. But the modern emphasis on its use in response to the widespread need to present Labor's story in action is most commendable." (From a report adopted by the American Federation of Labor Convention at Atlantic City, 1935).

9. See Chapter VII, Note 5.

10. "But it is the peculiarity of the epic poem to possess abundantly the power of extending its magnitude; for tragedy is not capable of imitating many actions that are performed at the same time, but that part only which is represented on the scene, and acted by the players. But in the epic, in consequence of its being a narration, many events may be introduced which have happened at the same time, which are properly connected with the subject, and from which the bulk of the poem is increased. Hence, this contributes to its magnificence, transports the hearer to different places, and adorns the poem with dissimilar episodes." (Aristotle: *The Causes and Progress of Poetry*).

11. Brecht's objections to the Aristotelian theory apply much more correctly to Gustav Freytag's revision of Aristotle. Freytag, the true ancestor of the modern "genteel" reviewer, tried to work out a theory of criticism which would banish from the stage anything that was topical or painful. He interpreted Aristotle anew, to make the point that

the object of drama is to impart *a feeling of security* as a release not through, but from, pity and terror. (See John Gassner: *Masters of the Drama*, p. 488).

The Greek tragic poets and Aristotle himself seemed well aware of the teaching function of drama. The Greek tragedies were not mere emotional symphonies in the style of William Saroyan; they developed a thesis and pointed a moral. The Athenians were accustomed to educate their sons by taking them to tragedies and comedies, which served as examples of virtue and vice. Although Aristotle's name is linked with the theory of catharsis, he also proposed the theory of *anagnorisis,* or "recognition," by which he meant a change *from ignorance to knowledge.* (See John Gassner: *Catharsis and the Theory of Enlightenment, One Act Play Magazine,* August, 1937.) Aristotle's views on didactic drama may be gathered from the following passage:

"For we are delighted on surveying very accurate images, the realities of which are painful to the view: such as the forms of the most contemptible animals, and dead bodies. The cause, however, of this is that learning is not only the delight to philosophers, but in like manner to other persons, though they partake of it in a small degree. For on this account, men are delighted in surveying images, because it happens that by surveying they learn and infer what each particular is." (Clark: *European Theories of the Drama*).

Just what Aristotle meant by his definitions continues to be a matter for discussion. Soviet scholars, for instance, consider that Attic tragedy was didactic. They look with some suspicion, however, on the lessons taught by the Greek theatre, even though they commend that theatre for its breadth of view. In their opinion neither Greek drama nor Aristotle could escape the "mental climate" of a slave State.

Aristotle, an owner of slaves, lauded the principles of a slaveholding society. He even described slaves as implements having human form. This was of course the ruling philosophy of his day. Soviet theorists contend that the same philosophy underlay the ancient Greek drama, just as "middle class liberalism" underlies the theatre of Broadway today.

If so, the ultimate moral of all the Attic tragedies was that it is useless to resist divine laws. Each man's fate, whether he be master or slave, is foreordained, and cannot be changed. (Such a philosophy was bound to be more congenial for masters than for slaves.) Slaves, incidentally, were permitted to attend the Attic plays—a privilege that might have been denied them if these plays ever depicted a rebellion as being successful.

According to the Soviet view, therefore, the type of emotional release achieved in the Greek tragedies was of a piece with the lesson taught by these tragedies: it swept all dangerous thoughts out of the mind, leaving the spectators content with what the gods had ordained.

12. This danger is also recognized by non-Epic theorists. Thus

Sheldon Cheney in *The Theatre* observes that "the French *pièce-bien-faite* is the perfect emotional tickler."

In a way the well-made play is simply too good to be true. Its inventors, Scribe and Sardou, were notoriously superficial playwrights; and the perfection of the well-made play is purchased, more often than not, at the expense of a thorough exposition of a complex subject.

This is not to deny that a play should be as well-constructed as possible for the sake of clarity. But the high tension of the average well-made Broadway play is sometimes no more than a device for keying up an emotion which is fundamentally extraneous to the theme of the play.

Tension was certainly not unknown to Shakespeare; but the dramatic suspense which he placed at the service of his themes was something different from the kind of synthetic frenzy which "puts across" too many plays today.

Edmund Fuller's *Epic Realism* (*One Act Play Magazine,* April, 1938) contains some of the typical objections to the Epic views on playwriting, including the belief that dramaturgy must be "emotional," not "logical." On the vexed point of the dramatist's emotions, George Jean Nathan writes, in *Materia Critica:*

"It is the mark of the first-rate playwright that his attitude toward his dramatic themes is, for all his affection and sympathy, platonic. Unlike the second-rate playwright who is ever passionately enamoured of and mentally seduced by his themes, this other remains mentally superior to those themes. . . . The notion, held by certain artists, that an artist can most convincingly record emotion when he himself is, from one romantic cause or another, afire with emotion is directly kin to the notion that a drunken man makes the best bartender."

13. Freud himself did not assert that there is a separate "unconscious mind" which is emotional in character as compared with the conscious, reasoning mind. He did not even argue that there is a more unconscious, more emotional half of the mind in contrast to the more conscious, more reasoning other half. His use of the term "unconscious mind" was distinctly by way of poetic illustration—a diagram to explain the mechanism of the psyche as a whole. The well-known imperfections of this mechanism have given rise to many conjectures about "dissociated" or "split" personalities, secondary and tertiary personalities, etc.

14. Thus, in showing the effect of the conveyor-system on workers in an automobile factory the method of psychological drama would be to build up a tense emotional relationship among certain workers, employers, etc., who are used to typify various aspects of the conveyor-system. The Epic writer would put into the foreground, not the psychology of these characters but the conveyor-system itself, of which human figures, in all their complexity, are only a part. This may seem more complicated than before. Actually it is simpler. It is more direct

and truthful to describe the conveyor-system bodily in this way than to describe it by indirection and in terms of psychology.

Psychological writing is not confined to the older school of playwrights. It is copied also by the newer dramatists, who disagree with the older men as to content, but accept the customary form without too much examination. Among progressive American dramatists Leopold Atlas in BUT FOR THE GRACE OF GOD (1937), Albert Bein in LET FREEDOM RING (1935), John Howard Lawson in MARCHING SONG (1936), Albert Maltz in BLACK PIT (1935), Clifford Odets in every play from AWAKE AND SING (1935) to NIGHT MUSIC (1940), John Wexley in THEY SHALL NOT DIE (1934)—in fact the whole younger movement in American playwriting—attempt to convince an audience, not with the clear description of a process and of the tactics of human beings involved in it, but with the machinery of psychological intensification. The buildup of emotion (as experienced by the characters) becomes the central aim, while the sociological process starts to drop out of sight, tending to become not much more than "atmosphere."

15. The difference between the utile and the picturesque setting was illustrated in the course of the Living Newspaper production of ONE-THIRD OF A NATION (1938). As designed by Howard Bay, a plot of grass, spread out on the stage like a small carpet, was used in order to demonstrate how rental values go up when land becomes crowded. This conventional scenic device was very effective dramatically. On the other hand the production also made use of a spectacular tenement-fire which was wholly illusory in technique. Although the fire excited the playgoers it demonstrated nothing. Instead of driving home the need for adequate housing (which was the theme of the production), it tended to give the audience a "catharsis," or emotional escape, from the dilemma set forth by the script.

16. See Chapter II, pp. 66–67.

17. "There may be noticed today, in this manner of stage construction, an extreme tendency towards simplification, which would prefer to dispense entirely with all the technical apparatus so expressive of the 19th century." (Joseph Gregor: *Weiner Szenische Kunst*).

18. Some of Piscator's requirements have been incorporated into a project, the *Totalbühne,* designed for him by Walter Gropius. It contains among other features an arena which revolves and may be used as a revolving stage; two other stages opposite the auditorium, a belt which turns around the auditorium, and walls on which moving pictures may be projected. On the whole a conservative project compared with the plans of Kiesler for an oval theatre and of Weininger for a spherical one!

19. See Chapter I, p. 21.

20. The expense of television broadcasting promises to be ruinous if the television companies continue to try Naturalistic or Symbolist

methods. Television will have to find a dramatic language which does not depend upon facsimile details or opulent stage pictures to be effective. Some variation of functionalism is the only path open to it, as it will discover after the usual waste of time and money.

21. See Chapter VI, p. 262.

22. Compare the structure of YELLOW JACK with that of Arnold Sundgaard's SPIROCHETE (1938), a Living Newspaper study of the problem of syphilis, produced at the Blackstone Theatre, Chicago, by the Federal Theatre.

23. The Microvivarium, invented by Dr. George Roemmert, casts on a screen images of living bacteria, millions of times enlarged.

24. A notable example of Epic technique in foreign films is the so-called "psychological attack" sequence of the Soviet film CHAPAYEV (Lenfilm, 1935). The White Guard troops are about to attack the Reds, who are entrenched and defending their positions with machine guns. The Reds are guerilla troops, untrained in formal fighting but highly dangerous on their own terms. The Whites, smartly uniformed and drilled, cannot be trained all over again for guerilla warfare. They make a curious attack, the officers smoking cigarettes, men advancing in parade formation, with flying colors as if for review. The Red machine guns turn loose and the paraders begin to fall like flies; but the advance continues as if nothing had happened. The lines of bayonets come ever closer; and in spite of the dead and wounded who are shot out of the ranks, the advancing troops give a terrifying semblance of beings not subject to death. Terror begins to seize the Red Partisans, and only a sudden awakening from the spell saves them. The episode is a striking example of the ability of a technical process to hold an audience spellbound, arousing thought and emotion at the same time.

25. See Chapter VI, Note 2.

REFERENCES

Erwin Piscator: *The Good Soldier Schweik.* Adapted from the translation by Eric Burroughs.

Erwin Piscator: *Das Politische Theater.* Adalbert Schultz, Berlin, 1929.

George Jean Nathan: *Testament of a Critic.* Alfred A. Knopf, New York, 1931.

Joseph Wood Krutch: *The American Drama Since 1918.* Random House.

Lucien Dubech: *Histoire générale illustrée du théâtre.* Librairie de France.

Bertolt Brecht: *Gesammelte Werke.* Malik-Verlag, London, 1938.

Richard Lockridge in the New York *Sun.* November 20, 1935.

Hallie Flanagan: *Introduction to Federal Theatre Plays.* Random House, New York, 1938.

Federal Theatre Plays. Random House, New York, 1938.

Arthur Arent: *The Technique of the Living Newspaper. Theatre Arts.* November, 1938.

Hallie Flanagan: *A Theatre Is Born. Theatre Arts.* November, 1931.

Ben Blake: *The Awakening of the American Theatre.* Tomorrow Publishers, New York, 1935.

Fannia M. Cohn: *Social Drama, a Technique for Workers' Education. Workers Education Bureau of America Quarterly.* October, 1935.

Archibald MacLeish: Foreword to *The Cradle Will Rock.* Random House, New York, 1938.

Thornton Wilder: *A Preface for Our Town.* New York *Times.* February 13, 1938.

Sir William Dampier: *A History of Science.* Macmillan, New York, 1936.

Alfred North Whitehead: *Science and the Modern World.* Macmillan.

Aristotle: *The Causes and Progress of Poetry.* From Clark: *European Theories of the Drama.* Appleton.

Goethe: *On Epic and Dramatic Poetry* (1797). From Clark: *Ibid.*

Gustav Freytag. From Clark: *Ibid.*

Sheldon Cheney: *The Theatre.* Tudor Publishing Company.

John Gassner: *Masters of the Drama.* Random House.

Eva Goldbeck: *Principles of "Educational Theatre." New Masses.* December 31, 1935.

P. Beaumont Wadsworth: *Piscator: Rebel. Theatre Guild Magazine.* June, 1930.

Joseph Gregor: *Wiener Szenische Kunst.* Wiener Drucke.

Harold Burris-Meyer: *Sound in the Theatre. Journal of the Acoustical Society of America.* January, 1940.

Julius Bab. From Dickinson: *The Theatre in a Changing Europe.* Henry Holt & Company.

John Mason Brown in the New York *Post.* April 5, 1937.

10

THEATRE IS REVELATION

THEATRE AND THOUGHT

THE modern era in theatre began fifty years ago when the Naturalistic form was established. In its own day Naturalism was a forward-looking, vigorous theatre. It did not hesitate to turn to life for confirmation of its beliefs; it did not fear to probe into any part of life, whether good or bad. But in time it ran down, became a technical habit rather than a method of dealing with reality. Decrepit, catch-penny, with a nose for petty facts which added up to nothing, it hung on to the letter of its credo long after it had lost the spirit of Naturalism. The time had come for a new stage form to replace it.

The new form arrived. Its adherents flung their banners to the breeze, inscribed with such words as "style," "beauty," "dreams," "poetry" and "inner truth." But the greatest, most stirring of these slogans was the one preferred by the artist Robert Edmond Jones—the word "revelation."

Why revelation? Because the new form must advance toward the task of revealing the deepest truths of existence. It must see deeply and clearly, it must soar far overhead, above the dull facts which blind us during our working hours. It must see beyond the disharmonies of prosaic life into the world of eternal values. The people of this new theatre renewed their trust in Dionysus, god of the drama, seeing in this faith an antidote to a stage practice that had grown utterly stale and unimaginative. Indeed they were now so skeptical of the older theatre's cautious, prosaic reasoning that they turned instead to intuition and pure feeling. Jones, for example, declared boldly, "Intuition is not inexact or vague. It is as exact and unerring as logic."

This was how a charter of freedom was established for the stage of our own day. The stage found a new vigor in moving, imaginative, colorful productions. The poetry of America began to reach the stage in images that were as moving as they were vivid. We looked confidently toward a future in which our theatre would prove as large, as heroic, as democratic, as the vision of a Whitman or of a Lincoln.

Then—something happened. Like the Naturalists before us, we saw the theatre lose greatness right under our eyes yet we could do nothing to stop that backward process. The very form which had liberated our theatre gave rise to a new kind of hokum. And all the old hokum began to return. What had become of the promised revelation? In 1931 one of our most seasoned critics, George Jean Nathan, exclaimed wrily, in his *Testament of a Critic,* "The hokum of long years' standing, whether dramatic or comic, has gone to the grave. The dawn of a new body of hokum that will galvanize our children and grandchildren is on its way."

It was not for a new body of hokum that our present-day American theatre people took arms against a decaying older theatre.

They did not devote themselves to building a theatre which would be nothing more than a place where, as Orson Welles once said, the public can come in out of the rain. They did not intend that their lyricism should become nothing more than a wrapper for stale clichés, superstitions, pseudo-scientific bunk, puerile glamor, cheap flag-waving, slipshod, mawkish thinking, or the condonement of all kinds of injustice. Least of all did they want to build a theatre which had no responsibility to its audiences. If they conceived of theatre as being "above the battle," it was not in order that the theatre might turn its back contemptuously on its audiences. On the contrary, they gave the theatre wings that it might be capable of the long view *for the sake of its audiences.*

What was the reason for the new, dismaying turn of affairs? The great reason, undoubtedly, was a rush of catastrophes outside the theatre—the bankruptcy of nations, unemployment, cleavages of thought, the rising tide of antagonisms which finally burst forth in a second World War. Our theatre had grown up in an interval of comparative peace. Under stress it began to show signs of weakness. On the stage itself this appeared as a falling away of

Pictures, Inc.

NÜRNBERG (1937). *Hitler: "Whoever wants to understand National Socialist Germany must know Wagner."*

constructive imagination, an impairment of clear vision. Constructive thought, soaring imagery, were replaced by hokum—the eternal bad thinking which is the darker side of theatre.

Dramatic thought never stands still. It is complex thought, with its constructive and civilized side always balancing its impulses toward frenzy and panic. When drama, temporarily, cannot deal with unaccustomed problems it reverts to more primitive methods of thought. We can see this contradiction in the earliest dramatic rituals, and we can see it in our own playhouses today.

TRIBAL FRENZY

There has been a tendency of late to describe primitive drama as a form of emotional release pure and simple. We are led to suppose that the archaic dramatic rites were a kind of emotional holiday for which such occasions as war, rain-making or hunting preparations furnished an excuse. The findings of anthropology do not support this view.

These rituals had an urgently practical meaning. They were intended to influence the outer world for the benefit of the tribe. The primitive dramatic ritual was a form capable of concentrating the will of the tribe upon important tasks: agriculture, hunting, fishing, war. Its costumes, settings and properties were taken from the natural world, which it mimicked. These first dramatic instruments were fashioned out of natural environment for the purpose of conquering that environment.

Because man in a savage or barbarous state did not have enough technology to control his environment, he used magic to make up what he lacked. It has taken us a very long time indeed to build up the amount of clear, logical thought which is at our service today (if we are permitted to use it). For primitive man so much clarity was not available. The American Indian of the southwest arid plains knew something about plowing and irrigation: he did not know how to build a Boulder Dam. When faced with a continuous drought which threatened his very existence, he could resort only to a specious device: the acting out of wish-fulfilment.

This activity employs logic of a sort—a fallacious "logic." Its practitioner believes in the power of sympathetic magic. If you want water for your crops, dress like a frog and make a noise like one; rain will surely come. Snakes ripple like water, therefore the Navajo Indians perform their rain dance with snakes.

The state of mind that accompanied these magic ceremonials was one of hysteria. More particularly, a crowd hysteria. The mere massing of the tribe created an electric tension, a mass emotion, which made any idea seem real just because a large number of people accepted it as real. Thus the Sioux Indians who performed a war dance whipped themselves up to the belief that they were practically invulnerable and certainly invincible.

Today we say: the purpose of these ceremonials was real, but their methods were fallacious. Their mode of influencing reality was certainly very crude. Most of us no longer share their type of thinking; we know that very different methods must be found to water the crops or to avoid casualties in war. The primitive view of the world seems to us insane—a form of paranoia. Man was the center of the universe, giving commands which nature was bound to obey. Belief was the result of mass hysteria, and the dramatic action, instead of following out a premise through its logical consequences, frequently drew conclusions that violated reason. These errors of judgment borrowed life, however, from the impact of emotion. And the emotion was produced by means of rituals of the most violent and brutal kind.

Recent dramatic theory has made much of the primitive origins of theatre. It has stressed the quality of orgiastic magic as a kind of sacred wellspring of the theatrical magic of today. Nevertheless we must use some discretion about this heritage which we have from the earliest days of theatre. Not all aspects of that form of drama were constructive. Indeed, the general record of primitive magic as given in the twelve volumes of Frazer's *Golden Bough* is overwhelmingly one of gloom and insane horror

It happens, in fact, that the blend of practical objective and sensual frenzy so typical of early theatre is nowhere better shown than in the archaic dramatic ritual of Greece, whose true character has almost been forgotten by recent writers on drama. The ritual of Dionysus, ancestor of the Attic theatre, was a ceremony of propitiation of the most important agricultural god of the Greeks; and the first site of the Attic drama was probably a threshing-floor. According to Frazer:

The god Dionysus or Bacchus is best known to us as the personification of the vine and of the exhilaration produced by the juice of the grape. His ecstatic worship, characterized by wild dances, thrilling music and tipsy excess, appears to have originated among the rude tribes of Thrace, who were notoriously addicted to drunkenness. Its mystic doctrines and extravagant rites were essentially foreign to the clear intelligence and sober temperament of the Greek race. . . . Like other gods of vegetation Dionysus was believed to have died a violent death, but to have been brought back to life again; and his sufferings, death and resurrection were enacted in his sacred rites. . . . Turning from the myth to the ritual, we find that the Cretans celebrated a biennial festival at which the passion of Dionysus was represented in every detail. All that he had done or suffered in his last moments was enacted before the eyes of his worshippers, who tore a live bull to pieces with their teeth and roamed the woods with frantic shouts. In front of them was carried a casket supposed to contain the sacred heart of Dionysus, and to the wild music of flutes and cymbals they mimicked the rattles by which the infant god had been lured to his doom. . . .

To save him from the wrath of Hera, his father Zeus changed the youthful Dionysus into a kid; and when the gods fled to Egypt to escape the fury of Tiphon, Dionysus was turned into a goat. Hence when his worshippers rent in pieces a live goat and devoured it raw, they must have believed that they were eating the body and blood of the god. The custom of tearing in pieces the bodies of animals and men and then devouring them raw has been practiced as a religious rite by savages in modern times. We need not therefore dismiss as a fable the testimony of antiquity to the observance of similar rites among the frenzied worshippers of Bacchus. . . . Meanwhile it remains to mention that in some places, instead of an animal, a human being was torn in pieces at the rites of Dionysus. This was the practice in Chios and Tenedos; and at Potniae in Boetia the tradition ran that it had formerly been the custom to sacrifice to the goat-smiting Dionysus a child, for whom a goat was afterwards substituted.

"The eternal theatre," writes Kenneth Macgowan, "was born beside altars." Such were the altars beside which it was born.

Let us have dramatic magic in the theatre by all means; but let us also be careful to define the meaning of dramatic magic in our own day. It is no longer our purpose to whip up audiences into a tribal frenzy. In the technique of primitive dance we can see starkly how the earliest drama mirrored the best as well as the most backward thought of its time. It has left us a wonderful heritage, to be sure, but not all of that heritage is unalloyed gold. We are not obliged to accept that part of it which is mere witch-doctor hysteria.

Is it too much to suggest, in the best interests of the stage and its audiences, that we perpetually take care lest we encourage the return of just such an orgiastic drama? The fact is that the belief in sympathetic magic has not vanished from the world. Science has a firm foothold in contemporary life, but it is far from being the undisputed standard of thought; and superstitions of all kinds are ready to claim us once again at the slightest opportunity.

PRIMITIVE THEATRE TODAY

There were glaring contradictions in the thought of primitive drama. Can we say that these contradictions have long since been removed? Is it fantastic to maintain that impulses of tribal frenzy can be found in the playhouses of our own day?

It happens to be true, however, that a kind of ruthless emotional excitement still exists and is still cultivated on our stages. Many qualified observers have been struck by its presence in modern theatres. It is so obvious, in fact, that it is usually taken as an essential part of theatregoing. Mrs. Anita Block is one of the few recent commentators who have felt that it is something which cannot simply be taken for granted, that it requires an explanation. She insists that it is caused by "those who have theatre to sell":

> Subjected to a barrage of the most tawdry ballyhoo, termed "publicity" by those who have theatre to sell, audiences in America are kept in a dither of excitement by the exploitation of the personal, the cheaply titillating and the sensational.

Archibald MacLeish places the blame on the "worldly audience," which he describes as a sort of collective "beast." This beast must be killed, he says; it must be replaced by men and women.

> The worldly audience is not human. It is not a collection of men and women sitting in their seats. It is something very different. It is a creature in its own dimensions. It answers to the definition of the Tory who said, "Your people, Sir, your people is a great beast." Your audience is a great beast. It is a beast sensual, cruel, and alert. It is a beast that waits in darkness as the spider waits, watching the stir within a little

shaft of light. It is a beast that hungers secretly as the panther hungers, stirring softly in the narrow room of its impatience. It is a beast that clamors greedily as monkeys clamor, barking voraciously from safety in the trees. It is a beast of one desire and that desire is *to feel.*

If you are courageous and sleep well you may turn softly when the lights are down in any Broadway theatre and see this monster. It is a monster of many faces which are all one face; of many bodies which are all one body. It is a monster with the faces of aging women, lewdness relaxing the corners of their loosened mouths, their collapsed breasts sighing "Make me feel." It is a monster with the bodies of tired men, their shoulders back against the pliant plush, their knees thrust forward for the thoughts to touch them. It is a monster with the eyes of the defeated young: the young girls cheated of the moment when the world should have been real; the young men cheated of themselves and impotent in everything but malice.

It is this monster, this audience both greedy and inert, both impotent and sensual, that must be killed. It must be killed because so long as it lives in the dark silence of its seats nothing true or noble can be shown upon the stage. It must be killed because it is greedy only for its own gratification and because, being greedy, it hates and will destroy what cannot be devoured. Most of all it hates and will destroy a work of art. For a work of art is not a prey it can devour. A work of art is not a morsel of indulgence to be sucked between the teeth. A work of art is a hard and tooth-breaking fact, by no nerves or blood-vessels to be metabolized into gratification and satiety. A work of art is a finality as actual as a man: more actual than most. A work of art is a finality with which a man can only make his peace: with which a man alone and never an audience can find a peace to make.

What is necessary therefore for the playwright who wishes to write truly and honestly and in form of art is to destroy this audience. Which means to destroy its quality of audience and change it back to men and women who will think and judge. What is necessary is to change the audience to men and women and compel these men and women to make terms with what they see. (Foreword to *The Cradle Will Rock*).

What MacLeish means by the necessity to "change the audience back to men and women" is clear enough. He evidently feels that an audience, as such, is inclined to let go its reasoning powers and to revert to tribal frenzy.

Now it is certainly true that the natural taste of great theatre and movie audiences have been undermined to some degree (though not permanently) by fatuous productions. As a result we have, all too often, the kind of playgoer whom Brecht has named "the modern primitive spectator." There is no lack of indolent or commercial-minded producers to give this sort of public "what the public wants."

But this state of affairs should be recognized for what it is—a vicious cycle. Whether a theatre audience reverts to tribal hysteria or other infantile forms of thought, depends upon the sort of appeal which the performance makes. An appeal to constructive thought will call out keen judgment; an appeal to thoughtlessness will evoke an unthinking behavior.

Surely we are not justified in the rather haughty belief that an audience is *necessarily* unthinking? Everyday experience shows that audiences are often wiser and more rational than their individual members—if they are not deliberately incited. Outside the theatre, any democratic American town meeting is a good example; and in the theatre itself, when superior plays are presented, the conduct of the audience as a rule needs no apology. Even in revolutionary times Stanislavsky found that rough peasants and soldiers followed the dramas of Chekhov with rapt attention. The widest possible American audiences—those of the movies—support good pictures, even though they can be made enthusiastic about pretentious shoddy.

In the long run it is not the public which is to blame for the survival of primitive frenzy in the theatre. There are others who are more directly responsible for the standards of theatre.

DOES THOUGHT BELONG ON THE MODERN STAGE?

"The stage," George Jean Nathan once wrote, "is not the place for consistent and resolute intelligence. The stage is the place, rather, for a deft and sagaciously deceptive simulacrum of intelligence." (*Materia Critica*).

This was penned as long ago as 1924. There are signs that its irony is lost on us today. We do not care as much as we used to whether there is room for "consistent and resolute intelligence" in the theatre.

A rather disturbing attitude seems to have crept into our theatre of late. It may be described as the belief that the stage is not really concerned with the truth or falsity, the greatness or pettiness, of any statement it chooses to make. All that really matters is the theatre's ability to "interest" its audiences. It is no longer our business to inquire whether a production reveals anything new or significant. The meaning of theatre consists, not in what it says, but how it says it. A play which manages to hypnotize its audiences, to make them weep over Hecuba (meaning that it impassions them over nothing), is now on a level with a play which has the clarity or imagination that comes of penetrating insight.

Our critics would deny that they have adopted any new standard. They would admit that, in their daily columns, the play of the century may get little more recognition than the play of the moment. They would argue that in the course of hurried daily reviewing there is no way to judge by lasting values. Yet we find that the weekly reviews, the monthly ones, and even books of criticism appearing at long intervals, differ little in their opinions from the day-by-day reviews.

Have our reviewers become so expert that their first verdicts are never changed by more considered thought? Would that it were so! But it seems more likely that the general level of criticism has dropped to that of day-by-day reviewing. The "I know what I like" attitude, friendly and genial as it usually is, does not tend to strengthen the more analytical side of the critic's work.

For example, conjectures about dramatic form tend to become abstract, with results that are sometimes surprising. In the course of some excellent statements on dramatic technique, John Mason Brown finally declares:

> Unless we comprehend the nature of the modern theatre's lies we can never fully appreciate the value of its truths. Its lies are constant reminders of the character of the medium in which its truths are advanced. . . .
>
> Playgoers, in other words, foregather in a mood of wilful self-deception. . . . When [dramatic production] is a virtuoso lie, told by playwrights or actors possessed of superlative powers of invention, one does not despise it, even if made conscious of its basic falsity. Instead one glories in the teller's skill as one does in the tall talk of a Paul Bunyan tale. The very audacity of its conception, the splendor of its means, the courage and magnificence of its exaggerations can be a source of pride as well as wonder, and joy as well as admiration.

At first glance, this way of putting the matter seems harmless enough. Yet is it not, at bottom, a peculiar, even unfortunate wording? Hitherto theatre has always been thought of as a true picture of life. Now we begin to look upon it as a *lie* which enables us to see the truth. Suppose the idea embodied in a production is basically false? Even then "one does not despise it." One continues to admire it just the same for its splendid, courageous and magnificent distortions, for its large-scale glibness in persuading us to accept falsehood in place of truth.

That is surely not what Brown intends. The tales of Paul Bunyan and similar inventions are not basically false, they are basically true. The Paul Bunyan yarns have a poetic form derived from homely lies spun by workers in American logging camps. These tales have life and power because they contain the true essence of the lumberjack's experience, given in a sort of homely exaggeration which is transparently honest. All this is very different from the pattern of so many contemporary plays which go through the motions of revealing something and yet wind up by distorting their material to fit some ancient cliché.

It is best not to confuse fantasies with falsehoods. The healthy theatres of every age have believed in fantasy, but only a sick theatre will accept lies as readily as truths. John Mason Brown is a very able critic, whose devotion to good drama cannot be questioned. He would undoubtedly fight against any theatre which he recognized as a lying theatre. Yet many of us seem to be moving imperceptibly into a position where we believe the theatre's way of saying something justifies anything it says, however trivial or distorted. What becomes of drama as revelation?

A theatre which fails to build up real integration begins to fall back on minor truths, half-truths and evasions. It appeals more and more to prejudice instead of to reason. Few of us may want that kind of theatre. But unless we are on our guard we are likely to have it just the same.

If our stage should lose its integrity the dramatic critics and instructors in drama will have their share of the blame along with the people of the stage itself. Not—let it be clearly understood—because these critics and teachers have no integrity of their own! This country is extremely fortunate in the calibre of its dramatic critics and instructors. Taken as a group they are men of broad sympathies, endowed with warm understanding and a sense of humor. But good intentions are not enough. In these times some-

Columbia

MR. SMITH GOES TO WASHINGTON (1939)

"Heir to the past so grand"

thing more analytical is needed than the vagueness of "I know what I like."

Theatre happens to be a public institution. Whoever makes use of it speaks from a lofty platform. Today, if ever, anyone who makes statements there would do well to ponder what his words mean to his countrymen. Audiences have the right to ask for mature imagination, careful thought, "consistent and resolute intelligence" in the theatre, all the more so when waves of hysteria assault them through the daily press and radio.

In controversial matters—and what is not controversial these days?—shall theatre feel it all the more necessary to make deep-going revelations? Or shall we decide that revelation as an ideal is a futile hope? That only a theatre of emotionalism makes sense any more?

"In the theatre," Arthur Hopkins once wrote, "I do not want the emotion that rises out of thought, but thought that rises out of emotion." Yet it was Hopkins himself who added that it is necessary to "abide by the conscious verdict, for, inevitably, all the unconscious reaction is wasted if the conscious ultimately rejects us." The emotional, abstract side of theatre has been fully appreciated and sufficiently extolled in our generation. Isn't it time to deal also with that side of theatre which is incisive and concrete?

PANEM ET CIRCENSES

One of the things that single out democratic theatre is the fact that it is still capable of revelation. Let us reflect that democracy can afford to reveal truths. Fascism cannot. The fascist ideal of theatre is the method of primitive emotional appeal. It is the method of turning away from concrete thought to abstract conjecture.

Is it only a coincidence that the Italian fascist "poet," Marinetti, who wrote that war is beautiful because of the stench of corpses,[1] should have lauded "pure abstraction" in the theatre? As early as 1915 he demanded in a manifesto:

> First the total abolition of the technique under the burden of which the "passatist" theatre is dying out. Second, to place upon the "boards" all the discoveries being made in the realms of the subconscious in ill-

defined forces, in pure abstractions, in pure cerebralism, pure fantasy. Third, the invasion of the auditorium and the spectators by the scenic action. Fourth, to fraternize warmly with the actors, who are among the only thinkers who flee every deforming cultural effort.

Fascism is very ready to talk in the theatre, to talk directly and energetically, but only in terms of "the subconscious, in ill-defined forces, in pure abstraction, in pure cerebralism, pure fantasy." It, too, treasures the artists of the theatre, the actors who (so it would like to believe) are among the few "thinkers" who run away from "deforming cultural effort."

Just what Marinetti means by all this has been more candidly explained by another dramatic luminary of our day. In the words of Adolf Hitler in *Mein Kampf:*

Propaganda is only another weapon, if a truly fearful one, in the hands of an expert. . . . The slighter its scientific ballast, and the more exclusively it considers the emotions of the masses, the more complete its success. . . . It must not objectively explore any truth that favors the other side.

Nobody knows better than Hitler how to sway the minds of an audience by means of a sensual appeal to prejudice. Uniforms, martial music, cheering and heiling, flags and searchlights, swastikas and slogans, passionate oratory filled with a barking, bellicose "idealism"—the Führer has learned how to make all these a substitute for rational thought.

In the beginning he was not so adept. He did not know, for instance, that mornings are not a good time for stealing away people's minds:

The same speech, the same speaker, the same subject have an entirely different effect at ten o'clock in the morning, at three o'clock in the afternoon or in the evening. I personally, when still a beginner, appointed meetings for the morning, and I remember especially one demonstration which we held as a protest "against the oppression of German territories" at the Münchner Kindl-Keller. . . . I arranged the meeting for a Sunday morning, at ten o'clock. The result was depressing, but at the same time extremely instructive: the hall filled, the impression truly overwhelming, but the atmosphere icy: nobody warmed up, and I personally as the speaker, deeply unhappy, felt that I was not able to establish any connection, not even the slightest contact with my listeners. . . . It seems that in the morning and even during the day men's will power revolts with the highest energy against an attempt at being forced under another's will and another's opinion. In the evening, however, they succumb more easily to the dominating force of a stronger will. For truly every such meeting presents a wrestling match between two opposed forces. The superior oratorical talent of a domineering apostolic nature will now succeed more easily in winning for the new will people who themselves have in turn experienced a weakening of their force of resistance in the most natural way, than people who still have full command of the energies of their minds and their will power. The same purpose serves also the artificially created and yet mysterious dusk of the Catholic churches, the burning candles, incense, censers, etc. (*Mein Kampf*).

The Führer's indebtedness to Richard Wagner dates from the time when, as a young man, he was carried away by a performance of LOHENGRIN given by a provincial troupe. Writes Hitler, "My youthful enthusiasm for the Baireuth master knew no bounds. Again and again I was drawn to his works. . . ." The operatic struttings, the heilings, even the *Deutschland erwache!* war-cry of the Third Reich, are among the properties inherited from Wagnerian theatrics. Those grandiose, if philistine, dreams had their appeal in tribal hysteria, not in the modern needs of civilized Germany. Their mood of lofty exhilaration is of the greatest service to Nazism, as Hitler himself has testified: "Whoever wants to understand National Socialist Germany must know Wagner." It is much easier to get a following with this heady impetus than on the basis of a clear-cut program which requires all sorts of commitments.

Let a doctrine be emotionally vague rather than clean-cut, and it can be reinterpreted and misinterpreted by every demagogue who has an axe to grind. The vague lyricism of Wagner has been appropriated to the uses of the new Germany. It is by no means certain that Richard Wagner—individualist, social reformer and author of *Art and Revolution*—would feel anything but torment at the Führer's homage. Yet it was Wagner's own descendants and in-laws who helped to turn the composer's abstract artistic work into a bulwark of Nazi policy. Madame Winifred Wagner has always maintained that Baireuth must be "a festival of pure art, away from the impression of day-to-day affairs." This exalted mood did not prevent her and her friends from welcoming Hitler to Baireuth as early as 1923. He was then an obscure agitator fulminating against the German republic; but the patrons of pure art hailed him as the coming savior of Germany. To this day Baireuth has remained a fortress of Hitlerism.

Assuredly the fascists know how to create mass delirium, how to make a lie stick (for a while) with emotional sweat. They have also learned how to give their theatrics a musicomedy modernism in properties, lighting and speeches that are as snappy as their uniforms. The lineage of their technique, however, dates far back, long before Wagner, to the *panem et circenses* of degenerate Imperial Rome, whose policy of "bread and circuses" helped to stupefy the world's first class of proletarians.[2]

When dramatic authorities speak of magic as the essence of drama, do they mean this sort of dementia? It is necessary to be careful how we define the word "magic" in the theatre. The kind of magic that can do without thought and requires only a feeling of certainty—is it not the essence, rather, of an ill, blind, socially destructive theatre?

This is an age of propaganda—propaganda for truth and propaganda for lies. When these two propagandas compete in the market place it is not easy for the average citizen to know which is which. But in the end the truth is distinguished from the lie, and for a simple reason. Life itself supports and fights for the truth, even under the most terrible adversity. "Truth crushed to earth will rise again." But a lie is a delicate thing, a fragile bloom which must be tended twenty-four hours a day. The circuses must not cease, the frenzy must not subside—or all is undone.

If we may paraphrase Hitler: the bigger the lie the more suddenly will the fabric of falsehood be rent to pieces. American democracy has a proper reply to the fascist philosophy about audiences. That reply was once formulated by Abraham Lincoln: "You can't fool all of the people all of the time."

When we understand how a socially destructive force makes deliberate use of hysteria in the theatre, we can understand also why healthy theatre is on guard against feelings which do not correspond to facts. We can understand why healthy theatre seems to be moving once more in the direction which Zola pointed out fifty years ago.

DRAMATIC AND SCIENTIFIC IMAGES

When Ibsen, Zola, Strindberg, Stanislavsky and the other great figures of the Naturalist theatre proposed to bring "life itself" to the stage, in what they conceived to be an objective, scientific spirit, they felt that they were making a new revelation of life on the stage. They were justified in that belief. The theatre of the Baroque-Romantic, which they replaced, no longer had any revelation to make; it has lost itself in meaningless routine.

With the disintegration of Naturalism, the power to reveal life passed to the Symbolists, who saw no particular gain in the methods of science. The very fact that the scientific ideal had been prized by the Naturalists seemed reason enough to consider it one of the mistakes which the theatre had outlived.

But in these dynamic times, theatre is again preparing for great changes. Need we overlook the value of objective thought or of anything else that may help to restore vigor to our theatre?

Surely theatre has no quarrel with objective thought, as such? Surely theatre can be opposed only to trivial or self-deceptive thought?

Objective thinking, at its best and keenest, is scientific. Why should the doors of the playhouse be closed in the face of science? May not an era of scientific thinking arrive in the theatre, as it has in many other important activities of mankind?

We need not all accept the belief of Zola or Brecht that the future of the stage *must* be scientific. At the same time we need not be equally dogmatic in asserting that there can be no place for scientific thought in the theatre.

Such an assertion flies in the face of stage history. The very first step away from primitive drama was in the direction of more extroverted, more logical thought.

What was it that made all the difference between the savage archaic rites of Dionysus and a performance of Aeschylus in the Attic theatre? The difference consisted in the fact that Aeschylus was not a frenzied savage running amuck to convince himself of a lie, but a thoughtful poet presenting a concept of nature and man, and presenting it with the greatest clarity, the keenest observation, of which he and his times were capable. Thought in the Greek theatre had become infinitely more incisive than in the archaic dance rituals. Above all it had become more capable of proceeding with unbiased logic. As Alfred North Whitehead has noted in *Science and the Modern World,*

> The pilgrim fathers of the scientific imagination as it exists today are the great tragedians of ancient Athens, Aeschylus, Sophocles, Euripides. Their vision of fate, remorseless and indifferent, urging a tragic incident to its inevitable issue, is the vision possessed by science. Fate in Greek tragedy becomes the order of nature in modern thought.

This, surely, is a creative relationship between science and the stage. Is there any reason why it should not continue?

It might be supposed that the advent of propaganda in the theatre has put an end to all hopes of an impartial, objective, open-minded technique of drama. But the fact is that the very development of the propagandist form opens the way to scientific advances in the theatre.

The moment that propagandist drama passes its initial stages, it must *of necessity* forsake its partisanship. Strange as this sounds, it is one of the historic lessons which the stage has learned in our day.

No theatre, perhaps, has had more experience with propaganda than the theatre of the Soviets. No other theatre, perhaps, has been more cocksure in its philosophy. Yet it is this very theatre which worries most about making its propaganda accord with objective reality. Just how successful it is in this aim remains an open question. Yet there seems little reason to doubt that the Soviet stage takes this aim quite seriously. It appears to realize that mere wishful thinking is unsafe. No one dares deceive himself, least of all in the world of today. It is said that Darwin, in writing his *Origin of Species,* was forever on the lookout for evidence that would *refute* the theory which had begun to take shape in his mind. So, too, there is the paradox that propaganda theatre, in order to win audiences, must cease to be a theatre of propaganda and become a theatre of *inquiry.*

If the Soviet theatre has understood this, it was the antifascist, Epic theatre of Germany which first brought that principle directly to the stage.

"Theatre is a tribunal," it declared. The stage, no less than any other public tribunal, must adhere to rules of evidence; the evidence must be sufficient and the verdict must be impartial. And the facts must be sifted not only by the playscript but by every other element of dramatic production, for all of these elements may add either to clarity or to confusion.

We may be grateful for this suggestion, even if we do not close our eyes to some of the many failings of the Epic method as hitherto practiced. We may condemn the pedanticism of Epic, its diffuseness, its glorification of undramatic dramaturgy, its over-suspicious attitude toward emotion on the stage. Yet there is something basically clean-cut and sound about the Epic technique which explains why it has found a counterpart in the Living Newspaper, whose idiom is as American as apple pie.

Americans, one of the most scientific people in the world, have a tendency to be moral rather than scientific in their judgments. Yet the morality of Americans is, in its own way, scientifically precise. We understand the meaning of fair play and a square deal; we know that in making moral judgments we must rise above prejudice of any kind. We are, after all, not so far removed from the sort of theatre which tries to do the same on a purely factual basis. From our own point of view we can even follow with understanding Brecht's plea for scientific method in the theatre:

> Until now the theatre has been a medium for the self-expression of the artist. . . . In contrast the work done by science has not been looked upon as the expression of individual talents. What matters in science is not the degree of individual talent, but the degree of general advance in the mastery of nature.
>
> Like the theatre, science works by constructing images of life. Scientific images seek to organize the factual world. Dramatic imagery has sought rather to construct an independent world of emotion—to organize subjective sensations. For this purpose neither accuracy nor responsibility are required.
>
> In recent decades, however, a new kind of theatre has developed—one which sets itself the goal of an accurate picture of the world. . . . The artist who belongs to this theatre no longer attempts to create *his own world*. . . . His purpose is to create images informative of the world rather than of himself.
>
> To create images capable of mastering objective fact is no simple task. The artist must refashion his whole method to suit a new purpose.
>
> The visionary ignores discoveries made by others; the desire for

experiment is not among the mental traits of the seer. Unlike the visionary and the seer, the artist in pursuit of a new goal finds no subliminal apparatus ready to serve him. The inner eye has never needed microscope or telescope. But the outer eye needs both.[3] (*Prospectus of the Diderot Society*).

While it is possible to show that Epic theatre is the predecessor of "learning plays" like the Living Newspaper or documentary films, there is no claim whatever that it is the ancestor of all the tendencies which, on stage or screen, approach life in a mood of factual inquiry. Epic looks upon itself as only one component of that new tendency in drama which moves to create "scientific images of the world."

Diverse as these new forms may be, they are united in their willingness to inquire into facts; and most of them are not afraid of an audience which comes armed with skepticism. They constitute a movement which is still below the surface of theatre and cinema today, but which is likely to come to the surface tomorrow. They see nothing incongruous about an art form which teaches its audiences. What experience is greater than a heightened awareness of life around us? What sensation is more thrilling than a wider and keener understanding of the outer world which surrounds us? Science has been a great revealing force outside the theatre. It is possible that in future it may play a part in the revelations which theatre will make.

It is true that some of the new technique of this kind—especially Living Newspaper and the documentaries, which deal directly with abstract facts—are still crude in their appeal. But theirs is the crudeness of a new style, not the primitivism of hysterical appeal. On the whole they have been received with remarkable enthusiasm by audiences used to a type of staging which is largely emotional and non-factual. There seems reason to believe that as factual technique grows more and more skillful and begins to combine its teaching qualities with the poetic qualities of older forms, its appeal to audiences will have the interest both of science and of art.

Perhaps there has been something artificial about the way in which art and science have been separated into watertight compartments up to now. In the case of drama, at any rate, it is impossible to exclude the influence of science.

Since earliest days the life of drama has been no different in its essentials from that of science. It has been motivated by the same needs, hampered by the same superstitions. It has been governed by the same laws. Today when drama proves something on the stage it does so with the most rigorous and beautiful logic. When science proves something in the laboratory, it acts out an absorbing and beautiful drama. Each has the power to reveal life in startling imagery.

It is reported that when Einstein formulated the theory of relativity the dramatic suspense under which he worked made him very ill. The famous science editor of the New York *Times,* William L. Laurence, is authority for the statement that such dramatic exhilaration is not at all unusual with men of science on the threshold of great scientific revelations; it is a state of mind which might almost be called typical. Whitehead has pictured as sheer drama the scene at the Royal Society in London when it was announced that photographs of the stars had substantiated the theory of relativity.

If, on the one hand, the dogged, fact-searching labor of science can rise to dramatic heights, on the other the passionate affirmations of drama can rise in the same way to the stark vision of science. Perhaps it is not enough to admit rather grudgingly that there is room for science in the theatre. At the moment we have a theatre which is, to its everlasting credit, attuned to a humanitarian ideal. How shall it keep all the values of idealism while carrying its ideals into reality? How shall it fill the measure of Walt Whitman's "genius of the modern, child of the real and ideal"? Science may be one of the answers.

ORDEAL

It may be that the theatre's revelation of life will in future be more and more scientific. Or perhaps the method of science will become only one part of the future technique of the theatre. We can be sure, in either case, that if it tries to reveal life accurately, usefully, with an imagination which is not dulled by self-interest, theatre will not find easy going.

Whether a new, adequate technique will have its opportunity to flower depends less on its own merits than on the danger of its suppression by forces outside the theatre. For whenever the forces of unreasoning hate and fear are let loose, the future of theatre is imperiled.

In the terrible struggle which rages over the world, propaganda has become a battle-front as important as any fought over with planes and tanks. The theatre is an advanced sector in that front. Ruthless efforts will be made to capture it, to force it to serve special interests. Theatre will be required to serve without thinking, and "consistent and resolute intelligence" may be more than ever at a discount. This regimentation of the theatre can come about with amazing swiftness.

In September 1937 there took place at Williamstown, Mass., before the Institute of Human Relations, a symposium on the social meaning of the American movies. Martin Quigley, publisher of the *Motion Picture Herald,* made the statement:

> There are those who damn the motion picture industry for an alleged lack of social consciousness, for failure to give pictorial expression to the great political, social and economic issues of the day.
>
> These critics deny or ignore the deliberately expressed policy of the entertainment film, which, simply stated, is to entertain.
>
> . . . Motion-picture executives do not envision themselves as teachers, statesmen, churchmen or economists. They are showmen; at least, they seek to be.

W. P. Montague, assignment editor of Paramount News, explained that even newsreels had to be treated as entertainment:

> The theatre managers who have to show our newsreels do not think their function is to educate. They go to great effort in their theatres to set up the desired atmosphere of romance, happiness, music and soft lights, and along comes a newsreel with the latest race riot, or something else that makes the audience hot.
>
> A disturbance may arise. Hissing may break out. Women feel they have to leave the theatre. And there goes the thousand-dollar effect that the manager has built up, destroyed by a newsreel.

These assurances that the movies cannot be anything but entertainment for entertainment's sake would be more convincing had not the movies already shown that they can, and do, turn into propaganda theatre at a moment's notice. The part played by the stage and screen in "selling" war propaganda in 1914–1918 is still fresh in the mind of the public. Less than three years following those statements by Mr. Quigley and Mr. Montague, some Hollywood producers, at least, were no longer worried about "making the audience hot."

Quite the reverse, in fact. A flood of new war propaganda pictures, crudely sensational, were being rushed to the screen. Writing in the New York *Times* of June 2, 1940, Bosley Crowther, the *Times* film critic, concluded apropos of Republic's WOMEN IN WAR:

> And so the hope is herewith expressed that the film-makers, for reasons other than purely economic ones, will steer fairly clear of war pictures, come whatever may, and that those which they do produce (as they inevitably will) may be reasonably free of wild sensationalism, hysteria and hateful fury. . . . We fear lest Hollywood, too, might get the notion that, by dressing its pictures in uniform, it can fool the public with some cheap theatrical tricks.

The vital and truthful theatre of the future will not betray its audiences. It will not trick its audiences into a sense of false security in the midst of catastrophic events by giving them "Olympian," art-for-art's sake productions when a useful and practical knowledge of the world is absolutely necessary. On the other hand it will not willingly become an instrument for recklessly stampeding public opinion without thought of consequences. It is easy enough to lead audiences into wishful thinking; but wishes are no substitute for careful judgment of reality. Problems of the gravest character lie before us. We shall not solve them by losing our heads en masse in a tribal frenzy.

Theatre is entering on a long struggle to maintain its integrity and freedom of thought, to hold on to its sacred duty of clarifying life. In the effort to remain clear in judgment, it will reach its greatest moral sensitivity, its most scientific accuracy, its most stirring imagination. It will rally around it devoted audiences who will share with it the most sublime of all experiences —that of learning truly from life.

Almost twenty years ago Kenneth Macgowan noted in the concluding chapter of his *Theatre of Tomorrow:*

> In the main I have tried to write of the coming theatre and its drama as if society were to go on with the same class divisions, class interests and class culture as exists today. My conclusions have rested on the implied basis of our leisure-class theatre. This seems something

less than sound, complete or safe. Revolution, economic or political, is either accomplished or imminent in much of Europe; and though it may be years before the bankruptcy of capitalism cuts across the imperial path of America, the upsetting of all our present aesthetic and moral values is something to be considered very seriously in any volume that tries to speak of the theatre of tomorrow. We cannot ignore the possibility that the whole aristocratic basis may be cut from under our present playhouse.

The storm is now upon us. The atmosphere of thought grows constricted; people throw away their minds and begin to shout the slogans of the market place. And what will happen to our theatre? Part of it, no doubt, will join the hue and cry, and cry louder than any. Another part will turn completely escapist. But the rest will go courageously through all that lies ahead. It will build the foundations of a future theatre worthy of the democratic American people.

NOTES

1. "*Guerra Bellissima.* War is beautiful when it fills the flowering meadow with the flaming orchids of grapeshot. . . . Then it makes a symphony of guns and cannon shots. . . . Songs of soldiers, odors of putrification." (From the *Gazetta del Popolo.* Quoted in *Ken,* April 7, 1938).

2. Even at the height of its power, Imperial Rome contained a large class of unemployed, known as the *proletarians.* The proletarians, who comprised at least half the population of the city, were a constant menace to the security of the ruling group. In order to prevent uprisings the poor were accorded free bread, augmented from time to time by State dinners on festive occasions. There was also a whole system of theatrical distraction. Triumphal processions took place after each imperial conquest, and showers of gold were thrown to the mob, making the "rabble" feel that it was part of the conquering military power of Rome. A huge circus of two hundred thousand seats, the Circus Maximus, was built, where wildly exciting and bloody spectacles could be presented on a grand scale.

Combats of gladiators (slave fighters), who attacked each other or were pitted against wild beasts, usually made up the program at the four great Roman circuses. It was also possible to turn some of the arenas into lakes with water from cisterns which had been built for that purpose. On the lakes small naval battles took place. These were not sham battles. Ships were burned and sunk and the crews (consisting of slaves) not infrequently drowned. Small wooden balls were flung to the audience during the performances. These balls were tokens which could be exchanged for clothing, roast meats and other gifts.

3. . . . "artificial instruments of cognition . . . extending a gigantic number of times the sphere of action of the natural organs of the body and the instruments of orientation. Micro-balances, the water-level, seismographs, the telephone, the telescope, the microscope, the ultra-microscope, the chronoscope, the Michelson grating, electrical thermometers, balometers, the photo-electrical element of Elster and Geitel, galvanoscopes and galvanometers, electrometers, the apparatus of Ehrenhaft and Millikan, etc., etc.,—all these immeasurably widen our natural sensual capacities, open new worlds, render possible the victorious advance of technique." (*Science at the Cross Roads*).

REFERENCES

George Jean Nathan: *Testament of a Critic.* Alfred A. Knopf, New York, 1931.

Sir George James Frazer: *The Golden Bough.* One volume edition. Macmillan, New York, 1922.

F. T. Marinetti: *The Futurist Synthetic Theatre* (1915).

Anita Block: *The Changing World of Plays and Theatre.* Little, Brown & Company.

Marc Blitzstein: *The Cradle Will Rock.* Random House, New York, 1938.

George Jean Nathan: *Materia Critica.* Alfred A. Knopf, New York, 1924.

John Mason Brown: *The Art of Playgoing.* W. W. Norton & Company.

Arthur Hopkins: *How's Your Second Act?* Samuel French.

Adolf Hitler: *Mein Kampf.* Reynal & Hitchcock, New York, 1940.

Otto D. Tolischus: *Wagner, Clue to Hitler.* New York *Times,* February 25, 1940.

Olin Downes: *On Misrepresenting Wagner.* New York *Times,* March 3, 1940.

Alfred North Whitehead: *Science and the Modern World.* Macmillan.

Bertolt Brecht: *Prospectus of the Diderot Society* (1937). Unpublished.

Science at the Crossroads. Gollancz, London, 1931.

Walt Whitman: *Song of the Redwood-Tree.* From *Leaves of Grass & Democratic Vistas.* J. M. Dent & Sons, New York, 1912.

Kenneth Macgowan: *The Theatre of Tomorrow.* Boni & Liveright.

GLOSSARY

A

Action: 1. the events, especially the physical events, in the course of a play; or one of such events. 2. the physical behavior of an actor in a play. 3. in the Stanislavsky system, the general pattern of behavior of a stage character, as related to the action of the whole play. See Chapter IV, p. 137.

Activism: the more realistic trend in the Expressionist movement. See Chapter VI, p. 251.

Adjustment: in the Stanislavsky system, the behavior of a stage character at specific moments, rather than his general behavior. See Chapter IV, p. 137.

Affective memory: in the Stanislavsky system, a recollection, emotionally colored, evoked in the actor.

Agitprop: 1. short for agitation-propaganda. 2. pertaining to mobile dramatic troupes which aim primarily at propagandizing their audiences. 3. pertaining to the plays or techniques used by such troupes.

Anagnorisis: the principle formulated by Aristotle, that drama is, among other things, a movement from what is unclear to what is clear. See Chapter IX, Note 11.

Apron: that part of the stage between the stage curtain, or the proscenium, and the audience. Also, *forestage.*

Architectonic: pertaining to the general field and principles of architecture.

Aristotelian unities: the principle, ascribed to Aristotle, that drama should have unity of place, of time (twenty-four hours) and of action.

Art Nouveau: in interior decoration, a period from about 1875 to 1900, associated with the names of Henri Van de Velde and Alfons Mucha. It seems to have been indebted to Japanese painting and to plant forms, and was characterized by a long, weakly curved line. Although it was a forerunner of present-day modernism, most examples of it strike the modern eye as crassly undeveloped.

Aside: a speech made to the audience by a stage character, as if thinking aloud. It is assumed that the speech is unnoticed by the other characters on stage.

Attic theatre: the theatre of ancient Athens and of Attica, its territory. About the fourth century B. C.

Automatism: the doctrine that works of art should be produced by artists without the use of any conscious thought. One of the basic principles of Surrealism. *Adj.* automatic.

B

Backdrop: a large taut curtain hanging in back of a stage setting. It usually has a sky or landscape painted on it, and is employed most often for exterior scenes. Its subsidiary use is to mask off the rear stage wall.

Barbizon school: a school of painters associated with the village of Barbizon, near Fontainebleau about 1850–1870. Its leaders were Corot, Rousseau, Millet, Daubigny. They painted peasant life, woods and fields in Naturalistic style with sincere sympathy rather than with virtuoso handling. Best known example of their work is "The Angelus," by Jean François Millet.

Baroque theatre: the later, more florid development of the theatre of the Renaissance, about 1600–1800. It was typically the court theatre of absolute monarchs like Louis XIV.

Batten: a long strip of lumber used for various purposes in handling scenery. In most theatres a series of battens hangs suspended from the gridiron, parallel with the proscenium. "Flown" scenery is attached to these battens.

Belascoism: the theatrical style of the American producer David Belasco. American Romantic Naturalism.

Bio-mechanics: a system of training for actors, invented by Vsevolod Meyerhold. Although the term sounds scientific, it appears to be unknown outside the theatre. Bio-mechanics is intended to teach an almost acrobatic control of the body as well as authority and precision in movement. See Chapter VIII, p. 345.

Blackout: the sudden putting-out of all stage lights.

Border: 1. a curtain or drop hung above the stage setting and parallel to the proscenium opening. It conceals the fly-loft and overhead rigging. 2. a line of stage lights hanging in the same position as a curtain border.

Boulevard dramatist: a French author of popular drama. The Boulevard du Crime was so called because, in the 19th century, it contained a row of the most popular Paris theatres.

Bugaku: one of the earliest forms of Japanese drama, about 850 A. D. It consisted of open-air pantomime dramas based on folklore, and used dance movements and, frequently, masks.

C

Camera angle: 1. in motion pictures, any angle from which the camera views a scene. 2. in stage usage, any view of the setting or actors which is not at a right angle to the line of vision of the audience, i. e. a setting may be considered to have a camera angle when its main lines are at an oblique angle to the proscenium opening.

Carpa: a mobile Mexican popular theatre on the order of the Italian Commedia dell' Arte.

Casting office: an agency which recommends actors to producing managers when a show is being cast.

Catharsis (κάθαρσις): According to Aristotle, the "purging" of the emotions of the playgoer. See Chapter IX, Note 11.

Chinoiserie: a form of Baroque or Rococo art using Chinese or Japanese themes.

Choral odes: in the Attic theatre, poems recited or sung by the chorus.

Cinematography: the art and science of motion picture photography.

Claque: those paid to applaud at a stage performance. *Chef de claque:* leader of the claque.

Classic: 1. a work of acknowledged excellence. 2. *Adj.* of ancient Greek or Roman origin. 3. *Adj.* based upon ancient Greek or Roman standards. Also, *neo-classic.*

Classicism: the principles of ancient Greek or Roman style.

Collective. N. a group of people working as a unit.

Color filter: 1. in stage lighting, any means, as colored glass or colored gelatine, used to change white light to colored light. 2. in monochrome motion pictures, a lens or other means used to eliminate any given color from the scene which is being photographed. 3. in polychrome motion pictures, a lens or other means used to isolate any given color so that the scene may be photographed and tinted in that color.

Comedians: the Italian Commedia dell' Arte, or its French counterpart.

Commedia dell' Arte: the popular theatre of the Italian Renaissance. It consisted generally of improvised farce-comedy staged by wandering players.

Commune: Following the defeat of the French Second Empire by the Prussians, the French National Assembly headed by Thiers (an interim government at Versailles, with a majority of monarchists), signed a humiliating peace with Bismarck. Paris, then a republican stronghold, rejected Thiers' order to surrender. Instead, on March 18, 1871, it set up a semi-socialist government known as the Commune. On the following May 29 the Paris militia, after desperate resistance, were overcome by the regular troops of Versailles. Thiers took a shocking revenge for the insurrection, executing thousands of working class men, women and children. *Adj.* Communard.

Company (*acting company*): a group of actors accustomed to performing together. Also, *troupe* (*acting troupe*).

Constructivism: 1. abstract sculpture based on structural principles. 2. non-representational stage settings composed of structural elements. See Chapter VIII, pp. 342–344.

Convention: 1. one of the two main theatrical styles. It emphasizes the presence of the stage platform, and the stage action is governed by more or less arbitrary rules, analogous to moves on a chessboard or to the rules of baseball. *Adj.* conventional. 2. an arbitrary rule observed in the staging or performance of a play, the rule being accepted by the audience as one of the conditions of the performance. The convention of the fourth wall, and the "aside," are examples.

Conventional: pertaining to stage conventions. See convention.

Conventional-illusory: a mixed dramatic style in which elements of illusion predominate.

Corral: yard or courtyard. In the 16th century plays in Spain were given in courtyards corresponding to the inn yards of Elizabethan England.

Cubism: in painting, a tendency supposed to have been derived from Cézanne and to have originated with Picasso. It is an attempt to analyze nature in terms of geometric forms, different facets sometimes being shown simultaneously.

Curtain raiser: a short play, when used to precede the performance of a longer play.

Cyclorama: a taut curtain hanging approximately in a semicircle at the rear of a stage setting. It is usually tinted a light blue color and is used to give the effect of sky or horizon. *Plaster cyclorama:* a wall, approaching a half-dome in shape, concave and coated with slightly roughened plaster, used in place of the ordinary canvas cyclorama. It gives a superior illusion of space or sky.

D

Dadaism: in art, a form associated with the work of Richard Hülsenbeck, Tristan Tzara, Hans Arp, Man Ray, Kandinsky, George Grosz and others, about 1916–1922. A forerunner of Surrealism, it made use of apparently nonsensical elements in order to mystify and annoy the more conservative art circles.

Decembrist: one who took part in the December 1825 revolt against Tsar Nicholas I of Russia. The Decembrist revolt was a "palace revolution," or uprising of the more progressive army officers and nobles. They wanted Russia to become industrialized and otherwise modern, and therefore demanded a constitutional government and other reforms. The attempt failed, five of its leaders were hanged and hundreds sent to Siberia.

Décor: stage settings, especially of the French and Russian decorative, "painty" type.

Dénouement: the outcome of the action of a play, following the climax and concluding the play.

Depth-stage: a stage whose settings and playing-areas are distinctly behind the proscenium, rather than one in which the forestage area is important. Most contemporary stages are depth-stages.

Deus ex machina (a god from the machine): a convention employed by the ancient Greek dramatists. A mechanical contrivance brought down a god from Olympus, who solved the problems presented by the dramatist.

Diagonal wall: the back wall of an interior stage setting, placed at an angle to the proscenium opening, rather than parallel with that opening.

Dialectics: in philosophy, a form of logical reasoning. An idea advanced as the truth (thesis) leads to another idea (antithesis) which is the negative of the first. Out of discussion a third, higher idea (synthesis) emerges. The synthesis in turn becomes the thesis, beginning another cycle.

Dialectic materialism: in philosophy, the application of dialectics to the concept of materialism. In contrast to idealism, it maintains that an objective, material universe exists apart from any ideas we may have about the universe. In contrast to simple materialism it maintains that the universe is subject to dialectic laws of change. Dialectic materialism is one of the theories advanced by Karl Marx. See *dialectics.*

Didactic drama: drama whose main object is to teach.

Diffusion disk: in motion pictures, an optical device for softening and diffusing the appearance of a scene or closeup.

Director: in American usage, one who is in charge of, and coordinates, the work of the actors, dramatist and technicians during the staging of a production. Also, *régisseur.*

Direct staging: a type of staging which is addressed to an alert and participating audience rather than to a passive and contemplative audience. It describes the psychology of most conventional staging.

Dissolve: in motion pictures, one of the means of transition from one scene to another, the second scene fading in simultaneously as the first fades out.

Documentary: N. a film which dramatizes a theme with the intent of providing information or education. It may use scenes taken from life (such as newsreels) or it may reconstruct such scenes with the aid of actors.

Dramatic metaphor: any poetic image on which a drama, action, rôle or setting may be based—considered apart from the more literal significance. (Thus the dramatic metaphor of ROMEO AND JULIET may be "springtime.") The dramatic metaphor is the most subjective element in dramatic characterization.

Dramatic pattern: the basic structure of a dramatic action, frequently identical in diverse plays. "Boy meets girl" is an example; so is "glamor versus menace," "love versus duty," etc.

Dramaturgy: the art of writing plays.

Dualism: in philosophy, the thesis that the universe is composed of two basic elements—matter and mind.

Dynamic: 1. energetic. 2. endowed with forceful, purposeful motion.

E

Eclectic: in art, marked by the use of already existing themes and methods, rather than by the creation of new ones. *N.* one who works in this way. *N.* eclecticism.

Economic determinism: the belief that economic motives are the most important determining factors in world history (though not necessarily in the history of individuals). One of the doctrines associated with the names of Karl Marx and Friedrich Engels.

Edit: in motion pictures, to cut and reassemble the sequences photographed by the camera men. This is in some ways the most important work done by the director. In the U.S., however, there is a growing tendency to put this work in the hands of a separate specialist.

Effect machine: 1. a stage apparatus used to imitate sounds such as wind, horses' hoofs, etc. 2. a light-projector, such as a stereopticon or magic lantern, used to project images of clouds, visions, etc.

Ekkyklema: See *exostra.*

Emotion: an aspect of consciousness having an intensity which in some way reflects or is associated with nervous or glandular alterations of the body in response to a stimulus. Leading authorities do not seem to agree on any more exact definition.

Emotionalism: over-susceptibility; excessive or unwarranted emotion.

Encyclopedist: one of the scholars who worked on the French Encyclopedia (1751–1765), which was of great importance in the establishment of democracy and of scientific enlightenment.

Entr'acte: 1. intermission. A wait, or period of audience relaxation, between acts. 2. a short performance of some kind given during this interval.

Epic theatre: a theatrical style in Germany between 1920–1932, as exemplified in the work of Bertolt Brecht and Erwin Piscator.

Estheticism: in philosophy, the consideration of the universe in terms of beauty.

Exostra: in the Attic theatre, a platform supposed to have been rolled or swung out of one of the doors of the *skene,* or scene building. It was used to display tableaus. Also, *ekkyklema.*

Exoticism: the charm of strange, far-off or foreign things or attributes.

Expressionism: an art movement, mainly in Germany before and after the first World War, characterized by violent subjective imagery. See Chapter VI, pp. 248–254.

Extroverted: See objective.

F

Fade out: in motion pictures, the gradual darkening and disappearance of a scene.

Filmic: pertaining to those principles or qualities which are unique to motion pictures.

Filmic time: time observance within a film story. Time in a film may be handled arbitrarily, in contrast with the passage of real time, over which we have no control. In a film it is possible to compress or expand any action beyond its normal span of time. For example: "Forty years pass" (actual timing, possibly five seconds). Stage time may also be handled arbitrarily but not with quite as much freedom. Example: "Mme. Butterfly waits all night" (actual timing, fourteen minutes).

Flash-back: in motion pictures, a sequence showing past events as if they were taking place once more in the mind of a film character; or a similar sequence arbitrarily inserted in order to recall a past episode to the audience.

Flat: one of the basic units in the building of stage settings. It consists of a rectangular wooden frame with canvas stretched over it. The canvas is painted to resemble sections of solid wall, etc.

Flies: the cubic area of the stage above the usual height of the settings. Close to the ceiling of the stage is the rigging loft, containing pulleys and ropes for "flying" (raising aloft) pieces of scenery which are not required on stage.

Flower path: the Japanese *hana-michi.* In the Japanese playhouses, a narrow acting platform running around the walls of the auditorium. See Chapter II, p. 55.

Fly gallery: a narrow balcony attached to one of the walls of the stage. It contains a pin-rail to which the ends of the batten ropes, or "lines," are brought. Flymen, operating from this gallery, raise or lower scenery by pulling on the lines.

Follow spot: a stage light kept trained on an actor as he moves around the stage.

Footlights: a row of lights at the front of the stage apron, to help illuminate the actors.

Forestage: See *apron.*

Formalism: 1. conventionalism. 2. Stylization. 3. in the Soviet theatre, any convention which tends to obscure or destroy the social significance of a production.

Fortuny lighting system: an indirect method of lighting the stage, named after its inventor, Mario Fortuny (1838–1874). The stage lights are thrown against colored silk bands, which color the lights and reflect them to the stage areas. The system appears to have some advantages over the ordinary one of projecting light directly through colored gelatine or glass mediums, but is not as practical.

Fourth wall: one of the descriptive terms applied to Naturalistic staging, which attempted to duplicate reality. When a Naturalistic interior is shown on the stage, it has a ceiling and three walls. The stage curtain corresponds to its fourth wall.

Frame: in motion pictures, a single exposure, one of the large number constituting a length of film. *Principle of the frame:* the theory, as advocated by Pudovkin, that the artistic composition of the individual frame is the very basis of the art of the cinema.

Freudism: the school of psychology founded by Sigmund Freud in the early 20th century. See *psychoanalysis.*

Frontispiece: the ornamented proscenium in English Restoration playhouses.

Front lights: all those stage lights whose beams are projected to the stage from positions in the auditorium.

Functionalism: in modern art, the belief that the artistic appearance of any object should conform to, and express, its function. An object should not merely have ornaments applied to it, or be disguised as something else. For example, in designing a racing-boat, functionalists will stress the slender, tapering lines which enable the boat to cut down the resistance of wind and water. *Adj.* functional.

Futurism: 1. in art, a broad movement aimed at departing from all past tradition and favoring new art forms derived from science and mass industry. 2. an art style with the same aim. It arose in Italy before the first World War, and was partly Dadaist in tendency.

G

Genre: a classification. *Adj.* in works of art, having as subject matter homely, low-class or everyday life.

Glory: in the Renaissance and Baroque theatres, a tableau of a god or gods descending on an elevator from the flies (in imitation of the Greek *deus ex machina*). The mechanism of the elevator was masked with painted clouds or sunbursts.

Gothic: in art, pertaining to Gothic culture during the Middle Ages, as exemplified in architecture by the pointed arch and foliated ornament; in literature by the legend of the Holy Grail, or the stories of Hamlet and Faust.

Grand Guignol: a Paris playhouse specializing, since 1897, in horror-melodrama.

Greek fate: predestination. One of the important items in the philosophy of the Greek tragic poets, whose dramas generally contained the moral that it is useless to struggle against fate.

Greenroom: a kind of backstage lounge or drawing room for actors and their friends.

Gridiron: a steel framework directly below the stage ceiling. From the gridiron, or "grid," hang the sets of ropes, or "lines," to which the stage battens are attached.

Groundcloth: a large piece of canvas or other material spread over the floor or acting area of a setting.

Ground plan: a diagram of a setting on the stage at the level of the stage floor.

Groundling: in the Elizabethan theatre, one of the less prosperous playgoers, who stood on the ground (the pit) in front of the stage during the performance.

H

Handicrafts: the productions of goods (as shoes, books), by individual craftsmen, working with hand tools, usually in their own homes, studios or shops.

Hanswurst Comedians: one of the German equivalents of the Italian Commedia dell' Arte. After Hans Wurst, a leading German farce character of the period.

Harlequinade: a pantomime in the style of the Commedia dell' Arte, so called after Harlequin, a character descended from the Italian farce character Arlecchino.

Hassidism: a revival of religious feeling among the Jews of the European ghettos beginning in the 18th century. It was fervid and mystic in character. See Chapter VII, p. 302.

Heavens: in the Elizabethan theatre, the wooden canopy over the outdoor stage.

Hegelian dialectics: in philosophy, a form of idealist dialectics proposed by Georg Hegel (1770–1831). Hegel applied dialectic logic to the concept of idealism, arriving at the conclusion that the universe is real only as a history of ideas. These ideas emanate from God and develop according to the dialectic laws ordained by Him. See *dialectics*.

Hellenic theatres: ancient Greek theatres of a period later than the Attic theatre.

Hellenist theatres: ancient theatres in the Greek tradition, especially those theatres of Africa and the Near East which followed that tradition.

Humanism: in pedagogy, the study of the pagan classic authors during the Italian Renaissance and afterwards; in contrast to Scholasticism, the study of Church authorities. Humanism claimed to take a more liberal view in education, devoting itself to human interests rather than to questions of religious dogma. *N.* Humanist.

I

Idealism: in philosophy, the belief either that there is no real world or that we can never know the real world; that we can know only our ideas about the world. Hence, that only ideas are real, and that life consists only of our ideas concerning it. *Adj.* idealistic.

Illusion: 1. one of the two main theatrical styles. It attempts to persuade an audience that the actions on stage have not been planned by theatre workers but are actually taking place in the natural world. It tries to make the audience feel that they are not in a theatre but have been transported to the scene of the events in the natural world. In contrast to the conventional style, which emphasizes the stage platform, illusion ignores the existence of the stage platform. *Adj.* illusory, illusionary. See Chapter I, pp. 26–27, Chapter II, p. 56. 2. a stage trick which deceives the senses of the audience.

Illusory-conventional: a mixed stage form in which the conventional elements predominate.

Impressionism: in painting, a general name for a number of related tendencies beginning about 1850 with Gustave Courbet and including Manet, Degas, Renoir, Seurat, Gauguin and Van Gogh. These painters, although distinctly individual, had a common tendency to rely upon a brilliant impression of the subject rather than a detailed, Naturalistic transcription. They also developed a full color-scale by means of the "cross-hatching" or juxtaposition of complementary colors.

Improvisation: 1. in acting, the playing of a role without rehearsal or dramatist's lines. 2. in the Stanislavsky system, the acting-out of scenes from the life of a stage character, in addition to the scenes written by the dramatist. The actor who plays the rôle imagines these scenes for himself and acts them out in order to clarify and enrich his conception of the rôle. See Chapter IV, p. 138.

Industrial revolution: the drastic change in manufacture caused by the introduction of machines operating in factory buildings under steam, electric or other power. This innovation made possible the production of goods on a mass scale at lower cost. In the early 19th century, especially in England, the new system of mass production began to replace the former system of handicraft production. See *handicrafts, mass production.*

Inner stage: in the Elizabethan theatre, the rearmost part of the stage, divided from the forestage by a curtain.

Interlude: in the Elizabethan theatre, a short farce sometimes played between the acts of longer plays.

Intermedio: in the Renaissance and Baroque theatres, and in the Commedia dell' Arte, a song or dance number between acts or scenes. Sometimes also *entr'acte* or *intermezzo.*

Introverted: See *subjective.*

Irising: in motion pictures, a transition from one scene to another made with the help of an iris shutter. On the screen the effect shows as a circular area which grows or diminishes in size.

Italian Comedy: the Commedia dell' Arte.

L

Light plot: the complete chart of stage lighting equipment, light cues and light changes used in a production.

Literalism: in art, the principle of making an exact replica of the subject. *Naturalism.*

Location: in motion pictures, an actual place used as background and environment for the actors, as compared with settings built on the studio grounds.

M

Machine for theatre: in scene design, the principle that a stage setting is a machine which functions during the period of a performance, serving the actors and the requirements of the script. In practice this idea leads to notable changes in scenic form. See Chapter VIII, pp. 351–353.

Mansion: in the medieval theatre, a stage setting usually resembling a building. These buildings represented palaces, castles, heaven, hell, etc. They were arranged in a circle, row or street, the dramatic action being carried from one mansion to another.

Masking: any scenery which serves to hide or screen off other parts of the stage from the view of the audience. Also, *masking piece.*

Masque: an allegorical dramatic entertainment popular in court society from the time of the Italian Renaissance until the 17th century in England. It included ballroom dancing, promenades and pageants.

Mass production: the production of goods (as shoes, books, railroad cars), in large numbers. See *industrial revolution.*

Mast: in the 19th century theatre, upright posts to which scenery flats were attached on stage. The masts slid along grooves in the stage floor, each mast being fixed to a chassis under the stage floor.

Materialism: in philosophy, the belief that the universe consists of matter and of the movement and modifications of matter. See *simple materialism, dialectic materialism.*

Mechanical materialism. See *simple materialism.*

Miracle play: in the Middle Ages, a play performed in liturgical drama.

Mise en scène: the completed work of the stage director, particularly as it shows in the groupings of the actors and their relation to the settings.

Montage: in motion pictures, the composition of a film by means of editing rather than by chronological order.

Morality play: in the late Middle Ages, a play such as EVERYMAN, dealing with vice and virtue, the characters being abstract examples of each, as Sin, Death, Joy, Friendship, Lust, etc.

Moyenageux: a coined word attributed to Théophile Gautier. It is an adjective derived from the French term *moyen âge,* or Middle Ages.

Multiple setting: a stage setting showing more than two places simultaneously. O'Neill's DESIRE UNDER THE ELMS requires a multiple setting showing several rooms in a farmhouse as well as the porch and front yard.

Musical comedy: light comedy set to music and containing dancing, singing and a chorus. The dramatic element is generally less important than the dance and song numbers.

Mystery play: in the later Middle Ages, the liturgical drama when performed by the laity. The word Mystery is derived in this case from the Latin word meaning servant or trade. The Mysteries were performed by the trade guilds.

Mysticism: in philosophy, the doctrine that true knowledge cannot be arrived at objectively, scientifically or logically, but must be felt through spiritual intuition.

N

Narrative: a story told in chronological rather than dramatic order.

Naturalism: in art, the principle of describing life in the form of vivid replica. In the theatre, this principle as exemplified in the work of Zola, Antoine, Brahm, Stanislavsky, etc.

Naturalist-Symbolist: the dramatic style dominant at present in the American theatre. A kind of simplified, attenuated and Romanticized Naturalism, combining elements of the Naturalistic and Symbolist styles.

Neo-classic: See *classic.*

Neo-conventional: modern conventional stage forms, such as Theatricalism. See *conventional.*

Neo-Gothic: in the tradition of Gothic art. Romantic. See Gothic, Romantic. See Chapter III, pp. 105–106.

Neo-Romanticism: art in the tradition of Romanticism, as Symbolism and Surrealism. See *Romanticism.*

New Stagecraft: a general term for certain stage forms which succeeded Naturalism. The term includes Symbolism, Neo-Romanticism, Expressionism, Theatricalism.

O

Objective: pertaining to a psychology or philosophy which is inclined to deal with the facts of outer reality rather than with inward thoughts or feelings. Extroverted.

Obscurantism: any form of mysticism whose effect is to hinder the advance of knowledge or learning.

Okribas (ὀκριβας): The Attic stage platform.

Opéra buffe: a form of light opera or musical comedy.

Optical printing: in motion pictures, a form of processing. The manipulation of film negatives by means of optical devices in order to obtain artistic or trick effects.

Oratorio: in church music, a composition in the form of opera but meant to be sung by a choir without acting, settings or costumes.

Orchestra: 1. the lower floor of a theatre auditorium. 2. a group of musicians playing mainly stringed instruments. 3. the Greek *orkestra.*

Orchestra rail: an ornamental railing separating the musicians' pit from the orchestra seats in a modern theatre.

Orkestra: in the ancient Greek theatre a level, circular area of ground at the foot of a hillside. The spectators chose seats on the hill, while the chorus performed in the *orkestra.*

P

Painted scenery: stage settings which rely for their effectiveness mainly upon painted drops, flats and set-pieces rather than upon three-dimensional constructions.

Pan: in motion pictures, short for panorama. The rotation of the camera horizontally. *v.* pan up: to enlarge the camera's field of vision by traveling from a near to a distant focus. *v.* pan down; to diminish the camera's field of vision by moving from a distant to a near focus.

Panorama: scenery painted on a long piece of canvas, held vertically, unrolled from a roller, or "drum" at one side of the stage and rolled upon a roller at the other side. It is generally used to give the effect of a moving panorama, as behind a train, boat or airplane setting.

Pantheism: 1. the worship of God as a universal spirit residing in each man and woman as well as in each object in nature. 2. a religious belief which accepts any and all gods.

Parallel: a support for stage platform, so made as to fold up when not in use.

Paranoia: a form of insanity characterized by chronic, systematized delusions such as delusions of grandeur.

Parquet: seats in the orchestra section, especially the rows which are not under the balcony.

Parterre: in the early French theatre, the pit or orchestra section.

Passion play: a dramatization of the martyrdom of Christ.

Periaktos: in the ancient Greek theatre, a scenic device consisting of a prism with three sides, each side painted to symbolize a different locale. The prism could be revolved to indicate changes of scene. *Pl. periaktoi.*

Permanent setting: 1. a setting which remains unchanged or unshifted during the whole action of a play. Also, *stationary setting.* 2. the term is sometimes applied to semi-permanent settings.

Perspective settings: in the Renaissance and Baroque theatres, settings mainly architectural in effect, painted according to the optical laws of diminution, foreshortening, and light and shade.

Pictorial: appealing to the eye.

Picture setting: a setting in which the emphasis is on pictorial quality. Together with the actors, this type of setting forms an animated picture framed by the proscenium. Examples are Romantic and Symbolist settings. Picture scenery tends to make use of stage depth rather than of the forestage.

Pièce-bien-faite: the well-made play.

Pit: 1. in English usage, the orchestra section of a theatre, especially the unreserved rear sections of the orchestra (stalls). 2. a space in front of the stage, sunk partly below the floor of the auditorium, and accommodating the musicians (orchestra pit).

Pitched floor: the floor of an auditorium, built on a slope upward and away from the stage.

Plastic stage: a stage whose settings seem sculpturally moulded and which emphasizes the values of light falling on the facets of construction. Also plastic setting. See Chapter V, pp. 190–191.

Platea: in the medieval theatre, the generalized playing area in front of the mansions. The mansions themselves represented definite locales.

Platform stage: a stage whose platform quality is emphasized in production, in contrast to a picture stage, where the emphasis is on the picture quality. Examples of platform stages are those of the Chinese and Japanese theatres, the Commedia dell' Arte, the stage of Shakespeare, etc.

Playing space: that part of the stage on which the actors perform, as distinct from the parts occupied by the setting. Also, *playing area.*

Playscript: a play in its written form, as prepared by the dramatist. Also, *script.*

Political theatre: a theatre devoted wholly or in part to productions dealing with current political questions. It is not necessarily a propaganda theatre.

Polytheism: the religious belief that the universe is ruled by numerous gods.

Portal: a formal, more or less permanent door or opening, architecturally related to the proscenium. It may occur in the proscenium thickness or in a second, temporary proscenium on the stage itself. Although unrelated to the setting, it may be used by the actors for their entrances and exits, if the style of the production is sufficiently conventional. Also, *portal door, portal opening.* 2. a second, or "false" proscenium, sometimes set up on the stage just back of the permanent proscenium of the theatre.

Post-Impressionism: in painting, a general term for a widely assorted number of tendencies beginning with Paul Cézanne and including Matisse, Braque, Picasso, Derain, Gleizes, Léger, Picabia, etc. It includes the separate currents of Fauvism, Cubism and Futurism. As compared with Impressionism it is further removed from nature, which it tends to explore in terms of geometrical or kinetic patterns.

Presentational staging: "presentational instead of representational." Any stage form which is anti-Naturalistic or against the idea of replica or facsimile. Neo-conventional. See also, *direct staging, representational staging.*

Primitive theatre: rudimentary theatre as known to savage tribes. It is remarkably similar all over the world and at different periods of history. Typically it consists of a ritual dance under religious auspices. The tribe surrounds, urges on or joins the performers, who wear animal, bird or ghost costumes and are often masked. The dancing, which usually imitates a specific animal or bird, is ecstatic, with a simple repeated rhythm generally tapped out on a drum.

Process: a series of natural or mechanical actions required for a stated result.

Processing: in motion pictures, the manipulation of film frames in the laboratory, either optically or chemically.

Producer: 1. the entrepreneur or owner of a play. 2. in English usage, the director or *régisseur.*

Projector: a stage lighting instrument used to project images or motion pictures on to a screen.

Prologue: 1. a special introductory scene at the beginning of a play. It may be only indirectly related to the main action or even entirely unrelated to it. 2. in earlier theatres, an introductory speech made by an actor before the beginning of the play.

Promptbook: the stage manager's or director's copy of the playscript, annotated with memoranda, cues, diagrams, cuts and additions, most of them entered during rehearsals. After the rehearsal period the stage manager's copy usually serves the stage manager or his assistant as a guide in prompting actors who forget lines or cues.

Prompter's box: the place occupied by the prompter. The duty of the prompter is to remind the actors of their lines or cues in case they forget. In European playhouses during performances the prompter sits at the very front of the apron, face to the stage, only his head above the stage floor; a low hood conceals him from the audience. The prompter's box is seldom met with in the modern American theatre.

Proscenium: the stage opening, often decorated and gilded. It is closed in by the curtain.

Proskenion: the façade of the *skenion,* or scene building, of the Attic theatre. It contained the entrance-doors of the stage characters.

Protagonist: the hero, or central figure, of a play.

Pseudo-classic: closely imitative of classic style. See classic, neo-classic.

Pseudo-Naturalistic: outwardly Naturalistic but usually Romantic in content. Examples are Belascoism and the average Hollywood film.

Psychoanalysis: a theory of psychology, especially of psychotherapy, associated with Freud. Its basic principle is the belief that suppressed desires are never eliminated but instead carry on their existence as fantasies in the depths of the mind, often causing mental disorders; and that such disorders may be relieved by a proper analysis of the mind of the patient.

Psychological Naturalism: Naturalism with a tendency to stress psychology in the stage characters and in the theme of the play. O'Neill's DIFF'RENT is an example.

Psychological theatre: any tendency in theatre which emphasizes the importance of the psychological factors.

Psychology: 1. the study of the functions of the mind. 2. mental behavior.

Q

Quantum theory: in physics, a theory advocated by Max Planck in 1901. It maintains that light is not radiated in continuous waves but consists of a succession of finite amounts, known as quanta.

R

Raked stage: a stage floor which slopes up from the apron or proscenium to the back wall. See Chapter VIII, pp. 349–350.

Ramp: in stage settings, a sloping platform.

Rationalism: in philosophy, the belief that truth can be attained only by logical reasoning, and that practical experience, although valuable, is not sufficient for that purpose.

Realism: defined in this book as the tendency to search out the principles and facts of outer reality. This tendency is considered apart from any stage form. An imaginative or even mystical form may also be realistic. See Chapter I, p. 26.

Regiebuch: a notebook used by the director while planning and rehearsing a production.

Régisseur: European term corresponding to the American term director.

Reinhardtism: the Symbolist-Theatricalist style, as exemplified in the methods of Max Reinhardt.

Relativity: a theory advanced by Albert Einstein in 1922. It maintains that the laws of physics are not absolute but must be considered relative to a changing universe.

Relief stage: a description applied to the stage of the Munich Artists' Theatre. In this theatre the actors played as much as possible on the forestage in front of a shallow setting. The effect was to bring out the actor "in relief" against the background. See Chapter VII, p. 289.

Replica: an exact copy, or duplicate.

Representational staging: any stage form having the ideal of reproducing or duplicating real life. *Naturalism.* See also, *illusion, presentational staging.*

Revolving platform: a stage floor capable of revolving on a central pivot. It is one of the methods of shifting scenery. Also, *turntable.*

Revue: a stage show containing music, dancing, a chorus and vaudeville features, with touches of topical satire and a plot that is generally unimportant.

Rococo: in art, the late period of the Baroque. An exceedingly ornate and fanciful style given to shell, scroll and rock motifs.

Roller: a heavy pole batten on which drops may be rolled or unrolled.

Romanticism: in art, a movement which originated in Germany in the 18th century and which stressed subjective emotional freedom. See Chapter III, pp. 106–107.

Romantic Naturalism: See *pseudo-Naturalistic.*

Rosse: crass. A term used to describe a rather coarse, melodramatic trend in Naturalistic drama. See Chapter IV, pp. 132–135. *N. rosserie.*

Runway: a narrow platform extending from the stage into an aisle of the auditorium, on the order of the Japanese flower path. See *flower path.*

S

Sardoudledom: a derisive term coined by George Bernard Shaw to describe the well-made play. After the French playwright Victorien Sardou (1831–1908), one of the originators of the well-made or tightly-knit play.

Scene dock: a place on, or next to, a stage, where scenery is kept when not in use.

Scenic imagery: the poetic metaphor on which the setting, or the pictorial side of the production as a whole, is based. Examples are: a locomotive visualized as an iron horse (CASEY JONES); a lighthouse visualized as a tower of light (THUNDER ROCK).

Scenic space: 1. the cubic volume of the stage area. 2. the same area, conceived as having a kind of architectural or emotional significance of its own—the dimensions of a stage world. See *depth stage.*

Scenic unit: one of the basic architectural forms used in the construction of stage settings—as the flat, the drop, the parallel, etc.

Screen: 1. a temporary partition, consisting often of light, folding flats. 2. a taut surface on which lantern slides or motion pictures can be flashed (projection screen).

Scrim drop: a drop made of scrim, or theatrical gauze, instead of canvas. It is used to produce hazy or misty effects. It is also used for magic effects, since it appears solid when lit from in front but is transparent when lit from in back.

"Searchlight" technique: the use of individual spotlights to pick out the actors in different areas of a comparatively unlit or underlit depth-stage. Examples are: the Berlin production of MASSE MENSCH; the Geddes HAMLET; the Orson Welles CAESAR.

Semi-permanent setting: a technical expedient for making quick shifts. Instead of designing entirely different settings for each locale of a many-scened play, the designer uses a single structure throughout, indicating changes of scene through minor changes in properties, lighting, drapery, etc. The use of the semi-permanent setting is widespread in the modern theatre. See Chapter VIII, p. 351. The designs for MEN IN WHITE (pp. 296–297) illustrate the use of the semi-permanent setting. Kenneth Macgowan's *The Theatre of Tomorrow* contains some excellent illustrations of this type of setting as used by Symbolist designers (pp. 43–45).

Sensory: pertaining to sensations or perceptions carried to the brain by the nerves.

Sensual: pertaining to the physical senses and their gratification.

Sequence: in motion pictures, the composition of a number of shots related to each other as a subdivision of the theme or action.

Set piece: a piece of two-dimensional painted scenery resting on the stage floor. It is usually irregular in outline and may represent a hedge, a low wall, etc.

Short: in motion pictures, a general term for a film on any subject when shorter than full length.

Shutter: in scene design, a sliding or swinging panel used to close an opening.

Sight line: a line of vision from any seat in the auditorium to the stage. It is the duty of the designer to make his stage settings valid for all seats in the auditorium. The director, also, must take care that all important actions, at least, are visible to every seat in the house.

Simple materialism: in philosophy, the belief that universal phenomena, including consciousness, can be fully explained on the basis of mechanical cause and effect. Also, *mechanical materialism.*

Sinking stage: a stage whose floor may be lowered mechanically to the basement. The stage floor is laid across the top of an elevator. Variations of this device are used for scene shifting in some of the larger European theatres.

Skene: in the Attic theatre, the "scene-building" behind the *orkestra* and opposite the seats of the amphitheatre. It was originally a one-story wooden structure used as a dressing room for the actors. Later, it is believed, it had two stories, with a long, narrow platform and entrance doors for the actors in front. Like the other architectural features of the ancient Greek theatre, the *skene* was eventually built of stone and ornamented.

Sky border: in the Baroque and Romantic theatres, one of a succession of borders used to mask the gridiron. Clouds were sometimes painted on these borders.

Sliding stage: See *truck.*

Socialist Realism: the Soviet ideal in stage technique. Its main principles are an orientation toward reality and a socialist philosophy. See Chapter VIII, pp. 336 ff., 358 ff.

Socialist Romanticism: recent Romantic tendencies in the Soviet theatre.

Social theatre: any form of theatre which takes an active interest in the sociological problems of its day.

Solipsism: in philosophy, the theory that the mind cannot grasp anything but its own thoughts or sensations; hence, that the universe exists only in one's own ego, or self. See *idealism*.

Soft focus lens: in motion pictures, a camera lens whose effect is to make scenes hazy in outline and misty in appearance. Most frequently used for Romantic closeups.

Spatial function: the function of extending through space. Dancers are said to function through space. The spatial functions of an old man may be said to be severely restricted in certain ways as compared with those of a young dancer. The particular way in which an environment occupies space may be called the spatial function of that environment. A plain extends horizontally; a cliff rises vertically. A corridor has a simple movement through space; a labyrinth has a very complex spatial movement.

Spartacist: pertaining to or a member of the Spartacist League, an association of communist war veterans in Germany, organized 1918.

Spine: in the Stanislavsky system, the dominant characterization used by an actor in portraying a stage character. See *action*.

Stage apparatus: any mechanical device used as an aid to stage production.

Stagecraft: the art and science of stage production.

Stage depth: the distance from the proscenium to the back wall of the stage.

Stage directions: instructions concerning actions, movements, sound effects, costumes or settings, as given in the playscript.

Stage manager: 1. one who is in charge of all technical activities and personnel routine on stage. During rehearsals he is the chief technical assistant of the director. After the play opens he remains on stage in charge of all performances. 2. in English usage, the *director*.

Stage space: the cubic volume of the stage area.

Stalls: in the British theatre, the cheaper, unreserved seats at the back of the orchestra; or the orchestra seats in general.

Stanislavsky system: a system of principles and practices formulated by Constantin Stanislavsky (1863–1938), for the training of actors. See Chapter IV, pp. 136–138.

Static: still, inert. Pertaining to things at rest, not in motion.

Stationary setting: See *permanent setting*.

Strolling players: a troupe of actors accustomed to setting up a temporary stage, giving performances and traveling further. Strolling players are an ancient institution and are still fairly common all over the world. The term does not apply to those companies, like American "barnstormers," who do not erect a stage of their own.

Student drama: dramatic productions by students at the universities. During the Middle Ages and early Renaissance such productions seem to have been common in Central Europe.

Sturm und Drang (Storm and Stress): in German literature, a period, about 1830, associated with the names of Herder, Goethe and Schiller. After the French revolution a period of "stormy and excessive" adjustment set in among German liberal writers; it culminated in the Romantic movement.

Style: in theatre, 1. a distinctive formula of stage production, including a specific philosophy accompanied by stated practices. Convention and illusion are the two dominant general styles in stage history. Subsidiary styles are the Baroque, Romantic, Naturalistic, etc. 2. the same in a lesser sense as applied to practices only.

Stylization: in theatre, neo-conventionalism, in a somewhat mannered treatment of individual stage productions. Characteristic of the work of Reinhardt and Tairov. See Chapter V, pp. 198 ff.

Subjective: pertaining to a psychology or philosophy which is inclined to view life in terms of inner thoughts, feelings or sensations. Introspective, introverted. *N.* subjectivism.

Surrealism: in art, a psychological approach with an emphasis on insanity, dreams and curiosities of thought. It began in Paris about 1923, and is exemplified in the work of Breton, Dali, Miro, Ernst, Giacometti, Arp, etc. See Chapter VI, pp. 255–261.

Symbolism: a theatrical style which originated in Paris at the Théâtre d'Art at the beginning of the 20th century, and which replaced Naturalism. It seeks to work with symbols of life rather than with "life itself," and is lyrical rather than prosaic. One of the main tendencies of the New Stagecraft. See *New Stagecraft.*

Symbolist-Theatricalist: any dramatic style or practice which combines elements of Symbolism and Theatricalism.

Synthesis: in staging, the principle advocated by Wagner, Craig, Appia and others that the art of the theatre is a separate and distinctive art made up of the harmoniously fused elements of acting, painting, lighting, music, dance, etc.

T

Tableau: in staging, a striking pictorial effect including both actors and setting. The actors usually "hold" the tableau for some moments without moving.

Tactics: in Epic acting, deliberate, planned procedure on the part of the stage character. See Chapter IX, pp. 414–418.

Technique: 1. the established procedure in the execution of any art. 2. the details of such procedure.

Technology: 1. the science of procedures involved in manufacture. 2. the same, with stress on the idea of perfecting inventions by means of continued study.

Theatricalism: a modern neo-conventional stage form based on the principle that "theatre is theatre, not life." See Chapter VII, pp. 283–285. See also *neo-conventionalism.*

Theatrics: the aggregate of stage practices, methods, instruments, etc.

Theatron (*θέατρον*): theatre, a place for seeing. Greek root of the word "theatre."

Theme: in dramaturgy, the topic of a play, as distinct from plot, action, thesis or viewpoint. A play may have the theme of war, marriage, old age, jealousy, childhood, birth, horse-racing, etc. *Adj.* thematic.

Trade guild: an association of master-craftsmen, such as mercers, butchers, weavers, etc.—characteristic of the Middle Ages.

Trap: removable section of the stage floor, giving access to the basement, for use in special circumstances of acting, setting or scene shifting.

Treadmill: a contrivance like an endless belt, sometimes employed on stage. It can carry scenery or actors across the stage, and is also useful for effects of marching troops, galloping horses, etc., since troops can march steadily or horses gallop wildly while remaining in the center of the stage.

Troupe (*acting troupe*): See *company* (*acting company*).

Truck: platform on casters or wheels. A device for shifting scenery. Scenery erected on a truck can be pushed on or off stage quickly and set up or dismantled at greater leisure. Also, *sliding stage, wagon stage.*

Turntable: See *revolving stage.*

Tyring-house: in the Elizabethan theatre, the dressing rooms backstage.

U

Ultra-realism: a term usually applied to Naturalism when excessively given to the doctrine of replica or facsimile.

Ultra-Symbolism: in the Symbolist stage form, the tendency to stress symbolic, mystic, or obscurantist ideas. Examples are Dadaism, Expressionism, Surrealism.

Unified lighting: the lighting of a stage setting in a well-composed manner.

V

Vehicle: a play which provides a good opportunity for showing the individual talent of an actor or actress.

Vorticism: in art, a variation of Expressionism.

W

Wagon stage: 1. in the medieval theatre, a variation of the mansion stage. (See *mansion*). Separate mansions or booths were built on wagons, which were drawn through the town, performing one scene after another in designated streets. 2. in the modern theatre, a method of scene shifting by means of trucks. See *truck.*

Well-made play: any play noteworthy for its technical skill in dramatic construction, expert machinery of plot, etc.—apart from its merit as art. See Chapter I, pp. 25–26. Also, *well-knit play, tightly-knit play.*

Work light: a single open lamp used on stage during rehearsals or when the stage is not in use. Also, *working light.*

X

X-rays (*X-ray border*): a line of stage lights usually hung just behind the proscenium opening, consisting of bulbs in polished metal receptacles, with colored mediums in front. The X-rays create an indefinite, diffused light suited to the demands of the central acting area

Z

Zionism: a movement having the aim of perpetuating Jewish culture and of re-establishing the Jews as an independent nation in Palestine. Founders of modern Zionism were Leo Pinsker (1821–1891) and Theodor Herzl (1860–1904).

BIBLIOGRAPHY

This bibliography is an introduction to writings on theatre as distinct from writings on drama (although many necessary books and articles on drama are included). It has seemed advisable to add some titles dealing with more general trends in art and literature.

While the list is by no means complete, the author considers it representative and ample enough to serve in encouraging more detailed studies of stage and screen form. For those interested in the almost untouched problems of science (including psychology) in the theatre, a few books on psychology and general science are included by way of suggestion.

Books cited in the text will also be found listed at the end of each chapter.

PRIMITIVE

Boas, Franz: *The Mind of Primitive Man.* Macmillan, New York, 1938.

Brown, Ivor: *First Player: The Origin of Drama.* William Morrow & Co., New York, 1928.

Catlin, G.: *North American Indians.* J. Grant, Edinburgh, 1926.

Covarrubias, Miguel: *The Theatre in Bali. Theatre Arts,* August, 1936.

Dengler, Hermann: *American Indians.* Albert and Charles Boni, New York, 1923.

Dramatic Arts of the American Indian. Theatre Arts, August, 1933.

Engels, Friedrich: *The Origin of the Family.* C. H. Kerr & Co., Chicago, 1902.

Frazer, Sir James George: *Aftermath.* Macmillan, London, 1936.

Frazer, Sir James George: *The Golden Bough.* One-volume edition. Macmillan, New York, 1922.

Frazer, Sir James George: *The Golden Bough.* 12 volumes. Macmillan, London, 1911–1926.

Freuchen, Peter: *Arctic Adventure.* Farrar & Rinehart, New York, 1935.

Frobenius, Leo and Fox, Douglas C.: *Prehistoric Rock Pictures in Europe and Africa.* Museum of Modern Art, New York, 1937.

Goris, R. and Spies, Walther: *The Island of Bali; Its Religion and Ceremonies.* Royal Packet Navigation Co., Batavia, 1931(?).

Gregor, Joseph: *Masks of the World.* B. T. Batsford, Ltd., London, 1936–1937.

Havemeyer, Loomis: *The Drama of Savage Peoples.* Yale University Press, New Haven, 1916.

Macgowan, Kenneth and Rosse, Hermann: *Masks and Demons.* Harcourt, Brace & Co., New York, 1923.

McKenney, Thomas L. and Hall, James: *The Indian Tribes of North America.* 3 volumes. J. Grant, Edinburgh, 1933–1934.

Montenegro, Roberto: *Mascaras Mexicanas.* De la Secretaria de Educacion, Mexico, 1926.

Osborn, Henry Fairfield: *Men of the Old Stone Age.* Charles Scribner's Sons, New York, 1919.

Ridgeway, William: *The Dramas and Dramatic Dances of Non-European Races.* Cambridge University Press, 1915.

Sweeney, James Johnson (editor): *African Negro Art.* Museum of Modern Art, New York, 1935.

Wissler, Clark: *Lore of the Demon Mask. Natural History,* July–August, 1928.

ORIENTAL

Arlington, L. C.: *The Chinese Drama.* Kelly & Walsh, Shanghai, 1930.

Bénazet, Alexandre: *Le théâtre au Japon.* E. Leroux, Paris, 1901.

Brinkley, F. (editor): *Japan.* 12 volumes. J. B. Millet Co., Boston, 1897–1901.

Buss, Kate: *Studies in the Chinese Drama.* Cape & Smith, New York, 1922.

Edwards, O.: *Japanese Plays and Playfellows.* William Heinemann, London, 1901.

Eisenstein, Sergei: *The Enchanter from the Pear Garden. Theatre Arts,* October, 1935.

Glaser, Curt: *Japanisches Theater.* Würfel Verlag, Berlin-Lankwitz, 1930.

Hasewaga, T. (editor): *Scènes du théâtre Japonais.* Tokio, 1900.

Hincks, Marcelle A.: *The Japanese Dance.* W. Heinemann, London, 1910.

Japanese Drama. Tourist Library No. 6. Board of Tourist Industry, Japanese Government Railway, 1935.

Kahle, P. E.: *Zur Geschichte des arabischen Schattentheaters in Egypten.* R. Haupt, Leipzig, 1909.

Kawatake, Shigetoshi: *Development of the Japanese Theatre Art.* Kokusai Bunka Shinkokai, Tokyo, 1935.

Keith, A. Berriedale: *The Sanskrit Drama.* Oxford University Press, New York, 1924.

Kincaid, Zoë: *Kabuki, the Popular Stage of Japan.* Macmillan, New York, 1925.

Kurth, Julius: *Sharaku.* R. Piper & Co., Munich, 1922.

Laufer, Berthold: *Oriental Theatricals. Field Museum of Natural History Guide.* Part 1. Chicago, 1923.

Levi, Sylvain: *Le Théâtre indien.* E. Bouillon, Paris, 1890.

Lombard, Frank Alanson: *An Outline History of the Japanese Drama.* Houghton, Mifflin Co., Boston, 1929.

Lozowick, Louis: *The Theatre of Turkestan. Theatre Arts,* November, 1933.

Martinovitch, Nicholas N.: *The Turkish Theatre.* Theatre Arts, Inc., New York, 1933.

Maybon, A.: *Le Théâtre japonais.* Laurens, Paris, 1925.

Miyamori, A.: *Masterpieces of Chikamatsu.* Kegan Paul, Trench, Trubner & Co., London, 1926.

Nogami, Prof. T.: *Japanese Noh Plays.* Tourist Library No. 2. Board of Tourist Industry, Japanese Government Railways, 1935.

Perzynski, Friedrich: *Japanische Masken, Nō Und Kyōgen.* 2 volumes. Walter de Gruyter & Co., Berlin, 1925.

Piper, Marie: *Das Japanische Theater: ein Spiegel des Volkes.* Societäts-Verlag, Frankfort-am-Main, 1937.

Piper, Marie: *Die Schaukunst der Japaner.* Walter de Gruyter & Co., Berlin, 1927.

Poupeye, Camille: *Le théâtre chinois.* Édition "Labor," Paris-Brussels, 1933.

Priest, Alan: *Japanese Costume.* Metropolitan Museum of Art, New York, 1935.

Ritter, Hellmut: *Türkische Schattenspiele: Karagos.* Orient Buchhandlung, Hanover, 1924.

Sadler, A. L.: *Japanese Plays.* Angus & Robertson Ltd., Sydney, 1934.

Seiroku Noma: *Old Japanese Masks.* Jurakusha, Tokyo, 1935.

Tcheng-Ki-Tong: *Le théâtre des Chinois.* Calmann Lévy, Éditeur, Paris, 1886.

Tchou-Kia-Kien: *Le théâtre chinois.* Brunoff, Paris, 1922.

Tresmin-Trémolières: *La Cité d'amour au Japon.* Librairie Universelle, Paris, (no date).

Waley, Arthur: *The Nō Plays of Japan.* Alfred A. Knopf, New York, 1922.

Yacovleff, A. and Tchou-Kia-Kieu: *The Chinese Theatre.* Stokes, New York, 1922.

Zucker, Adolf Eduard: *The Chinese Theatre.* Little, Brown & Co., Boston, 1925.

Zung, Cecilia S. L.: *The Secrets of the Chinese Drama.* Kelly & Walsh, Ltd., Hong Kong, 1937.

CLASSIC

Allen, James Turney: *Stage Antiquities of the Greeks and Romans and Their Influence.* Longmans, Green & Co., New York, 1927.

Aristophanes: *The Eleven Comedies.* Horace Liveright, New York, 1930.

Bieber, Margarete: *Die Denkmäler zum Theaterwesen im Altertum.* Vereinigung Wissenschaftlicher Verläge, Berlin and Leipzig, 1920.

Bieber, Margarete: *History of the Greek and Roman Theatre.* Princeton University Press, 1939.

Bodensteiner, Ernst: *Szenische Fragen im griechischen Drama.* B. G. Teubner, Leipzig, 1893.

Böttiger, Carl August: *Les Furies.* A. Delalain, Paris, 1802.

Butcher, S. H.: *Aristotle's Theory of Poetry and Fine Art.* Macmillan, New York, 1907.

Capps, E.: *Vitruvius and the Greek Stage.* University of Chicago Press, 1893.

Cornford, F. M.: *The Origin of Attic Comedy.* E. Arnold, London, 1914.

Dorpfeld, W. and Reisch, E.: *Das grieschische Theater.* Barth & Von Hirst, Athens, 1896.

Duff, J. Wright: *A Literary History of Rome.* E. Benn, Ltd., London, 1928.

Emmanuel, M.: *The Antique Greek Dance.* J. Lane Co., New York, 1916.

Fiechter, E. R.: *Die baugeschichtliche Entwicklung des antiken Theaters.* O. Beck, Munich, 1914.

Flickinger, R. C.: *The Greek Theatre and Its Drama.* University of Chicago Press, 1926.

Frickenhaus, August Heinrich: *Die altgriechische Bühne.* K. J. Trubner, Strassburg, 1917.

Gardner, Ernest Arthur: *Excavations at Megalopolis. Athenaeum,* Vol. 90, I: 507–711. *American Architect,* 29:7.

Grysar, C. J.: *Der Römische Mimus.* Wiener Akademie der Wissenschaften, December, 1854.

Grysar, C. J.: *Über die Pantomimen der Römer.* Rheinisches Museum für Philologie, February, 1934.

Gsell, Stéphane: *Les Monuments antiques de l'Algérie.* A. Fontemoing, Paris, 1901.

Haigh, A. E.: *The Attic Theater.* Clarendon Press, Oxford, 1907.

Haigh, A. E.: *The Tragic Drama of the Greeks.* Clarendon Press, Oxford, 1925.

Harrison, Jane Ellen: *Ancient Art and Ritual.* Henry Holt & Co., New York, 1913.

Harrison, Jane Ellen: *Themis.* Cambridge University Press, 1912.

Hense, Otto: *Die Modificirung der Maske in der griechischen Tragödie.* G. Ragoczy, Freiburg, 1905.

Körting, Gustav Carl Otto: *Geschichte des griechischen und römischen Theaters.* F. Schöningh, Paderborn, 1897.

Lord, Louis E.: *Aristophanes.* Longmans, Green & Co., New York, 1925.

Mahr, August C.: *The Origin of the Greek Tragic Form.* Prentice-Hall, New York, 1938.

Murray, Gilbert: *Euripides and His Age.* Henry Holt & Co., New York, 1913.

Murray, Gilbert: *The Plays of Euripides.* Longmans, Green & Co., New York, 1906.

Navarre, Octave: *Le Théâtre grec.* Payot, Paris, 1925.

Nietzsche, Friedrich: *Ecce Homo: The Birth of Tragedy.* Modern Library, New York, 1937.

Oates, Whitney J. and O'Neill, Eugene, Jr.: *The Complete Greek Drama.* 2 volumes. Random House, New York, 1939.

Opitz, R.: *Schauspiel und Theaterwesen der Griechen und Römer.* Richter, Leipzig, 1889.

Owen, A. S.: *Aristotle on the Art of Poetry.* Clarendon Press, Oxford, 1931.

Petersen, E.: *Die attische Tragödie als Bild-und Bühnen-Kunst.* F. Cohen, Bonn, 1915.

Pickard-Cambridge, A. W.: *Dithyramb, Tragedy and Comedy.* Clarendon Press, Oxford, 1927.

Puchstein, Otto: *Die griechische Bühne.* Weidmann, Berlin, 1901.

Rizzo, G. E.: *Il teatro greco di Siracusa.* Bestetti e Tumminelli, Milan, 1923.

Robert, Karl: *Die Masken der neueren attischen Komödie.* M. Niemeyer, Halle a. S., 1911.

Saint-Saëns, Charles Camille: *Note sur les décors de théâtre dans l'antiquité romaine.* L. Baschet, Paris, 1886.

Showerman, Grant: *Eternal Rome.* Yale University Press, New Haven, 1924.

Sittl, K.: *I Personaggi dell' Atellana. Rivista di storia antica,* 1, 3, 1895.

Smyth, H. W.: *Aeschylean Tragedy.* University of California Press, 1924.

Versakis, F.: *Das Scenengebäude des Dionysos-Theaters.* Kaiserlich deutsches archäologisches Institut, Berlin, 1910.

Vitruvius: *De Architectura.* Cristoforo di Pensa, da Mandello, Venice, 1496.

Vitruvius, Pollio: *Ten Books of Architecture.* Harvard University Press, Cambridge, 1914.

Weissmann, K.: *Die scenische Aufführung der griechischen Dramen.* Ch. Kaiser, Munich, 1893.

Wieseler, Friedrich: *Theatergebäude und Denkmäler des Bühnenwesens bei der Griechen und Römern.* Vandenhoeck & Ruprecht, Göttingen, 1851.

MEDIEVAL

Bruggermann, Fritz: *Vom Schembartlaufen.* Bibliographisches Institut, Leipzig, 1936.

Chambers, E. K.: *The Medieval Stage.* 2 volumes. Clarendon Press, Oxford, 1903.

Coffman, G. R.: *A New Approach to Medieval Latin Drama. Modern Philology,* 1925, XXII, 3.

Coffman, G. R.: *A Note Concerning the Cult of St. Nicholas at Hildesheim.* Manley Anniversary Studies, 1922.

Cohen, Gustave: *Histoire de la mise en scène dans le théâtre religieux français du moyen age.* Champion, Paris, 1926.

Cohen, Gustave: *Le livre de conduite du régisseur et le compte des dépenses pour le mystère de la Passion joué à Mons en 1501.* H. Champion, Paris, 1925.

Cohen, Gustave: *Le Théâtre en France au moyen age.* 2 volumes. Rieder et Cie., Paris, 1928.

de Coussemaker, Charles E.: *Drames liturgiques du moyen âge.* Rennes, 1860.

Cripps-Day, F. H.: *History of the Tournament in England and France.* B. Quaritch, Ltd., London, 1918.

Dacier, E.: *La Mise en scène à Paris au xvii siècle. Mémoires de la Société d'Histoire de Paris,* Paris, 1901.

Disher, Maurice Willson: *Clowns and Pantomimes.* Houghton, Mifflin Co., Boston, 1925.

Froning, Richard: *Das Drama des Mittelalters.* Union deutsche Verlagsgesellschaft, Stuttgart, 1891–1892.

Gasté, A.: *Drames liturgiques de la cathédrale de Rouen. Annales de la Faculté des Lettres de Caen,* 1888.

Jubinal, Michel L. A.: *Mystères inédits du xv siècle.* Paris, 1837.

Lacroix, Paul: 1. *Science et lettres au moyen âge.* 2. *Vie militaire et religieuse au moyen âge.* 3. *Les Arts au moyen âge.* 4. *Moeurs, usages et costumes au moyen âge.* Didot, Paris, 1869–1873.

Lancaster, Henry C.: *Mémoire de Mahélot.* E. Champion, Paris, 1920.

Migne, Jacques Paul: *Patrologiae cursus completus.* Paris, 1844.

Milchsack, Gustav: *Die Oster- und Passionsspiele.* Wolfenbuettel, 1880.

Mone, Franz Joseph: *Schauspiele des Mittelalters.* C. Macklot, Karlsruhe, 1846.

Petit de Julleville, Louis: *La Comédie et les moeurs en France au moyen âge.* Hachette et Cie., Paris, 1880–1886.

Petit de Julleville, Louis: *Les Mystères.* Hachette et Cie., Paris, 1880–1886.

Pollard, A. W.: *English Miracle Plays, Moralities and Interludes.* Clarendon Press, Oxford, 1904.

Rigal, Eugène: *La Mise-en scène dans les tragédies du xvi siècle. Revue d'histoire litt. de la France,* 1905, XII, 1.

Rigal, Eugène: *Le Théâtre français avant la période classique.* Hachette et Cie., Paris, 1901.

Wilhelm Thellen: Ein Hübsch Spiel. Insel-Verlag, Leipzig, (no date).

Young, Karl: *The Drama of the Medieval Church.* 2 volumes. Clarendon Press, Oxford, 1933.

BAROQUE

Beijer, Agne: *The Drottningholm Theatre Museum. Theatre Arts,* March, 1934.

da Bibiena, Ferdinando: *Direzioni della prospettiva teorica.* 1732.

da Bibiena, Ferdinando: *Disegni delle scene.* 1714.

da Bibiena, Giuseppe Galli: *Architetture e prospettiva.* Augustae, 1740.

Boswell, Eleanore: *The Restoration Court Stage.* Harvard University Press, Cambridge, 1932.

Brown, Frank C.: *Elkanah Settle: His Life and Works.* University of Chicago Press, 1910.

Campbell, Lily B.: *Scenes and Machines of the English Stage During the Renaissance.* Cambridge University Press, 1923.

Celler, Ludovic: *Les Décors, les costumes et la mise-en-scène au xvii siècle.* Liepmannsohn, Paris, 1869.

Celler, Ludovic: *Les origines de l'opéra.* Didier, Paris, 1868.

Chiaramonti, Scipione: *Delle scene e teatri.* 1675.

Designs by Inigo Jones for Masques and Plays at Court. Publications of the Walpole Society, Vol. XII, 1924.

Despois, Eugène André: *Le Théâtre français sous Louis XIV.* Hachette & Cie., Paris, 1882.

Diderot, Denis: *Encyclopédie.* Pellet, Geneva, 1777–1779.

Dobrée, Bonamy: *Restoration Tragedy.* Oxford University Press, New York, 1927.

Downes, John: *Roscium Anglicanus.* J. W. Jarvis & Son, London, 1886.

Frischauer, Paul: *Beaumarchais.* Viking Press, New York, 1936.

Fülöp-Miller, René: *Macht und Geheimnis der Jesuiten.* Grethlein & Co., Leipzig, 1929.

Gay, John: *The Beggars' Opera.* William Heinemann, London, 1923.

Gregor, Joseph: *Wiener Szenische Kunst.* Wiener Drucke, Vienna, 1923.

Hotson, Leslie: *The Commonwealth and Restoration Stage.* Harvard University Press, Cambridge, 1928.

Jouvet, Louis: *Molière. Theatre Arts,* September, 1937.

Lacroix, Paul: 5. *Lettres, sciences et arts au xviii siècle.* 6. *Institutions, usages et costumes au xvii siècle.* 7. *Institutions, usages et costumes au xviii siècle.* Didot, Paris, 1875–1880.

Lope de Vega, Three Hundred Years After. Theatre Arts, September, 1935.

Lowe, Robert William: *Apology for the Life of Mr. Colley Cibber.* J. C. Nimmo, London, 1889.

Lowe, Robert William: *Thomas Betterton.* K. Paul, Trench, Trubner & Co., Ltd., London, 1891.

Magrini, A.: *De Teatro Olimpico.* A spese dell' Accademia Olimpica, Padua, 1847.

Matthews, Brander: *Molière, His Life and Works.* Scribner's, New York, 1910.

McAfee, Helen: *Pepys on the Restoration Stage.* Yale University Press, New Haven, 1916.

Moland, Louis: *Molière et la comédie italienne.* Paris, 1867.

Montenari, Giovanni: *Del Teatro Olympico.* G. Conzatti, Padua, 1733.

Mourey, Gabriel: *Le Livre des fêtes françaises.* Librairie de France, Paris, 1930.

Nethercot, Arthur H.: *Sir William D'Avenant.* University of Chicago Press, 1939.

Nicoll, Allardyce: *A History of Early Eighteenth Century Drama, 1700–1750.* University Press, Cambridge, 1925.

Nicoll, Allardyce: *A History of Restoration Drama, 1660–1700.* Macmillan, New York, 1923.

Nicoll, Allardyce: *Stuart Masques and the Renaissance Stage.* Harcourt, Brace & Co., New York, 1938.

Palmer, John: *Molière.* Brewer & Warren, New York, 1930.

Pepys, Samuel: *Diary.* 2 volumes. J. M. Dent, London and Toronto, 1933.

Piranesi, Giovanni Battista: *Le Magnificenze di Roma.* G. Bouchard, 1751.

Piranesi, Giovanni Battista: *Opere varie di architettura e perspettiva.* Rome, 1756(?).

Piranesi, Giovanni Battista: *Teatro di Ercolano.* Rome, 1756(?).

Pozzo, Andrea: *Prospettiva dei pittori e architetti.* 1692–1700.

Pozzo, Andrea: *Rules and Examples of Perspective Proper for Painters and Architects.* London, 1707.

Rennert, Hugo Albert: *The Spanish Stage in the Time of Lope de Vega.* Hispanic Society of America, New York, 1909.

Riccoboni, Luigi: *Histoire du théâtre italien.* Delormel, Paris, 1728.

Sabbattini, Nicola: *Practica di fabricar scene, e machine ne teatre.* Facsimile, German translation. Gesellschaft der Bibliophilen, Weimar, 1926.

Serlio, Sebastiano: *Architettura.* G. D. Scamozzi, Venice, 1584.

Serlio, Sebastiano: *The First Five Bookes of Architecture.* S. Stafford, London, 1611.

Settle, Elkanah: *Notes and Observations on the Empress of Morocco: Being a defense against Dryden.* London, 1674.

Smith, Winifred: *Italian Actors of the Renaissance.* Coward-McCann, New York, 1930.

Sullivan, Mary: *The Court Masks of James I.* Putnam's Sons, New York, 1913.

Summers, Montague (editor): *The Empress of Morocco.* Macmillan, London.

Summers, Montague: *The Playhouse of Pepys.* Macmillan, New York, 1935.

Summers, Montague: *The Restoration Theatre.* Macmillan, New York, 1934.

Symonds, John Addington: *The Renaissance in Italy.* 2 volumes. Scribner's, New York, 1906.

Vasari, Giorgio: *Lives of the Painters.* J. M. Dent, London, 1900.

de Voltaire: *Letters Concerning the English Nation, by Mons. de Voltaire.* Peter Davis, London, 1926.

Zucker, Paul: *Die Theaterdekoration des Barock.* Rudolf Kaemmerer, Berlin, 1925.

Zucker, Paul: *Die Theaterdekoration des Klassizismus.* Rudolf Kaemmerer, Berlin, 1925.

COMMEDIA

Baschet, Armand: *Les Comédiens italiens à la cour de France.* E. Plon, Paris, 1882.

Beaumont, Cyril W.: *History of Harlequin.* C. W. Beaumont, London, 1926.

Beijer, Agne and Duchartre, P. L.: *Recueil de plusieurs fragments des premières Comédies Italiennes.* Duchartre & Von Bugenhoudt, Paris, 1928.

Brunelleschi, Umberto: *Les Masques et les personnages de la comédie italienne.* Paris, 1913.

Constantini, Angelo: *The Birth and Death of Scaramouch.* C. W. Beaumont, London, 1924.

Constantini, Angelo: *La Vie de Scaramouche.* Paris, 1695.

Croce, Bendetto: *Commedia dell' Arte. Theatre Arts,* December, 1933.

Dieterich, A.: *Pulcinella.* B. G. Teubner, Leipzig, 1897.

Driessen, O.: *Der Ursprung des Harlekin. Forschungen zur Neuren Literaturgeschichte,* XXV, 1904.

Duchartre, Pierre: *Italian Comedy.* The John Day Co., New York, 1928.

Faust, Camille: *Le Théâtre, le cirque, le music hall et les peintures du xviii siècle à nos jours.* E. Flammarion, Paris, 1926.

Hiler, Hilaire and Moss, Arthur: *Slapstick and Dumb-bell.* Paris, 1924.

Lea, K. M.: *Italian Popular Comedy.* 2 volumes. Clarendon Press, Oxford, 1934.

Marchini-Capasso, O.: *Goldoni e la commedia dell' arte.* Naples, 1912.

Mic, Constantin: *La Commedia dell' Arte.* J. Schiffrin, Paris, 1927.

Petit de Julleville, Louis: *Les Comédiens en France au moyen âge.* Hachette et Cie., Paris, 1880–1886.

Petit de Julleville, Louis: *Répertoire du théâtre comique en France au moyen âge.* Hachette et Cie., Paris, 1886.

Petraccone, Enzo: *La Commedia dell' Arte: storia, tecnica, scenari.* Naples, 1927.

della Porta, Giovanni Battista: *Delle Commedie.* Naples, 1726.

Sand, Maurice: *The History of the Harlequinade.* J. B. Lippincott Co., Philadelphia, 1915.

Sand, Maurice: *Les Masques et bouffons de la comédie italienne.* Paris, 1860.

Scherillo, Michele: *La Commedia dell' Arte in Italia.* E. Loescher, Turin, 1884.

Scherillo, Michele: *The Genealogy of Pulcinella. The Mask,* III, Florence.

Smith, Winifred: *Commedia dell' Arte.* Columbia University Press, New York, 1912.

Uraneff, Vadim: *Commedia dell' Arte and American Vaudeville. Theatre Arts,* October, 1923.

Vail, R. W. G.: *Random Notes on the History of the Early American Circus* American Antiquarian Society, Worcester, 1934.

TUDOR

Adams, John C.: *Shakespeare's Stage. Theatre Arts,* October, 1936.

Adams, J. Q.: *Shakespearean Playhouses.* Houghton, Mifflin Co., Boston, 1917.

Baker, George Pierce: *The Development of Shakespeare as a Dramatist.* Macmillan, New York, 1917.

Boas, Frederick S.: *An Introduction to Tudor Drama.* Oxford University Press, New York, 1933.

Boas, Frederick S.: *Marlowe and His Circle.* Clarendon Press, Oxford, 1929.

Bradbrook, Muriel Clara: *Themes and Conventions of Elizabethan Tragedy.* University Press, Cambridge, 1935.

Bradly, Ann (editor): *Shakespeare Criticism.* Oxford University Press, 1935.

Brandes, Georg: *William Shakespeare.* Macmillan, London, 1904.

Brooke, C. F. Tucker: *The Tudor Drama.* Houghton, Mifflin Co., Boston, 1911.

Chambers, E. K.: *The Elizabethan Stage.* 4 volumes. Clarendon Press, Oxford, 1923.

Chambers, E. K.: *William Shakespeare.* 2 volumes. Oxford University Press, 1930.

Dowden, Edward: *Shakespeare, His Mind and Art.* Harper's, New York, 1918.

Granville-Barker, Harley: *Prefaces to Shakespeare.* Sidgwick & Jackson, London, 1933.

Gregg, W. W.: *Dramatic Documents from the Elizabethan Playhouses.* 2 volumes. Clarendon Press, Oxford, 1931.

Gregor, Joseph: *Shakespeare.* Phaidon-Verlag, Vienna, 1935.

Isaacs, J.: *Shakespeare in the Theatre.* Clarendon Press, Oxford, 1927.

Lawrence, W. J.: *The Elizabethan Playhouse and Other Studies.* J. P. Lippincott Co., Philadelphia, 1912.

Lawrence, W. J.: *New Light on the Elizabethan Theatre. Fortnightly Review,* May, 1916.

Lawrence, W. J.: *Night Performances in the Elizabethan Theatres. Englische Studien,* Leipzig, 1915.

Lawrence, W. J.: *The Physical Conditions of the Elizabethan Public Playhouse.* Harvard University Press, Cambridge, 1927.

Lawrence, W. J.: *Pre-Restoration Stage Studies.* Harvard University Press, Cambridge, 1927.

Lee, Sidney: *Life of William Shakespeare.* Macmillan, New York, 1929.

Lee, Sidney: *Shakespeare's England.* Clarendon Press, Oxford, 1932.

Matthews, Brander: *Shakespeare as a Playwright.* Scribner's, New York, 1913.

Morgan, Appleton: *The Shakespearean Myth.* Robert Clarke & Co., Cincinnati, 1886.

Morrow, Donald: *Where Shakespeare Stood.* Casanova Press, Milwaukee, 1935.

Odell, George C. D.: *Shakespeare from Betterton to Irving.* 2 volumes. Scribner's, New York, 1920.

Poel, William: *Shakespeare and the Theatre.* Sidgwick & Jackson, London, 1913.

Reed, A. W.: *Early Tudor Drama.* Methuen & Co., London, 1926.

Reynolds, G. F.: *Some Principles of Elizabethan Staging. Modern Philology,* January–February, 1905.

Reynolds, G. F.: *What We Know of the Elizabethan Stage. Modern Philology,* November, 1911.

Rhodes, R. Crompton: *The Stagery of Shakespeare.* Cornish Bros. Ltd., Birmingham, 1922.

Smirnov, A. A.: *Shakespeare: A Marxist Interpretation.* Critics Group, New York, 1936.

Symonds, John Addington: *Shakespeare's Predecessors.* Scribner's, New York, 1900.

Theatre Arts Prints. III. *Shakespeare and His Times.* Theatre Arts, Inc., New York, 1935.

Thorndike, Ashley H.: *Shakespeare's Theatre.* Macmillan, New York, 1916.

Welsford, Enid: *The Court Masque.* Cambridge University Press, 1927.

Wilson, J. Dover: *The Essential Shakespeare.* At the University Press, Cambridge, 1935.

Wilson, J. Dover: *What Happens in Hamlet.* At the University Press, Cambridge, 1937.

ROMANTIC

Burlingame, Edward L. (editor): *The Art Life and Theories of Richard Wagner.* Henry Holt & Co., New York, 1889.

Carson, William G. B.: *The Theatre on the Frontier.* University of Chicago Press, 1932.

Cole, Arvin Neil: *Eugène Scribe and the French Theatre 1815–1860.* Cambridge, 1924.

Brandes, Georg: *Wolfgang Goethe.* Little, Brown & Co., Boston, 1924.

Dunlap, William: *History of the American Theatre.* R. Bentley, London, 1833.

Grube, Max: *Geschichte der Meininger.* Deutsche Verlags-Anstalt, Stuttgart, 1926.

Henderson, Myrtle E.: *A History of the Theatre in Salt Lake City.* Evanston, Illinois, 1934.

Hugo, Victor: *Préface de Cromwell and Hernani.* Scott, Foresman & Co., Chicago, 1900.

Leverton, Garrett H.: *The Production of Later Nineteenth Century American Drama.* Teachers College, Columbia University, New York, 1936.

Logan, Olive: *Before the Footlights and Behind the Scenes.* Parmelee & Co., Philadelphia, 1870.

Löhle, Franz: *Theater-Catechismus.* Piloty & Löhle, Munich, (no date).

Matthews, Brander: *The Theatres of Paris.* Sampson Low, Marston, Searle and Rivington, London, 1880.

Moynet, M. J.: *L'Envers du théâtre.* Hachette et Cie., Paris, 1873.

Moynet, George. *La Machinerie théâtrale: trucs et décors.* À la librairie illustrée, Paris, 1893.

Muncker, Franz: *Richard Wagner.* Buchnersche Verlagsbuchhandlung, Bamberg, 1891.

Palache, John Garber: *Gautier and the Romantics.* Viking Press, New York.

Paris-Théâtre (periodical). Paris.

Saintsbury, George Edward Bateman: *Romance. Encyclopaedia Britannica,* 1937.

von Schlegel, August Wilhelm: *Lectures on Dramatic Art and Literature.* G. Bell & Sons, London, 1894.

Wagner, Richard: *Die Kunst und die Revolution.* In *Gesammelte Schriften und Dichtungen,* Volume 3. Fritsche, Leipzig, 1872.

NATURALISTIC

Antoine, André: *Mes souvenirs sur le Théâtre-Libre.* A. Fayard, Paris, 1921.

Antoine, André: *Recollections of the Théâtre-Libre. Theatre Arts,* March, 1925.

Bab, Julius: *Neue Wege Zum Drama.* Oesterheld & Co., Berlin, 1911.

Bab, Julius: *Wesen und Weg der Berliner Volksbühnenbewegung.* E. Wasmuth, Berlin, 1919.

Балухатов, С. Д. (ред.) (Balikhatov, S. D., editor): *Чайка* (*The Seagull, from Stanislavsky's Notebook*). Iskustvo, Leningrad-Moscow, 1938.

Barnouw, A. J.: *Herman Heijermans. Theatre Arts*, February, 1925.

Belasco, David: *Six Plays*. Little, Brown & Co., Boston, 1929.

Benoist-Hanappier, Louis: *De Drame naturaliste*. Felix Alcan, Paris, 1905.

Berg, Leo: *Der Naturalismus*. Pösal, Munich, 1892.

Пьесы А. П. Чехова (*The A. P. Chekhov Album*). Album Solntsa Rossi vii, 1914.

Chekhov, Anton: *Letters of Anton Chekhov to His Family and Friends*. Macmillan, New York, 1920.

Clark, Barrett H.: *Four Plays of the Free Theatre*. Appleton, New York, 1915.

Darzens, Rodolphe: *Le Théâtre-Libre illustré*. 2 volumes. E. Dentu, Paris, 1889–1890.

Doell, Otto: *Die Entwicklung der Naturalistischen Form in Jüngstdeutschen Drama*. H. Gesenius, Halle, 1910.

Flores, Angel (editor): *Henrik Ibsen*. Critics Group Series No. 6, New York, 1937.

Gosse, Edmund: *Henrik Ibsen*. Scribner's, New York, 1908.

Grau, Robert: *The Stage in the Twentieth Century*. Broadway Publishing Co., New York, 1912.

Hecht, Ben and MacArthur, Charles: *The Front Page*. Covici-Friede, New York, 1928.

Josephson, Matthew: *Zola and His Time*. Book League, New York, 1928.

Lafargue, Paul: *Émile Zola*. Critics Group Series No. 4, New York, 1937.

McGill, V. J.: *August Strindberg*. Brentano's, New York, 1930.

Moses, Montrose J.: *Henrik Ibsen, the Man and His Plays*. Little, Brown & Co., Boston, 1920.

Sayler, Oliver M.: *Inside the Moscow Art Theatre*. Brentano's, New York, 1925.

Sayler, Oliver M.: *The Moscow Art Theatre. Theatre Arts*, October, 1920.

Sayler, Oliver M.: *The World's First Theatre: Moscow Art Theatre. The Drama*, June, 1919.

Shaw, George Bernard: *Quintessence of Ibsenism*. B. R. Tucker, Boston, 1891.

Stanislavsky, Constantin: *My Life in Art*. Little, Brown & Co., Boston, 1924.

Thalasso, A.: *Le Théâtre-Libre. Mercure de France*, Paris, 1909.

Toumanova, Princess Nina Andronikova: *Anton Chekhov, the Voice of Twilight Russia*. Columbia University Press, New York, 1937.

Waxman, S. M.: *Antoine and the Théâtre-Libre*. Harvard University Press, Cambridge, 1926.

Winter, William: *The Life of David Belasco.* 2 volumes. Jefferson Winter, Staten Island, New York, 1918.

Zola, Émile: *Le Naturalisme au théâtre.* E. Fasquelle, Paris, 1881.

Zucker, Adolf E.: *Ibsen the Master Builder.* Henry Holt & Co., New York, 1929.

NEW STAGECRAFT, EUROPE

Alexandre, Arsène: *L'Art décoratif de Léon Bakst.* M. de Brunoff, Paris, 1913.

Ansky, S.: *The Dybbuk.* Boni & Liveright, New York, 1926.

Adolphe Appia. Art. Institut Orell, Füsli, Zurich, 1929.

Adolphe Appia. Theatre Arts (special number), August, 1932.

Appia, Adolphe: *Art vivant ou nature morte?.* Bottega di Poesia, Milan, 1923.

Appia, Adolphe: *Comment reformer nôtre mise en scène. La Revue,* Paris, 1 Juin, 1904.

Appia, Adolphe: *Directions for the Staging of Tristan and Isolde.* Translated by Lee Simonson. *Theatre Workshop,* April–July, 1937.

Appia, Adolphe: *La Mise en scène du drame wagnérien.* L. Chailley, Paris, 1895.

Appia, Adolphe: *Die Musik und die Inscenierung.* F. Bruckmann, Munich, 1899.

Appia, Adolphe: *L'Oeuvre d'art vivant.* Atar, Paris and Geneva, 1921.

Aronson, Boris: *L'Art de théâtre.* Paris, 1928.

Bakshy, Alexander: *The Path of the Modern Russian Stage.* C. Palmer & Hayward, London, 1918.

Bakshy, Alexander: *The Russian Dramatic Stage. The Drama,* Chicago, February, 1919.

Bamah Theatre Art Journal (periodical). Bamah, Tel-Aviv, Palestine, 1937.

Barr, Alfred H., Jr. (editor): *Fantastic Art, Dada, Surrealism.* Museum of Modern Art, New York, 1936.

ר.בן־ארי (Ben-Ari, R.): הבימה (*The Moscow Theatre Habimah*). L. M. Stein, Publisher, 913 West Van Buren St., Chicago.

Bickley, Francis: *J. M. Synge and the Irish Dramatic Movement.* Houghton, Mifflin Co., Boston, 1912.

Bourgeois, Maurice: *John Millington Synge and the Irish Theatre.* Macmillan, London, 1913.

Boyd, Ernest: *Contemporary Drama of Ireland.* Little, Brown & Co., Boston, 1917.

Boyd, Ernest: *Ireland's Literary Renaissance.* John Lane, New York, 1916.

Bragaglia, Anton Giulio: *Del Teatro teatrale.* Edizioni Tiber, Rome, 1926.

Bragaglia, Anton Giulio: *La Maschera Mobile.* F. Campitelli, Foligno, 1926.

Carter, Huntly: *The New Spirit in Drama and Art.* Mitchell Kennerley, New York, 1913.

Carter, Huntly: *The New Spirit in the European Theatre 1914–1924.* George H. Doran, New York, 1925.

Carter, Huntly: *The Theatre of Max Reinhardt.* F. & C. Palmer, London, 1914.

Cheney, Sheldon: *The New Movement in the Theatre.* Mitchell Kennerley, New York, 1914.

Cheney, Sheldon: *The Open Air Theatre.* Mitchell Kennerley, New York, 1918.

Cheney, Sheldon: *Stage Decoration.* The John Day Co., New York, 1928.

Cheney, Sheldon: *The Theatre, Three Thousand Years of Drama, Acting and Stagecraft.* Tudor Publishing Co., New York, 1935.

Chiti, Remo: *I Creatori del Teatro Futurista: Marinetti, Corradini, Seltimelli.* A. Quattrini, Florence, 1915.

Cogniat, Raymond: *Décors de theatre.* Chroniques du Jour, Paris, 1930.

Copeau, Jacques: *The Theatre du Vieux-Colombier. The Drama,* February, 1918.

Craig, Edward Gordon: *Books and Theatres.* Dent, London, 1926.

Craig, Edward Gordon: *Fourteen Notes.* University of Washington Bookstore, 1931.

Craig, Edward Gordon (editor): *The Mask* (periodical). Florence.

Craig, Edward Gordon: *On the Art of the Theatre.* T. N. Foulis, Edinburgh, 1905.

Craig, Edward Gordon: *A Production, 1926.* Oxford University Press, New York, 1930.

Craig, Edward Gordon: *Scene.* Oxford University Press, New York, 1923.

Craig, Edward Gordon: *The Theatre Advancing.* Little, Brown & Co., Boston, 1919.

Craig, Edward Gordon: *Towards a New Theatre.* Dent, London, 1913.

The Designs of Leon Bakst for the Sleeping Princess. Benn, London, 1923.

Das Deutsche Bühnenbild. Leonhard Preiss Verlag, Berlin, 1938.

Deutsche Theater-Ausstellung, Magdeburg 1927. Mitteldeutschen Ausstellungsgesellschaft, Magdeburg, 1928.

Das Deutsche Theater in Berlin. Monographs on Max Reinhardt with contributions by William Archer, Georg Brandes, M. Maeterlinck. G. Müller, Munich, 1909.

Dickinson, Thomas Herbert: *Insurgent Theatre.* B. W. Huebsch, New York, 1917.

Dobrée, Bonamy: *Timotheus, the Future of the Theatre.* K. Paul, Trench, Trubner & Co., London, 1925.

Dukes, Ashley: *The Youngest Drama.* Sergel, London, 1924.

Elaborate Simplicity of Jacques Copeau's New Theatre. Current Opinion, January, 1918.

Evreinov, Nikolai: *The Theatre of the Soul.* Hendersons, London, 1915.

Fischel, Oskar: *Das moderne Bühnenbild.* E. Wasmuth, Berlin, 1923.

Flanagan, Hallie: *Shifting Scenes.* Coward, McCann, New York, 1928.

Frank Waldo: *The Art of the Vieux-Colombier. Nouvelle Revue Française,* Paris, 1918.

Fuchs, Georg: *Die Revolution des Theaters.* Georg Müller, Munich and Leipzig, 1909.

Fuchs, Georg: *Die Schaubühne der Zukunft.* Schuster & Loeffler, Berlin (no date).

Fuerst, Walter René and Hume, Samuel J.: *Twentieth Century Stage Decoration.* Alfred A. Knopf, New York, 1929.

Fülop-Miller, René and Gregor, Joseph: *The Russian Theatre.* Lippincott, Philadelphia, 1930.

George, Waldemar: *Boris Aronson.* Chroniques du Jour, Paris, 1928.

Goldberg, Isaac: *The Drama of Transition.* Stewart Kidd, Cincinnati, 1923.

Gorelik, Mordecai: *Man in a White Collar. Theatre Arts,* November, 1936.

Gregory, Lady Isabella Augusta: *Our Irish Theatre.* Putnam's, New York, 1913.

Habimah. Bamah, Palestine, 1937.

Hagemann, Carl: *Moderne Bühnenkunst.* 2 volumes. Schuster & Loeffler, Berlin, 1916–1918.

Herald, Heinz and Stern, Ernst: *Reinhardt und seine Bühne.* Eysler & Co., Berlin, 1920.

Hume, Samuel J. and Fuerst, Walter René: *Twentieth Century Stage Decoration.* A. A. Knopf, London, 1928.

International Theatre Exposition (catalogue). *The Little Review,* New York, 1926.

Internationale Ausstellung für Theaterkunst (catalogue). Gesellschaft der Freunde der National-bibliothek, Vienna, 1936.

Jacobsohn, Siegfried: *Max Reinhardt.* Reiss, Berlin, 1910.

Kerber, Erwin: *Salzburg and Its Festivals.* R. Piper & Co., Munich, 1936.

Komisarjevsky, Theodore: *Myself and the Theatre.* Dutton, New York, 1930.

Komisarjevsky, Theodore and Simonson, Lee: *Settings and Costumes of the Modern Stage.* The Studio Publications, New York, 1933.

Levy, Julien: *Surrealism.* Black Sun Press, New York, 1936.

Lewisohn, Ludwig: *Modern Drama.* Huebsch, New York, 1915.

Littmann, Max: *Das Künstler-Theater.* L. Werner, Munich, 1909.

Macgowan, Kenneth and Jones, Robert Edmond: *Continental Stagecraft.* Harcourt, Brace & Co., New York, 1922.

Macgowan, Kenneth: *The Theatre of Tomorrow.* Boni & Liveright, New York, 1921.

MacClintock, Lander: *Contemporary Drama of Italy.* Little, Brown & Co., Boston, 1920.

Malone, Andrew E.: *The Irish Drama.* Scribner's, New York, 1929.

The Mask (periodical). Florence.

Meyerhold, Vsevolod: *Contribution à l'histoire et à la technique du théâtre.* Korniloff et Cie., Moscow.

Moderwell, Hiram Kelly: *The Theatre of Today.* John Lane, New York, 1914.

Das Moskauer Jüdische Akademische Theater. Verlag der Schmiede, Berlin, 1928.

Moussinac, Léon: *La Décoration théâtrale.* F. Rieder & Cie, Paris, 1922.

Moussinac, Léon: *Tendances nouvelles du théâtre.* F. Rieder & Cie., Paris, 1922.

Niessen, Carl: *Das Bühnenbild.* K. Schroeder, Bonn, 1924.

Poupeye, Camille: *La mise en scène théâtrale d'aujourdhui.* Édition L'Equerre, Brussels, 1927(?).

Propert, W. A.: *The Russian Ballet in Western Europe 1909–1920.* John Lane, London and New York, 1921.

Read, Herbert: *Surrealism.* Harcourt, Brace & Co., New York, 1936.

Ricci, C.: *La Scenografia Italiana.* Fratelli Treves, Milan, 1930.

Rose, Enid: *Gordon Craig and the Theatre.* Sampson Low, London, 1931.

Rothe, Hans: *Max Reinhardt, 25 Jahre Des Deutsches Theater.* R. Piper & Co., Munich, 1930.

Rouché, Jacques: *L'Art théâtrale moderne.* Bloud & Gay, Paris, 1924.

Rutherston, Albert: *Decoration in the Art of the Theatre. The Monthly Chapbook,* No. 2, London, 1919.

Sayler, Oliver M. (editor): *Max Reinhardt and His Theatre.* Brentano's, New York, 1924.

Scenedekorativ Konst (catalogue). Drottningholms Teatermuseum, 1936.

Scheffauer, Herman George: *The New Vision in the German Arts.* Huebsch, New York, 1924.

Sheringham, George: *Design in the Theatre.* The Studio, London, 1927.

Starkie, Walter: *Luigi Pirandello.* Dutton, New York, 1927.

Stavba. Special theatre edition. Prague, 1936.

Steinhauer, H.: *Das Deutsche Drama 1880–1933.* W. W. Norton & Co., New York, 1938.

Stern, Ernst and Herald, Heinz: *Reinhardt und seine Bühne.* Eysler, Berlin, 1919.

Stragnell, Gregory: *A Psychopathological Study of Franz Molnar's Liliom. The Psychoanalytic Review,* January, 1922.

The Studio (periodical). London.

Tairov, Alexander: *Das Entfesselte Theater.* Gustav Kiepenheuer, Potsdam, 1927.

Theatre Arts Prints. II. Modern Stage Design. Theatre Arts, Inc., New York, 1929.

Le Théâtre de chambre. Art et Action, Paris, 1932.

Toller, Ernst: *Masse-Mensch.* Gustav Kiepenheuer, Potsdam, 1922.

Toller, Ernst: *Seven Plays.* J. Lane, London, 1935.

Tucker, S. Marion: *Twenty-Five Modern Plays.* Harper's, New York, 1931.

Van Wyck, Jessica Davis: *Designing Hamlet with Appia. Theatre Arts,* January, 1925.

Vernon, Frank: *The Twentieth Century Theatre.* Houghton, Mifflin Co., Boston, 1924.

Vittorini, Domenico: *The Drama of Luigi Pirandello.* University of Pennsylvania, 1936.

Wagner, Ludwig: *Der Szeniker Ludwig Sievert.* Bühnenvolksbundverlag, Berlin, 1926.

Whitworth, Geoffrey: *Theatre in Action.* Studio Publications, New York, 1938.

Wiegand, Charmion von: *Ernst Toller. New Theatre,* August, 1936.

Yeats, William Butler: *Plays and Controversies.* Macmillan, London, 1923.

NEW STAGECRAFT, UNITED STATES

American Stage Designs (catalogue). Bourgeois Galleries, New York, 1919.

Anderson, John: *The American Theatre.* The Dial Press, New York, 1936.

Anderson, Maxwell: *The Essence of Tragedy.* Anderson House, Washington, D.C., 1939.

Art and Decoration. Stage Settings, special number. New York, November, 1930.

Barnes, Djuna: *Mordecai Gorelik. Theatre Guild Magazine,* February, 1931.

Brown, John Mason: *The Modern Theatre in Revolt.* W. W. Norton & Co., New York, 1929.

Brown, John Mason: *Two on the Aisle.* W. W. Norton & Co., New York, 1938.

Brown, John Mason: *Upstage.* W. W. Norton & Co., New York, 1930.

Cheney, Sheldon: *The Art Theatre.* Alfred A. Knopf, New York, 1917.

Clark, Barrett H.: *New Trends in the Theatre. The Forum,* November, 1924.

Clurman, Harold: *The Conductor Speaks.* New York *Times,* March 3, 1940.

Connelly, Marc: *The Green Pastures*. Farrar & Rinehart, New York, 1930.

Deutsch, Helen and Hanau, Stella: *The Provincetown, A Story of the Theatre*. Farrar & Rinehart, New York, 1931.

Duncan, Isadora: *My Life*. Garden City Publishing Co., Garden City, New York, 1927.

Flexner, Eleanor: *American Playwrights 1918–1938*. Simon & Shuster, New York, 1938.

Geddes, Norman Bel: *A Project for the Divine Comedy*. Boni & Liveright, New York, 1927.

Gorelik, Mordecai: *The Conquest of Stage Space*. *Theatre Arts*, March, 1934.

Gorelik, Mordecai: *The Group Theatre*. *Contempo*, September, 1931.

Gorelik, Mordecai: *Some Observations on the New Stagecraft*. *The Arts*, April, 1926.

Gregor, Joseph and Fülöp-Miller, René: *Das Amerikanische Theater und Kino*. Amalthea-Verlag, Vienna, 1931.

Hopkins, Arthur: *How's Your Second Act?*. Samuel French, New York, 1931.

Jones, Robert Edmond: *Art in the Theatre*. *Yale Review*, October, 1927.

Jones, Robert Edmond: *Drawings for the Theatre*. Theatre Arts, Inc., New York, 1925.

Jones, Robert Edmond: *Exhibition of Stage Designs* (catalogue). Bourgeois Galleries, New York, 1925.

Jones, Robert Edmond: *Exhibition of Stage Models and Designs* (catalogue). Bourgeois Galleries, New York, 1920.

Kaufman, George S. and Connelly, Marc: *Beggar on Horseback*. Boni & Liveright, New York, 1924.

Krutch, Joseph Wood: *The American Drama Since 1918*. Random House, New York, 1939.

Lawson, John Howard: *Processional*. Thomas Seltzer, New York, 1925.

Macgowan, Kenneth: *Footlights Across America*. Harcourt, Brace & Co., New York, 1929.

Mackay, Constance d'Arcy: *The Little Theatre in the United States*. Henry Holt & Co., New York, 1917.

Mantle, Burns: *Contemporary American Playwrights*. Dodd, Mead & Co., New York, 1938.

Mitchell, Lee: *The Space Stage Defined*. *Theatre Arts*, July, 1936.

Mitchell, Roy: *Creative Theatre*. John Day, New York, 1929.

Oenslager, Donald: *Scenery Then and Now*. W. W. Norton & Co., New York, 1936.

O'Neill, Eugene: *Nine Plays*. Random House, New York, 1932.

Reed, Joseph Verner: *The Curtain Falls*. Harcourt, Brace & Co., New York, 1935.

Rosse, Hermann: *Designs and Impressions*. Ralph Fletcher Seymour, Chicago, 1920.

Sayler, Oliver M.: *Our American Theatre.* Brentano's, New York, 1923.

Winther, Sophus Keith: *Eugene O'Neill.* Random House, New York, 1934.

SOVIET

Afinogenov, Alexander (editor): *Театр и Драматургия* (*Theatre and Dramaturgy*) (periodical). Moscow.

Н. П. Акимов (*N. P. Akimov*). Academia, Leningrad, 1927.

Амаглобели, Серго (Amglobeli, Sergo): *Грузинский Театр* (*The Georgian Theatre*). Moscow, 1930.

Бартошевкча, А. А. (Bartoshevkcha, A. A.): *Акимов* (*Akimov*). Leningrad, 1933.

Большой Драматический Театр (*The Grand Dramatic Theatre*). Edition of the Gorky Grand Dramatic Theatre, Leningrad, 1935.

Бригада Художников (*Brigade of Artists*) (periodical). Moscow.

Carter, Huntly: *Historical Sketch of the Theatre in Soviet Russia. Fortnightly Review,* March, 1922.

Carter, Huntly: *The New Spirit in the Russian Theatre.* Brentano's, New York, 1929.

Carter, Huntly: *The New Theatre and Cinema of Soviet Russia.* International Publishers, New York, 1925.

Cherniavsky, L. N. (editor): *The Moscow Children's Theatre.* Moscow-Leningrad, (no date).

Crawford, J.: *Moscow to Broadway. Drama,* March, 1923.

Dana, Henry W. L.: *Handbook on Soviet Drama.* American-Russian Institute, New York, 1938.

Данилин, Ю. (Danilin, Yuri): *Театральная Жизнь в Эпоху Парижской Коммуны* (*Theatrical Life in the Period of the Paris Commune*). State Publishing House of Art and Literature, Moscow, 1936.

Данилов, С. С. (Danilov, S. S.): *Ревизор на Сцене* (*Revisor on the Stage*). Goslitizdat, Leningrad, 1934.

Derjavine, Constantin: *A Century of the State Dramatic Theatre 1832–1932.* State Publishing House, Leningrad, 1932.

Eastman, Max: *Artists in Uniform.* Alfred A. Knopf, New York, 1934.

Flanagan, Hallie: *A Skit by the Blue Blouse. Theatre Guild Magazine,* January, 1930.

Freeman, Joseph: *An American Testament.* Farrar & Rinehart, New York, 1936.

Freeman, Joseph; Kunitz, Joshua; and Lozowick, Louis: *Voices of October.* Vanguard Press, New York, 1930.

Gorelik, Mordecai: *The Horses of Hamlet. Theatre Arts,* November, 1932.

Gorelik, Mordecai: *Soviet Scene Design. New Theatre and Film,* April, 1937.

Gorelik, Mordecai: *Theatre Outpost, U.S.S.R. Theatre Arts,* January, 1933.

Горьковец (newspaper of the Moscow Art Theatre). Moscow.

Gregor, Joseph and Fülöp-Miller, René: *The Russian Theatre.* Lippincott, Philadelphia, 1930.

Гвоздев, А. А. (Gvozdev, A. A.): *Художник в Театре* (*The Artist in the Theatre*). Ogiz-Izogiz, Leningrad-Moscow, 1931.

Гвоздев, А. А. (Gvozdev, A. A.): *Ревизор в Театре Имени Мейерхольда* (*Revisor at Meyerhold's Theatre*). Academia, Leningrad, 1927.

Гвоздев, А. А. (Gvozdev, A. A.): *Театр Имени Вс. Мейерхольда* (*The Theatre of V. Meyerhold*). Academia, Leningrad, 1927.

Houghton, Norris: *Moscow Rehearsals.* Harcourt, Brace & Co., New York, 1936.

International Literature (periodical). Moscow.

International Theatre (periodical). Moscow.

Leyda, Jay (editor): *The Soviet Theatre Speaks for Itself. Theatre Arts* special number, September, 1936.

Literature of the World Revolution (periodical). Moscow.

Литовский, О. С. (Litovsky, O. S.): *В Поисках Нового Героя* (*In Quest of a New Hero*). Moscow, 1933.

London, Kurt: *The Seven Soviet Arts.* Yale University Press, New Haven, 1938.

Lozowick, Louis: *Meyerhold's Theatre. Hound & Horn,* October–December, 1930.

Markov, Pavel A.: *The Soviet Theatre.* Victor Gollancz, London, 1934.

Маслеников, Н. (Maslenikov, N.): *Художник в Театре* (*The Artist in the Theatre*). Teakinopechat, Moscow, 1930.

Meyerhold Orders Music. Theatre Arts, September, 1936.

Мокульский, С. (Mokulsky, S.): *История Западно-Европейского Театра* (*History of the West European Theatre* volume 1). Goslitizdat, Moscow, 1936.

Moscow *Daily News* (journal). Moscow.

Moscow News (periodical). Moscow.

Moskvin, I.: *The Soviet Theatre.* Foreign Languages Publishing House, Moscow, 1939.

Рабочий и Театр (*The Worker in the Theatre*) (periodical). Moscow.

Sayler, Oliver M.: *The Russian Theatre.* Brentano's, New York, 1922.

Sayler, Oliver M.: *The Russian Theatre under the Revolution.* Little, Brown & Co., Boston, 1920.

Sayler, Oliver M.: *Theory and Practice in Russian Theatres. Theatre Arts,* July, 1920.

Schiller, F. P.: *Engels as a Literary Critic.* State Publishing House, Moscow, 1933.

Soviet Travel (periodical), special theatre number. Moscow, 1934.

The Theatre in the U.S.S.R. Voks, Vol. VI, Moscow, 1934.

Цехновицер, О. (Tsekhnovitser, Orest): *Празднества Революции* (*Festivals of the Revolution*). Ogiz Priboi, Leningrad, 1931.

Тверской, К. К. (Tverskoy, K. K.): *М. З. Левин* (*M. Z. Levin*). Academia, Leningrad, 1927.

Творчество Масс (*Mass Creativity*). (Newspaper of the Theatre of People's Art). Moscow.

USSR in Construction (periodical). Moscow.

Валентина Ходасевич (*Valentina Khodasevich*). Academia, Leningrad, 1927.

Всеволодский-Гернгросс, В. (Vsevolodsky-Gerngross, V.): *Краткий Курс Истории Русского Театра* (*History of the Russian Theatre*). Goslitizdat, Moscow, 1936.

Wiener, Leo: *Contemporary Drama in Russia.* Little, Brown & Co., Boston, 1924.

EPIC

Blitzstein, Marc: *The Cradle Will Rock.* Random House, New York, 1938.

Brecht, Bertolt: *Gesammelte Werke.* Malik-Verlag, London, 1938.

Brecht, Bertolt: *Mann ist Mann.* Propylaen-Verlag, Berlin, 1926.

Brecht, Bertolt: *Prospectus of the Diderot Society.* 1937 (unpublished).

Federal Theatre (periodical). New York.

Federal Theatre Plays. Random House, New York, 1938.

Fuller, Edmund: *Epic Realism. One Act Play Magazine,* April, 1938.

Gassner, John: *Catharsis and the Theory of Enlightenment. One Act Play Magazine,* August, 1937.

Gorelik, Mordecai: *Epic Realism. Theatre Workshop,* April–July, 1937.

Grosz, George: *Hintergrund.* Malik-Verlag, Berlin, 1928.

Гвоздев, А. А. (Gvosdev, A. A.): *Театр Послевоенной Германии* (*The Theatre of Post-War Germany*). Leningrad, 1933.

Ihering, Herbert: *Regisseure und Bühnenmaler.* Berlin, 1921. Goldschmidt-Gabrielli, Berlin-Wilmersdorf, 1921.

Ihering, Herbert: *Reinhardt, Jessner, Piscator oder Klassikertod.* Ernst Rowohlt Verlag, Berlin, 1929.

Piscator, Erwin: *Das Politische Theater.* Adalbert Schultz, Berlin, 1929.

Wadsworth, P. Beaumont: *Piscator: Rebel. Theatre Guild Magazine,* June, 1930.

Whitman, Willson: *Bread and Circuses.* (Federal Theatre). Oxford University Press, New York, 1937.

GENERAL

d'Ancona, Alessandro: *Origini del teatro in Italia.* Florence, 1877.

Archer, William: *The Old Drama and the New.* Dodd, Mead & Co., New York, 1927.

Baker, Henry Barton: *History of the London Stage.* E. P. Dutton & Co., 1904.

Beerbohm, Max: *Around Theatres.* Alfred A. Knopf, New York, 1930.

Benjamin, Walter: *Ursprung des Deutschen Trauerspieles.* Ernst Rowohlt, Berlin, 1927.

The Billboard (periodical). New York.

Blake, Ben: *The Awakening of the American Theatre.* Tomorrow Publishers, New York, 1935.

Block, Anita: *The Changing World in Plays and Theatre.* Little, Brown & Co., Boston, 1939.

Blum, Léon: *Au théâtre.* Ollendorf, Paris, 1905.

Brandes, Georg: *Main Currents in Nineteenth Century Literature.* 6 volumes. Boni & Liveright, New York, 1924.

Brown, Allen A.: *Catalogue of Books Relating to the Stage.* Boston Public Library, 1919.

Brown, Benjamin Williams: *Theatre at the Left.* The Booke Shop, Providence, R. I., 1938.

Brown, John Mason: *The Art of Playgoing.* W. W. Norton & Co., New York, 1936.

Brown, John Mason: *Letters from Greenroom Ghosts.* Viking Press, New York, 1934.

Brown, John Mason: *The Modern Theatre in Revolt.* W. W. Norton & Co., New York, 1929.

Die Bühne (periodical). Vienna.

Burian, Emil F. and Kouřil, Miroslav: *Dejte nám divadlo.* Prague, 1939.

de Cahusac, Louis: *La Danse ancienne et moderne.* La Haye, 1754.

Carskadon, T. R.: *Report on Television. Theatre Arts,* June, 1937.

Chandler, Frank Wadleigh: *The Contemporary Drama of France.* Little, Brown & Co., Boston, 1921.

Cheney, Sheldon: *The Theatre: Three Thousand Years of Drama, Acting and Stagecraft.* Longmans, Green & Co., New York, 1929.

Clark, Barrett H.: *European Theories of the Drama.* Appleton, New York, 1918.

Cohen, Fannia M.: *How One Big Trade Union Has Dramatized Labor Problems. Workers Education News,* May 18, 1935.

Cohen, Fannia M.: *Meeting Our Problem. Workers Education Bureau of America Quarterly,* January, 1935.

Cohen, Fannia M.: *Social Drama, a Technique for Workers' Education. Workers Education Bureau of America Quarterly,* October, 1935.

Croce, Bendetto: *Ariosto, Shakespeare and Corneille.* G. Allen & Unwin, London, 1920.

Cue (periodical). New York.
Dělnické Divadlo (periodical). Prague.
Dickinson, Thomas H. (editor): *The Theatre in a Changing Europe.* Henry Holt & Co., New York, 1937.
Drama (periodical). London.
The Drama (periodical). New York.
Dubech, Lucien: *Histoire générale illustrée du théâtre.* 5 volumes. Librairie de France, Paris, 1931–1934.
Dukes, Ashley: *Nazi Theatre. Theatre Arts,* January, 1934.
Duncan, Isadora: *Art of the Dance.* Theatre Arts, Inc., New York, 1928.
Dunlap, William: *History of the American Theatre.* R. Bentley, London, 1833.
Equity (periodical of the Actors Equity Association). New York.
Flanagan, Hallie: *Shifting Scenes of the Modern European Theatre.* Coward-McCann, New York, 1928.
Flanagan, Hallie: *A Theatre Is Born. Theatre Arts,* November, 1931.
Fournel, V.: *Curiosités théâtrales, anciennes et modernes.* Garnier Frères, Paris, 1859.
Független Szinpad (periodical). Budapest.
Gamble, William Burt: *Stage Scenery.* List of references. New York Public Library, 1917.
Gassner, John: *Masters of the Drama.* Random House, New York, 1940.
Geddes, Virgil. *Left Turn for American Drama.* Brookfield Pamphlets, No. 5. Brookfield Players, Inc., Brookfield, Ct., 1934.
Geddes, Virgil: *The Theatre of Dreadful Nights.* Brookfield Pamphlets, No. 3. Brookfield Players, Inc., Brookfield, Ct., 1934.
Gilder, Rosamond: *A Theatre Library* (bibliography). Theatre Arts, Inc., New York, 1932.
Gilder, Rosamond: *Enter the Actress.* Houghton, Mifflin Co., New York, 1931.
Gilder, Rosamond and Freedley, George: *Theatre Collections in Libraries and Museums.* Theatre Arts, Inc., 1936.
Gilder, Rosamond: *The World in the Mirror of the Theatre. Theatre Arts,* August, 1937.
Golden, John and Shore, Viola Brothers: *Stage-Struck John Golden.* Samuel French, New York, 1930.
Gorelik, Mordecai: *Theatre Is a Weapon. Theatre Arts,* June, 1934.
Granville-Barker, Harley: *The Study of Drama.* University Press, Cambridge, 1934.
Granville-Barker, Harley: *The Exemplary Theatre.* Little, Brown & Co., Boston, 1922.
Gregor, Joseph: *Monumenta Scenica.* 12 portfolios. National Library and R. Piper & Co., Vienna and Munich, 1925–1930.
Gregor, Joseph: *Weltgeschichte des Theaters.* Phaidon-Verlag, Zurich, 1933.

Harding, Alfred: *Revolt of the Actors.* W. Morrow & Co., New York, 1929.

Hartt, Rollin L.: *The People at Play.* Houghton, Mifflin Co., Boston, 1909.

Hood, Richard: *The Actors Present War.* The Theatre Arts Committee and the Hollywood League for Democratic Action, May, 1940.

Hornblow, Arthur: *A History of the Theatre in America.* J. B. Lippincott, Philadelphia, 1919.

Hughes, Glenn: *The Story of the Theatre.* Samuel French, New York, 1928.

Huneker, James Gibbons: *Iconoclasts.* Scribner's, New York, 1905.

Isaacs, Edith J. R. (editor): *Theatre: Essays on the Arts of the Theatre.* Little, Brown & Co., New York, 1927.

Jewish Theatre Museum (catalogue). New York, 1926.

Kennard, Joseph Spencer: *The Italian Theatre.* 2 volumes. W. E. Rudge, New York, 1932.

Kirstein, Lincoln: *Dance.* G. P. Putnam's Sons, New York, 1936.

Komedie (periodical). Prague.

Levinson, André: *La Danse au théâtre.* Bloud & Gay, Paris, 1924.

Mantzius, Karl: *A History of Theatrical Art.* 6 volumes. Duckworth, London, 1903–1921.

Matthews, Brander: *French Dramatists of the Nineteenth Century.* Scribner's, New York, 1905.

Matthews, Brander: *A Study of the Drama.* Houghton, Mifflin Co., Boston, 1910.

May, Earl Chapin: *The Circus from Rome to Ringling.* New York, 1932.

McKechnie, Samuel: *Popular Entertainment through the Ages.* Frederick A. Stokes Co., London, 1931.

Miller, Anna Irene: *The Independent Theatre in Europe.* Ray Long & Richard R. Smith, New York, 1931.

Moses, Montrose and Brown, John Mason: *The American Theatre as Seen by Its Critics.* W. W. Norton & Co., New York, 1934.

Nathan, George Jean: *Materia Critica.* Alfred A. Knopf, New York, 1924.

Nathan, George Jean: *Testament of a Critic.* Alfred A. Knopf, New York, 1931.

Newman, Ernest: *Stories of the Great Operas.* Garden City Publishing Co., Garden City, New York, 1928.

New Theatre (periodical). New York.

New Theatre and Film (periodical). New York.

New Theatre News. Bulletin of the New Theatre League. New York.

Nicoll, Allardyce: *British Drama.* Crowell, New York, 1925.

Nicoll, Allardyce: *The Development of the Theatre.* Harcourt, Brace & Co., New York, 1927.

Nicoll, Allardyce: *The English Theatre.* Thomas Nelson & Sons, London, 1936.

Nicoll, Allardyce: *Masks, Mimes and Miracles.* Harcourt, Brace & Co., New York, 1931.

Nicoll, Allardyce: *The Theory of Drama.* G. G. Harrap, London, 1931.

O'Casey, Sean: *I Knock at the Door.* Macmillan, New York, 1939.

Odell, George C. D.: *Annals of the New York Stage.* 11 volumes. Columbia University Press, New York, 1927–1939.

One Act Play Magazine (periodical). New York.

Pack, Richard and Marvin, Mark: *Censored!* National Committee against Censorship of Theatre Arts, New York, 1935.

Petit de Julleville, Louis: *Histoire du théâtre en France.* 2 volumes. Hachette et Cie., Paris, 1880–1886.

Pougin, Arthur: *Dictionnaire historique et pittoresque du théâtre et des arts.* Paris, 1885.

Program D37 (periodical of the Burian D37 Collective). Prague.

Quinn, Arthur Hobson: *A History of the American Drama. From the Civil War to the Present Day.* F. S. Crofts & Co., New York, 1936.

Ricci, Corrado: *La Scenografia italiana.* Fratelli Treves, Milan, 1930.

Ridå (periodical). Stockholm.

Ring, Herman A.: *Teaterns Historia.* 2 volumes. Koersners, Stockholm, 1898.

Rolland, Romain: *The People's Theatre.* Henry Holt & Co., New York, 1918.

Scenen (periodical). Stockholm.

Shaw, George Bernard: *Dramatic Opinions and Essays.* 2 volumes. Brentano's, New York, 1907.

Simonson, Lee: *The Stage Is Set.* Harcourt, Brace & Co., New York, 1932.

Sinclair, Upton: *Mammonart.* Upton Sinclair, Pasadena, 1925.

Sobel, Bernard (editor): *The Theatre Handbook.* Crown Publishers, New York, 1940.

South American Theatre. Theatre Arts special number, May, 1938.

Les spectacles à travers les âges. 3 volumes. Aux Éditions du Cygne, Paris, 1932.

Stage (periodical). New York.

Stevens, Thomas Wood: *The Theatre from Athens to Broadway.* D. Appleton & Co., New York, 1932.

Svenska Teater Förbundets Medlems Blad (periodical). Stockholm.

TAC (periodical). New York.

Teatern (periodical). Stockholm.

Das Theater (periodical). Berlin.

Theater der Welt (periodical). Vienna.

Theater Illustrierte (periodical). Zurich.

Le Théâtre (periodical). Paris.

Theatre Art International Exhibition (catalogue). Museum of Modern Art, New York, 1934.

Theatre Arts (periodical). New York.

Theatre Arts Prints. I. *The Greeks to Our Day.* John Day Co., New York, 1929. II. *Modern Stage Design.* Theatre Arts, Inc., New York, 1935. III. *Shakespeare and His Times.* Theatre Arts, Inc., New York, 1935.
Theatre Guild Magazine (periodical). New York.
Theatre Workshop (periodical). New York.
Toller, Ernst: *I Was a German.* Morrow & Co., New York, 1934.
Usigli, Rodolfo: *México en el Teatro.* Imprenta Mundial, Mexico City, 1932.
Variety (periodical). New York.
Woollcott, Alexander: *Enchanted Aisles.* Putnam, New York, 1924.
Workers' Theatre (periodical). New York.
Young, Stark: *The Flower in Drama.* Scribner's, New York, 1923.
Young, Stark: *The Theatre.* Doran, New York, 1927.
Young, Stark: *Theatre Practice.* Scribner's, New York, 1926.

TECHNICAL

Abraham, Pierre: *Le Physique au théâtre.* Coutan-Lambert, Paris, 1933.
Anderson, John: *Box Office.* Cape & Smith, New York, 1929.
Archer, William: *Play-making: a Manual of Craftsmanship.* Small, Maynard & Co., Boston, 1912.
Baird, John F.: *Make-Up.* Samuel French, New York, 1930.
Baker, George Pierce: *Dramatic Technique.* Houghton, Mifflin Co., Boston, 1919.
Barber, Philip W.: *The Scene Technician's Handbook.* Whitlock's, New Haven, 1928.
Bates, Esther Willard: *The Church Play and Its Production.* Baker & Co., Boston, 1938.
Bax, Peter: *Stage Management.* Dickson, London, 1936.
Benson, Sir Frank: *I Want to Go on the Stage.* Ernest Benn, London, 1931.
Bernhardt, Sarah: *The Art of the Theatre.* Geoffrey Bles, London, 1924.
Bernheim, Alfred L.: *The Business of the Theatre.* Actors Equity Association, New York, 1932.
Boleslavsky, Constantin: *Acting: The First Six Lessons.* Theatre Arts, Inc., New York, 1933.
Bosworth, Halliam. *Technique in Dramatic Art.* Macmillan, New York, 1934.
Boyd, A. K.: *The Technique of Play Production.* Harrap, London, 1934.
Brandon-Thomas, Jevan: *Practical Stagecraft for Amateurs.* Harrap, London, 1936.
Brickell, Herschel L. (editor): *Our Theatre Today.* Samuel French, New York, 1936.
Brown, Gilmor and Garwood, Alice: *General Principles of Play Direction.* Samuel French, New York, 1936.

Burris-Meyer, Harold: *Research in Sound in the Theatre.* Report No. 3. Stevens Institute of Technology, Hoboken, N.J., 1940.

Burris-Meyer, Harold: *Sound Control Apparatus for the Theater. Journal of the Acoustical Society of America,* July, 1940.

Burris-Meyer, Harold and Cole, Edward: *Scenery for the Theatre.* Little, Brown & Co., Boston, 1938.

Calvert, Louis: *Problems of the Actor.* Holt, New York, 1918.

Campbell, Wayne: *Amateur Acting and Play Production.* Macmillan, New York, 1931.

Careers in the Theatre. The Institute for Research, Chicago, 1939.

Carroll, Sydney W.: *Acting for the Stage.* Pitman, London, 1938.

Chalmers, Helena: *The Art of Make-Up.* Appleton, New York, 1930.

Clark, Barrett H.: *How to Produce Amateur Plays.* Little, Brown & Co., Boston, 1925.

Cole, Edward C.: *A Stage Manager's Manual.* Yale University Theatre, New Haven, 1937.

Coquelin, Constant: *Art of the Actor.* George Allen & Unwin, London, 1932.

Crawford, Lane: *Acting, Its Theory and Practice.* Constable, London, 1930.

Crocker, Carlotte; Fields, Victor A.; and Broomall, Will: *Taking the Stage.* Pitman, New York, 1939.

Crump, Leslie: *Directing for the Amateur Stage.* Dodd, Mead & Co., New York, 1935.

D'Angelo, Aristides: *The Actor Creates.* Samuel French, New York, 1939.

Dean, Alexander: *Little Theatre Organization and Management.* Appleton, New York, 1926.

Dolman, John Jr.: *The Art of Play Production.* Harper's, New York, 1928.

Donnet, Alexis: *Architectonographie des théâtres.* Lacroix & Baudry, Paris, 1840–1857.

Downs, Harold (editor): *Theatre and Stage.* 2 volumes. Pitman, London, 1934.

Ervine, St. John: *How To Write a Play.* G. Allen & Unwin, London, 1928.

Eustis, Morton: *B'way, Inc.* Dodd, Mead & Co., New York, 1935.

Eustis, Morton: *Players at Work.* Theatre Arts, Inc., New York, 1937.

Franklin, Miriam A.: *Rehearsal.* Prentice-Hall, New York, 1938.

Fuchs, Theodore: *Stage Lighting.* Little, Brown & Co., Boston, 1929.

Gamble, William Burt: *The Development of Scenic Art and Stage Machinery.* New York Public Library, 1920.

Gamble, William Burt: *The Development of Scenic Art and Stage Design* (supplement). New York Public Library, 1928.

Geddes, Norman Bel; Simonson, Lee; and others: *Architecture for the New Theatre.* Theatre Arts, Inc., New York, 1935.

Gorelik, Mordecai: *I Design for the Group Theatre. Theatre Arts,* March, 1939.

Gorelik, Mordecai: *Scenic and Dramatic Form. The Arts,* November, 1923.

Harden, Edwin Lyle: *Practice in Dramatics.* Baker, Boston, 1936.

Hartmann, Louis: *Theatre Lighting.* Appleton, New York and London, 1930.

Heffner, Hubert C.; Selden, Samuel; and Sellman, Hunton D.: *Modern Theatre Practice.* Crofts & Co., New York, 1935.

Hicks, Seymour: *Acting.* Cassell, London, 1931.

Hochdorf, Max: *Die Deutsche Bühnengenossenschaft.* Gustav Kiepenheuer Verlag, Potsdam, 1921.

Houghton, Norris: *The Designer Sets the Stage.* 1. *Norman Bel Geddes, Vincente Minelli* (October, 1936). 2. *Lee Simonson, Donald Oenslager* (November, 1936). 3. *Robert Edmond Jones, Mordecai Gorelik* (December, 1936). 4. *Jo Mielziner, Aline Bernstein* (January, 1937). *Theatre Arts,* 1936–1937.

Hughes, Glenn: *The Penthouse Idea* (pamphlet). Dramatists Play Service, New York, (no date).

Isaacs, Edith J. R. (editor): *Architecture for the New Theatre,* Theatre Arts, Inc., New York, 1935.

Извеков, Н. П. (Izvekov. N. P.): *Сцена* (*Stage*). Moscow, 1935.

Jones, Leslie Allen: *Painting Scenery.* Baker & Co., Boston, 1935.

Jones, Leslie Allen: *Scenic Design and Model Building.* Baker & Co., Boston, 1939.

Journal of the Acoustical Society of America. Menasha, Wis.

Kouřil, Miroslav and Burian, Emil F.: *Divadlo Práce* (*Theatre of Labor*). Prague, 1938.

Kranich, Friedrich: *Das Bühnentechnik der Gegenwart.* 2 volumes. R. Oldenbourg, Munich and Berlin, 1929–1933.

Krows, Arthur Edwin: *Equipment for Stage Production.* Appleton, New York, 1928.

Krows, Arthur Edwin: *Playwriting for Profit.* Longmans, Green & Co., New York, 1928.

Laumann, E. M.: *La Machinerie au théâtre depuis les Grecs jusqu'à nos jours.* Firmin-Didot, Paris, 1897.

Lawson, John Howard: *Theory and Technique of Playwriting.* G. P. Putnam's Sons, New York, 1936.

Lessing, Gotthold Ephraim: *Hamburgische Dramaturgie.* G. I. Göschen, Leipzig, 1856.

Mackay, Constance D'Arcy: *Costume and Scenery for Amateurs.* Henry Holt & Co., New York, 1932.

Mackay, Edward J. and Alice: *Elementary Principles of Acting.* Samuel French, New York, 1934.

Mather, Charles Chambers; Spaulding, Alice Howard; and Skillen, Melita: *Behind the Footlights.* Silver, Burdett & Co., *New York,* 1935.

Matthews, Brander: *Principles of Playmaking.* Scribner's, New York, 1919.

Maule, Donovan: *The Stage as a Career.* Pitman, London, 1932.

McCandless, Stanley R.: *A Method of Lighting the Stage.* Theatre Arts, Inc., New York, 1932.

McCandless, Stanley R.: *A Syllabus of Stage Lighting.* Whitlock's Book Store, New Haven, 1931.

McCleery, Albert and Glick, Carl: *Curtains Going Up.* Pitman Publishing Corp., New York and Chicago, 1939.

Mitchell, Roy: *The School Theatre.* Brentano's, New York, 1925.

Napier, Frank: *Curtains for Stage Settings.* Frederick Muller, London, 1937.

Napier, Frank: *Noises Off.* Frederick Muller, London, 1936.

Nelms, Henning: *Lighting the Amateur Stage.* Theatre Arts, Inc., New York, 1931.

Parsons, Charles S.: *Amateur Stage Management and Production.* Pitman, London, 1931.

Parsons, Charles S.: *A Guide to Theatrical Make-Up.* Pitman, London, 1932.

Pichel, Irving: *On Building a Theatre.* Theatre Arts Monographs No. 1. Theatre Arts, Inc., 1920.

Pichel, Irving: *Modern Theatres.* Harcourt, Brace & Co., New York, 1925.

Polunin, Vladimir: *The Continental Method of Scene Painting.* C. W. Beaumont, London, 1927.

Ряжский, Ник. (Riazhsky, N.): *Оборудование Клубной Сцены* (*Equipping the Non-Professional Stage*). Goslitizdat, Moscow, 1935.

Richards, Mary: *Practical Play Production.* Evans Brothers, London, 1937.

Ridge, C. Harold and Aldred, F. S.: *Stage Lighting.* Pitman, London, 1935.

Rose, Arthur: *Stage Effects.* G. Routledge, London, 1928.

Rosenstein, Sophie; Haydon, Larrae A.; and Sparrow, Wilbur: *Modern Acting: A Manual.* Samuel French, New York, 1936.

Sachs, Edwin O.: *Modern Opera Houses and Theatres.* 2 volumes. B. T. Batsford, London, 1897.

Schonberger, Emanuel D.: *Play Production for Amateurs.* Nelson & Co., New York, 1938.

Selden, Samuel: *A Player's Handbook.* Crofts, New York, 1934.

Selden, Samuel and Sellman, Hunton D.: *Stage Scenery and Lighting.* F. S. Crofts, New York, 1936.

Sexton, Randolph Williams: *American Theatres of Today.* Architectural Book Publishing Co., New York, 1930.

Simonson, Lee: *Down to the Cellar. Theatre Arts,* April, 1922.

Smith, André: *The Scenewright.* Macmillan, New York, 1926.

Smith, Milton: *The Book of Play Production.* Appleton-Century, New York, 1926.

Smith, Solomon Franklin: *Theatrical Management in the West and South for Thirty Years.* Harpers, New York, 1868.

Southern, Richard: *Stage-Setting.* Faber & Faber, London, 1927.

Speaight, Robert: *Acting.* Cassell, London, 1939.

Stanislavsky, Constantin: *An Actor Prepares.* Theatre Arts, Inc., New York, 1936.

Strauss, Ivard: *Paint, Powder and Make-Up.* Sweet & Son, New Haven, 1936.

Strenkovsky, Serge: *The Art of Make-Up.* Dutton, New York, 1937.

Talma, François Joseph: *Reflections on the Actor's Art.* Columbia University Press, New York, 1915.

Theatre Lighting, Past and Present (catalogue). Ward Leonard Electric Co., Mt. Vernon, N.Y., 1923.

Throckmorton, Cleon: *Catalogue of the Theatre* (catalogue). New York.

To Architects: Stop! Look! Listen! Theatre Arts, January, 1939.

Traube, Shepard: *So You Want to Go into the Theatre?* Little, Brown & Co., Boston, 1936.

Urban, Joseph: *Theatres.* Theatre Arts, Inc., New York, 1929.

von Engel, Alfred: *Bühnenbeleuchtung.* Hochmeister & Thal, Leipzig, 1926.

Waugh, Frank Albert: *Outdoor Theatres.* R. G. Badger, Boston, 1917.

Das Werk, special theatre number. Zurich, November, 1936.

White, Edwin C.: *Problems of Acting and Play Production.* Pitman, London, 1939.

Zakhava, Boris E.: *Principles of Directing. Theatre Workshop,* April–July, 1937.

Zinkeisen, Doris: *Designing for the Stage.* The Studio, London, 1938.

COSTUME

Aria, E.: *Costume: Fanciful, Historical and Theatrical.* Macmillan, London, 1906.

Baxter, Thomas: *Egyptian, Grecian and Roman Costume.* H. Setchel & Son, London, 1814.

von Boehn, Max: *Das Beuwerk der Mode.* F. Bruckmann, Munich, 1928.

von Boehn, Max: *Die Mode.* 6 volumes. F. Bruckmann, Munich, 1919.

Fischel, Oskar: *Chronisten der Mode.* Müller & Co., Potsdam, 1923.

Fischer, Carlos: *Les costumes de l'opéra.* Librairie de France, Paris, 1931.

Gregor, Joseph: *Wiener Szenische Kunst: Das Bühnenkostum.* 2 volumes. Amalthea-Verlag, Zurich, 1924–1925.

Grimball, Elizabeth B. and Wells, Rhea: *Costuming a Play.* The Century Co., New York, 1925.

Heuzey, Léon Alexandre: *Histoire de costume antique.* H. Champion, Paris, 1922.

Hiler, Hilaire: *From Nudity to Raiment.* Educational Press, New York, 1930.

Hottenroth, Friedrich: *Trachten, Hans-, Feld- und Kriegsgeräthschaften der Völker alter und neuer Zeit.* 2 volumes. G. Weise, Stuttgart, 1883–1886.

Kohler, Carl: *A History of Costume.* Harrap, London, 1929.

Kohler, Carl: *Praktische Kostum-Kunde.* Bruckmann, Munich, 1926.

Komisarjevsky, Theodore: *The Costume of the Theatre.* Geoffrey Bles, London, 1931.

Kretschmer, Albert and Rohrbach, Carl: *The Costumes of All Nations.* H. Sotheran & Co., London, 1882.

Lens, André: *Le Costume des peuples de l'antiquité.* Privately printed, Liége, 1776.

Mutzel, Hans: *Vom Lendenschurz zur Modetracht.* Widder, Berlin, 1925.

Parry, Albert: *Tattoo.* Simon and Schuster, New York, 1933.

Parsons, F. A.: *Art of Dress.* Doubleday, Doran & Co., New York, 1928.

Petrizky, Anatol: *Ukranian: Theater Trachten.* Staatsverlag der Ukraine, 1929.

Planché, James Robinson: *A Cyclopedia of Costume or Dictionary of Dress.* 2 volumes. Chatto & Windus, London, 1876–1879.

Quicherat, Jules E. J.: *Histoire de costume en France.* Paris, 1877.

Racinet, M. Auguste: *Le Costume Historique.* Paris, 1888.

Rosenberg, Adolph: *Geschichte des Kostums.* E. Wasmuth, Berlin, 1905.

Saunders, Catherine: *Costume in Roman Comedy.* Columbia University Press, New York, 1909.

Saunders, Dorothy L.: *Costuming the Amateur Show.* Samuel French, New York, 1938.

von Sichart, Emma: *Praktische Kostum Kunde.* 2 volumes. Bruckmann, Munich, 1933.

Tilke, Max: *Orientalische Kostume in Schnitt und Farbe.* E. Wasmuth, Berlin, 1923.

Walkup, Fairfax Proudfit: *Dressing the Part.* F. S. Crofts & Co., New York, 1938.

West, Robert: *Der Stil im Wandel der Jahrhunderte.* Kurt Wolff, Berlin, 1934.

Young, Agnes Brooks: *Stage Costuming.* Macmillan, New York, 1927.

PUPPETS

Altherr, Alfred (editor): *Marionetten.* E. Rentsch, Erlenbach-Zurich, 1926.

Anderson, Madge: *Heroes of the Puppet Stage.* Harcourt, Brace & Co., London, 1924.

Beaumont, Cyril W.: *Puppets and the Puppet Stage.* The Studio, London, 1939.

von Boehn, Max: *Dolls and Puppets.* Harrap, London, 1932.
von Boehn, Max: *Puppen und Puppenspiele.* F. Bruckmann, Munich, 1929.
Brown, Forman: *The Pie-Eyed Piper.* Greenberg, New York, 1933.
Bufano, Remo: *Magic Strings.* Macmillan, New York, 1939.
Bufano, Remo: *A Puppet Showman.* Appleton-Century Co., New York, 1933.
Bufano, Remo: *The Show Book of Remo Bufano.* Macmillan, New York, 1929.
Darah Bharata. Commissie Voor de Volkslectuur, Batavia, 1919.
Gorelik, Mordecai: *Remo Bufano. The Arts,* January, 1926.
Gröber, Karl: *Kinderspielzeug aus alter Zeit.* Deutscher Kunstverlag, Berlin, 1928.
Gröber, Karl: *Das Puppenhaus.* Verlag der Eiserne Hammer, Leipzig, 1935(?).
Joseph, Helen Haiman: *A Book of Marionettes.* The Viking Press, New York, 1931.
Kennard, Joseph Spencer: *Masks and Marionettes.* Macmillan, New York, 1935.
Lehmann, Ernst: *Das Handpuppenspiel.* Ludwig Voggenreiter, Potsdam, 1934.
Magnin, Charles: *Histoire des marionettes en Europe.* M. Levy Frères, Paris, 1862.
McPharlin, Paul L. (editor): *Puppetry* (yearbook). Marionette Fellowship of America, Detroit, 1931.
Munger, Martha Perrine: *The Book of Puppets.* Lothrop, Boston, 1934.
Niessen, Carl: *Das Rheinische Puppenspiel.* Fritz Klopp, Bonn, 1928.
Das Puppentheater (periodical). Leipzig, 1925–1931.
Rabe, Johs. E.: *Kasper Putschenelle.* Quickborn, Hamburg, 1924.
Rehm, Hermann Siegfried: *Das Buch der Marionetten.* Frensdorf, Berlin, 1903(?).
Rohden, Peter Richard: *Das Puppenspiel.* Hanseatische Verlangstalt, Hamburg, 1922.
Sarg, Tony: *Marionette Book.* Viking Press, New York, 1930.
Театр Детской Книги (*The Theatre of the Child's Book*). Moscow, 1934.
Верховский, Н. (ред.) (Verkhovsky, N.) (editor): *Кукольные Театры* (*Puppet Theatres*). Leningrad, 1934.
Weismantel, Leo: *Werkbuch der Puppenspiele.* Verlag des Bühnenvolksbundes, Frankfort-am-Main, 1924.

CINEMA

Adam, T. R.: *Motion Pictures in Adult Education.* American Association for Adult Education, New York, 1940.
Arnheim, Rudolf: *Film.* Faber & Faber, London, 1933.

Arossev, A.: *Soviet Cinema.* VOKS, Moscow, 1935(?).

Bardèche and Brasillach: *The History of Motion Pictures.* W. W. Norton & Co., New York, 1938.

Bloem, Walter S.: *The Soul of the Moving Picture.* Dutton, New York, 1924.

Blumer, Herbert: *Movies and Conduct.* Macmillan, New York, 1933.

Brunel, Adrian: *Film Production.* Newnes, London, 1936.

Buchanan, Andrew: *The Art of Film Production.* Pitman, London, 1937.

Buckle, Gerard Fort: *The Mind and the Film.* George Routledge & Sons, London, 1926.

Cinema Quarterly (periodical). London.

Cowan, Lester (editor): *Recording Sound for Motion Pictures.* McGraw-Hill Book Co., New York, 1931.

Dale, Edgar: *The Content of Motion Pictures.* Macmillan, New York, 1935.

Dale, Edgar (editor): *Motion Pictures in Education.* H. W. Wilson, New York, 1937.

Eisenstein, Sergei: *Film Forms: New Problems. New Theatre,* April, May and June, 1936.

Elliott, Eric: *Anatomy of Motion Picture Art.* Pool, Territet, Switzerland, 1928.

Ernst, Morris L. and Lorentz, Pare: *Censored.* Cape & Smith, New York, 1930.

Experimental Cinema (quarterly). Philadelphia, 1930–1934.

Faure, Elie: *The Art of Cineplastics.* The Four Seas Company, Boston, 1923.

Federal Writers Project: *Bibliography of the Film.* H. W. Wilson and the Museum of Modern Art Film Library, New York, 1939.

Film Art (quarterly). London.

Films (quarterly). New York.

Freeburg, Victor Oscar: *The Art of Photoplay Making.* Macmillan, New York, 1918.

Freeburg, Victor Oscar: *Pictorial Beauty on the Screen.* Macmillan, New York, 1923.

Gregor, Joseph and Fülöp-Miller, René: *Das Amerikanische Theater und Kino.* Amalthea-Verlag, Vienna, 1931.

Hampton, Benjamin B.: *A History of the Movies.* Covici, Friede, New York, 1931.

Heygate, John: *Talking Picture.* J. Cape, London, 1936.

Hunter, William: *Scrutiny of Cinema.* Wishart, London, 1932.

Jacobs, Lewis: *The Rise of the American Film.* Harcourt, Brace & Co., New York, 1939.

Journal of the Society of Motion Picture Engineers (periodical). Easton, Pa.

Kennedy, J. P.: *The Story of the Films.* A. W. Shaw & Co., New York, 1927.

Lenin, Nikolai: *On Cinema. New Theatre,* January, 1935.

Leyda, Jay: *Backgrounds of Film Reality* (unpublished).

Leyda, Jay and Ellis, Peter: *A Guide to the Social Study of the Film* (bibliography). *Theatre Workshop,* April–July, 1937.

Lindsay, Vachel: *The Art of the Moving Picture.* Macmillan, New York, 1922.

Lorentz, Pare: *The River.* Stackpole, New York, 1938.

Marion, Frances: *How to Write and Sell Film Stories; with a Complete Shooting Script for Marco Polo by Robert E. Sherwood.* Covici, Friede, New York, 1937.

Martin, Olga J.: *Hollywood's Movie Commandments.* H. W. Wilson, New York, 1937.

Milne, Peter: *Motion Picture Directing.* Falk Publishing Co., New York, 1922.

Moussinac, Léon: *Panoramique du cinéma.* Au Sans Pareil, Paris, 1929.

Munterberg, Hugo: *The Photoplay; a Psychological Study.* Appleton, New York, 1916.

Naumburg, Nancy (editor): *We Make the Movies.* W. W. Norton & Co., New York, 1937.

Nicoll, Allardyce: *Film and Theatre.* Thomas Y. Crowell, New York, 1933.

Nilsen, Vladimir: *The Cinema as a Graphic Art.* Newnes, London, 1938.

Patterson, Frances Taylor: *Motion Picture Continuities.* Columbia University Press, New York, 1929.

Pearlman, William J. (editor): *The Movies on Trial.* Macmillan, New York, 1936.

Pitkin, Walter B. and Marston, William M.: *The Art of Sound Pictures.* D. Appleton & Co., New York, 1930.

Potamkin, Harry Alan: *The Eyes of the Movie.* International Pamphlets, New York, 1934.

Pudovkin, V. I.: *Film Technique.* George Newnes, Ltd., London, 1929.

Ramsaye, Terry: *A Million and One Nights.* 2 volumes. Simon & Shuster, New York, 1926.

Rotha, Paul: *Documentary Film.* W. W. Norton & Co., New York, 1939.

Rotha, Paul: *Movie Parade.* The Studio Publications, New York, 1936.

Seldes, Gilbert: *The Movies Come from America.* Scribner's, New York, 1937.

Shand, Philip Morton: *Modern Picture Houses and Theatres.* J. B. Lippincott, Philadelphia, 1930.

Sinclair, Upton: *Upton Sinclair Presents William Fox.* Upton Sinclair, Los Angeles, 1933.

Spottiswoode, Raymond: *A Grammar of the Film; an Analysis of Film Technique.* Faber & Faber, London, 1935.

Swope, John: *Camera Over Hollywood.* Random House, New York, 1939.

Thorpe, Margaret Farrand: *America at the Movies.* Yale University Press, New Haven, 1939.

Il Ventuno (quarterly). Rome.

Watts, Stephen (editor): *Behind the Screen; How Films Are Made.* Arthur Barker, London, 1938.

Zucker, Paul and Stindt, G. O.: *Lichtspielhäuser Tonfilmtheater.* Wasmuth, Berlin, 1931.

SCIENCE

d'Abro, A.: *The Evolution of Scientific Thought from Newton to Einstein.* Boni & Liveright, New York, 1927.

Boas, Franz: *Race, Language and Culture.* Macmillan, New York, 1940.

Bragg, William: *The Universe of Light.* Macmillan, New York, 1933.

Butler, Samuel: *Evolution Old and New.* Hardwicke & Bogue, London, 1879.

Carrel, Alexis: *Man the Unknown.* Harper & Bros., New York, 1935.

Cohen, Morris R.: *Reason and Nature.* Harcourt, Brace & Co., New York, 1931.

Dampier, Sir William: *A History of Science.* Macmillan, New York, 1936.

Darwin, Charles: *The Descent of Man.* Appleton, New York, 1909.

Darwin, Charles: *The Origin of Species.* Appleton, New York, 1909.

Eddington, Arthur Stanley: *The Nature of the Physical World.* University Press, Cambridge, 1928.

Eddington, Arthur Stanley: *New Pathways in Science.* Macmillan, New York, 1935.

Graubard, Mark: *Genetics and the Social Order.* Tomorrow Publishers, New York, 1935.

Heidel, William Arthur: *The Heroic Age of Science.* Williams and Wilkins, Baltimore, 1933.

Hogben, Launcelot: *Science for the Citizen.* Alfred A. Knopf, New York, 1938.

Millikan, Robert Andrews: *The Electron.* University of Chicago Press, Chicago, 1924.

Rose, William (editor): *An Outline of Modern Knowledge.* Victor Gollanez, London, 1931.

Science at the Cross Roads. Victor Gollancz, London, 1931.

Sullivan, J. W. N.: *The Bases of Modern Science.* E. Benn, London, 1928.

Thomson, J. Arthur: *The Outline of Science.* G. P. Putnam's Sons, New York, 1937.

Whitehead, Alfred North: *Science and the Modern World.* Macmillan, New York, 1925.

PSYCHOLOGY

Adler, Alfred: *The Practice and Theory of Individual Psychology.* Harcourt, Brace & Co., New York, 1932.

Adler, Alfred: *Problems of Neurosis.* K. Paul, Trench, Trubner & Co., London, 1929.

Adler, Alfred: *Social Interest.* G. P. Putnam's Sons, New York, 1939.

Adler, Alfred: *Understanding Human Nature.* Greenberg, New York, 1927.

Angell and Thompson: *Organic Effects of Agreeable and Disagreeable Stimuli. Psychological Review,* New York, 1896.

Binet, A. and Vaschide, N.: *L'Influence de travail des emotions sur la pression du sang. L'Année Psychologique,* Paris, 1896.

Boas, Franz: *Anthropology and Modern Life.* W. W. Norton & Co., New York, 1924.

Burrow, T.: *The Social Basis of Consciousness.* Harcourt, Brace & Co., New York, 1927.

Cannon, W. B.: *Bodily Changes in Pain, Hunger, Fear and Rage.* Appleton, New York, 1929.

Caudwell, Christopher: *Illusion and Reality.* Macmillan, New York, 1937.

Freud, Sigmund: *Delusion and Dream.* Moffat, Yard & Co., New York, 1917.

Freud, Sigmund: *The Interpretation of Dreams.* Macmillan, New York, 1920.

Freud, Sigmund: *Totem and Taboo.* Moffat, Yard & Co., New York, 1919.

Freud, Sigmund: *Wit and Its Relation to the Unconscious.* Moffat, Yard & Co., New York, 1917.

Graves, T. S.: *The Literal Acceptance of Stage Illusion. South Atlantic Quarterly,* Durham, N.C., Vol. 23.

Horney, Karen: *The Neurotic Personality in Our Time.* W. W. Norton & Co., New York, 1937.

Hull, Clark L.: *Hypnosis and Suggestibility.* Appleton-Century Co., New York, 1933.

James, William: *The Physical Basis of Emotions. Psychological Review,* 1884.

James, William: *The Varieties of Religious Experience.* Longmans, Green & Co., New York, 1928.

Jelliffe, Smith Ely: *The Technique of Psychoanalysis.* Nervous and Mental Disease Publishing Co., New York and Washington, 1918.

Jung, C. G.: *Psychology of the Unconscious.* Moffat, Yard & Co., New York, 1919.

Marston, W. M.: *Emotions of Normal People.* Harcourt, Brace & Co., New York, 1928.

Marston, W. M.: *Motor Consciousness as a Basis for Emotion. Journal of Abnormal and Social Psychology*. Boston, September, 1927.

Pavlov, Ivan Petrovich: *Conditioned Reflexes*. Oxford University Press, London, 1928.

Pavlov, Ivan Petrovich: *Work of the Digestive Glands*. C. Griffin & Co., London, 1902.

Pfister, Oskar: *The Psychoanalytic Method*. Moffat, Yard & Co., New York, 1919.

Prince, Morton: *The Dissociation of a Personality*. Longmans, Green & Co., New York, 1906.

Prinzhorn, Hans: *Bildnerei der Geisteskranken*. Julius Springer, Berlin, 1922.

Watson, John Broadus: *Behaviorism*. W. W. Norton & Co., New York, 1925.

Wechsler, David: *The Measurement of Emotional Reaction*. Columbia University Thesis Publications, New York, 1925.

White, William A.: *Mechanisms of Character Formation*. Macmillan, New York, 1920.

Wundt, Wilhelm: *Outlines of Psychology*. A. Kröner, Leipzig, 1907.

MISCELLANEOUS

Aronson, Joseph: *The Encyclopedia of Furniture*. Crown Publishers, New York, 1938

Barr, Alfred H., Jr. (editor): *Picasso: Forty Years of His Art*. Museum of Modern Art, New York, 1939.

Bayer, Herbert; Gropius, Walter; and Gropius, Ise: *Bauhaus*. Museum of Modern Art, New York, 1938.

Beard, Charles and Mary: *The Rise of American Civilization*. Macmillan, New York, 1930.

Beard, Charles A. (editor): *Whither Mankind*. Longmans, Green & Co., New York, 1928.

Benjamin, Walter: *The Work of Art in the Era of Mechanical Reproduction* (unpublished).

Bouhler, Philipp: *Parteitag der Ehre*. 73 Bilddokumente vom Reichsparteitag zu Nürnberg, 1936. Verlag und Vertriebs-Gesellschaft, Berlin, 1936.

Cahill, Holger: *New Horizons in American Art*. Museum of Modern Art, New York, 1936.

Cheney, Sheldon: *The New World Architecture*. Tudor Publishing Co., New York, 1935.

Cheney, Sheldon and Cheney, Martha: *Art and the Machine*. Whittlesey House, New York, 1936.

le Corbusier: *Précisions*. Crès & Cie., Paris, 1930.

le Corbusier: *Towards a New Architecture*. John Rodker, London, 1931.

le Corbusier: *Une Maison—un palais*. Crès & Cie., Paris, 1928.

le Corbusier and Jeanneret: *L'Architecture vivante.* Éditions Albert Morance, Paris, 1938.
Cross, Arthur Lyon: *A History of England and Greater Britain.* Macmillan, New York, 1923.
Einstein, Carl: *Die Kunst des 20 Jahrhunderts.* Propylaen-Verlag, Berlin, 1931.
Geddes, Norman Bel: *Horizons.* Little, Brown & Co., Boston, 1933.
Gleizes, Albert and Metzinger, Jean: *Cubism.* Unwin, London, 1913.
Gropius, Walter: *Bauhausbauten Dessau.* Albert Langen, Munich, 1930.
Hitler, Adolf: *Mein Kampf.* Reynal & Hitchcock, New York, 1940.
Kreymborg, Alfred: *Our Singing Strength.* Coward McCann, New York, 1929.
Lavine, Harold and Wechsler, James: *War Propaganda in the United States.* Yale University Press, New Haven, 1940.
Minotaure (periodical). Paris.
Moholy-Nagy, László: *The New Vision.* Brewer, Warren & Putnam, New York, 1928.
Ozenfant, Amadée: *Foundations of Modern Art.* John Rodker, London, 1931.
Pater, Walter: *The Renaissance.* Macmillan, London, 1873.
Rousseau, Jean Jacques: *Confessions.* 2 volumes. The Nonesuch Press, London, 1938.
Robinson, James Harvey and Beard, Charles A.: *The Development of Modern Europe.* 2 volumes. Ginn & Company, Boston, 1908.
Ruhle, Otto: *Illustrierte Kultur- und Sittengeschichte des Proletariats.* Neuer Deutscher Verlag, Berlin, 1930.
Strachey, G. L.: *Landmarks in French Literature.* Henry Holt & Co., New York, 1912.
Terrasse, Charles: *French Painting in the XXth Century.* Hyperion Press, London, Paris, New York, 1939.
Theimer, Walter: *The Penguin Political Dictionary.* Penguin Books, Harmondsworth, Middlesex, England, 1939.
Ticknor, George: *History of Spanish Literature.* Houghton, Mifflin Co., Boston, 1891.
Whitman, Walt: *Leaves of Grass & Democratic Vistas.* J. M. Dent & Sons, New York, 1912.
Yeats, William Butler: *The Shadowy Waters.* Dodd, Mead & Co., New York, 1921.

INDEX OF PLAYS

Film plays are in *italics*

GENERAL INDEX

This index does not include play titles. See Index of Plays, page 537.